EDUCATIONAL TESTING AND MEASUREMENT

EDUCATIONAL TESTING AND MEASUREMENT

CLASSROOM APPLICATION AND PRACTICE

FIFTH EDITION

TOM KUBISZYN
Practice Directorate, American Psychological Association

GARY BORICH
The University of Texas at Austin

HarperCollins*CollegePublishers*

Executive Editor: Christopher Jennison
Project Coordination, Text and Cover Design: Interactive Composition Corporation
Electronic Production Manager: Eric Jorgensen
Manufacturing Manager: Hilda Koparanian
Electronic Page Makeup: Interactive Composition Corporation
Printer and Binder: RR Donnelley & Sons Company
Cover Printer: Phoenix Color Corp

Educational Testing and Measurement
Classroom Application and Practice
Fifth Edition

Library of Congress Cataloging-in-Publication Data

Kubiszyn, Tom.
Educational testing and measurement : classroom application and practice / Tom Kubiszyn and Gary Borich. — 5th ed.
p. cm.
Includes bibliographical references and index.
ISBN 0–673–99734–0
1. Educational tests and measurements—United States. I. Borich, Gary D. II. Title.
LB3051.K8 1995
371.2′6′0973—dc20 95–10668
CIP

95 96 97 98 9 8 7 6 5 4 3 2 1

CONTENTS

CHAPTER 11

CHAPTER 12

CHAPTER 13

CHAPTER 17

CHAPTER 18

PREFACE

In the Preface to the first edition of *Educational Testing and Measurement*, we stated our goal: to present complex test and measurement content in a friendly, non-intimidating, and unique manner. We hoped to fill a need we noted while teaching undergraduate and graduate measurement courses. This need was for a textbook that kept its audience—classroom teachers—fully in mind while presenting often abstract and sometimes difficult concepts and procedures in an accessible manner. Too often, we thought, measurement texts appeared to be written in a dry, overly theoretical or technical fashion, and provided too little rationale or practice with application of concepts. So, rather than overwhelm students with jargon and statistical theory, we focused on the application of theory with a friendly, conversational style. At the same time, we provided sufficient theory to ensure that students will understand the foundations of measurement and avoid an oversimplified approach.

The first four editions of this text were well received, and this positive response has led us to conclude that our approach was an appropriate one. Furthermore, recent developments in testing and measurement indicate that both educators and the general public have become increasingly aware of and involved with educational testing issues.

In this, our fifth edition, we would like to reaffirm our commitment to improving the student's ability to make sound educational decisions in an increasingly complex, technical, and demanding environment. But we also promise to continue with the accessible writing style that has been a major reason for the success of this text. We believe that this revision represents another improvement in making measurement concepts readily available to the classroom teacher.

In preparing this edition, we have added many new features. As with past editions, we have included early in the text a discussion of contemporary issues that are significantly influencing educational testing today, and will continue to do so for the foreseeable future. Perhaps the most far reaching of these is the issue of performance assessment. No longer will the general public settle for student evaluations based only upon multiple-choice and other objective item formats. Increasingly, the public and legislators are clamoring for more widespread use of performance-based assessment in hopes of obtaining more accurate evaluations of a child's educational skill acquisition, integration, and application. While the overall validity and reliability of such assessments remain a matter of debate, the classroom teacher must be trained in these evaluation techniques, while continuing to be trained in other more traditional measurement approaches. Toward this end we have completely revised and expanded our chapter on performance assessment to include portfolio and authentic assessment approaches. We also linked relevant sections of several other chapters to this important trend.

As an outgrowth of the demand for performance-based assessment, today's teacher is faced with the task of combining grades for performance assessments with grades from conventional tests, homework and classroom assignments, and other achievement measures into a single, valid, end-of-grading-period mark. As a result, we have revised the last half of Chapter 10 to train the teacher in psychometrically sound approaches to weighting and combining grades from seemingly disparate sources efficiently and accurately.

Throughout our text we have added references reflecting other contemporary measurement trends, tying these to day-to-day decision making for the classroom teacher. In view of the widespread movement toward "full inclusion" of special learners with severe and/or multiple disabilities into the regular classroom, our chapter on testing and measuring the special learner has been modified and expanded to prepare the regular classroom teacher to play an integral role in the evaluation of the special learner. Also addressed is the concurrent trend toward provision of services to children with "504 only" disabilities, the result of recent interpretations of Section 504 of the Rehabilitation Act. These children, too, will receive services primarily or entirely in the regular classroom, and thus the regular teacher will be called on to evaluate their progress.

Furthermore, both "full inclusion" and "504 only" special learners often take medications that can affect their school learning and behavior. Prescribers are increasingly recognizing the need to evaluate the safety and efficacy of these medications with school-based data. Thus, the classroom teacher will increasingly be called on to collect these data in the future. Accordingly, a new section has been added to our chapter on special learners which includes examples of questionnaires often used for this purpose, to prepare the teacher for this new and important role.

As has been the case with past revisions, there has been remarkable change in the personal computer since the fourth edition was published. We have therefore revised and updated our chapter on measurement applications of the personal computer. We have added several new sections describing how measurement practice can be improved by utilizing multimedia, electronic bulletin boards, LANS (Local Area Networks), the Internet (i.e., the information superhighway), and CD-ROM and CD-R (i.e., CD-ROM that can be recorded upon). We have also explained why full utilization of the opportunity afforded by some of these advances (e.g., CD-ROM, multimedia, Internet) requires upgrading or replacing even relatively new (2–3 years old) personal computer systems. Within the IBM compatible area, for example, entry level "platforms" now contain powerful 486DX and Pentium processors, have 8 and 16 megs of memory, and 400–500 meg hard drives. This is a far cry from the XT, AT, 386SX and 386DX processors with one meg or less of memory and a 40 meg hard drive that were considered entry level when our last edition was published.

As with earlier editions, readers will find at the conclusion of each chapter a step-by-step summary in which all important concepts in the chapter are identified for review. Additionally, we have prepared several new discussion questions and/or exercises for each chapter. These discussion questions and exercises should help students learn how to apply the concepts presented and, along with the *Instructor's*

Manual, should help instructors identify organized activities and assignments that can be integrated into their class presentations. Discussion questions and exercises marked with an asterisk have answers listed in Appendix D.

We have divided our text into 22 chapters according to measurement concepts that are of immediate practical value for the classroom teacher. We have tried to select topics and organize our writing to help the teacher, especially the beginning teacher, deal with the prevailing problems of testing students and measuring their behavior. The topics we have chosen, their natural sequencing according to the real-life tasks of teachers, the step-by-step summaries of major concepts, and our discussion questions and exercises all work, we believe, to make this text a valuable tool and an important resource for observing, measuring, and understanding life in the classroom.

ACKNOWLEDGMENTS

We would like to express our appreciation to the following instructors for their constructive comments on this revision: Susan Barnes, Southwest Texas State University; Claire R. Barrett, Seton Hall University; William Bechtol, Southwest Texas State University; Lowell Bynum, Southwest Texas State University; Bonnie Cramond, University of Georgia; Donald J. Dessart, University of Tennessee; Victor Dupuis, Pennsylvania State University; Charles Good, West Chester University; Gerhard Lang, Montclair State College; Ben Layne, Georgia State University; and Bruce G. Rogers, University of Northern Iowa. Thanks to Jason Millman, Cornell University; David Payne, University of Georgia; Glen Nicholson, University of Arizona; Carol Mardell-Czudnowski, Northern Illinois University; and James Collins, University of Wyoming, for their constructive comments on earlier versions of the manuscript. Also, thanks to Marty Tombari for his contributions to Chapter 9 and other examples, illustrations, and test items in this volume, and to Ann Schulte for her contributions to Chapter 17. Finally, we would like to thank our editors at HarperCollins for their helpful comments.

— *Tom Kubiszyn/Gary Borich*

CHAPTER 1

An Introduction to Educational Testing and Measurement

Chances are that some of your strongest childhood and adolescent memories include test taking in school. More recently, you probably remember taking a great number of tests in college. If your experiences are like those of most who come through our educational system, you probably have very strong or mixed feelings about tests and testing. Indeed, some of you may swear that you will never test your students when you become teachers. If so, you may feel that test results add little to the educational process and fail to reflect learning, or that testing may turn off students. Others may feel that tests are necessary and vital to the educational process. For you, they may represent irrefutable evidence as to whether learning has occurred. Rather than view tests as deterrents that turn off students, you may see them as motivators that stimulate students to study and provide them with feedback about their achievement.

Between these extremes may lie a third group, those who see tests as necessary to the educational process but who question the status and power often afforded tests and test scores. It is within this group that the authors of this text may best be classified. We see tests as tools that can effectively enhance the educational process, but only if they are well designed and properly used. Tools can be used and abused, and we are acutely aware that both poorly designed tools and well-designed tools in the hands of ill-trained or inexperienced users can be dangerous. It was in hopes of minimizing abuse of tests that we decided to write this text. We will discuss test use and test abuse more thoroughly later in the text, but for now let us restate our position:

1. Tests are necessary in order for teachers to determine whether students are learning.
2. To be potentially useful, tests must be well designed.
3. Even well-designed tests can be abused.

Thus, our goals for this text are to:

1. Sensitize you to current and future trends in education, which strongly suggest that test use is unlikely to decrease and may actually increase;

2. Teach you how to construct well-designed tests that yield valid and reliable measures of how well you teach and how well your students learn; and
3. Help you learn to use test results appropriately and effectively and to know the advantages and limitations of tests and test scores.

Let's now turn to some recent, current, and future trends in testing and measurement in the classroom so you will see why we chose these goals for our text.

RECENT TRENDS IN CLASSROOM MEASUREMENT

Beginning in the late 1960s, a fairly strong anti-test sentiment began to develop in our country. Over the next two decades many scholarly papers and popular articles questioned or denounced testing for a variety of reasons. Some decried tests as weapons willfully used to suppress minorities. To others, tests represented simplistic attempts to measure complex traits or attributes. Still others questioned whether the traits or attributes tested could be measured, or whether these traits or attributes even existed! From the classroom to the Supreme Court, testing and measurement practice came under close scrutiny. It seemed that tests were largely responsible for many of our society's ills.

Initially it looked as though the anti-test movement might succeed in abolishing testing in education—and there was professional and lay support for such a move. Today, it appears that this movement was part of a swinging pendulum. Calls for the abolition of testing and grading gradually subsided, and by the 1980s more tests than ever were being administered. Advocates and critics of testing now seem to have taken more moderate stances. Advocates, rather than stubbornly trying to convince critics that test scores represent scientific evidence that should be challenged only by those thoroughly steeped in test theory and construction, have begun instead to respond to the concerns voiced by the general public. The result has been that test advocates have come to be much more tempered and realistic in their attempts to convince others of the utility of test scores. Indeed, it is now common practice for measurement experts and instructors to emphasize that *all* test scores are at best *estimates* that are subject to greater or lesser margins of error. In addition, there has been a shift from the past emphasis on multiple-choice, true-false, and matching item formats for tests. More and more calls are being heard and heeded for tests that assess higher level thinking skills than are typically measured by such item formats. Extended essays, portfolios, and performance assessments (all discussed in detail later in this text) are increasingly being utilized in contemporary assessment efforts in addition to traditional multiple-choice items. Advocates argue strongly that, in spite of their shortcomings, these types of assessments, when not abused, often represent the most objective, valid, and reliable information that can be gathered about individuals.

On the other hand, while critics continue to raise important issues related to testing, they have come to realize that abolishing testing will not be a panacea for the problems of education and contemporary society. Even the most outspoken critics of testing would have to agree that in our everyday world decisions must be made. If tests were eliminated, these decisions would still be made, but would be based on nontest data that might be subjective, opinionated, and biased. For example, you may have dreaded taking the

Scholastic Assessment Test (SAT) during your junior or senior year in high school. You may have had some preconceived, stereotyped notions about the test. However, the SAT had no preconceived, stereotyped, or prejudiced notions about you! Advocates and many critics of testing would now agree that it is not the tests themselves that are at fault, but the people who abuse them. We hope you will be a much wiser, informed, and more careful user of test data after reading this text.

CURRENT AND FUTURE TRENDS IN EDUCATIONAL MEASUREMENT

With the passage of Public Law 94–142, all persons of school age with disabilities were guaranteed the right to a free and appropriate public education. A decade later Public Law 99–457 extended this right to preschool age children. Furthermore, this education was to be provided in "the least restrictive environment." This requirement led to the concept of "mainstreaming," or incorporating exceptional children into the regular classroom, which in turn was one of the ways the regular classroom teacher was impacted by this legislation. Special learners were no longer isolated in self-contained classrooms. More recently, the more active and encompassing term "full inclusion," described more fully in Chapter 20, has come to replace mainstreaming as the preferred way to provide special learners, even those with severe disabilities, with learning and social opportunities within the regular classroom environment.

The implications of PL 94–142, PL 99–457, and full inclusion on the testing and measurement skills of teachers will be discussed more thoroughly in Chapter 20. For now, suffice it to say that full implementation of the law will require more, rather than less, testing. Furthermore, testing will increasingly have to be modified to adapt to the needs of special learners. Testing of special learners within the regular classroom will be required to help determine whether a student is in need of special education, to adhere to each student's Individual Educational Plan (IEP), to evaluate each special learner's progress toward the goals established in the IEP, and to meet the law's accountability requirements. This may seem to place an additional burden on regular classroom teachers, and it does. Classroom teachers will now be required to spend increased time in the instruction and evaluation of special learners included in their classrooms. This issue will be addressed in Chapter 20. In Chapter 21 we will describe how the teacher may employ rapidly developing personal computer (PC) technology to minimize the added burden of full inclusion.

The public's demand for accountability also suggests an increase in test use in the future. Since education is supported by taxpayers, educators must be responsive to the demands of taxpayers. With declining test scores, grade inflation, and decreasing confidence in public education, school boards and the general public are becoming more and more concerned that they "get what they pay for." Yearly achievement test scores are one way that these accountability demands are currently being met. Most school districts already administer yearly standardized achievement tests to ascertain their district's position compared with other districts. Along with this movement, however, has come controversy.

Interpreting Tests: The Lake Wobegon Effect

In author Garrison Keiller's (1985) fictional town at Lake Wobegon, all students score above the national average. How can this happen? At first, it seems a statistical impossibility. If the average is the sum of all the test scores divided by the number of students who took the test, then about half must score below average. Right? . . . Right! Well, then, what is the explanation? We could simply remind you that the novel is fiction and let it go at that, but by now you know we would not do that. Here goes.

First, a standardized test uses a norms table to determine score rankings. The table is compiled from the scores of students who took the test years earlier when the test was being developed or revised. In reality, none of the scores of the students who take a standardized test after it is distributed will affect the norms table. Thus, in theory, it is possible for all students who take a test to score above average, or even above the ninetieth percentile, when they are very different from the group on which the test was normed. Indeed, as teachers and district administrators become more familiar with a particular test it becomes increasingly enticing to "teach to the test," a practice that should be condemned, but too frequently is condoned either directly or indirectly. This is most likely to occur when standardized test scores become the basis for teacher evaluations, teacher salaries, allocating tax dollars, or local real estate assessments, or when political rather than pedagogical considerations are allowed to become of paramount concern. The important point is that scoring above the average on a standardized test may not necessarily mean a student is doing well. It may mean the teacher has been teaching to the test rather than teaching the critical thinking, independent judgment, and decision-making skills that are more closely related to performance in the real world. This is one of the reasons why the performance assessment trends we describe in Chapter 9 have become so popular.

In 1991, the *New York Times* reported that the city's "much maligned public school students had scored above the national average, first on a standardized math test and, then, on an annual reading exam" (quoted in *Newsweek*, July 8, 1991). This seems like impressive information, and as *Newsweek* reported, New York City school officials were quick to take credit for the results. However, in June, 1991, the National Assessment of Educational Progress (NAEP) issued a report which indicated that half the nation's eighth-graders were performing at just above a fifth-grade level in math, with only 14 percent of the eighth-graders scoring at the seventh-grade level or above. New York City's results on this test were comparable to those of the entire nation.

How can two reports yield such alarmingly discrepant results? Which report is to be believed, if either? If neither is accurate, then what are we to believe? These questions are being asked increasingly today, and the coverage given to this issue by the media illustrates the concern and confusion that current standardized testing procedures generate.

Developments at the National Level

Where will all this lead? Perhaps it will lead to the creation of a single, national set of tests for the various academic subjects, as called for by former President Bush in April, 1991. In contrast, there currently exist literally dozens of standardized tests in various subjects that districts are free to choose from in order to evaluate their educational programs. If you were a district administrator, would you choose a test that would make your district look bad, one that would make it look good, or one that accurately reflects student achievement, regardless of how the district looks? If you make the correct choice, are you prepared to find a job elsewhere next year if your district doesn't look good? Perhaps the growing discontent with current standardized test procedures will lead to more rigorous monitoring of test administration and reporting by school districts, and penalties for districts or individuals teaching to the test. We should also expect national tests to contain fewer multiple-choice items and to be more heavily weighted with open-ended, essay, and performance items, which allow for more thorough evaluation of thought processes, but which also will be much more difficult to score. Movement in this direction has already occurred.

The National Assessment of Educational Progress (NAEP) is an independent and comprehensive assessment system used to evaluate progress toward the six National Educational Goals established by former president Bush and the nation's governors at an historic Education Summit in 1989 (see Table 1.1). The NAEP is employed by the National Education Goals Panel, an independent bi-partisan panel charged with reporting on progress towards the National Educational Goals. The 1992 NAEP included two-thirds multiple-choice items with the remaining one-third being open-ended questions. While performance assessment is not simply open-ended questions, the intent of the NAEP is to begin with open-ended items and move more toward authentic perfor-

TABLE 1.1
National Educational Goals (Goals 2000)

1. By the year 2000, all children in America will start school ready to learn.
2. By the year 2000, the high school graduation rate will increase to at least 90 percent.
3. By the year 2000, American students will leave grades four, eight, and twelve having demonstrated competency in challenging subject matter, including English, mathematics, science, history, and geography; and every school in America will ensure that all students learn to use their minds well, so they may be prepared for responsible citizenship, further learning, and productive employment in our modern economy.
4. By the year 2000, U.S. students will be first in the world in science and mathematics achievement.
5. By the year 2000, every adult American will be literate and will possess the knowledge and skills necessary to compete in a global economy and exercise the rights and responsibilities of citizenship.
6. By the year 2000, every school in America will be free of drugs and violence and will offer a disciplined environment conducive to learning.

* For more information contact the National Education Goals Panel; 1850 M Street, NW, Suite 270; Washington, D.C. 20036.

mance assessment items in the future. Indeed, the 1992 Resolutions of the National Education Goals Panel on the Future of the NAEP reported "NAEP should provide leadership in developing assessments that incorporate performance assessment tasks" (1992, p.1).

Issues related to these developments, both pro and con, will be covered in detail in this text. Particular attention is given to the recent trend towards performance or portfolio assessment, also referred to as "authentic" assessment in Chapter 9. While many regard this trend as "the answer" to complex measurement issues and problems, you will see that performance assessment, like other forms of assessment, is another tool that also may be used or abused.

Whatever the outcome, it is clear that testing will not go away. The real question is: How will tests of the future be constructed, administered, scored, and interpreted? Whatever the changes, you will be well prepared for them as a result of completing your measurement course and mastering and applying the principles provided in this text. This is because the principles you will learn in this text have withstood the test of time. Your knowledge of the theory and applications presented in this text will enable you to teach from a secure and stable knowledge base and respond to whatever new assessment practices develop in the future.

Are Teachers Accountable for Test Administration Errors?

Is what we just said stated too strongly? Are we alarmists? Are individual teachers rather than school districts ever really held accountable for errors in test administration and/or interpretation? "Students implicate Round Rock teachers" was a recent headline in an Austin, Texas daily newspaper (*Austin American-Statesman*, September 29, 1994). The article went on to state that students testified that three district teachers "pointed out answers, urged pupils to look over questions again, and made gestures to indicate whether answers were correct." The article later stated that the superintendent said "disciplinary action was taken against. . . (the teachers). . . but would not elaborate because it was a personnel matter." While their positions were not terminated and they were not sued, the teachers' names were published in the local paper, and they did incur whatever discipline the superintendent handed out.

One of the attorneys representing the teachers said the teachers were only guilty of "unintentional mistakes," which may be true, especially if they did not take a tests and measurements course during their pre-service training. He went on to state that these kinds of violations of standardized testing procedure were "minor, approaching trivial." As you will see in Chapter 18 such violations may not be trivial. They can be serious, since, as you will learn, they can undermine the very reason districts undergo the considerable expense and effort involved in administering standardized tests. This point was not lost on the district's coordinator of student assessment who said "everyone has been reminded in many ways that they need to be very, very careful in following test procedures and practicing good, professional ethics." This is just one example from one school district.

Competency Testing: Students and Teachers

The trend toward competency testing for high-school graduates is another indication of the increasing role of testing in education today (NAEP, 1987). The competency testing movement developed in response to the public pressure that was placed on educators to demonstrate that our schools were actually teaching the skills and competencies necessary to survive in contemporary society. This trend is closely tied to specific measurement practices that will be discussed in more detail later in the text.

Another current trend in our educational system is toward competency testing for teachers. In the early 1980s a number of states passed legislation requiring teachers to take paper-and-pencil tests measuring their teaching and subject matter competencies. Some states required only incoming teachers to pass such tests, while other states mandated that both established and new teachers qualify. The competency testing movement was spawned by demands from the general public that teachers and schools be held increasingly accountable for widespread deficiencies in basic skills of high-school graduates.

Much controversy still surrounds the use of these tests. No one wants to see poorly trained, incompetent, or ineffective teachers in the classroom. However, the development of a cost-effective, valid, and reliable paper-and-pencil method of measuring the complex set of skills and traits that go into being an effective classroom teacher remains elusive. Currently, such tests are not ordinarily used to prohibit a teacher from teaching, or to terminate an experienced teacher. Instead, they often are used to document minimum levels of competency in various content areas for career ladder enhancement (Holmes, 1986). Possibly, with the increasing emphasis on performance-based assessment of students (several types of which will be described in Chapter 9), reliable and valid standardized, performance-based assessments for teachers will be developed. If such procedures are developed, they may provide for a more valid assessment of teaching competency than paper-and-pencil measures alone.

Performance Testing

A small revolution is under way in how testing is defined and actually implemented. No longer do test scholars cling to the notion that accurate assessments of behavior can be derived only from formal tests, such as multiple-choice, true-false, matching, short answer, and essay examinations. Recently added to this list of testing formats are performance examinations that ask the learner to carry out the activities actually used in the real world (such as measuring the tensile strength of a building material, estimating the effects of pollutants on aquatic life, or designing circuitry for a microprocessor). Assessment techniques might include having students videotape portions of their own projects, conducting interviews with the student in order to probe for understanding and thinking abilities, or making a visual inspection of the product in order to determine whether it has the required characteristics for successful operation. These forms of assessment are intended to remove existing pressures to test solely for facts and skills, and to provide a stimulus to introduce more extended thinking and reasoning activities in the curriculum (Resnick & Resnick, 1989). We will have more to say about performance-based assessment in Chapter 9.

In summary, some of the anti-test sentiment that once seemed to pervade education has passed, but changes in measurement practice have occurred and will continue in the future. Educators are devising new forms of testing and, more than ever, understand that test data, fallible as they may be, are more objective when used properly than any of the alternatives. Educators realize that they must make decisions and that properly used test data can enhance their ability to make sound decisions. Increasing demands for accountability are also being made by the general public. By and large, the public tends to respect and accept test data to judge accountability. Remember, the taxpaying public, through school boards and voting behavior, controls educational programs and the purse strings of these programs. The accountability movement grew in reaction to the public's increasing disenchantment with education. As long as the public continues to be disenchanted with education, calls for accountability and testing will be heard. Since the public's disenchantment with current education is not likely to subside quickly, you are likely to see strong demands for accountability and testing in the future.

EFFECTS ON THE CLASSROOM TEACHER

The likelihood that test use will increase in the foreseeable future implies that the average teacher ought to have a good working knowledge of testing and measurement practice. However, teachers traditionally have not been well trained in test construction and use. Many teachers see no need for training in testing and measurement practice because they feel testing is supplemental to the instructional process. Indeed, many prospective teachers have been heard to say things like "If I need to know about tests I'll go to the counselor!" Perhaps the trend toward seemingly ever-increasing "specialists" in education has fostered or reinforced such beliefs. Nevertheless, regardless of how a teacher feels about the relationship of tests to instruction, regardless of whether a counselor—who is often scarce in elementary schools—is available, and regardless of whether test data were collected by "specialists," one fact stands out: *It is frequently the classroom teacher who must administer and then organize and interpret standardized and teacher-constructed test data to curious and sometimes hostile parents and other concerned parties.* Figure 1.1 illustrates many sources of pressure influencing a teacher's use of tests. It is intended to convince you of the seriousness with which you should consider your knowledge or lack of knowledge of testing and measurement.

After years of consulting and teaching experience in the public schools, we have concluded that discussing test results with parents is frequently an anxiety provoking experience for teachers. Lacking appropriate training, some teachers are tempted to try to avoid interpretation entirely by dismissing test data as "unimportant" or "inaccurate," not realizing that such data are often very important and thought to be quite accurate by parents. The following dialogue occurred when one of the authors had a conference with his son's second-grade teacher in September.

TEACHER: Hi, I'm Jeff's second-grade teacher. What can I do for you so early in the year?

AUTHOR: Jeff says he's in the low reading group, and I am curious about why he is. Could you explain that to me?

FIGURE 1.1
Some of the Many Forces Influencing the Teacher's Use of Tests.

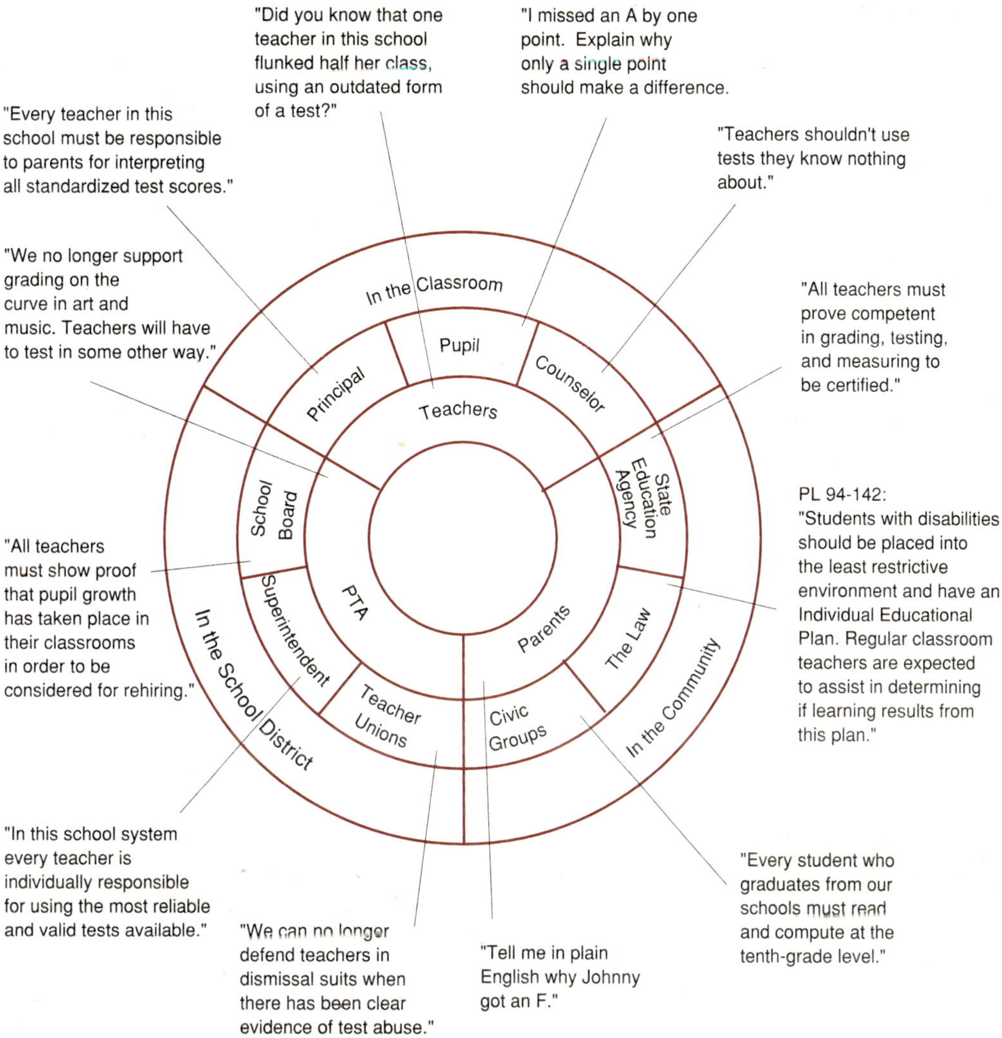

TEACHER: Oh, don't worry—we don't label kids at this school. I think that would be a terrible injustice.

AUTHOR: I see, but could you explain why Jeff is in the "Walkers" instead of the "Runners"?

TEACHER: Oh, those are just names, that's all.

AUTHOR: Are both groups at the same level in reading?

TEACHER: They're both at the first-grade level, yes.

AUTHOR: I'm beginning to catch on. Are they reading in the same-level books in the same reading series?

TEACHER: Of course not! Some children are further along than others—that's all—but the kids don't know.

AUTHOR: Let me guess; the "Runners" are further ahead?

TEACHER: Yes, they're in book 9.

AUTHOR: And the "Walkers" are in . . .

TEACHER Book 5. But they are grouped for instructional purposes—I have twenty-five students, you know!

AUTHOR I'm confused. Jeff's reading scores on the California Achievement Test last May were above the ninetieth percentile.

TEACHER: (*chuckles to herself*) I can understand your confusion. Those test scores are so hard to understand. Why, even we professionals can't understand them.

AUTHOR: A score at the ninetieth percentile means the score was higher than the scores of 90 percent of the students who took the test all across the country.

TEACHER: Oh, really? It is very complicated. As I said, even professional educators don't understand testing.

AUTHOR: Some do, Mrs. B.

Had the teacher understood the data she was dealing with, an obviously embarrassing situation might have been avoided. Similar experiences are unfortunately experienced by many classroom teachers.

Another often overheard statement is "I don't even have time to teach; how can I learn about test construction and interpretation?" We are well aware that teachers and most other professionals have become increasingly burdened by paperwork and bureaucratic requirements. However, the trends discussed earlier point toward comparable or increased levels of test use in the future. And the public will be keeping an increasingly watchful eye on the users of these data! Thus, it appears that more than ever, teachers of the future will need adequate training in testing and measurement practice. Ignoring or denying the need for proper training in this area will make neither this need nor the watchful eye of the public go away. Given the time constraints under which the average teacher must operate, it appears wiser to seek such training now, before you begin teaching. The alternative may be to attend what might seem like an endless series of workshops later on, while you also have your class of students and all the attendant responsibilities.

In short, it looks like tomorrow's teachers will be increasingly exposed to testing and test data. With increasing public pressure for accountability, it does not appear likely that the average teacher will be able to get ahead or even get by without a good working knowledge of tests and measurement practice. With practicing teachers getting more and more involved with paperwork, prospective teachers should acquire this working knowledge before beginning to teach. We sincerely hope that this text will help you acquire the knowledge and the skills necessary to construct good tests and to use test data knowledgeably and professionally. Hopefully, unlike the three teachers who unwittingly prompted their students during a test, you can avoid the embarrassment of seeing your name in the paper.

ABOUT THE TEXT

When you talk to teachers who have completed courses in testing and measurement, you often find that they are somewhat less than inspired by their courses. In fact, talking with such veterans may have made you a little reluctant to register for this course. Nevertheless, here you are! The authors have taught testing and measurement courses for many years and, quite frankly, are accustomed to hearing the course content described as "dry, but necessary." Too many times, however, we have heard "The course is dry, but necessary—I think!" Since a fair amount of straightforward, technical information is presented, we could understand calling a course in testing and measurement "dry." Indeed, this is almost how we feel about some of the content when we teach it! Thus, hearing "dry, but necessary" from students did little more than confirm our own feelings. But, to hear "dry, but necessary—I think!" made us think and led us to evaluate our courses to determine the cause for this uncertainty. Remember, we stated earlier that we feel knowledge of tests and measurement practice is vital to today's teacher—yet somehow this was not coming across to some of our students.

We considered many different potential problems and each of us came to the same conclusion: Although each of us had used several different textbooks, we were never really satisfied with them. There are several introductory testing and measurement texts available, but each seemed to be lacking in one major respect. They all did a fine job of relating information and explaining concepts, but seemed to fall short in *applying these facts and concepts to real-world situations*. We found that we were supplementing the texts with anecdotes and suggestions based on our own experiences in the public schools. However, it still appeared that many prospective teachers had difficulty relating the real-world examples to the facts and concepts detailed in the text. Our conclusion was that what is needed is a text that emphasizes the relationship of the necessary facts and concepts to real-world situations. With this aim in mind we wrote this text. Only you can tell whether we have succeeded. We invite your comments and suggestions.

WHAT IF YOU'RE "NO GOOD IN MATH"?

Since tests yield numerical scores and test theory is based on statistical principles, it is no surprise that many who feel weak in math have great reservations about being able to succeed in a course in tests and measurements. If you fall into this category, rest assured that many of your fears are groundless or exaggerated. In our experience, fewer than 1 percent of the students who have completed the tests and measurements courses we have taught have done poorly solely because of a "weak" math background.

Naturally, knowledge of the basic mathematical functions—addition, subtraction, multiplication, and division—is a necessity. Mix these with fractions, decimals, and a sprinkling of algebra and you are all set! If you are still doubtful, work your way through the review of math skills provided in Appendix A. This review and accompanying self-check test should also prove useful to you if you feel a little "rusty" in math—a fairly common experience in this age of electronic calculators and computers. All operations necessary to complete the calculations in this text are covered in this review. We think you will agree that our review of math skills in Appendix A will be all that's needed.

SUMMARY

In this chapter we have introduced you to issues related to educational testing and measurement and have described the orientation of the text. Its major points are:

1. Test use is more likely to increase than decrease in the foreseeable future.
2. The public has begun clamoring for evidence that schools and teachers are in fact educating children and relies on test scores for such evidence.
3. Since test use is likely to increase, the burden of interpreting test results likely will fall more and more on the classroom teacher.
4. Recently, the trend in testing has been away from the traditional multiple-choice type test and toward more open-ended, performance-based tests.
5. The classroom teacher who is trained in educational testing procedures will be able to use test results more efficiently and effectively and will be less likely to abuse test results.
6. This text is oriented toward the application of measurement principles to real-world situations.

For Discussion

1. Thinking back to your own high-school days, what were some of the factors that "turned you off" about tests?
2. Were these factors connected with the tests themselves, or were they the result of how the tests were used?
3. Point out some societal trends (for example, changing demographics, increased population, or increasing adult literacy) occurring in your city, state, or region that will likely make testing and measurement in our schools more complicated and important in the future.

4. Imagine the modern American high school 20 years from now. Identify several ways in which testing and measurement will have changed since the time you were attending high school.

5. You notice that one student is "different" from the rest of the class. The student is a behavior problem, and you feel he or she needs special attention. You say so to your principal, expecting the principal to transfer the student to a special class. However, the principal says, "We have to collect the data first—get started." What kind of data do you believe the principal would want you to collect? How likely is it that the child will actually be taken out of your class?

6. Review the National Education Goals. Which of these have the greatest impact on measurement practice? Why?

CHAPTER 2

The Purpose of Testing

In the classroom, decisions are constantly being made. As a teacher you may decide:

John, Don, Marie, and Jeri are ready to advance to level 7 in reading, but Chris and Linda are not.

Mark receives an A; Mary receives a C.

Ed has difficulty discriminating between long and short vowel sounds.

My teaching method is not effective for this group of students.

Arthur is a social isolate.

Mike's attitude toward school has improved.

Mary should be moved to a higher reading group.

Mrs. Morrison's class is better at math concepts than my class.

Donna is a "slow learner."

On what basis do teachers make decisions such as these? In some cases the teacher relies solely on personal judgment. In other cases the teacher relies solely on measurement data. In still other cases the teacher combines measurement data with judgment or subjective data. Which approach is best?

Anti-test advocates suggest that testing should be done away with. Unfortunately, decisions will still have to be made. Teachers, as human beings, are subject to "good and bad days," biases, student and parent pressures, faulty perceptions, and a variety of other influences. In other words, relying solely on a teacher's judgment means relying on a subjective decision-making process. Naturally, no teacher would intentionally make a "wrong" decision about a student. However, all of us make mistakes.

Tests represent an attempt to provide objective data that can be used with subjective impressions to make better, more defensible decisions. This is the purpose of testing, or *why* we test. Tests are not subject to the ups and downs or other influences that affect teachers. And subjective impressions can often place in perspective important aspects of a decision-making problem for which no objective data exist. Thus, it seems likely that a combination of subjective judgments and objective data will result in more appropriate rather than less appropriate decisions. Reliance on measurement data alone can even prove to be detrimental to decision making. Although such data are objective, we must remember that they are only *estimates* of a student's behavior. Test data are never 100 percent accurate!

In summary, we test to provide objective information, which we combine with our subjective, commonsense impressions to make better educational decisions. However, suggesting that better educational decisions are made by combining objective measurement data and subjective impressions assumes that:

measurement data are valid;

the teacher or individual interpreting such data understands the uses and limitations of such data.

Unfortunately, too often one or both of these assumptions are violated in the decision-making process. Obviously, when this happens, the resultant educational decisions may be invalid.

TESTING, ACCOUNTABILITY, AND THE CLASSROOM TEACHER

It is no longer surprising to say that the American public has become disenchanted with education. Reduced school budgets, defeated bond issues, and the elimination of special programs are all too common occurrences on today's educational scene. The reasons for this disenchantment are many and complex, but at least some can be traced to poor decision making in our schools—decision making not just at the classroom level, but at the grade, school, district, and national levels as well. Nevertheless, the most frequently made decisions are the everyday decisions of the classroom teacher, which also form the cornerstone for other decisions at higher levels of the educational structure. If the cornerstone is weak, the structure itself cannot be sound.

At the classroom level, the extent to which unsound educational decision making occurs is not yet known. However, the everyday decisions of classroom teachers are coming under closer and closer scrutiny. Classroom teachers are increasingly being asked questions like:

PARENT: On what grounds was Jane moved to the slower reading group?

PRINCIPAL: What method are you using to measure student achievement in social studies?

COUNSELOR: How is it that you've determined Tom is a behavior problem?

Individuals asking such questions are asking teachers for the data on which these decisions were based. With mounting accountability pressures it is no longer sufficient to rely solely on judgment to make such decisions. Indeed, such decisions should never be made based on judgments alone.

What does the teacher do? Give up? Complain? Yearn for the "good old days"? We hope not! Yet, the answers to these and many other questions need to be provided if education is to improve. In many cases, it will be classroom teachers who will be asked to answer these questions. It seems likely that those who can understand and respond to such questions will swim in the educational sea, while those who cannot will sink. In other words, a good working knowledge and understanding of testing and measurement is no longer just a useful skill in education, but one that is necessary for survival. The successful teacher of tomorrow not only will have to report test data to parents, principals, counselors, academic review committees, and even the courts, but will have to interpret test data and be fully aware of the uses and limitations of such data. One of the first steps toward acquiring the ability to interpret test data is to understand the different types of educational decisions that are made from measurement data.

Types of Educational Decisions

Measurement data enter into decisions at all levels of education, from those made by the individual classroom teacher to those made by the State Commissioner of Education. There are several ways of categorizing these decisions. We have found the following classification approach, suggested by Thorndike, Cunningham, Thorndike, and Hagen (1991), useful for understanding the various types of decisions that can be made in schools. The categories range from specific everyday in-class decision making to much less frequent administrative decisions. The categories of decisions discussed below are instructional, grading, diagnostic, selection, placement, counseling and guidance, program or curriculum, and administrative policy.

INSTRUCTIONAL DECISIONS. Instructional decisions are the nuts-and-bolts types of decisions made by all classroom teachers. In fact, these are the most frequently made decisions in education. Examples of such decisions include deciding to:

spend more time in math class on addition with regrouping

skip the review you planned before the test

stick to your instructional plan

Since educational decisions at lower levels have a way of affecting decisions at higher levels, it is important that these types of decisions be sound ones. Deciding more time should be spent on addition with regrouping when it doesn't need to be wastes valuable instructional time and may have very noticeable effects on classroom management. Students may get turned off, tune you out, or act up. And such problems may not be confined to the classroom. A student's home life, interactions with peers, and even lifelong ambitions can be affected by these seemingly small misjudgments at the classroom level.

You may expect similar detrimental effects when you present material too quickly. Moving too quickly almost invariably results in skill deficiencies in some students. You can be sure that many of the Johnnys and Janes who can't read were unable to master various reading skills in school because their teachers moved through the curricula too quickly for them to acquire the needed skills.

It seems reasonable to suggest that instructional decisions will become part of the accountability picture in the near future. If so, classroom teachers will have to do more than say they "felt" it was time to move ahead in the curriculum or that they had "always kept the same schedule." Remember, your judgments or impressions are fallible and the students you teach may not be aware of your "schedule."

GRADING DECISIONS. Educational decisions based on grades are also made by the classroom teacher, but much less frequently than instructional decisions. Grades are usually assigned about every six weeks, and the teacher often considers test scores and other data in making decisions about who gets A's, B's, and so on. If test data are used, naturally it is important that such data be acquired from appropriate tests, including performance assessments, which will be described in detail in Chapter 9. As with instructional decisions, teacher-made tests are usually the most appropriate for grading decisions.

Other factors, such as attendance, ability, attitude, behavior, and effort, are sometimes graded also. A common mistake is to combine one or more of these with achievement data to decide on grades. Although each of these factors represents an area of legitimate concern to classroom teachers, and although assigning grades for one or more of these factors is perfectly acceptable, these grades should be kept separate from grades for achievement. These issues will be discussed at length in Chapter 10. Methods used to measure nonachievement factors will be presented in Chapter 11.

Grade inflation—or the tendency for teachers to assign higher grades today than in the past for the same level of performance—has become a matter of considerable public concern. Consequently, it will be no surprise if grading decisions and policies come under increasing public scrutiny and become subject to accountability procedures as well. For most students, grading decisions are probably the most influential decisions made about them during their school years. All students are familiar with the effects grades have on them, their peers, and their parents. The teacher who adheres to an acceptable grading policy, who uses data obtained through appropriate measurement instruments, and who knows the uses and limitations of such data will be the teacher who makes sound grading decisions, most likely will be fair in assigning grades, and most likely will be able to defend the grades that are assigned.

DIAGNOSTIC DECISIONS. Diagnostic decisions are those made about a student's strengths and weaknesses and the reason or reasons for them. For example, you may know Martha is having trouble in reading. When you determine *why* she is having trouble you are making a diagnostic decision. Such decisions should be based on test data. In the past, diagnostic decisions often have been delegated to specialists. However, with the passage of PL 94–142 and the recent movement toward full inclusion of even severely challenged special learners in the regular classroom, the regular classroom teacher can increasingly be expected to make diagnostic decisions. We will discuss the role of the regular classroom teacher in providing test data and in making decisions for the challenged child in Chapter 20, but for now it should be obvious that the teacher who uses appropriate tests and properly interprets the data they yield will make better diagnostic decisions.

However, the regular classroom teacher also makes diagnostic decisions about regular learners, which are usually based on a teacher-made test. For example, a teacher may notice in test results that Dick can successfully subtract four-digit numbers from four-digit numbers, but not if carrying is involved. Given this information, the teacher decides that Dick does not fully understand the carrying process. The teacher has made a diagnostic decision based on information yielded by an informal, teacher-made test.

The three types of decisions listed above—instructional, grading, and diagnostic—are types of educational decisions every classroom teacher must make. The five remaining types of decisions are made by specialists, administrators, or committees composed of teachers, specialists, and administrators. Their decisions are typically based on standardized rather than teacher-made tests. Although teachers are not directly involved in the decisions based on standardized test data, it is a fact that teachers are often called upon to interpret the results of standardized tests for parents and students since the tests are part of a student's cumulative work record. Standardized testing will be discussed in Chapters 18 and 19. For now, let's get familiar with the types of decisions in which standardized tests play a role.

SELECTION DECISIONS. Selection decisions involve test data used in part for accepting or rejecting applicants for admission into a group, program, or institution. The SAT that you probably took before being admitted to college and the Graduate Record Examination (GRE) that you will be required to take if you intend to go to graduate school are examples of standardized tests that are used to help make selection decisions. At the elementary- and secondary-school level, teachers are often asked to assist with the testing of pupils for selection into remedial programs that are designed to improve educational opportunities for economically disadvantaged pupils.

PLACEMENT DECISIONS. Placement decisions are made after an individual has been accepted into a program. They involve determining where in a program someone is best suited to begin work. For example, you may have had to take an English test prior to first-year college registration to determine whether you were ready for first-year college English courses, needed remedial work, or were ready for intermediate or advanced courses. Standardized achievement test data are often used in elementary and secondary schools for placing students in courses that are at their current level of functioning.

COUNSELING AND GUIDANCE DECISIONS. Counseling and guidance decisions involve the use of test data to help recommend programs of study that are likely to be appropriate for a student. For example, in your junior or senior year in high school you probably took the Differential Aptitude Test (DAT) or some similar aptitude test battery. Partly on the basis of your scores, your guidance counselor may have recommended that you consider one or more career paths or apply to a particular set of colleges.

PROGRAM OR CURRICULUM DECISIONS. Program or curriculum decisions are usually made at the school-district level after an evaluation study comparing two or more programs has been completed. Your district's decision to abandon a traditional math program in favor of a "new math" program is an example of a program or curriculum decision. Teachers are often required to participate in these studies and even to help collect test data for them.

ADMINISTRATIVE POLICY DECISIONS. Administrative policy decisions may be made at the school-district, state, or national level. Based at least in part on measurement data, these decisions may determine the amount of money to be channeled into a school or district, whether a school or district is entitled to special funding, or what needs to be done to improve a school, district, or the nation's achievement scores.

Thus far we have considered the purposes of testing, or why we test. Next, let's consider two other aspects of educational measurement: how we measure and what we measure.

A Pinch of Salt

Jean-Pierre, the master French chef, was watching Marcel, who was Jean-Pierre's best student, do a flawless job of preparing the master's hollandaise sauce. Suddenly, Jean-Pierre began pummeling Marcel with his fists. "Fool!" he shouted. "I said a pinch of salt, not a pound!" Jean-Pierre was furious. He threatened to pour the sauce over Marcel's head, but before he could, Marcel indignantly emptied the whole salt container into the pot.

"There, you old goat, I only added a pinch to begin with, but now there is a pound of salt in the sauce—and I'm going to make you eat it!"

Startled by his student's response, Jean-Pierre regained his composure. "All right, all right. So you didn't add a pound, but you certainly added more than a pinch!"

Still upset, Marcel shouted, "Are you senile? You were watching me all the time and you saw me add only one pinch!" Marcel pressed his right thumb and index finger together an inch from the master's nose to emphasize his point.

"Aha! You see! There you have it!" Jean-Pierre said elatedly. "That is not the way to measure a pinch. Only the tips of the thumb and index finger make contact when you measure a pinch!"

Marcel looked at the difference between his idea of a "pinch" of salt and the master's. Indeed, there was quite a difference. Marcel's finger and thumb made contact not just at the fingertips, but all the way down to the knuckle. At Jean-Pierre's request, they both deposited a "pinch" of salt on the table. Marcel's pinch contained four or five times as much salt as Jean-Pierre's.

Who is correct? Is Marcel's pinch too much? Is Jean-Pierre's pinch too little? Whose method would you use to measure a pinch of salt? Perhaps relying on an established standard will help. *Webster's New Collegiate Dictionary* defines a pinch this way: "As much as may be taken between the finger and the thumb." If *Webster's* is our standard of comparison, we may conclude that both Jean-Pierre and Marcel are correct. Yet, we see that Marcel's pinch contains a lot more salt than Jean-Pierre's. It seems we have a problem. Until Marcel and Jean-Pierre decide on who is correct and adopt a more specific or standard definition of a "pinch," they may never resolve their argument. Furthermore, if we were to try to match the recipes they develop for their culinary masterpieces, we might never succeed unless we know which measuring method to use.

This measurement problem resulted from the lack of a clear, unambiguous method of measurement. Who is to say Jean-Pierre's method is better than Marcel's or vice versa? In Jean-Pierre's eyes, his method is correct and Marcel's is not. In Marcel's eyes, his method is correct and Jean-Pierre's is not. According to *Webster's*, both are correct. A clear and unambiguous method of measuring a "pinch" would resolve the problem. It seems reasonable to suggest that any time measurement procedures—that is, *how* we measure—are somewhat subjective and lack specificity, similar interpretive problems may arise.

"Pinching" in the Classroom

Mr. Walsh assigns his history grades based entirely on his monthly tests and a comprehensive final examination. He takes attendance, comments on homework assignments, encourages classroom participation, and tries to help his students develop positive attitudes toward history, but none of these is considered in assigning grades. Mr. Carter, another history teacher, assigns grades in the following manner:

Monthly tests	20%
Comprehensive final	20%
Homework	10%
Attendance	20%
Class participation	15%
Attitude	15%

Both teachers assign roughly the same numbers of A's, B's, C's, D's, and F's each semester. Does an A in Mr. Walsh's class mean the same thing as an A in Mr. Carter's class? Obviously, Mr. Walsh "pinches" more heavily when it comes to test data than does Mr. Carter (100% versus 40%). On the other hand, Mr. Carter "pinches" more heavily on attendance and participation in assigning grades than does Mr. Walsh (35% versus 0%).

Which method is correct? In interpreting grades earned in each class, would you say that students who earn A's in either class are likely to do equally well on history tests constructed by a third teacher? Should Mr. Walsh "pinch," that is, assign grades, more like Mr. Carter, or should Mr. Carter assign grades more like Mr. Walsh? Obviously, there are no easy answers to these questions. The differences in how Jean-Pierre and Marcel measure a "pinch" of salt result from the lack of a clear, unambiguous definition of a "pinch." Similarly, the differences in how Mr. Walsh and Mr. Carter measure learning in history result from the lack of a clear, unambiguous definition of what constitutes a grade. As a result, their grades represent somewhat different aspects of their student's performance. The way they "pinch" or how they measure differs.

For Jean-Pierre and Marcel, there is a relatively easy way out of the disagreement. Only their method of measurement or how they measure is in question, not what they are measuring. It would be easy to develop a small container, a common standard, that could then be used to uniformly measure "pinches" of salt. In the classroom, the task is more difficult for Mr. Walsh and Mr. Carter. What is in question is not only their measurement method, or *how* they weigh components of a grade, but what they are measuring.

Much of what we measure or attempt to measure in the classroom is not clearly defined. For example, think of how many different ways you have heard *learning*, *intelligence*, or *adjustment* defined. Yet, we constantly attempt to assess or measure these traits. Furthermore, the methods we use to measure these often ill-defined traits are not very precise. But even good methods cannot accurately measure ill-defined or undefined traits.

Only when both what to measure and how to measure have been considered, specified, and clearly defined can we hope to eliminate the problems involved in measuring and interpreting classroom information. The task is formidable. We cannot hope to solve it entirely, but we can minimize the subjectivity, the inaccuracy, and the more common interpretative errors often inherent in classroom measurement. Achieving these goals will go far toward helping us "pinch" properly. Sound measurement practice will benefit you professionally. Moreover, it will benefit most those unwitting and captive receptors of measurement practice, your students.

The examples presented are intended to alert you to two general problems encountered in classroom measurement:

1. Defining what it is that you want to measure, and
2. Determining how to measure whatever it is that you are measuring.

WHAT TO MEASURE

Defining what to measure may, at first glance, not appear like much of a problem, but consider the following example:

> Mrs. Norton taught first-year math in a small private high school comprised of high-achieving students. She prided herself on her tests, which stressed the ability to apply math concepts to real-life situations. She did this by constructing fairly elaborate word problems. When she moved to another part of the state, she went to work in an inner-city high school teaching an introductory math skills course. Realizing that her new students were not nearly as "sharp" as her private-school students, she "toned down" her tests by substituting simpler computations in her word problems. Even with this substitution, 29 of her 31 students failed this "easier" test. Dejected, she substituted even simpler computations into her next test, only to have 30 out of 31 fail. She concluded that her students "totally lack even basic math skills," and applied for a transfer.

Think about these questions:

Do you agree with Mrs. Norton's conclusion? If so, why? If not, why not?

Are there any possible alternative conclusions?

What might she have done differently?

We disagree with Mrs. Norton. While it may be that some of her students lack or are weak in basic math skills, there seems to be little conclusive evidence that all, or even most, lack these skills. There may be another explanation for her students' poor performance.

Her tests were originally designed to measure the ability of her high-achieving private-school students to *apply* their skills to real-life situations. This is what she wanted to measure.

In her public-school skills class, *what* Mrs. Norton wanted to measure was a bit different. What she wanted to measure was not the ability to *apply* skills (at least not at first) but whether the skills were ever acquired. How she measured must also be considered. Her tests consisted of fairly elaborate word problems. They may have been tests of reading ability as much as tests of math applications. Their reading level may have been appropriate for her "bright" students but too advanced for her new students. Since her tests measured skill application and reading ability rather than skill acquisition, how Mrs. Norton measured also was not appropriate. Assuming you are convinced it is important to define *what* you are measuring, let's look in more detail at what we mean by determining *how* to measure.

HOW TO MEASURE

Mrs. Norton got into trouble mainly because she wasn't sure what she was measuring. At least by giving a written test she had the right idea about one aspect of how to measure basic math skills . . . or did she? How else could basic math skills be measured? An oral test, you say? But in a class of 31 students? Any other ideas? What about a questionnaire without any math problems, just questions about math skills to which students respond yes or no to indicate whether they *believe* they have acquired a certain skill? How about simply observing your students in the process of completing a math problem? Or how about requiring your students to complete a practical project requiring math skills?

The techniques mentioned above are all possible measurement methods, some for measuring basic math skills, others for measuring attitudes toward math. Questionnaires, oral responses, observation, and projects are common methods of measurement. These and a variety of performance assessment techniques, including portfolios, will be discussed later in this text. For now, simply be aware that there are alternatives to written tests and that how we measure is often determined by what we measure. Let's return to Mrs. Norton and the most commonly used form of measurement, the written test.

Written Tests

The test Mrs. Norton used was heavily verbal, which suggests that it relied almost exclusively on words to ask questions. Although the answers to her questions may have been numerical, the questions themselves were word problems. While there is probably no better way to measure basic math skills than through a written test, was the written test that Mrs. Norton used the best type of written test? We would say no and suggest that her test should have looked more like the following instead of consisting of only word problems:

(1) $\begin{array}{r} 1431 \\ +\ 467 \\ \hline \end{array}$ (2) $\begin{array}{r} 798 \\ -\ 581 \\ \hline \end{array}$ (3) $\begin{array}{r} 125 \\ \times\ 7 \\ \hline \end{array}$ (4) $21 \div 11 =$

The advantages of a basic math skills test with items similar in format to those above include the following:

They do not rely on reading ability.

Basic skills are measured directly.

More items can be included in the same amount of test time.

All these points are important. The first two help ensure that the test measures what it is supposed to measure. The last improves the test's reliability, or the consistency of the scores it yields over time. Furthermore, inspecting a student's written work on such a test can help you diagnose errors in the process used by students to arrive at an answer.

So, you see, there can be different types of written tests. The point of our discussion about Mrs. Norton is simply that *how* you measure must always match *what* you measure. Whether you give word problems, use number formats, or provide real-world examples depends on whether you are measuring problem-solving ability, knowledge of facts or processes, application, and so on. Table 2.1 defines some common types of written tests.

In this section we have considered the importance of knowing what we want to measure and how we want to measure. We also saw that determining what and how may not be as simple as it appears. However, both considerations are vitally important in classroom measurement, since failing to be clear about them is likely to result in invalid measurement.

TABLE 2.1
Types of Written Tests

Type of Written Test	*Description*
Verbal	Emphasizes reading, writing, or speaking. Most tests in education are verbal tests.
Nonverbal	Does *not* require reading, writing, or speaking ability. Tests composed of numerals or drawings are examples.
Objective	Refers to the scoring of tests. When two or more scorers can easily agree on whether an answer is correct or incorrect, the test is an objective one. True-false, multiple-choice, and matching tests are the best examples.
Subjective	Also refers to scoring. When it is difficult for two scorers to agree on whether an item is correct or incorrect, the test is a subjective one. Essay tests are examples.
Teacher-made	Tests constructed entirely by teachers for use in the teachers' classrooms.
Standardized	Tests constructed by measurement experts over a period of years. They are designed to measure broad, national objectives, and have a uniform set of instructions that are adhered to during each administration. Most also have tables of norms, to which a student's performance may be compared to determine where the student stands in relation to a national sample of students at the same grade or age level.
Power	Tests with liberal time limits that allow each student to attempt each item. Items tend to be difficult.
Speed	Tests with time limits so strict that no one is expected to complete all items. Items tend to be easy.

SUMMARY

This chapter has introduced you to *why* we test, *what* we test, and *how* we test. Its major points are:

1. The purpose of testing is to collect objective information that may be used in conjunction with subjective information to make better educational decisions.
2. In our age of increasing demands for accountability, it has become imperative that teachers be able to understand and demonstrate the role that objective test data can play in educational decision making.
3. Classroom teachers are responsible for the bulk of educational decision making, such as everyday instructional decisions, grading decisions, and diagnostic decisions. Such decisions are often based, or ought to be based, on information obtained from teacher-made tests.
4. Other, less frequent kinds of educational decisions are usually made by administrators or specialists other than the classroom teacher. These include decisions about selection, placement, counseling and guidance, programs and curriculum, and administration. Such decisions are usually based on information obtained from standardized tests.
5. Measurement problems may be expected any time testing procedures lack definition or specificity, or when we fail to specify clearly the trait we are measuring.
6. Specifying or defining *what* we want to measure often determines *how* the trait should be measured.

For Discussion

1. Identify some of the ways we measure "pinches" of achievement, intelligence, and classroom conduct.
2. Make a list of all the different kinds of behaviors you will need to measure, formally or informally, during your first month of teaching. Identify two different ways of measuring each of these behaviors.
3. List some of the instructional, grading, and diagnostic decisions you will be expected to make during your first month of teaching. Identify which category each decision represents.
4. Using Mrs. Norton's problem as a guide, make up some examples in your own subject area that illustrate mismatches between what is being tested and how it is being tested.

CHAPTER 3

Norm-Referenced and Criterion-Referenced Tests

In Chapter 2 we stated that the purpose of testing is to provide objective data that can be used along with subjective impressions to make better educational decisions. In this chapter we will discuss the two main types of tests used to make educational decisions and the different types of information that each test yields.

DEFINING NORM-REFERENCED AND CRITERION-REFERENCED TESTS

One type of information tells us where a student stands compared to other students. In other words, certain kinds of test data help us determine a student's "place" or "rank." This is accomplished by comparing the student's performance to a norm or average of performances by other, similar students. A test that yields this kind of information is called a *norm-referenced test* (NRT) because the information it conveys refers to the performance of a large sample of pupils representative of those we are testing. Such information is useful *only* for certain types of decisions, which we will discuss later in this chapter.

A second type of information provided by tests tells us about a student's level of proficiency in or mastery of some skill or set of skills. This is accomplished by comparing a student's performance to a standard of mastery called a *criterion*. A test that yields this kind of information is called a *criterion-referenced test* (CRT) because the information it conveys refers to a comparison with a criterion or absolute standard. Such information helps us decide whether a student needs more or less work on some skill or set of skills. It says nothing about the student's place or rank compared to other students and, hence, it too is useful *only* for certain types of decisions. Figure 3.1 illustrates the relationship of NRT's and CRT's to the purpose of testing.

As you may have guessed, it is important to identify the type of information you need *before* you administer a test. If you fail to do so, you may have test data but be unable to use the data to make necessary decisions. Unfortunately, teachers often know little more about a student after testing than they did before testing. In our technically oriented society, test scores have sometimes become ends in themselves while the meaning of the test scores has tended to be ignored. With methods of measurement sometimes comes the illu-

FIGURE 3.1
Relationships Among the Purpose of Testing, Information Desired, and the Type of Test Required

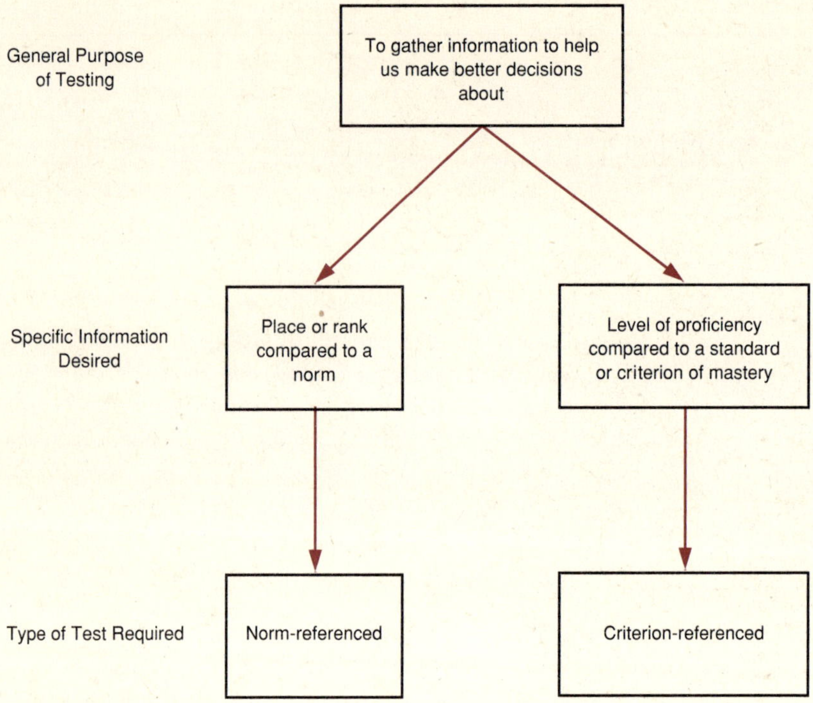

sion that the scores themselves are what is important, not the judgment criteria by which the scores must be interpreted and made meaningful for decision making. In such cases teachers, parents, and others may be quick to denounce or blame the test, often suggesting that such test abuse "proves" that test data are useless. In reality, all it indicates is that the teacher selecting the test either failed to identify the specific information desired *before* administering the test or failed to carefully match the test to this purpose. A similar situation can occur when existing test data are used or interpreted inappropriately. Consider the following:

Pat, the counselor, was checking her records when she heard a knock at the door. It was Mary, the sixth-grade teacher.

PAT: Come in. What can I do for you?

MARY: I just stopped by to get the latest test information you have on Danny. As you know, he's going to be in my class this year after being in remedial classes for the last five years. Mrs. French, his teacher last year, said you have all the test information on him.

PAT: Well, I'd be glad to help out. In fact, I was just reviewing his folder.

MARY: Great! Can I see it?

PAT: Well, his Math Cluster score on the Woodcock-Johnson is at the sixth percentile, and his Reading Cluster is at the first percentile. Good luck with him.

MARY: Boy, he sure is low. I guess that's why he's been in the remedial classroom for so long.

PAT: You've got it!

MARY: Okay. Well, really that's about what I was expecting. Now what about his skill levels?

PAT: What do you mean?

MARY: You know, his academic skill levels.

PAT: Oh, his grade levels! Now let's see, his math grade equivalent is 2.6, and his reading grade equivalent is even lower, 1.7.

MARY: Well . . . that's not really what I need to know. I know he's way below grade level, but I'm wondering about his skills—specific skills, that is. You know, like what words he can read, what phonetic skills he has, whether he can subtract two-digit numbers with regrouping . . . things like that.

PAT: (*becoming a bit irritated*) Mary, what more do you need than what I've given you? Don't you know how to interpret these scores? Perhaps you should have taken a tests and measurements course in college.

MARY: (*beginning to get frustrated*) Pat, I *have* taken a tests and measurements course and I do know what those scores mean, but they only compare Danny to other students. I'm not interested in that. I want to know what he can and can't do, so I can begin teaching him at the proper skill level.

PAT: (*shaking her head*) Look, he's at a first-grade level in reading and second-grade level in math. Isn't that enough?

MARY: But what level of mastery has he demonstrated?

PAT: Mastery? He's years behind! He has mastered very little of anything.

MARY: This has been a very enlightening conversation. Thank you for your time.

It appears there is a communication gap between Mary and Pat. Pat has provided a lot of test data to Mary, and yet Mary doesn't seem to care about it. Pat is frustrated, Mary is frustrated, and little that may be of help to Danny has been accomplished. Why? Just what is the problem? Is it Pat or is it Mary? Or is it something else?

Take another look at the situation. Do you think Mary was being unreasonable? Why did Pat seem satisfied that she had provided the necessary data? Should Mary's course in tests and measurements have helped her "understand" the test data better? What if Danny's mother were asking the questions instead of Mary—would the outcome have been different? Finding answers to these questions may help us. Let's consider each of these in turn.

Was Mary being unreasonable? Mary's questions were specific: Does he have phonetic skills? Can he subtract two-digit numbers with regrouping? Certainly these are not unreasonable questions. She was probably expecting answers that were fairly specific. Maybe something like "yes" or "no" or maybe something like "about 80 percent of the time" or "about 20 percent of the time." Responses like these would have helped her plan instruction for Danny. She would know which skills he had mastered, which he was a little deficient in, and which would require a lot of work. However, the grade-equivalent and percentile scores that Pat reported provided her with none of this information. No wonder she was frustrated.

Then why was Pat reporting these scores? Obviously, they were close at hand, and she probably thought she *was* conveying useful information. Actually, she was conveying useful information; it just wasn't very useful in this particular case. In relaying this information to Mary, she may have thought she was answering her questions.

Does Mary need another course in tests and measurements? Maybe, but we don't really know. Mary seems to have a perfectly adequate understanding of the information that grade-equivalent scores convey. If we agree that her questions were reasonable, is it necessarily a lack of understanding of test scores that prevented her from making use of the data Pat provided? Or could it be that the information provided failed to answer her questions? The latter explanation appears most satisfactory. Indeed, as you will discover shortly, it seems that it is Pat, not Mary, who would benefit most from a tests and measurements course.

Would things be different if a parent questioned? Maybe. Teachers may respond differently to other teachers than to parents. In some cases inquisitive parents can be intimidated by authoritative-sounding test scores and jargon. But is a parent-teacher conference supposed to cloud or sidestep issues, rather than deal with them directly? We think not. If a parent were as concerned as Mary was about certain skills, that parent would probably end up feeling as frustrated as Mary. While Mary might go home and complain to a friend or husband, a parent might complain to a principal or a superintendent!

Mary's questions, whether raised by her or a parent, are legitimate. Pat probably could answer these questions if she thought about them. However, she seems to think that the test scores she reported are acceptable substitutes for direct answers to questions about specific skills.

Then what is the problem? The problem appears to be Pat's, not Mary's. Her questions refer to competencies or mastery of skills. Referring back to Figure 3.1, we can conclude that she was interested in information about Danny's *level of proficiency*. Pat's answers refer to test performance compared to other students, which, according to Figure 3.1, means information about Danny's *place or rank compared to others*. Answers to Mary's questions can come only from a test designed to indicate whether Danny exceeded some standard of performance taken to indicate mastery of some skill. If a test indicated that Danny could subtract two-digit numbers with regrouping, he would probably be considered to have "mastered" this skill, at least if, say, 80 percent or more correct was the standard for having attained mastery. In other words, he would have exceeded the standard or criterion of "80 percent mastery of subtraction of two-digit numbers with regrouping." Recall that a criterion-referenced test is a test designed to measure whether a student has mastered a skill, where the definition of mastery depends on the level or criterion of performance set.

The information Pat was providing was normative or comparative rather than mastery information. Grade-equivalent scores only allow you to make decisions involving comparisons between a child's performance and that of the typical or average performance of a child in a "norm" group. Danny's grade-equivalent score of 1.7 in reading indicates that Danny's reading ability is equivalent to that of the average first-grader after seven months in the first grade. It says nothing about which words he knows, nor does it give any information about the process he uses to read new words, nor does it indicate how long it takes Danny to comprehend what he reads or to learn the meaning of new words. All this score indicates is that his ability to read is below that of the average fifth-grader and equivalent to that of an average first-grader after seven months of school. In short, grade-equivalent scores, and a variety of other scores obtained from standardized, norm-referenced tests, allow one to make only general, comparative decisions, not decisions about mastery of specific skills. Unfortunately, situations like the one described above occur every day. Only by becoming knowledgeable about the information yielded by CRT's and NRT's can we avoid these situations.

Recall that in the previous chapter we talked about eight types of decisions for which test data are used. Of these eight we decided that for instructional and grading decisions a teacher-made test was most appropriate. We said that both teacher-made and standardized tests are useful in diagnostic decisions and that standardized tests are most appropriate for selection, placement, counseling and guidance, program or curriculum evaluation, and administrative policy decisions. Most teacher-made tests should be of the mastery type, since these are most useful for instructional decisions—the type of decision most frequently made.

Mary's questions were related to instructional decisions. She was interested in Danny's skill levels. The information Pat was providing came from a norm-referenced, standardized test. If Mary had been interested in where Danny stands compared to national norms, then Pat's information would have been perfectly appropriate. However, she was apparently not all that interested in his position relative to others; she was interested in what he knew or what he had mastered. Most often in the classroom we are concerned with mastery information. Although we are constantly reminded of where our class, school, or district stands in comparison to national norms, these reminders are usually of secondary importance to the classroom teacher. Of prime importance in the classroom is whether our students are mastering what we teach—whether they are reaching the goals and objectives set for them. Daily decisions to reteach, review, or push ahead depend on whether mastery is occurring. What better way to measure whether our students have mastered an objective than to test them to see if they can perform the learning outcome specified, under the conditions or with the materials specified, and at or above the standard of performance specified for them.

COMPARING NORM-REFERENCED AND CRITERION-REFERENCED TESTS

As you may have guessed, criterion-referenced tests must be very specific if they are to yield information about individual skills. This is both an advantage and a disadvantage. Using a very specific test enables you to be relatively certain that your students have mastered or failed to master the skill in question. The major disadvantage of criterion-referenced tests is that many such tests would be necessary to make decisions about the multitude of skills typically taught in the average classroom.

The norm-referenced test, in contrast, tends to be general. It measures a variety of specific and general skills at once, but fails to measure them thoroughly. Thus, you are not as sure as you would be with a criterion-referenced test that your students have mastered the individual skills in question. On the other hand, you get an estimate of ability in a variety of skills in a much shorter time than you could through a battery of criterion-referenced tests. Since there is a trade-off in the uses of criterion- and norm-referenced measures, there are situations in which each is appropriate. Determining the appropriateness of a given type of test depends on the purpose of testing.

Finally, the difficulty of items in NRT's and CRT's also differs. In the NRT, items vary in level of difficulty from those that almost no one answers correctly to those that almost everyone answers correctly. In the CRT, the items tend to be equivalent to each other in difficulty. Following a period of instruction students tend to find CRT items easy and answer most correctly. In a CRT, about 80 percent of the students completing a unit of instruction are expected to answer each item correctly, while in an NRT about 50 percent are expected to do so. Table 3.1 illustrates differences between NRT's and CRT's.

DIFFERENCES IN THE CONSTRUCTION OF NORM-REFERENCED AND CRITERION-REFERENCED TESTS

In the following chapters we will describe in detail test planning, construction, and evaluation procedures. The procedures outlined in the test planning and test construction phases are, for the most part, equally appropriate whether you are using a norm-referenced test or a criterion-referenced test. However, because of differences in the difficulty level of the items and the amount of variability in student scores, different evaluation procedures must be used in selecting test items. These will be described further in Chapter 8. At this point, we will simply describe some of the general differences in the construction of these two items, which are designed to measure a student's knowledge about the Gulf War in 1991:

Item 1. During the Gulf War against Iraq, which of the following were employed by Iraq against Coalition forces?

a. Biological weapons
b. Nuclear weapons
c. Scud missiles
d. Naval bombardment

Item 2. During the Gulf War more Iraqi tanks were destroyed by this aircraft than by all other aircraft combined.

a. F14 Tomcat
b. F16 Hornet
c. A6 Intruder
d. A10 Thunderbolt

Well, what are the correct answers? Most would answer item 1 correctly (i.e., Scud missiles), and probably only military buffs would answer item 2 correctly (i.e., A10 Thunderbolt). The second item involves a subtle point that is probably of interest only to

TABLE 3.1
Comparing NRT's and CRT's

Dimension	*NRT*	*CRT*
Average number of students who get an item right	50%	80%
Compares a student's performance to	The performance of other students.	Standards indicative of mastery.
Breadth of content sampled	Broad, covers many objectives	Narrow, covers a few objectives
Comprehensiveness of content sampled	Shallow, usually one or two items per objective.	Comprehensive, usually three or more items per objective.
Variability	Since the meaningfulness of a norm-referenced score basically depends on the relative position of the score in comparison with other scores, the more variability or spread of scores, the better.	The meaning of the score does not depend on comparison with other scores: It flows directly from the connection between the items and the criterion. Thus, variability may be minimal.
Item construction	Items are chosen to promote variance or spread. Items that are "too easy" or "too hard" are avoided. One aim is to produce good "distractor options."	Items are chosen to reflect the criterion behavior. Emphasis is placed upon identifying the domain of relevant responses.
Reporting and interpreting considerations	Percentile rank and standard scores used (relative rankings).*	Number succeeding or failing or range of acceptable performance used (e.g., 90% proficiency achieved, or 80% of class reached 90% proficiency).

*For a further discussion of percentile rank and standard scores, see Chapters 12 and 13.

military strategists and historians. Such an item might prove useful in discriminating among individuals who have mastery of specific details of the Gulf War, such as in a class in military history. However, for a high-school or junior-high unit on American history, this level of specificity would be unnecessary. Item 1, which assesses general knowledge about the Gulf War, would be most appropriate for a criterion-referenced test, since it measures general facts about the war, whereas item 2 would be most appropriate for a norm-referenced test or a more advanced course, since it attempts to make more subtle distinctions among the facts. Due to its difficulty and specificity, few junior or senior high students would answer item 2 correctly, even if they showed mastery of other aspects of the unit.

Let's complicate matters, however: Item 2 *might* be included in a criterion-referenced test in a military history class. Students of military history might be expected to be familiar with the intricacies and specifics of weaponry employed during the Gulf War. In such a class we would expect the content of the item to represent basic knowledge extensively addressed in text and lecture. In other words, test items are not norm-referenced or criterion-referenced by nature. They need to be considered in terms of the audience for whom they are being prepared.

SUMMARY

In this chapter we have introduced norm-referenced and criterion-referenced tests. The major points covered are:

1. A norm-referenced test (NRT) indicates how a pupil's performance compares to that of other pupils.
2. A criterion-referenced test (CRT) indicates how a pupil's performance compares to an established standard or criterion thought to indicate mastery of a skill.
3. What type of test you use depends on the purpose of the testing, which should be determined before you administer the test.
4. Information from NRT's is usually not as useful for classroom decision making as information from CRT's.
5. In addition to differing in regard to what a pupil's performance is compared to, NRT's and CRT's differ in the following dimensions:
   a. item difficulty
   b. content sampling (breadth and depth)
   c. variability of scores
   d. item construction
   e. reporting and interpreting considerations

For Discussion

1. Identify five characteristics that distinguish a norm-referenced from a criterion-referenced test.
2. Describe several testing decisions for which you would want to use a norm-referenced test and several situations in which you would want to use a criterion-referenced test.

3. A parent calls you and wants to set up a conference to discuss Johnny's potential for getting into the college of his choice. Which type of test score, NRT or CRT, should you be prepared to discuss first? Why?
4. Another parent calls and wants to discuss why Sally received a D in math this grading period. Which type of test score, NRT or CRT, should you be prepared to discuss first? Why?
5. Imagine that you have been randomly chosen to be evaluated by your school district's Office of Evaluation. They ask you for your students' scores on an achievement test. What type of test scores, NRT or CRT, would be most indicative of your success as a teacher?

CHAPTER 4

Instructional Goals and Objectives

In Chapter 2 we discussed what, how, and especially why we measure. Chapter 3 elaborated on how we measure. In this chapter and the several that follow we will look more closely at what and how we measure. We have discussed the importance of defining what we want to measure and now will learn how to determine if what we actually measure is what we want to measure. A model for classroom measurement will be presented that can help you determine when students have attained the instructional objectives you set for them.

We will not be concerned with the differences between educational goals and objectives, or even the differences among different kinds of objectives. What we will be concerned with is the fact that all teachers have some objectives in mind when they teach. Usually these are both long- and short-term objectives. An example of a long-term objective would be:

The student will master all phases of addition.

With this long-term objective are several short-term objectives, which might include such objectives as;

The student will add correctly one-, two-, three-, and four-digit numbers without regrouping.
The student will add correctly two-digit numbers with regrouping.
The student will add correctly three-digit numbers with regrouping.

Regardless of whether we are talking about long- or short-term objectives, it is important to know when your students have mastered your objectives. Remember Mrs. Norton? One of her objectives was probably "The student will master basic math skills." Like any good teacher, she tried to determine through a test whether her students mastered this objective. The problem was that her test did not measure mastery of basic math skills. It measured the ability to *apply* math skills and to *read* and to *comprehend* word problems. In short, she knew what she wanted to measure, but her test did not actually measure it. This is another way of saying that her test lacked *validity*. More specifically, it lacked *content validity*. She knew what she wanted to measure, but how she did so was inappropriate.

In the classroom, content validity is of utmost importance. Simply stated, content validity describes the extent to which a test actually measures the teacher's instructional objectives. Later in this chapter we will introduce procedures for examining a test to determine whether it has content validity. Since most educational decisions are based on classroom achievement tests, we cannot overemphasize the importance of constructing tests that have content validity. If you construct content-valid tests, you will be on your way to making sound instructional decisions and having valid evidence to support your decisions should they ever be questioned.

A THREE-STAGE MODEL OF CLASSROOM MEASUREMENT

Most classroom instruction takes place with some objective in mind. One way to determine whether the objective has been reached is through a test. The three-stage classroom measurement model in Figure 4.1 depicts these relationships. We will illustrate this model by describing how a criterion-referenced test is constructed.

The first stage in the model is the first step in constructing a criterion-referenced test. It is also the first step in sound instructional planning. For our purposes we will use as examples only a few of the many possible objectives in a unit on writing instructional objectives. Some of these objectives might be:

The student will discriminate learning activities from learning outcomes.

FIGURE 4.1
The Three-Stage Classroom Measurement Model

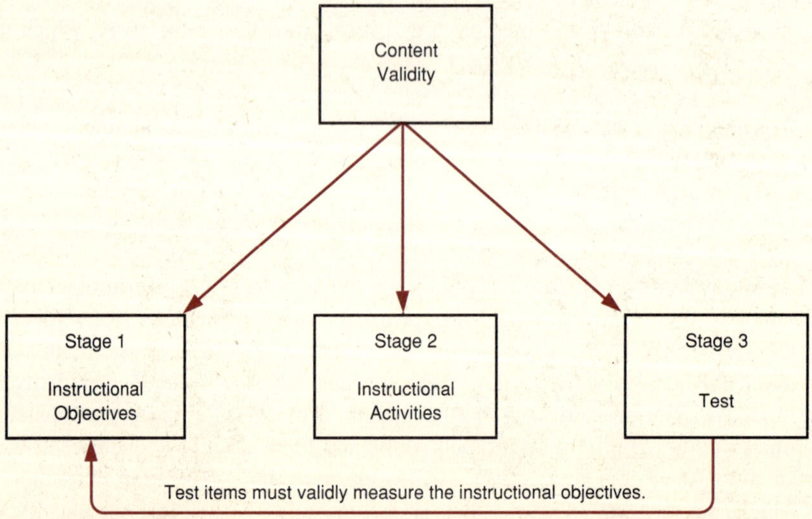

The student will discriminate observable learning outcomes from unobservable learning outcomes.

The student will construct well-written instructional objectives.

Each of these objectives would fit in Stage 1 of the model.

In Stage 2, instructional activities designed to develop student mastery of these objectives would be implemented. For example:

Objective:

The student will discriminate learning activities from learning outcomes.

Instructional Activity:

Define and provide examples of learning activities and learning outcomes. Point out similarities and differences between the two.

Naturally, the instructional procedures will vary depending on the content and type of learning outcomes desired. Courses in teaching methods are most concerned with the structure of the procedures in Stage 2 of this model. For our purposes, however, we are more concerned with determining the effectiveness of the procedures, not necessarily the nature of the procedures themselves. Thus, it is Stages 1 and 3 that will be of most interest.

In constructing a criterion-referenced test, our task is made easier if we develop clear and measurable instructional objectives. In Chapter 5 we will learn how to do this. Once we have measurable instructional objectives, our task is to construct several items to validly measure each objective. Typically, this means about three to ten items per objective. Furthermore, we normally define mastery not as perfect performance but as 70, 80, or 90 percent correct performance. A student who answers four out of five or eight out of ten items that validly measure an objective generally is considered to have mastered the objective. The following is an example of a five-item test to measure the first objective.

Objective:

The student will discriminate learning activities from learning outcomes.

TEST ITEM: Indicate which terms in the following list are learning activities by placing an A in the space to the left of the term, and indicate which are learning outcomes by placing an O in the space.

________ 1. Practice multiplication tables.
________ 2. List the parts of a carburetor.
________ 3. Recall the main events in a story.
________ 4. Listen to a foreign language tape.
________ 5. Memorize the names of the first five United States presidents.

Answers: 1. A; 2. O; 3. O; 4. A; 5. A.

These response alternatives are content-valid measures of the objective. They ask the student to do exactly what the objective requires. There are certainly other equally valid ways of measuring this objective, but the response alternatives listed above are appropriate. If a student answers four out of five or five out of five correctly on this criterion-referenced test, the teacher could feel reasonably secure in concluding that the student has mastered the objective. These types of tests are called criterion-referenced because a specific level of acceptable performance called the criterion is established directly from the instructional objectives. As we shall see, we are less confident of the mastery of specific objectives when a norm-referenced test is employed.

Regardless of the type of achievement test you select, the issue of content validity is of paramount concern. Keep the three-stage model in mind when you select or develop an achievement test, and you are likely to be aware of the issue of content validity.

Well, now that we have an overall framework for thinking about classroom measurement, let's get into test construction itself. Keep in mind that any good classroom test begins with your objectives, Stage 1 of our three-stage measurement model. Much of the remainder of this chapter and the next will be devoted to considering instructional objectives and ways of ensuring the content validity of items intended to measure instructional objectives.

WHY OBJECTIVES? WHY NOT JUST WRITE TEST ITEMS?

What if you don't believe that instructional objectives are necessary? What if you feel that they are a waste of time? What if you don't feel you will need to use or construct instructional objectives in your teaching career? Many believe that objectives for classroom instruction are unnecessary, limiting, too time-consuming, and mechanistic. If you agree, then learning to write instructional objectives may be a frustrating, difficult task. If we told you they're necessary and you're better off learning to write them, you probably would not believe us. We *do* feel it is important for teachers to be able to write measurable instructional objectives, but we also understand and respect your right to hold another opinion. You should, however, take the time to consider the place of instructional objectives in the overall instructional process. Consider the situation described below and then decide whether it's worthwhile to take the time to learn to write instructional objectives.

Two Schools: Their Objectives

Getting off the bus at her destination, Maude was immediately taken by the name of the first of the two schools she was about to visit: the Center for Self-Actualization and Humanistic Experiences. Maude was awestruck. At last she would see what education really should be about—free from dry, mechanical methods and curricula, and characterized by the teachers' loving acceptance and excitement and the students' sense of freedom. To her surprise, the door was open, so Maude walked in and was greeted with a warm smile and hug from the "facilitator."

"Is that another name for teacher?" Maude asked.

"Heavens, no!" said the facilitator. "I only facilitate learning, I don't teach. For your information, use of the words *teacher* and *educator* are forbidden here at the Center; we are all facilitators." Maude was confused, but decided not to press the issue.

The students were engaged in a variety of activities or lack of activities. One was reading a book; another worked with an abacus; a third was asleep on a couch; others were talking, playing, and generally having what appeared to Maude to be a pretty good time. Maude was encouraged by the facilitator to "experience" the students. Almost unanimously the students felt the Center was "fun." One said, "You never have to do nuthin' around here."

Concerned, Maude questioned the facilitator about this comment. The facilitator's reply was that freedom of choice is strongly encouraged at the Center. All students are free to choose what to do or not to do.

"But are they learning anything?" Maude asked.

"They are learning that they are free and independent human beings," said the facilitator. "When they are ready, they will choose to learn on their own. Now, if you'll excuse me, I have an appointment with my aroma therapist." At a loss for words and feeling troubled, Maude said goodbye and left the Center for Self-Actualization and Humanistic Experiences.

The Center for Accelerated Education was Maude's next stop. After knocking on the door she was greeted by a rather stern-faced middle-aged man who was wearing a "Better Living Through Behaviorism" button on his lapel. A "behavioral engineer," he called himself. He said hello and handed Maude a list of "behaviors" that the students would be engaging in for the next thirty minutes or so and told her to feel free to "collect data." He then picked up a box of plastic strips—"tokens," he called them—muttered something about a "reinforcement schedule" and "consequating appropriate behaviors," and walked off toward his "subjects."

The students at the Center for Accelerated Education sat in individual cubicles or carrels. Each student had a contract specifying what was expected of him or her. Privileges, such as free time, and rewards from the "reinforcer menu" were earned by performing on-task behavior (like sitting quietly in a cubicle, working on a worksheet, or reading). The behavioral engineer circulated around the room, periodically "reinforcing" on-task behavior with tokens and also providing tokens for each completed worksheet. Students demonstrating off-task and disruptive behavior relinquished tokens or, in extreme cases, were required to spend several minutes in the time-out room. The time-out room was "devoid of all potential reinforcers," according to the behavioral engineer. In other words, it was a barren room—no windows, tables, or anything interesting.

When Maude asked whether the pupils were learning, the behavioral engineer pointed to the stacks of completed worksheets almost filling a large storeroom.

"Let's see you get that much learning from the kids at the Center for Self-Actualization and Humanistic Experiences," chuckled the behavioral engineer.

More confused and concerned than she had been before she entered, Maude decided not to press the issue and to engage in some exiting behaviors.

As you probably guessed, both the Center for Self-Actualization and Humanistic Experiences and the Center for Accelerated Education are, we hope, exaggerations. They represent extremes in educational theory. On the one hand, the "hands-off" approach is characteristic of nondirective, discovery approaches to learning. On the other hand, the regimented approach is characteristic of a directive, guided approach to learning. Which approach is better? We don't know, and probably no one knows. Fortunately, most educational institutions operate with some combination of directive and nondirective approaches.

Instruction is not a rigid, easily defined procedure. It tends to be different things to different people. No one will ever be completely happy with any one approach to instruction since no *one* approach is really a single method but a combination of methods. As a result, specific educational goals and objectives are unlikely to be approved or supported by everyone. So where do the goals and objectives come from, and who decides on the goals and objectives of education? The answer is that society, government, school boards, school administration, teachers, students, and parents all, to some extent, set educational goals and objectives.

Where Do Goals Come From?

Educators must be responsive to societal needs and pressures. This is especially true for public-school educators, since the purse strings that make public education a reality are controlled by all who make up our society. If a superintendent or school board implements educational policies or procedures that are too far removed from what the community wants and needs, the superintendent may find himself or herself looking for work elsewhere, and board members may not be reelected.

We frequently make the mistake of thinking that it is the administration that is completely responsible for the curriculum implemented in a given school or district. This is only partially true. Ultimately, the general public, or society, sets the goals for education. Figure 4.2 illustrates with a specific example the flow from goals to objectives in education. This illustration shows how public pressure for a back-to-basics movement can reach the classroom.

We may also view this process as a funneling or narrowing of focus, with the often ambiguous wants and needs of society gradually translated into manageable "bits" called instructional objectives, as shown in Figure 4.3.

FIGURE 4.2
Back to Basics: The Flow of Goals to Objectives

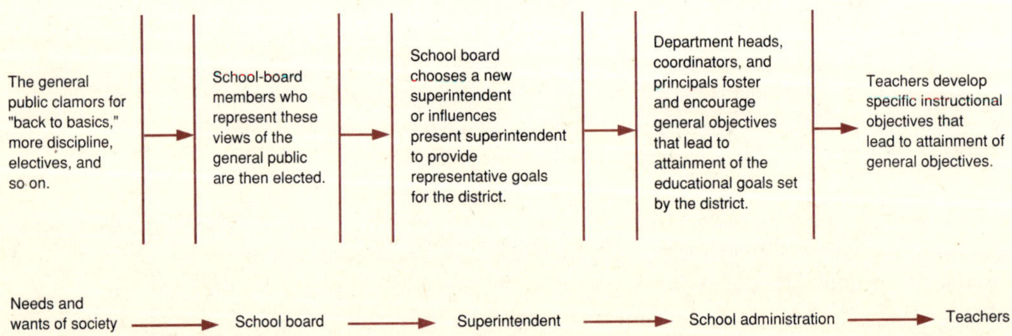

Are There Different Kinds of Goals and Objectives?

What do you think are the instructional goals and objectives of the schools Maude visited? Well, you probably can't say precisely, but you could probably look at a list of objectives and decide which would be accepted by the Center for Self-Actualization and Humanistic Experiences or by the behaviorist Center for Accelerated Education. Look at the objectives in the following exercise and indicate the school with which they would most likely be associated.

EXERCISE: Write H for Humanistic or B for Behavioristic in the blank to the left of each objective to indicate which school they would probably go with.

________ 1. With 80 percent accuracy, subtract two-digit numbers from three-digit numbers without borrowing.
________ 2. Identify initial consonant sounds correctly 90 percent of the time when listening to an audiocassette.
________ 3. Enjoy the beauty of nature.
________ 4. Interpret *The Lion, the Witch, and the Wardrobe*.

FIGURE 4.3
The Funneling of Societal Wants into Objectives

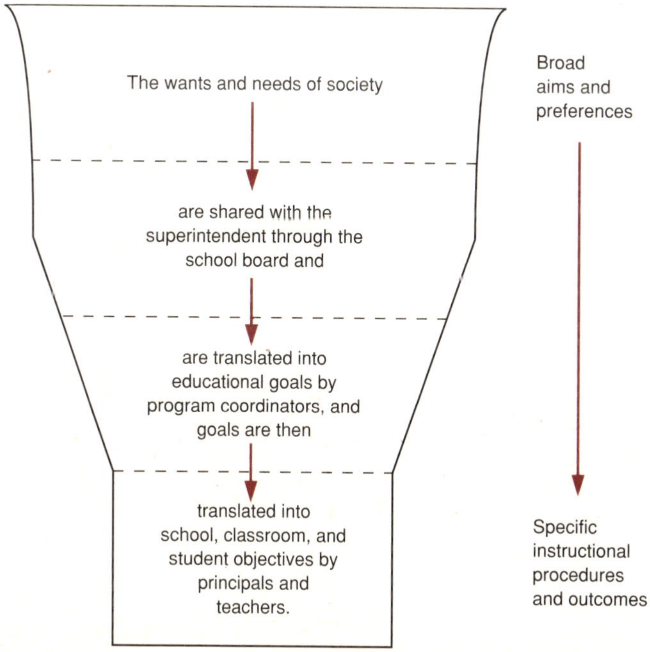

_______ 5. Type at least 25 words per minute with no more than two errors, using a manual typewriter.
_______ 6. Visit the zoo and discuss what was of interest.
_______ 7. Be creative.
_______ 8. Be spontaneous.
_______ 9. List the days of the week in proper order, from memory, with 100 percent accuracy.

This exercise points out the difference between two types of educational objectives: behavioral (specific) and expressive (general). A behavioral objective is a precise statement of behavior to be exhibited; the criterion by which mastery of the objective will be judged; and, at times, a statement of the conditions under which the behavior must be demonstrated. Objectives 1, 2, 5, and 9 are examples. As you can see, they are specific statements or "bits" of *observable* behavior with specific conditions under which the behavior is to be observed and the level of performance attained. Using these objectives, two or more observers would likely agree about whether a student was, for example, able to list the days of the week in proper order, from memory, with 100 percent accuracy.

An expressive objective is somewhat different. Behaviors are *not* usually specified, *nor* is a criterion performance level generally stated. What is stated in an expressive objective is the experience or educational activity to be undertaken. The outcome of the activity is not detailed in specific terms, but in general terms such as *interpret* or *analyze*. Examples of expressive objectives would include items 4 and 6 from the above list. They specify an activity or experience and a broad educational outcome.

Now you might ask, "What about items 3, 7, and 8?" They do *not* describe a specific observable behavior, conditions, and criterion level of performance, and they do *not* describe an educational activity or experience. What do they describe? They describe broad, hard-to-define entities. We would have little agreement among individuals trying to define enjoyment, creativity, and spontaneity. These may be best classified as broad goals, rather than objectives, because they are the end result of perhaps a complete educational program.

Educational goals reflect the general needs of society. As a result, most goals, if stated in general terms, tend to be accepted or adopted by most educators and educational institutions. Regardless of whether a program is directive or nondirective, behavioral or humanistic, rigid or flexible, various general goals will be held in common. When we get more specific, often at the local school level, disagreements over methods used to reach these goals arise. For example, the two schools described above would probably agree that creativity is an important goal for education but disagree as to how creativity should be fostered or developed. One school may feel creativity is best developed through structured experiences. Another school may feel creativity is best developed in an open, unstructured environment.

As a result, sometimes different methods are employed to reach the same goal. But it is important to realize that, in addition to having a goal, any method must also have some implicit or explicit steps thought necessary to achieve the goal. Such steps may vary in specificity but are present in any logically constructed instructional program. For example, in the Center for Self-Actualization and Humanistic Experiences the facilitators most certainly had some steps in mind in trying to foster creativity. It is unlikely that they expected creativity to develop without any guidance. If they did, why would they see a need for their Center? The expressive objectives mentioned might be one of the steps they would use. Others might include:

Make all students feel welcome.

Encourage students to try out new activities and methods of expression.

Encourage students to express all ideas, regardless of how inappropriate they may seem.

Statements such as these help define the atmosphere or philosophy of the Center, but are they instructional objectives? Some would say yes, and some would say no. We would say no, since they do not meet our criteria for instructional objectives. That is, they do not (1) specify student behaviors and do not (2) specify observable, measurable behaviors. This is not to say that they are unimportant, but for our purposes instructional objectives must specify observable, overt student behavior. The test of this is whether two independent observers would agree as to the presence or absence of the student behavior in question. Would two or more observers agree that "expression of student ideas is always encouraged, regardless of how inappropriate they may seem"? Some probably would agree and some would not. Thus, this statement would not qualify as an instructional objective according to our criteria. But consider this statement: "During each period the students will write an alternative ending to each assigned short story." Here it seems more likely that observers would agree as to whether students displayed this behavior. It is student-oriented, and it is easily observed.

Thus far, we have discussed the difference between specific instructional objectives and general expressive objectives. These tend to reflect a school's educational philosophy. We have also mentioned general goals that tend to reflect the overall needs of society. From this point on, we will focus on specific instructional objectives, but we will also consider another type of objective called a *general* or *program objective*. Although these are usually formulated at the school-district level, they are sometimes confused with classroom instructional objectives. Table 4.1 illustrates the difference among educational goals, program objectives, and instructional objectives.

Since the average classroom teacher will have little input into the formulation of either educational goals or general educational program objectives, we will not concern ourselves further with these. For the remainder of this chapter and in the next we will focus on those objectives that classroom teachers must formulate themselves. In other words, we will concentrate on instructional objectives. Instructional objectives can make a teacher's day-to-day job easier, save time, and result in more effective instruction.

TABLE 4.1
Goals, Program Objectives, and Instructional Objectives

Category	*Description*	*Examples*
Goals	Broad statements of very general educational outcomes that: Do *not* include specific levels of performance Tend to change infrequently and in response to societal pressure	Become a good citizen Be competent in the basic skills areas Be creative Learn problem solving Appreciate art Develop high-level thinking skills
General educational program objectives	More narrowly defined statements of educational outcomes that: Apply to specific educational programs May be formulated on an annual basis Are developed by program coordinators, principals, and other high school administrators	By the end of the academic year, students receiving Chapter 1 reading program services will realize achievement gains of at least .8 of a grade level, as measured by the Iowa Test of Basic Skills.
Instructional objectives	Specific statements of learner behavior or outcomes that are expected to be exhibited by students after completing a unit of instruction. A unit of instruction may, for example, mean: A six-week lesson on "Foreign Culture" A one-week lesson on "Deciduous Trees" A class period on "Subtracting with Borrowing" A five-minute lesson on "Cursive Letters: Lowercase b" These objectives are often included in teacher manuals, and more and more frequently instructional objectives are also being included for specific lessons. Unfortunately, they are *not* always well written and do *not* always "fit" a particular class or style. Thus, instructional objectives often have to be formulated by classroom teachers to "fit" their individual classrooms.	By Friday, the students will be able to recite the names of the months in order. The student will be able to take apart and reassemble correctly within 45 minutes a disk drive with the tools provided.

HOW CAN INSTRUCTIONAL OBJECTIVES MAKE A TEACHER'S JOB EASIER?

When we were first learning about goals and objectives, we also wondered how instructional objectives can make a teacher's job easier. How can something that takes time to prepare actually save time, and how does that make a teacher's job easier?

You've probably heard the old saying that it takes money to make money. It's true. An equally relevant, but far less popular expression is that it takes time to save time. In other words, taking time to plan and to organize will save you time in the long run. Planning your lessons, getting organized, and being efficient all take time but can save time later.

Research has identified several factors that are associated with effective, successful teaching. Among these are organization and clarity, which typically go hand in hand. While it is possible to be clear without being organized, and vice versa, it is unlikely. Unfortunately, we spend a lot of time "spinning our wheels" because we do not have clear objectives for ourselves, or for our students. In other words, we often don't know where we're going so we don't know when we get there. Using instructional objectives helps minimize this floundering by clearing the way. Thus, we know where we're going and when we get there. The result is increased efficiency and effectiveness in teaching and learning.

SUMMARY

This chapter introduced you to educational goals and objectives. Its major points are:

1. *Content validity* describes the extent to which a test measures or matches the teacher's instructional objectives.
2. There are three stages involved in classroom measurement:

   a. constructing instructional objectives,

   b. implementing instructional activities, and

   c. testing to measure the attainment of the instructional objectives.

   Each of these must match with the others for measurement to be valid.
3. Instructional activities tend to vary across educational institutions, ranging from flexible to rigid.
4. These instructional activities tend to be determined by instructional objectives, which tend to be derived from educational goals, which tend to reflect societal attitudes and values.
5. One type of instructional objective is the behavioral objective. It specifies an observable, measurable behavior to be exhibited, the conditions under which it is to be exhibited, and the criterion for mastery.

6. Another type of instructional objective is the expressive objective. It specifies an educational activity but does not specify the particular outcome of the activity.

7. Instructional objectives help the teacher clarify and organize instruction, enabling the teacher to save time in the long run.

For Discussion

1. Compare and contrast the following:

   a. behavioral and expressive objectives

   b. program objectives and instructional objectives

   c. educational goals and instructional objectives

2. A teacher is complaining about having to write instructional objectives. He just cannot see any benefit they may have and feels they are too time-consuming. Role-play with another student and describe how well-written objectives can make teaching more effective.

*3. Identify which of the following are expressive (E) and which are behavioral (B) objectives.

   B a. Properly use and adjust a microscope.

   E b. Understand the nature of plant growth.

   B c. Know how to drive a car.

   E d. Appreciate the role of physics in everyday life.

   B e. Be able to divide fractions.

   B f. Be able to dissect a starfish.

   E g. Understand the importance of eating the right foods.

   B h. List the parts of the abdomen.

4. Convert the following goals to general objectives:

   a. Become a good citizen.

   b. Be creative.

   c. Appreciate art.

   d. Know math.

   e. Develop musical ability.

*5. Match the following general objectives to the most content-valid method of testing.

Objectives	*Testing method*
________ 1. From memory, describe the main figures in classical music.	a. Copy by hand at least two classical compositions.
________ 2. Match the classical composers with their compositions.	b. Associate the composers listed with their compositions.
________ 3. Identify the titles and composers of the classical pieces discussed in class, after listening to no more than two minutes of each piece.	c. Chronicle the lives of three European composers who lived between 1500 and 1875.
________ 4. Play two classical compositions on the piano by the end of the semester.	d. After listening to this tape, identify the composer.
	g. Play two classical selections of your choice.

*Answers to questions 3 and 5 appear in Appendix D.

CHAPTER 5

Measuring Learning Outcomes

In Chapter 4 we considered the differences between goals and objectives and some reasons instructional objectives are helpful to the teacher. Next we will consider a method for actually writing instructional objectives.

WRITING INSTRUCTIONAL OBJECTIVES

An instructional objective should be a clear and concise statement of the skill or skills that your students will be expected to perform after a unit of instruction. It should include the level of proficiency to be demonstrated and the special conditions under which the skill must be demonstrated. Furthermore, an instructional objective should be stated in observable, behavioral terms, in order for two or more individuals to agree that a student has or has not displayed the learning outcome in question. In short, a complete instructional objective includes:

An observable behavior (action verb specifying the learning outcome)

Any special conditions under which the behavior must be displayed

The performance level considered sufficient to demonstrate mastery

The following series of exercises should help you become familiar with each of these components. With practice, they should lead to your mastery in writing instructional objectives.

Identifying Learning Outcomes

An instructional objective must include an action verb that specifies a learning outcome. However, not all action verbs specify learning outcomes. Learning outcomes are often confused with learning activities. Try to determine which of the following examples represent learning outcomes and which represent learning activities:

1. The child will identify pictures of words that sound alike by the end of the semester.
2. The child will demonstrate an appreciation of poetry.
3. The student will subtract one-digit numbers with 80% accuracy.
4. The student will show a knowledge of correct punctuation.
5. The student will practice the multiplication tables.
6. The student will sing "The Star-Spangled Banner."

In the first four objectives the action words *identify*, *demonstrate*, *subtract*, and *show* all point to outcomes, or end products of units of instruction. However, *practice*, the action word in 5, only implies an activity that will *lead* to a learning outcome. Thus, 5 has no learning outcome; it is a learning activity. The means rather than the end is identified. Objective 6 is a little troublesome, too. Is *sing* an outcome or an activity? It's hard to say without more information. If your goal is to have a stage-frightened pupil sing in public, this may be a learning outcome. However, if singing is only practice for a later performance, it is a learning activity. The following exercise should help you discriminate between learning outcomes and learning activities. Look at the examples of outcomes and activities, then work through the exercise and check your answers.

Learning Outcomes (Ends)	**Learning Activities (Means)**
identify	study
recall	watch
list	listen
write	read

EXERCISE: Distinguish learning outcomes from learning activities by marking an O next to outcomes and an A next to activities.

_______ 1. Fixing a car radio

_______ 2. Reciting the four components of a good essay

_______ 3. Adding signed numbers correctly

_______ 4. Practicing the violin

_______ 5. Recalling the parts of speech

_______ 6. Outlining the main theme in *The House of the Seven Gables*

_______ 7. Reciting the alphabet

_______ 8. Punctuating an essay correctly

Answers: 1. O; 2. O; 3. O; 4. A; 5. O; 6. O; 7. A; 8. O.

If an activity implies a specific product or result, we have considered it an outcome. What we want our instructional objective to include is the *end* product of the instructional procedure. It is on this end product that we will base our test item. If you find your objective includes a learning activity (means) and not an outcome (end), rewrite it so that the product of the intended activity is stated. Next, let's consider two types of learning outcomes: those that are observable and directly measurable, and those that are not.

Identifying Observable and Directly Measurable Learning Outcomes

At this stage, your task is to determine whether the outcome is stated as a measurable, observable behavior or an unmeasurable, unobservable behavior. That is, would two or more individuals observing a student agree that the student had demonstrated the learning outcome? Sometimes we need to replace the unobservable behavior with an observable indicator of the learning outcome. For example, if our objective is:

The student will show a knowledge of punctuation

then the learning outcome, "show a knowledge of punctuation," is unmeasurable. How would we know whether knowledge was shown? Ask the student? Would we assume that if a student was present for a lecture or read the appropriate section of a text, knowledge followed? Probably not. Instead we would need some indication that would serve to demonstrate evidence of knowledge. For example, to indicate knowledge of punctuation, a student would have to "insert commas where appropriate" in sentences, "list the rules governing the use of colons or semicolons," and so on. Thus, there are actually *two* kinds of instructional objectives commonly found in method textbooks, in teachers manuals, and in school memos and directives. The first are more correctly called *instructional goals* because they are broad, often difficult-to-measure statements of instructional intent (know math and reading, appreciate music, and so forth). Only the second deserve the title "instructional objectives" because they are specific, measurable statements of the *outcomes* of instruction that indicate whether instructional intents have been achieved (add two-digit numbers with regrouping, independently pick up a musical instrument and play it, and so on).

For the purpose of classroom instruction, we are most concerned with instructional objectives, as these are the "meat and potatoes" of a teacher's everyday life. When a teacher writes or comes across an instructional goal, the task, for instructional purposes, is to select an indicator of the goal and write an appropriate objective around the indicator. There is an added bonus to such practice: Constructing the test is then much easier. Imagine how difficult it would be to evaluate objectively whether a student "shows a knowledge of punctuation." On the other hand, it is fairly easy to determine whether a student is able to "insert commas where appropriate in sentences."

Let's practice identifying observable learning outcomes. Study the following examples of observable and unobservable outcomes, work through the exercise, then check your answers.

Observables	**Unobservables**
list	value
recite	appreciate
build	know
draw	understand

EXERCISE: Distinguish observable learning outcomes from unobservable outcomes by marking O next to observables and U next to unobservables.

_______ 1. Circle the initial sound of words.
_______ 2. Be familiar with the law.
_______ 3. Add two-digit numbers on paper.
_______ 4. Understand the process of osmosis.
_______ 5. Enjoy speaking French.
_______ 6. Change the spark plugs on an engine.
_______ 7. Recite the names of the characters in *Tom Sawyer*.
_______ 8. Really understand set theory.
_______ 9. Appreciate art deco.
_______ 10. Recite a short poem from memory.

Answers: 1. O; 2. U; 3. O; 4. U; 5. U; 6. O; 7. O; 8. U; 9. U; 10. O.

Stating Conditions

An instructional objective describes any special conditions in which the learning will take place. If the observable learning outcome is to take place at a particular time, in a particular place, with particular materials, equipment, tools, or other resources, then the conditions must be stated explicitly in the objective, as the following examples show:

Given a calculator, multiply two-digit numbers, correct to the nearest whole number.

Given a typed list, correct any typographical errors.

Given a list of six scrambled words, arrange the words to form a sentence.

EXERCISE: Write conditions for the following learning outcomes:

1. Given _____, change the oil and oil filter.
2. Given _____, identify the correct temperature.
3. Given _____, add three-digit numbers.

Possible Answers: 1. a foreign automobile; 2. a thermometer; 3. an electronic calculator.

Stating Criterion Levels

An instructional objective indicates how well the behavior is to be performed. For any given objective a number of test items will be written. The criterion level of acceptable performance specifies how many of these items the student must get correct for him or her to have passed the objective. The following are examples of objectives with criterion stated:

Given 20 two-digit addition problems, the student will compute all answers correctly.

Given 20 two-digit addition problems, the student will compute 90 percent correctly.

EXERCISE: Write criterion levels of acceptable performance for the following objectives.

1. Given ten words, circle those that contain a silent "e" with _____% accuracy.
2. The student will swim freestyle for 100 yards in less than _____.
3. The good student must be able to leap tall buildings _____.

Possible Answers: 1. 80; 2. 60 seconds; 3. in a single bound.

Remember, criterion levels need not always be specified in terms of percentages of items answered correctly. They may also be stated as:

number of items correct

number of consecutive items correct (or consecutive errorless performances)

essential features included (as in an essay question or paper)

completion within a prescribed time limit (where speed of performance is important)

completion with a certain degree of accuracy

Now that you have worked through these exercises, you have some idea of what is necessary for a complete instructional objective. The following are examples of complete instructional objectives:

With a ball-point pen, write your name, address, birthdate, telephone number, and grade with 100 percent accuracy.

Without reference to class notes, describe correctly four out of five alternative sources of energy discussed in class.

The student will reply in grammatically correct French to 95 percent of the French questions spoken orally during an examination.

Given a human skeleton, the student will identify at least 40 of the bones correctly.

To this point we have shown you how to:

discriminate learning outcomes from learning activities

discriminate observable/measurable learning outcomes from unobservable/unmeasurable learning outcomes

state conditions

state criterion levels

Before moving on to our next topic, let's consider one more issue related to the construction of instructional objectives,

Keeping It Simple and Straightforward

We often make the mistake of being too "sophisticated" in measuring learning outcomes. As a result, we often resort to indirect or unnecessarily complex methods to measure learning outcomes. If you want to know whether students can write their name, ask them to write their name—but not blindfolded! Resist the temptation to be tricky. Consider the following examples:

The student will show his or her ability to recall characters of the book *Tom Sawyer* by painting a picture of each.

Discriminate between a telephone and a television by drawing an electrical diagram of each.

Demonstrate that you understand how to use an encyclopedia index by listing the page a given subject can be found on in the *Encyclopedia Britannica*.

In the first example, painting a picture would likely allow us to determine whether the pupils could recall the characters in *Tom Sawyer*, but isn't there an easier (and less time-consuming) way to measure recall? How about asking the students to simply list the characters? If your objective is to determine recall, listing is sufficient.

For the second example, another unnecessarily complex task is suggested. Instead, how about presenting students with two illustrations, one of a telephone, the other of a television, and simply ask them to tell you (orally or in writing) which is which?

Finally, the third example is on target. The task required is a simple and efficient way of measuring whether someone can use an encyclopedia index.

The next step is to practice writing objectives on your own. Return to the exercises when you have trouble, and be sure you include the three components in each objective. Remember, the three components are:

observable learning outcome

conditions

criterion level

Once you have written an instructional objective, it is always a good idea to analyze it to make sure that the necessary components are included. Determining whether an observable learning outcome has been stated is usually the initial step. The Checklist for Written Objectives in Figure 5.1 addresses this point and provides you with a step-by-step method to analyze and improve written objectives.

We are now ready to consider the third stage of the classroom measurement model introduced in Chapter 4—matching a test item to the instructional objective.

MATCHING TEST ITEMS TO INSTRUCTIONAL OBJECTIVES

In matching test items to instructional objectives, there is one basic rule to keep in mind: *The learning outcome and conditions specified in the test question must match the learning outcome and conditions described in the objective.* This rule will ensure that the test you are developing will have content validity. Because content validity is so important, let's go through some exercises to be sure we actually can match correctly. The following exercises illustrate the two steps involved in matching items to objectives.

STEP 1: Identify the learning outcome called for by the objective. Check to determine if your item requires the same learning outcome.

EXERCISE: For the following, employ step 1 and decide whether the learning outcomes match.

	Match? Yes	Match? No
1. *Objectives:* Recall the names of the capitals of all 50 states. *Test Item:* List the capitals of Texas, New York, California, and Rhode Island.	______	______
2. *Objective:* Discriminate fact from opinion in the President's most recent state of the union address. *Test Item:* Given a text of the state of the union address, list three examples of facts and three examples of opinion.	______	______
3. *Objective:* The student will write complete instructional objectives, including behavior, conditions, and criteria. *Test Item:* Describe why instructional objectives must contain an observable behavior, conditions, and criteria.	______	______
4. *Objective:* Using your text as a reference, recognize the names of the various components of the central nervous system.	______	______

FIGURE 5.1
Checklist for Written Objectives

	Yes	No
1. Are the objectives composed of only learning outcomes and *not* learning activities?	_____	_____
a. If yes, go to step 2.		
b. If no, eliminate the learning activities or replace them with the learning outcomes.		
2. Are the learning outcomes stated in overt observable terms?	_____	_____
a. If yes, go to step 3.		
b. If no, replace the unobservable outcomes with indicators of the outcomes. Remember, because this almost always results in more specific objectives, you may have to write several overt objectives to adequately "sample" the covert learning outcome.		
3. Now that you have all overt learning outcomes listed, are they the simplest and most direct ways to measure the learning outcomes?	_____	_____
a. If yes, you now have a useful list of instructional objectives that will serve as a basis for a content-valid test.		
b. If no, rewrite the indirect or complicated means of measurement so that they are as simple and direct as possible. Once you have done so, you have the basis for a content-valid test.		

Test Item: From memory, list the various components of the central nervous system.

5. *Objective:* Given a written story, list the main events in chronological order. _____ _____
   Test Item: From the story provided, list the main events in chronological order.

Answers: Items 1, 2, and 5 have learning outcomes that match; items 3 and 4 do not have learning outcomes that match.

STEP 2: Identify the learning conditions that are called for by the objective. Check to determine if your item requires the same learning conditions.

EXERCISE: For the following, assume step 1 has been performed. Employ step 2.

	Match? Yes	No
1. *Objective:* Using your map as a guide, make a freehand drawing of Australia. *Item:* Without using your map, draw the continent of Australia.	_______	_______
2. *Objective:* Given a complete instructional objective, write a test item that matches the objective's learning outcome and conditions. *Item:* Write an item that matches the learning outcome and conditions of the following objective: "The student will add on paper 10 two-digit numbers without regrouping within one minute with 80 percent accuracy."	_______	_______
3. *Objective:* Given a list of words, the student will circle the nouns with 90 percent accuracy. *Item:* Give ten examples of nouns and ten examples of verbs.	_______	_______
4. *Objective:* Using their own nondigital watches, the students will tell time to the quarter hour with 90 percent accuracy. *Item:* Look at the digital clock on my desk and write down the correct time when I ask.	_______	_______
5. *Objective:* The student will sing "The Star-Spangled Banner" in front of the class with the aid of a record. *Item:* Sing "The Star-Spangled Banner" in front of the class.	_______	_______

Answers: Item 2 has matching conditions; items 1, 3, 4, and 5 do not have matching conditions.

In summary, ensuring content validity is as simple as making sure that both the learning outcomes and conditions called for by your test items match the learning outcomes and conditions called for by your instructional objectives. Remember, your goal is to measure achievement, not to trick your students or to have them guess what kind of answer you are looking for. The best way to measure achievement is to ask your students to demonstrate mastery of a skill under the conditions you specify in your instructional objectives. With time, steps 1 and 2 will become second nature. Until then, subject your items to these steps to ensure their content validity.

TAXONOMY OF EDUCATIONAL OBJECTIVES

We've now considered methods not only to analyze objectives already written, but to write instructional objectives and to match test items to instructional objectives. In the rest of this chapter we will consider different levels at which objectives and test items may be written and a method for test construction that will help us write items at these levels.

Cognitive Domain

The *level* of an objective refers to the cognitive, mental, or thought complexity called for by the objective. For example, the objective "The student will list from memory the names of at least three of the last four United States presidents" is a relatively straightforward cognitive task. It involves only recall of the information. Such an objective would be considered lower-level. On the other hand, an objective such as "Given an eyewitness account of an event, separate fact from opinion with at least 75 percent accuracy" is a relatively complex cognitive task. It requires the ability to analyze an eyewitness account and apply some criteria in determining whether statements are observable and objective or subjective and based on inference. Such an objective would be considered higher-level.

One method of categorizing objectives according to cognitive complexity was devised by Bloom, Englehart, Hill, Furst, and Krathwohl (1956). It is a taxonomy of educational objectives for the cognitive domain and delineates six levels of cognitive complexity ranging from the knowledge level (simplest) to the evaluation level (most complex). As illustrated in Figure 5.2, the levels are presumed to be hierarchical. That is, higher-level objectives are assumed to include, and be dependent on, lower-level cognitive skills. Each level of the taxonomy has different characteristics. Each of these is described next with examples of action verbs usually indicative of the different levels.

KNOWLEDGE. Objectives at the knowledge level require the students to remember. Test items ask the student to recall or recognize facts, terminology, problem-solving strategies, or rules. Some action verbs that describe learning outcomes at the knowledge level are:

define	list	recall
describe	match	recite
identify	name	select
label	outline	state

Some example objectives are:

The student will recall the four major food groups without error, by Friday.

From memory, the student will match each United States general with his most famous battle, with 80 percent accuracy.

FIGURE 5.2
Taxonomy of Educational Objectives: Cognitive Domain

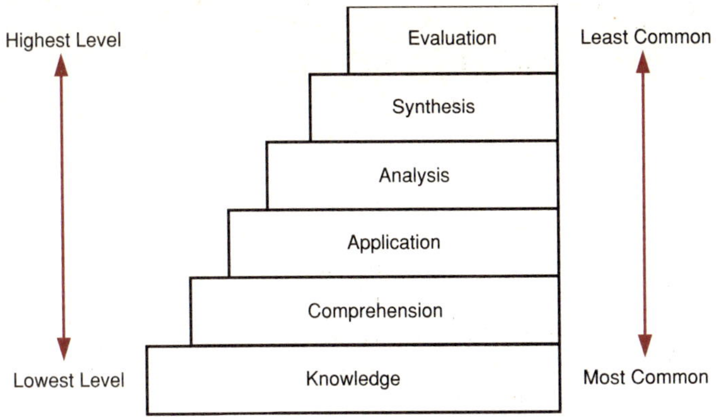

COMPREHENSION. Objectives at this level require some level of understanding. Test items require the student to change the form of a communication (translation), to restate what has been read, to see connections or relationships among parts of a communication (interpretation), or to draw conclusions or consequences from information (inference). Some action verbs that describe learning outcomes at the comprehension level are:

convert	explain	infer
defend	extend	paraphrase
discriminate	estimate	predict
distinguish	generalize	summarize

Some example objectives are:

By the end of the semester, the student will summarize the main events of a story in grammatically correct English.

The student will discriminate between the "realists" and the "naturalists," citing examples from the readings.

APPLICATION. Objectives written at this level require the student to use previously acquired information in a setting other than that in which it was learned. Application differs from comprehension in that questions requiring application present the problem in a different and often applied context. Thus, the student can rely on neither the question nor the context to decide what prior learning information must be used to solve the problem. Some action verbs that describe learning outcomes at the application level are:

change	modify	relate
compute	operate	solve
demonstrate	organize	transfer

develop	prepare	use
employ	produce	

Some example objectives are:

On Monday, the student will tell the class what he or she did over the holiday.

Given fractions not covered in class, the student will multiply them on paper with 85 percent accuracy.

ANALYSIS. Objectives written at the analysis level require the student to identify logical errors (for example, point out a contradiction or an erroneous inference) or to differentiate among facts, opinions, assumptions, hypotheses, or conclusions. Questions at the analysis level often require the student to draw relationships among ideas or to compare and contrast. Some action verbs that describe learning outcomes at the analysis level are:

break down	distinguish	point out
deduce	illustrate	relate
diagram	infer	separate out
differentiate	outline	subdivide

Some example objectives are:

Given a presidential speech, the student will be able to point out the positions that attack an individual rather than his or her program.

Given absurd statements (for example: A man had flu twice. The first time it killed him. The second time he got well quickly.), the student will be able to point out the contradiction.

SYNTHESIS. Objectives written at the synthesis level require the student to produce something unique or original. Questions at the synthesis level require students to solve some unfamiliar problem in a unique way, or combine parts to form a unique or novel whole. Some action verbs that describe learning outcomes at the synthesis level are:

categorize	create	formulate
compile	design	rewrite
compose	devise	summarize

Some example objectives at the synthesis level are:

Given a short story, the student will write a different but plausible ending.

Given a problem to be solved, the student will design on paper a scientific experiment to address the problem.

EVALUATION. Instructional objectives written at this level require the student to form judgments about the value or worth of methods, ideas, people, or products that have a specific purpose. Questions require the student to state the basis for his or her judgments (for example, what external criteria or principles were drawn upon to reach a conclusion). Some action verbs that describe learning outcomes at the evaluation level are:

appraise	criticize	support
compare	defend	validate
contrast	justify	
conclude	interpret	

Some example objectives at the evaluation level are:

Given a previously unread paragraph, the student will judge its value according to the five criteria discussed in class.

Given a description of a country's economic system, the student will defend it, basing arguments on principles of socialism.

Affective Domain

The Affective Taxonomy, which describes objectives that reflect underlying *emotions*, *feelings*, or *values* rather than cognitive or thought complexity, has been developed by Krathwohl, Bloom, and Masia (1964). This taxonomy describes a process by which another person's, group's, or society's ideas, beliefs, customs, philosophies, attitudes, etc., are gradually accepted and internalized by a different person, group, or society. This process usually begins with a minimal, partial, or incomplete acceptance of an alternative point of view and culminates with the complete integration of this point of view into an individual's personal belief system.

For example, an individual who naively believed in early 1985 that the return of Halley's Comet in 1986 would cause the end of life on earth may at first have found it difficult even to listen to, *receive*, or *attend* to information that indicated that the comet's return would have no significant or lasting effect on life on earth. Instead, the individual may have ignored such information, attempting instead to convince others of the earth's impending doom. However, with the passage of time throughout the year, and with increased media and educational reports about the event, the individual may have increasingly listened to such information and even considered, discussed, or *responded* to explanations regarding the earth's safety due to the comet's distance from earth, its lack of mass, the protection afforded by the earth's atmosphere, etc. Eventually, the individual likely began to *value* the argument that the comet would have little or no effect on life on earth and ceased preaching the earth's demise. Finally, after trying unsuccessfully even to see the comet on numerous occasions during its closest approach to earth, the individual may have accepted and *organized* the arguments against the total destruction of the human race to the extent that these have come to be internalized and now *characterize* the individual's *value complex*. This would be evident by the individual's calm acceptance of near approaches by celestial bodies in the future and efforts to reassure others of their safety in the face of such events.

The preceding italicized words indicate the five categories or levels of the Affective Domain. Each of these is described further under the following heads, and sublevels within each of these levels are italicized also. As with the cognitive taxonomy, the levels and sublevels are generally considered to be hierarchical.

RECEIVING (ATTENDING). Progressing through this level requires that a student have at least an *awareness* of some stimulus. Once this has occurred, a *willingness* at least to listen or attend to the stimulus must be present (i.e., tolerance). A student will next be able to *attend selectively* to various aspects of the context within which the stimulus exists, differentiating those which are relevant to the stimulus from those which are not.

RESPONDING. Student responses at this level indicate more than passive listening/attending; they require active participation. In the most basic form of responding, a student will at least *acquiesce* to a teacher's or other's request, although given a choice the student might choose some other activity. More complete responding would be indicated by a student's *willingness* to engage in an activity, even when allowed a choice. The highest level within this category is indicated by *satisfaction* after engaging in a response. The student not only participates, but it is evident that the student enjoys the activity.

VALUING. At this level students judge an activity as to its worthiness and tend to do so consistently enough that the pattern is recognizable to others. The most basic sublevel involves the *acceptance* of a belief, idea, attitude, etc. The individual may not be willing to defend publicly the idea, but has internalized it. When a student actively pursues an idea, the student is demonstrating a preference for it, the next sublevel of valuing. Finally, after becoming convinced of the validity of an idea, a student expresses commitment to the idea. At this point the student demonstrates conviction, pursuing the goal or idea diligently.

ORGANIZATION. As ideas are internalized they become increasingly interrelated and prioritized. That is, they become organized into a value system. This requires first that a student *conceptualize* a value by analyzing interrelationships and drawing generalizations that reflect the valued idea. It may be noted that such an activity is cognitive. However, it is classified here because such conceptualizing would only be undertaken after an idea or philosophy was valued. Next, values that have been conceptualized are subject to the *organization of a value system.* That is, the valued ideas are arranged to foster their consistency and compatibility with each other.

CHARACTERIZATION BY A VALUE OR VALUE COMPLEX. Students operating at this level behave in a way that is consistent with their value system, avoiding hypocrisy and behaving consistently with an underlying philosophy "automatically." The first sublevel is characterized by a *generalized set.* This means the individual is predisposed to perceive, process, and react to a situation in accordance with an internalized value system. The next level, *characterization,* is evident in the consistency between an individual's thoughts and behaviors. Such individuals would never say "Do as I say, not as I do."

Now that you are familiar with the Affective Taxonomy you may ask, "What do I do with it in the classroom?" First of all, it is probably unrealistic to expect a classroom teacher to structure experiences over a one-year period that would lead a student through all five levels. Indeed, there are many who would argue that few human beings ever reach a point in their lives where they function at the fifth, or even the fourth, level. Nonetheless, this taxonomy has important implications for instructional activities and for methods to evaluate instructional activities.

Let's look at an example. Suppose most of the children in your class say they "hate" history and avoid all stimuli related to history. Asking those students to write a paper describing the importance of history courses in the public-school curriculum would likely be a frustrating experience for them and for you, since those students are not even at the *receiving/attending* level when it comes to history. You might spend a good deal of time developing a reliable scoring scheme for such a paper and grading the papers only to find that the students failed to see any value in history courses in general or the topic of the paper. Thus, it would be more appropriate, given this example, to develop activities and ways to evaluate these activities that are aimed initially at the *receiving/attending* level; progressing to the *responding* level only after the students have demonstrated their willingness to consider history as an important part of the curriculum and after they have demonstrated the ability to attend selectively to history when distracting stimuli are present; and progressing to the *valuing* level only after the students have demonstrated their willingness to deal objectively with history and/or their satisfaction with history as a subject. While individualizing instruction in this way may not always be completely practical, the Affective Taxonomy will at least provide you with a framework to allow you to better assess "where they are" regarding various topics. This should help you keep your expectations for the class realistic and keep you from pushing for "too much too soon," perhaps frustrating yourself and the class in the process. Practically speaking, it is probably unrealistic to expect students to progress much beyond the *valuing* level as a result of their elementary and secondary school experiences.

The Psychomotor Domain

In addition to the cognitive and affective taxonomies, a taxonomy of psychomotor behaviors has been developed by Harrow (1972). This domain includes virtually all behaviors: speaking, writing, eating, jumping, throwing, catching, running, walking, driving a car, opening a door, dancing, flying an airplane, etc. The psychomotor domain has proved most difficult to classify into taxonomic levels since all but the simplest reflex actions involve cognitive, and often affective, components. Nonetheless, Harrow's taxonomy is presented because it does again provide a framework within which to consider the design of instructional activities and methods to evaluate the activities. This taxonomy may prove especially useful to teachers in the lower elementary grades and teachers of physical education, dance, theater, and other courses that require considerable movement. The Psychomotor Taxonomy listed under the following headings ranges from the lowest level of observable reflexive behavior to the highest level, representing the most complex forms of nonverbal communication.

REFLEX MOVEMENTS. Reflex movements are involuntary movements that either are evident at birth or develop with maturation. Sublevels include *segmental reflexes*, *intersegmental reflexes*, and *suprasegmental reflexes*.

BASIC-FUNDAMENTAL MOVEMENTS. Basic-fundamental movements are inherent in more complex or skilled motor movements. Sublevels include *locomotor movements*, *nonlocomotor movements*, and *manipulative movements*.

PERCEPTUAL ABILITIES. Perceptual abilities refer to all the abilities of an individual that send input to the brain for interpretation, which in turn affects motor movements. Sublevels include *kinesthetic*, *visual*, *auditory*, *tactile discrimination*, and *coordinated abilities*.

PHYSICAL ABILITIES. Physical abilities are the characteristics of an individual's physical self which, when developed properly, enable smooth and efficient movement. Sublevels include endurance, strength, flexibility, and agility.

SKILLED MOVEMENTS. Skilled movements are the result of learning, often complex learning. They result in efficiency in carrying out a complex movement or task. Sublevels include *simple*, *compound*, and *complex adaptive skills*.

NONDISCURSIVE COMMUNICATION. Nondiscursive communication is a form of communication through movement. Such nonverbal communication as facial expressions, postures, and expressive dance routines are examples. Sublevels include *expressive movement* and *interpretive movement*.

THE TEST BLUEPRINT

Thus far we've devoted a good deal of time to writing and analyzing objectives and showing you how to match test items to objectives. We also need to spend some time discussing a technique to help you remember to write objectives and test items at different levels. This technique is referred to as a *test blueprint*. Much like a blueprint used by a builder to guide building construction, the test blueprint used by a teacher guides test construction. The test blueprint is also called a table of specifications.

The blueprint for a building ensures that the builder will not overlook details considered essential. Similarly, the test blueprint ensures that the teacher will not overlook details considered essential to a good test. More specifically, it ensures that a test will sample whether learning has taken place across the range of (1) content areas covered in class and readings and (2) cognitive processes considered important. It ensures that your test will include a variety of items that tap different levels of cognitive complexity. To get an idea of what a test blueprint helps you avoid, consider the following:

> Joan was nervous. She knew she had to do very well on the comprehensive final in order to pass American History: 1945–1995. To make matters worse, her teacher was new and no one knew what his final exams were like.
>
> "Well," she told herself. "There's really no point in worrying. Even if I don't do well on this test, I have learned to analyze information and think critically—the discussions were great. I've studied the text and lessons very hard and managed to cover every topic very thoroughly beginning with the end of World War II in 1945 through the debate on health care reform. I realize I missed the class dealing with the late 1960s and early 1970s, but that stuff only covered a few pages in the text anyway, and we only spent one class on it!"
>
> Feeling more relaxed and confident, Joan felt even better when she saw that the entire final was only one page long. After receiving her copy, Joan began shaking. Her test is reproduced on the top of page 67.

American History: 1945–1995

Name:________________________________ Date:__________

It has been a long year and you have been good students. This test is your reward.

1. On what date did American soldiers first begin to fight in Vietnam? _______
2. How many years did Americans fight in Vietnam? _______
3. What was the capital of South Vietnam? ___________
4. On what date did Richard Nixon become president? ________
5. Who was Richard Nixon's vice president during his second administration? ___________________
6. What is Vietnam's largest seaport? ______________
7. Who was the president of South Vietnam? ________________
8. On what date did Americans begin to leave Vietnam? ________

Have a good summer!

We wish we could safely say that things like this never happen, but they do! Chances are you have had a similar experience—perhaps not as extreme, but similar. This test is not a comprehensive assessment of American History: 1945–1995. It is not comprehensive; it focuses on events that occurred during the Vietnam War. It fails to sample representatively content presented in the text and omits content presented in class, except for one class. Finally, it fails to tap any higher-level thinking processes. Each question requires rote memorization at the knowledge level. A test blueprint, as shown in Table 5.1, helps us avoid falling into this or similar traps in test construction.

A test blueprint is essential to good test construction. It not only ensures that your test will sample all important content areas and processes (levels of cognitive complexity), but is also useful in planning and organizing instruction. The blueprint should be assembled *before* you actually begin a unit. Table 5.1 illustrates a test blueprint appropriate for a unit on instructional objectives being taught in an education course.

Let's consider each component of the blueprint. Once we understand how the components are interrelated, the significance of a test blueprint will become more clear.

Content Outline

The content outline lists the topic and the important objectives included under the topic. It is for these objectives that you will write test items. Try to keep the total number of objectives to a manageable number, certainly no more than about 15 for any one unit. Otherwise, you will end up with too many test items.

Categories

The categories serve as a reminder or a check on the "cognitive complexity" of the test. Obviously many units over which you want to test will contain objectives that do not go

TABLE 5.1
Test Blueprint for a Unit on Instructional Objectives

	Categories					
Content Outline	*Knowledge*	*Comprehension*	*Application*	*Analysis*	*Total*	*Percentage*
	Number of Items					
1. Role of Objectives						
a. The student can state purposes for objectives in education.	4				4	12%
b. The student can describe a classroom system model and the role of objectives in it.		1			1	3%
2. Writing Objectives						
a. Given a general educational goal, the student will write an instructional objective that specifies that goal.			5		5	14%
b. The student can match instructional objectives with their appropriate level in the cognitive domain.		5			5	14%
c. The student can identify the three parts of an objective: behavior, conditions, criteria.		5			5	14%
d. The student can distinguish learning activities from learning outcomes when given examples of each.		10			10	29%
3. Decoding Ready-Made Objectives						
a. Given instructional objectives in need of modification, the student will rewrite the objective so that it is a suitable instructional objective.				5	5	14%
Total	4	21	5	5	35	
Percentage	12%	60%	14%	14%	100%	

beyond the comprehension level. However, the outline can suggest that you try to incorporate higher levels of learning into your instruction and evaluations. In the cells under these categories, report the number of items in your tests that are included in that level for a particular objective. For example, five items are to be constructed to measure comprehension-level objective 2b in Table 5.1.

Number of Items

Fill in the cells in Table 5.1 using the following procedure:

1. Determine the classification of each instructional objective.
2. Record the number of items that are to be constructed for the objective in the cell corresponding to the category for that objective.
3. Repeat steps 1 and 2 for every objective in the outline.
4. Total the number of items for the instructional objective, and record the number in the *Total* column.
5. Repeat steps 1 through 4 for each topic.
6. Total the number of items falling into each category and record the number at the bottom of the table.
7. Compute the column and row percentages by dividing each total by the number of items in the test.

Functions

The information in Table 5.1 is intended to convey to the teacher the following:

How many items are to be constructed for which objectives and content topics.

Whether the test will reflect a balanced picture of what was taught.

Whether all topics and objectives will be assessed.

Seldom can such "balance" be so easily attained. The little extra time required to construct such a blueprint for your test (and your instruction!) will quickly repay itself. You will not only avoid constructing a bad test, but will have to make fewer and less extensive revisions of your test. You'll also have a sense of satisfaction from realizing you've constructed a representative test.

Since test blueprints are so important to test construction (not to mention instructional planning!), we have included a second example of a test blueprint in Table 5.2. This table illustrates a test blueprint appropriate for an elementary unit on subtraction without borrowing.

This concludes our introduction to test planning and instructional objectives. In the next two chapters we'll consider the actual process by which objective and essay test items are constructed. Soon you'll be able to construct not just a representative test, but a *good* representative test!

TABLE 5.2
Test Blueprint for a Unit on Subtraction Without Borrowing

Content Outline	*Knowledge*	*Comprehension*	*Application*	*Total*	*Percentage*
1. The student will discriminate the subtraction sign from the addition sign.	1			1	4%
2. The student will discriminate addition problems from subtraction problems.	2			2	8%
3. The student will discriminate correctly solved subtraction problems from incorrectly solved subtraction problems.		4		4	16%
4. The student will solve correctly single-digit subtraction problems.			6	6	24%
5. The student will solve correctly subtraction problems with double-digit numerators and single-digit denominators.			6	6	24%
6. The student will solve correctly double-digit subtraction problems.			6	6	24%
Total	3	4	18	25	
Percentage	12%	16%	72%		100%

SUMMARY

Chapter 5 introduced you to the first two steps in test construction, writing instructional objectives, and preparing a test blueprint. Its major points are:

1. A complete instructional objective includes:
   a. An observable behavior or learning outcome,
   b. Any special conditions under which the behavior must be displayed, and
   c. A performance level considered to be indicative of mastery.
2. Learning outcomes are ends (products); learning activities are the means (processes) to the ends.
3. Objectives may be analyzed to determine their adequacy by:
   a. Determining whether a learning outcome or learning activity is stated in the objective,

b. Rewriting the objective if a learning outcome is not stated,

c. Determining whether the learning outcomes are stated in measurable or unmeasurable terms, and

d. Determining whether the objective states the simplest and most direct way of measuring the learning outcome.

4. Learning outcomes and conditions stated in a test item must match the outcomes and conditions stated in the objective if the item is to be considered a valid measure of or match for the objective.

5. The taxonomy of educational objectives for the cognitive domain helps categorize objectives at different levels of cognitive complexity. There are six levels: knowledge, comprehension, application, analysis, synthesis, and evaluation.

6. A test blueprint, including instructional objectives covering the content areas to be covered and the relevant cognitive processes, should be constructed to guide item writing and test construction.

7. The test blueprint conveys to the teacher the number of items to be constructed per objective and their level in the taxonomy and whether the test represents a balanced picture based on what was taught.

For Practice

1. For the same content area, make up two objectives each at the knowledge, comprehension, application, analysis, synthesis, and evaluation levels of the taxonomy of cognitive objectives. Select verbs for each level from the lists provided. Try to make your objectives cover the same subject.

2. Exchange the objectives you have just written with a classmate. Have him or her check each objective for (1) an observable behavior, (2) any special conditions under which the behavior must be displayed, and (3) a performance level considered sufficient to demonstrate mastery. Revise your objectives, if necessary.

3. Now take your list of objectives and arrange them into the format of a test blueprint (see Table 5.1). To construct a test blueprint, determine some general content headings under which your specific objectives can be placed. List these with your objectives vertically down the left side of the page. Next, across the top of the page, indicate the levels of behavior at which you have written your objectives. In the cells of the table, place the number of items you would write for each objective if you were to prepare a 100-item test over this content. Total the items and compute percentages, as indicated in Table 5.1.

*4. Column A on the following page contains instructional objectives. Column B contains levels of cognitive learning outcomes. Match the levels in Column B with the most appropriate objective in Column A. Write in the space next to the numbers in Column A the letter that indicates the highest level of cognitive outcome implied. Column B levels *can* be used more than once.

Column A	Column B
_____1. Given a two-page essay, the student can distinguish the assumptions basic to the author's position.	a. Knowledge
_____2. The student will correctly spell the word mountain.	b. Comprehension
_____3. The student will convert the following English passage into Spanish.	c. Application
_____4. The student will compose new pieces of prose and poetry according to the classification system emphasized in lecture.	d. Analysis
_____5. Given a sinking passenger ship with 19 of its 20 lifeboats destroyed, the captain will decide who is to be on the last lifeboat on the basis of perceptions of their potential worth to society.	e. Synthesis
	f. Evaluation

*5. Using the following test blueprint or table of specifications for a unit on mathematics, answer the following questions:

a. How many questions will deal with long division at the comprehension, application, and analysis levels?

b. What percentage of the test questions will deal with multiplication and division?

Major areas	*Minor areas*	*Knowledge*	*Comprehension*	*Application*	*Analysis*	*Synthesis*	*Evaluation*	*Total*	*Percentage*
Addition	Whole numbers	2	1	2				5	
	Fractions	1	1	2	1			5	20%
Subtraction	Whole numbers	1	1	2	1			5	
	Fractions	1	1	2	1			5	20%
Multiplication	Tables	2	2					4	
	Whole numbers			2	2	1		5	
	Fractions	1	1	2	1	1		6	30%
Division	Long division	1	2	1				4	
	Whole numbers	1	1	2	1			5	
	Fractions	1	2	2	1			6	30%

*Answers to questions 4 and 5 appear in Appendix D.

CHAPTER 6

Writing Objective Test Items

Thus far, we have discussed how to establish general goals for instruction and how to develop instructional objectives derived from these goals. We have also discussed using the test blueprint to ensure an adequate sampling of the content area and accurate matching of test items to instructional objectives. We are now ready to put some "meat" on this test "skeleton." In this chapter we will discuss objective test items and how to construct them. Objective test items include items with the following formats: true-false, matching, multiple-choice, and completion or short answer. The essay item, because of its special characteristics and scoring considerations, will be treated in Chapter 7.

WHICH FORMAT?

Once you have reached the item-writing stage of test construction, you will have to choose a format or combination of formats to use for your test. Although your choice can be somewhat arbitrary at times, this is not always the case. Often your decision has already been made for you, or more correctly, you may have at least partially made the decision when you wrote the objective or objectives. In many instances, however, you will have a choice among several item formats. For example, consider the following objectives and item formats:

OBJECTIVE 1: Given a story, the student can recognize the meaning of all new words.

TEST ITEM: Circle the letter that represents the correct meaning of the following words

1. intention
   a. desire
   b. need
   c. direction
   d. command

2. crisis
   a. feeling
   b. message
   c. pending
   d. critical

OBJECTIVE 2: The student can associate the characteristics of leading characters with their names.

TEST ITEM: The first column below is a list of the names of the main characters in *Huckleberry Finn.* Descriptions of the main characters are listed in the second column. In the space provided, write the letter of the description that matches each character.

Characters	**Descriptions**
_____ 1. Tom	a. Cruel
_____ 2. Becky	b. Always by himself, a loner
_____ 3. Jim	c. Popular, outgoing, fun-loving
_____ 4. Huck	d. Always critical
_____ 5. Mrs. Watson	e. Sneaky, lying, scheming
	f. Kind, gentle, loving
	g. Dull, slow-moving

OBJECTIVE 3: The student can write a plausible alternative ending to a story.

TEST ITEM: You have just read the story *Huckleberry Finn.* In 40 words, write a different ending to the story that would be believable.

OBJECTIVE 4: The students will recognize whether certain events occured.

TEST ITEM. Below is a list of incidents in *Huckleberry Finn.* Circle T if it happened in the story and F if it did not.

1. The thieves were killed in the storm on the river.	T	F
2. Jim gained his freedom.	T	F
3. Tom broke his leg.	T	F

Objective 1 was measured using a multiple-choice format. We might also have tested this objective using a true-false or matching format. Similarly, objective 2 lends itself to a multiple-choice as well as a matching format. Since in many circumstances alternative item formats may be appropriate, the choice between them will be made on the basis of other considerations. For example, time constraints or your preference for, or skill in, writing different types of items will undoubtedly influence your choice of item format. However, objective 3 requires an essay item. There is no way this objective can be measured with an objective item. Similarly, objective 4 lends itself almost exclusively to a single format. Perhaps other formats would work, but the true-false format certainly does the job. In short, there are times our objectives tell us which format to use. At other times we must consider other factors. Now let's look more closely at the different item formats.

True-False Items

True-false items are popular probably because they are quick and easy to write, or at least they seem to be. Actually, true-false items do take less time to write than good objective items of any other format, but *good* true-false items are not all that easy to write. Consider the following true-false items. Use your common sense to help you determine which are good items and which are poor.

EXERCISE: Put a G in the space next to the items you believe are good true-false items and a P next to the items you feel are poor.

________ 1. High-IQ children always get high grades in school.

________ 2. Will Rogers said, "I never met a man I didn't like."

________ 3. If a plane crashed on the Mexican-American border, half the survivors would be buried in Mexico and half in the United States.

________ 4. The use of double negatives is not an altogether undesirable characteristic of diplomats and academicians.

________ 5. Prayer should *not* be outlawed in the schools.

________ 6. Of the objective items, true-false items are the least time-consuming to construct.

________ 7. The trend toward competency testing of high-school graduates began in the late 1970s and represents a big step forward for slow learners.

Answers: 1. P; 2. G; 3. P; 4. P; 5. P; 6. G; 7. P.

In item 1, the word *always* is an absolute. To some extent, true-false items depend on absolute judgments. However, statements or facts are seldom *completely* true or *completely* false. Thus, an alert student will usually answer "false" to items that include *always, all, never,* or *only.*

To avoid this problem, avoid using terms like *all, always, never,* or *only.* Item 1 could be improved by replacing always with a less absolute term, perhaps *tend.* Thus, item 1 might read:

High-IQ children tend to get high grades in school.

Item 2 is a good one. To answer the item correctly, the students would have to know whether Will Rogers made the statement. Or do they? Consider the following situation:

> Mrs. Allen, a history teacher and crusader against grade inflation, couldn't wait to spring her latest creation on her students. She had spent weeks inserting trick words, phrases, and complicated grammatical constructions into her 100-item true-false test. In order to ensure low grades on the test, she allowed only 30 minutes for the test. Although her harried students worked as quickly as they could, no one completed more than half the items, and no one answered more than 40 items correctly. No one, that is, except Tina. When Tina handed her test back to Mrs. Allen after 2 minutes, Mrs. Allen announced, "Class, Tina has handed in her test! Obviously, she hasn't read the questions and will earn a zero!" However, when she scored the test, Mrs. Allen was shocked to see that in fact Tina had answered 50 items correctly. She earned the highest score on the test without even reading Mrs. Allen's tricky questions. Confused and embarrassed, Mrs. Allen told the class they would have no more true-false tests and would have essay tests in the future.

This points to the most serious shortcoming of true-false items: With every true-false item, regardless of how well or poorly written, the student has a 50 percent chance of guessing correctly even without reading the item! In other words, on a 50-item true-false test, we would expect individuals who were totally unfamiliar with the content being tested to answer about 25 items correctly. However, this doesn't mean you should avoid true-false items entirely, since they are appropriate at times. Fortunately, there are ways of reducing the effects of guessing. Some of these are described next and another will be presented in Chapter 8.

1. Encourage *all* students to guess when they do not know the correct answer. Since it is virtually impossible to prevent certain students from guessing, encouraging all students to guess should equalize the effects of guessing. The test scores will then reflect a more or less equal "guessing factor" *plus* the actual level of each student's knowledge. This will also prevent test-wise students from having an unfair advantage over non-test-wise students.
2. Require revision of statements that are false. With this approach, space is provided for students to alter false items to make them true. Usually the student also underlines or circles the false part of the item. Item 1 is revised below along with other examples.

T	F	High-IQ children <u>always</u> get high grades in school. *tend to*
T	F	Panama is <u>north</u> of Cuba. *south*
T	F	<u>September</u> has an extra day during leap year. *February*

With such a strategy full credit is awarded only if the revision is correct. The disadvantage of such an approach is that more test time is required for the same number of items and scoring time is increased.

Item 3 is a poor item, but Mrs. Allen would probably like it because it is a trick question. "Survivors" of a plane crash are *not* buried! Chances are that you never even noticed the word *survivors* and probably assumed the item referred to fatalities. Trick items may have a place in tests of critical reading or visual discrimination (in which case they would no longer be trick questions), but seldom are they appropriate in the average classroom test. Rewritten, item 3 might read:

If a plane crashes on the Mexican-American border, half the fatalities would be buried in Mexico and half in the United States.

Item 4 is also poor. First of all, it includes a double negative—*not* and *undesirable*. Items with a single negative are confusing enough. Negating the first negative with a second wastes space and test-taking time and also confuses most students. If you want to say something, say it positively. The following revision makes this item slightly more palatable.

The use of double negatives is an altogether desirable trait of diplomats and academicians.

We said slightly more palatable because the item is still troublesome. The world *altogether* is an absolute, and we now know we should avoid absolutes, since there usually are exceptions to the rules they imply. Thus, when we eliminate *altogether* the item reads:

The use of double negatives is a desirable trait of diplomats and academicians.

However, the item is still flawed because it states an opinion, not a fact. Is the item true or false? The answer depends on whom you ask. To most of us, the use of double negatives is probably undesirable, for the reasons already stated. To some diplomats, the use of double negatives may seem highly desirable. In short, true-false statements should normally be used to measure knowledge of factual information. If you must use a true-false item to measure knowledge of an opinionated position or statement, state the referent (the person or group that made the statement or took the position), as illustrated in the following revision:

According to the National Institute of Diplomacy, the use of double negatives is a desirable trait of diplomats and academicians.

Item 5 further illustrates this point. It is deficient because it states an opinion. It is neither obviously true nor obviously false. The revision below includes a referent which makes it acceptable.

The American Civil Liberties Union (ACLU) has taken the position that prayer should *not* be outlawed in the schools.

Notice the word *not* in item 5. When you include a negative in a test item, highlight it in italics, underlining, or uppercase letters so the reader will not overlook it. Remember that, unlike Mrs. Allen, you intend to determine whether your students have mastered your objective, not to ensure low test scores.

Item 6 represents a good item. It measures factual information, and the phrase "Of the objective items" qualifies the item and limits it to a specific frame of reference.

The last item is deficient because it is double-barreled. It is actually two items in one. When do you mark *true* for a double-barreled item? When both parts of the item are true? When one part is true? Or only when the most important part is true? The point is that items should measure a single idea. Double-barreled items take too much time to read and comprehend. To avoid this problem, simply construct two items, as we have done here:

The trend toward competency testing of high-school graduates began in the late 1970s.
The trend toward competency testing represents a big step forward for slow learners.

Better? Yes. Acceptable? Not quite. The second item is opinionated. According to whom is this statement true or false? Let's include a referent.

According to the Office of Education, the trend toward competency testing of high-school graduates is a big step forward for slow learners.

Whose position is being represented is now clear, and the item is straightforward.

Suggestions for Writing True-False Items

1. The desired method of marking *true* or *false* should be clearly explained before students begin the test.
2. Construct statements that are definitely true or definitely false, without additional qualifications. If opinion is used, attribute it to some source.
3. Use relatively short statements and eliminate extraneous material.
4. Keep true and false statements at approximately the same length, and be sure that there are approximately equal numbers of true and false items.
5. Avoid using double-negative statements. They take extra time to decipher and are difficult to interpret.
6. Avoid the following:
   a. verbal clues, absolutes, and complex sentences
   b. broad general statements that are usually not true or false without further qualifications
   c. terms denoting indefinite degree (for example, *large, long time, regularly*), or absolutes (for example, *never, only, always*)
   d. placing items in a systematic order (for example, TTFF, TFTF, and so on)
   e. taking statements directly from the text and presenting them out of context

Matching Items

Like true-false items, matching items represent a popular and convenient testing format. Just like good true-false items, though, good matching items are not as easy to write as you might think. Imagine you are back in your tenth-grade American History class and the following matching item shows up on your test. Is it a good matching exercise or not? If not, what is wrong with it?

DIRECTIONS: MATCH A AND B.

A	B
1. Lincoln	a. President during the twentieth century
2. Nixon	b. Invented the telephone
3. Whitney	c. Delivered the Emancipation Proclamation
4. Ford	d. Recent president to resign from office
5. Bell	e. Civil-rights leader
6. King	f. Invented the cotton gin
7. Washington	g. Our first president
8. Roosevelt	h. Only president elected for more than two terms

See any problems? Compare those you have identified with the list of faults and explanations below.

HOMOGENEITY. The lists are *not* homogeneous. Column A contains names of presidents, inventors, and a civil-rights leader. Unless specifically taught as a set of related public figures or ideas, this example represents too wide a variety for a matching exercise. To prevent this from happening you might title your lists (for example, "United States Presidents"). This will help keep irrelevant or filler items from creeping in. If you really want to measure student knowledge of presidents, inventors, and civil-rights leaders, then build three separate matching exercises. Doing so will prevent implausible options from being eliminated by the student. When students can eliminate implausible options they are more likely to guess correctly. For example, the student may not know a president who resigned from office, but may know that Washington and Lincoln were presidents, and that neither was recent. Thus, the student could eliminate two options, increasing the chance of guessing correctly from one out of eight to one out of six.

ORDER OF LISTS. The lists should be reversed; that is, column A should be column B, and column B should be column A. This is a consideration to save time for the test taker. We are trained to read from left to right. When the longer description is in the left-hand column the student only reads the description once and glances down the list of names to find the answer. As the exercise is now written, the student reads a name and then has to read through all or many of the more lengthy descriptions to find the answer, a much more time-consuming process.

EASY GUESSING. There are equal numbers of options and descriptions in each column. Again, this increases the chances of guessing correctly through elimination. In the preceding exercise, if a student did not know who invented the cotton gin but knew which of the names went with the other seven descriptions, the student would arrive at the correct answer through elimination. If there are at least three more options than descriptions, the chances of guessing correctly in such a situation are reduced to one chance in four. Alternatively, the instructions for the exercise may be written to indicate that each option *may* be used more than once.

POOR DIRECTIONS. Speaking of directions, those included above are much too brief. Matching directions should specify the basis for matching. For example:

> DIRECTIONS: Column A contains brief descriptions of historical events. Column B contains the names of presidents. Indicate which man was president when the historical event took place by placing the appropriate letter to the left of the number in column A.

The directions also do not indicate *how* the matches should be shown. Should lines be drawn? Should letters be written next to numbers, or numbers next to letters? Failure to indicate how matches should be marked can greatly increase your scoring time.

TOO MANY CORRECT RESPONSES. The description "President during the twentieth century" has three defensible answers: Nixon, Ford, and Roosevelt. You say you meant Henry Ford, inventor of the Model T, not Gerald Ford! Well, that brings us to our final criticism of this matching exercise.

AMBIGUOUS LISTS. The list of names is ambiguous. Franklin Roosevelt or Teddy Roosevelt? Henry Ford or Gerald Ford? When using names, always include first and last names to avoid such ambiguities.

Now that we have completed our analysis of this test item, we can easily conclude that it needs revision. Let's revise it, starting by breaking the exercise into homogeneous groupings.

> DIRECTIONS: Column A describes events associated with United States presidents. Indicate which name in column B matches each event by placing the appropriate letter to the left of the number of column A. Each name may be used only once.

Column A	*Column B*
_____ 1. Only president not elected to office	a. Abraham Lincoln
_____ 2. Delivered the Emancipation Proclamation	b. Richard Nixon
_____ 3. Only president to resign from office	c. Gerald Ford
_____ 4. Only president elected for more than two terms	d. George Washington
_____ 5. Our first president	e. Franklin Roosevelt
	f. Theodore Roosevelt
	g. Thomas Jefferson
	h. Woodrow Wilson

We can make one more clarification. It is a good idea to introduce some sort of order—chronological, numerical, or alphabetical—to your list of options. This saves the reader time. Students usually go through the list several times in answering a matching exercise, and it is easier to remember a name's or date's location in a list if it is in some sort of order. Thus, we can arrange the list of names in alphabetical order to look like this:

Column A	*Column B*
_____ 1. Only president not elected to office	a. Gerald Ford
_____ 2. Delivered the Emancipation Proclamation	b. Thomas Jefferson
_____ 3. Only president to resign from office	c. Abraham Lincoln
_____ 4. Only president elected for more than two terms	d. Richard Nixon
_____ 5. Our first president	e. Franklin Roosevelt
	f. Theodore Roosevelt
	g. George Washington
	h. Woodrow Wilson

Our original exercise contained two items relating to invention. If we were determined to measure only knowledge of inventors through a matching exercise, we would want to add at least one more item. Normally, at least three items are used for matching exercises. Such an exercise might look like the following:

> DIRECTIONS: Column A lists famous inventions and column B famous inventors. Match the inventor with the invention by placing the appropriate letter in the space to the left of the number in column A. Each name may be used only once.

Column A	*Column B*
_____ 1. Invented the cotton gin	a. Alexander Graham Bell
_____ 2. One of his inventions was the telephone	b. Henry Bessemer
_____ 3. Famous for inventing the wireless	c. Thomas Edison
	d. Guglielmo Marconi
	e. Eli Whitney
	f. Orville Wright

Notice we have complete directions, there are three more options than descriptions, the lists are homogeneous, and the list of names is alphabetically ordered. But what about the final item remaining from our original exercise? Let's say we want to determine whether our students know that Martin Luther King, Jr., was a civil-rights leader. We can construct another matching exercise with one column listing the names of civil-rights leaders and another listing civil-rights accomplishments. However, an alternative would be simply to switch item formats. Usually, single items that are removed from matching exercises because of nonhomogeneity are easily converted into true-false, completion, or, with a little more difficulty, multiple-choice items. For example:

True-False

T F Martin Luther King, Jr., was a civil-rights leader.

Completion

The name of the black civil-rights leader assassinated in 1968 was__________________.

Multiple-Choice

Which of the following was a civil-rights leader?
a. Jefferson Davis
b. Martin Luther King, Jr.
c. John Quincy Adams
d. John Wilkes Booth

Suggestions for Writing Matching Items

1. Keep both the list of descriptions and the list of options fairly short and homogeneous—they should both fit on the same page. Title the lists to ensure homogeneity, and arrange the descriptions and options in some logical order. If this is impossible you're probably including too wide a variety in the exercise. Try two or more exercises.
2. Make sure that all the options are plausible distractors for each description to ensure homogeneity of lists.
3. The list of descriptions should contain the longer phrases or statements, while the options should consist of short phrases, words, or symbols.
4. Each description in the list should be numbered (each is an item), and the list of options should be identified by letter.
5. Include more options than descriptions. If the option list is longer than the description list, it is harder for students to eliminate options. If the option list is shorter, some options must be used more than once. Always include some options that do not match any of the descriptions, or some that match more than one, or both.
6. In the directions, specify the basis for matching and whether options can be used more than once.

Multiple-Choice Items

Another popular item format is the multiple-choice question. Practically everyone has taken multiple-choice tests at one time or another, but probably more often in high school and college than elementary school. This doesn't mean that multiple-choice items are not appropriate in the elementary years; it suggests only that one needs to be cautious about using them with younger children.

Multiple-choice items are unique among objective test items because they enable you to measure at the higher levels of the taxonomy of educational objectives. Our discussion of multiple-choice items will be in two parts. The first part will consider the mechanics of multiple-choice item construction applied to knowledge-level questions. The second part will deal with the construction of higher-level multiple-choice items. As before, let's start by using common sense to identify good and poor multiple-choice items in the following exercise:

EXERCISE: Place a G next to a good item and a P next to a poor item.

________ 1. U.S. Grant was an

a. president.

b. man.

c. alcoholic.

d. general.

________ 2. In what year did humans first set foot on the moon?

a. 1975

b. 1957

c. 1969

d. 1963

________ 3. The free-floating structures within the cell that synthesize protein are called

a. chromosomes.

b. lysosomes.

c. mitochondria.

d. free ribosomes.

________ 4. The principal value of a balanced diet is that it

a. increases your intelligence.

b. gives you something to talk about with friends.

c. promotes mental health.

d. promotes physical health.

e. improves self-discipline.

________ 5. Some test items

a. are too difficult.

b. are objective.

c. are poorly constructed.

d. have multiple defensible answers.

________ 6. Which of the following are not associated with pneumonia?

a. quiet breathing

b. fever

c. clear chest X ray

d. a and c

e. b and c

________ 7. When 53 Americans were held hostage in Iran,

a. the United States did nothing to try to free them.

b. the United States declared war on Iran.

c. the United States first attempted to free them by diplomatic means and later attempted a rescue.

d. the United States expelled all Iranian students.

________ 8. The square root of 256 is

a. 14.

b. 16.

c. 4×4.

d. both a and c.

e. both b and c.

f. all of the above.

g. none of the above.

________ 9. When a test item and the objective it is intended to measure match in learning outcome and conditions, the item

a. is called an objective item.

b. has content validity.

c. is too easy.

d. should be discarded.

Go over the exercise again. Chances are you'll find a few more problems the second time. Here's the answer key and a breakdown of the faults found in each item.

Answers: 1. P; 2. G; 3. P; 4. P; 5. P; 6. P; 7. P; 8. P; 9. G.

Most students would probably pick up on the "grammatical clue" in the first item. The article "an" eliminates options a, b, and d immediately, since "U.S. Grant was an man," "an president," or "an general" are not grammatically correct statements. Thus, option c is the only option that forms a grammatically correct sentence. Inadvertently providing students with grammatical clues to the correct answer is very common in multiple-choice items. The result is decreased test validity. Students can answer items correctly because of knowledge of grammar, not content.

Replacing "an" with "a/an" would be one way to eliminate grammatical clues in your own writing. Other examples would be "is/are," "was/were," "his/her," and so on. As an alternative, the article, verb, or pronoun may be included in the list of options, as the following example illustrates:

Poor: Christopher Columbus came to America in a

a. car.
b. boat.
c. airplane.
d. balloon.

Better: Christopher Columbus came to America in

a. a car.
b. a boat.
c. an airplane.
d. a balloon.

Let's return to the first item again and replace "an" with "a/an":

U.S. Grant was a/an

a. president.
b. man.
c. alcoholic.
d. general.

There! We've removed the grammatical clue, and we now have an acceptable item, right? Not quite. We now have an item free of grammatical clues, but it is still seriously deficient. What is the correct answer?

This item still has a serious flaw: multiple defensible answers. In fact, all four options are defensible answers! U.S. Grant was a president, a man, a general, and, as historians tell us, an alcoholic. Including such an item on a test would contribute nothing to your understanding of student knowledge. But what can you do when you have an item with more than one defensible answer? The answer, of course, is to eliminate the incorrect but defensible option or options.

Let's assume item 1 was written to measure the following objective:

The student will discriminate among the United States presidents immediately before, during, and immediately after the United States Civil War.

We could modify item 1 to look like this:

U. S. Grant was a

a. general.
b. slave.
c. pirate.
d. trader.

This item is fine, from a technical standpoint. The grammatical clue has been eliminated and there is but one defensible answer. However, it does not match the instructional objective; it is not very valuable as a measure of student achievement of the objective. We could also modify the item to look like this:

Of the following, who was elected president after the Civil War?

a. U. S. Grant
b. Andrew Johnson
c. Abraham Lincoln
d. Andrew Jackson

This item is technically sound, and all response alternatives are relevant to the instructional objective. It meets the two main criteria for inclusion in a test: The item is technically well constructed, and it matches the instructional objectives.

We said item 2 was good, but it can still stand some improvement. Remember when we recommended arranging lists for matching items in alphabetical or chronological order? The same holds true for multiple-choice items. To make a good item even better, arrange the options in chronological order. Revised, the item should look like this:

In what year did humans first set foot on the moon?

a. 1957
b. 1963
c. 1969
d. 1975

The major deficiency in item 3 is referred to as a "stem clue." The statement portion of a multiple-choice item is called the *stem,* and the correct answer and incorrect choices are called *options* or *response alternatives*. A stem clue occurs when the same word or a close derivative occurs in both the stem and options, thereby clueing the test taker to the correct answer. In item 3 the word *free* in the option is identical to *free* in the stem. Thus, the wise test taker has a good chance of answering the item correctly without mastery of the content being measured. This fault can be eliminated by simply rewording the item without the word *free*.

The structures within the cell that synthesize protein are called

a. chromosomes.
b. lysosomes.
c. mitochondria.
d. ribosomes.

Item 4 is related to the "opinionated" items we considered when we discussed true-false items. Depending on the source, or referent, different answers may be the "right" answer. To Person X, the principal value may be to promote physical health; to Person Y, the principal value may be to improve self-discipline. As stated earlier, when you are measuring a viewpoint or opinion, be sure to state the referent or source. To be acceptable the item should be rewritten to include the name of an authority:

The USDA feels the principal value of a balanced diet is that it

a. increases your intelligence.
b. gives you something to talk about.
c. promotes mental health.
d. promotes physical health.
e. improves self-discipline.

Item 5 is, of course, meaningless. It has at least two serious faults. To begin with, the stem fails to present a problem, and it fails to focus the item. What is the item getting at? The test taker has no idea what to look for in trying to discriminate among the options. The only way to approach such an item is to look at each option as an individual true-false item. This is very time-consuming and frustrating for the test taker. Be sure to focus your multiple-choice items by presenting a problem or situation in the stem.

Like item 1, item 5 also has more than one defensible answer. However, option d seems to control this problem. But if more than a single option is defensible, then how can you mark as incorrect someone who chooses a, b, or c and not d? Sometimes, however, you may wish to construct items that have two defensible answers. Is there any way to avoid the problem just mentioned? Fortunately, there is a way to avoid the problem, as illustrated in item 6:

Which of the following are not associated with pneumonia?

a. quiet breathing
b. fever
c. clear chest X ray
d. a and c
e. b and c

Where the possibility of more than one answer is desirable, use an option format like that just shown. This approach avoids the wording problems we ran into in item 5. We would caution, however, that "a and b," "b and c," and so on should be used sparingly.

Now, how about the rest of item 6; is it okay? No; again a grammatical clue is present. The word *are* indicates a plural response is appropriate. Thus, options a, b, and c can automatically be eliminated, leaving the test taker with a 50 percent chance of guessing correctly. This fault can be corrected by using the same approach we used with item 1, where we substituted "a/an" for "an." Of course, in this instance we would substitute "is/are" for "are." Rewritten, the item looks like this:

Which of the following is/are not associated with pneumonia?

a. quiet breathing
b. fever
c. clear chest X ray
d. a and c
e. b and c

All set? Not yet! Remember what we said about negatives? Let's highlight the "not" with uppercase letters, italics, or underlining to minimize the likelihood of someone misreading the item. After this revision we have an acceptable multiple-choice item.

Two very common faults in multiple-choice construction are illustrated by item 7. First, the phrase "the United States" is included in each option. To save space and time, add it to the stem. Second, the length of options could be a giveaway. Multiple-choice item writers have a tendency to include more information in the correct option than in the incorrect options. Test-wise students take advantage of this tendency, since past experience tells them that longer options are more often than not the correct answer. Naturally, it is impossible to make all options exactly the same length, but try to avoid situations where correct answers are more than one and a half times the length of incorrect options. Eliminating the redundancies in the options and condensing the correct option, we have:

When 53 Americans were held hostage in Iran, the United States

a. did nothing to try to free them.
b. declared war on Iran.
c. undertook diplomatic and military efforts to free them.
d. expelled all Iranian students.

Item 8 has some problems, too. First, let's consider the use of "all of the above" and "none of the above." In general, "none of the above" should be used sparingly. Some item writers tend to use "none of the above" only when there is no clearly correct option presented. However, students can quickly catch on to such a practice and guess that "none of the above" is the correct answer without knowledge of the content being measured.

As far as "all of the above" goes, we cannot think of *any* circumstances in which its use may be justified. Thus, our recommendation is to avoid this option entirely.

The use of "both a and c" and "both b and c" was already discussed in relation to item 6. In that item, their use was appropriate and justifiable, but here it is questionable.

Again, let us see just what it takes to arrive at the correct choice, option e. Presumably, the item is intended to measure knowledge of square roots. However, the correct answer can be arrived at without considering square roots at all! A logical approach to this item, which would pay off with the right answer for someone who doesn't know the answer, might go something like this:

> Sure wish I'd studied the square-root table. Oh, well, there's more than one way to get to the root of the problem. Let's see, 14 might be right, 16 might be right, and 4 × 4 might be right. Hmmm, both a and c? No, that can't be it because I know that 4 × 4 = 16 and not 14. Well, both b and c have to be it! I know it's not "none of the above" because the teacher never uses "none of the above" as the right answer when she uses "both a and c" and "both b and c" as options.

Thus, when using "both a and c" and "both b and c," be on the alert for logical inconsistencies that can be used to eliminate options. Naturally, this problem can be minimized by using such options sparingly. Also try to monitor your item construction patterns to make sure you're not overusing certain types of options.

Finally, we come to a good item. Item 9 is free of the flaws and faults we've pointed out in this section. There are a lot of things to consider when you write items, and keeping them all in mind will help you write better items. But it's virtually impossible for anyone to write good items *all* the time. So, when you've written a poor item, don't be too critical of yourself. Analyze it, revise or replace it, and learn from your mistakes.

Higher-Level Multiple-Choice Questions

Good multiple-choice items are the most time-consuming kind of objective test items to write. Unfortunately, most multiple-choice items are also written at the knowledge level of the taxonomy of educational objectives. As a new item writer (and, if you're not careful, as an experienced item writer) you will have a tendency to write items at this level. In this section we will provide you with suggestions for writing multiple-choice items to measure higher-level thinking.

The first step is to write at least some objectives that measure comprehension, application, analysis, synthesis, or evaluation to ensure that your items will be at the higher-than-knowledge level—*if your items match your objectives!* The following objectives measure behavior at the knowledge level:

> The student will name, from memory, the first three presidents of the United States by next Friday.

> Given a color chart, the students will identify each of the primary colors.

Objectives such as these will generate multiple-choice items that will measure only memorization. By contrast, the following objectives measure at higher than the knowledge level:

> Given a copy of the President's state of the union address, the student will be able to identify one example of a simile and one of a metaphor.

The student will be able to solve correctly three-digit addition problems without regrouping.

With objectives such as these, higher-level multiple-choice items would have to be constructed to match the objectives. Some suggestions for other approaches to measuring at higher than the knowledge level follow.

USE PICTORIAL, GRAPHICAL, OR TABULAR STIMULI. Pictures, drawings, graphs, tables, and so on, require the student to think at the application level of the taxonomy of educational objectives and may involve even higher levels of cognitive processes. Also, the use of such stimuli can often generate several higher-level multiple-choice items rather than a single higher-level multiple-choice item, as Figure 6.1 illustrates.

Other items based on the map in Figure 6.1 could be:

1. Approximately how many miles is it from Dube to Rog?
   a. 100 miles b. 150 miles
   c. 200 miles d. 250 miles
2. In what direction would someone have to travel to get from Wog to Um?
   a. northwest b. northeast
   c. southwest d. southeast

A variation on this same theme is to include several pictorial stimuli to represent options and build several stems around them. The following items would be appropriate for a plane geometry class:

_______ 1. Which of the figures is a rhombus?
_______ 2. Which of the figures is a parallelogram?
_______ 3. Which of the figures is a trapezoid?

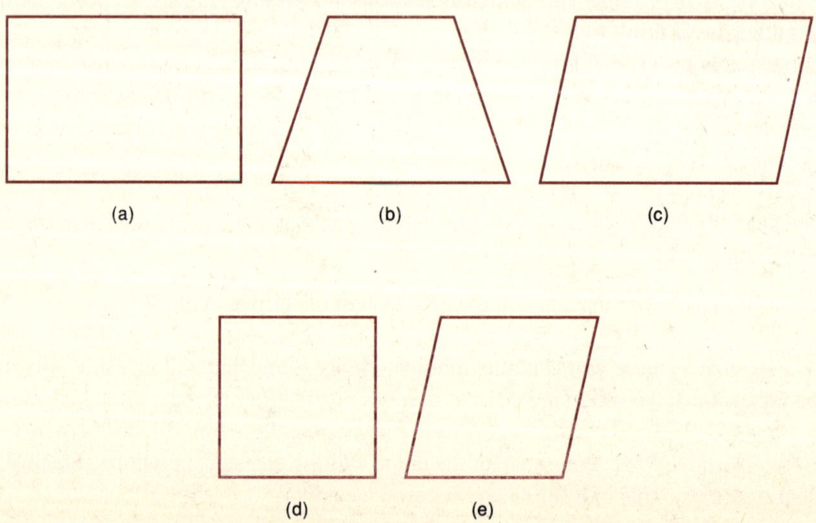

FIGURE 6.1
Use of Pictorial Stimulus to Measure High-Level Cognitive Processes

In the following questions you are asked to make inferences from the data which are given you on the map of the imaginary country, Serendip. The answers in most instances must be probabilities rather than certainties. The relative size of towns and cities is not shown. To assist you in the location of the places mentioned in the questions, the map is divided into squares lettered vertically from A to E and numbered horizontally from 1 to 5.

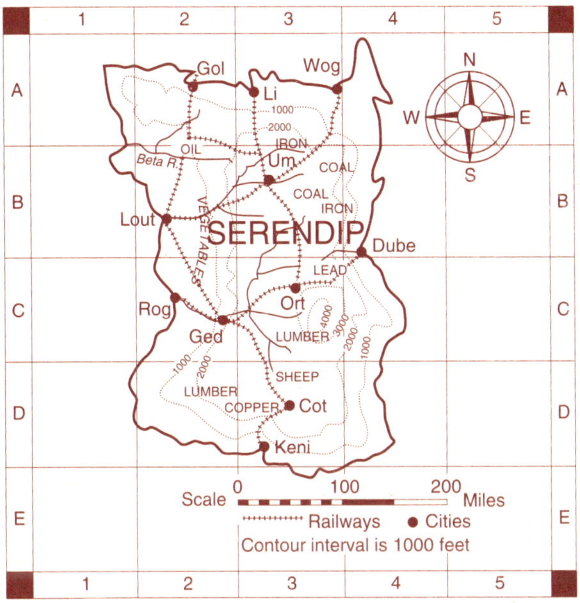

Which of the following cities would be the best location for a steel mill?

(A) Li (3A)
(B) Um (3B)
(C) Cot (3D)
(D) Dube (4B)

Naturally, it would be important to include several more stimulus pictures than items in order to minimize guessing.

USE ANALOGIES THAT DEMONSTRATE RELATIONSHIPS AMONG TERMS. To answer analogies correctly students must not only be familiar with the terms, but be able to *understand* how the terms relate to each other, as the following examples show:

1. Man is to woman as boy is to
    a. father.
    b. mother.
    c. girl.
    d. boy.

2. Physician is to humans as veterinarian is to
   a. fruits.
   b. animals.
   c. minerals.
   d. vegetables.

REQUIRE THE APPLICATION OF PREVIOUSLY LEARNED PRINCIPLES OR PROCEDURES TO NOVEL SITUATIONS. To test whether students really comprehend the implications of a procedure or principle, have the students use the principle or procedure with new information or in a novel way. This requires that the student do more than simply "follow the steps" in solving a problem. It asks the student to demonstrate an ability to go beyond the confines within which a principle or procedure was originally learned.

1. In class we discussed at length Darwin's notion of the "survival of the fittest" within the animal world. Which of the following best describes how this principle applies to the current competitive residential construction industry?
   a. Those builders in existence today are those who have formed alliances with powerful financial institutions.
   b. Only those builders who emphasize matching their homes to the changing structure of the family will survive in the future.
   c. The intense competition for a limited number of qualified home buyers will eventually "weed out" poorly managed construction firms.
   d. Only those home builders who construct the strongest and most durable homes will survive in the long term.
2. (*Follows a lesson on division which relied on computation of grade-point averages as examples.*) After filling up his tank with 18 gallons of gasoline, Mr. Watts said to his son, "We've come 450 miles since the last fillup. What kind of gas mileage are we getting?" Which of the following is the best answer?
   a. 4 miles per gallon.
   b. 25 miles per gallon.
   c. Between 30 and 35 miles per gallon.
   d. It can't be determined from the information given.

These examples are intended to stimulate your creativity—they are by no means exhaustive of the many approaches to measuring higher-level cognitive skills with multiple-choice items. Rather than limit yourself to pictorial items and analogies, use them where appropriate and also develop your own approaches. Remember the main point: Be sure your items match your objectives. Do not write higher-level items if your objectives are at the knowledge level. Doing so will impair your test's content validity. In Chapter 9 we will consider yet another way you can measure higher-level thinking skills, called *performance-based* assessment.

Suggestions for Writing Multiple-Choice Items

Here are some guidelines for writing multiple-choice tests:

1. The stem of the item should clearly formulate a problem. Include as much of the item as possible, keeping the response options as short as possible. However, include only the material needed to make the problem clear and specific. Be concise—don't add extraneous information.
2. Be sure that there is one and only one correct or clearly best answer.
3. Be sure wrong answer choices (distractors) are plausible. Eliminate unintentional grammatical clues, and keep the length and form of all the answer choices equal. Rotate the position of the correct answer from item to item randomly.
4. Use negative questions or statements only if the knowledge being tested requires it. In most cases it is more important for the student to know what a specific item of information *is* rather than what it is not.
5. Include from three to five options (two to four distractors plus one correct answer) to optimize testing for knowledge rather than encouraging guessing. It is not necessary to provide additional distractors for an item simply to maintain the same number of distractors for each item. This usually leads to poorly constructed distractors that add nothing to test validity and reliability.
6. To increase the difficulty of a multiple-choice item, increase the similarity of content among the options.
7. Use the option "none of the above" sparingly and only when the keyed answer can be classified unequivocally as right or wrong. Don't use this option when asking for a best answer.
8. Avoid using "all of the above." It is usually the correct answer and makes the item too easy for students with partial information.

Thus far, we have considered true-false, matching, and multiple-choice items. We have called these items *objective* items, but they are also referred to as *recognition* items. They are recognition items because the test taker needs only to "recognize" the correct answer. Contrast this with "recall" or "supply" formats such as essays and completion items. With essays and completion items it is much more difficult to guess the right answer than with true-false, matching, or multiple-choice items.

Nevertheless, we will classify completion items with true-false, matching, and multiple-choice items. We call items written in these formats *objective items* because of the way they are scored, which tends to be fairly straightforward and reliable. This is in contrast to essays, which we will call *subjective,* because their somewhat less reliable scoring makes them more prone to bias.

Completion Items

Like true-false items, completion items are relatively easy to write. Perhaps the first tests classroom teachers construct and students take are completion tests. Like items of all other formats, though, there are good and poor completion items. Work through the following exercise, again relying on your common sense to identify good and poor items. After having worked through the three previous exercises, you are probably now adept at recognizing common item-writing flaws.

EXERCISE: Put a G in the space next to the items you feel are good, and a P next to the items you feel are poor.

_______ 1. The evolutionary theory of [Darwin] is based on the principle of [survival of the fittest].

_______ 2. Columbus discovered America in [1492].

_______ 3. The capital of Mexico is [Mexico City].

_______ 4. In what year did Gerald Ford become president of the United States? [1973]

_______ 5. [Too many] blanks cause much frustration in [both test takers and test scorers].

_______ 6. [Armstrong] was the first American to [walk on the moon].

Answers: 1. P; 2. P; 3. P; 4. G; 5. P; 6. P.

The first item probably reminds you of many you have seen. It is a good rule of thumb to avoid using more than one blank per item. The item writer had a specific evolutionary theorist in mind when writing this item, but the final form of the item is not at all focused toward one single theorist. Thus, there are a variety of possible *correct* answers to this item. Not only are such items disturbing and confusing to test takers, they are very time-consuming and frustrating to score. An acceptable revision might look like this:

The evolutionary theory of Darwin is based on the principle of [survival of the fittest].

If you marked item 2 with a G, you were probably in the majority. This is a standard type of completion item that is frequently used. It is also the kind of item that can generate student-teacher conflict. Granted, "1492" is probably the answer most students who studied their lesson would write. But how would you score a response like "a boat," or, "the fifteenth century," or "a search for India?" These may not be the answers you wanted, but they are correct answers.

This illustrates the major disadvantage of completion items and gives you some idea on a much smaller scale of the kinds of difficulties encountered in scoring essay items as well. Unless you take pains to be *very* specific when you word completion items, you will come across similar situations frequently. In general, it's better to be very specific in writing completion items. Item 2 could be made specific by adding the words "the year," as illustrated here:

Columbus discovered America in the year [1492].

In this form the item leaves little to be interpreted subjectively by the student. The test taker doesn't spend time thinking about what the question is "really" asking, and the test scorer doesn't spend time trying to decide how to score a variety of different, but correct, answers. For once everybody's happy.

Item 3 is a similar case. Consider the following dialogue as heard by one of the authors in a teachers' lounge at an elementary school:

MISS RIGIDITY: (*to no one in particular*) Smart-aleck kids nowadays! Ask them a simple question and you get a smart-aleck answer. Kids today don't give you any respect.

MISS FEELINGS: I hear some frustration in what you're saying. Anything I can do?

MISS RIGIDITY: No, there's nothing you can do, but listen to this. On the last test one of the questions was "The largest city in Puerto Rico is _____." Simple enough, right? Well, not for Sally! Instead of answering "San Juan," she answered "the capital city." Smart-aleck kid. We'll see how smart she feels when she gets no credit for that ridiculous answer.

MISS FEELINGS: What I hear you saying is that you feel Sally may not have known that San Juan is the largest city in Puerto Rico.

MISS RIGIDITY: Of course she doesn't know—otherwise she would have given the correct answer. That's the whole point!

AUTHOR: (*never known for his tactfulness*) She *did* give a correct answer. Your question wasn't specific enough.

MISS RIGIDITY: I've been using this same test for years, and there are always one or two kids who give me the same answer Sally did! And they are always kids who lack respect!

AUTHOR: How do you know they lack respect?

MISS RIGIDITY: Because they always argue with me when they get their tests back. In fact, they say the same thing you did! You're as bad as they are!

MISS FEELINGS: I'm hearing some frustration from both of you . . .

How could this have been avoided? Let's look at Miss Rigidity's item again.

The largest city in Puerto Rico is _____.

Since San Juan *is* the largest city in Puerto Rico and *is* the capital city of Puerto Rico as well, then "the largest city in Puerto Rico is the capital city." There are at least two defensible answers. Just as in true-false, matching, and multiple-choice items, we should strive to avoid multiple defensible answers in completion items. But how can this be avoided? Again, be specific. Made more specific, Miss Rigidity's item looks like this:

The name of the largest city in Puerto Rico is [San Juan].

Of course, you could have students who carry things to an extreme. For example, some might claim the following is a defensible answer:

The name of the largest city in Puerto Rico is [familiar to many people].

Thus, only you, as the classroom teacher, can determine which answers are defensible and which are not. Your job will be to determine which responses are logical derivations of your test item and which responses are creative attempts to cover up for lack of mastery of content. Keep an open mind, and good luck! Don't be like Miss Rigidity!

We can clean up item 3 in much the same fashion as we did Miss Rigidity's item. Revised in this way, item 3 looks like this:

The name of the capital city of Mexico is [Mexico City].

Adding "name of the" to the original item minimizes your chances of students responding that the capital of Mexico is "a city," "very pretty," "huge," "near central Mexico," and so forth.

Item 4 is an example of a well-written completion item. It is specific, and it would be difficult to think of defensible answers other than "1973."

Both the fifth and sixth items illustrate a case of having too many blanks, which prevent the item from taking on any single theme. Blanks are contagious—avoid using more than one.

Suggestions for Writing Completion or Supply Items

1. If at all possible, items should require a single-word answer, or a brief and definite statement. Avoid statements that are so indefinite that they may be logically answered by several terms.

   Poor item: World War II ended in _____.

   Better item: World War II ended in the year _____.
2. Be sure the question or statement poses a problem to the examinee. A direct question is often more desirable than an incomplete statement (it provides more structure).
3. Be sure the answer that the student is required to produce is factually correct. Be sure the language used in the question is precise and accurate in relation to the subject matter area being tested.
4. Omit only key words; don't eliminate so many elements that the sense of the content is impaired.

   Poor item: The _____ type of test item is usually more _____ than the _____ type.

   Better item: The supply type of test item is usually graded less objectively than the _____ type.

5. Word the statement such that the blank is near the end of the sentence rather than near the beginning. This will prevent awkward sentences.
6. If the problem requires a numerical answer, indicate the units in which it is to be expressed.

You've now used common sense and an increased level of "test-wiseness" to analyze and think about different types of objective test items. In Chapter 7 we will extend our discussion to essay items. Before we move on to essays, however, let's consider one more topic related to item writing, one that applies equally to objective and essay items. This topic is gender and racial bias in test items.

GENDER AND RACIAL BIAS IN TEST ITEMS

An important but often overlooked aspect of item writing involves gender or racial bias. Over the last decades many have become increasingly aware of, and sensitive to, such issues. Professional item writers take great care to eliminate or minimize the extent to which such biases are present in their test items. The classroom teacher would be wise to follow their lead.

One example of gender bias is the exclusive use of the male pronoun *he* in test items. Since the item writer may use it unconsciously, it does not necessarily follow that the item writer has a sexist attitude. However, this does not prevent the practice from offending a proportion of the population. Similarly, referring exclusively in our items only to members of a single ethnic group will likely be offensive to individuals of different ethnicity. Again, such a practice may be almost unconscious and may not reflect a racist attitude, but this will not prevent others from taking offense to it.

To avoid such bias, you should carefully balance your references in items. That is, always check your items to be sure that fairly equal numbers of references to males and females are made. Obviously, equal care and time should be devoted to ensure that ethnic groups are appropriately represented in your items. Such considerations are especially relevant when items are being written at higher than the knowledge level. Since such items often are word problems involving people, gender and racial bias can easily creep in. The checklist in Chapter 8 will help remind you to be on the watch for such bias.

Remember, our goal is to measure learning in as valid and reliable a fashion as possible. When emotions are stimulated by gender-biased or racially biased items, these emotions can interfere with valid measurement, leaving us with results that are less useful than they would be otherwise. Given all the care and time we have taken to learn to develop good tests, it makes good sense to take just a bit more to avoid racial and gender bias in our items.

In this chapter we have provided you with a good deal of information related to item writing. Much of this information is condensed in the summary, and some general guidelines for item writing are also included. Following these guidelines you will find a summary of the advantages and disadvantages of various item formats. This section should help you make decisions about the type of format to use for your test items. Remember, you will write poor items until the recommendations we have provided become second nature, which comes only with practice.

GUIDELINES FOR WRITING TEST ITEMS

1. Begin writing items far enough in advance that you will have time to revise them.
2. Match items to intended outcomes at the proper difficulty level to provide a valid measure of instructional objectives. Limit the question to the skill being assessed.
3. Be sure each item deals with an important aspect of the content area and not with trivia.
4. Be sure that the problem posed is clear and unambiguous.
5. Be sure that each item is independent of all other items. The answer to one item should not be required as a condition for answering the next item, nor should a hint to one answer be unintentionally embedded in another item.
6. Be sure the item has one correct or best answer on which experts would agree.
7. Prevent unintended clues to the answer in the statement or question. Grammatical inconsistencies such as *a* or *an* give clues to the correct answer to those students who are not well prepared for the test.
8. Avoid replication of the textbook in writing test items; don't quote directly from textual materials. You're usually not interested in how well the student memorized the text. Besides, taken out of context, direct quotes from the text are often ambiguous.
9. Avoid trick or catch questions in an achievement test. Don't waste time testing how well the students can interpret your intentions.
10. Try to write items that require higher-level thinking.

ADVANTAGES AND DISADVANTAGES OF DIFFERENT OBJECTIVE-ITEM FORMATS

True-False Tests

Advantages

Because T-F questions tend to be short, more material can be covered than with any other item format. Thus, T-F items tend to be used when a great deal of content has been covered.

T-F questions take less time to construct. But avoid taking statements directly from the text and modifying them slightly to create an item.

Scoring is easier with T-F questions. But avoid having students write "true" or "false" or a "T" or "F." Instead have them circle "T" or "F" provided for each item.

Disdvantages

T-F questions tend to emphasize rote memorization of knowledge, although sometimes complex questions *can* be asked using T-F items.

T-F questions presume that the answer to the question or issue is unequivocally true or false. It would be unfair to ask the student to guess at the teacher's criteria for evaluating the truth of a statement.

T-F questions allow for and sometimes encourage a high degree of guessing. Generally, longer examinations are needed to compensate for this.

Matching Tests

Advantages

Matching questions are usually simple to construct and to score.

Matching items are ideally suited to measure associations between facts.

Matching questions can be more efficient than multiple-choice questions because they avoid repetition of options in measuring associations.

Matching questions reduce the effects of guessing.

Disdvantages

Matching questions sometimes tend to ask students *trivial* information.

They emphasize memorization.

Most commercial answer sheets can accommodate no more than five options, thus limiting the size of any particular matching item.

Multiple-Choice Tests

Advantages

Multiple-choice questions have considerable versatility in measuring objectives from the knowledge to the evaluation level.

Since writing is minimized, a substantial amount of course material can be sampled in a relatively short time.

Scoring is highly objective, requiring only a count of the number of correct responses.

Multiple-choice items can be written so that students must discriminate among options that vary in degree of correctness. This allows students to select the best alternative and avoids the absolute judgments found in T-F tests.

Since there are multiple options, effects of guessing are reduced.

Multiple-choice items are amenable to item analysis (see Chapter 8), which permits a determination of which items are ambiguous or too difficult.

Disdvantages

Multiple-choice questions can be time-consuming to write.

If not carefully written, multiple-choice questions can sometimes have more than one defensible correct answer.

Completion Tests

Advantages

Construction of a completion question is relatively easy.

Guessing is eliminated since the question requires recall.

Completion questions take less time to complete than multiple-choice items, so greater amounts of content can be covered.

Disdvantages

Completion questions usually encourage a relatively low level of response complexity.

The responses can be difficult to score since the stem must be general enough so as not to communicate the correct answer. This can lead unintentionally to more than one defensible answer.

The restriction of an answer to a few words tends to measure the recall of specific facts, names, places, and events as opposed to more complex behaviors.

SUMMARY

This chapter introduced you to four types of objective test items: true-false, matching, multiple-choice, and completion. The major points are:

1. Choice of item format is sometimes determined by your instructional objectives. At other times the advantages and disadvantages of the different formats should influence your choice.

2. True-false items require less time to construct than other objective items, but they are most prone to guessing, as well as a variety of other faults. These include absolutes in wording, double negatives, opinionated and double-barreled statements, excessive wordiness, and a tendency to reflect statements taken verbatim from readings.

3. Matching items are fairly easy to construct but tend to be subject to the following faults: lack of clarity and specificity in directions, dissimilar and nonordered lists, and reversal of options and descriptions.

4. Multiple-choice items are the most difficult of the objective items to construct. However, higher-order multiple-choice items lend themselves well to measuring higher-level thinking skills. They are subject to several faults, including grammatical cues or specific determiners, multiple defensible answers, unordered option lists, stem clues, opinionated statements, failure to state a problem in the stem, redundant wording, wordiness in the correct option, use of "all of the above," and indiscriminate use of "none of the above."

5. Completion items rival true-false items in ease of construction. Since answers must be supplied, they are least subject to guessing. On the other hand, they require more scoring time than other objective formats. Common faults include too many blanks, lack of specificity (too many responses), and failure to state a problem.

6. To avoid gender and/or racial biases in test items, avoid using stereotypes and be sure to make equal reference to both males and females and to various ethnic groups.

For Practice

1. Write a behavioral objective in some area with which you are familiar. Using this objective as your guide, write a test item using each of the four test item formats (true-false, matching, multiple-choice, and completion) discussed in this chapter.

2. Exchange your test items with a classmate. Have him or her check the appropriateness of each of your items for a match with the appropriate objective and against the criteria and guidelines given in this chapter for each test item format. List and correct any deficiencies.

*3. Each of the following items is defective in some way(s). Identify the principal fault or faults in each item and rewrite the item so that it is fault-free.

1. "The Time Machine" is considered to be a

   a. adventure story.

   b. science fiction story.

   c. historical novel.

   d. autobiography.

2. Thaddeus Kosciusko and Casimer Pulaski were heroes in the Revolutionary War. What was their country of origin?

   a. Great Britain

   b. Poland

   c. France

   d. Italy

3. The use of force to attain political goals is never justifiable. (True or false)

4. The microcomputer was invented in _____.

5. _____ spent his life trying to demonstrate that _____.

6.

_____	1. Discovered the Zambezi River	a. Webb
_____	2. First female governor	b. Armstrong
_____	3. Invented the cotton gin	c. Minuit
_____	4. First to swim the English Channel	d. Livingstone
_____	5. Purchased Manhattan Island	e. Whitney
_____	6. First to walk on the moon	f. Edison
		g. Cortez
		h. Keller
		i. Rhodes

*Answers for question 3 appear in Appendix D.

CHAPTER 7

Writing Essay Test Items

9:00 A.M., Tuesday, October 20

"I can't believe it! I just *can't* believe it!" Donna thought to herself. "How can he do this to us?" Donna was becoming more and more upset by the second, as were many of the other students in Mr. Smith's government class. They were taking the midterm exam, on which 50 percent of their grade would be based. Before the exam, the students spent two classes discussing this issue. All other classes that semester dealt with a rather mechanical review of the federal government. The exam consisted of a single essay item:

Why should presidents be limited or not be limited to two consecutive terms in office? (100 points)

Does this ring a bell? Test questions that do not reflect classroom emphases can frustrate test takers. "How could he do it?" Well, there are probably several answers to this question, and we could only speculate about the reasons for Mr. Smith's question. Just as we could generate a variety of explanations for Mr. Smith's test item, students could generate a variety of answers to his question! Let's look at his question again.

> Why should presidents be limited or not be limited to two consecutive terms in office? (100 points)

What answer is he looking for? Again, only Mr. Smith knows for sure. "Come on," some of you may say. "He's not looking for any specific answer—he wants you to take a position and defend it, to test your knowledge and writing ability, that's all!" Well, if that's the case, why didn't he phrase the test item something like this:

> In class and in your assigned readings, arguments both for and against giving presidents the opportunity to complete more than two consecutive terms in office were presented.

> Take a stand either for or against two consecutive terms in office. Use at least three points made in class or in your readings to support your position. Both the content and organization of your argument will be considered in assigning your final grade. Use no more than one page for your answer. (28 points)

This item *focuses* the task for the student—he or she has a clearer idea of what is expected, and, therefore, how he or she will be evaluated. Remember, your goal is not to see whether students can guess correctly what you are expecting as an answer. Your goal is to assess learning—to determine whether your instructional objectives have been met.

In the remainder of this chapter we will discuss various aspects of essay item construction. While this will go far in helping you avoid writing deficient essay items, we will also discuss several other equally important issues related to essay items. We will begin with a general discussion of what an essay item is, describe the two major types of essay items and their relationships to instructional objectives, identify the major advantages and disadvantages of essay items, provide you with suggestions for writing essay items, and discuss various approaches to scoring essays. With this comprehensive treatment, we hope to increase your awareness of the complexities of essay items and thereby minimize the likelihood that you will write poorly constructed, ambiguous essay items.

WHAT IS AN ESSAY ITEM?

An essay item is one for which the student supplies, rather than selects, the correct answer. It demands that the student compose a response, often extensive, to a question for which no *single* response or pattern of responses can be cited as correct to the exclusion of all other answers. The accuracy and quality of such a response can often be judged only by a person skilled and informed in the subject area being tested.

Like objective test items, essay items may be well constructed or poorly constructed. The well-constructed essay item aims to test complex cognitive skills by requiring the student to organize, integrate, and synthesize knowledge, to use information to solve novel problems, or to be original and innovative in problem solving. The poorly constructed essay item may require the student to do no more than recall information as it was presented in the textbook or lecture. Worse, the poorly constructed essay may not even let the student know what is required for a satisfactory response.

The potential of the essay item as an evaluation device depends not only upon writing appropriate questions that elicit complex cognitive skills, but also upon being able to structure the situation so that other factors do not obscure the intent of the item. Differences in knowledge of factual material are often hidden by differences in ability to use and organize those facts. The time pressures of a test situation can cause students to demonstrate less than optimum communication skills. The way the item is constructed determines to a large extent the types of learning outcomes being tested. Consider the following two essay items:

QUESTION 1. What methods have been used in the United States to prevent industrial accidents?

What learning outcomes are being tested? To provide an acceptable answer, a student need only recall information. The item is at the knowledge level; no higher-level mental processes are tapped. It would be easy and much less time-consuming to score a series of objective items covering this same topic. This is not abuse of the essay item, but it is a misuse. Now consider the second question:

QUESTION 2. Examine the data provided in the table on causes of accidents. Explain how the introduction of occupational health and safety standards in the United States account for changes in the number of industrial accidents shown in the following table.

Causes of Accidents and Rate for Each in 1960 and 1980

	Accident Rate per 100,000 Employees	
Cause of Accident	*1960*	*1980*
1. Defective equipment	135.1	16.7
2. Failure to use safety-related equipment	222.8	36.1
3. Failure to heed instructions	422.1	128.6
4. Improperly trained for job	598.7	26.4
5. Medical or health-related impairment	41.0	13.5

This question requires that the student recall something about the occupational health and safety standards. Then, the student must relate these standards to such things as occupational training programs, plant safety inspections, the display of warning or danger signs, equipment manufacturing, codes related to safety, and so forth, which may have been incorporated in industrial settings between 1960 and 1980.

In short, the student must use higher-level mental processes to answer this question successfully. The student must be able to analyze, infer, organize, apply, and so on. No objective item or series of items would suffice. This is an *appropriate* use of the essay item. However, not all essays are alike. We will consider two types of essay items: extended response and restricted-response items.

Extended-Response Items

An essay item that allows the student to determine the length and complexity of response is called an *extended-response essay item*. This type of essay is most useful at the synthesis or evaluation levels of the cognitive taxonomy. Because of the length of this type of item and the time required in organizing and expressing the response, the extended-response item is sometimes better as a term paper assignment or a take-home test. The extended-response item is often of value more in assessing communication ability than in assessing achievement.

EXAMPLE: Compare and contrast the presidential administrations of Carter and Reagan. Consider economic, social, and military policies. Avoid taking a position in support of either president. Your response will be graded on objectivity, accuracy, organization, and clarity.

Restricted-Response Items

An essay item that poses a specific problem for which the student must recall proper information, organize it in a suitable manner, derive a defensible conclusion, and express it within the limits of the posed problem is called a *restricted-response essay item.* The statement of the problem specifies response limitations that guide the student in responding and provide evaluation criteria for scoring.

EXAMPLE: List the major political similarities and differences between U.S. participation in the Korean War and World War II. Limit your answer to one page. Your score will depend on accuracy, organization, and brevity.

ESSAY ITEMS AND INSTRUCTIONAL OBJECTIVES

Essays may be used to measure general or specific outcomes of instruction. The restricted-response item is most likely to be used to assess knowledge, comprehension, and application types of learning outcomes.

EXAMPLE: The Learning to Like It Company is proposing a profit-sharing plan for its employees. For each 1 percent increase in production compared to the average production figures over the last ten years, workers will get a 1 percent increase in pay.

1. List the advantages and disadvantages to the workers of such a profit-sharing plan.
2. List the advantages and disadvantages to the corporation of such a profit-sharing plan.

Multiple-choice items may also be effectively used for these learning outcomes, except when recall of information rather than recognition is desired. Restricted response items may also be used for instructional objectives requiring students to be able to apply skills in new situations, to state testable hypotheses, or to formulate conclusions.

To assess the ability to evaluate, to organize, and to select viewpoints, an extended-response essay is more appropriate.

EXAMPLE: Describe the two views of the creation of the universe that your text describes. Select the view you think is most probable and defend your selection. Be sure to discriminate between fact and opinion in your defense.

The following are some of the learning outcomes for which essay items may be put to use:

Analyze relationships

Arrange items in sequence

Compare positions

State necessary assumptions

Identify appropriate conclusions

Explain cause-and-effect relations

Formulate hypotheses

Organize data to support a viewpoint

Point out strengths and weaknesses

Produce a solution for a problem

Integrate data from several sources

Evaluate the quality or worth of an item, product, or action

Create an original solution, arrangement, or procedure

Thus far we've discussed essay items in terms of appropriateness, specificity, range of response, and relationship to instructional objectives. These are all important to the appropriate use of essay tests, but now we must also consider specifics—the nuts and bolts of essay item construction.

The next section provides generally accepted suggestions for essay item construction and use, followed by examples of poorly written and well-written essay items. If it seems as though we are spending a lot of time dealing with what you may have thought was a simple topic, you're right. Our reasons for doing so are twofold. First, essay item writing is not simple or easy. It is a higher-level cognitive skill. As with all higher-level skills, it requires awareness of issues and knowledge of specifics, as well as lots of practice for mastery. Second, there is probably no other item type that is misused or abused as often as the essay item.

SUGGESTIONS FOR WRITING AND USING ESSAY ITEMS

1. Have clearly in mind what mental processes you want the student to use before starting to write the question. Refer to the processes described in Chapter 5 about the taxonomy of educational objectives for the cognitive domain. If you want students to analyze, judge, or think critically, what mental processes involve analysis, judgment, or critical thinking? Once you've determined this, use the appropriate verbs in your question.

   Poor Item: Criticize the following speech by our President.

   Better Item: Consider the following presidential speech. Focus on the section dealing with economic policy and discriminate between factual statements and opinions. List these statements separately, label them, and indicate whether each statement is or is not consistent with the President's overall economic policy.

2. Write the question in such a way that the task is clearly and unambiguously defined for the student. Tasks should be explained (1) in the overall instructions preceding the test items and/or (2) in the test items themselves. Include instructions for the type of writing style desired (for example, technical vs. prose); whether spelling and grammar will be counted; and whether organization of the response will be an important scoring element. Also, indicate the level of detail and supporting data required.

   Poor Item: Discuss the value of behavioral objectives.

   Better Item: Behavioral objectives have enjoyed increased popularity in education over the past several years. In your text and in class the advantages and disadvantages of behavioral objectives have been discussed. Take a position for or against the use of behavioral objectives in education and support your position with at least three of the arguments covered in class or in the text.

   Poor Item: What were the forces that led to the outbreak of the Civil War?

   Better Item: Compare and contrast the positions of the North and South at the outbreak of the Civil War. Include in your discussion economic conditions, foreign policies, political sentiments, and social conditions.

3. Start essay questions with such words or phrases as *compare, contrast, give reasons for, give original examples of, predict what would happen if,* and so on. Don't begin with such words as *what, who, when,* and *list,* since these words generally lead to tasks that require only recall of information.

   Poor Item: List three reasons behind America's withdrawal from Vietnam.

   Better Item: After more than ten years of involvement, the United States withdrew from Vietnam in 1975. Predict what would have happened if America had *not* withdrawn at that time and had *not* increased significantly its military presence above 1972 levels.

4. A question dealing with a controversial issue should ask for and be evaluated in terms of the presentation of evidence for a position, rather than the position taken. It is not defensible to demand that a student accept a specific conclusion or solution, but it is reasonable to appraise how well he or she has learned to utilize the evidence upon which a specific conclusion is based.

   Poor Item: What laws should Congress pass to improve the medical care of all citizens in the United States?

   Better Item: Some feel that the cost of all medical care should be borne by the federal government. Do you agree or disagree? Support your position with at least three logical arguments.

5. Avoid using optional items. That is, require all students to complete the same items. Allowing students to select three of five, four of seven, and so forth decreases test validity, as well as decreases your basis for comparison among students.

6. Establish reasonable time and/or page limits for each essay item to help the student complete the entire test and to give indications of the level of detail you have in mind for each item. Indicate such time limits either within the statement of the problem or close to the number of the question.

7. Restrict the use of essays to those learning outcomes that cannot be satisfactorily measured by objective items.
8. Be sure each question relates to an instructional objective.

Not all of the above suggestions may be relevant for each item you write. However, the suggestions are worth going over even *after* you've written items, as a means of checking and, when necessary, modifying your items. With time you will get better and more efficient at writing essay items.

WHY USE ESSAY ITEMS?

We've already mentioned some of the benefits of using essay items, and the following list summarizes the advantages of essays over objective items.

Advantages of the Essay Item

MOST EFFECTIVE IN ASSESSING COMPLEX LEARNING OUTCOMES. To the extent that instructional objectives require the student to organize information constructively to solve a problem, analyze and evaluate information, or perform other high-level cognitive skills, the essay test is an appropriate assessment tool.

RELATIVELY EASY TO CONSTRUCT. Although essay tests are relatively easy to construct, the items should not be constructed haphazardly; consult the table of specifications, identify only the topics and objectives that can best be assessed by essays, and build items around those and only those.

EMPHASIZE COMMUNICATION SKILLS AS ESSENTIAL IN COMPLEX ACADEMIC DISCIPLINES. If developing communication skills is an instructional objective, it can be tested with an essay item. However, this assumes that the teacher has spent time in teaching communication skills pertinent to the course area, including special vocabulary and writing styles, as well as providing practice with relevant arguments for and against controversial points.

GUESSING IS ELIMINATED. Since no options are provided, the student must supply rather than select the proper response.

Naturally, there is another side to the essay coin. These items also have limitations and disadvantages.

Disadvantages of the Essay Item

DIFFICULT TO SCORE. It is tedious to wade through pages and pages of student handwriting. Also, it is difficult not to let spelling and grammatical mistakes influence grading or to let superior abilities in communication cover up for incomplete comprehension of facts.

SCORES ARE UNRELIABLE. It is difficult to maintain a common set of criteria for all students. Two persons may disagree on the correct answer for any essay item; even the same person will disagree on the correctness of one answer read on two separate occasions.

LIMITED SAMPLE OF TOTAL INSTRUCTIONAL CONTENT. Fewer essay items can be attempted than any objective type of item; it takes more time to complete an essay item than any other type of item. Students become fatigued faster with these items than with objective items.

BLUFFING. It is no secret that longer essays tend to be graded higher than short essays, regardless of content! As a result, students may bluff.

The first two limitations are serious disadvantages. Fortunately, we do have some suggestions that have been shown to make the task of scoring essays more manageable and reliable. These will be discussed shortly. First, however, we will consider several situations in which the use of essay items is most appropriate.

WHEN SHOULD ESSAY QUESTIONS BE USED?

While each situation must be considered individually, there are certain situations that lend themselves well to the use of essay items. Among them are situations in which:

1. The instructional objectives specify high-level cognitive processes—they require supplying information rather than simply recognizing information. These processes often cannot be measured with objective items.
2. Only a few tests or items need to be graded. If you have 30 students and design a test consisting of six extended-range essays, you will spend a great deal of time scoring. Use essays when class size is small, or use only one or two essays in conjunction with objective items.
3. Test security is a consideration. If you are afraid test items will be passed on to future students and consequently decide not to reuse a test, it is better to use an essay test. In general, a good essay test takes less time to construct than a good objective test.

SCORING ESSAYS

As mentioned earlier, essays tend to be difficult to score reliably. That is, the *same* essay answer may be given an A by one scorer and a B or C by another scorer. Or, the *same* answer may be graded A on one occasion, but B or C on another occasion by the *same* scorer! As disturbing and surprising as they may seem, these conclusions have long been supported by research findings (Coffman, 1971). Why does this happen, and what can be done to avoid such scoring problems?

Why Are Essay Scores Unreliable?

To understand the difficulties involved in scoring essays reliably, it is necessary to consider the difficulty involved in constructing good essay items. As you saw earlier, the clearer your instructional objective, the easier the essay item is to construct. Similarly, the clearer the essay item in terms of task specification, the easier it is to score reliably. Make sense? If you're not sure, look at the next two examples of essay items and decide which would likely be more reliably scored.

> EXAMPLE 1: Some economists recommend massive tax cuts as a means of controlling inflation. Identify at least two assumptions on which such a position is based, and indicate the effect that violating each assumption might have on inflation. Limit your response to one-half page. Organize your answer according to the criteria discussed in class. Although spelling, punctuation, and grammar will not be counted in your grade, try to attend to these factors to the best of your ability. (8 points)

> EXAMPLE 2: What effect would massive tax cuts have on inflation? (100 points)

Which did you select? If you chose the first one, you are catching on.

Example 2 is a poor essay question. It is unstructured and unfocused; it fails to define response limits; and it fails to establish a policy for grammar, spelling, and punctuation. Thus, depending on the scorer, a lengthy answer with poor grammar and good content might get a high grade, a low grade, or an intermediate grade. Different scorers would probably all have a different idea of what a "good" answer to the question looks like. Questions like this trouble and confuse scorers and invite scorer unreliability. They do so for the same reasons that they trouble and confuse test takers. Poorly written essay items hurt both students and scorers.

But the first example is different. The task is spelled out for the student; limits are defined; and the policy on spelling, punctuation, and grammar is indicated. The task for the scorer is to determine whether the student has included (1) at least two assumptions underlying the proposition, and (2) the likely effect on inflation if each assumption is violated. Granted, there may be some difficulty agreeing how adequate the statements of the assumptions and effects of violating the assumptions may be, but there is little else to quibble over. Thus, there are *fewer* potential sources of scorer error or variability (that is, unreliability) in this question than in the second. Remember, essay scoring can never be as reliable as scoring an objective test, but it doesn't have to be little better than chance.

How to Improve Scoring Reliability (and Save Time!)

To improve essay scoring reliability: write good essay items, use several restricted-range items rather than a single extended-range item, and use a predetermined scoring scheme.

WRITE GOOD ESSAY ITEMS. Poorly written questions are one source of scorer unreliability. Questions that do not specify response length are another important source of unreliability. In general, long (say, two-page) essay responses are more difficult to score reliably than restricted-range essay responses (say, one-half page). This is due to student fatigue and subsequent clerical errors, as well as a tendency for grading criteria to vary from response to response, or, for that matter, from page to page or paragraph to paragraph in the same response.

USE SEVERAL RESTRICTED-RANGE ITEMS RATHER THAN A SINGLE EXTENDED-RANGE ITEM. Writing good items and using restricted-range essays rather than extended-range essays will help improve essay scoring reliability. However, as we mentioned, sometimes extended-range essays are desirable and/or necessary. What do you do then? Use a predetermined scoring scheme.

USE A PREDETERMINED SCORING SCHEME. This point is an important one. All too often essays are graded without the scorer having specified in advance what he or she is looking for in a "good" answer. In scoring an essay, you are making an evaluation. In making an evaluation, criteria are necessary. If a teacher does not determine and specify the relevant criteria beforehand, the reliability of scoring will be greatly reduced.

If the relevant criteria are not readily available for the teacher to refer to in scoring each question, the following may happen:

1. The criteria themselves may change (teacher grades harder or easier after a number of papers, even if the papers do not change).
2. The ability of the teacher to consistently keep these criteria in mind will be influenced by fatigue, distractions, frame of mind, and so on.

Since teachers and other essay scorers are only human, it is likely they will be subject to these factors. Referring to a predetermined set of criteria minimizes this likelihood. What do such criteria look like? Scoring criteria may vary from fairly simple checklists to elaborate combinations of checklists and rating scales. How elaborate your scoring scheme is depends on what you are trying to measure. If your essay item is a restricted-response item simply assessing mastery of factual content, a fairly simple listing of essential points would suffice. Table 7.1 illustrates this type of scoring scheme. For most restricted-response items a similar scoring scheme would probably suffice. However, when items are measuring synthesis and evaluation skills, more complex schemes are necessary. Tuckman (1975) has identified three components that we feel are useful in evaluating high-level essay items: content, organization, and process. Let's consider these in more detail.

Scoring Criteria for High-Level Essay Items

CONTENT. Although essays often are not used to measure factual knowledge as much as thinking processes, the information included in an essay—the content—can and should be scored specifically for its presence and accuracy and not the way it is organized or otherwise used. This is what you would do in scoring the sample essay in the previous section. You are simply trying to determine whether a student has acquired prerequisite knowledge with such content criteria.

ORGANIZATION. Does the essay have an introduction, body, and conclusion? Let the students know that you will be scoring for organization to minimize rambling. Beyond the three general organizational criteria mentioned, you may want to develop specific criteria for your class. For example: Are recommendations, inferences, and hypotheses supported? Is it apparent which supporting statements go with which recommendation? Do

TABLE 7.1
An Essay Item Appropriate for a Tenth-Grade American Government Course, Its Objective, and a Simple Scoring Scheme

Scoring Scheme	*Description*
Objective	The student will be able to name and describe at least five important conditions that contributed to the industrial revolution, drawn from among the following: Breakdown of feudal ideas and social boundaries (rise of ordinary people) Legitimization of individualism and competition Transportation revolution, which allowed for massive transport of goods (first national roads, canals, steamboats, railroads, etc.) New forms of energy (e.g., coal) that brought about factory system Slow decline of death rates due to improved hygiene and continuation of high birthrates resulted in rise in population Media revolution (printing press, newspapers, telegraph, etc.) Migration to urban areas
Test item	Name and describe five of the most important conditions that made possible the industrial revolution. (10 points)
Scoring criteria	1 point for each of the seven factors named, to a maximum of 5 points. 1 point for each appropriate description of the factors named, to a maximum of 5 points. No penalty for spelling, punctuation, or grammatical error. No extra credit for more than five factors named or described. Extraneous information will be ignored.

progressions and sequences follow a logical or chronological development? You should also decide on a spelling and grammar policy and develop these criteria, alerting the students before they take the test.

PROCESS. If your essay item tests at the application level or above, the most important criteria for scoring are those that reflect the extent to which these processes have been carried out. Each process (application, analysis, synthesis, and evaluation) results in a solution, recommendation, or decision and some reasons for justifying or supporting the final decision, and so on. Thus, the process criteria should attempt to assess both the adequacy of the solution or decision and the reasons behind it.

When an essay requires a solution or conclusion, the solution or conclusion should be evaluated in terms of the following:

ACCURACY/REASONABLENESS. Will it work? Have the correct analytical dimensions been identified? Scorers must ultimately decide for themselves what is accurate but should be prepared for unexpected, but accurate, responses.

COMPLETENESS/INTERNAL CONSISTENCY. To what extent does it sufficiently deal with the problem presented? Again, the scorer's judgment will weigh heavily, but points should be logically related and cover the topics as fully as required by the essay item.

ORIGINALITY/CREATIVITY. Again, it is up to the scorer to recognize the unexpected and give credit for it. That is, the scorer should expect that some students will develop new ways of conceptualizing questions, and credit should be awarded for such conceptualizations when appropriate.

Your criteria should be made known to students. This will maximize their learning experience. Knowing how you are going to score the test, students will be able to develop better and more defensible responses. Table 7.2 illustrates the application of these criteria to an extended-range essay item.

As the scorer reads through each response, points are assigned for each of the three major criteria of the scoring scheme. As you can probably guess, there are some disadvantages to this approach. It is likely to be quite laborious and time-consuming. Furthermore, undue attention may be given to superficial aspects of the answer. When used properly, however, such a scoring scheme can yield reliable scores for extended-range essay answers. Another advantage of this approach is that constructing such a detailed scoring scheme *before* administering the test can often alert the teacher to such problems in the item as unrealistic expectations for the students or poor wording. A third advantage is that discussion of a student's grade on such an item is greatly facilitated. The student can see what aspects of his or her response were considered deficient.

Keep in mind that Table 7.2 represents a scoring scheme for an extended-range essay item. When reliability is crucial, such a detailed scheme is vital. Scoring schemes for restricted-range items would be less complex, depending on what components of the answer the teacher felt were most critical. The point we have been making is that using some kind of scoring scheme is helpful in improving the reliability of essay scoring.

Another method that has gained considerable acceptance—although it runs contrary to our position that scoring criteria should be written down beforehand—is the rating method.

THE RATING METHOD. With the rating method, the teacher generally is more interested in the overall quality of the answer than in specific points. Rating is done by simply sorting papers into piles, usually five, if letter grades are given. After sorting, the answers in each pile are re-read and an attempt is made to ensure that all the A papers are of comparable quality (that is, that they do not include B and C papers) and so forth. This step is very important, since the problem of changing criteria mentioned above is always present in rating answers. It helps minimize the likelihood, for example, that an A paper gets sorted into the C pile because it was graded early while the teacher was maintaining "strict" criteria.

This method is certainly an improvement over simply reading each answer and assigning a grade based on some nebulous, undefined rationale. However, as we mentioned before, this method is still subject to the problem of unintentionally changing the criteria.

TABLE 7.2
An Essay Item Appropriate for a High-School American History Course, Its Objectives, and a Detailed Scoring Scheme

Scoring Scheme	*Description*
Objectives	The student will be able to explain the forces that operated to weaken Southern regional self-consciousness between the Civil War and 1900. The student will consider these forces and draw an overall conclusion as to the condition of Southern self-consciousness at the turn of the century.
Test item	The Civil War left the South with a heritage of intense regional self-consciousness. In what respects, and to what extent, was this feeling weakened during the next half century, and in what respects, and to what extent, was it intensified? Your answer will be graded on content and organization and on the accuracy, consistency, and originality of your conclusion and the quality of your argument in support of your conclusion. Be sure to identify at least seven weakening factors and seven strengthening factors. Although spelling, punctuation, and grammar will not be considered in grading, do your best to consider them in your writing. Limit your answer to two (2) pages. (32 points)
Detailed scoring criteria	*Content* 1 point for each weakening factor mentioned, to a maximum of 7 points. 1 point for each strengthening factor mentioned—all factors must come from the following list: Forces weakening Southern regional self-consciousness: Growth of railroads and desire for federal subsidies Old Whigs join Northern businessmen in Compromise of 1877 Desire for Northern capital to industrialize the South Efforts of magazines and writers to interpret the South The vision of the New South Aid to Negro education by Northern philanthropists New state constitutions stressing public education Supreme Court decisions affecting Negro rights Tom Watson's early Populist efforts Booker T. Washington's "submissiveness" The Spanish-American War The "white man's burden"

Continued

TABLE 7.2 Continued

Scoring Scheme	*Description*
	After 1890, new issues did not conform to a North-South political alignment
	World War I
Detailed scoring criteria	Forces strengthening Southern regional self-consciousness:
	Destruction caused by the war and its long-range effects
	Reconstruction policy of Congress
	One-crop economy, crop-lien system, and sharecropping
	Carpetbaggers, Ku Klux Klan, Redshirts
	Waving the bloody shirt
	Memories of the lost cause
	Glorifying the prewar tradition
	Continuing weakness of Southern education compared with the rest of the Union
	Populism
	Jim Crow laws after 1890
	Solid South
	14 points possible
	Organization
	0 to 6 points assigned, depending on whether the essay has an introduction, body, and conclusion.
	6 points possible
	Process
	1. Solution: 0 to 6 points depending on whether the solution is:
	a. Accurate (0 to 2 points)
	Does the solution/conclusion fit?
	b. Internally consistent (0 to 2 points)
	Does the solution/conclusion logically flow?
	c. Originality/creativity (0 to 2 points)
	Is the solution/conclusion novel or creative?
	2. Argument: 0 to 6 points, depending on whether the argument is:
	a. Accurate (0 to 2 points)
	Dependent on whether the argument fits the situation.
	b. Internally consistent (0 to 2 points)
	Is the argument logical?
	c. Original/creative (0 to 2 points)
32 points possible	Is the argument unique or novel in its approach?

OTHER SUGGESTIONS. We have been discussing ways to improve essay scoring reliability. Remember our first three suggestions?

1. Write good essay items.
2. Use restricted-range rather than extended-range items, if appropriate.
3. Use a predetermined scoring scheme.

Now let's consider several other suggestions to improve essay scoring reliability.

4. Use the scoring scheme consistently.

In other words, don't favor one student over another or get stricter or more lax over time. How can you do this?

5. Remove or cover the names on the papers before beginning scoring.

In this way you are more likely to rate papers on their merits, rather than on your overall impression of the student.

6. Score *each* student's answer to the same question before going on to the next answer.

In other words, do *all* of the answers to the first question before looking at the answers to the second. Why? First, you want to avoid having a student's score on an earlier question influence your evaluation of his or her later questions; and second, it is much easier to keep scoring criteria for one question in mind than it is to keep scoring criteria for all the questions in mind.

7. Try to keep scores for previous items hidden when scoring subsequent items, for the same reason already mentioned.
8. Try to re-evaluate your papers before returning them. When you come across discrepant ratings, average them.

Well, there you have it! Eight suggestions for improving reliability of essay scoring. If you use essay items, try to incorporate as many of these suggestions as possible.

SUMMARY

Chapter 7 introduced you to the major issues related to the construction and scoring of essay items. Its major points are:

1. Essay items require that the student supply rather than select a response. The length and complexity of the response may vary, and essay items lend themselves best to the assessment of higher-level cognitive skills.
2. There are two main types of essay items that are differentiated by length of response: extended-response and restricted-response essay items.
   a. The extended-response item usually requires responses more than a page in length and may be used to assess synthesis and evaluation skills.
   b. The restricted-response item is usually answered in a page or less. It is often used to measure comprehension, application, and analysis.

3. The type of item written is determined by the cognitive skills called for in the instructional objective.

4. Suggestions for writing essay items include the following:
   a. Identify the cognitive processes you want the student to use before you write the item.
   b. State the task clearly (that is, focus the item), including any criteria on which the essay will be graded.
   c. Avoid beginning essay items with *what*, *who*, *when*, and *list*, unless you are measuring at the knowledge level.
   d. Ask for presentation of evidence for a controversial position, rather than asking the student simply to take a controversial position.
   e. Avoid using optional items.
   f. Establish reasonable time and/or page limits for each item.
   g. Use essays to measure learning outcomes that cannot be measured by objective items.
   h. Be sure the item matches the instructional objective.

5. Advantages of essay items over objective items include the following:
   a. Essays enable you to assess complex learning outcomes.
   b. Essays are relatively easy to construct.
   c. Essays enable you to assess communication skills.
   d. Essays eliminate student guessing.

6. Disadvantages of essay items include:
   a. Longer scoring time
   b. Scoring unreliability
   c. Limited content sampling
   d. Susceptible to bluffing

7. Essay items should be used when:
   a. Objectives specify higher-level cognitive processes and objective items are inappropriate.
   b. Few tests or items are necessary.
   c. Test security is in question.

8. Essay scoring reliability may be improved by:
   a. Writing good essay items.

b. Using restricted-range rather than extended-range essays whenever appropriate.

c. Using a predetermined scoring scheme.

d. Implementing the scoring scheme consistently with all students.

e. Removing or covering names on papers to avoid scoring bias.

f. Scoring all responses to one item before scoring the next item.

g. Keeping scores from previous items hidden when scoring subsequent items.

h. Rescoring all papers before returning them and averaging discrepant ratings.

9. Essays may be scored according to:

   a. Simple scoring schemes that assign credit for content.

   b. Detailed scoring schemes that assign credit for content, organization, process, and any other factors that the scorer deems desirable.

   c. The rating method, in which grades are assigned on the basis of a global impression of the whole response.

For Practice

1. Write an essay test item using both an extended-response format and a restricted-response format. Your extended-response question should be targeted to measure a synthesis or evaluation objective, while your restricted response question should be targeted to measure a comprehension, application, or analysis objective.

2. Prepare a scoring guide for your restricted-response essay item using the format shown in Table 7.1.

3. Describe five scoring procedures from among those discussed in this chapter that will help ensure the reliability of scoring your essay question.

4. Give some pros and cons of the rating method, in which grades are assigned on the basis of global impressions of the whole response.

CHAPTER 8

Administering, Analyzing, and Improving the Test

Over the last several chapters we have discussed various aspects of test planning and item construction. If you have written instructional objectives, constructed a test blueprint, and written items that match your objectives, then more than likely you will have a good test. All the "raw material" will be there. However, sometimes the raw material, as good as it may be, can be rendered useless because of poorly assembled and administered tests. By now you know it requires a substantial amount of time to write objectives, put together a test blueprint, and write items. It is worth a little more time to properly assemble or package your test so that your efforts will not be wasted. Our goal for this chapter is to provide some suggestions to help you avoid common pitfalls in test assembly, administration, and scoring. Later in the chapter we will discuss considerations and techniques of test analysis. First, let's consider test assembly.

ASSEMBLING THE TEST

At this point let's assume you have:

1. Written measurable instructional objectives;
2. Prepared a test blueprint, specifying the number of items for each content and process area;
3. Written test items that match your instructional objectives.

Once you have completed these activities you are ready to:

1. Package the test
2. Reproduce the test

These components constitute what we are calling *test assembly*. Let's consider each a little more closely.

Packaging the Test

There are several packaging guidelines worth remembering, including grouping together items of similar format, arranging test items from easy to hard, properly spacing items, keeping items and options on the same page, placing illustrations near the descriptive material, checking for randomness in the answer key, deciding how students will record their answers, providing space for the test taker's name and the date, checking test directions for clarity, and proofreading the test before you reproduce and distribute it.

GROUP TOGETHER ALL ITEMS OF SIMILAR FORMAT. If you have all true-false items grouped together, all completion items together, and so on, then students will not have to "switch gears" to adjust to new formats. This will enable them to cover more items in a given time than if item formats were mixed throughout the test. Also, by grouping items of a given format together, only one set of directions per format section is necessary—another time-saver.

ARRANGE TEST ITEMS FROM EASY TO HARD. Arranging test items according to level of difficulty should enable more students to answer the first few items correctly, thereby building confidence and, hopefully, reducing test anxiety.

SPACE THE ITEMS FOR EASY READING. If possible, try to provide enough blank space between items so that each item is distinctly separate from others. When items are crowded together, students may inadvertently perceive a word, phrase, or line from a preceding or following item as part of the item in question. Naturally, this interferes with a student's capacity to demonstrate his or her true ability.

KEEP ITEMS AND OPTIONS ON THE SAME PAGE. There are few things more aggravating to a test taker than to have to turn the page to read the options for multiple-choice or matching items, or to finish reading a true-false or completion item. To avoid this, do not begin an item at the bottom of the page unless you will have at least an inch left *after completing* the item. Not only will this help eliminate having to carry items over to the next page, it will also minimize the likelihood that the last line or two of the item will be cut off when you reproduce the test.

POSITION ILLUSTRATIONS NEAR DESCRIPTIONS. Place diagrams, maps, or other supporting material immediately above the item or items to which they refer. In other words, if items 9, 10, and 11 refer to a map of South America, locate the map above items 9, 10, and 11—not between 9 and 10 or between 10 and 11 and not below them. Also, if possible, keep any such stimuli and related questions on the same page to save the test taker time.

CHECK YOUR ANSWER KEY. Be sure the correct answers follow a fairly random pattern. Avoid true-false patterns such as T F T F, etc., or T T F F, etc., and multiple-choice patterns such as D C B A D C B A, etc. At the same time, check to see that your correct answers are distributed about equally between true and false and among multiple-choice options.

DETERMINE HOW STUDENTS RECORD ANSWERS. Decide whether you want to have students record their answers on the test paper or on a separate answer sheet. In the lower elementary grades, it is generally a good idea to have students record answers on the test papers themselves. In the upper elementary and secondary grades, separate answer sheets can be used to facilitate scoring accuracy and to cut down on scoring time. Also, in the upper grades, learning to complete separate answer sheets will make students familiar with the process they will use when taking standardized tests.

PROVIDE SPACE FOR NAME AND DATE. Be sure to include a blank on your test booklet and/or answer sheet for the student's name and the date. This may seem an unnecessary suggestion, but it is *not* always evident to a nervous test taker that a name should be included on the test. Students are much more likely to remember to put their names on tests if space is provided.

CHECK TEST DIRECTIONS. Check your directions for each item format to be sure they are clear. Directions should specify:

1. The numbers of the items to which they apply
2. How to record answers
3. The basis on which to select answers
4. Criteria for scoring

PROOFREAD THE TEST. Proofread for typographical and grammatical errors before reproducing the test and make any necessary corrections. Having to announce corrections to the class just before the test or during the test will waste time and is likely to inhibit the test takers' concentration.

Before reproducing the test, it's a good idea to check off these steps. The checklist in Figure 8.1 can be used for this purpose.

Reproducing the Test

Most test reproduction in the schools is done on ditto or photocopying machines. As you well know, the quality of such copies can vary tremendously. Regardless of how valid and reliable your test might be, poor copies will make it less so. Thus, it makes sense to take the following practical steps to ensure that the time you spend constructing a valid and reliable test does not end in illegible copies.

KNOW THE DITTO OR PHOTOCOPYING MACHINE. Be sure you or the person you designate to do the reproduction understands how to operate the ditto or photocopying machine. There is some variation across models, and a few minutes of "practice" on a new machine is a worthwhile investment.

MAKE EXTRA COPIES. Always make at least five extra copies of each page of the test when you use ditto machines, since they have a tendency to count pages they fail to print.

SPECIFY COPYING INSTRUCTIONS. If someone else will do the reproducing, be sure to specify that the dittos are for a test and not simply an enrichment exercise. Ask the clerk or aide to inspect every tenth copy for legibility while running the copies and to be alert for blank or half-dittoed pages while collating, ordering, and stapling multi-page tests.

AVOID COMMON PITFALLS. If your test is to be dittoed, avoid:

1. Fine print;
2. Finely detailed maps or drawings;
3. Barely legible masters or originals—if you can barely read the original, you can't later blame the ditto machine.

FIGURE 8.1
Test Assembly Checklist

Put a check in the blank to the right of each statement after you've checked to see that it applies to your test.

	Yes	No
1. Are items of similar format grouped together?	___	___
2. Are items arranged from easy-to-hard levels of difficulty?	___	___
3. Are items properly spaced?	___	___
4. Are items and options on the same page?	___	___
5. Are diagrams, maps, and supporting material above designated items and on the same page with items?	___	___
6. Are answers random?	___	___
7. Have you decided whether an answer sheet will be used?	___	___
8. Are blanks for name and date included?	___	___
9. Have the directions been checked for clarity?	___	___
10. Has the test been proofread for errors?	___	___
11. Do items avoid racial and gender bias?	___	___

FILE ORIGINAL TEST. Finally, retain the original or master in case you want to reuse the test, or items within the test. Be sure you tell your clerk or aide to return the original to you—otherwise it may end up thrown away.

ADMINISTERING THE TEST

The test is ready. All that remains is to get the students ready and hand out the tests. Here is a series of suggestions to help your students psychologically prepare for the test:

MAINTAIN A POSITIVE ATTITUDE. Try to induce a positive test-taking attitude. Of course, this consideration must be kept in mind long before the test is actually distributed. It helps to keep the main purposes of classroom testing in mind—to evaluate achievement and instructional procedures and to provide feedback to yourself and your students. Too often tests are used to punish ("Well, it's obvious the class isn't doing the readings, so we'll have a test today"), or are used indiscriminately ("It's Tuesday, I guess I may as well give my class a test"), or inappropriately ("I need a good evaluation from the principal; I'll give my class an easy test"). To the extent that you can avoid falling victim to such testing traps, you will be helping induce and maintain a positive test-taking atmosphere.

MAXIMIZE ACHIEVEMENT MOTIVATION. Try *not* to minimize the achievement aspect of the test. While you do not want to immobilize your students with fear, you do want them to try to do their best on the test. Encourage them to do so. If a student's grade will be influenced, avoid making comments such as "We're just going to have an easy little quiz today; it's no big deal." Such an approach will probably minimize anxiety in very nervous test takers, which might improve their performance, but it may also serve to impair the test performance of students who need to take tests seriously in order to be motivated enough to do their best. In your class you will likely have both types of students. Keep your general statement about the test accurate. The test is something to be taken seriously and this should be clear to the class. Remember, you can always make reassuring or motivational comments individually to students.

EQUALIZE ADVANTAGES. Try to equalize the advantages test-wise students have over non-test-wise students. Since you are interested in student achievement, and not how test-wise a student is (unless you are teaching a course in test-taking skills), the results will be more valid if the advantages of test-wiseness are minimized. You can do so by instructing the class when it is best to guess or not guess at an answer, and remind them about general test-taking strategies (for example: "Don't spend too much time on any difficult items"; "Try all items, then return to those you are unsure of"; "Cross off options you've ruled out on matching or multiple-choice items"; "Check your answers for accuracy before turning in the test").

You may even want to take guessing into consideration when scoring the test. If time allows each student to attempt every item, a total score that is equal to the number of right answers may be perfectly adequate. In this case, students should be told to make an "educated" guess, even if they are not certain of the answer. However, the case may arise in which different students will attempt different numbers of items. This sometimes occurs when the test has a strict time limit, which may prevent some students from finishing. In this situation you may want to discourage guessing, that is, discourage the random filling out of unfinished answers seconds before the time limit is up.

A correction-for-guessing formula can be used to penalize the student for answering questions to which he or she does not know the answer. A student's score which has been corrected for guessing will be equal to the number of questions answered incorrectly divided by the number of answer choices for an item minus 1 and, then, this amount subtracted from the total number of right answers. Or:

$$\text{Score} = \text{Total Right} - \frac{\text{Total Wrong}}{\text{Number of Answer Choices} - 1}$$

For example, in a 50-item multiple-choice test where there are 4 possible answers and a student gets 44 answers correct, the student's score would be 44 – 6/3 = 42. The student's score, corrected for guessing, is 42. When this formula is used, students should be encouraged to make "educated" guesses.

AVOID SURPRISES. Be sure your students have sufficient advance notice of a test. "Pop" quizzes have little beneficial effect on overall academic achievement. They are especially problematic in junior high and high school where students have five or six different teachers. If each teacher gave pop quizzes, students would be hard pressed to be well prepared for each class each day. This is not to say that you should avoid frequent quizzes, however. When students are tested frequently, learning or study takes place at more regular intervals rather than massed or crammed the night before a test. Retention is generally better following spaced rather than massed learning.

CLARIFY THE RULES. Inform students about time limits, restroom policy, and any special considerations about the answer sheet *before* you distribute the tests. Students often tune out the instructor after they receive their tests and may miss important information.

ROTATE DISTRIBUTION. Alternate beginning test distribution at the left, right, front, and back of the class. This way, the same person will not always be the last one to receive the test.

REMIND STUDENTS TO CHECK THEIR COPIES. After handing out the tests, remind students to check page and item numbers to see that none has been omitted, and remind them to put their names on their papers.

MONITOR STUDENTS. While students are completing their tests, monitor them. While it would be nice to trust students not to look at each other's papers, it is not realistic. Inform students about penalties for cheating, and implement the penalties when cheating occurs. It is distasteful to do so, but so is cheating. After students learn they can't "get away with it," there should be little need for the penalties.

MINIMIZE DISTRACTIONS. Try to keep noise and distractions to a minimum—for obvious reasons.

GIVE TIME WARNINGS. Give students a warning 15, 10, and 5 minutes before the time limit is up, so they are not caught by surprise at the deadline.

COLLECT TESTS UNIFORMLY. Finally, have a uniform policy on collecting the tests. Indicate whether you want all papers or only some returned, where they are to be placed, and so forth. This not only saves time, but minimizes lost papers.

SCORING THE TEST

We discussed specific scoring recommendations for various types of objective test formats in Chapter 6 and for essay items in Chapter 7. Following are some general suggestions to save scoring time and improve scoring accuracy and consistency.

PREPARE ANSWER KEY. Prepare your answer key in advance, which will save time when you score the test and will help you identify questions that need rewording or need to be eliminated. Also, when constructing the answer key, you should get an idea of how long it will take your students to complete the test and whether this time is appropriate for the time slot you have allocated to the test.

CHECK ANSWER KEY. If possible, have a colleague check your answer key to identify alternative answers or potential problems.

SCORE BLINDLY. Try to score "blindly." That is, try to keep the student's name out of sight to prevent your knowledge about, or expectations of, the student from influencing the score.

CHECK MACHINE-SCORED ANSWER SHEETS. If machine scoring is used, check each answer sheet for stray marks, multiple answers, or marks that may be too light to be picked up by the scoring machine.

CHECK SCORING. If possible, double-check your scoring. Scoring errors due to clerical error occur frequently. There is no reason to expect that you will not make such errors.

RECORD SCORES. Before returning the scored papers to students, be sure you have recorded their scores in your record book! (Forgetting to do this has happened at least once to every teacher.)

ANALYZING THE TEST

Just as you can expect to make scoring errors, you can expect to make errors in test construction. *No* test you construct will be perfect—it will include inappropriate, invalid, or otherwise deficient items. In the remainder of this chapter we will introduce you to a technique called *item analysis*. Item analysis can be used to identify items that are deficient in some way, thus paving the way to improve or eliminate them, with the result being a better overall test. We will make a distinction between two kinds of item analysis, quantitative and qualitative. As you will see, qualitative item analysis is something with which you are already familiar. Quantitative item analysis is likely to be something new. Finally, we will discuss how item analysis differs for norm- and criterion-referenced tests, and we provide you with several modified norm-referenced analysis methods to use with criterion-referenced tests.

Quantitative Item Analysis

As mentioned, quantitative item analysis is a technique that will enable us to assess the quality or utility of an item. It does so by identifying *distractors* or response options that are not doing what they are supposed to be doing. How useful is this procedure for a completion or an essay item? Frankly, it is not very useful for these types of items, but qualitative item analysis is. On the other hand, quantitative item analysis is ideally suited for examining the usefulness of multiple-choice formats. The quantitative item analysis procedures that we will describe are most appropriate for items on a norm-referenced test. As you will see, we are interested in spreading out students, or discriminating among them, with such a test. When dealing with a criterion-referenced test, qualitative and modified quantitative item analysis procedures are most appropriate.

Unfortunately, there is some terminology or jargon associated with quantitative item analysis that must be mastered. Figure 8.2, Item Analysis Terminology, defines these terms. Study the definitions in the box and refer to them throughout this section.

Now that you have reviewed the terms and definitions, let's see how they apply to multiple-choice items. Consider the following example.

Suppose your students chose the options to a four-alternative multiple-choice item the following numbers of times: Three students chose option A; none chose B; eighteen chose the correct answer, C (marked with an asterisk); and nine chose D.

A	*B*	*C**	*D*
3	0	18	9

How does that help us? We can see immediately that B was not a very good option or distractor, since no one chose it. Also we can see that more than half the class answered the item correctly. In fact, by employing the following formula, we can compute p, the item's difficulty index, which is the first step in item analysis.

$$\text{p} = \frac{\text{Number of students selecting correct answer}}{\text{Total number of students attempting the item}}$$

$$\text{p} = \frac{18}{30} = .60$$

From this information we learn that the item was moderately difficult (60 percent of the class got it right) and that option B ought to be modified or replaced. This is useful information, but we can learn (and need to know) more about this item. Were the students who answered it correctly those who did well on the overall test? Did the distractors fool those who did well or poorly on the test? The answers to these questions are important, because they tell us whether the item discriminated between students who did well and those who did not do well on the overall test. A little confused? Let's look at it another way:

QUESTION: Why do we administer tests?

ANSWER: To find out who has mastered the material and who has not (that is, to discriminate between these two groups).

FIGURE 8.2
Item Analysis Terminology

Quantitative item analysis	A numerical method for analyzing test items employing student response alternatives or options.
Qualitative item analysis	A non-numerical method for analyzing test items not employing student responses, but considering test objectives, content validity, and technical item quality.
Key	Correct option in a multiple-choice item.
Distractor	Incorrect option in a multiple-choice item.
Difficulty index (p)	Proportion of students who answered the item correctly.
Discrimination index (D)	Measure of the extent to which a test item discriminates or differentiates between students who do well on the overall test and those who do not do well on the overall test. There are three types of discrimination indexes: 1. *Positive discrimination index*—those who did *well* on the overall test chose the correct answer for a particular item more often than those who did poorly on the overall test. 2. *Negative discrimination index*—those who did *poorly* on the overall test chose the correct answer for a particular item more often than those who did well on the overall test. 3. *Zero discrimination index*—those who did well and those who did poorly on the overall test chose the correct answer for a particular item with equal frequency.

QUESTION: Will a test discriminate between these groups better if each item on the test discriminates between those who did and did not do well on the test overall?

ANSWER: Absolutely! If more students who do *well* on the test overall answer an item correctly—positive discrimination index—that item helps the overall discrimination ability of the test. If this is true for all items (they are all positively discriminating), the test will do a good job of discriminating between those who know their stuff and those who don't. To the extent that students who do *poorly* on the overall test answer individual items correctly—negative discrimination index—the test loses its ability to discriminate.

QUESTION: How can I tell whether the key for any question is chosen more frequently by the better students (i.e., the item is positively discriminating) or the poorer students (i.e., the item is negatively discriminating)?

ANSWER: Follow the procedure described next.

DISCRIMINATION INDEX. To determine each item's discrimination index (D), complete the following steps:

1. Arrange the papers from highest to lowest score.
2. Separate the papers into an upper group and a lower group based on total test scores. Do so by including half of your papers in each group.
3. For each item, count the number in the upper group and the number in the lower group that chose each alternative.
4. Record your information for each item in the following form (the following is data from the previous example; again the asterisk indicates the keyed option):

Example for Item X
(Class size = 30)

Options	*A*	*B*	*C**	*D*
Upper	1	0	11	3
Lower	2	0	7	6

5. Compute D, the discrimination index, by plugging the appropriate numbers into the following formula:

$$D = \frac{(\text{Numbers who got item correct in upper group}) - (\text{Number who got item correct in lower group})}{\text{Number of students in either group (if group sizes are unequal, choose the higher number)}}$$

Plugging in our numbers we arrive at

$$D = \frac{11 - 7}{15} = .267$$

Our discrimination index (D) is .267, which is positive. More students who did well on the overall test answered the item correctly than students who did poorly on the overall test. Now, let's put it all together for this item.

Difficulty index (p) = .60

Discrimination index (D) = .267

An item with p = .60 and D = .267 would be considered a moderately difficult item that has positive (desirable) discrimination ability. When p levels are less than about .25, the item is considered relatively difficult. When p levels are above .75, the item is considered relatively easy. Test construction experts try to build tests that have most items between p levels of .20 and .80, with an average p level of about .50. All other factors being equal, the test's discrimination ability is greatest when the overall p level (difficulty) is about .50.

How high is a "good" discrimination index? Unfortunately, there is no single answer. Some experts insist that D should be at least .30, while others believe that as long as D has a positive value, the item's discrimination ability is adequate. Further complicating the issue is the fact that D is related to p. Just as a test tends to have maximum discrimination ability when p is around .50, so too does an individual item. It can be difficult to obtain discrimination indices above .30 when items are easy or difficult. Naturally, you want your items to have as high a discrimination index as possible, but our recommendation is that you consider seriously any item with a positive D value. Based on this information, we would conclude that, in general, the item is acceptable. But, we must also look at the item analysis data further to see if any distractors need to be modified or replaced.

We noted earlier that B would need to be replaced, since no one chose it. But what about A and D? Are they acceptable? The answer is yes, but can you figure out why? Because *more* people in the lower group chose them than people in the upper group. This is the opposite of what we would want for the correct answer, and it makes sense. If we want more students who do well on the overall test to choose the correct answer, then we also must want more students who do poorly on the overall test to choose the distractors. Let's look at the responses for another item.

Example for Item Y
(Class size = 28)

Options	*A**	*B*	*C*	*D*
Upper	4	1	5	4
Lower	1	7	3	3

The following questions will help guide us through the quantitative item analysis procedure.

1. What is the difficulty level?

$$p = \frac{\text{Number selecting correct answer}}{\text{Total number taking the test}}$$

$$p = \frac{5}{28} = .18$$

2. What is the discrimination index?

$$D = \frac{\text{Number correct (upper)} - \text{Number correct (lower)}}{\text{Number in either group}}$$

$$D = \frac{4 - 1}{14} = .214$$

3. Should this item be eliminated? No, since it is positively discriminating. However, it is a difficult item; only 18 percent of the class got it right.
4. Should any distractor be eliminated or modified? Yes; distractors C and D have attracted *more* students who did *well* on the test overall. If these distractors are modified or replaced, a good item will be made even better. Remember, in order for an item to discriminate well, more students who do well on the test should choose the correct answer than students who do poorly (the correct answer should be positively discriminating) *and* fewer students who do well on the test should choose each distractor than students who do poorly (the distractors should be negatively discriminating).

Example for Item Z
(Class Size = 30)

Options	*A*	*B**	*C*	*D*
Upper	3	4	3	5
Lower	0	10	2	3

Again, let's ask the four basic questions:

1. What is the difficulty level?

$$p = \frac{\text{Number selecting correct answer}}{\text{Total number taking the test}}$$

$$p = \frac{14}{30} = .467 \text{ (moderately difficult)}$$

2. What is the discrimination index?

$$D = \frac{\text{Number correct (upper)} - \text{Number correct (lower)}}{\text{Number in either group}}$$

$$= \frac{4 - 10}{15} = \frac{-6}{15} = -.40 \text{ (negatively discriminating)}$$

3. Should this item be eliminated? Yes! The item is moderately difficult (approximately 47 percent of the class got it right), but it discriminates *negatively* (D = −.40). Remember, one of the reasons for testing is to discriminate between those students who know their stuff and those who do not. On this item more students who knew their stuff (who did *well* on the overall test) chose the *incorrect* options than the correct answer. If the test were made mostly of or entirely of items like this, the students who score high on the test, who answered the most items correctly, might be those who did not know their stuff. This is clearly what we want to avoid. Thus, an item that discriminates negatively should be eliminated.

4. Should any distractor(s) be modified or eliminated? Since we have already decided to eliminate the item, this is a moot question. However, let's look at the distractors anyway. In the case of options A, C, and D, more students who did well on the test chose each of these options than students who did poorly on the test. Each distractor discriminates positively. We want our distractors to discriminate *negatively*. Thus, this item has nothing going for it, according to our quantitative item analysis. The correct answer, which should discriminate positively, discriminates negatively. The distractors, which should discriminate negatively, discriminate positively!

In addition to helping us decide which items to eliminate from a test before it is again administered, quantitative item analysis also enables us to make other decisions. For example, we can use quantitative item analysis to decide whether an item is miskeyed, whether responses to the item are characterized by guessing, or whether the item is ambiguous. To do so, we need only consider the responses of students in the upper half of the class. Let's see how.

MISKEYING. When an item is miskeyed, most students who did well on the test will likely select an option that is a distractor, rather than the option that is keyed. Consider the following miskeyed item:

Who was the first astronaut to set foot on the moon?

a. John Glenn
b. Scott Carpenter
c. Neil Armstrong
*d. Alan Sheppard

Analyzing the responses for the *upper* half of the class, we find the following distribution:

	A	*B*	*C*	*D**
Upper half	1	1	9	2

Anytime most students in the upper half of the class fail to select the keyed option, consider whether your item is miskeyed. Remember, just as you are bound to make scoring errors, you are bound to miskey an item occasionally.

GUESSING. When guessing occurs, students in the upper half of the class respond in more or less random fashion. This is most likely to occur when the item measures content that is (1) not covered in class or the text, (2) so difficult that even the upper-half students have no idea what the correct answer is, or (3) so trivial that students are unable to choose from among the options provided. In such cases, each alternative is about equally attractive to students in the upper half, so their responses tend to be about equally distributed among the options. The following choice distribution would suggest that guessing occurred:

	A	*B*	*C**	*D*
Upper half	4	3	3	3

AMBIGUITY. So far we have discussed using quantitative item analysis to identify miskeying and guessing. We did so by looking at response distributions for the upper group. With miskeying, the upper group chooses a distractor more frequently than the key. With *guessing*, each option is chosen with about equal frequency. Ambiguity is suspected when, among the upper group, one of the distractors is chosen with about the same frequency as the correct answer. The following distribution suggests this item is ambiguous:

	A	*B*	*C*	*D**
Upper half	7	0	1	7

In this item, students who do well on the test but miss the item are drawn almost entirely to one of the distractors. However, quantitative analysis data can only *suggest* ambiguity. In the preceding item, there is no way for us to tell whether the "good" students chose distractor A because the item is deficient, or whether it was because they were distracted by an option that was plausible, but not as correct as the key.

The only way to determine whether the root of the problem is lack of mastery or a poorly written item is through qualitative item analysis. Before leaving quantitative item analysis, however, a final point should be made. As you are by now aware, there can be considerable time and effort invested in quantitative item analysis by a teacher. This can be a "turnoff" to some, resulting in a teacher failing to use this very useful test analysis tool. Fortunately, with the advent of personal computers and item analysis computer software, the actual time spent in quantitative item analysis by the teacher may now be significantly reduced. We will discuss personal computers and measurement-related software in Chapter 21 and will identify specific computer programs you can use for doing quantitative item analysis.

We will turn to qualitative item analysis next. However, first review what we have learned about the application of quantitative item analysis by studying Figure 8.3, the Quantitative Item Analysis Checklist.

Qualitative Item Analysis

As noted earlier, you already know something about qualitative item analysis. It's something you can and ought to do with items of *all* formats. Essentially, when we talk about qualitative item analysis, we are talking about matching items and objectives and editing poorly written items. These are activities we've discussed in Chapters 5, 6, and 7 in relation to improving the content validity of a test. We refer to them again simply because it is appropriate to edit or rewrite items and assess their content validity after a test, as well as before a test.

Let's face it. In spite of our best intentions, we end up pressed for time as the day for the test approaches. What do we do? Probably we work more quickly to assemble the test—overlooking such things as grammatical cues, specific determiners, double negatives, multiple defensible answers, and items that fail to match instructional objectives.

As a result, these faults creep into the final version of the test. It would be nice if quantitative item analysis pointed out such problems, but it does not. Quantitative item analysis is useful but limited. It points out items that have problems but doesn't tell us what

FIGURE 8.3
Quantitative Item Analysis Checklist

1. Item number ________
2. Difficulty level: $p = \frac{\text{No. correct}}{\text{Total}} =$ ________
3. Discrimination index: ________

$$D = \frac{\text{Number correct (upper)} - \text{Number correct (lower)}}{\text{Number of students in either group}} =$$ ________

4. Eliminate or revise item? Check:
   a. Does key discriminate positively? ________
   b. Do distractors discriminate negatively? ________
   If you answer yes to both a and b, no revision may be necessary. If you answer no to a *or* b, revision is necessary. If you answer no to a *and* b, eliminate the item.
5. Check for miskeying, ambiguity, or guessing. Among the choices for the *upper group only*, was there evidence of:
   a. miskeying (more chose distractor than key)? ________
   b. guessing (equal spread of choices across options)? ________
   c. ambiguity (equal number chose one distractor and the key)? ________

these problems are. It is possible that an item that fails to measure or match an instructional objective could have an acceptable difficulty level, an answer that discriminates positively, and distractors that discriminate negatively. In short, quantitative item analysis is fallible. To do a thorough job of test analysis, one must use a combination of quantitative and qualitative item analysis, and not rely solely on one or the other. In other words, there is no substitute for carefully scrutinizing and editing items and matching test items with objectives.

Item Analysis Modifications for the Criterion-Referenced Test

The statistical test analysis method discussed earlier, called quantitative item analysis, applies most directly to the norm-referenced test. We know from Chapter 2, however, that the classroom teacher will typically use criterion-referenced tests rather than norm-referenced tests. Well, then, we can just use these same procedures for our teacher-made, criterion-referenced tests. Right? Wrong!

As we will discover in later chapters, variability of scores is crucial to the appropriateness and success of norm-referenced item analysis procedures. In short, these procedures depend on the variability or spread of scores (i.e., low to high) if they are to do their jobs correctly. In a typical teacher-made criterion-referenced test, however, variability of scores would be expected to be small, assuming instruction is effective and the test and its objectives match. Thus, the application of quantitative item analysis procedures to criterion-referenced measures is not appropriate, since by definition most students will answer these items correctly (i.e., there will be *minimal* variability or spread of scores). In this section we will describe several ways in which these procedures can be modified when a criterion-referenced, mastery approach to test item evaluation is employed. As you will see, these modifications are straightforward and easier to use than the quantitative procedures described earlier.

USING PRE- AND POST-TESTS AS UPPER AND LOWER GROUPS. The following approaches require that you administer the test as a "pre-test" prior to your instruction and as a "post-test" after your instruction. Ideally, in such a situation the majority of students should answer most of your test items incorrectly on the pre-test and correctly on the post-test. By studying the difference between the difficulty (p) levels for each item at the time of the pre- and post-tests, we can tell if this is happening. At pre-test the p level should be low (e.g., .30 or lower), and at post-test it should be high (e.g., .70 or higher). In addition, we can consider the pre-test results for an item as the lower group (L) and post-test results for the item as the upper group (U), and then we can perform the quantitative item analysis procedures previously described to determine the discrimination direction for the key and the distractors.

EXAMPLE 1: Analyze the following results.

	Numbers of students choosing option (n = 25)	
Option	***At pre-test (Lower or L)***	***At post-test (Upper or U)***
A	9	1
B	7	1
C	3	2
D* (key)	6	21

Step 1

Compute p levels for both tests.

	Pre-test	Post-test
p = No. choosing correctly/Total number	$\frac{6}{25} = .24$	$\frac{21}{25} = .84$

This is what we would hope for in a criterion-referenced test; most students should answer the item *incorrectly* on the pre-test and *correctly* on the post-test. In this case it was an improvement from 24 percent to 84 percent.

Step 2

Determine the discrimination index (D) for the key.

$$D = \frac{\text{Number correct (Post-)} - \text{Number correct (Pre-)}}{\text{Number in either group}}$$

$$D = \frac{21 - 6}{25} = \frac{15}{25} = .60$$

This indicates that the keyed correct option has a *positive* discrimination index, which is what we want.

Step 3
Determine whether each option separately discriminates *negatively.*

Option A: $D = \frac{1 - 9}{25} = \frac{-8}{25} = -.32$

Option A discriminates *negatively*, which is what we want; more students chose this option on the pre-test (L) than the post-test (U).

Option B: $D = \frac{1 - 7}{25} = \frac{-6}{25} = -.24$

Option B also discriminates *negatively.*

Option C: $D = \frac{2 - 3}{25} = \frac{-1}{25} = -.04$

Option C also discriminates negatively, albeit weakly.

In summary, our modified quantitative item analysis procedures indicate the following:

1. There was a sizeable increase in p value from pre-test to post-test.
2. The D index for the key was positive.
3. The distractors all discriminated negatively.

If a criterion-referenced test item manifests these features, it has passed our "test" and probably is a good item with little or no need for modification. Contrast this conclusion, however, with the following item from the same test.

EXAMPLE 2: Analyze the results in the table below.

Numbers of students choosing option (n = 25)

Option	***At Pre-test (L)***	***At Post-test (U)***
A*	23	24
B	1	1
C	1	0
D	0	0

For this item, the pre-test p level was .92 and the post-test level was .96—an increase of only .04, hardly an increase at all. In addition, the majority of students answered this item *correctly* on the pre-test. We want *most* students to answer incorrectly at the pre-test and correctly at the post-test!

Furthermore, the D index for the key is only .04:

$$D = \frac{24 - 23}{25} = \frac{1}{25} = .04$$

While this index is positive, and *might* be acceptable in a norm-referenced test, it is *not* acceptable for a criterion-referenced test.

OK, so what D value is acceptable? Unfortunately, there is no easy answer to this question. We would suggest, however, that you look for D values of .40 or greater. This would mean that almost twice as many students are answering the item correctly on the post-test than on the pre-test.

Finally, let's investigate our distractors. The D values for both options B and D are .00.

$$\text{Option B:}\quad D = \frac{1 - 1}{25} = \frac{0}{25} = .00$$

$$\text{Option D:}\quad D = \frac{0 - 0}{25} = \frac{0}{25} = .00$$

Neither of these options are useful; they both fail to differentiate between pre- and post-test. These options require modification or elimination.

Let's look at option C.

$$\text{Option C:}\quad D = \frac{0 - 1}{25} = \frac{-1}{25} = -.04$$

This option does discriminate negatively, but weakly. Modifications to this option may increase its ability to discriminate negatively.

To evaluate this item overall, let's subject it to our three-step analysis:

1. Is there a substantial increase in p value (.40 or more) between pre- and post-test?
   p increased from .92 to .96, hardly substantial.
2. Was D greater than .40 for the key?
   D was only .04.
3. Did all distractors discriminate negatively?
   Options B and D had zero discrimination ability; option C discriminated negatively, but only weakly.

Thus, the item in Example 2 failed all the tests. Rather than modify the item, it is probably more efficient to replace it with another.

Less technical variations of modified quantitative item analysis procedures for criterion-referenced tests follow. The next two methods also have the advantage of applying to true-false, matching, and completion tests rather than just multiple-choice tests.

COMPARING THE PERCENTAGE ANSWERING EACH ITEM CORRECTLY ON BOTH PRE- AND POST-TEST. If your test is sensitive to your objectives (and assuming you teach to your objectives), the majority of learners should receive a low score on the test prior to your instruction and a high score afterward. This method can be used to determine whether this is happening.

Subtract the percentage of students passing each item before your instruction from the percentage of students passing each item after your instruction. The more positive the difference, the more you know the item is tapping the content you are teaching. This method is similar to step 1 as described in the preceding section.

For example, consider the following percentages for five test items:

Item	Percentage passing Pre-test	Percentage passing Post-test	Difference
1	16	79	+63%
2	10	82	+72%
3	75	75	+ 0%
4	27	91	+64%
5	67	53	−14%

Notice that item 3 registers no change in the percentage of students passing from before to after instruction. In fact, a high percentage of students got the item correct without any instruction! This item may be eliminated from the test, since little or no instruction pertaining to it was provided *and* most students already knew the content it represents.

Now, look at item 5. Notice the percentage is negative. That is, 14 percent of the class actually changed from getting the item *correct* before instruction to getting it *wrong* after. Here, either the instruction was not related to the item, or it actually confused some students who knew the correct answer beforehand. A revision of the item, the objective pertaining to this item, or the related instruction would be in order.

DETERMINING THE PERCENTAGE OF ITEMS ANSWERED IN THE EXPECTED DIRECTION FOR THE ENTIRE TEST. Another, slightly different approach is to determine whether the entire test reflects the change from fewer to more students answering items correctly from pre- to post-test. This index uses the number of items each learner failed on the test prior to instruction *but* passed on the test after instruction. Here is how it is computed.

STEP 1: Find the number of items each student *failed* on the pre-test, *prior* to instruction, but *passed* on the post-test, *after* instruction.

Item	Bobby at pre-test	Bobby at post-test
1*	Incorrect	Correct
2	Correct	Correct
3*	Incorrect	Correct
4	Correct	Incorrect
5	Incorrect	Incorrect

The asterisks indicate just the items counted in step 1 for Bobby. This count is then repeated for each student.

STEP 2: Add the counts in step 1 for all students and divide by the number of students.

STEP 3: Divide the result from step 2 by the number of items on the test.

STEP 4: Multiply the result from step 3 by 100.

Let's see how this would work for a 25-item test given to five students before and after instruction.

STEP 1: Find the number of items that students answered incorrectly prior to instruction but correctly after instruction.

Mary	18
Carlos	15
Sharon	22
Amanda	20
Charles	13

STEP 2: $$\frac{18 + 15 + 22 + 20 + 13}{5} = 17.6$$

STEP 3: $$\frac{17.6}{25} = .70$$

STEP 4: $.70 \times 100 = 70\%$

Seventy percent of the items on the test registered a positive change after instruction, where a positive change is defined as failing an item before instruction and passing it afterward. The greater the overall positive percentage of change, the more your test is likely to match your instruction and to be a content-valid test.

Limitations of These Modifications. One limitation of these modified quantitative item analysis procedures is that it is difficult, especially at first, to write items that virtually everyone will be successful on only after a unit of instruction. Thus, you may find that in your initial efforts, 40 percent of your students answer an item correctly on the pre-test and only 60 percent answer an item correctly on the post-test. This is less than optimal, but it may be a good "first try." Another limitation is that if the unit of instruction is brief, there may be some "contamination" of the post-test by a student's recollection of responses made during the pre-test. A third limitation is that we are taking a procedure that was developed for a single administration of a norm-referenced test and applying it to a criterion-referenced test administered to the same group at two different times. Lastly, these modifications require two test administrations (pre and post), which will reduce the amount of time you devote to instruction.

In conclusion, it would be a mistake to apply the quantitative item analysis procedures appropriate for norm-referenced measures uncritically to criterion-referenced tests. At the same time, it would be a mistake to reject their utility. Their utility is probably strongest when tests or test items are in their early stages of use and development, and the methods are used along with qualitative item analysis.

We have discussed quantitative and qualitative item analysis, how they apply to norm-referenced tests, and how these procedures must be modified to apply more specifically to the typical classroom test. What's left is returning the test to the students, something we like to call *debriefing*.

DEBRIEFING

Take a moment to think back to the times a test on which you did well was returned. Remember the happy, satisfied feeling you had? You felt good about yourself, your teacher, and the test. Of course, it was a good test because it proved that you knew your stuff. Now take a minute to think back to the times a test on which you did poorly was returned. Remember the unhappy, unsatisfied feeling you had? Were you angry or resentful? It's likely you weren't feeling very fond of yourself, your teacher, or the test—especially the test. Any time you give a test, it's likely that some students will do poorly and feel unhappy or angry as a result.

Teachers adopt their own ways of coping with complaints about a test. These range from "Your score is final, and that's it" to "I'll give everybody 10 extra points so that no one fails." We feel that neither of these positions is defensible. The first position denies or ignores reality. It is not just possible, but probable, that your test has deficiencies. Refusing to examine the test with your students robs you of the opportunity to get feedback that you can use to improve or fine-tune your test before you use it again. Furthermore, such an approach serves to antagonize and alienate students. Awarding extra credit or a make-up test may calm the angry students who did poorly but may be unfair to those who did well. As with the first approach, it robs you of the opportunity to get feedback on, and make appropriate modifications to, your test. Rather, we advocate having concern for the quality of your test and showing this concern by going over the test with your students each time you use it. Your students can actually save you time and effort by screening your test and identifying those items that are worth subjecting to the time consuming processes of quantitative and qualitative item analysis.

If you are truly interested in improving the validity and reliability of your test, you can subject each item to both kinds of item analysis. Your reward will be a better test. Or you can find out which items your students found problematic and subject only those few items to analysis. Again, your reward will be a better test. The choice is yours, but, of course, we hope you choose to go over the test with your students later. Should you do so, consult the following suggested debriefing guidelines.

Debriefing Guidelines

Before handing back answer sheets or grades:

DISCUSS PROBLEM ITEMS. Discuss any items you found problematic in scoring the test. This sets the stage for rational discussion and makes for more effective consideration of the item(s) in question. Also, you are more likely to have the attention of the students than you would if they were looking over their answer sheets or thinking about the grades they received.

LISTEN TO STUDENT REACTIONS. Ask for student reactions to your comments and *listen* to their reactions. Again, you are setting the stage for rational discussion of the test by letting the students know you are interested in their feedback. Remember, your goal is to improve the validity and reliability of your test by improving on its weaknesses. When you or your students begin to respond emotionally, defensiveness is likely to replace listening and issues of power and control replace rational discussion. In short, improving the test may seem less important than asserting your authority. You will have plenty of opportunities to assert your authority and few opportunities to improve your test. Try to keep these issues separate, and use the few opportunities you do have for test improvement as advantageously as you can.

AVOID ON-THE-SPOT DECISIONS. Tell your students that you will consider their comments, complaints, and suggestions, but you will not make any decisions about omitting items, partial credit, extra credit, and so forth until you have had time to study and think about the test data. You may want to make it clear that soliciting their comments is only for the purpose of preparing the next test, not for reconsidering grades for the present test.

BE EQUITABLE WITH CHANGES. If you decide to make changes, let your students know that any changes in scoring will apply to all students, not just those who raise objections.

After handing back answer sheets or grades:

ASK STUDENTS TO DOUBLE-CHECK. Ask students to double-check your arithmetic, and ask any who feel clerical errors have been made to see you as soon as possible. Here you are presenting yourself as human by admitting that you can make errors.

ASK STUDENTS TO IDENTIFY PROBLEMS. If time permits, ask students to identify the items they find problematic and why they are so. Make note of the items and problems. Such items may then be discussed or worked into some new instructional objectives.

We have been suggesting that you use the time you spend returning your test as an opportunity to improve your test. To the extent that you can elicit relevant and constructive feedback from your class, you will be likely to reach this goal. In trying to remain emotionally detached from your test and nondefensive, it is useful to keep a few points in mind:

1. Your test will include at least some items that can be improved. You are human!
2. Students are criticizing your skill as a test constructor, not you as a person. Admittedly, though, frustrated students can get too personal. When this happens, try to remember what's behind it—frustration with your test.
3. The quality of an item is not necessarily related to the loudness with which complaints are made. At times, items that students loudly protest are indeed poor items. At other times, they are simply difficult or challenging items. Use quantitative item analysis to determine which is the case.
4. When it appears necessary to rescore a test or award credit, keep in mind that research has shown that rescoring tends to be highly related to the original scoring. Thus, although some individual scores may change, one's rank in relation to others is not likely to change much. For all their protest, students seldom really gain much other than letting off steam.

5. Finally, keep in mind that the most important objectives for debriefing are to improve your test and to gain insight into the effectiveness and thoroughness of your instruction and to plan new objectives that can address the problems students had in learning the test content.

THE PROCESS OF EVALUATING CLASSROOM ACHIEVEMENT

Many of the various components of testing that have been presented in the last several chapters are specific and technical. You may wonder how important they are. Unfortunately, none of the major steps we have focused on can be considered optional because they are all components of a single process—the process of evaluating classroom achievement. It is important to keep this in mind since valid and reliable measurement of classroom achievement depends on *each* and *all* components. Remember, the general public is clamoring for accountability, and one of the factors for which teachers are likely to be held more and more accountable is classroom achievement. Spend the time now to master the skills involved in validly and reliably measuring classroom achievement. You will reap the benefits later. The process of measuring classroom achievement is depicted in Figure 8.4, which summarizes all of the important components of achievement testing that we have discussed thus far.

There's nothing for you to do now but go out and do it. If you've studied and worked at these chapters, you are ahead in the test construction game. What that means for you is better tests that cause fewer students and parents to complain and that are more valid and reliable measurements of achievement.

SUMMARY

In Chapter 8 many issues related to test assembly, administration, scoring, and analysis were covered. Major points mentioned are:

1. When assembling a test:
   a. Group all items of same or similar formats together.
   b. Arrange items so that item difficulty progresses from easy to hard.
   c. Space items to eliminate overcrowding.
   d. Keep items and options on the same page.
   e. Place contextual material above the items to which they refer.
   f. Arrange answers in a random pattern.
   g. Decide how students are to record answers.
   h. Be sure to include a space for the student's name.
   i. Be sure directions are specific and accurate.
   j. Proofread your master copy before reproducing it.

FIGURE 8.4
The Process of Measuring Achievement in the Classroom

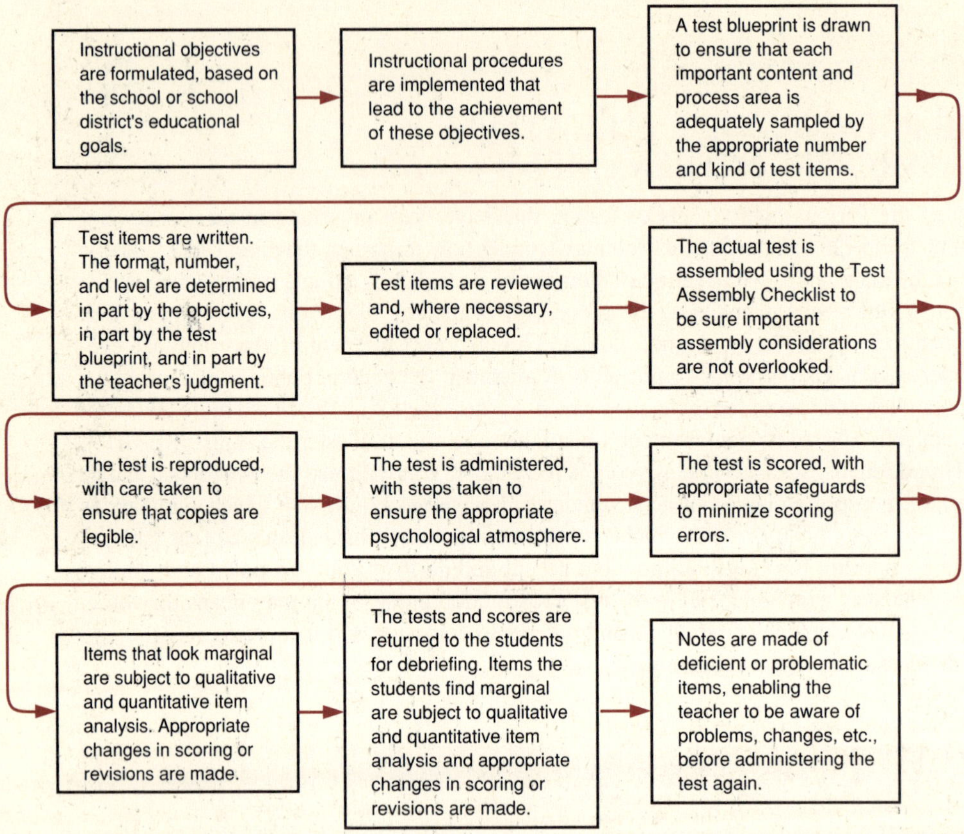

2. Care must be taken in reproducing the test to avoid illegible copies that would impair test validity.
3. In administering a test, make an effort to:
   a. Induce a positive test-taking attitude.
   b. Maximize the achievement nature of the test.
   c. Equalize the advantages test-wise students have over non-test-wise students.
   d. Avoid surprise tests.
   e. Provide special instructions before the tests are actually distributed.
   f. Alternate your test distribution procedures.
   g. Have students check that they have the entire test.

   h. Keep distractions to a minimum.
   i. Alert students to the amount of time left toward the end of the test.
   j. Clarify test collection procedures before handing out the test.

4. In scoring the test, try to:
   a. Have the key prepared in advance.
   b. Have the key checked for accuracy.
   c. Score blindly.
   d. Check for multiple answers if machine scoring is used.
   e. Double-check scores, if scored by hand.
   f. Record scores before returning the tests.
5. Quantitative item analysis is a mathematical approach to assessing an item's utility.
6. An item's difficulty level (p) is computed by dividing the number of students who answered correctly by the total number of students who attempted the item.
7. An item's discrimination index (D) is computed by subtracting the number of students who answered correctly in the low-scoring half of the class from the number of students who answered correctly in the high-scoring half of the class, and dividing the remainder by the number of students in the upper or lower group.
8. Keyed correct options should discriminate positively (positive D value), and incorrect options should discriminate negatively (negative D value).
9. Quantitative item analysis helps us decide whether to retain or eliminate an item, which distractor(s) should be modified or eliminated, whether an item is miskeyed, whether guessing occurred, and whether ambiguity is present.
10. Qualitative item analysis is a nonmathematical approach to assessing an item's utility.
11. Qualitative item analysis is performed by checking an item's content validity and inspecting it for technical faults, as outlined in Chapters 5, 6, and 7.
12. Do not apply to criterion-referenced tests the quantitative item analysis procedures that have been developed and proved using norm-referenced tests, without appropriate caution and modification.
13. Several modifications of traditional norm-referenced item analysis procedures appropriate for criterion-referenced tests were discussed; they vary in their complexity.
14. These modifications to the usual quantitative item analysis procedures should be coupled with the qualitative item analysis procedures discussed in Chapters 5, 6, and 7 to properly evaluate the criterion-referenced, teacher-made test.

15. After the test has been scored, but before you give students their scores:
    a. Discuss any items considered to be problematic.
    b. Listen to student concerns, trying to stay unemotional.
    c. Let students know you will consider their comments but will not make any decisions affecting their scores until you have had time to reflect on their comments.
    d. Let students know that any changes made will apply equally to all students.
16. After the students are given their scores, ask them to check for clerical errors.

For Practice

*1. Compute p, the difficulty index, for the following items. Interpret your results. (The asterisk indicates the correct option.)

Options

A	*B**	*C*	*D*
10	5	8	0

Options

A	*B*	*C**	*D*
4	2	16	3

*2. Compute D, the discrimination index, for the following items. Interpret your results.

(Class size = 40)
Options

	A	*B*	*C*	*D**
Upper half	3	0	7	10
Lower half	5	4	9	2

(Class size = 30)
Options

	*A**	*B*	*C*	*D*
Upper half	3	5	7	0
Lower half	8	5	1	1

*3. Identify which of the following items are likely to be miskeyed, which are likely to be susceptible to guessing, and which are probably ambiguous.

	*A**	*B*	*C*	*D*
a. Upper half	8	0	7	2

	A	*B*	*C**	*D*
b. Upper half	10	2	4	3

	A	*B**	*C*	*D*
c. Upper half	3	11	3	10

	*A**	*B*	*C*	*D*
d. Upper half	9	8	11	9

	*A**	*B*	*C*	*D*
e. Upper half	0	1	6	2

*4. Do a complete item analysis for the following item data. Use the Quantitative Item Analysis Checklist as your guide, answering each of the questions indicated.

(Class size = 20)
Options

	*A**	*B*	*C*	*D*
Upper half	3	2	3	2
Lower half	2	3	1	4

*Answers for these questions appear in Appendix D.

CHAPTER 9

Performance-Based Assessment

In Chapter 6 (Writing Instructional Objectives), you learned that there are a variety of skills that children acquire in school. Some of these require learners to acquire information by memorizing vocabulary, multiplication tables, dates of historical events, and so on. Other skills involve learning action sequences or procedures to follow when performing mathematical computations, dissecting a frog, focusing a microscope, handwriting, or typing. In addition, you learned that students must acquire concepts, rules, and generalizations which allow them to understand what they read, analyze and solve problems, carry out experiments, write poems and essays, and design projects to study historical, political, or economic problems.

Some of these skills are best assessed with paper and pencil tests. But other skills—particularly those involving independent judgment, critical thinking, and decision-making—are best assessed with performance tests. Although paper and pencil tests currently represent the principal means of assessing these more complex cognitive outcomes, in this chapter we will study other ways of measuring them in more authentic contexts.

PERFORMANCE TESTS: DIRECT MEASURES OF COMPETENCE

In earlier chapters you learned that many educational tests measure learning indirectly. That is, they ask questions, the responses to which *indicate* that something has been learned or mastered. Performance tests, on the other hand, use direct measures of learning rather than indicators that simply suggest cognitive, affective, or psychomotor processes have taken place. In the field of athletics, diving and gymnastics are examples of performances which judges rate directly. Their scores are pooled and used to decide who, for example, earns a medal, wins first, second, third, etc., or qualifies for district or regional competition. Likewise, at band contests judges directly see and hear the competence of trombone or violin players and pool their ratings to decide who makes the state or district band and who gets the leading chairs.

Teachers can use performance tests to assess complex cognitive learning, as well as attitudes and social skills in academic areas such as science, social studies, or math. When doing so, they establish situations which allow them to observe and to rate learners directly as they analyze, problem solve, experiment, make decisions, measure, cooperate with others, present orally, or produce a product. These situations simulate real-world activities, as might be expected in a job, in the community, or in various forms of advanced training, for example, in the military, a technical institute, on the job training, or in college.

Performance tests also allow teachers to observe achievements, mental habits, ways of working, and behaviors of value in the real world that conventional tests may miss and in ways that an outside observer would be unaware that a "test" is going on. Performance tests can include observing and rating learners as they carry out a dialogue in a foreign language, conduct a science experiment, edit a composition, present an exhibit, work with a group of other learners in designing a student attitude survey, or use equipment. In other words, the teacher observes and evaluates student abilities to carry out complex activities which are used and valued outside the immediate confines of the classroom.

PERFORMANCE TESTS CAN ASSESS PROCESSES AND PRODUCTS

Performance tests can be assessments of processes, products, or both. For example, at the Darwin School in Winnipeg, Manitoba, teachers assess the reading process of each student by noting the percentage of words read accurately during oral reading, the number of sentences read by the learner that are meaningful within the context of the story, and the percentage of story elements which the learner can talk about in his or her own words after reading.

At the West Orient School in Gresham, Oregon, fourth-grade learners assemble a portfolio of their writing products. These portfolios include rough as well as final drafts of poetry, essays, biographies, and self-reflections. Several math teachers at Twin Peaks Middle School in Poway, California require their students to assemble math portfolios which include the following products of their problem-solving efforts: long-term projects, daily notes, journal entries about troublesome test problems, written explanations of how they solved problems, and the problem solutions themselves.

Social studies learning processes and products are assessed in the Aurora, Colorado Public Schools by having learners engage in a variety of projects built around the following question: "Based on your study of Colorado history, what current issues in Colorado do you believe are the most important to address, what are your ideas about the resolutions of those issues, and what contributions will you make toward the resolutions?" (Pollock, 1992). Learners answer these questions in a variety of ways involving individual and group writing assignments, oral presentations, and exhibits.

PERFORMANCE TESTS CAN BE EMBEDDED IN LESSONS

The examples of performance tests given above involved performances which occurred outside the context of a lesson and which were completed at the end of a term or during an examination period. Many teachers use performance tests as part of their lessons. In fact, some proponents of performance tests hold that the ideal performance test is a good teaching activity (Shavelson & Baxter, 1992). Viewed from this perspective, a well-constructed performance test can serve as a teaching activity as well as an assessment.

For example, Figure 9.1 illustrates a performance activity and assessment that was embedded in a unit on electricity in a general science class (Shavelson & Baxter, 1992, p. 22). During the activity the teacher observes and rates the learners on the method they used to solve the problem, the care with which they measured, the manner of recording

FIGURE 9.1
An Example Performance Activity and Assessment

HANDS-ON ELECTRIC MYSTERIES INVESTIGATION

Find out what is in the six mystery boxes A, B, C, D, E, and F. They have five different things inside, shown below. Two of the boxes will have the same thing. All of the others will have something different inside.

Two batteries:

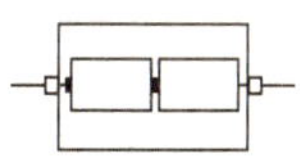

A wire:

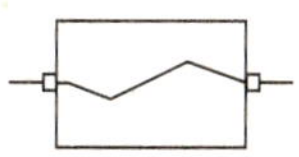

A bulb:

A battery and a bulb:

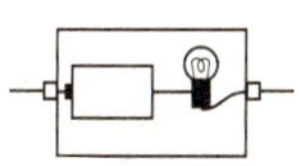

Nothing at all:

You can use your bulbs, batteries, and wires any way you like. Connect them in a circuit to help you figure out what is inside.

When you find out what is in a box, fill in the spaces on the following pages.

Box A: Has ____________________ inside.

Draw a picture of the circuit that told you what was inside Box A.

How could you tell from your circuit what was inside Box A?

____

____

____

Do the same for Boxes B, C, D, E, and F.

____

____

From Shavelson and Baxter (1992), p.22.

results, and the correctness of the final solution. This type of assessment provides immediate feedback on how learners are performing, reinforces hands-on teaching and learning, and underscores for learners the important link between teaching and testing. In this manner, it moves the instruction toward higher order and more authentic behavior.

Other examples of lesson-embedded performance tests might include observing and rating the following as they are actually happening: typing, preparing a microscope slide, reading out loud, programming a calculator, giving an oral presentation, determining how plants react to certain substances, designing a questionnaire or survey, solving a math problem, developing an original math problem and a solution for it, critiquing the logic of an editorial, or graphing information.

PERFORMANCE TESTS CAN ASSESS AFFECTIVE AND SOCIAL SKILLS

Teachers across the country are using performance tests not only to assess higher-level cognitive skills but also noncognitive outcomes, such as self-direction, ability to work with others, and social awareness (Redding, 1992). This concern for the affective domain of learning reflects an awareness by educators that the skilled performance of complex tasks involves more than the ability to recall information, form concepts, generalize, and problem solve. It also includes the mental and behavioral habits or characteristics evident in individuals who successfully perform such complex tasks, also known as habits of mind, and interpersonal or social skills.

The Aurora Public Schools in Colorado have developed a list of learning outcomes and their indicators for learners in grades K–12. These are shown in Figure 9.2. For each of these 19 indicators a four category rating scale has been developed to serve as a guide for teachers who are unsure of how to define "assumes responsibility" or "demonstrates consideration." While observing learners during performance tests in social studies, science, art, or economics, teachers are alert to recognize and rate those behaviors that suggest learners have acquired the outcomes.

Teachers in the Aurora Public Schools are encouraged to use this list of outcomes when planning their courses. They first ask themselves what key facts, concepts, and principles should all learners remember? In addition, they try to fuse this subject area content with the five district outcomes by designing special performance tests. For example, a third grade language arts teacher who is planning a writing unit might choose to focus on indicators 8 and 9 to address district outcomes related to "collaborative worker," indicator 1 for the outcome of self-directed learner, and 13 for the outcome "quality producer." She would then design a performance assessment which allows learners to demonstrate learning in these areas. She might select other indicators and outcomes for subsequent units and performance tests.

In summary, performance tests represent an addition to the measurement practices reviewed in previous chapters. Paper and pencil tests are the most efficient, reliable, and valid instruments available for assessing knowledge, comprehension, and some types of application. But when it comes to assessing complex thinking skills, habits of mind, and

FIGURE 9.2
Learning Outcomes of Aurora Public Schools

A Self-Directed Learner

1. Sets priorities and achievable goals.
2. Monitors and evaluates progress.
3. Creates options for self.
4. Assumes responsibility for actions.
5. Creates a positive vision for self and future.

A Collaborative Worker

6. Monitors own behavior as a group member.
7. Assesses and manages group functioning.
8. Demonstrates interactive communication.
9. Demonstrates consideration for individual differences.

A Complex Thinker

10. Uses a wide variety of strategies for managing complex issues.
11. Selects strategies appropriate to the resolution of complex issues and applies the strategies with accuracy and thoroughness.
12. Accesses and uses topic-relevant knowledge.

A Quality Producer

13. Creates products that achieve their purpose.
14. Creates products appropriate to the intended audience.
15. Creates products that reflect craftsmanship.
16. Uses appropriate resources/technology.

A Community Contributor

17. Demonstrates knowledge about his or her diverse communities.
18. Takes action.
19. Reflects on his or her role as a community contributor.

social skills, performance tests can, if properly constructed, do a better job. On the other hand, if not properly constructed, performance assessments can have some of the same problems with scoring efficiency, reliability, and validity as traditional approaches to testing. This chapter will guide you through a process which will allow you to properly construct performance tests in your classroom.

DEVELOPING PERFORMANCE TESTS FOR YOUR LEARNERS

As we learned in the previous section, performance assessment has the potential to improve both instruction and learning. But as we have also learned, there are both conceptual and technical issues associated with the use of performance tests that teachers must resolve before these assessments can be effectively and efficiently used. In this chapter we will discuss some of the important considerations in planning and designing a performance test and how to score performance tests, including student portfolios. In the next chapter we will describe how you can include the scores from performance tests in your six-week and semester grades.

Step 1. Deciding What to Test

The first step in developing a performance test is to create a list of objectives which specifies the knowledge, skills, habits of mind, and indicators of these outcomes which will be the focus of your instruction.

There are three general questions to ask when deciding what to teach:

- What knowledge or content (i.e., facts, concepts, principles, rules) is essential for learner understanding of the subject matter?
- What intellectual skills are necessary for the learner to use this knowledge or content?
- What habits of mind are important for the learner to successfully perform with this knowledge or content?

Instructional objectives which come from answering question 1 are usually measured by paper and pencil tests (discussed in Chapters 6 and 7). Objectives derived from answering questions 2 and 3, although often assessed with objective or essay-type questions, can be more authentically assessed with performance tests. Thus, your assessment plan for a unit should include both paper and pencil tests to measure mastery of content and performance tests to assess skills and habits of mind. Let's see what objectives for these latter outcomes might look like.

PERFORMANCE OBJECTIVES IN THE COGNITIVE DOMAIN. Designers of performance tests usually ask the following questions to help guide their initial selection of objectives:

- What kinds of essential tasks, achievements, or other valued competencies am I missing with paper and pencil tests?
- What accomplishments of those who practice my discipline (historians, writers, scientists, mathematicians) are valued but left unmeasured by conventional tests?

Typically two categories of performance skills are identified from such questions:

1. Skills related to acquiring information, and
2. Skills related to organizing and using information

Figure 9.3 contains a suggested list of skills for acquiring, organizing, and using information. As you study this list, consider which skills you might use as a basis for a performance test in your area of expertise.

The following are some example objectives for performance tests from a consideration of the performance skills described in Figure 9.3.

1. Write a summary of a current controversy drawn from school life and tell how a courageous and civic-minded American you have studied might decide to act on the issue.
2. Draw a physical map of North America from memory and locate 10 cities.
3. Prepare an exhibit showing how your community responds to an important social problem of your choosing.
4. Construct an electrical circuit using wires, a switch, a bulb, resistors, and a battery.
5. Describe two alternative ways to solve a mathematics word problem.
6. Identify the important variables which affected recent events in our state, and forecast how these variables will affect future events.
7. Design a free-standing structure in which the size of one leg of a triangular structure must be determined from the other two sides.
8. Program a calculator to solve an equation with one unknown.
9. Design an exhibit showing the best ways to clean up an oil spill.
10. Prepare a visual presentation to the city council requesting increased funding to deal with a problem in our community.

PERFORMANCE OBJECTIVES IN THE AFFECTIVE AND SOCIAL DOMAIN. Performance assessments not only require curriculum to teach thinking skills but also to develop positive dispositions and "habits of mind." Habits of mind include such behaviors as constructive criticism, tolerance of ambiguity, respect for reason, and appreciation for the significance of the past. Performance tests are ideal vehicles for assessing habits of mind and social skills (for example, cooperation, sharing, and negotiation). Thus, in deciding what objectives to teach and measure with a performance test, you should give consideration to affective and social skill objectives. Following are some key questions to ask for including affective and social skills in your list of performance objectives:

FIGURE 9.3
Skills for Acquiring, Organizing, and Using Information

Skills in acquiring information	Skills in organizing and using information
Communicating explaining modeling demonstrating graphing displaying writing advising programming proposing drawing **Measuring** counting calibrating rationing appraising weighing balancing guessing estimating forecasting **Investigating** gathering references interviewing using references experimenting hypothesizing	**Organizing** classifying categorizing sorting ordering ranking arranging **Problem Solving** stating questions identifying problems developing hypotheses interpreting assessing risks monitoring **Decision Making** weighing alternatives evaluating choosing supporting defending electing adopting

- What dispositions, habits of mind, or values characterize successful individuals in the community who work in your academic discipline?
- What are some of the qualities of mind or character traits which good scientists, writers, reporters, historians, mathematicians, musicians, etc. have?
- What will I accept as evidence that my learners have or are developing these qualities?
- What social skills for getting along with others are necessary for being successful as a journalist, weather forecaster, park ranger, historian, economist, mechanic, etc.?
- What evidence will convince my learners' parents that their children are developing these skills?

Figure 9.4 displays some examples of habits of mind which could be the focus of a performance assessment in science, social studies, and mathematics.

FIGURE 9.4
Example Habits of Mind in Performance Assessment

In SCIENCE (from Loucks-Horsley, et al., 1990. *Elementary School Science for the '90's*, p. 41).

- ☐ Desiring knowledge. Viewing science as a way of knowing and understanding.
- ☐ Being skeptical. Recognizing the appropriate time and place to question authoritarian statements and "self-evident truths."
- ☐ Relying on data. Explaining natural occurrences by collecting and ordering information, testing ideas, and respecting the facts that are revealed.
- ☐ Accepting ambiguity. Recognizing that data are rarely clear and compelling, and appreciating the new questions and problems that arise.
- ☐ Willingness to modify explanations. Seeing new possibilities in the data.
- ☐ Cooperating in answering questions and solving problems. Working together to pool ideas, explanations and solutions.
- ☐ Respecting reason. Valuing patterns of thought that lead from data to conclusions and, eventually, to the construction of theories.
- ☐ Being Honest. Viewing information objectively, without bias.

Continued

FIGURE 9.4 Continued

In SOCIAL STUDIES (from Parker, 1990. *Renewing the Social Studies Curriculum*, p. 74).

- ☐ Understanding the significance of the past to their own lives, both private and public, and to their society.
- ☐ Distinguishing between the important and inconsequential to develop the "discriminating memory" needed for a discerning judgment in public and personal life.
- ☐ Preparing to live with uncertainties and exasperating, even perilous, unfinished business, realizing that not all problems have solutions.
- ☐ Appreciating the often tentative nature of judgments about the past, and thereby avoiding the temptation to seize upon particular "lessons" of history as cures for present ills.

In MATHEMATICS (from Willoughby, 1990. *Mathematics Education for a Changing World*, p.14).

- ☐ Appreciating that mathematics is a discipline that helps solve real-world problems.
- ☐ Seeing mathematics as a tool or servant rather than something mysterious or mystical to be afraid of.
- ☐ Recognizing that there is more than one way to solve a problem.

Once you have completed Step 1, you will have identified the important knowledge, skills, and habits of mind, which will be the focus of your instruction and assessment. The next step is to design the task or context in which these outcomes will be assessed.

Step 2. Designing the Assessment Context

The purpose of Step 2 is to create an authentic task, simulation, or situation which will allow learners to demonstrate the knowledge, skills, and attitudes that they have acquired. Ideas for these tasks may come from newspapers, reading popular books, or interviews with professionals as reported in the media (for example, an oil tanker runs aground and creates an environmental crisis, a drought occurs in an underdeveloped country causing famine, a technological breakthrough presents a moral dilemma). The tasks should center on issues, concepts, or problems which are important to your context area. In other words, they should be the same issues, concepts, and problems that important people who are working in the field face every day.

Here are some questions to get you started on Step 2, suggested by Wiggins (1992):

- What does the "doing of mathematics, history, science, art, writing, and so forth" look and feel like to professionals who make their living working in these fields in the real world?
- What are the projects and tasks performed by these professionals that can be adapted to school instruction?
- What are the roles—or habits of mind—that these professionals acquire that learners can re-create in the classroom?

The tasks you create may involve debates, mock trials, presentations to a city commission, re-enactments of historical events, science experiments, job responsibilities (for example, a travel agent, weather forecaster, park ranger), etc. Regardless of the specific context, they should present the learner with an authentic challenge.

For example, consider the social studies performance test below (adapted from Wiggins, 1992):

> You and several travel agent colleagues have been assigned the responsibility of designing a trip to China for 12–14-year-olds. Prepare an extensive brochure for a month-long cultural exchange trip. Include itinerary, modes of transportation, costs, suggested budget, clothing, health considerations, areas of cultural sensitivity, language considerations, and other information necessary for a family to decide if they want their child to participate.

Notice that this example presents learners with:

1. A hands-on exercise or problem to solve, which produces
2. An observable outcome or product (typed business letter, a map, graph, piece of clothing, multi-media presentation, poem, etc.), such that the teacher
3. Can observe and assess not only the product but also the process used to get there.

Designing the content for a performance test involves equal parts of inspiration and perspiration. While there is no formula or recipe to follow which guarantees a valid performance test, the criteria below can help guide you in revising and refining the task.

THE REQUIREMENTS FOR TASK MASTERY SHOULD BE CLEAR WITHOUT REVEALING THE SOLUTION. While your tasks should be complex, the final product should be clear. Learners should not have to question whether they are finished, or have provided what you want. They should, however, have to think long and hard about how to complete the task. As you refine the task, make sure you can visualize what mastery of the task looks like and identify the skills that can be inferred from it.

THE TASK SHOULD REPRESENT A SPECIFIC ACTIVITY FROM WHICH GENERALIZATIONS ABOUT THE LEARNER'S KNOWLEDGE, THINKING ABILITY, AND HABITS OF MIND CAN BE MADE. What performance tests lack in breadth of coverage, they make up in depth. In other words, they allow you to observe a wide range of behavior in a narrow domain of skill. Thus, the type of tasks you choose should be complex enough and rich enough in detail to allow you to draw conclusions about transfer and generalization to other tasks. Ideally, you should be able to identify about eight to ten important performance tasks for an entire course of study (one or two a unit) which assess the essential performance outcomes you wish your learners to achieve.

THE TASKS SHOULD BE COMPLEX ENOUGH TO ALLOW FOR MULTI-MODAL ASSESSMENT. Most assessment tends to depend on the written word. Performance tests, however, are designed to allow learners to demonstrate learning through a variety of modalities. In science, for example, one could make direct observations of students while they investigate a problem using laboratory equipment, have students give oral explanations of what they did, require them to record procedures and conclusions in notebooks, prepare an exhibit of their project, and solve short-answer paper and pencil problems. This will be more time consuming than a multiple-choice test but will provide unique information about your learners' achievement untapped by other assessment methods. Shavelson & Baxter (1992) have shown that performance tests allow teachers to draw different conclusions about a learner's problem-solving ability than do higher-order multiple-choice tests or restricted-response essay tests which ask learners to analyze, interpret, and evaluate information.

THE TASKS SHOULD YIELD MULTIPLE SOLUTIONS WHERE POSSIBLE, EACH WITH COSTS AND BENEFITS. Performance testing is not a form of practice or drill. It should involve more than simple tasks for which there is one solution. Performance tests should be nonalgorithmic (the path of action is not fully specified in advance), complex (the total solution cannot be seen from any one vantage point), and involve judgment and interpretation.

THE TASKS SHOULD REQUIRE SELF-REGULATED LEARNING. Performance tests should require considerable mental effort and place high demands on the persistence and determination of the individual learner. The learner should be required to use cognitive strategies to arrive at a solution rather than depend on coaching at various points in the assessment process.

Step 3. Specifying the Scoring Rubrics

One of the principal limitations of performance tests is the time required to score them. Just as these tests require time and effort on the part of the learner, they demand similar commitment from teachers when scoring them. True-false, multiple-choice, and fill-ins are significantly easier to score than projects, portfolios, or performances. In addition, these latter accomplishments force teachers to make difficult choices over how much qualities such as effort, participation, and cooperation, count in the final score.

Given the challenges confronting teachers who use performance tests, there is a temptation to limit the scoring criteria to those qualities of performance which are easiest to rate rather than the most important required for doing an effective job. Resorting to scoring what is easiest or least controversial can turn a well-thought-out and authentic performance test into an inaccurate one. Thus, your goal when scoring performance tests is to do justice to the time spent developing them and the effort expended by students taking them. You can accomplish this by developing carefully constructed scoring systems, called *rubrics*.

By giving careful consideration to rubrics, you can develop a scoring system for performance tests which minimizes the arbitrariness of your judgments while holding learners to high standards of achievement. Here are some of the important considerations in developing rubrics for a performance test.

DEVELOP RUBRICS FOR A VARIETY OF ACCOMPLISHMENTS. In general, performance tests require four types of accomplishments from learners:

Products:	Poems, essays, charts, graphs, exhibits, drawings, maps, etc.
Complex cognitive processes:	Skills in acquiring, organizing, and using information (see Figure 9.3).
Observable performance:	Physical movements as in dance, gymnastics, or typing; oral presentations; use of specialized equipment as in focusing a microscope; following a set of procedures as when dissecting a frog, bisecting an angle, or following a recipe.
Habits of mind and social skills:	Mental and behavioral habits, group work, and recognition skills.

As this list suggests, the effect of your teaching may be realized in a variety of ways.

CHOOSE A SCORING SYSTEM BEST SUITED FOR THE TYPE OF ACCOMPLISHMENT YOU WANT TO MEASURE. In general, there are three categories of rubrics to use when scoring performance tests: checklists, rating scales, and holistic scoring. Each has certain strengths and limitations, and each is more or less suitable for scoring products, cognitive processes, performances, and social skills.

CHECKLISTS. Checklists contain lists of behaviors, traits, or characteristics that can be scored as either present or absent. They are best suited for complex behaviors or performances which can be divided into a series of clearly defined, specific actions. Dissecting a frog, bisecting an angle, balancing a scale, making an audio tape recording, or tying a shoe are behaviors that require sequences of actions which can be clearly identified and listed on a checklist. Checklists are scored on a yes/no, present or absent, 0 or 1 point basis and should provide the opportunity for observers to indicate that they had no opportunity to observe the performance. Some checklists also include frequent mistakes that learners make when performing the task. In such cases, a score of +1 may be given for each positive behavior, −1 for each mistake, and 0 for no opportunity to observe. Figures 9.5 and 9.6 show checklists for using a microscope and a calculator.

FIGURE 9.5
Checklist for Using a Microscope

No opportunity to observe	Observed	
☐	☐	Wipes slide with lens paper
☐	☐	Places drop or two of culture on slide
☐	☐	Adds few drops of water
☐	☐	Places slide on stage
☐	☐	Turns to low power
☐	☐	Looks through eyepiece with one eye
☐	☐	Adjusts mirror
☐	☐	Turns to high power
☐	☐	Adjusts for maximum enlargement and resolution

RATING SCALES. Rating scales are typically used for those aspects of a complex performance which do not lend themselves to yes/no or present/absent type judgments. The most common form of a rating scale is one which assigns numbers to categories of performance. Figure 9.7 shows a rating scale for judging elements of writing in a term paper. This scale focuses the rater's observations on certain aspects of the performance (accuracy, logic, organization, style, etc.) and assigns numbers to five degrees of performance.

Most numeric rating scales use an analytical scoring technique called *primary trait scoring* (Sax, 1989). This type of rating requires that the test developer first identify the most salient characteristics or primary traits of greatest importance when observing the product, process, or performance. Then, for each trait, the developer assigns numbers (usually 1–5) which represent degrees of performance.

Figure 9.8 displays a numerical rating scale which uses primary trait scoring to rate problem solving (Szetela & Nicol, 1992). In this system, problem solving is subdivided into the primary traits of understanding the problem, solving the problem, and answering the problem. For each trait, points are assigned to certain aspects or qualities of the trait. Notice how the designer of this rating scale identified both characteristics of effective and ineffective problem solving.

FIGURE 9.6
Checklist for Using an Electronic Calculator

No opportunity to observe	Observed	
☐	☐	Knows how to turn calculator on
☐	☐	Can "key in" ten numbers consecutively, without hitting adjacent keys
☐	☐	Can quickly add three 2-digit numbers, without error
☐	☐	Knows how to position keyboard and to rest arm and elbow for maximum comfort and accuracy
☐	☐	Knows how to reposition display screen to reduce reflection and glare, when necessary
☐	☐	Pushes keys with positive, firm motions
☐	☐	Can *feel* when a key touch is insufficiently firm to activate calculator

Usually, two key questions are addressed when designing scoring systems for rating scales using primary trait scoring:

1. What are the most important characteristics which show a high degree of the trait?
2. What are the errors most justifiable for achieving a lower score?

Answering these questions can prevent raters from assigning higher or lower scores on the basis of performance that may be trivial or unrelated to the purpose of the performance test, such as the quantity rather than quality of a performance. One of the advantages of rating scales is that they focus the scorer on specific and relevant aspects of a performance. Without the breakdown of important traits, successes, and relevant errors provided by these scales, a scorer's attention may be diverted to aspects of performance which are unrelated to the purpose of the performance test.

HOLISTIC SCORING. Holistic scoring is used when the rater is more interested in estimating the overall quality of the performance and assigning a numerical value to that quality than assigning points for the addition or omission of a specific aspect of performance. Holistic scoring is typically used in evaluating extended essays, term papers, or some artistic performances such as dance or musical creations.

FIGURE 9.7
Rating Scale for Themes and Term Papers That Emphasizes Interpretation and Organization

	1	2	3	4	5
Quality and accuracy of ideas	Very limited investigation; little or no material related to the facts.		Some investigation and attention to the facts are apparent.		Extensive investigation; good detail and representation of the facts.
Logical development of ideas	Very little orderly development of ideas; presentation is confusing and hard to follow.		Some logical development of ideas, but logical order needs to be improved.		Good logical development; ideas logically connected and build upon one another.
Organization of ideas	No apparent organization. Lack of paragraphing and transitions.		Organization is mixed; some of the ideas not adequately separated from others with appropriate transitions.		Good organization and paragraphing; clear transitions between ideas.
Style, individuality	Style bland and inconsistent, or "borrowed."		Some style and individuality beginning to show.		Good style and individuality; personality of writer shows through.
Wording and phrasing	Wording trite; extensive use of clichés.		Some word choices awkward.		Appropriate use of words and phrasing work to sharpen ideas.

For example, a rater might decide to score an extended essay question or term paper on an A–F rating scale. In this case, it would be important for the rater to have a model paper which exemplifies each score category. After having created or selected these models from the set to be scored, the rater again reads each paper and then assigns each to one

FIGURE 9.8
Analytic Scale for Problem Solving

Understanding the problem

0 - No attempt
1 - Completely misinterprets the problem
2 - Misinterprets major part of the problem
3 - Misinterprets minor part of the problem
4 - Complete understanding of the problem

Solving the problem

0 - No attempt
1 - Totally inappropriate plan
2 - Partially correct procedure but with major fault
3 - Substantially correct procedure with major omission or procedural error
4 - A plan that could lead to a correct solution with no arithmetic errors

Answering the problem

0 - No answer or wrong answer based upon an inappropriate plan
1 - Copying error, computational error, partial answer for problem with multiple answers; no answer statement; answer labeled incorrectly
2 - Correct solution

of the categories. A model paper for each category (A–F) helps to assure that all the papers assigned to a given category are of comparable quality.

Holistic scoring systems can be more difficult to use for performances than for products. For the former, some experience in rating the performance, for example, dramatic rendition, oral interpretations, debate, etc., may be required. In these cases, audio or video tapes from past classes can be helpful as models representing different categories of performance.

COMBINING SCORING SYSTEMS. As suggested above, good performance tests require learners to demonstrate their achievements through a variety of primary traits, for example, cooperation, research, delivery, etc. Several ratings, therefore, may need to be combined from checklists, rating scales, and holistic impressions to arrive at a total assessment. Figure 9.9 shows how scores across several traits for a current events project might be combined to provide a single performance score.

FIGURE 9.9
Combined Scoring Rubric for Current Events Project

Checklist (Assign 1 or 0 points) Total Points (5)

_____ Interviewed four people
_____ Cited current references
_____ Typed
_____ No spelling errors
_____ Included title and summary page

Rating Circle numbers which best represent quality of the presentation.
Total points (9)

Persuasiveness

1	**2**	**3**
Lacks enthusiasm	Somewhat unanimated	Highly convincing

Delivery

1	**2**	**3**
Unclear, mumbled a lot	Often failed to look at audience, somewhat unclear	Clear, forceful delivery

Sensitivity to audience

1	**2**	**3**
Rarely looked at or noticed audience	Answered some questions, not always aware when audience didn't understand	Encouraged questions, stopped and clarified when saw that audience didn't understand

Holistic Rating Total Points (3)
What is your overall impression of the quality of the project?

1	**2**	**3**
Below average	Average	Clearly outstanding

Total Points (17)

TABLE 9.1
The Strength of Three Performance-Based Scoring Systems According to Five Measurement Criteria

	Ease of Construction	*Scoring Efficiency*	*Reliability*	*Defensibility*	*Feedback*	*More Suitable For*
Checklists	low	moderate	high	high	high	procedures
Rating Scales	moderate	moderate	moderate	moderate	moderate	attitudes, products, social skills
Holistic Scoring	high	high	low	low	low	products and processes

COMPARING THE THREE SCORING SYSTEMS. Each of the three scoring systems has its particular strengths and weaknesses. Table 9.1 serves as a guide in choosing a particular scoring system for a given type of performance, according to the following criteria:

1. ***Ease of construction.*** Refers to the time involved in generating a comprehensive list of the important aspects or traits of successful and unsuccessful performance. Checklists, for example, are particularly time-consuming, while holistic scoring is not.
2. ***Scoring efficiency.*** Refers to the amount of time required to score various aspects of the performance and sum these scores into an overall score.
3. ***Reliability.*** The likelihood of two raters independently coming up with a similar score; or the likelihood of the same rater coming up with a similar score on two separate occasions.
4. ***Defensibility.*** Refers to the ease with which you can explain your score to a student or parent who challenges it.
5. ***Quality of feedback.*** Refers to the amount of information that the scoring system gives to learners or parents concening strengths and weaknesses of their performance.

LIMIT THE NUMBER OF POINTS THAT THE ASSESSMENT OR COMPONENT OF THE ASSESSMENT IS WORTH TO THAT WHICH CAN BE RELIABLY DISCRIMINATED. For example, 25 points assigned to a particular product or procedure assumes that the rater can discriminate 25 degrees of quality. When faced with more degrees of quality than can be detected, a typical rater may assign some points arbitrarily, reducing the reliability of the assessment.

On what basis should points be assigned to a response on a performance test? On the one hand, you want a response to be worth enough points to allow you to differentiate subtle differences in response quality. On the other hand, you want to avoid assigning too many points to a response, the complexity of which does not lend itself to complex discriminations. Thus, assigning one or two points to a math question requiring complex problem solving would not allow you to differentiate among outstanding, above average, average, and poor responses. Yet, assigning 30 points to this same answer would seriously challenge your ability to distinguish a rating of 15 from a rating of 18. Two considerations can help in making decisions about the size and complexity of a rating scale.

The first is that a scoring model can be prepared wherein the rater specifies the exact performance—or examples of acceptable performance—that corresponds with each scale point. The ability to successfully define distinct criteria can then determine the number of scale points that are defensible. A second consideration is that, although it is customary for homework, paper and pencil tests, and report cards to use a 100 point (percent) scale, scale points derived from performance assessments do not need to add up to 100. In the next chapter we will indicate how to assign marks to performance tests and how to integrate them with other aspects of an overall grading system (for example, homework, paper and pencil tests, classwork, etc.) including student portfolios.

Step 4. Specifying Testing Constraints

Should performance tests have time limits? Should learners be allowed to correct their mistakes? Can they consult references or ask for help from other learners? Were these questions asked of a multiple-choice test, most test developers would respond negatively without much hesitation. But performance tests confront the designer with the following dilemma: If performance tests are designed to confront learners with real-world challenges, why shouldn't they be allowed to tackle these challenges as real-world people do?

In the world outside of the classroom, mathematicians make mistakes and correct them, journalists write first drafts and revise them, weather forecasters make predictions and change them. These workers can consult references to help them solve problems and consult with colleagues. Why then shouldn't learners who are working on performance tests which simulate similar problems be allowed the same working (or testing) conditions? But even outside the classroom, professionals have constraints on their performance, such as deadlines, limited office space, outmoded equipment, etc. So how does a teacher decide which conditions to impose during a performance test? Before examining this question, let's look at some of the typical conditions imposed on learners during tests. The following are among the most common forms of test constraints:

1. ***Time.*** How much time should a learner have to prepare, rethink, revise, and finish a test?
2. ***Reference material.*** Should learners be able to consult dictionaries, textbooks, notes, etc., as they take a test?
3. ***Other people.*** May learners ask for help from peers, teachers, experts, etc., as they take a test or complete a project?

4. ***Equipment.*** May learners use computers, calculators, etc., to help them solve problems?
5. ***Prior knowledge of the task.*** How much information on what they will be tested should learners receive in advance?
6. ***Scoring criteria.*** Should learners know the standards by which the teacher will score the assessment?

Wiggins (1992) recommends that teachers take an "Authenticity Test" to decide which of the above constraints to impose on a performance assessment. His "Authenticity Test" involves answering the following questions:

1. What kinds of constraints authentically replicate the constraints and opportunities facing the performer in the real world?
2. What kinds of constraints tend to bring out the best in apprentice performers and producers?
3. What are the appropriate or authentic limits one should impose on the availability of the six resources listed above?

Objective tests, by the nature of the questions asked, require numerous contraints during the testing conditions. Performance tests, on the other hand, are direct forms of assessment in which real-world conditions and constraints play an important role in demonstrating the competencies desired.

PORTFOLIO ASSESSMENT

According to Paulson & Paulson (1991), portfolios "tell a story." The theme of the story is determined from answering the student question "What have I learned during this period of instruction and how have I put it into practice?" Some portfolios represent the student's own selection of products—scripts, musical scores, sculpture, videotapes, research reports, narratives, models, and photographs—that represent the learner's attempt to construct his or her own meaning out of what has been taught. Other portfolios are preorganized by the teacher to include the results of specific products and projects, the exact nature of which may be determined by the student.

Whether portfolio entries are preorganized by teachers or left to the discretion of the learner, several questions must be answered prior to the portfolio assignment. These are:

- What are the criteria for selecting the samples that go into the portfolio?
- Will individual pieces of work be evaluated as they go into the portfolio or will all the entries be evaluated collectively at the end of a period of time—or both?
- Will the amount of student growth, progress, or improvement over time be graded?
- How will different entries, such as videos, essays, artwork, and reports, be compared and weighted?

- What role will peers, parents, other teachers, and the student himself or herself have in the evaluation of the portfolio?

Shavelson, Gao, & Baxter (1991) suggest that at least eight products or tasks over different topic areas may be needed to measure performance from portfolios. Therefore, portfolios are usually built and assessed cumulatively over a period of time. These assessments determine the quality of individual contributions to the larger portfolio at various intervals throughout a period of instruction and of the entire portfolio at the end of instruction. Various schemes have been devised for evaluating portfolios. Most involve a recording form in which the specific entries representing student performance are cumulatively rated over a course of instruction. This form also includes the criteria with which each entry is to be evaluated beforehand and an overall rating scale for rating each entry against the criteria given.

Frazier & Paulson (1992) and Hebert (1992) report successful ways in which peers, parents, and the students themselves have participated in portfolio evaluations. Figure 9.10 represents one example of a portfolio assessment intended for use as a cumulative record of accomplishment over an extended course of study.

Many teachers are using portfolios as a means of increasing students' reflections about their own work and encouraging the continuous refinement of portfolio entries. Portfolios have the advantage of containing multiple samples of student work completed over time that can represent finished as well as works in progress. Entries designated "works in progress" are cumulatively assessed at regular intervals on the basis of student growth or improvement and the extent to which the entry increasingly matches the criteria given.

A FINAL WORD

Performance assessments create challenges that objective and essay tests do not. Performance grading requires greater use of judgment than do true-false or multiple-choice questions. These judgments will be more indicative of your learners' performance if (1) the performance to be judged (process and product) is clearly specified, (2) the ratings or criteria in making the judgments are determined beforehand, and (3) more than a single rater independently grades the performance and an average is taken.

Using video or audio tapes can enhance the validity of performance assessments when direct observation of performance is required. Furthermore, performance assessments need not take place at one time for the whole class. Learners can be assessed at different times, individually or in small groups. For example, learners can rotate through classroom learning centers and be assessed when the teacher feels they are acquiring mastery.

Finally, don't lose sight of the fact that performance assessments are meant to serve and enhance instruction rather than being simply an after-the-fact test given to assign a grade. When tests serve instruction, they can be given at a variety of times and in as many settings and contexts as instruction requires. Some performance assessments can sample the behavior of learners as they receive instruction or be placed within on-going classroom activities rather than consume extra time during the day.

FIGURE 9.10
Example Portfolio Assessment Form

<table>
<tr><td>Student: Julia Coe
Grade: 8 Date: 4/16
Rater: Ms. Hartley</td><td>A1 Understanding of Task
SOURCES OF EVIDENCE
• Explanation of task
• Reasonableness of approach
• Correctness of response</td><td>A2 How—Quality of Approaches/Procedures
SOURCES OF EVIDENCE
• Demonstrations
• Descriptions (oral or written)
• Drafts, scratch work, etc.</td><td>A3 Why—Decisions Along the Way
SOURCES OF EVIDENCE
• Revisions in approach
• Explanations (oral or written)
• Validation of final solution</td></tr>
<tr><td>ENTRY 1
Title: Photosynthesis
D (I) A O
Demonstration Investigation Application Other</td><td>4 Good Oral Presentation</td><td>2 Graphing Procedures not uniform</td><td>3 Logical conclusions with supporting data</td></tr>
<tr><td>ENTRY 2
Title: Game of Chance
D I (A) O
Demonstration Investigation Application Other</td><td>3 Practical example</td><td>2 Lacks some sources from text</td><td>4 Shows careful thinking</td></tr>
<tr><td>ENTRY 3
Title:
D I A O
Demonstration Investigation Application Other</td><td></td><td></td><td></td></tr>
<tr><td>ENTRY 4
Title:
D I A O
Demonstration Investigation Application Other</td><td></td><td></td><td></td></tr>
<tr><td>ENTRY 5
Title:
D I A O
Demonstration Investigation Application Other</td><td></td><td></td><td></td></tr>
<tr><td>Overall Ratings →</td><td>Understanding of Task Final Rating
1 Totally misunderstood
2 Partially understood
3 Understood
4 Generalized, applied, extended</td><td>How–Quality of Approaches/Procedures Final Rating
1 Inappropriate or unworkable approach/procedure
2 Appropriate approach/procedure some of the time
3 Workable approach/procedure
4 Efficient or sophisticated approach/procedure</td><td>Why–Decision Along the Way Final Rating
1 No evidence of reasoned decision-making
2 Reasoned decision-making possible
3 Reasoned decisions/adjustments inferred with certainty
4 Reasoned decisions/adjustments shown/explicated</td></tr>
</table>

Adapted from the Vermont Mathematics Portfolio (1992) *Looking Beyond "The Answer,"* the report of Vermont's Mathematics Portfolio Assessment Program, pub year 1990–1991, Montpelier, Vermont, Department of Education.

SUMMARY

This chapter introduced you to performance-based assessment. Its main points are:

1. The four steps to constructing a performance assessment are deciding what to test, designing the assessment context, specifying the scoring rubrics, and specifying the testing constraints.
2. Some questions to ask in designing the performance assessment context are (1) what does the "doing of math, history . . . " etc. look and feel like to professionals, (2) what projects and tasks are performed by these professionals, and (3) what roles— or habits of mind— do professionals assume?
3. A good performance assessment includes a hands-on exercise or problem, an observable outcome, and a process that can be observed.
4. A performance test can require five types of accomplishments from learners: products, complex cognitive processes, observable performance, habits of mind, and social skills. These performances can be scored with checklists, rating scales, or holistic scales.
5. "Rubrics" are scoring standards composed of model answers which are used to score performance tests. They are samples of acceptable responses against which the rater compares a student's performance.
6. Primary trait scoring is a type of rating that requires that the test developer first identify the most relevant characteristics or primary traits of importance.
7. Checklists contain lists of behaviors, traits, or characteristics which can be scored as either present or absent. They are best suited for complex behaviors or performances that can be divided into a series of clearly defined, specific actions.
8. Rating scales assign numbers to categories representing different degrees of performance. They are typically used for those aspects of a complex performance, such as attitudes, products, and social skills, which do not lend themselves to yes/no or present/absent type judgments.
9. Holistic scoring estimates the overall quality of a performance by assigning a single numerical value to represent a specific category of accomplishment. They are used for measuring both products and processes.
10. Constraints which must be decided on when constructing and administering a performance test are amount of time allowed, use of reference material, help from others, use of specialized equipment, prior knowledge of the task, and scoring criteria.
11. Student portfolios tell a story with the students' own contributions of what was learned during a period of instruction.

For Discussion and Practice

*1. Compare and contrast some of the reasons given to explain why we give conventional tests with those given to explain why we give performance assessments.

*2. In your own words, explain how performance assessment can be a tool for instruction.

*3. Using an example from your teaching area, explain the difference between a direct and an indirect measure of behavior.

4. Describe some "habits of mind" that might be required by professionals working in your teaching area and their importance in the workplace.

*5. Describe how at least two school districts have implemented performance assessments. Indicate the behaviors they assess and by what means they are measured.

6. Would you agree or disagree with the statement that "an ideal performance test is a good teaching activity"? With a specific example in your teaching area, illustrate why you believe as you do.

7. Provide at least two learning outcomes and how you would measure them in your classroom that could indicate that a learner is (1) self-directed, (2) a collaborative worker, (3) a complex thinker, (4) a quality producer, and (5) a community contributor.

*8. Describe what is meant by a "scoring rubric."

9. In your own words, how would you answer a critic of performance tests who says they do not measure generalizable thinking skills outside the classroom?

10. Identify several habits of mind and/or social skills for a unit you will be teaching that would be important to using the content taught in the real world.

11. Create a performance test of your own choosing that: (1) requires a hands-on problem to solve, (2) results in an observable outcome for which (3) the process used by learners to achieve the outcome can be observed.

12. For the performance assessment above, describe and give an example of the accomplishments—or rubrics—you would use in scoring the assessment.

13. For this same assessment, compose a checklist, rating scale, or holistic scoring method by which a learner's performance would be evaluated. Explain why you chose the scoring system you did, which may include a combination of the above methods.

14. For your performance assessment above, describe the constraints you would place upon your learners pertaining to the time to prepare for and complete the activity; references that may be used; people who may be consulted, including other students; equipment allowed; prior knowledge about what is expected; and points or percentages you would assign to various degrees of their performance.

---

*Answers for questions 1, 2, 3, 5, and 8 appear in Appendix D.

CHAPTER 10

Marks and Marking Systems

After you have administered your test, you score it and assign a grade to the test. This grade is not what we will be referring to in this chapter. In this chapter we will discuss several issues related to the assignment of *marks*—cumulative grades that reflect academic achievement at the end of a six- or nine-week marking period, semester, or school year.

WHAT IS THE PURPOSE OF A MARK?

Marks are assigned to provide feedback about student *achievement*. We will reiterate this point several times in this chapter, not because it is so difficult, but because it is so often forgotten. All too often marks have been assigned as rewards and punishments. This is not what they are intended for.

Why Be Concerned About Marking?

Marks have become an accepted and expected aspect of our culture. Students come to realize very early in their educational careers that they will be graded or marked depending on their performance in school. Parents of students, having been graded themselves, realize that the marks a student receives may well affect their child's educational, occupational, and financial status by opening or closing various opportunities. Parents know that children are compared with each other through their marks. Thus, marks have considerable meaning for both child and parent.

Educators also are strongly influenced by marks, often relegating pupils to faster or slower tracks, depending on their marks. Since marks carry a great deal of importance for many people, it seems sensible that care and objectivity be exercised in assigning marks. Unfortunately, this is often not the case. Rather than being assigned accurately, in hopes of presenting as valid a picture of student achievement as possible, marks are sometimes assigned in haste, or according to nebulous, undefined, and little understood "marking systems." Different marking systems have different advantages and disadvantages—some of which the average teacher often does not know. We will acquaint you with various marking systems so that you may choose the system that best fits your situation. In general, such systems compare students with other students or with established standards of knowledge, or are based on aptitude, effort, and improvement.

What Should a Mark Reflect?

What a mark should reflect depends on the subject or topic being marked. We generally talk about marks in relation to reading achievement, math achievement, and so on. However, marks are also assigned in areas like conduct, study skills, and responsibility. When marks are related to academic subjects, marks should reflect *academic achievement,* and nothing more!

Marks are assigned to provide feedback about academic achievement in order for students to be compared according to their achievement. If marks reflect *only* academic achievement and are assigned consistently according to a system, such marks may be compared with considerable validity (as long as the system according to which the marks are assigned is made clear). But when a single mark represents a hodgepodge of factors (for example, achievement, attitude, attendance, punctuality, or conduct) or systems (for example, comparisons with other students, comparisons with standards of effort, or improvement), interpretation or comparison of such marks becomes a hopeless task. Unfortunately, the latter case characterizes some marking practices today. Different schools employ different marking systems and weigh various nonachievement factors in assigning marks, making direct and meaningful comparisons of grades from two schools difficult at best.

We are *not* suggesting that information about nonachievement factors, such as conduct, punctuality, and so forth, should not be reported or is unimportant. We *are* suggesting that such information should *not* be mixed with test scores and other indicators of academic achievement in a single grade. In other words, don't mix apples with oranges in a single mark for an academic subject. All this may seem perfectly obvious, but strange things happen when marks are assigned. It's all too tempting to use marks as vehicles to reach, or try to reach, other ends. Consider the following dialogue:

PARENT: Mr. Stokes, Jack got a D in reading this six weeks, but he's had A's in reading all year. I don't understand. He seems to be reading better all the time, but I'm no teacher. What can I do to help him?

TEACHER: One thing you can do is tell him to stop looking out the window during oral reading. Some of these fifth-graders seem to think that what is going on outside is more important than reading!

PARENT: Do you mean Jack is being disruptive in class?

TEACHER: Yes, he looks out the window, then the next thing you know another one does, then another . . .

PARENT: Have you asked him why he's doing it?

TEACHER: Of course, but it's always the same excuse—"I'm bored, listening to the others read aloud what I've already read to myself."

PARENT: I see, but what about his reading ability—has it declined?

TEACHER: Oh, no! Jack's one of the top readers in the class—there's nothing he can't read.

PARENT: So he's a top reader, but he got a D in reading for not paying attention—is that it?

TEACHER: Mrs. Burns! What do you think I am? I grade on achievement—not on conduct!

PARENT: Why *did* he get the D, then? It sounds as though he was punished for not paying attention.

TEACHER: You've got it wrong. He failed to turn in two homework assignments. That's an automatic D in all my classes. Someone's got to teach these kids responsibility.

PARENT: Mr. Stokes, I know that Sarah Smith failed to turn in two homework assignments, and she got an A.

TEACHER: That's different; she pays attention during oral reading. So, it's obvious that she's getting more out of the class. She also tries harder, even though she's not as smart as Jack.

PARENT: Mr. Stokes, you certainly are an exceptional teacher.

TEACHER: Thank you, Mrs. Burns, but it won't work—Jack's D still stands.

Unfortunately, this type of dialogue is not uncommon. We agree with the teacher in that we feel grades should be based on achievement, not conduct. However, it is quite clear that Jack's D is unrelated to reading achievement. By the teacher's own admission, Jack is reading well, but his classroom *behavior* is not congruent with Mr. Stokes's expectations, and he failed to turn in some homework assignments—another behavioral deficiency that Mr. Stokes equates with poor reading achievement. To what is Mr. Stokes comparing Jack's reading achievement? We can't be sure, although effort and aptitude were mentioned.

It appears that the main function of the marks in this case is punishment. Rather than providing feedback to the student about *reading* achievement, Mr. Stokes is punishing Jack for off-task behavior during class and for less-than-perfect compliance with his homework expectations. The major problem we see here is that the main function of grades—to provide feedback about achievement—has been lost in Mr. Stokes's zeal to change Jack's behavior. In too many cases, a single grade is used to report achievement, conduct, homework compliance, tardiness, and so on. This would be *less* of a problem if it were done consistently across schools. However, different schools weight each of these differently. The real point is that as long as grades continue to be based on factors other than achievement, we are robbing ourselves of the effective use of the main purpose of grading—evaluating achievement. Let's consider the different marking systems employed in schools.

MARKING SYSTEMS

Various types of marking systems have been used in the schools. They may be considered along two dimensions:

1. Type of comparison involved
2. Type of symbol used

Types of Comparisons

Often the type of symbol a teacher uses is determined at the school or district level—the teacher has little to say about whether an A–F, E–G–S–U, or numerical marking system is employed. However, the classroom teacher often has more flexibility and autonomy in deciding how to assign the marks. That is, teachers often have considerable control over *how* they decide who gets an A or B. As mentioned earlier, marks are based on comparisons, usually from among comparisons of students with:

1. Other students
2. Established standards
3. Aptitude
4. Actual versus potential effort
5. Actual versus potential improvement

Each of these systems has advantages and limitations. Our aim is to acquaint you with these so you may choose wisely. Whichever system you choose to employ, be sure to indicate it on the report card. Remember, the function of marking is to provide feedback on achievement. However, a grade of B based on effort versus a grade of B based on comparisons to established standards can reflect very different absolute levels of achievement. Indicating your marking system will minimize potential misinterpretations of a student's level of achievement.

COMPARISONS WITH OTHER STUDENTS. Certainly you have had instructors who have graded "on the curve." It almost sounds illegal, shady, or underhanded. It seems at times that this is some mysterious method by which test grades are transformed into semester marks. Basically, all that the expression "grading on the curve" means is that your grade or mark depends on how your achievement compares with the achievement of other students in your class. You may recall from Chapter 3 that such an approach is also called norm-referenced. Certain proportions of the class are assigned A's, B's, etc., regardless of their absolute level of performance on a test. In such a system, a student who misses 50 percent of the items on a test might get an A, F, or any other grade on the test depending on how his or her score of 50 percent compared with the scores of the other students in the class. If the score was higher than those of 95 percent of the students, the student would likely get an A. Sometimes districts or schools encourage grading on the curve by specifying the percentages of students who will be assigned various grades. The following distribution is an example:

Grade	Percentage of Students
A	10
B	25
C	40
D	20
F	5

The main advantage of such a system is that it simplifies marking decisions. The student is either in the top 10 percent or he or she doesn't get an A. There is no apparent need for deliberation or agonizing over what cut-off scores should determine if students get this grade or that.

There are several disadvantages in such a system. First, this type of marking system fails to consider differences due to the overall ability level of the class. Imagine the disappointment that would result if such a system were imposed on a class of intellectually gifted students—none of whom had ever earned less than a B. Suddenly 65 percent would be transformed into C through F students. Regardless of achievement, in such a system some students will always get A's, and some will always get F's.

Another problem involves the percentages—why not 5 percent A's, or 15 percent A's? These percentages are set rather arbitrarily. Furthermore, what does it mean when a student gets an A? Has the student mastered all course content? Or was the student lucky enough to be in with a class of slow learners? Such a system says nothing about *absolute* achievement, which makes comparisons across grades and schools difficult.

Finally, consider the teacher in such a system. No matter how well or poorly the teacher teaches, his or her students always get the same percentage of grades. There is little, if any, reward available through seeing grades on the whole improve following improved teaching. As a result a teacher may not feel quite as motivated to improve teaching

COMPARISON WITH ESTABLISHED STANDARDS. In this marking system, it is possible for all students to get A's or F's or any other grade in between. How much the rest of the students in the class achieve is irrelevant to a student's grade. All that is relevant is whether a student attains a defined standard of achievement or performance. We labeled this approach *criterion-referenced* in Chapter 3. In such a system, letter grades may be assigned based on the percentage of test items answered correctly, as the distribution below illustrates:

Grade	Percentage of items answered correctly
A	85
B	75
C	65
D	55
F	Less than 55

Thus, a student who answers 79 percent of the test items correctly earns a B, regardless of whether the rest of the class did better, worse, or about the same. Obviously, such a system requires some prior knowledge of what level of achievement or performance is reasonable to expect and the difficulty of the test.

There are several advantages to such a system. First, it is possible, in theory, for all students to obtain high grades if they put forth sufficient effort (assuming the percentage cut-offs are not unreasonably high). Second, assignment of grades is simplified. A student either has answered 75 percent of the items correctly or hasn't. As with comparison with other students, there is no apparent need to deliberate or agonize over assigning grades. Finally, assuming that ability levels of incoming students remain fairly constant and that tests remain comparable in validity and difficulty, teachers who work to improve teaching effectiveness should see improvement in grades with the passage of time. Presumably, this would help motivate teachers to continue working to improve their effectiveness.

As you might expect, such a system also has its drawbacks. Establishing a standard is no small task. Just what is reasonable for an A may vary from school to school and from time to time, as a result of ability levels, societal pressures, and curriculum changes. Furthermore, should the same standards be maintained for a gifted or a special education class as for an average class? Another problem is that the public and administrators often have difficulty "adjusting" to a marking system that potentially allows everyone to make an A. It is a curious fact of life that everyone presses for excellence in education, but many balk at marking systems that make attainment of excellence within everyone's reach.

COMPARISONS WITH APTITUDE. Aptitude is another name for potential or ability. In such systems students are compared neither to other students nor to established standards. Instead, they are compared to themselves. That is, marks are assigned depending on how closely to their potential students are achieving. Thus, students with high aptitude or potential who are achieving at high levels would get high grades, since they would be achieving at their potential. Those with high aptitude and average achievement would get lower grades, since they would be achieving below their potential. But students with average aptitude and average achievement would get high grades, since they would be considered to be achieving at their potential. Such a system sounds attractive to many educators. However, serious problems exist, as Table 10.1 shows.

Table 10.1 illustrates that the concept of assigning grades based on the congruence of a student's achievement with the student's aptitude is quite sensible for high-aptitude students. Look at what happens for the low-aptitude students, however. If a student's aptitude is low enough, the student would have a hard time achieving below his or her potential. Thus the student always would be achieving at or above the expected level. Would this be fair to the moderate- and high-ability students? Perhaps more important, can you see how such a system would greatly complicate interpreting grades? For example, a C for a high-aptitude student might indicate 70 percent mastery, while for an average-aptitude student it might indicate 60 percent, and perhaps 50 percent mastery for the low-aptitude student. The same grade may mean very different things in terms of absolute achievement.

Other drawbacks of such a system relate to statistical considerations beyond the scope of this text that affect the reliability of such comparisons. Another is the tendency for the achievement scores of slow learners to increase and the achievement scores of fast learners to decrease when tested again. Technically this phenomenon is called the *regression toward the mean effect*—the more extreme an achievement score, the more it can be expected to "regress" or fall back toward the average or mean of all students at another testing. Finally, such a system requires more complex recordkeeping than the first two systems discussed. Such a system, as appealing as it is at first glance, is not practical.

TABLE 10.1
The Relationships Among Aptitude, Achievement, and Marks in Marking Systems Based on Comparisons of Achievement with Aptitude

Aptitude Level	*Achievement Level*	*Marks*
High	High	High
	Average	Average
	Low	Low
Average	High	High
	Average	High
	Low	Average
Low	High	High
	Average	High
	Low	High

COMPARISON OF ACHIEVEMENT WITH EFFORT. Systems that compare achievement with effort are similar to those that compare achievement with aptitude. Students who get average test scores but have to work hard to get them are given high marks. Students who get average scores but do not have to work hard to get them are given lower grades.

Several problems plague marking systems that are based on effort. First, we have no known measure of effort. Unlike aptitude, for which reliable and valid measures exist, effort is at best estimated by informal procedures. Second, within such a system children are punished for being bright and catching on quickly, while other children are rewarded for taking a long time to master concepts. Third, there is the old problem of the marks not representing academic achievement. Effort may cover up academic attainment, making marks all the more difficult to interpret. Finally, recordkeeping is once again complex.

The advantage cited for grading based on effort is that it serves to motivate the slower or turned-off students, but it may also serve to turn off the brighter students who would quickly see such a system as unfair. Whatever the case, the primary function of marking—to provide feedback about academic achievement—is not well served by such a system.

COMPARISON OF ACHIEVEMENT WITH IMPROVEMENT. Such systems compare the amount of improvement between the beginning (pre-test) and end (post-test) of instruction. Students who show the most progress get the highest grades. An obvious problem occurs for the student who does well on the pre-test. Improvement for such a student is likely to be less overall than for a student who does poorly on the pre-test. In fact, some bright students have been known to "play dumb" on pre-tests when such systems are in force. Other shortcomings of such systems include the statistical problems we mentioned before in regard to comparisons with aptitude (that is, unreliability of such comparisons and regression toward the mean) and unwieldy recordkeeping.

Which System Should You Choose?

We have seen that each system has significant drawbacks as well as advantages. Which should you choose? In our opinion, comparisons with established standards would best suit the primary function of marking—to provide feedback about academic achievement. Once standards are established, comparisons among schools and students may be more easily made. It seems to us that such a system has the best chance of reducing misinterpretation of marks.

In reality, many schools and districts have adopted multiple marking systems, such as assigning separate grades for achievement and effort or achievement, effort, and improvement. Others are now considering separate grades for paper-and-pencil tasks and performance-based assessments, such as those we have considered in Chapter 9. As long as the achievement portion of the grade reflects only achievement, such systems seem to be reasonable. Two disadvantages of such systems are worth noting, however. First, they double or triple the number of grades to be assigned and interpreted, leading to an increase in recordkeeping and interpretation time. Second, unless the purpose of each grade is explained very clearly on the report card, marking systems are often difficult for parents to decipher.

Types of Symbols

Within marking systems, a variety of symbols has been used. Some of the more common types are discussed in this section.

LETTER GRADES. Using letter grades is the most common symbol system. Many American schools use the letters A–F to report marks. Often, plus and minus symbols are used to indicate finer distinctions between the letter grades. This system, along with its variations (E, G, S, U), has several advantages that have led to its widespread adoption and continuing popularity.

First, the letter system is widely understood. Students, teachers, parents, administrators, and employers understand, at least in a general sense, that grades of A represent excellent or exceptional performance and grades of D or F represent marginal or poor performance. Second, such a system is compact, requiring only one or two spaces to report a summary mark of an entire semester's work. Third, such a system has just about the optimal number of levels of judgment humans can effectively exercise (Miller, 1956). It can have as few as 5 or as many as 15 if plus and minus signs are used.

Limitations of the system are worth considering. First, the specific meaning of letter grades varies from class to class and from school to school. Different schools and districts tend to use different marking systems and, as will be discussed later in this chapter, also tend to combine and weight the components of a mark differently. Consequently, a grade of A in one school or district may represent performance similar to a grade of B or even C in another.

Second, letter grades fail to indicate clearly the student's actual level of mastery. There is often a considerable difference between the achievement of a "low-B" student and that of a "high-B" student. Finally, because of this, averaging of letter grades often results in a loss of information or misinterpretation of the student's actual achievement. When averaging letter grades, it is necessary to go back to the actual numerical grades to obtain the "correct" average.

NUMERICAL GRADES. The numerical symbol system is another type of mark commonly used in the schools. Such systems usually employ 100 as the highest mark, and report cards often carry letter grade equivalents for the range of numerical grades. For example:

Numerical grade	Letter grade
90–100	A
80–89	B
70–79	C
60–69	D
Below 60	F

Numerical grades have three main advantages. First, like letter grades, they provide a convenient summary mark for a semester's or year's work. Second, unlike letter grades, numerical grades are easily averaged to obtain the "correct" final marks. Third, they are widely understood—most pupils and parents realize there are substantial differences between a mark of 95 and one of 75.

There are also disadvantages to such a system. First, the discriminations are finer than humans can really make (Miller, 1956). No one can make 40 reliable distinctions between grades from 61 to 100. Another way of saying this is that it is not possible to determine the real difference between a grade of 67 and a grade of 68 or between a grade of 95 and a grade of 96. Second, as with letter grades, we are never sure just what a grade means, since standards may vary considerably from school to school.

OTHER SYMBOLS. Pass-fail (P–F) grading reached its popularity peak in the 1970s. Fewer schools exclusively employ this approach today because of its shortcomings. One shortcoming is that such symbols do not provide enough information: P could mean the student exhibited anywhere from exceptional to marginal performance in the class. This makes it difficult for employers and admissions officers to evaluate applicants. Students themselves have complained about the same lack of information—they really do not know how well they did. Finally, students tend to do the minimum necessary to earn a P under such systems. When used, pass-fail approaches should at least elaborate the strengths and weaknesses upon which the mark was based.

CHECKLISTS. A common adjunct to a letter, numerical, or pass-fail symbol system is a checklist. Since these symbol systems may fail to define just what a student can or cannot do, many report cards now include skill checklists to go along with their grade symbols for each subject. Checklists are also used to provide information about nonacademic aspects of the child. For example, checklists often are provided to identify problems in the areas of conduct, social skills, responsibility, and organization. Properly utilized checklists represent useful supplements to letter or numerical grades and can convey much more detailed information about the student without contaminating or confusing the interpretation of a student's overall achievement level.

As mentioned at the beginning of this chapter, districts and schools usually decide which symbol system teachers must use. In such situations you have little choice but to employ the required system. It is more likely, though, that you will have some say about how the marks are actually assigned (that is, what you will compare student achievement with). Now that you have been exposed to the pros and cons of various systems, you should be able to make better use of any marking or symbol system you are required—or choose—to use. However, there are a number of technical considerations regarding the combining and weighting of the components of a mark that must be considered before we leave this topic. The following discussion covers points that, unfortunately, most classroom teachers are unaware of regarding marks. Master the points and procedures covered, and you will have yet another important tool to add to your growing expertise in classroom measurement and evaluation.

COMBINING AND WEIGHTING THE COMPONENTS OF A MARK

As we mentioned, the classroom teacher seldom has control over the symbol system employed but may have latitude insofar as deciding on the type of comparison used to assign marks at the end of a marking period. But how does a teacher go about combining the grades from two quizzes, one major test, a performance assessment, several homework assignments, and a term paper into a mark without allowing one or more of these factors to influence the final mark too heavily or lightly? Recall the example at the beginning of this chapter. Mr. Stokes said that Jack's failure to turn in two homework assignments earned him "an automatic D," regardless of Jack's achievement on tests, oral reading, papers, etc. While Mr. Stokes later contradicted himself on this point, there are some teachers who do adhere to such or similar practices. This would be an example of allowing a component of a mark to influence that mark *too heavily.* Remember that the main purpose of marks is to provide feedback about student achievement.

It goes without saying that such feedback is beneficial only if it is accurate. To attain this goal, each component of a final mark (tests, quizzes, homework assignments, papers, etc.) should affect the final mark *only to the appropriate extent.* At first glance it might seem simple enough to do this by weighting components considered more important (e.g., a final test grade) more heavily than components considered less important (e.g., homework grades) in computing the final mark. While differential weighting of components is an important step in arriving at an accurate, fair, and just final mark, it is only *one* step of several that must be taken, and taken carefully, to prevent a final mark from misrepresenting student achievement. Unfortunately, failure to recognize this fact is widespread in classrooms today. As a result, feedback provided about student achievement through final marks is often distorted. It may be argued that distorted feedback is more troublesome than no feedback at all. To sensitize you to the complexity of what appears to be a simple issue, consider the following scenario.

Who Is the Better Teacher?

Mr. Nickels and Ms. Dimes, history teachers at different high schools in the same district, decided prior to the school year to collaborate in developing their instructional objectives, methods, tests, quizzes, and assignments for the upcoming school year. Since they always had similar students in the past, in terms of background and aptitude, they saw no problem in reducing their workload by using the same objectives, methods, and measurement instruments for both of their classes. They did have some concerns about students from the different schools "finding out" that they were using the same materials and sharing them, but they decided that this potential problem could be avoided by administering the quizzes and tests at the same time and by giving out assignments on the same day. Pleased that they had ironed out all the wrinkles, they agreed to meet at the end of the semester to compare marks. They expected that the marks would be about the same, on the average, for both classes, since the marking symbols and the marking system they were required to use by the district were the same in both of their schools, and they both considered quizzes and test grades to be more important than homework or term paper grades. Therefore, they agreed to weight their students' quiz and test grades twice as heavily in computing their final marks.

Mr. Nickels and Ms. Dimes both prided themselves on their ability and dedication as teachers. They decided that this would be a good opportunity to determine who was the "better" teacher. Since their classes would be similar, and since they would both be using the same objectives, methods, measurement instruments, and weights for the various components that would go into their students' marks, they agreed that any significant difference in the marks earned by their classes "must" reflect differences in teaching ability and/or effectiveness. To spice things up a bit, they agreed to wager a cheeseburger on the outcome. The competition was on, and both Mr. Nickels and Ms. Dimes anticipated their own students earning the higher marks. Each teacher expected to earn a cheeseburger at the end of the semester.

At their end-of-semester meeting, however, Mr. Nickels was shocked to find that on the average Ms. Dimes's students earned marks that were one-half to a full letter grade higher than those earned by his students. Not panicking, he applied what he had learned in his college tests and measurements class. Mr. Nickels compared aptitude test scores for the two classes, hoping that by chance there would be some difference in aptitude between these two classes and their previous classes. He expected he would find significantly higher aptitude scores for Ms. Dimes's class, which would explain why their semester marks were higher than those of his class. After comparing aptitude scores for the two classes, however, Mr. Nickels found them to be quite comparable. "I could have told you that," responded Ms. Dimes somewhat haughtily.

Unwilling to concede and suspicious by nature, Mr. Nickels next suggested that Ms. Dimes must have "fixed" things by changing the curriculum—perhaps only covering two-thirds of the material he covered. This would have enabled her students to have more time to master the material and thereby earn higher grades. Offended by this challenge to her integrity, Ms. Dimes tossed her objectives, curriculum guide, and all the semester's assignments, quizzes, and tests to Mr. Nickels. "Read 'em and weep!" she exclaimed. And Mr. Nickels did . . . at first. After comparing the materials piece by piece with his own, he found them to be identical. Next, however, he laboriously compared the test and quiz grades for both classes, since this is what both he and Ms. Dimes agreed would be the major basis for the marks of their students. To his relief he discovered that the scores from both classes on the tests and quizzes *were about the same*.

"Look here, Ms. Dimes! The test and quiz grades for both classes are the same—you must have made a mistake in computing your marks," said Mr. Nickels. "Impossible, I triple-checked all my computations," stated Ms. Dimes firmly. However, when she compared the grades herself she agreed that Mr. Nickels was correct. The test and quiz grades were similar, yet she had assigned marks that on the average were one-half to a full letter grade higher than those assigned by Mr. Nickels.

Both teachers were confused. Not only were they unable to settle their bet, they were puzzled as to how such a situation could occur. They decided to review the procedures they used to combine and weight the marks their pupils had obtained. What they learned from this review is described in the next section.

Combining Grades from Quizzes, Tests, Papers, Homework, etc., into a Single Mark

Let's consider a set of grades earned by a typical student in Mr. Nickels's class, who earned a mark of B, and a set of grades of a typical student in Ms. Dimes's class, who also earned a B over the semester (see Table 10.2). Remember, both teachers used the same measurement instruments and applied the same scoring schemes to these instruments. Also, consistent with good measurement practice, they included only *achievement* factors in assigning their marks, not *nonachievement* factors, such as attendance, conduct, appearance, effort, etc.

Simply looking at the data in Table 10.2 indicates that student performance was different in an important way. Ms. Dimes's student obtained very low test and quiz grades but had very high homework and term paper grades, while Mr. Nickels's student displayed an opposite tendency. Yet both earned about the same number of overall points out of a possible 170, and both received B's. Since both teachers emphasize test and quiz grades over homework and term paper grades, this doesn't make sense, especially when one considers that Ms. Dimes's student had the lowest grade on one quiz and the second-lowest grade on the final test—and yet still earned a mark of B! To understand how this happened we must consider how the obtained component scores were combined and weighted by the teachers.

Ms. Dimes, doing what most teachers commonly do in such situations, simply assigned double weight to the quiz and test scores and then added the scores:

$$(76 \times 2) + (5 \times 2) + (7 \times 2) + 25 + 25 = 226$$

TABLE 10.2
Grades of Nickels's and Dimes's Students

Semester Test (75-100)	*Student (Nickels)* 86	*Student (Dimes)* 76
Quiz no. 1 (5–10)	9	5
Quiz no. 2 (5–10)	9	7
Homework (15–25)	18	25
Paper (15–25)	18	25
Total points earned	140	138

NOTE: The lowest and highest scores for each component are in parentheses.

Next she divided this number by the total number of points possible [(100 × 2) + (10 × 2) + (10 × 2) + 25 + 25 = 290] to arrive at the percentage of points earned by this student:

(226/290) × 100 = 78%

Since the district mandated that students who earn 78–88.99 percent of possible points be assigned a B, she assigned a mark of B to this student and followed the same procedure for all her students. Thus, even though Ms. Dimes herself believes that test and quiz performance is most important, and "weighted" these scores to reflect this belief, this student ended up with a grade of B in spite of having the lowest grade on one of the quizzes and close to the lowest grade on the final test! Unknowingly and unintentionally, Ms. Dimes is employing a combining and weighting procedure that contradicts her beliefs and her intent.

Mr. Nickels assigned the *same weight* to the various components as did Ms. Dimes. However, he recalled that in his tests and measurements class his instructor emphasized the importance of considering the *variation,* or *range,* of the scores, not just the scores themselves, in combining component scores into a *composite score*. Mr. Nickels also recalled that the reason for this is that *it is the extent of the variability of the scores of each component that determines largely the extent of the component's contribution to the composite score, NOT simply the weight attached to the component.*

Notice that each of the grade components was scored using scales of different ranges. The range is obtained by subtracting the lowest score from the highest score. A more accurate estimate of variation, called the standard deviation (covered in Chapter 13), is actually preferable to the range when combining component scores into a composite score. However, the range is an adequate estimate for most classroom purposes and is less time-consuming and easier to compute than the standard deviation. Here are the ranges for the five score components:

	Range
Semester test	100 − 75 = 25
Quiz no. 1	10 − 5 = 5
Quiz no. 2	10 − 5 = 5
Homework	25 − 15 = 10
Paper	25 − 15 = 10

After determining the range for each of the components, Mr. Nickels avoided the problem Ms. Dimes had by realizing he had to *equate the variability of each component before he could double the weights of the quizzes and the tests.* Since the semester test had the greatest range, 25 points, he did so by multiplying the quizzes by 5, the homework grade by 2.5, and the paper grade by 2.5. This procedure *equated* the variability of the scores (i.e., all components then had a range of 25 points). Only then did he *weight* the scores by multiplying the quiz and test scores by 2. Table 10.3 illustrates the procedure followed by Mr. Nickels. The maximum number of points possible, *after equating and weighting,* is 525 (200+100+100+62.5+62.5=525). Dividing the points earned by the points possible gives us this student's percentage:

(442/525) × 100 = 84.19%

TABLE 10.3
Weighting Procedure Followed by Mr. Nickels

	Score	×	Equating factor	=	Equated score	×	Weight	=	Weighted score
Semester test	86	×	1		86	×	2		172
Quiz no. 1	9	×	5		45	×	2		90
Quiz no. 2	9	×	5		45	×	2		90
Homework	18	×	2.5		45	×	1		45
Paper	18	×	2.5		45	×	1		45
Total									442

Recalling that the district's policy is to assign marks of B to all students who earn between 78 percent and 88.99 percent of possible points, Mr. Nickels assigned a mark of B to this student—the same mark assigned by Ms. Dimes to her student, in spite of this student's significantly better test and quiz performance.

Which procedure best achieved the goals of the teacher, that is, to weight test and quiz performance twice as heavily as homework and term paper performance? Which procedure do you think is more fair? Which procedure is less likely to result in a storm of protest from the students, who will invariably compare their scores and marks?

Let's consider one more example. This time let's compare the effects of Mr. Nickels's *correct* procedure on the mark earned by Ms. Dimes's student, as shown in Table 10.4. Dividing the total points earned after equating and weighting (397) by the total points possible (525) gives us the percentage of points earned:

$$(397/525) \times 100 = 75.6\%$$

According to the district's policy, this student mark would be a C. Clearly, it is more fair that this student, who has such low test and quiz grades, be assigned a lower semester mark than a student whose test and quiz grades are significantly higher.

We hope that this example has sensitized you to a potential problem in assigning semester or grading period marks. When developing a composite mark from scores with different ranges or variation, remember to *equate before you weight* to avoid the problem encountered by Ms. Dimes.

However, in the face of the increasing demands placed on today's classroom teacher, finding the time to go through the procedures outlined above may prove to be frustrating. Furthermore, in the above examples we have only considered a limited sample of mark components: test, quiz, homework, and paper. Today, most teachers also have to include marks for performance assessments, portfolios, and notebooks in their composite semester or other marking period summary marks. As important as it may be to accurate measurement, remembering to equate all these components before you weight may be lost in the face of the other important instructional, administrative, and legal considerations (see Chapter 1) that today's classroom teacher is faced with. To guard against such an oversight we will next present equating procedures that are less computationally complex, less time-consuming and, we believe, more congruent with the typical teacher's intuitive marking practices.

TABLE 10.4
Effect of Mr. Nickels's Correct Procedure on Ms. Dime's Student's Mark

	Score	×	*Equating factor*	=	*Equated score*	×	*Weight*	=	*Weighted score*
Semester test	76	×	1		76	×	2		152
Quiz no. 1	5	×	5		25	×	2		50
Quiz no. 2	7	×	5		35	×	2		70
Homework	25	×	2.5		62.5	×	1		62.5
Paper	25	×	2.5		62.5	×	1		62.5
Total									397.0

EQUATING BEFORE WEIGHTING IN THE BUSY CLASSROOM: COMBINING PERFORMANCE AND TRADITIONAL ASSESSMENT SCORES INTO A SINGLE MARK

The approaches we present in this section represent compromises between the equating approach taken by Mr. Nickels and the non-equating approach taken by Ms. Dimes. Technically, even Ms. Dimes' approach is a compromise since, from a statistical perspective, the standard deviation rather than the range is the preferred variability measure to be used in developing a composite score or mark. We believe that the methods below represent an efficient way for busy teachers to incorporate equating considerations (although they are approximations) into their marking procedures. By presenting these methods we hope to minimize the likelihood that equating will be overlooked completely.

Performance and portfolio assessments require a substantial commitment of teacher time and learner-engaged time. Consequently, a teacher who decides to use them should ensure that the performance assessment has substantial weight in the six-week or final report card grade. The following equating methods lend themselves well to the relatively straightforward inclusion of these important, additional measures to the traditional test, quiz, homework, and paper components of a mark.

Front-end Equating

This approach requires that you immediately convert all grades assigned to a 100 point scale (i.e., a percentage) by dividing the number of points obtained on every component by the total number of points possible and multiplying by 100. For example, a student who obtains 37 of 50 possible points on a performance assessment would be assigned a grade of 74.

$$(37/50) \times 100 = 74\%$$

FIGURE 10.1

Three Examples of Different "Front-End" Ways to Equate and Weigh a Six-Week Mark Based on Grades from a 100 Point Scale
Marking Formula Example #1:

This formula is known as the "One, Two, Three Times Plan."

Homework and classwork:

All grades recorded for homework and classwork will be totaled and averaged. The average grade will count once (one-sixth of the six-week mark).

Example homework and classwork grades:
84, 81, 88, 92, 96, 85, 78, 83, 91, 79, 89, 94 = 1040/12 = 86.6 = 87 average

Quizzes:

All of the quizzes are totaled and averaged. This average grade will count two times (one-third of the six-week mark).

Example quiz grades:
82, 88, 80, 91, 78, 86 = 505/6 = 84.2 = 84 average

Performance Assessments:

All of the performance assessments will be totaled and averaged. This average grade will count three times (one-half of the six-week mark).

Example performance assessment grades:
81, 91, 86, = 258/3 = 86 average

Then, the six-week mark would be computed as follows:
87 (one time) + 84 + 84 (two times) + 86 + 86 + 86 (three times) = 513/6 = 85.5 = 86 the six-week mark.

Continued

This is a very common practice followed by many teachers. If all components (e.g., tests, quizzes, etc.) are similarly converted then all grades will be on the same 100 point scale. Each component will then have the same potential range of 100 points; you have thereby equated the scores without having to go through Mr. Nickels more time-consuming (but more technically correct) procedure.* Computing the composite mark, then, simply involves averaging the grades for each component, multiplying these averages by the

*This approach and the following approach are intended to promote comparable variation in scale scores across components that will be combined into a final mark. They assume that the variation of actual scale scores for each component will be approximately the same, that is, that you use the full or comparable portions of the scale across components.

FIGURE 10.1 Continued

Marking Formula Example #2:

This formula is known as the "Percentages Plan."

A teacher determines a percentage for each component. For example, homework and classwork will count for 20% of the grade; quizzes will count for 40% of the grade; and performance assessments will count for 40% of the grade.

Using the same scores as listed above, a student's mark would be computed as follows:
20% of the 86.6 for homework and classwork is 17.3.
40% of the 84.2 for quizzes is 33.7, and
40% of the 86 for performance assessments is 34.4

17.3 + 33.7 + 34.4 = 85.4 = 85 as the six-week mark

(This mark differs from the mark obtained from Example #1 because the "weight" put on each component differs in the two examples).

Marking Formula Example #3:

This formula is known as the "Language Arts Plan."

A language arts teacher determines that the publishing, goal meeting, journal, and daily process grades each count one-fourth (25%) of the six-week mark.

A language arts mark will be computed as follows:
The publishing grade, issued at the end of the six week period, is 88.
The goal meeting grade, issued at the end of the six week period, is 86.
The journal grades are: 82 + 92 + 94 + 90 + 88 + 86 = 532/6 = 88.7 = 89.
The daily process grades are: 78 + 82 + 86 + 94 + 94 + 91 = 525/6 = 87.5 = 8

The six week mark would be: 88 + 86 + 89 + 88 = 351/4 = 87.75 = 88.

weight assigned to the component, and adding these products to determine the final grade. Figure 10.1 provides examples of three formulae to accomplish this.

Back-end Equating

With the "back-end" approach you decide how many points each component of your marking system is worth on a case-by-case basis. You may want some tests to be worth 40 points, some 75, some 14, and so on, since the total point value should depend on the complexity of the items and the number of discriminations you can reliably make, rather than a multiple of 5 or 10, as is common practice. Similarly, some homework assignments may be worth 10 points, or 7 points; portfolios may be worth 23 points, or 64 points, and so on. The "front-end" approach requires you to convert these scores to percentages before combining them. As we shall see, this approach addresses this consideration at the "back-end" rather than the beginning of the process. Both approaches will lead to the same outcome, so experiment with both until you find one that best "fits your style." Here are the procedures involved in setting up a "back-end" marking scheme for a six-week marking period.

STEP 1: Identify the components of your marking system and assign each component a weight. Recall that a weight is the percentage of total points a particular component carries. For example:

Component	**Weight**
Homework	15%
Objective Tests	20%
Performance Tests	20%
Portfolio	20%
Classroom Work	15%
Notebook	10%
	100%

STEP 2: Record the actual points earned out of the total possible in the grade book. Leave a column for totals. These scores are illustrated in Figure 10.2. As you can see, each component and each separate assignment have varying numbers of points possible to be earned. Assign possible points for each component based on the length of the assignment, your ability to make reliable distinctions, etc.

STEP 3: Total the actual points earned for each component and divide this by the possible points and multiply by 100. The results represent the percentage of points earned for each particular component. In our example from Figure 10.2, Cornell and Rosie earned the following total points:

	Cornell	*Rosie*
Homework	50/70 = 71%	55/70 = 79%
Objective Tests	45/60 = 75%	35/60 = 58%
Performance Tests	33/40 = 83%	39/40 = 98%
Portfolio	18/20 = 90%	15/20 = 75%
Classroom Work	39/50 = 78%	37/50 = 74%
Notebook	5/10 = 50%	8/10 = 80%

FIGURE 10.2
Sample Grade Recording Sheet, First Six Weeks

Component	Homework							Objective Tests			Performance Tests			Portfolio	Classwork						Notebook
Dates	8/20	9/7	9/14	9/20	9/28	10/6	Total	9/17	10/7	Total	9/23	10/8	Total	10/7	9/2	9/6	9/14	9/23	10/5	Total	10/8
Cornell	10/10	8/10	14/15	10/10	8/15	0/10	50/70	20/30	25/30	45/60	15/20	18/20	33/40	18/20	9/10	7/15	10/10	9/10	4/5	39/50	5/10
Rosie	10/10	5/10	12/15	8/10	12/15	8/10	55/70	15/30	20/30	35/60	20/20	19/20	39/40	15/20	8/10	14/15	0/10	10/10	5/5	37/50	8/10

STEP 4: Multiply each of these percentages by the weights assigned, as shown below, and then sum these products.

	Cornell	*Rosie*
Homework	71 × .15 = 10.6	79 × .15 = 11.8
Objective Tests	75 × .20 = 15.0	58 × .20 = 11.6
Performance Tests	83 × .20 = 16.6	98 × .20 = 19.6
Portfolio	90 × .20 = 18.0	75 × .20 = 15.0
Classroom Work	78 × .15 = 11.7	74 × .15 = 11.1
Notebook	50 × .10 = 5.0	80 × .10 = 8.0
Totals	76.9	77.1

STEP 5: Record the six-week mark either as a letter grade (e.g., A = 90–100, B = 80–89.99, etc.), or as the total (i.e., percentage) for each subject, depending on your district's policy.

SUMMARY

This chapter introduced you to various issues related to marks and marking systems. Its major points are:

1. Marks are used to provide information about student achievement.
2. Marks should reflect academic achievement and nothing more. Grades for attitude, effort, improvement, conduct, and so on should be recorded separately from marks.
3. Marks often reflect factors other than achievement and are often assigned according to a variety of marking systems. This makes valid comparisons of marks across schools, and even across teachers, difficult at best.
4. Several types of marking systems are employed in the schools today. These involve comparison of a student with:
   a. Other students (grades depend on how well the student did compared with other students)
   b. Established standards (grades depend on how well a student's performance compares with pre-established standards)
   c. Aptitude (grades depend on how consistent a student's actual achievement is with his or her achievement potential)
   d. Effort (grades depend on how hard the student works)
   e. Improvement (grades depend on how much progress a student makes over the course of instruction)
5. Each system has its advantages and disadvantages, but marking based on comparisons with established standards seems to fit best the main function of marks—to provide feedback about academic achievement.

6. The symbols most commonly used in marking systems are letter grades (A–F, E–U) and numerical grades (0–100). Such symbol systems are often combined with checklists to provide specific information about such factors as skill level, conduct, and attitude.

7. When combining grades from quizzes, tests, papers, homework, etc., that have different ranges or variation, and which are not on 100 point scales, equate the variability of each component before weighting and computing the final mark.

8. A practical alternative to this technique is to use the "front-end" or "back-end" equating approaches. These approaches yield approximate but similar outcomes, and are less time-consuming ways to equate scores from quizzes, tests, homework, performance assessments, portfolios, and notebooks.

For Practice

1. List the pros and cons of each of the following types of marking systems:
   a. Comparison with other students
   b. Comparison with established standards
   c. Comparison of achievement with one's own aptitude
   d. Basing grades on effort
   e. Basing grades on improvement

2. Create a numerical scale for measuring effort and another for measuring improvement. Indicate, for each level of the scale, the type of behavior(s) you are looking for. What might be another way of measuring these two qualities?

3. Choose the most appropriate marking system from among the following pairs of symbol systems and give reasons for your choices.
   a. A–F and 0–100
   b. 0–100 and P–F
   c. E–U and P–F

4. The school in which you will teach will probably have an established marking system to report subject matter grades. With what behaviors might you augment this marking system to report to students and parents additional information which you feel is important? How would you measure these additional behaviors?

*5. Using the following scores obtained from a single student, use both the "front-end" and "back-end" methods to determine an overall mark: Quiz, 10 out of 15; test, 32 out of 50; paper, 8 out of 10; homework, 80 out of 100; portfolio, 9 out of 10. You decided that the quiz, test, paper, homework, and portfolio would be weighted 15, 30, 30, 10, and 15 percent of the final mark respectively. What is the final numerical mark? What letter grade would be assigned if A=90 – 100%, B=80 – 89.99%; C=70 – 79.99%, D=65 – 69.99%, and F=64.99% and below? Why does the same numerical mark result from both the "front-end" and "back-end" approaches?

---

* Answer for question 5 appears in Appendix D.

CHAPTER 11

Measuring Attitudes and Social Behavior

"Just thinking about it makes me mad," said Bob. "I hate this class. The only reason I'm here is that the counselor told me to take it. Even though I like my other classes, this one ruins the whole semester for me. The teacher is OK, but the materials are useless, and the text is a waste of time. Sometimes I don't even attend class or do the readings. I told the teacher about my feelings. I thought she would see that some changes were needed. Guess what she said? She said that things wouldn't get better until my attitude changed! To top it off, she said she had suspected I had a bad attitude all along and listening to me just confirmed her suspicions. But it's *her* attitude that's bad. She has had a bad attitude about *me* all along and listening to her just confirmed *my* suspicions."

Have you ever felt like Bob? Well, most of us have at one time or another. No student enjoys, or is even neutral about, every class, teacher, or text. Similarly, no teacher is fortunate enough to have only interested and motivated students. Therefore, sometimes students are likely to develop negative attitudes about some classes, and sometimes teachers are likely to develop negative attitudes about some students. These are simply facts of life, but many such problems can and should be resolved. One of the first steps toward resolving attitude problems is learning what attitudes are and what they are not.

In the situation just described, what do you think an attitude is? The teacher could tell Bob had a bad attitude from what she saw and heard. Bob could tell the teacher's attitude was negative from what he saw and heard. Seeing, looking, hearing, saying—these are what the teacher and Bob focused on to conclude that the other had a bad or negative attitude. In other words, based on what you see or hear, you draw conclusions about someone's attitude. You determine someone's attitude about something or someone from what they do or say. But just what are attitudes? Before defining what attitudes are, let's be sure we know what they are not. Attitudes are *not:*

descriptions of behaviors (you cannot see or hear them directly)

descriptions of what a person knows or understands

right or wrong, in a moral or ethical sense (although behaviors generated by attitudes may be!)

necessarily related to intelligence, age, ethnicity, or social or financial status

directly measurable or observable

Attitudes *are:*

descriptions of how people typically feel about or react to other people, places, things, or ideas

Attitudes can be thought of as fairly consistent and stable ways that people feel, behave, and are predisposed to feel and behave in the presence of various stimuli.

HOW ARE ATTITUDES CLASSIFIED?

In our example, we referred to positive attitudes and negative attitudes. Others refer to attitudes as appropriate or inappropriate or as good or bad. However, we prefer to use *positive/negative,* since these terms do not necessarily imply value judgments about the attitude itself, at least not as clearly as do *good/bad,* or *appropriate/inappropriate.* We want to avoid making value judgments, since it is often not very clear whether attitudes are justified or sensible, especially for the individual in question.

Thus, we will classify attitudes as either positive or negative. But to do so, we need to decide on just what kinds of indicators or behaviors we will use to identify positive attitudes and negative attitudes. Fortunately, we can do this quite easily by considering what individuals with differing attitudes do or say in the presence of some stimulus. Consider the following:

Lisa and Lorrie are pupils in the fourth grade. As their teacher, you've noticed that Lisa:

has never missed math class

has never been late for math class

frequently is the first one to complete the math lesson

frequently is the first to finish math tests

often asks for extra math work

smiles often during math class

seldom, if ever, requires reminders to stay on task in math class

often tells you how much she likes math class

is often seen and heard explaining math concepts and procedures to classmates

You've noticed that Lorrie:

frequently misses math class

frequently is late for math class

is usually the last to finish math lessons, on those few occasions she does finish

has not finished a math test yet

has never asked for extra math work

constantly has a frown on her face during math class

needs constant reminders to stay on task during math

has told you several times how much she hates math

is often seen and heard telling classmates how much she hates math

Obviously, in this case the stimulus (math class) evokes different kinds of behaviors in Lisa and Lorrie. Those exhibited by Lisa may be called *approach* behaviors. Those exhibited by Lorrie may be called *avoidance* behaviors. Approach behaviors are those that result in more frequent, closer, or more intense contact with the stimulus. Such behaviors are considered to indicate a positive attitude toward the stimulus. Avoidance behaviors result in less frequent, more distant, or less intense contact with the stimulus. Such behaviors are considered to indicate a negative attitude toward the stimulus.

So far, we have considered what attitudes are—descriptions of how people typically feel about or react to other people, places, things, or ideas—and how attitudes are classified—positive if they lead to increased contact with the stimulus or negative if they lead to decreased contact with the stimulus.

WHY MEASURE ATTITUDES?

Attitude measurement can help most classroom teachers:

1. Identify early in the school year those students who are turned on or turned off to school, certain subjects, or certain teachers. Once this information is collected, the teacher may implement strategies to best utilize and challenge the turned-on students (those with positive attitudes) and to better motivate the turned-off students (those with negative attitudes).
2. Assess general changes that may take place in attitudes over time. Obviously, the teacher would prefer that students with positive attitudes get even more positive or at least maintain the same positive attitude. On the other hand, the teacher would like to see students with negative attitudes develop more positive attitudes, or at least not develop more negative attitudes.
3. Determine the effect on student attitudes of specific aspects of the school or classroom experience. For example, it would be worthwhile to know whether a

> social studies unit on cultural differences alters student attitudes toward classmates from different cultures. All too often curricular or instructional innovations are implemented without really attempting to assess the effect they have on attitudes *as well as* on achievement.

Since attitudes are not directly measurable, what we will consider next are ways of measuring behaviors that are associated with positive or negative attitudes.

MEASURING ATTITUDES

Recall our example in which both the teacher and the student drew inferences about each other's attitudes on the basis of what they saw and heard, that is, on what they observed. Indeed, one common way we assess attitudes is through observation. In the next section we will discuss two methods of carrying out observations. Afterward we will consider several paper-and-pencil methods used to measure attitudes.

Observation

Observation can be classified into two categories, *structured* and *unstructured.* For our purposes, the difference between these two methods of assessing attitudes lies in the extent of the preparation we go through to "plan" an observation, and to record what we observe. Let's consider each method individually and then consider the pros and cons of observation as a means of assessing attitudes.

UNSTRUCTURED OBSERVATION. As the name implies, unstructured observation is open-ended. Essentially all that is done to prepare for an observation session is that the teacher identifies the time and place for the observation and how long it will last. Thus, very little preparation time is required. The teacher then observes the behavior of the pupils, recording as much as possible, or whatever appears to be useful, important, or unusual. Afterward, an attempt is made to infer student attitudes based on the information recorded. The following illustrates data produced from an unstructured observation on the playground.

Class:	Fourth grade
Date:	March 26
Time:	10:25 A.M.
Place:	Playground
Activity:	Recess

> *Notes:* Sunny, cool, lots of energy, Jim on fringe of activity. Paul and Barb arguing, Mike running and yelling, Jim joins Dorothy and Mike on swings, Paula asks about math assignment, Jim leaves swing and wanders by self, Paul playing ball with Pat, Paula tells Mark about math assignment, much activity, but beginning to slow down, bell, time to line up, Paula is first, Jim last.

Once the data are recorded, the teacher's task is to make some sense of it. From this record, what conclusions can be drawn about student attitudes? Well, it seems that Paula is exhibiting approach behaviors (remember those?) related to math, and Jim exhibits avoidance behaviors related to his peers. Beyond these conclusions, little else that is useful is available. Unfortunately, this is often the case when unstructured observation is employed. Why is this so? Think for a moment about why the observation was conducted—to make inferences about student attitudes. But attitudes toward or about what or whom? About school? About math? About peers? About teachers? About playground equipment? Identifying the purpose of the observation too often is overlooked in unstructured observation.

When we specify the purpose of the observation *before* doing the observation, the task of the observer is focused. Now, rather than trying to record everything or all the important incidents, the observer can zero in on specific approach and avoidance behaviors that indicate positive and negative attitudes toward whatever or whomever has been identified. Thus, although focusing on *one aspect* of the playground interaction runs the risk of the observer overlooking potentially interesting events, the benefits in terms of reliability and relevance of the data obtained are substantial. In reality, clearly identifying the purpose of the observation is the first step in conducting a *structured* observation. Our recommendation is that you refrain from unstructured observation sessions and focus instead on structured observation sessions to measure student attitudes.

STRUCTURED OBSERVATION. A structured observation requires more preparation time, often substantially more than an informal or unstructured observation session. It is necessary to determine *why* you are observing, *what* you expect to see or think you might see, and *how* you will record what you see. The following steps are useful in preparing for a structured observation session:

1. Indicate why you are observing, for example:
   To determine whether students feel good about the new math curriculum
   To see whether cliques in the classroom have become more accepting of new students
   To determine whether students feel more positive about reading after your Fun-in-Reading program
2. Assemble an outline of approach and avoidance behaviors appropriate to why you are observing. To develop an appropriate list of approach and avoidance behaviors, it is often helpful to simply watch what a student does who is turned on or turned off to the person, thing, or activity in question and note the behaviors exhibited. For example, if you want to assess attitude toward reading following the Fun-in-Reading program, the following might be appropriate for an observation during free time:

Approach	Avoidance
Looks at books on table	Moves away from books on table
Picks up books on table	Makes faces when looking at books
Reads book(s)	Tells others not to read
Tells others about a book recently read	Expresses dislike for reading

3. If possible, list behaviors in terms of likelihood of occurrence, to save time scanning the list and recording the behavior. For example, "read books" would be further down the list than "looks at books on table" and "picks up books on table," since before you read a book you must first look at it and then pick it up. However, it is possible that someone could look at a book, pick it up, and then not read it, so these behaviors are more likely.
4. Decide how to record the behaviors you observe. Two common methods are illustrated in Figure 11.1.
   a. Frequency approach: Place a checkmark to the right of the behaviors listed each time they occur.
   b. Rating approach: Arrange five columns labeled "Always," "Often," "Sometimes," "Seldom," or "Never" to the right of the behavior, and then put a check in the appropriate column for each behavior to indicate the approximate frequency of occurrence.

The second checklist is most useful when the teacher is not able to devote sufficient attention to a student or students long enough to obtain valid frequency counts. Here, the teacher checks the appropriate column after observing for a while. Naturally, such an approach increases the chances of error. However, it is substantial improvement over an unstructured observation. If you have the opportunity, use the frequency approach, but the rating approach is normally an acceptable compromise.

The Likert Scale

This paper-and-pencil method of assessing attitudes was developed by and named after Rensis Likert (1932). The Likert scales have become one of the most widely used methods of attitude assessment. Likert scales consist of a series of attitude statements about some person, group, or thing. Respondents indicate the extent to which they agree or disagree with each statement, and the overall score then suggests whether the individual's attitude is favorable or unfavorable. Figure 11.2 illustrates a very brief Likert scale that might be used to assess attitudes toward a tests and measurement course.

SCORING LIKERT SCALES. To complete this scale, students would simply circle the appropriate letter for each item. In order to score the scale, weights are assigned to each letter, depending on whether the item is worded positively or negatively.

For example, the weights assigned to the options for item 1, which is worded negatively, would be:

SA = 1
A = 2
U = 3
D = 4
SD = 5

The weights assigned to the options for item 2, which is worded positively, would be:

SA = 5
A = 4
U = 3
D = 2
SD = 1

FIGURE 11.1
Two Checklists for a Structured Observation to Assess Attitudes Toward Reading

Checklist 1 (Frequency Approach)

Name ______________________________ *Date* _______ *Time* _______

Behaviors	*Frequency*
1. Looks at books on table	________
2. Picks up books on table	________
3. Reads books	________
4. Tells others about books read	________
5. Moves away from books on table	________
6. Makes faces when looking at books	________
7. Tells others not to read	________
8. Expresses dislike for reading	________

Checklist 2 (Rating Approach)

Name ______________________________ *Date* _______ *Time* _______

Behaviors	*Always*	*Often*	*Sometimes*	*Seldom*	*Never*
1. Looks at books on table					
2. Picks up books on table					
3. Reads books					
4. Tells others about books read					
5. Moves away from books on table					
6. Makes faces when looking at books					
7. Tells others not to read					
8. Expresses dislike for reading					

FIGURE 11.2
A Five-Item Likert Scale to Assess Attitudes Toward a Tests and Measurement Course

DIRECTIONS: Indicate the extent to which you agree or disagree with each statement by circling the appropriate letter to the right of each statement.

	Strongly Agree	*Agree*	*Uncertain*	*Disagree*	*Strongly Disagree*
1. I have a hard time keeping awake in class.	SA	A	U	D	SD
2. This course should be required for teachers.	SA	A	U	D	SD
3. I like learning to write objective test items.	SA	A	U	D	SD
4. I daydream a lot in class.	SA	A	U	D	SD
5. I often feel like coming to this class.	SA	A	U	D	SD

An individual's score for each item, then, would be the value assigned to the choice selected. For example, if an individual circled SA for item 1 (negatively worded), his or her score for that item would be 1. If the same individual circled SA for item 2 (positively worded), his or her score for that item would be 5. Figure 11.3 illustrates the attitude scale depicted in Figure 11.2 with items marked as either positive or negative, options circled, and weights assigned for the choices.

Scoring of the scale would simply require summing up the weights for the options selected and then dividing the total by the number of items. This provides the student's *mean attitude score.* The mean attitude score for our hypothetical student is 2.0 because $(2 + 2 + 1 + 1 + 4) \div 5 = 2.0$. Next, we would have to conclude whether the student's responses reflected a positive or negative attitude toward the course. Higher weights are associated with positive attitudes, and lower weights with negative attitudes. As a general rule, we draw the line at a mean rating of 3.0. That is, if the score is equal to or greater than 3.0, a positive attitude exists, and if the score is less than 3.0, as was the case for our hypothetical student in Figure 11.3, then a negative attitude exists. Let's look at one more example of scoring a Likert scale before moving on to a discussion of its advantages and disadvantages and some suggestions for writing attitude statements. Figure 11.4 on page 206 again represents the Likert scale presented in Figure 11.2, but with another set of responses circled. This time, try to score the scale yourself, and conclude whether the mean attitude score represents a positive or negative attitude.

FIGURE 11.3
Sample Likert Scale with Items Labeled as Positive or Negative, Options Circled, and Weights Assigned to Choices

	Strongly Agree	*Agree*	*Uncertain*	*Disagree*	*Strongly Disagree*
1. I have a hard time keeping awake in class. (Negative)	SA (1	(A) 2	U 3	D 4	SD 5)
2. All teachers should have to take a course like this one. (Positive)	SA (5	A 4	U 3	(D) 2	SD 1)
3. I like learning to write objective test items. (Positive).	SA (5	A 4	U 3	D 2	(SD) 1)
4. I daydream a lot in class. (Negative)	(SA) (1	A 2	U 3	D 4	SD 5)
5. I often feel like coming to this class. (Positive)	SA (5	(A) 4	U 3	D 2	SD 1)

What did you conclude? What is the hypothetical student's score? Does the score indicate a positive attitude? Check your answers against the solution provided.

Item	Positive/negative	Weight of option selected
1	Negative	5
2	Positive	4
3	Positive	5
4	Negative	4
5	Positive	1
	Total	19
		$19 \div 5 = 3.8$

Since 3.8 is greater than 3.0, we would conclude that this student exhibits a positive attitude toward the course.

ADVANTAGES AND DISADVANTAGES OF LIKERT SCALES. The following are probably the most salient advantages and disadvantages of Likert scales:

Advantages

1. Quick and economical to administer and score

FIGURE 11.4
Sample Likert Scale with Options Circled

	Strongly Agree	*Agree*	*Uncertain*	*Disagree*	*Strongly Disagree*
1. I have a hard time keeping awake in class.	SA	A	U	D	(SD)
2. All teachers should have to take a class like this one.	SA	(A)	U	D	SD
3. I like learning to write objective test items.	(SA)	A	U	D	SD
4. I daydream a lot in class.	SA	A	U	(D)	SD
5. I often feel like coming to this class.	SA	A	U	D	(SD)

2. Adapts easily to most attitude measurement situations
3. Provides direct and reliable assessment of attitudes when scales are well constructed
4. Lends itself well to item analysis procedures

Disadvantages

1. Easily faked where individuals want to present a false impression of their attitudes (this can be offset somewhat by developing a good level of rapport with the respondents and convincing them that honest responses are in their best interests)
2. Intervals between points on the scale do not represent equal changes in attitude for all individuals (that is, the differences between SA and A may be slight for one individual and great for another)
3. Internal consistency of the scale may be difficult to achieve (care must be taken to have unidimensional items aimed at a single person, group, thing, or organization)
4. *Good* attitude statements take time to construct (it is usually best to begin by constructing several times as many attitude statements as you will actually need, then selecting only those that best assess the attitude in question)

The last point, that attitude statements are time-consuming to construct, bears elaboration. In Chapter 6 you learned how to avoid common errors in constructing objective test items. Fortunately, many of the same guidelines apply to the construction of attitude statements, so it is not likely that you will have to start from scratch in learning how to write attitude statements.

Next we provide some suggestions for writing attitude statements. While some of these suggestions are straightforward, others are not. Examples of poorly written and well-written attitude statements are provided to clarify the suggestions.

Suggestions for Writing Attitude Statements

1. Write simple, clear, and direct sentences. Keep in mind that your goal is to assess *attitude* in as valid and reliable a fashion as possible. You are *not* trying to assess another person's intellectual ability, vocabulary, or reading comprehension or to demonstrate your own!

   Poor Item: In any kind of choice situation, we are likely to discover that different individuals will think and express themselves in ways that are idiosyncratic to them, and we should be willing to tolerate different kinds of behavioral manifestations, which by inference are related to their unobservable cognition and affect.
   Better Item: We should be tolerant of different kinds of behavior.

2. Write short statements. A general rule is that attitude statements should rarely, if ever, exceed 20 words. The item above is a good example of excessive wordiness. Another follows:

   Poor Item: When a person finds himself or herself in a situation in which he or she can take advantage of another person, he or she can usually be expected to do so.
   Better Item: Basically, people can't be trusted.

3. Avoid negatives, especially double negatives. The use of negatives like no, not, and none and especially the use of two negatives in one sentence confuses the reader.

   Poor Item: There isn't a teacher in this school that does not respect student rights.
   Better Item: Teachers in this school respect student rights.

4. Avoid factual statements. Remember that you are attempting to assess affective responses, not cognitive responses.

   Poor Item: Career education programs require considerable developmental funds to begin.
   Better Item: The price tag for starting up career education programs is too high to be warranted.

5. Avoid reference to the past. Unless you are for some reason interested in retrospective accounts of *past* attitudes (which are likely to be less reliable than present-day attempts at attitude assessment), phrase your statements in the present tense.

   Poor Item: I have always gotten good grades when I wanted to.
   Better Item: I get good grades when I want to.

6. Avoid absolutes like *all, none, always,* and *never.* At best, such terms add little or nothing to the statement. At worst, they add either confusion or certainty.
   Poor Item: I never met a person I didn't like.
   Better Item: I like most people I meet.
7. Avoid nondistinguishing statements. Such statements fail to discriminate between various attitude positions. In other words, they are statements with which most people either agree or disagree.
   Poor Item: I would rather go to school than do anything else.
   Better Item: School is one of my favorite activities.
8. Avoid irrelevancies. Such statements fail to address the real issue in question.
   Poor Item: My morning walk to school is pleasant.
   Better Item: I look forward to walking to school in the morning.
9. Use *only, merely,* and *just* sparingly. Although such terms do not always introduce ambiguity, in many instances they do. It is usually better to avoid them.
   Poor Item: Organized religion is the only way people can express their faith.
   Better Item: Organized religion is the best way for people to express their faith.
10. Use one thought per statement. If double-barreled statements are written, respondents will not know which part of the statement to respond to.
    Poor Item: A good teacher knows the subject matter and treats students fairly.
    Better Item: A good teacher treats students fairly.

FIGURE 11.5
Suggestions to Follow in Writing Attitude Statements

In developing an attitude statement, try to:

WRITE	simple, clear, and direct sentences or short statements
AVOID	negatives, especially double negatives
	factual statements
	reference to the past
	absolutes (*all, always, none, never*)
	nondistinguishing statements
	irrelevancies
USE	*only, merely, just,* and so on, sparingly
	one thought per statement
	equal numbers of positive and negative statements

Now you have some suggestions for writing attitude statements. Figure 11.5 summarizes the suggestions to follow in writing attitude statements. However, these suggestions will be ineffective unless you thoroughly sample the *relevant* aspects of the attitudes to be measured. In other words, it is useful to consider several different kinds of statements that will enable you to tap the attitude in question adequately and avoid tapping irrelevant aspects of attitudes. You do this by focusing your Likert scale.

Focusing Your Likert Scale

Writing good attitude statements takes time. It makes sense to focus your writing on those aspects of the attitude in question that are relevant. What are they? The following suggestions should help you determine them:

1. List the attitudinal area in question (for example, attitudes toward space exploration).
2. List relevant approach and avoidance behaviors (as you did in the second step in developing a structured observation checklist). The list would include behaviors that lead to:
   a. Increased or decreased contact with the person, object, or group in question, or
   b. Exhibitions of support or disdain for the person, object, or group. (For example, approach behaviors may include the following: talks about the benefits of space exploration, takes a trip to the Kennedy Space Center, reads books about space exploration, and sends contributions to NASA. Avoidance behaviors could include: talks about the costs of space exploration, avoids the Kennedy Space Center while traveling down Florida's east coast, never reads books about space exploration, and is against public funding of NASA.)
3. Write your attitude statements. A good way to begin is to lump them into two categories, those that someone might:
   a. Say to indicate approach or avoidance tendencies ("A trip to the Kennedy Space Center would be interesting," "A trip to the Kennedy Space Center would be boring"), or
   b. Do to indicate approach or avoidance tendencies ("I intend to write a letter to the editor decrying the cost of space exploration," "I intend to write a letter to the editor extolling the benefits of space exploration").
4. Write several such statements for each approach or avoidance behavior listed in step 2.
5. Use the suggestions given for writing attitude statements to avoid common flaws.

You are now ready to begin constructing your own Likert scales. As with any skill, practice will be necessary if you want to be good at it. Thus far, we have discussed the Likert scale, which is only one of several paper-and-pencil attitude assessment approaches. In the next section, we will introduce two other commonly used attitude measures: the two-point scale and the bipolar adjective scale.

The Two-Point Scale

The two-point scale is simply a variation of the Likert scale. The only real differences between this scale and the Likert scale lie in the response options and in the scoring of the scale. Rather than selecting from among five degrees of agreement or disagreement, the respondent must choose between two options: yes to agree, or no to disagree. For this reason, this type of scale is often referred to as a *forced-choice scale*. In essence, the respondent is forced into an all or none indication of agreement or disagreement. Figure 11.6 is an example of a two-point scale measuring attitudes toward two-point scales.

ADVANTAGES AND DISADVANTAGES OF TWO-POINT SCALES. The two-point scale has several advantages. It is simpler and more straightforward, responses are less likely to be inaccurately indicated, and many times a clearer indication of attitudinal preference is obtained than from the Likert scale. Its main disadvantage is that such a scale can rub people the wrong way. Most people do not have clear yes or no, black or white perceptions or attitudes, and they sometimes resent scales that suggest the world operates in such simplistic terms. Such individuals may purposely respond inaccurately in protest of such scales, damaging the validity of the attitude assessment. Problems like this can be defused somewhat by addressing the issues *before* administering the scale and giving individuals whose views differ the opportunity to voice their objections.

SCORING TWO-POINT SCALES. Coming up with an attitude score for a two-point scale follows much the same process as was used in scoring a Likert scale. The difference is that weights of $+1$ and -1 are assigned to the options depending on whether the statement contains positive or negative wording. After summing and averaging the weights for the entire scale, decisions are made as to whether the score indicates a positive or negative attitude according to the following rule.

Rule: If the average is greater than zero, a positive attitude is reflected. If the score is less than or equal to zero, a negative attitude is reflected.

Figure 11.7 illustrates the two-point scale presented in Figure 11.6 with options circled and scoring completed.

Adding up the weights of the options selected, we have:

FIGURE 11.6
A Two-Point Scale Measuring Attitudes Toward Two-Point Scales

DIRECTIONS: Circle *yes* or *no* to indicate whether you agree or disagree with each statement.

1. Two-point scales are underutilized.	yes	no
2. I prefer Likert scales to two-point scales.	yes	no
3. When I teach, I will use two-point scales.	yes	no
4. Likert scales are easier to use than two-point scales.	yes	no

FIGURE 11.7
A Scored Two-Point Scale with Weights Assigned to Options

DIRECTIONS: Circle *yes* or *no* to indicate whether you agree or disagree with each statement.

1. Two-point scales are underutilized.	(yes) (+ 1)	no (– 1)
2. I prefer Likert scales to two-point scales.	(yes) (– 1)	no (+ 1)
3. When I teach, I will use two-point scales.	(yes) (+ 1)	no (– 1)
4. Likert scales are easier to use than two-point scales.	yes (– 1)	(no) (+ 1)

(1)	+1
(2)	−1
(3)	+1
(4)	+1
	+2

Dividing by the number of items, we have:

$$2 \div 4 = .5$$

According to our rule, since .5 is greater than zero, this respondent has a positive attitude toward two-point scales.

The Bipolar Adjective Scale

The bipolar adjective scale differs from the previous two scales mainly because it does not use attitude statements. Instead, a word or phrase referring to the person, object, or group in question is presented, along with a list of adjectives that have opposite bipolar meanings. By circling one of the seven choices in the scale, respondents indicate the degree to which they feel the adjective represents their attitude. Figure 11.8 illustrates a bipolar adjective scale.

As you may have guessed, the major task in constructing a bipolar adjective scale is the selection of adjectives. A handy source of such adjectives is Osgood, Suci, and Tannenbaum (1957), which provides a lengthy list of bipolar adjectives. However, you are encouraged to think of adjectives that will be particularly relevant to what *you* want to measure. Many times this is better than borrowing from the lists of others.

Scoring the scale can be done in two ways. The first way is very similar to the procedures outlined for the Likert and two-point scales. Weights could be assigned, depending on whether the positive adjective was on the left (1 would get a weight of 7, and 7 a weight of 1) or on the right (1 would get a weight of 1, and 7 a weight of 7). The weights

FIGURE 11.8
A Bipolar Adjective Scale

DIRECTIONS: Circle one of the numbers between each pair of adjectives to best indicate how closely one of the adjectives describes your attitude about essay questions.

Essay questions

good	1	2	3	4	5	6	7	bad
unpleasant	1	2	3	4	5	6	7	pleasant
fair	1	2	3	4	5	6	7	unfair
ugly	1	2	3	4	5	6	7	beautiful
meaningful	1	2	3	4	5	6	7	meaningless
unimportant	1	2	3	4	5	6	7	important
positive	1	2	3	4	5	6	7	negative
painful	1	2	3	4	5	6	7	pleasurable

would then be summed and averaged, and a score of 3.5 or more would be indicative of a positive attitude. However, there are so many numbers involved that such an approach may become cumbersome, and the likelihood of clerical errors is greater. Consequently, we recommend an alternative procedure to score a bipolar adjective scale:

1. Assign weights of 7, 6, 5, 4, 3, 2, 1 to each option, regardless of whether the positive or negative adjective is on the left.
2. Sum all the scores (weights) for the pairs with the positive adjective on the left.
3. Sum all the scores (weights) for the pairs with the negative adjective on the left.
4. Subtract the score for the left-negative adjective pairs from the score for the left-positive adjective pairs.
5. Divide the score by the number of adjective pairs.
6. Make a decision as to the direction of the attitude according to the following rule: If the average is greater than zero, a positive attitude is reflected. If the average is equal to or less than zero, a negative attitude is reflected.

Figure 11.9 illustrates the bipolar adjective scale presented in Figure 11.8, with choices circled and scoring completed. Adding up the weights for the left-positive adjectives we have 2 + 2 = 4. Adding up the weights for the left-negative items we

FIGURE 11.9
A Scored Bipolar Adjective Scale (Weights Assigned to Choices Are in Parentheses)

Essay questions

good	1	2	3	4	5	(6 circled)	7	bad
(positive)	(7)	(6)	(5)	(4)	(3)	(2)	(1)	
unpleasant	(1 circled)	2	3	4	5	6	7	pleasant
(negative)	(7)	(6)	(5)	(4)	(3)	(2)	(1)	
fair	1	2	3	4	5	(6 circled)	7	unfair
(positive)	(7)	(6)	(5)	(4)	(3)	(2)	(1)	
ugly	1	2	3	(4 circled)	5	6	7	beautiful
(negative)	(7)	(6)	(5)	(4)	(3)	(2)	(1)	

have $7 + 4 = 11$. Subtracting the left-negative sum from the left-positive sum, we have $4 - 11 = -7$. Dividing this score by the number of adjective pairs, we have $-7 \div 4 = -1.75$. Since -1.75 is less than zero, according to our rule these responses indicate a negative attitude toward essay questions.

MEASURING SOCIAL BEHAVIORS

Thus far we have discussed the use of observation and paper-and-pencil questionnaires to assess or make inferences about attitudes. At times, however, we are interested in the behaviors themselves rather than the attitudes they may represent. We may be interested in what a student does rather than why he or she does it. The use of structured observation lends itself well to the assessment of behaviors in such cases. However, just as unstructured observation is not recommended for attitudinal measurement, it also is not recommended for measuring social behaviors.

Although both teacher-made and standardized structured observation checklists have been used for many years, the typical classroom teacher often finds them too cumbersome and unwieldy for everyday use. What is a less cumbersome way for teachers to record student behavior? The answer is a compromise between the open-ended unstructured observation and the focused structured observation. We will refer to this compromise as the *anecdotal record.*

Anecdotal Records

Anecdotal records are sequential, usually brief reports that record a teacher's observation of a student's social behavior. Such records are kept both for the benefit of the present teacher—so that better understanding of a student may be attained—and for the benefit of future teachers—so that they will have a better understanding of the student. However, most of what school personnel call anecdotal records are *not* all that useful. In fact, most of what are called anecdotal records may better be called *pseudoanecdotal records*. Such records are often *not* sequential and are subjective, judgmental, and, too frequently, negatively phrased *opinions* about, rather than observations of, a student. The main difference between an anecdotal record and a pseudoanecdotal record is the presence or absence of statements referring to observed behaviors and the sequential or nonsequential character of the records. Consider the following examples:

Example of Anecdotal Record

Jack has really not applied himself all year. He seems to have adequate social skills but can't overcome his laziness. I really tried to motivate him this year, but he was uncooperative. I wish his next teacher luck.

Example of Anecdotal Record

September 14. Jack returned from lunch talking with Mark and Jay. After the bell rang, Mark and Jay stopped talking, but Jack continued asking them questions. I asked the class to take out their math books. Everyone did except Jack, who said he was "too tired for math." I ignored his comment and began the lesson. Jack had his book open and was participating in the lesson within two minutes from the time we started the lesson. This is the third time this week an incident similar to this has occurred.

September 17. Today, Jack returned after lunch by himself. After the bell rang he was among the first to take out math books and went directly to work.

September 18. Jack, Mark, and Jay returned from lunch together. Jack and Jay continued talking after the bell. I asked the class to take out their books and all did, except Jack who continued to ask Jay questions for about three minutes. He then said, "Math is a drag." No one in the class responded, and he opened his book and went to work.

What is the difference between the two examples? In the second example (anecdotal record), only observable behaviors are described. The teacher does not speculate about why Jack does what he does, but describes what Jack was doing. In the first example (pseudoanecdotal record), the teachers speculates about the causes of Jack's behavior ("laziness," "he is uncooperative") and fails to describe any of the behaviors that are presumed to be caused by his personality or character traits. We are not suggesting that such comments or speculations are always incorrect, but how can one be sure the teacher is right?

Human behavior is complex and often difficult to explain. More important, the causes of human behavior are probably multiple. Rather than get involved in trying to explain behavior and never knowing whether you are right, it seems far more profitable and realistic to stick to descriptions of behavior. If you limit your records to descriptions of *observable* behavior, you are reporting, not interpreting, human behavior. Psychiatrists and psychologists are the experts in interpreting human behavior, and even they frequently disagree about why someone does what he or she does. Rather than get involved in the business of interpretation, stick to reporting. If Johnnie walks into class five minutes late and throws his book on the floor, describe his behavior in your anecdotal record. Avoid speculating about the causes of his behavior.

"Well, then," you may ask, "why bother?" For a couple of reasons. First, when you document a sequential description of behaviors over several days, it becomes possible to notice behavior patterns—patterns that perhaps may be altered and result in a decrease in undesirable or disruptive behavior. Anecdotal records can make your classroom management tasks easier. In the second example, it became evident, thanks to the anecdotal records, that Jack's behavior after lunch was markedly different depending on whether he was engaged in conversation with Mark and Jay. When he was, his behavior after the bell was inappropriate. When he was *not,* his behavior was appropriate. As a result of this finding, you can develop a procedure to increase the likelihood of Jack engaging in appropriate behavior. The sequential descriptions of Jack's after-lunch behavior (anecdotal records) enabled you to identify a behavioral pattern that can be altered.

Wouldn't a teacher notice such a pattern simply by being aware? Perhaps. But writing about an incident and disciplining ourselves to describe only observable behavior are different from simply being aware. When we observe and try to synthesize everything we see happening, we can easily become overwhelmed by the amount of data we have access to (just like using an unstructured observation). As a result, we naturally limit the information we process. We risk making a decision on information that is too limited. And our memories are quite fallible. Trying to recall previous incidents over several days is difficult. Patterns fall victim to forgetting.

A second reason to keep a file of anecdotal records is to document your own and your student's responses to particular problems. Anecdotal records provide you with written, objective accounts of classroom incidents that you can refer to if needed. The following is a typical situation in which such documentation would be helpful:

> Mark has turned in less than 5 percent of his homework and in-school science assignments. You assign him a failing grade in science. His parents contact your principal and several school-board members, demanding that you be fired for not letting them know about the problem sooner. You have anecdotal records describing Mark's behavior and documenting the telephone calls you made to Mark's parents requesting a parent conference.

Another technique we employ to assess behavior is called a *sociogram.* This technique is used to measure social behavior and is discussed in the following section.

Measuring Social Interaction

Before we describe how to measure social interaction, consider the following interchange between Mr. and Mrs. White and their son's fifth-grade teacher, Mr. Kelley:

MR. WHITE: Thank you for taking time out to meet with us today.

MR. KELLEY: I'm pleased you both could make it.

MRS. WHITE: We're worried about our son Johnny. He just doesn't seem to have many friends around the house. We are afraid he is becoming a "loner." Is he like that at school?

MR. KELLEY: Uh . . . well . . . Johnny always does his work—he's never been a behavior problem.

MR. WHITE: We're happy to hear that, but what about socially? Does he have a friend or group of friends he pals around with?

MR. KELLEY: Oh, I've seen him talking with some of the other kids. He's never gotten in trouble, though!

MRS. WHITE: Please. We're worried about his social development. We know he is a good student and that he has good conduct. We can see that from his report card. What we want to know is how well he "fits in" socially. Can you tell us that?

MR. KELLEY: I'm a teacher, not a sociologist. I have twenty-eight other kids to worry about and so much paperwork you wouldn't believe it. All I know is that he's not a troublemaker and he gets good grades.

MRS. WHITE: But could we just get an idea of how Johnny is getting along with his classmates?

MR. KELLEY: If you want, come by during recess and lunch and watch. You're welcome to!

MR. WHITE: But couldn't you find out some other way? Is observation the only way to tell whether kids are developing socially?

MR. KELLEY: (*looking annoyed*) What else is there?

Is there no way other than through observation to obtain the information these parents wanted? While observation is one way to obtain information on social development or group behavior, a sociogram is another.

SOCIOGRAMS. A sociogram is one type of sociometric measure. *Sociometry* is the measurement of interaction patterns in groups. In the classroom, the following steps may be followed in developing a sociogram:

1. On a sheet of paper, ask each child to nominate two of his or her peers for a given activity (for example, "With whom would you like to play at recess?").
2. Construct a table to record "choosers" and "chosens," and record the choices on it. Such a table is illustrated in Table 11.1. In this table, choosers are listed vertically and their two choices are indicated by X's under the names of the students they chose (for example, Don chose Bob and Bill). By inspecting the row of totals, you discover the number of times each student was chosen—an index of popularity for the activity chosen.
3. Based on your table of choices, develop a sociogram, a graphical representation of the choice patterns in the group. A sociogram representing

TABLE 11.1
Table Illustrating First and Second Choices

		Chosen							
		Don	*Maria*	*Pat*	*Joan*	*Bob*	*Bill*	*Mary*	*Ted*
Choosers	Don					X	X		
	Maria			X	X				
	Pat		X					X	
	Joan			X				X	
	Bob	X					X		
	Bill	X				X			
	Mary		X		X				
	Ted		X					X	
Totals		2	3	2	2	2	2	3	0

the choice pattern from Table 11.1 is illustrated in Figure 11.10 on page 218. The sociogram is constructed by drawing arrows among the circles to indicate the direction of the choices.

4. Interpret the sociogram, which is done by inspecting the choice patterns and looking for cliques, cleavages, stars, mutual choices, and isolates. These terms are defined as follows:
   a. *Cliques*—Pupils select only each other and avoid selecting others in the group. In our example, Don, Bill, and Bob represent a clique.
   b. *Cleavage*—Two or more groups in the class fail to nominate each other. In our example there is a cleavage, a split between Don, Bill, and Bob, and Pat, Joan, Maria, Mary, and Ted.
   c. *Stars*—Pupils most frequently selected. In our example there is no single star. Instead, both Maria and Mary may be considered stars, since each was chosen three times.
   d. *Mutual choices*—Two individuals who select each other. Don and Bill, Don and Bob, Bob and Bill, Joan and Mary, and Pat and Maria all represent mutual choices.
   e. *Isolates*—Individuals not selected by any other pupil. In our example, Ted would be the isolate.

After the sociogram has been interpreted, decisions can be made about possible interventions. For example, steps may be taken to get Ted more involved in the class, or an effort may be made to weaken the clique or bridge the cleavage. Care should be taken in interpreting sociograms, however. While they do have certain advantages, they also have their limitations, and these should be kept in mind when using sociograms. Some of these are listed next.

FIGURE 11.10
Sociogram Representing Choice Pattern in Table 11.1

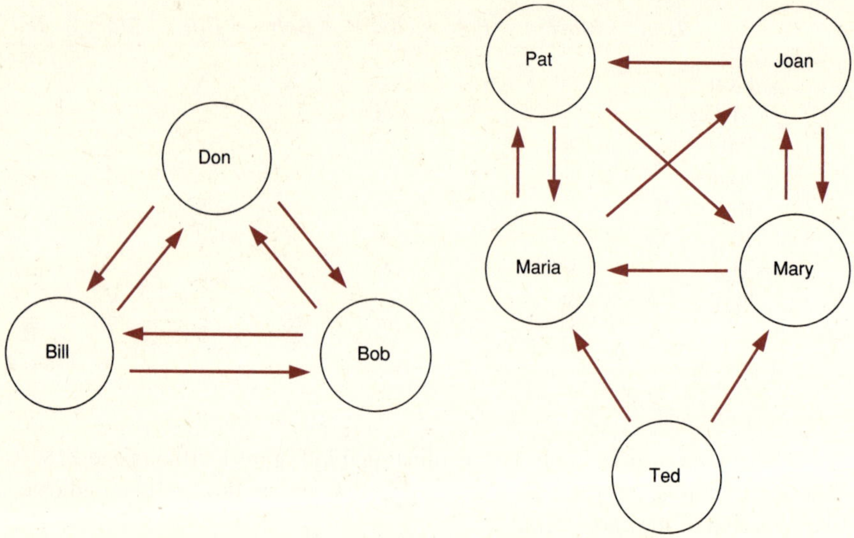

THE LIMITATIONS OF SOCIOGRAMS. Sociograms have their limitations as well, as listed below:

1. Only choices, not the reasons for the choices, are indicated.
2. Mutual choices and cliques do not necessarily indicate social acceptance or integration. For example, they may indicate common difficulties in being accepted or integrated into the class or some common advantage, depending on the situation. If the question "With whom would you like to sit during the math test?" were asked, the responses might indicate a hope to accidentally or intentionally "share" answers.
3. It is tempting to assume that isolates are actually rejected by the other pupils. Rather than being seen as undesirable, isolates may simply be new, shy, or not chosen for some other relatively minor reason. In general, however, isolates do tend to be less popular socially than nonisolates.
4. Popularity or isolation often depends on the situation. As mentioned before, choices may change depending on the kind of questions asked.
5. Finally, with a class of 25 to 30 pupils, a sociogram can be quite complicated and time-consuming to construct. In general, use of a sociogram at the beginning and end of the school year, with perhaps one more administration at midyear, is about the extent to which the average teacher can use this method of measurement.

While the techniques presented in this chapter will certainly not be used as frequently as teacher-made tests, they clearly have a role in the classroom to assess attitudes and social behavior. Use them to increase your understanding of your pupils and to further their development, and you will have moved a step closer to educating the whole child.

SUMMARY

Chapter 11 introduced you to a variety of teacher-made assessment instruments to measure attitudes, behaviors, and social interaction. Its major points are:

1. Attitudes are descriptions of how people typically feel about or react to other people, places, things, or ideas.
2. Attitudes are not directly measurable and are inferred from observable behaviors.
3. Attitudes are classified as positive or negative. Positive attitudes are inferred from approach behaviors—those that result in more frequent, closer, or more intense contact with the stimulus. Negative attitudes are inferred from avoidance behaviors—those that result in less frequent, more distant, or less intense contact with the stimulus.
4. Attitudes may be assessed through unstructured (open-ended) and structured (focused) observation. Structured observation is recommended.
5. The steps involved in conducting a structured observation are:
   a. Indicate why you are observing.
   b. Outline relevant behaviors.
   c. List behaviors, with those more likely to occur listed first.
   d. Decide how you will record your observations.
6. Attitudes may also be assessed with questionnaires: Likert scales, two-point scales, and bipolar adjective scales.
7. Likert scales consist of attitude statements to which respondents indicate the degree to which they agree or disagree with the statements, usually on a five-point scale.
8. Two-point scales are very similar to Likert scales, except that responses are made on a two-point scale. Respondents are "forced" to indicate their agreement or disagreement—they cannot take a neutral position as they could with a Likert scale.
9. Attitude statements should be short and written simply and clearly. They should avoid negatives (and especially double negatives), factual statements, reference to the past, absolutes, nondistinguishing statements, and irrelevancies. They should use *only, merely, just,* etc., sparingly. They should have one thought per statement, and equal numbers of positive and negative statements.

10. The steps involved in developing a Likert or two-point scale are:
    a. List the attitudinal area in question.
    b. List relevant behaviors.
    c. Write attitude statements to reflect these behaviors (what someone would say or do).
    d. Write several statements for each behavior.
    e. Edit your statements to avoid technical flaws.
11. The bipolar adjective scale consists of a stimulus word or phrase and a list of several pairs of adjectives with opposite meanings. The respondent circles numbers from 1 to 7 to indicate the degree to which each adjective pair best represents his or her attitudes.
12. Social behaviors may be measured through unstructured or structured observation and anecdotal records.
13. Anecdotal records are brief sequential reports of observations of a student's behavior, not presumed reasons for the student's behavior.
14. Social behavior or social interaction may be measured with a sociogram, a graphical representation of social patterns in a specific situation.
15. To develop a sociogram:
    a. Ask each child to nominate one or two of his or her peers.
    b. Tabulate choices.
    c. Graphically depict the choices.
    d. Interpret the choice patterns to identify cliques, cleavage, stars, mutual choices, and isolates.
16. Sociograms only indicate choice patterns, not the reasons for the choices.

For Practice

1. Make a list of observable approach and avoidance behaviors for a subject area you will be teaching. Arrange these in either a checklist or rating scale format.
2. Now develop a Likert scale for measuring student attitude in this same subject area.
3. Construct a bipolar adjective scale using ten bipolar adjectives of your own choosing. Try to make these adjectives as specific and meaningful as possible in regard to the attitude you are measuring.
4. Make up a sociometric table similar to Table 11.1 using fictitious names. Now randomly place X's throughout the table. Practice converting the resulting data into a sociogram similar to that shown in Figure 11.10. Identify stars, mutual choices, and isolates.
5. The principal of a certain junior high school schedules assemblies every Friday during the last period. For some time a few teachers have been telling him that

the assemblies are not well received by the students or faculty. The principal asks for evidence that their opinion is shared by others. Develop an observation checklist. List eight behaviors that you might observe from which you could infer something about the students' attitude toward assemblies. Include four approach and four avoidance behaviors.

*6. Compute this person's attitude score for the following scale measuring attitude toward your class.

a. I should have taken a different course.	SA	A	U	(D)	SD
b. I have a hard time keeping awake.	SA	A	U	(D)	SD
c. Class time should be lengthened.	SA	A	(U)	D	SD
d. I like writing objectives.	SA	(A)	U	D	SD
e. I daydream a lot in class.	SA	A	U	D	(SD)

*7. You are interested in determining attitudes toward utility companies, and you have generated the following list of behaviors that you feel will be helpful in assessing these attitudes. Classify these behaviors as either approach or avoidance behaviors by placing AP (for approach) or AV (for avoidance) in the blank to the left of the behavior.

_____ a. Complaining about rising utility bills

_____ b. Volunteering to work for the utility company

_____ c. Picketing the central office

_____ d. Painting the glass on your electric meter black

_____ e. Paying utility bills the same day you are billed

_____ f. Including a $5.00 tip with each electric payment

_____ g. Writing a letter to your congressperson, supporting utility rate hikes

_____ h. Defending utility companies in a debate

_____ i. Paying your utility bill in pennies

*8. The following statements were written as part of an attitude scale. In one sentence, explain what is wrong with each statement.

a. Mathematics in my school is fun to take, and my teacher teaches it well.
b. Classrooms in an open-education system often are without walls.
c. Last year I had some boring math assignments.
d. There is nothing I would rather do than make attitude scales.
e. I am often seized by an inexorable urge to engage in irrelevant rumination in math.

*Answers for questions 6, 7, and 8 appear in Appendix D.

CHAPTER 12

Summarizing Data and Measures of Central Tendency

For many, the term *statistics* forebodes evil. It is probably one of the most misunderstood terms in education. A statistician, or statistical expert, is stereotypically seen as a social isolate who lacks a sense of humor, speaks in strange tongues, and knows how to make numbers say whatever he or she desires them to say. Indeed, in some doctoral programs, courses in statistics are acceptable as substitutes for foreign languages! Having taught statistics courses, both authors are keenly aware of the anxiety and/or resentment many students feel when they are required or encouraged to take their first statistics course. As we mentioned in Chapter 1, however, fewer than 1 percent of the students we have taught fail courses in tests and measurement because of statistics. Then why are students so anxious about statistics?

The answer, we believe, lies in the misconceptions students have about statistics and statisticians. Let's clarify some things. We do not intend that you become full-fledged statisticians after completing this section of the text. In fact, a complete course of graduate study is usually necessary before one can call oneself a statistician. Perhaps you know students who suffered through an introductory statistics course. Will you have to undergo the trauma they may have undergone? Again, the answer is no. Even courses in introductory statistics treat this topic in much greater depth than is necessary for a course in tests and measurement. If you did well on the self-test and review in Appendix A, you have little to fear. If you failed to do well, brush up on the fundamentals presented in Appendix A until you do perform well. After you completed the review it should have been apparent that the four basic functions—addition, subtraction, multiplication, and division—will suffice for the statistics we will deal with. Master these operations, and with a little work (and an open mind), mastery of statistics at the tests and measurement level will soon follow.

WHAT ARE STATISTICS?

Thus far we have been talking about statistics in general. In reality, there are two types of statistics: descriptive and inferential. For our purposes we will deal entirely with the "easy" side of statistics, descriptive statistics. Inferential statistics are more complicated and are best taught in more advanced courses.

Descriptive statistics are simply numbers, for example, percentages, numerals, fractions, and decimals. These numbers are used to describe or summarize a larger body of numbers. For example, if you wanted to give someone an indication of how your grades have been in college, you could list all your courses and the grade you received in each course, or you could simply report your grade point average (GPA). Both approaches have advantages and disadvantages, of course, but we think you will agree that reporting your GPA would normally be the most useful approach. In this example, the GPA is a descriptive or summary statistic, since it describes or summarizes extensive data.

In the classroom the typical teacher has from 25 to 30 pupils. When a test is administered to the class, 25 to 30 test scores result. If a teacher gives ten tests over the year, 250 to 300 test scores result. Naturally, these scores would be recorded in the teacher's grade book, but when it comes time to report grades to parents at the end of the year, are they *all* reported? Obviously not. Instead, teachers report descriptive or summary statistics—that is, grades—probably without realizing they are reporting statistics!

Anytime you deal with averages (GPA, batting averages), rates (death rates, birthrates), or other numbers used to describe or summarize a larger body of numbers, you are dealing with descriptive or summary statistics. All of us deal with statistics daily. One of our goals for this chapter is to make you better users and consumers of such information. We hope to do this by going a little beyond commonsense statistics and looking at statistics and their uses more systematically.

WHY STATISTICS?

As we said, the term *statistics* is frequently misunderstood. Although some people want nothing to do with statistics, statistics are important and appear to be an increasingly important aspect of our personal as well as professional lives. Anytime you read, hear, or see "a 70 percent chance of rain" or "82 percent of doctors surveyed recommend" or "an EPA average of 32 miles per gallon," you are being exposed to statistics. Exposure to statistics will not go away. The ability to understand and profit from everyday statistics is well within your reach. You will become a better interpreter of educational data (and thus a better teacher) by mastering the statistical concepts presented in this section of the text. You will also become a better consumer of everyday data presented in advertising, public relations, opinion polls, and so forth. Much of what you learn in teacher training may seem to have little application outside the classroom. This is not the case for statistics. Master the concepts in this chapter and they will serve you throughout your personal and professional life.

With increasing calls for accountability, it will become all the more important that classroom teachers understand the statistics reported to them and the statistics they report to others. Needless to say, the teacher who understands the uses and limitations of various kinds of statistical data will have a decided advantage over the teacher who lacks such understanding. While your professional survival and development may not depend entirely upon a working knowledge of statistics, they may certainly be enhanced by it.

TABULATING FREQUENCY DATA

The classroom teacher normally deals with a large amount of data, usually in the form of test scores. As more and more scores accumulate, it gets more and more difficult to make sense of the data. It becomes more and more difficult to answer questions such as:

How many people are above average?

How many scored above the cut-off passing score?

Did most of the class do well on the test?

What is the highest or lowest score?

Keeping these questions in mind, consider the following set of scores obtained by 25 sixth-grade children on a math test:

36	63	51	43	93
54	48	84	36	45
57	45	48	96	66
54	72	81	30	27
45	51	47	63	88

Without doing anything to these test scores, are you able to answer the above questions? Naturally, you cannot answer the first two questions until you compute the average score and establish the cut-off or passing score. But what about the last two questions?

You can eventually answer these questions, but it takes a lot of time to do so. In arriving at answers to the last two questions, you probably resorted to some sort of strategy to organize the data so they make sense. For example, to determine whether "most of the class did well" you may have crossed off and counted the number of scores in the 80's and 90's.

Whatever the strategy you used, you used it because the 25 scores, as they stood, were difficult to make sense of or to interpret. Next, we will consider several systematic ways of making sense of an unwieldy group of numbers. We will be organizing or introducing some sort of order to unorganized, unordered test scores. The first method is to simply list the scores in ascending or descending numerical order.

The List

Let's list our set of 25 scores in descending order:

96	72	54	48	43
93	66	54	47	36
88	63	51	45	36
84	63	51	45	30
81	57	48	45	27

Introducing some order or "sense" into this group of scores makes trends, patterns, and individual scores easier to find and to interpret. At a glance we can now determine the highest score, lowest score, and even the middle score. We can easily see that only five students scored above 80 on the test. Thus, listing has helped us organize this set of scores. But what if we had 50 scores, or 100 scores, or 1,000 scores?

As the number of scores increases, the advantage of simply listing scores decreases. Many scores will repeat themselves several times. It becomes more and more difficult to make sense of data when the number of scores would require a lot of paper. Also, when you list data there are usually many missing scores (for example, 95, 94, 92, 91, 90, 89,

86, and so on, in the above example). Failure to consider these missing scores can sometimes result in a misrepresentation of the data.

To sum up, a simple list summarizes data conveniently if N, the number of scores, is small. If N is large, however, lists become difficult to interpret. Trends are not always very clear, numbers tend to repeat themselves, and there are usually a lot of missing scores. Next, we will consider *a simple frequency distribution*. This approach to tabulating data considers all scores, including those that are missing.

The Simple Frequency Distribution

Inspecting the simple frequency distribution in Table 12.1 may cause as much, or more, confusion as the original group of 25 unorganized scores. Usually, for classroom purposes, a simple frequency distribution is too unwieldy. Unless your tests yield a narrow spread of scores, simple frequency distributions tend to be so lengthy that it is difficult to make sense of the data, which is what we are trying to do. Seldom will a simple frequency distribution prove useful in the average classroom.

In summary, a simple frequency distribution will summarize data effectively *only* if the spread of scores is small. If there is a large amount of variation in test scores, a simple frequency distribution usually results in a table similar to Table 12.1, full of zeros in the frequency column and with so many categories that it becomes difficult to interpret the data. Fortunately, a variation of the simple frequency distribution, called the *grouped frequency distribution,* eliminates these shortcomings and can be quite useful in the classroom. Let's consider this variation.

The Grouped Frequency Distribution

The grouped frequency distribution method of tabulating data is very similar to the simple frequency distribution, except that ranges or intervals of scores are used for categories rather than considering each possible score as a category. The following is a grouped frequency distribution for the 25 scores we've been talking about:

Interval	*f*
91–97	2
84–90	2
77–83	1
70–76	1
63–69	3
56–62	1
49–55	4
42–48	7
35–41	2
28–34	1
21–27	1

Contrast this grouped frequency distribution with the simple frequency distribution and with the listing of scores. The grouped frequency distribution has two major advan-

TABLE 12.1
Simple Frequency Distribution

X (score)	*f (frequency)*	*X (score)*	*f (frequency)*
96	1	61	0
95	0	60	0
94	0	59	0
93	1	58	0
92	0	57	1
91	0	56	0
90	0	55	0
89	0	54	2
88	1	53	0
87	0	52	0
86	0	51	2
85	0	50	0
84	1	49	0
83	0	48	2
82	0	47	1
81	1	46	0
80	0	45	3
79	0	44	0
78	0	43	1
77	0	42	0
76	0	41	0
75	0	40	0
74	0	39	0
73	0	38	0
72	1	37	0
71	0	36	2
70	0	35	0
69	0	34	0
68	0	33	0
67	0	32	0
66	1	31	0
65	0	30	1
64	0	29	0
63	2	28	0
62	0	27	1

tages over the listing and the simple frequency distribution. It compresses the size of the table and makes the data much more interpretable. At a glance it becomes apparent that most of the class (as indicated by the numbers in the frequency column) obtained scores of 55 or below. If we add the numbers in the *f* column, we can see specifically that 15 (4 + 7 + 2 + 1 + 1 = 15) of the 25 students in the class scored 55 or below. That is, 4 students scored between 49 and 55, 7 scored between 42 and 48, 2 scored between 35 and 41, 1 scored between 28 and 34, and 1 scored between 21 and 27.

Since most of the class scored 55 or lower, one interpretation the grouped frequency distribution helps us make is that the test may have been too difficult. However, at least three other possible interpretations are suggested: Perhaps the students simply failed to prepare for the test; perhaps the students need more instruction in this area because they are "slower" than the teacher expected them to be; perhaps the instruction was ineffective or inappropriate.

Whichever of these interpretations is correct is irrelevant to us at the moment. What is important is that once we construct a grouped frequency distribution, it quickly becomes apparent that the class did not do well on the test. We may have arrived at the same conclusion after looking at the listing of scores or simple frequency distribution, but it certainly would take longer. Thus, a grouped frequency distribution does help us make sense of a set of scores. But there are also disadvantages to using a grouped frequency distribution.

The main disadvantage of a grouped frequency distribution is that information about individual scores is lost. As a result, the information we deal with becomes less accurate. Consider the interval of scores 49–55 in the previous grouped frequency distribution. We see that four scores fell in this interval. However, exactly what were these scores? Were they 49, 51, 53, and 55? Or were they 49, 50, 51, and 54? Or were all four scores 49? Or were two scores 52 and two scores 53? Or 51? The four scores could be any conceivable combination of scores. Without referring to the original list of scores, we cannot tell.

Thus, while a grouped frequency distribution compresses table size and makes data easier to interpret, it does so at the expense of accuracy and information about individual scores. Usually, the advantages of constructing grouped frequency distributions are great enough to offset the disadvantages. Next, we will consider the steps involved in actually constructing a grouped frequency distribution.

Steps in Constructing a Grouped Frequency Distribution

STEP 1. Determine the range of scores (symbolized by R). The range (or spread) of scores is determined by subtracting the lowest score (L) from the highest score (H).

Formula	***Application***
$R = H - L$	$R = H - L$
	$R = 96 - 27$
	$R = 69$

The range of scores for the 25 sixth-graders is 69.

STEP 2. Determine the appropriate number of intervals. The number of intervals or categories used in a grouped frequency distribution is somewhat flexible or arbitrary. Different authorities will suggest that you select from among 5, 10, or 15 intervals, or 8, 10, 12, or 15 intervals, and so on. In our example we used 11 intervals. Well, then, what is "correct"?

As we said, this decision is somewhat arbitrary. In making such decisions, though, be sure to *use as many categories or intervals as are necessary to demonstrate variations in the frequencies of scores.* In other words, if you decide to use 5 intervals and find that for an N of 25 scores there are frequencies of 5 in each interval, the number of intervals is too small. Increasing the number of intervals to 10 in this case should result in different frequencies for each interval. Selecting too many intervals is also a possibility. Generally, if you find more than one interval with zero in the frequency column you have decided on too many intervals. If this all sounds confusing, that's because in some ways it is. The bottom line is that sometimes it is necessary to experiment a little. You may have to vary the number of intervals until you find the number you feel best represents your data. Generally, it is best to begin with 8 or 10 intervals when constructing a grouped frequency distribution for a group of 25 to 30 scores, the typical number of scores resulting from a classroom test. Increase the number of intervals for larger score sets.

STEP 3. Divide the range by the number of intervals you decide to use and round to the nearest odd number. This will give you i, the interval width.

Formula	*Application*
$i = \dfrac{R}{\text{Number of intervals}}$	$i = \dfrac{69}{10}$
	$= 6.9$ (rounded to nearest odd number = 7)

The width of the interval is 7. If we decided to use 8 for our number of intervals we would arrive at a wider interval width, or *i*.

Formula	*Application*
$i = \dfrac{R}{\text{Number of intervals}}$	$i = \dfrac{69}{8}$
	$= 8.6$ (rounded to nearest odd number = 9)

If we decide to use 15 intervals, we would arrive at a narrower interval width than we would with 10 or 8 intervals.

Formula	*Application*
$i = \dfrac{R}{\text{Number of intervals}}$	$i = \dfrac{69}{15}$
	$= 4.6$ (rounded to nearest odd number = 5)

You can see there is an inverse relationship between the number of intervals and the width of each interval. That is, as fewer intervals are used, the width of each interval increases; as more intervals are used, the interval width decreases. Also, keep in mind that as *i*, the interval width, increases, we lose more and more information about individual scores.

STEP 4. Construct the interval column making sure that the lowest score in each interval, called the lower limit (LL), is a multiple of the interval width (*i*). The upper limit of each interval (UL) is one point less than the lower limit of the next interval. All this means is that the lowest score of each interval should be a value that is equal to the interval width times 1, 2, 3, etc. With an interval width of 7, the LL of each interval could be 7, 14, 21, etc. (7 × 1; 7 × 2; 7 × 3). However, we eliminate those intervals below and above the intervals that included or "capture" the lowest and highest scores. Consider the following sets of intervals for which the highest score was 96 and the lowest score was 27:

Lower limit	*Upper limit*	
112	118	
105	111	
98	104	
91	97	←Highest score captured; eliminated all intervals above.
84	90	
77	83	
70	76	
63	69	
56	62	
49	55	
42	48	
35	41	
28	34	
21	27	←Lowest score captured; eliminate all intervals below.
14	20	
7	13	

We retain only the intervals 21–27 through 91–97. Thus, the interval column of our grouped frequency distribution should look like this:

Intervals
91–97
84–90
77–83
70–76
63–69
56–62
49–55
42–48
35–41
28–34
21–27

STEP 5. Construct the *f*, or frequency, column by tallying the number of scores that are captured by each interval.

Intervals	*Tally*	*f*
91–97	ll	2
84–90	ll	2

Intervals	*Tally*	*f*
77–83	|	1
70–76	|	1
63–69	|||	3
56–62	|	1
49–55	||||	4
42–48	~~||||~~ ||	7
35–41	||	2
28–34	|	1
21–27	|	1

Next, simply eliminate the tally column and you have a grouped frequency distribution.

However, didn't we decide we wanted 10 intervals? How is it we ended up with 11? The answer to the first question is yes, but it is not unusual to end up with one more or one less interval than you intended. This happens because of what we often end up doing at step 3. We round to the nearest odd number. The inaccuracy we introduce by rounding to the nearest odd number is multiplied by the number of intervals (since in effect we do this for each interval). The result is that the range from the upper limit of the highest interval to the lower limit of the lowest interval is greater than the range from the highest score to the lowest score. In our example:

Upper limit of highest interval	97
Lower limit of lowest interval	−21
	76

High score	96
Low score	−27
	69

Notice the difference between 76 and 69. The extra interval is needed to include the extra values. Fortunately, ending up with one more or one less interval than we intended is not a serious problem. We need only be aware of it, not unduly concerned with it.

Before we leave grouped frequency distributions, let's clarify one more point. In step 3 we said "round to the nearest odd number." There is no sound mathematical reason for this recommendation. Rather, it is to simplify determining the midpoint of the interval. While the midpoint is of little importance for grouped frequency distributions, it is important in the construction of a *frequency polygon,* a graphical representation of a grouped frequency distribution, which we will consider next.

GRAPHING DATA

"A picture is worth a thousand words" is a well-worn expression, but especially applicable to statistics. Some of you may have the ability to extract meaning from groups of numbers, but others, the authors included, need to see graphical representations before such data can be meaningful. In any case, a graph will almost always clarify or simplify the information

FIGURE 12.1
Histogram Based on a Grouped Frequency Distribution

Intervals	*f*
91–97	2
84–90	2
77–83	1
70–76	1
63–69	3
56–62	1
49–55	4
42–48	7
35–41	2
28–34	1
21–27	1

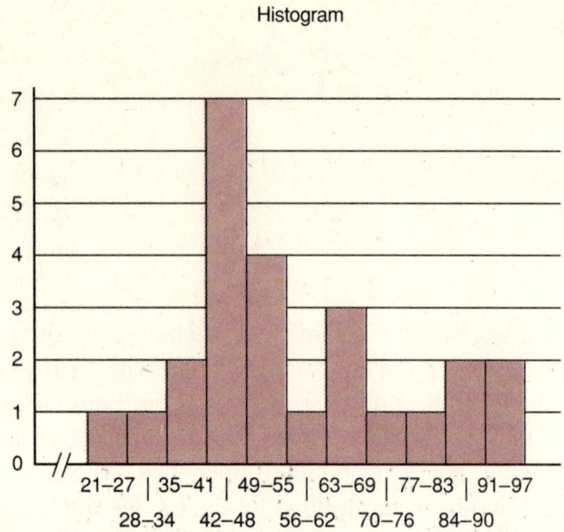

presented in a grouped frequency distribution. There are three types of graphs we will consider: the *bar graph,* or *histogram;* the *frequency polygon;* and the *smooth curve.*

The Bar Graph, or Histogram

The bar graph, or histogram, is the type of graph used most frequently to convey statistical data. The histogram in Figure 12.1 is based on the grouped frequency distribution used earlier to represent the scores of 25 sixth-graders.

In constructing a histogram, or bar graph, several guidelines should be followed, which are listed in Figure 12.2.

The interpretation of bar graphs is straightforward. The higher the column, the greater the number of scores falling in that interval. The lower the column, the fewer the number of scores falling in that interval.

The Frequency Polygon

Technically, a frequency polygon is best used for graphically representing what are called *continuous data,* such as test scores. Continuous data usually represent entities that can be expressed as fractions or parts of whole numbers, for example, achievement test scores and grade point averages. Histograms are best used for graphically representing *discrete* or *noncontinuous data.* Discrete or noncontinuous data represent entities that usually cannot be expressed as fractionated parts of anything and, hence, signify different dimensions, for example, Catholics, Protestants, and Jews. However, we need not be overly concerned with discriminating between continuous and discrete data, because much overlap exists in the actual ways these two types of graphs are used.

FIGURE 12.2
Guidelines for Constructing a Histogram

1. The vertical axis should be two-thirds to three-fourths as long as the horizontal axis to help prevent misrepresenting the data.

2. Scores are listed along the horizontal axis and increase from left to right. Frequencies are listed along the vertical axis and increase from bottom to top.

3. Double slash marks (//) are used to indicate breaks in the sequence of numbers (horizontal axis) or in the sequence of frequencies (vertical axis).

4. Points in the scales along the axes are expanded or compressed so that the range of scores and frequencies fit within the "two-thirds to three-fourths" guideline given above.

5. If an interval or intervals with frequencies of zero occur, these *must not* be omitted from the horizontal axis. To do so misrepresents the data. The following example illustrates this point:

Interval	*f*
50–59	10
40–49	5
30–39	0
20–29	5
10–19	0

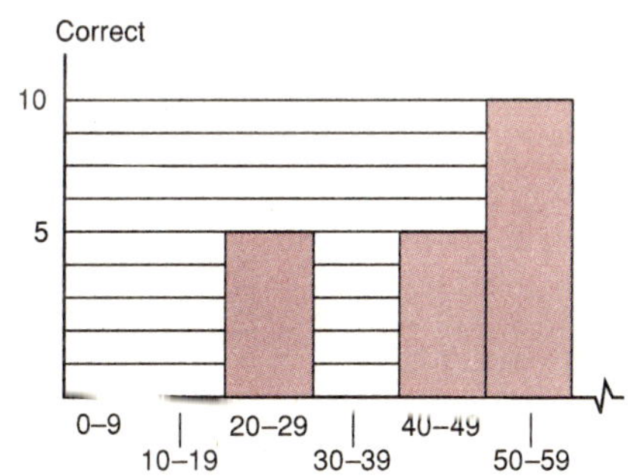

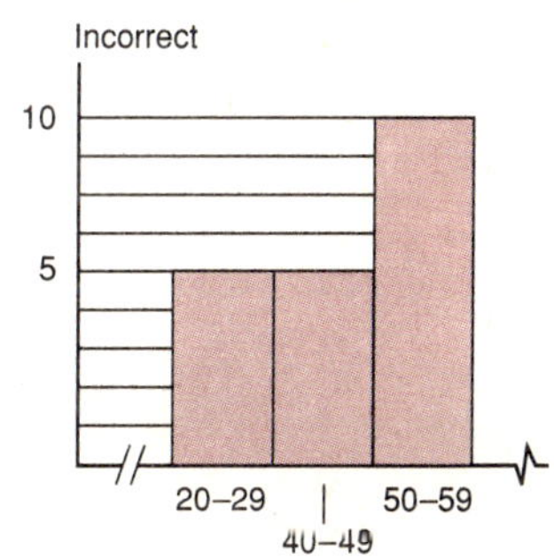

For our purposes, what is the critical difference between a histogram and a frequency polygon? The answer is that a frequency polygon is an alternative way of representing a grouped frequency distribution. It uses straight lines to connect the midpoint (MP) of each interval rather than bars or columns to show the frequency with which scores occur. The grouped frequency distribution with midpoints and the frequency polygon shown in Figure 12.3 represent the same group of scores we have been considering.

Interpretation of the frequency polygon is similar to that of the histogram. The higher or lower the dots, the greater or lesser the number of scores in the interval.

FIGURE 12.3
A Grouped Frequency Distribution and Frequency Polygon

Intervals	*MP*	*f*
91–97	94	2
84–90	87	2
77–83	80	1
70–76	73	1
63–69	66	3
56–62	59	1
49–55	52	4
42–48	45	7
35–41	38	2
28–34	31	1
21–27	24	1

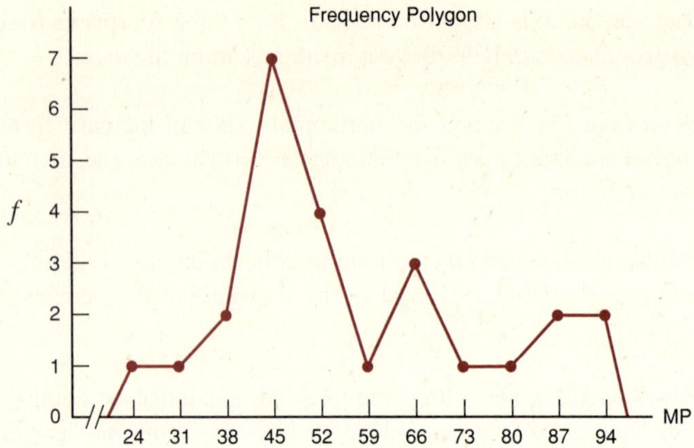

Comparing the frequency polygon with the histogram demonstrates the same pattern of scores. This is a perfectly logical finding, since they were both constructed from the same grouped frequency distribution, except that we add a midpoint column to construct a frequency polygon.

Determining the MP is straightforward and results in a whole number if the interval width is an odd number. Its determination results in a fractional number if the interval width is an even number. In either case, the midpoint is simply the middle score in each interval. If you mistrust your ability to determine the middle score in an interval, you can check yourself mathematically. Simply add the lower limit (lowest score in the interval) to the upper limit (highest score in the interval) and divide the sum of these two scores by 2.

Formula

$$MP = \frac{LL + UL}{2}$$

Application

Top interval

$$MP = \frac{91 + 97}{2} = \frac{188}{2} = 94$$

Second from top

$$MP = \frac{84 + 90}{2} = \frac{174}{2} = 87$$

Guidelines for constructing a frequency polygon appear in Figure 12.4. Notice that they are similar to those for histograms.

FIGURE 12.4
Guidelines for Constructing a Frequency Polygon

1. Construct the vertical axis two-thirds to three-fourths as long as the horizontal axis.

2. List scores along the horizontal axis, increasing from left to right, and list frequencies along the vertical axis, increasing from bottom to top.

3. Double slash marks (//) are used to indicate breaks in the sequence of numbers between scores and/or frequencies and zero points.

4. Points in the scales along the axes are expanded or compressed to fit the two-thirds to three-fourths guideline.

5. When intervals of zero frequency occur, the midpoints *must not* be omitted from the horizontal axis, and the lines connecting the dots must be brought down to the baseline to represent zero frequencies.

6. The lines should also be brought down to the baseline halfway into the intervals above and below the highest and lowest intervals, as noted in the diagram below:

Interval	*MP*	*f*
50–59	55	10
40–49	45	5
30–39	35	0
20–29	25	5

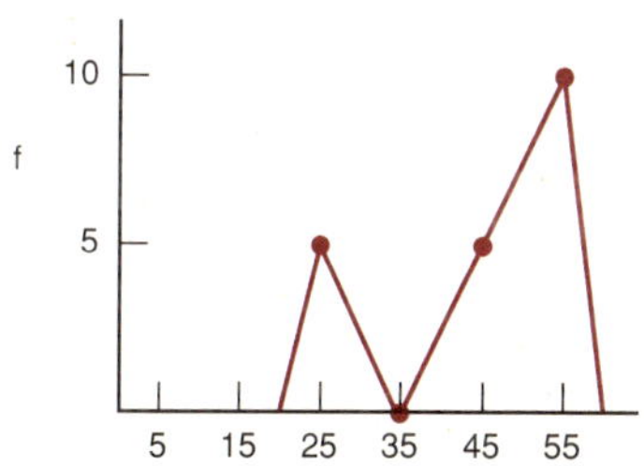

This guideline represents more of an aesthetic than a statistical consideration. A frequency polygon "tied" to the baseline has a better or more complete appearance, as shown below.

Incorrect
Frequency Polygon "Floating"

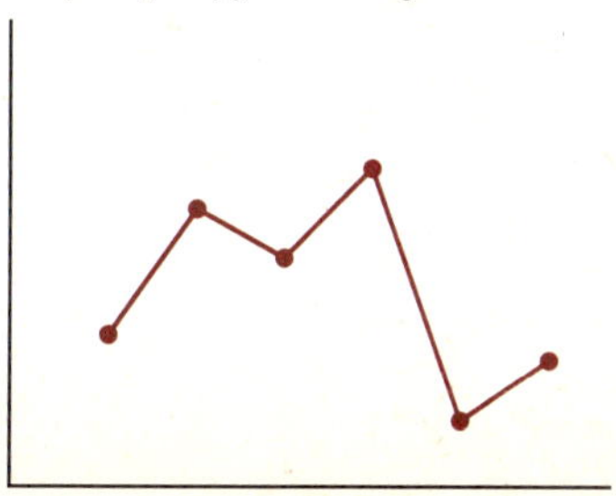

Correct
Frequency Polygon "Tied Down"

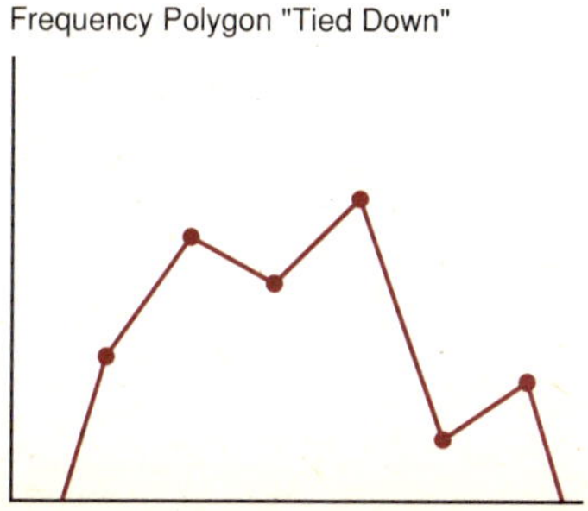

The Smooth Curve

Thus far we have discussed two graphical ways of depicting data represented by a grouped frequency distribution, the histogram and the frequency polygon. Our topic for this section, the *smooth,* or *smoothed,* curve, is not really an appropriate way to represent data from grouped frequency distributions, since an accurate smooth curve requires that advanced mathematical calculations be computed. Nevertheless, we will make great use of a smooth curve as a general representation of groups of scores. An example of a smooth curve is provided in the following graph:

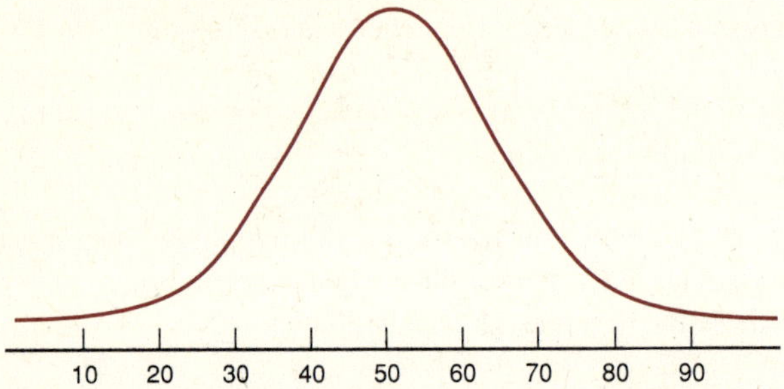

This curve represents a set of data. Note that it closely resembles a frequency polygon except that the *f,* or frequency, axis is omitted, and curved rather than straight lines are used. Although the *f* column is omitted, we can still make decisions about the frequency of occurrence of certain scores on the basis of the height of the curve. That is, scores in the 40–60 range were obtained by large numbers of students, while very few students obtained scores below 20 and/or above 80. With a histogram or frequency polygon we could determine *exactly* how many students scored between 40 and 60 or above 80 and/or below 20 by referring to the *f* axis. However, we are willing to sacrifice this accuracy when dealing with smooth curves because we use these curves to depict the *shape* of a distribution rather than to accurately represent the data.

Smooth curves can easily be developed from existing histograms or frequency polygons by connecting the high points of the bars or midpoints of the intervals, as shown in Figure 12.5.

Follow these two guidelines in constructing smooth curves:

1. Be sure your score axis increases from left to right.
2. Be sure the "tails" or ends of the curves come close to, but do not touch, the baseline.

Remember, although we use smooth curves to give us an idea of the shape of a distribution, they also enable us to make general statements about the frequency of scores. The higher the curve, the more frequently the same scores occur. The lower the curve, the less frequently the same scores occur. Next, let's consider two major characteristics of distributions: symmetry and skewness.

SYMMETRICAL AND ASYMMETRICAL DISTRIBUTIONS. There are two major types of distributions: symmetrical and asymmetrical. In a symmetrical distribution each half or

FIGURE 12.5
Smooth Curves

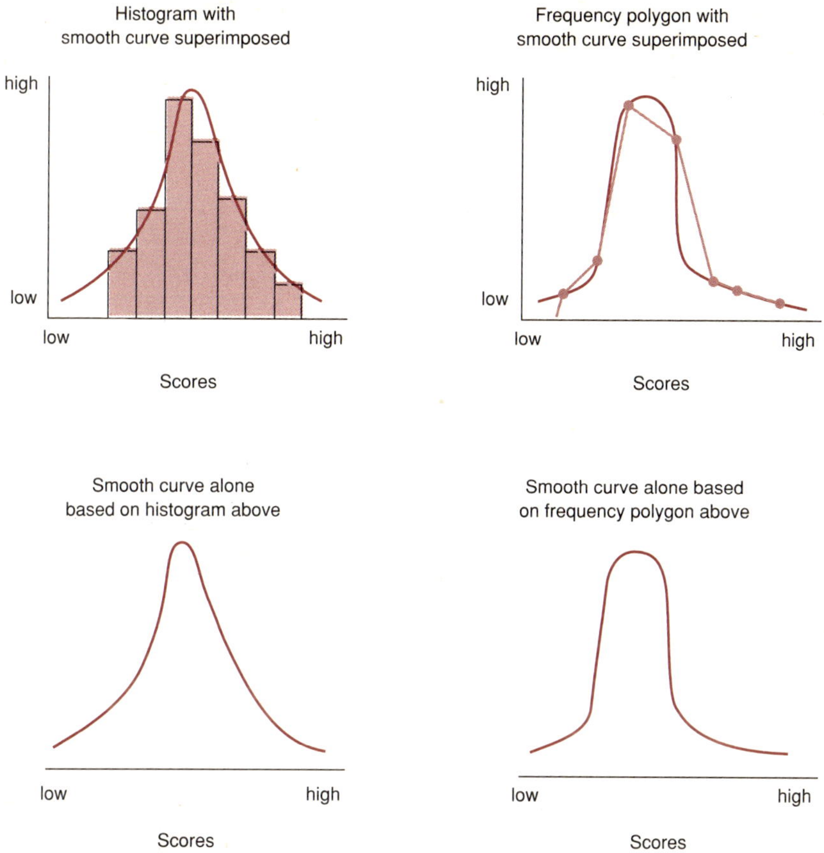

side of the distribution is a mirror image of the other side. An asymmetrical distribution, on the other hand, has nonmatching sides or halves. Both types of distributions are illustrated in the following graphs:

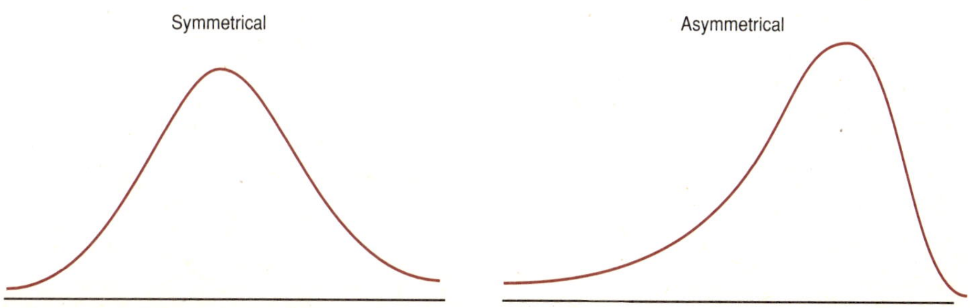

Symmetrical distributions can come in a variety of configurations. As illustrated, they may appear peaked, flattened, or somewhere in between:

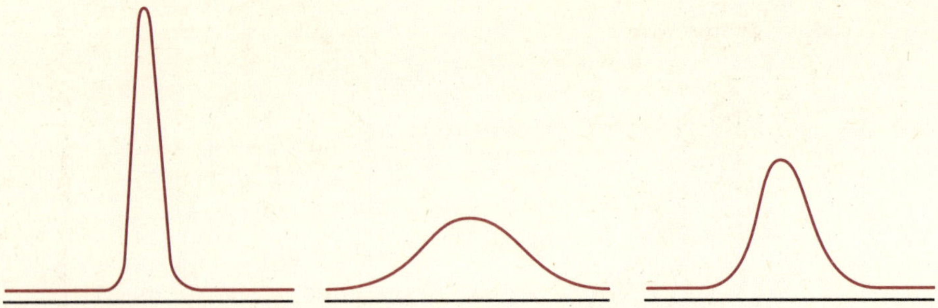

All three of these are symmetrical distributions. The distribution on the right, however, has special significance. It is a special kind of symmetrical distribution called a normal distribution. It has some unique characteristics that make it the most important distribution in statistics. Practice drawing this distribution. You will be called on to draw it many times before leaving this section of the book. Technically, the normal distribution follows very precise mathematical rules, but as long as you can approximate the illustration you need not worry about its precise mathematical properties. We will have more to say about the normal curve later.

POSITIVELY AND NEGATIVELY SKEWED DISTRIBUTIONS. There are also two types of skewness: positive skewness and negative skewness. A positively skewed distribution results from an asymmetrical distribution of scores. In this case, the majority of scores fall below the middle of the score distribution. There are many low scores, but few high scores. A positively skewed distribution is illustrated as follows:

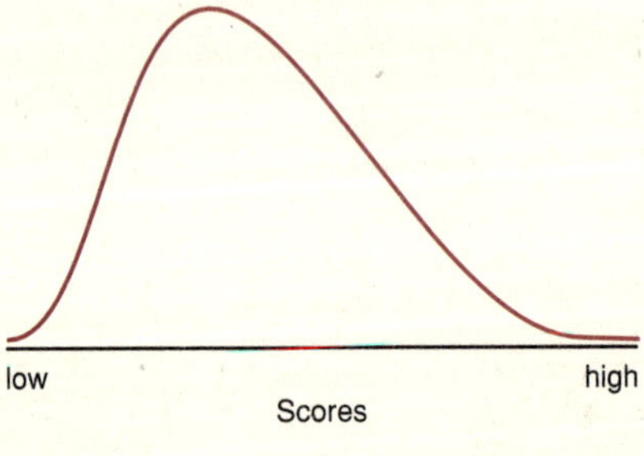

In a classroom testing situation a positively skewed distribution indicates the class did poorly on the test (a majority of low scores and few high scores). The reasons for such poor performance could include that the test was too difficult, teaching was ineffective, the students didn't study, or not enough time was allowed. A positively skewed distribution does *not* tell you why the class did poorly; it only informs you of the fact that they did.

A negatively skewed distribution also results from an asymmetrical score distribution. In this type of distribution the majority of scores fall *above* the middle of the score distribution. There are many high scores, but few low scores. A negatively skewed distribution is illustrated as follows:

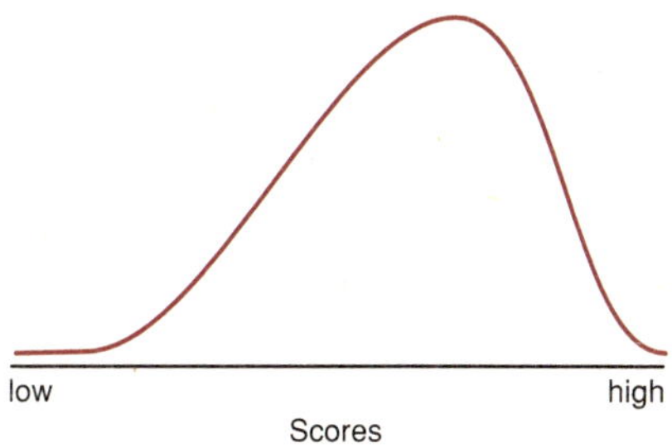

One interpretation attached to a negatively skewed distribution is that the class did well on the test (a majority had high scores and few had low scores). Again, there could be many reasons for this. The test may have been too easy, too much time may have been allowed, the class may be exceptionally bright, and so forth. Distributional shapes only describe data. They do not explain why the data take their shape.

We have discussed the what and why of statistics and have described methods for tabulating and depicting data. Next, we will discuss what are probably the most widely used (and frequently misunderstood) summary statistics, *measures of central tendency.*

MEASURES OF CENTRAL TENDENCY

There are three measures of central tendency: the mean, the median, and the mode. We will define each in turn, give an example or examples of its computation, and discuss its characteristics. The main point to remember about these measures is that they represent our best bet when we must rely on a single score to represent an entire distribution. Since we have three measures of central tendency, it may occur to you that each is more or less applicable in different situations. But before we go any further, test yourself to see if you are on top of the statistical jargon we have already presented. If you can define the terms listed in Figure 12.6, the Jargon Checklist, you are in good shape. If not, review these terms and commit them to memory to build your vocabulary and to prepare yourself to learn more terms later.

The Mean

Have you ever computed your grade average in elementary school, your GPA in college, your field-goal average in basketball, or any other average? The mean is nothing more than the average of a group of scores.

$$\text{Average} = \text{Mean}$$

FIGURE 12.6
Jargon Checklist

Statistics	Frequency (f)
List	Midpoint (MP)
Simple frequency distribution	Histogram
Grouped frequency distribution	Frequency polygon
N	Smooth curve
Range (R)	Symmetrical distribution
Interval (i)	Normal distribution
Lower limit (LL)	Positively skewed distribution
Upper limit (UL)	Negatively skewed distribution

The symbol we will use for the mean is $\overline{X}$ (pronounced "X bar"). Some texts use M rather than $\overline{X}$ to symbolize the average or mean score, but most use $\overline{X}$, and so will we. Just in case you have forgotten how, we will compute a mean (our sneaky way of introducing a formula with a couple of other unfamiliar symbols). The formula and its plain English interpretation appear here:

Formula	***Plain English version***
$\overline{X} = \dfrac{\Sigma X}{N}$	$\text{Average} = \dfrac{\text{Sum of all the scores}}{\text{Total number of scores}}$

The formula looks impressive. But as you can see, it (like all mathematical formulas) is only a shorthand way of describing the process you go through to compute an average. Let's have a closer look at the terms in the formula:

$\overline{X}$	Symbol for the mean or arithmetic average
Σ	Sigma symbol used in mathematics that tells you to sum up whatever follows it
X	Symbol we will use from now on to represent a test score
N	Total number of scores in a distribution

Thus, ΣX tells you to sum up the test scores, and $\Sigma X/N$ tells you to sum up the test scores and divide this value by the total number of scores in the distribution. Let's work an example for the following set of scores: 90, 105, 95, 100, and 110.

Example	*Application*
$\overline{X} = \frac{\Sigma X}{N}$	$\overline{X} = \frac{\Sigma X}{N}$

$$\overline{X} = \frac{90 + 105 + 95 + 100 + 110}{5}$$

$$\overline{X} = \frac{500}{5}$$

$$\overline{X} = 100$$

The mean has several characteristics that make it the measure of central tendency most frequently used. One of these characteristics is stability. Since each score in the distribution enters into the computation of the mean, it is more stable over time than other measures of central tendency, which consider only one or two scores.

Another characteristic is that the sum of each score's distance from the mean is equal to zero. Presently, this is probably quite meaningless to you. However, it is a key concept in more advanced statistical operations. We will discuss this characteristic and its importance shortly.

A third characteristic of the mean is that it is affected by extreme scores. This means that a few very high scores in a distribution composed primarily of low scores (a positively skewed distribution) or a few very low scores in a distribution composed primarily of high scores (a negatively skewed distribution) will "pull" the value of the mean down or up toward the extreme score or scores. Table 12.2 illustrates this point. Since the mean is affected by extreme scores, it is usually not the measure of choice when dealing with skewed distributions. In such cases a measure that is more resistant to extreme scores is required. Our next topic for discussion, the median, represents such a measure.

The Median

The median is the second most frequently encountered measure of central tendency. The median is the score that splits a distribution in half: 50 percent of the scores lie above the median, and 50 percent of the scores lie below the median. Thus, the median (abbreviated MDN) is also known as the fiftieth percentile. You may also think of the median as the middle score, since it falls in the middle of the distribution of scores.

For classroom purposes the methods used to determine the median are simple. When the score distribution contains an odd number of scores, the median is the score that has equal numbers of scores above and below it. The following example describes the steps involved in determining the median when N, the total number of scores in the distribution, is odd.

TABLE 12.2
The Effect of Extreme Scores on the Mean

Original Set of Scores	*Add an Extremely Low Score*	*Add an Extremely High Score*
90	90	90
105	105	105
95	95	95
100	100	100
+110	110	110
$\Sigma X=500$	**+20**	**+200**
	$\Sigma X=520$	$\Sigma X=700$
$\bar{X}=\frac{\Sigma X}{N}$	$\bar{X}=\frac{\Sigma X}{N}$	$\bar{X}=\frac{\Sigma X}{N}$
$\bar{X}=\frac{500}{5}$	$\bar{X}=\frac{520}{6}$	$\bar{X}=\frac{700}{6}$
$\bar{X}=100$	$\bar{X}=86.67$	$\bar{X}=116.67$

EXAMPLE: Determine the median for the following set of scores: 90, 105, 95, 100, and 110.

Steps:

1. Arrange the scores in ascending or descending numerical order (don't just take the middle score from the original distribution).
2. Circle the score that has equal numbers of scores above and below it; this score is the median.

Application:

110
105
(100) = MDN
95
90

When N is even, the procedure is only a bit more complicated. In this case, select the *two* scores in the middle that have equal numbers of scores above and below them. Taking the average of these two scores will give you the median. These steps are illustrated in the following example.

EXAMPLE: Determine the median for the following set of scores: 90, 105, 95, 100, 110, and 95.

Steps:

1. Arrange the scores in numerical order.
2. Circle the *two* middle scores that have equal numbers of scores above and below them.
3. Compute the average of these two scores to determine the median.

Application:

110
105
(100
95) 2 middle scores $\frac{95 + 100}{2} = \frac{195}{2} = 97.5 = \text{MDN}$
95
90

Notice that step 1 is the same regardless of N. *Always* arrange your data in numerical order before determining the median. Next, let's consider one more example of determining the MDN when N is even.

EXAMPLE: Determine the median for the following set of scores: 90, 105, 95, 100, 110, and 100.

Steps:

1. Arrange the scores in numerical order.
2. Circle the *two* middle scores that have equal numbers of scores above and below them.
3. Compute the average of these two scores to determine the median.

Application:

110
(105
100) 2 middle scores $\frac{100 + 100}{2} = \frac{200}{2} = 100 = \text{MDN}$
100
95
90

In this case the median is a whole number and the same value as the two middle scores, a common occurrence. These methods are useful for classroom purposes, although more complex computational methods also exist.

The main characteristic of the median is that it is not affected by extreme scores. This is because only the middle or two middle scores are considered in determining the median. Let's consider the following examples:

Original set of scores	*Substitute an extremely high score*	*Substitute an extremely low score*
X	X	X
110	**600**	110
105	105	105
(100)	(100)	(100)
(100)	(100)	(100)
95	95	90
90	90	**5**
$MDN = \frac{100 + 100}{2}$	$MDN = \frac{100 + 100}{2}$	$MDN = \frac{100 + 100}{2}$
$= 100$	$= 100$	$= 100$

Since the median is not affected by extreme scores, it represents central tendency better than the mean when distributions are skewed. In skewed distributions the mean is "pulled" toward the extremes, so that in some cases it may give a falsely high or falsely low estimate of central tendency. Since the median, on the other hand, is the score above and below which half the scores lie, it always indicates the center of the distribution, as illustrated by the following diagrams:

Positively skewed distribution

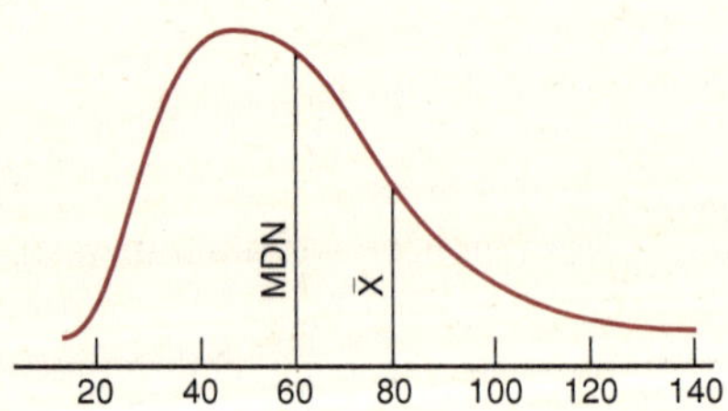

Negatively skewed distribution

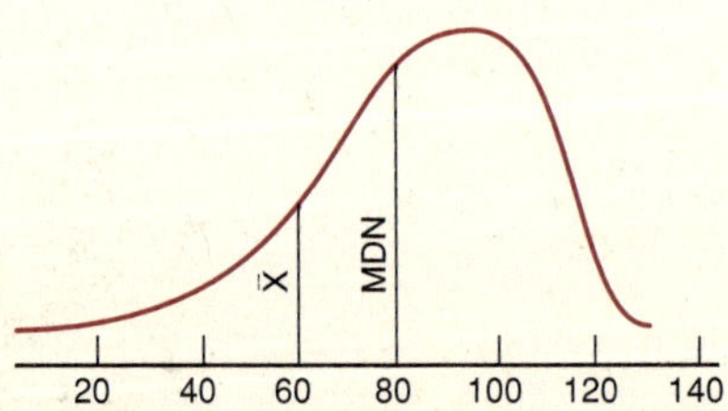

In the positively skewed distribution the few scores of 100 or above pull the $\overline{X}$ toward them. The mean presents the impression that the typical student scored about 80 and passed the test. However, the MDN shows that fully 50 percent of the students scored 60 or below. In other words, not only did the typical students fail the test (if we consider the middle student typical), but the *majority* of students *failed* the test.

In the negatively skewed distribution the few scores of 40 or below pull the mean down toward them. Thus, the mean score gives the impression that the typical student scored about 60 and failed the test. Again, the median contradicts this interpretation. It shows that fully 50 percent of the students scored 80 or above on the test and that actually the *majority* of students *passed* the test.

As you can see, it is important that the median be considered when skewed distributions are involved. Too often, however, only the average or mean is reported when statistics are presented, without regard for the shape of the distribution.

PERCENTILE. Now that we have introduced the idea of the median as the fiftieth percentile, it is only a small step to finding out how to determine the score that represents any desired percentile in a frequency distribution. Although a percentile is not considered a measure of central tendency unless it is the fiftieth percentile, the calculation of other percentiles is very similar to that of the median. A percentile is a score below which a certain percentage of the scores lie. In the case of the median, we saw that 50 percent of the cases were lower (and higher) than the median. Percentiles divide a frequency distribution into 100 equal parts. Percentiles are symbolized $P_1, P_2, \ldots, P_{99}$. P_1 represents that score in a frequency distribution below which 1 percent of the scores lie. P_2 represents that score in a frequency distribution below which 2 percent of the scores lie. P_{99} represents that score in a frequency distribution below which 99 percent of the scores lie. A score can be calculated for each percentile from P_1 to P_{99} in a manner similar to the way the median—or fiftieth percentile—was calculated for a distribution with an even number of scores. That is:

1. Arrange the scores in numerical order.
2. Counting up from the bottom, find the point below which the desired percentage of scores falls.
3. Circle the two scores that surround this point.
4. The average of this pair of scores will be the percentile of interest.

For example, for the following data, P_{25} would be determined in the following manner:

115
110
110
110
105
100
100
95
95
$P_{25} \ldots$ (95, 90 circled) $\frac{95 + 90}{2} = 92.5$
90
90
85

Finally, we will consider the last of the measures of central tendency—the mode.

The Mode

The mode is the least reported measure of central tendency. The *mode,* or *modal score,* in a distribution is the score that occurs most frequently. However, a distribution may have one score that occurs most frequently (unimodal), two scores that occur with equal frequency and more frequently than any other scores (bimodal), or three or more scores that occur with equal frequency and more frequently than any other scores (multimodal). If *each* score in a distribution occurs with equal frequency, the distribution is called a rectangular distribution, and it has *no mode.*

The mode is determined by tallying up the number of times each score occurs in a distribution and selecting the score that occurs most frequently. The following examples are illustrative:

EXAMPLE: What is the mode of this score distribution: 90, 105, 95, 100, and 100?

X	*Tally*	
105	I	
100	II	Mode = 100
95	I	This is a unimodal distribution.
90	I	

EXAMPLE: What is the mode for this set of scores: 90, 110, 95, 100, 110, 90, 105, 100, 110, and 95?

X	*Tally*	
110	III	
105	I	
100	II	Mode = 110
95	II	This is a unimodal distribution.
90	II	

EXAMPLE: What is the mode for this set of scores: 6, 9, 1, 3, 4, 6, and 9?

X	*Tally*	
9	II	
6	II	
4	I	Modes = 6 and 9
3	I	This is a bimodal distribution.
1	I	

The mode has the advantage of being easy to determine. If you know how to count you can determine a mode! However, it is the least used of the measures of central tendency because of a serious shortcoming. The mode is the least stable measure of central tendency. A few scores can influence the mode considerably. Consider the following:

Original set of scores

X	*Tally*
105	I
100	II
95	I
90	I

Mode = 100

Add a few scores (e.g., 90, 70, 70, 70, and 90)

X	*Tally*
105	I
100	II
95	I
90	III
70	III

Modes = 70 and 90

Because of this unfortunate characteristic, the mode usually is not used as the only measure of central tendency. An exceptional case, however, is the normal distribution because in a normal distribution all three measures of central tendency have the same value.

The Measures of Central Tendency in Various Distributions

As was mentioned, the mean, median, and mode all have the same value in a normal distribution, which is illustrated here:

$\overline{X}$ = 40
MDN = 40
Mode = 40

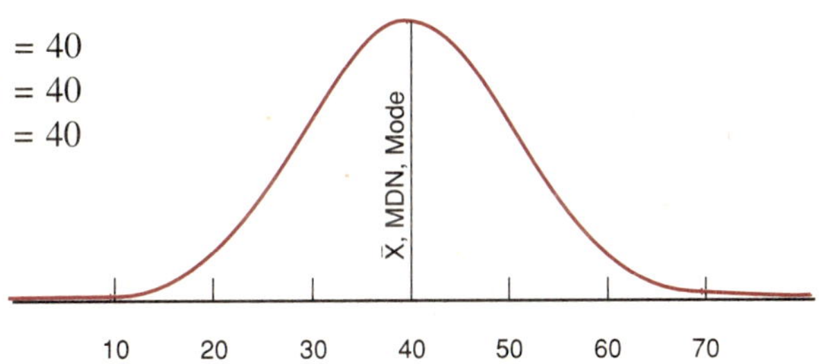

In a positively skewed distribution, the mean ($\overline{X}$) usually has the highest value of all the measures of central tendency, the mode the lowest, and the median the middle or intermediate value.

$\overline{X}$ = 40
MDN = 35
Mode = 30

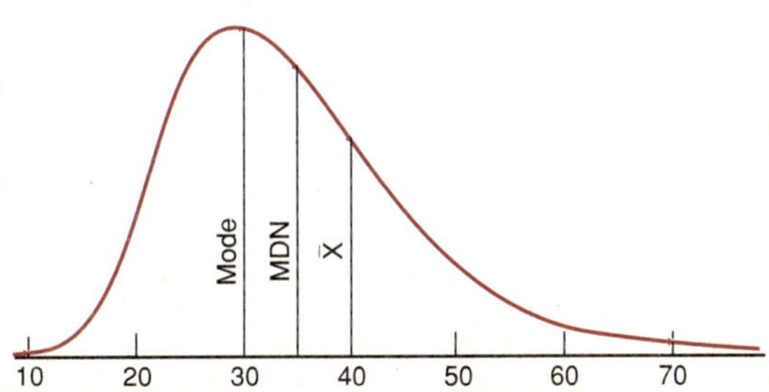

Just the opposite occurs in a negatively skewed distribution. In a negatively skewed distribution, the mean usually has the lowest value, the mode the highest, and the median the middle or intermediate value.

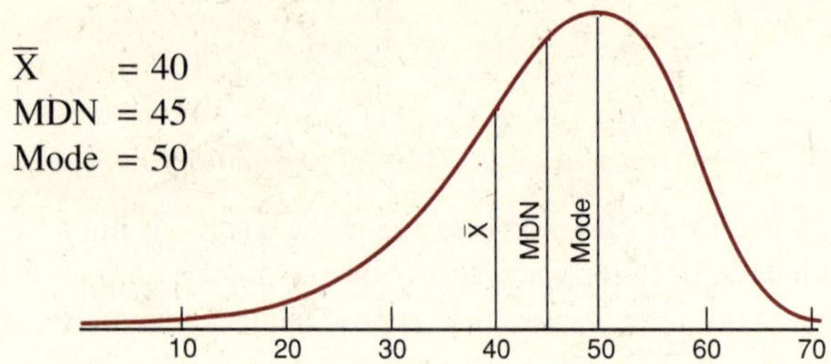

Knowing the relationships of the measures of central tendency to these distributions enables you to place these measures in their appropriate position when a distribution's shape is known. The opposite is also true. Knowing the values of the measures of central tendency enables you to determine the shape of the distribution. For example, if the $\overline{X}=47$, MDN = 54, and mode = 59, what is the shape of the distribution? You know it is not normal (since the values are different). But, before you *guess* at whether it's positively or negatively skewed, take the uncertainty or guesswork out of the question. How? The answer to this and many other questions concerning statistical principles is to draw a picture.

EXAMPLE: What is the shape of a distribution with a mean of 47, median of 54, and mode of 59?

Steps:

1. Examine the relationship among the three measures of central tendency.
2. Draw a picture (baseline first); then mark the measures of central tendency in the appropriate spaces. Draw in the curve. Remember the high point of the curve is the mode.
3. Answer: negatively skewed.

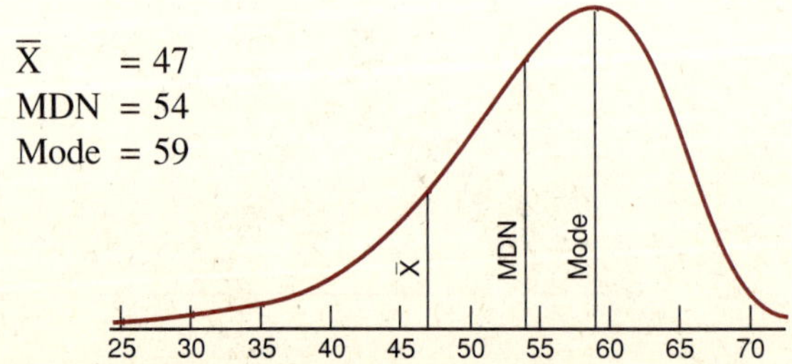

Application:

We've been discussing estimates of one important aspect of a distribution. Estimates of central tendency represent good bets about the single value that best describes a distribution. But some good bets are better than others. In the next chapter we will consider statistics that indicate how adequate our good bets really are. These are estimates of variability.

SUMMARY

This chapter introduced you to various methods of tabulating and graphing data and to the measures of central tendency. Its major points are:

1. Descriptive statistics are numbers used to describe or summarize a larger body of numbers.
2. Data are tabulated to introduce some order to the data and make them more interpretable. Three methods of tabulating data are listing, simple frequency distributions, and grouped frequency distributions.
3. While each method has its advantages and disadvantages, the grouped frequency distribution is usually most appropriate for classroom use.
4. The following steps are followed in constructing a grouped frequency distribution:
    a. Determine the range.
    b. Determine the number of intervals.
    c. Divide the range by the number of intervals and round to the nearest odd number to get the interval width (i).
    d. Develop the interval column, being sure the lower limit of each interval is a multiple of i.
    e. Tally the scores in each interval to get f, the frequency column.
5. Data from grouped frequency distributions may be graphically represented by histograms or frequency polygons.
6. Histograms, or bar graphs, use columns of varying height to represent the frequencies in each interval.
7. Frequency polygons use straight lines to connect the midpoints of each interval, which vary in height depending on the frequency of scores in the interval.
8. The following general guidelines apply to the construction of both histograms and frequency polygons:
    a. Make sure the vertical axis is two-thirds to three-quarters as long as the horizontal axis.
    b. List scores along the horizontal axis, frequencies along the vertical axis.

c. Use double slash marks (//) to indicate breaks in any number sequences.

d. Do *not* omit intervals with frequencies of zero.

9. A smooth curve is usually drawn to represent a distribution's shape, although decisions about frequency of occurrence of scores or scores in intervals can be made by looking at the height of the curve. The *f* axis is omitted in a smooth curve.
10. In a symmetrical distribution, each half or side of the distribution is a mirror image of the other, unlike in an asymmetrical distribution.
11. A normal distribution is a special type of symmetrical distribution.
12. An asymmetrical distribution in which most scores are low is called a positively skewed distribution. The tail in such a distribution is toward the high scores.
13. An asymmetrical distribution in which most scores are high is called a negatively skewed distribution. The tail in such a distribution is toward the low scores.
14. One of the measures of central tendency (mean, median, and mode) is used to represent a distribution when a single value must be used. Such a measure is our "best bet" about the overall distribution.
15. The mean, or the arithmetic average, of a set of scores is determined by summing all the scores and dividing by the number of scores.
16. The mean has several important characteristics. Of the measures of central tendency it is the most stable, the sum of the deviations of each score from the mean always equals zero, and it is affected by extreme scores.
17. Since the mean is affected by extreme scores, it is not the measure of central tendency of choice for skewed distributions.
18. The median is the score that splits a distribution in half. It is also known as the middle score, or the fiftieth percentile.
19. The median is determined by finding the score or value that has equal numbers of scores above or below it.
20. The most important characteristic of the median is that it is not affected by extreme scores. Thus, it is the measure of central tendency of choice in a skewed distribution.
21. The mode is the score in a distribution that occurs most frequently.
22. The mode is determined by counting the number of times scores occur and selecting the score(s) that occur(s) most frequently. A distribution may have more than one mode.
23. The major characteristic of the mode is its instability. Seldom is the mode, by itself, acceptable as a measure of central tendency.
24. In a normal distribution, the mean, median, and mode have the same value.

25. In a positively skewed distribution, the mean has the highest and the mode the lowest value of the measures of central tendency. The median has an intermediate value.

26. In a negatively skewed distribution, the mean has the lowest value and the mode the highest value of the measures of central tendency. Again, the median has an intermediate value.

For Practice

*1. An achievement test designed to measure the level of arithmetic achievement among students in the middle of the third grade is administered to three classes of equal size: one first-grade class, one third-grade class, and one fifth-grade class. The test is administered in the middle of the school year. Other things being equal, what sort of distribution would you predict for each of the three classes? Sketch a distribution of the shape you would expect for each grade. On each of your three sketches, indicate the probable location of the three measures of central tendency.

*2. Mr. Martin's best reading group obtained the following scores on an achievement test:
85, 90, 90, 92, 94, 94, 96, 97, 97, 98

Mr. Scott's best reading group obtained the following scores on the same achievement test:
61, 85, 90, 90, 92, 93, 94, 97, 97, 97

For each group, determine the following:

a. N =

b. R =

c. X

d. MDN =

e. Mode =

f. Why is there so much difference in means?

g. Which measure of central tendency should be used to compare these distributions?

*3. For the following group of 30 scores, construct three grouped frequency distributions with different numbers of intervals. Graph your data, using both a histogram and a frequency polygon. Decide which frequency distribution best represents the data.
60, 60, 63, 68, 70, 72, 75, 75, 75, 76, 76, 77, 78, 80, 83, 83, 84, 88, 93, 93, 93, 94, 94, 94, 94, 95, 97, 98, 100, 100

*4. Match the terms in column B with the characteristics listed in column A. The options from column B may be used more than once.

	Column A	*Column B*
_____	1. Least stable measure of central tendency	a. Mean
_____	2. More than one possible in same distribution	b. Median
_____	3. Most influenced by extreme scores	c. Mode
_____	4. Also known as the fiftieth percentile	
_____	5. Measure of choice in skewed distributions	

*5. Find P_{25} and P_{50} in the following distribution of scores:
115, 112, 110, 108, 106, 104, 100, 100, 98, 96, 96, 94, 93, 91, 90, 88

*6. Indicate the type of distribution to which each of these sets of data refer:

a.	b.	c.
$\overline{X} = 78.37$	$\overline{X} = 374.3$	$\overline{X} = 109.5$
MDN = 78.37	MDN = 379.7	MDN = 107.4
Mode = 78.37	Mode = 391.3	Mode = 107.4

*7. For the following sets of data, which method of tabulating data would be most appropriate? Why?

a. 70, 70, 70, 71, 72, 72, 73, 73, 73, 73, 74

b. 39, 47, 67, 51, 92, 60, 75

c. 35, 88, 85, 45, 49, 52, 69, 71, 49, 50, 90, 72, 79, 36, 43, 52, 92, 81, 80, 47, 55, 60, 72, 94, 91, 53, 48, 72

---

*Answers for these questions appear in Appendix D.

CHAPTER 13

Variability, the Normal Distribution, and Converted Scores

In Chapter 12 we learned that measures of central tendency can be used to describe a distribution. However, an estimate of the variability, or spread, of scores is needed before we can compare scores within and between distributions. For example, suppose we have the following data: $\overline{X} = 160$, MDN = 170, Mode = 180. After drawing a curve, we know that the distribution is negatively skewed. What we don't know is how spread out, dispersed, or variable the scores are. For this we would at least need to know the range of obtained scores. Were all the scores between 100 and 200? 50 and 250? 150 and 190? Without an estimate of variability, we don't know which of the following three negatively skewed distributions best fits the data:

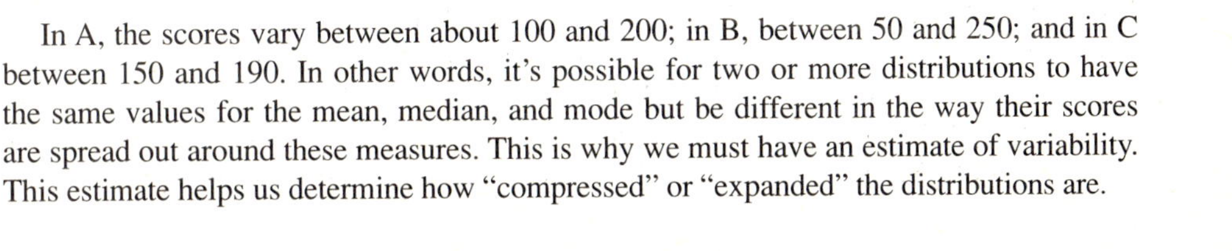

In A, the scores vary between about 100 and 200; in B, between 50 and 250; and in C between 150 and 190. In other words, it's possible for two or more distributions to have the same values for the mean, median, and mode but be different in the way their scores are spread out around these measures. This is why we must have an estimate of variability. This estimate helps us determine how "compressed" or "expanded" the distributions are.

THE RANGE

The easiest estimate of variability to compute is one we've already been exposed to: the range (R). The range is determined by subtracting the lowest score from the highest score.* This is what you did as the first step in constructing a grouped frequency

---

*Sometimes the range is defined as the lowest score subtracted from the highest score plus 1. This is called the *inclusive range*. It is the statistic most often referred to in introductory statistics texts and is based upon mathematical concepts that need not concern us here.

distribution. Ease of computation does not offset the major drawbacks of the range as an estimate of variability, however. Since the range is dependent only on the low and high scores, it is often unstable and is useful only for gross ballpark estimates of variability. If an extreme score is present, R can be very misleading. Consider the following example:

DIRECTIONS: Compute the range for the following set of data: 11, 11, 11, 11, 12, 12, 13, 14, 14, 14, 15, 15, 15, 15, 16, 17, 18, 18, 18.

$$R = H - L$$
$$R = 18 - 11$$
$$R = 7$$

Now substitute one extreme score, 96, for one of the scores of 18 and compute the range: 11, 11, 11, 11, 12, 12, 13, 14, 14, 14, 15, 15, 15, 15, 16, 17, 18, 18, 96.

$$R = H - L$$
$$R = 96 - 11$$
$$R = 85$$

This single extreme score increased R by 78 points and gives the impression that there is a large spread of scores when, with the exception of the single extreme score, there is actually very little.

THE SEMI-INTERQUARTILE RANGE (SIQR)

The semi-interquartile range (SIQR) compensates for the sensitivity of the range to extreme scores by preventing extreme scores from influencing its computation. The SIQR computation is determined by the middle 50 percent of the scores in a distribution. The lower 25 percent and upper 25 percent do not enter into its final computation. The formula for the SIQR is presented here:

$$SIQR = \frac{Q_3 - Q_1}{2}$$

In this formula Q_3 stands for the third quartile and Q_1 stands for the first. Quartiles, like the median, are points in a distribution below which a certain percentage of scores lie. In fact the median, or fiftieth percentile, is the same as Q_2, or the second quartile.

Q_1 is the point below which 25 percent of the scores lie, and Q_3 is the point below which 75 percent of the scores lie. The same process we used in Chapter 12 to determine a percentile is used to determine Q_1 and Q_3 as illustrated by the following example:

EXAMPLE: Determine the semi-interquartile range for the following set of scores: 85, 115, 90, 90, 105, 100, 110, 110, 95, 110, 95, 100.

Process:

1. Determine Q_1 and Q_3 by employing the steps used to determine the median (Q_2) for a distribution with an even number of scores.
   a. Arrange scores in numerical order.
   b. Counting up from the bottom, find the points *below which* 25 percent of the scores and 75 percent of the scores fall.
   c. Circle the two scores that "surround" these points.
   d. The averages of each of these two pairs of scores are Q_1 and Q_3.

115
Q_3 . . . (110, 110) $\frac{110 + 110}{2} = 110$
105
100
100
Q_3 . . . (95, 90) $\frac{95 + 90}{2} = 92.5$
90
85

2. Plug Q_1 and Q_3 into the formula and determine the SIQR.

Formula	***Application***
$\text{SIQR} = \frac{Q_3 - Q_1}{2}$	$\text{SIQR} = \frac{110 - 92.5}{2}$
	$= \frac{17.5}{2}$
	$= 8.75$

Although the SIQR has the advantage of not being influenced by extreme scores, it has the disadvantage of being determined ultimately by only *half* the scores in a distribution. Anytime all scores in a distribution do not enter the computation of a statistic, an element of error is introduced. Thus, although the SIQR is a better estimate of variability than the range, it is not as good, or as stable, as the estimate of variability known as the standard deviation. The standard deviation, like the mean, considers all scores in its computation. As a result, it is the most commonly used estimate of variability. When the SIQR is reported it usually accompanies the median, which is not surprising since they share part of the same computational process. Next we will consider the standard deviation.

THE STANDARD DEVIATION

As mentioned, the standard deviation (SD) includes all scores in a distribution in its computation. The mean must be computed before the SD can be computed. Thus, you normally see the SD reported as the estimate of variability that accompanies the mean in describing a distribution.

Remember, we said an estimate of variability tells us how poor our best bet is as a single value with which to describe a distribution. Consider the following three distributions:

A	B	C
38	20	25
34	20	24
26	20	23
24	20	22
20	20	21
20	20	19
16	20	18
14	20	17
6	20	16
2	20	15
$\Sigma X = 200$	$\Sigma X = 200$	$\Sigma X = 200$

$$\overline{X}_A = \frac{\Sigma X}{N} = \frac{200}{10} = 20 \qquad \overline{X}_B = \frac{\Sigma X}{N} = \frac{200}{10} = 20 \qquad \overline{X}_C = \frac{\Sigma X}{N} = \frac{200}{10} = 20$$

Although the distributions are composed of many different scores, they all have the same mean value. In distribution B, this best bet is right on the mark. Our mean value of 20 perfectly represents each and every score in the distribution, simply because each score in the distribution is 20. What about our best bets in A and C? How good or poor are they?

From these cases we can easily see that the mean is a better estimate of the scores in distribution C than in distribution A. We know this because none of the scores in C is more than 5 points away from the mean. In distribution A, on the other hand, six of the ten scores are 6 or more points away from the mean. Using this information, we can conclude that there is less variability, spread, or dispersion of scores in C. But just how much less variable is C than A? And what if there were less of a discrepancy in scores between A and C? How could we determine which was more or less variable?

With only this information, it would be difficult, if not impossible, to answer these questions. We need a reliable index of variability that considers all scores. Let's develop one by putting down on paper what we did when we compared A and C.

First, we looked at each distribution to see how far away each score was from the mean. We can do this more formally by subtracting the mean from each score ($X - \overline{X}$). We'll call this distance the score's *deviation* from the mean and use the symbol x (lowercase) to represent such deviation scores. Thus, $X - \overline{X} = x$, which is illustrated here:

A		C	
$X - \overline{X}$ =	x	$X - \overline{X}$ =	x
38 − 20 =	18	25 − 20 =	5
34 − 20 =	14	24 − 20 =	4
26 − 20 =	6	23 − 20 =	3
24 − 20 =	4	22 − 20 =	2
20 − 20 =	0	21 − 20 =	1
20 − 20 =	0	19 − 20 =	−1
16 − 20 =	−4	18 − 20 =	−2
14 − 20 =	−6	17 − 20 =	−3
6 − 20 =	−14	16 − 20 =	−4
2 − 20 =	−18	15 − 20 =	−5

This is just what we did before, except it was done in our heads. Since we want a single number or index to represent the deviations, why don't we just sum the x column, being careful to note the sign of the number, and then average the result? Let's do this:

A	C
x = 18	x = 5
14	4
6	3
4	2
0	1
0	−1
−4	−2
−6	−3
−14	−4
−18	−5
$\frac{\Sigma x}{N} = 0$	$\frac{\Sigma x}{N} = 0$

Because the positive and negative numbers cancel each other out, the sum of both x columns is zero. Remember the characteristics of the mean? One of these stated that the sum of the deviations from the mean always equals zero. Now you can see what is meant by this characteristic. This characteristic holds true for all shapes and sizes of distributions without exception. Thus, we cannot use Σx or even the average deviation, $\Sigma x/N$ as our index of variability, as promising as these two indices might appear at first glance. Fortunately, mathematics provides us with a way out of this dilemma. An index of variability based on deviation scores that we can use is computed in much the same fashion. There are two differences, however. First, let's square all the individual deviation scores and then sum them, as illustrated here:

A			C		
$X - \overline{X} =$	x	x^2	$X - \overline{X} =$	x	x^2
$38 - 20 =$	18	324	$25 - 20 =$	5	25
$34 - 20 =$	14	196	$24 - 20 =$	4	16
$26 - 20 =$	6	36	$23 - 20 =$	3	9
$24 - 20 =$	4	16	$22 - 20 =$	2	4
$20 - 20 =$	0	0	$21 - 20 =$	1	1
$20 - 20 =$	0	0	$19 - 20 =$	-1	1
$16 - 20 =$	-4	16	$18 - 20 =$	-2	4
$14 - 20 =$	-6	36	$17 - 20 =$	-3	9
$6 - 20 =$	-14	196	$16 - 20 =$	-4	16
$2 - 20 =$	-18	324	$15 - 20 =$	-5	25
		$1144 = \Sigma x^2$			$110 = \Sigma x^2$

The next step is to find the average of the sum of the squared deviation scores:

A

$$\frac{1144}{10} = 114.4$$

C

$$\frac{110}{10} = 11.0$$

These estimates of variability are useful in more advanced statistical computations and have a special name. The average of the sum of the squared deviation scores is called the *variance*. By themselves these estimates are not very useful because they represent squared units, not the units we started with. To return these values to units representative of our original data we must extract their square roots:

A

$$\sqrt{114.4} = 10.7$$

C

$$\sqrt{11.0} = 3.32$$

These values—10.7 for distribution A and 3.32 for distribution C—are the indices we've been looking for. They are based on *all* the scores in a distribution and are on the *same scale* of units as our original set of data. These values are the standard deviations for distributions A and C. The following formula is simply a shorthand mathematical way of representing what we have just done for distributions A and C:

$$SD = \sqrt{\frac{\Sigma(X - \overline{X})^2}{N}} \quad \text{or, since } X - \overline{X} = x, \quad SD = \sqrt{\frac{\Sigma x^2}{N}}$$

These formulas are equivalent. In other words, they tell you that to find the standard deviation you must square each deviation score, sum the squares of the deviation scores, divide this value by the number of scores in the distribution, and find the square root of this value. Just to be sure you understand the process we will work one more example, listing each of the steps.

The Deviation Score Method for Computing the Standard Deviation

EXAMPLE: Determine the standard deviation for the following set of scores: 92, 100, 90, 80, 94, 96.

Process:

1. Determine the mean.

$$\begin{array}{r} 100 \\ 96 \\ 94 \\ 92 \\ 90 \\ 80 \\ \hline 552 = \Sigma X \end{array} \qquad \overline{X} = \frac{\Sigma X}{N} \qquad \overline{X} = \frac{552}{6} \qquad \overline{X} = 92$$

2. Subtract the mean from each raw score to arrive at the deviation scores. (As a check on your computations, sum the x column to see if it equals zero.)

$$\begin{array}{rcr} \overline{X} - \overline{X} & = & x \\ 100 - 92 & = & 8 \\ 96 - 92 & = & 4 \\ 94 - 92 & = & 2 \\ 92 - 92 & = & 0 \\ 90 - 92 & = & -2 \\ 80 - 92 & = & -12 \\ \hline & & 0 = \Sigma x \end{array}$$

3. Square each deviation score and sum the squared deviation scores.

$X - \overline{X} =$	x	x^2
$100 - 92 =$	8	64
$96 - 92 =$	4	16
$94 - 92 =$	2	4
$92 - 92 =$	0	0
$90 - 92 =$	−2	4
$80 - 92 =$	−12	144
		$232 = \Sigma x^2$

4. Plug the Σx^2 into the formula and solve for the SD.

$$SD = \sqrt{\frac{\Sigma x^2}{N}} = \sqrt{\frac{232}{6}} = \sqrt{38.67} = 6.22$$

The Raw Score Method for Computing the Standard Deviation

The following formula is another, easier way of representing what we have just done for distributions A and C. It is called the *raw score* formula for the standard deviation, since it uses only the raw scores and does not require the more laborious process of finding deviations from the mean. Here is the raw score formula for calculating SD:

$$SD = \sqrt{\frac{\Sigma X^2 - (\Sigma X)^2/N}{N}}$$

where:

ΣX^2 = each raw score squared and then summed

$(\Sigma X)^2$ = the square of the sum of the raw scores (i.e., add the scores, then square the total)

N = the number of pupils

Both the more cumbersome deviation method and the shorter raw score method of computing the standard deviation will give you the same result; keep in mind that the raw score formula will be easier to use. Just to be sure you understand the process of obtaining a standard deviation, we will work one more example, using the raw score formula.

EXAMPLE: Determine the standard deviation for the following set of scores: 10, 12, 15, 13, 20, 14, 15, 14, 18, 13.

Process:

1. Determine the square of each raw score.

X	X^2
10	100
12	144
15	225
13	169
20	400
14	196
15	225
14	196
18	324
13	169

2. Sum both the raw scores (X) and the *squared* scores (X^2).

X	X^2
10	100
12	144
15	225
13	169
20	400
14	196
15	225
14	196
18	324
13	169
$\Sigma X = 144$	$\Sigma X^2 = 2{,}148$

3. Square the sum of the raw scores.

$$(\Sigma X)^2 = 144^2 = 20{,}736$$

4. Find N, the number of scores.

$$N = 10$$

5. Plug ΣX^2, $(\Sigma X)^2$, and N into the formula and solve for the SD.

$$SD = \sqrt{\frac{\Sigma X^2 - (\Sigma X)^2 / N}{N}}$$

$$= \sqrt{\frac{2148 - (20{,}736)/10}{10}}$$

$$= \sqrt{\frac{2{,}148 - 2{,}074}{10}}$$

$$= \sqrt{\frac{74}{10}}$$

$$= \sqrt{7.4}$$

$$= 2.72$$

Since the SD is an estimate of score variability or spread, it stands to reason that large SD values indicate greater score variability than do small SD values. In other words, when the SD is small, scores tend to cluster closely around the mean. Such a distribution is said to be *homogeneous* and tends to have a compressed shape, whether it is symmetrical or skewed. Three examples of *homogeneous* distributions with compressed shapes are pictured here:

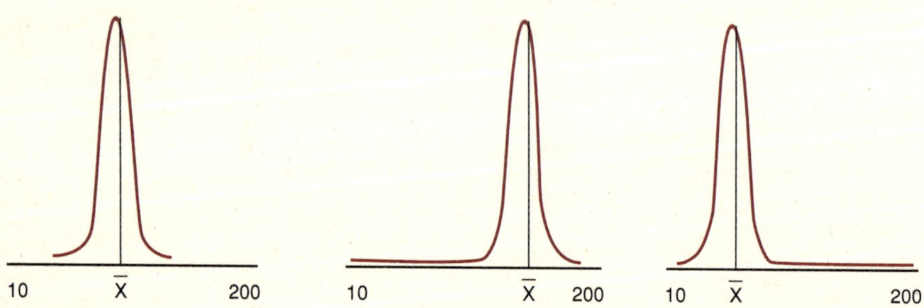

In these examples the $\overline{X}$ is a very good bet as the single value that best represents all the scores in each distribution. Our best bet is much poorer when distributions have large standard deviations. Such distributions have a lot of variability or spread of scores and all have an expanded appearance. These are called *heterogeneous distributions*. Three examples follow.

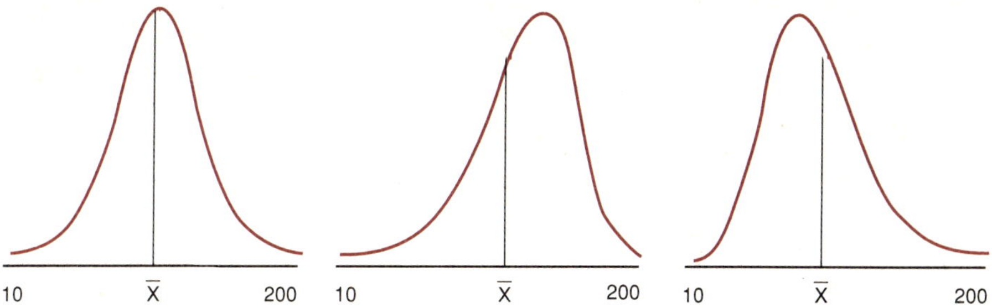

To sum up, measures of central tendency help us determine whether a distribution is symmetrical or skewed. Measures of variability help us determine more precisely whether these distributions appear compressed (small SD) or expanded (large SD). The SD also has a very important role in a special kind of symmetrical distribution. This is called the *normal distribution,* and it is to this topic that we now turn.

THE NORMAL DISTRIBUTION

The normal distribution is a special kind of symmetrical distribution that represents specific mathematical properties. This distribution has special importance for us because it is the model we use to make comparisons among scores or to make other kinds of statistical decisions. It is important, however, to note that the normal distribution is hypothetical. No distribution of scores matches the normal distribution perfectly. However, many distributions or scores in education *come close* to the normal distribution, and herein lies its value. The following example shows a distribution of Stanford-Binet IQ scores for a large number of students:

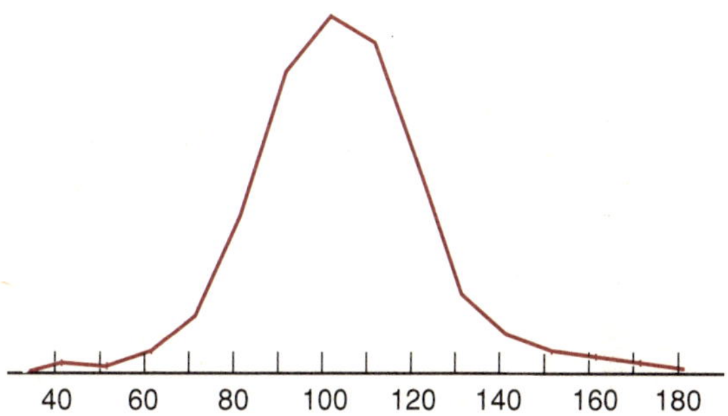

Looking at this figure you can see that although the IQ distribution differs somewhat from the symmetrical, normal distribution, it is close enough that we do not lose too much accuracy by using the normal distribution as a model for the actual distribution.

Many other characteristics of individuals also come close enough to the normal distribution for it to be used as a model for these distributions. Besides IQ, examples of these include most kinds of achievement and physical characteristics (for example, height and weight). The accuracy we sacrifice by employing a slightly inaccurate model is offset by the advantages of being able to make statistical and measurement decisions based on a *single* standard for comparison, the normal distribution. Before we can make such decisions, though, we must become familiar with the fixed properties of the normal distribution.

Properties of the Normal Distribution

The curve drawn here represents the normal distribution. Notice in the curve that the mean, median, and mode all coincide. This, of course, will occur whenever a distribution is normal. The percentages show how many cases fall under portions of the curve.

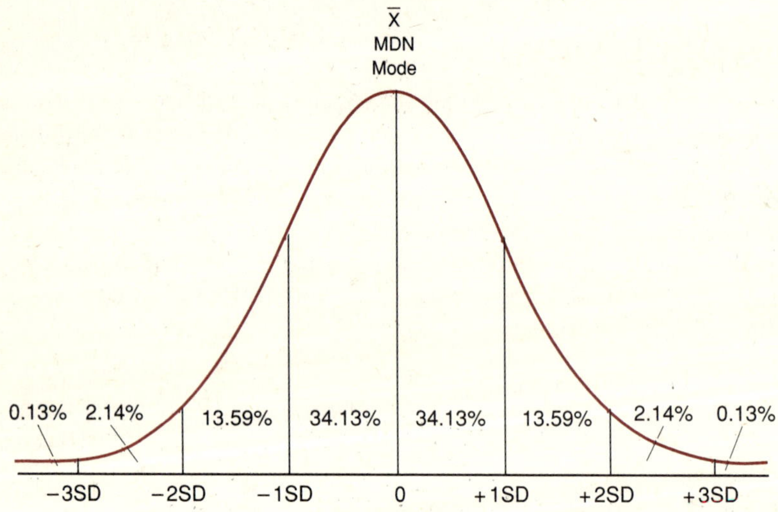

Percent of Cases Under Portions of the Normal Curve

Now add up the percentages you see above the baseline between three SD units below and three SD units above the mean. Notice that more than 99.9 percent or almost all scores in the normal distribution fall between three standard deviation units below the mean and three standard deviation units above the mean. Now look at the area of the curve between the mean and one SD above the mean. The 34.13 percent you see in this area indicates the percentage of cases that fall between the mean value and the value of the mean *plus* the value of one standard deviation unit in a large distribution of scores. For example, if we were using the normal curve as a model for a distribution with a mean of 61 and a standard deviation of 7, we would expect 34.13 percent (about 34 percent or 1/3) of the scores in this distribution to fall between 61 and 68, as the following illustration shows:

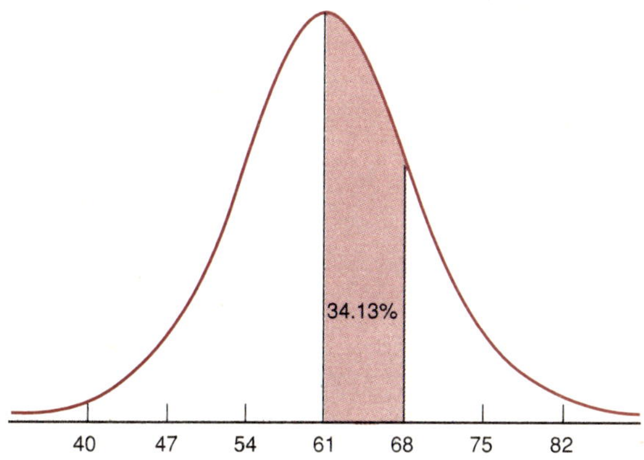

Notice also that for a distribution with a mean equal to 61 and a standard deviation equal to 7, seven points are added for each standard deviation unit above the mean (68, 75, 82), and seven points are subtracted from the mean for each standard deviation unit below the mean (54, 47, 40). Thus, we can see that about 68 percent or about 2/3 of the scores in this distribution fall between 54 and 68, as shown here:

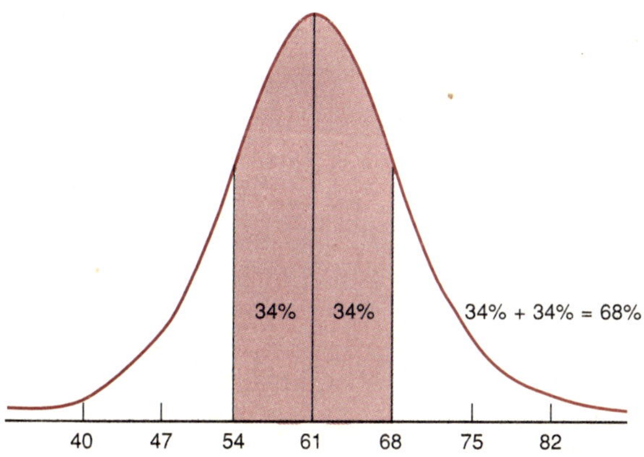

The interval between the mean and 75 represents what percentage of scores? We know what percentage of cases fall in each interval of the normal curve, so we can easily find the answer. The answer is about 48 percent, as shown in the following illustration:

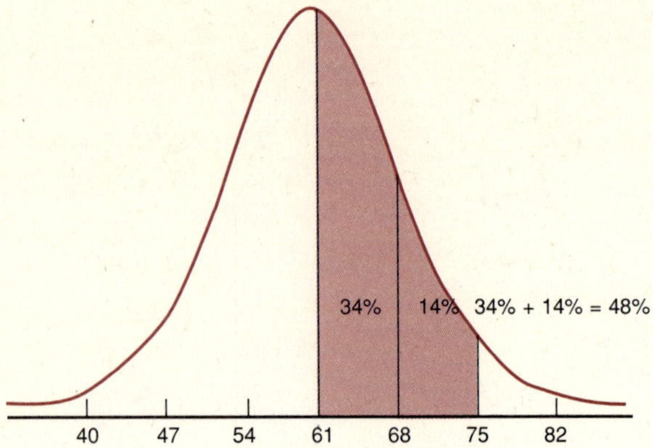

We can also use the normal curve to determine the percentage of scores above or below a certain score. The interval above 47 represents what percentage of scores? The answer, 98 percent, is illustrated next:

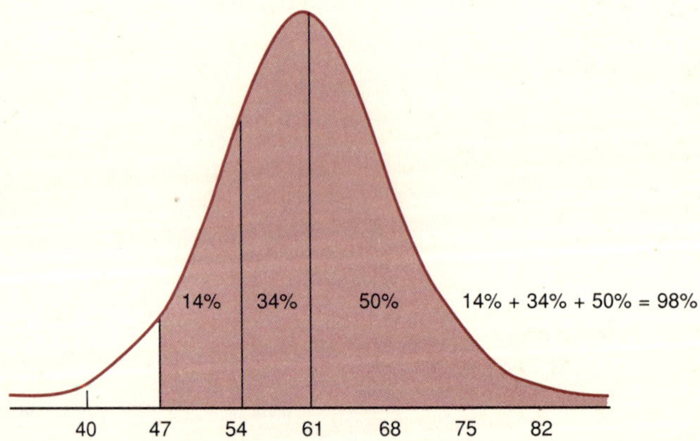

The interval below 68 represents what percentage of scores? The answer is about 84 percent, as shown in the following illustration:

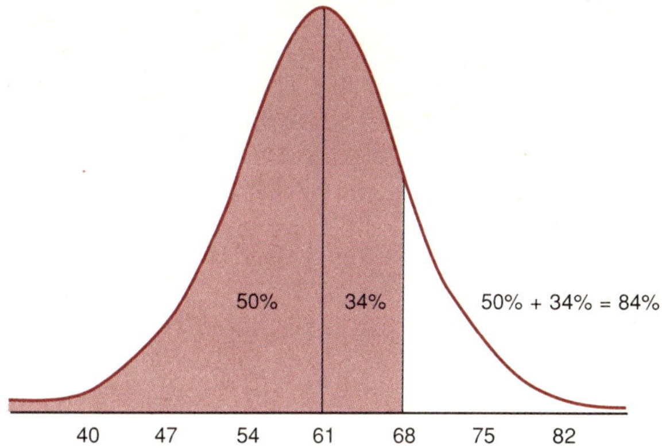

In other words, in a distribution with a mean of 61 and a standard deviation of 7, a score of 68 is at the eighty-fourth percentile. Recall that a percentile, like a quartile, is the point *below* which a given percentage of scores lie. So, if you wanted to determine the score at the sixteenth percentile, you would find that score below which there is 16 percent of the area under the normal curve, as illustrated here:

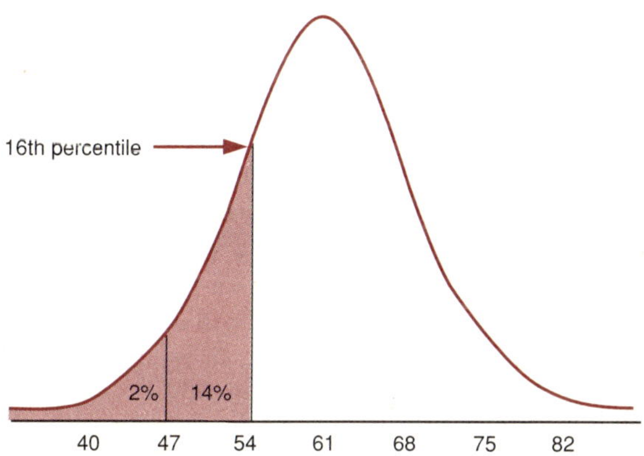

Assuming that test scores for a group of students were normally distributed—that is, if they conformed to a normal curve or close approximation of it—the standard deviation of that group could be converted to numbers and percentages of students scoring above or below certain score points. Before illustrating this concept, however, we must know how to accomplish this conversion.

CONVERTED SCORES

Thus far, we have talked about scores that come directly from tests. These actual or obtained scores are called *raw* scores. Consider the following:

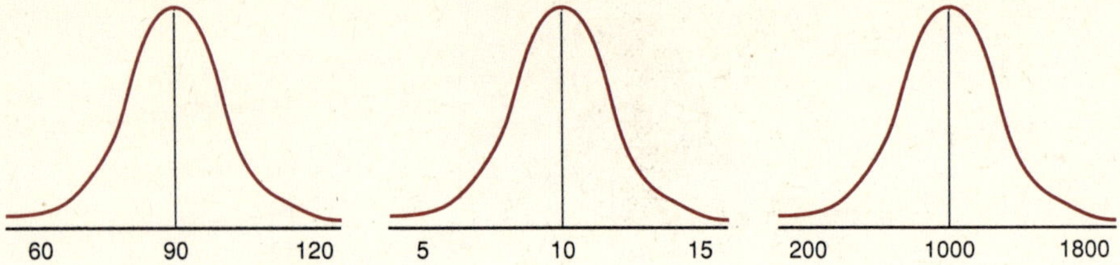

In these illustrations all three distributions have the same shape, but their means and standard deviation are different, which is often what happens because tests have different ranges of scores. The example illustrates what we are up against when we try to compare scores from different tests. The following example shows the process necessary to compare scores from distributions with different means and standard deviations.

> John obtained a score of 85 on his psychology midterm and 90 on his history midterm. On which test did he do better compared to the rest of the class?

At first glance you might say he did better in history. Well, this may be true, but how do you know? If you did say history, chances are you're treating these raw scores as percentages. Most of us are accustomed to test scores being converted to percentages before they are reported to us—but this is not always the case. John's score of 85 *may* mean he answered 85 out of 100 correctly, or it *may* mean he answered 85 out of 85 correctly, or 85 out of 217! Similarly, his history score may indicate he answered 90 out of 100, 90 out of 90, or 90 out of 329 items correctly. The point is that without additional information, we can't say which of these scores is higher or lower. With only raw scores reported, we *cannot* determine whether these scores are low, high, or intermediate. We need more information. Raw scores, by themselves, are *not* interpretable. This is an important but often overlooked point. Let's add some information.

The information we have—the raw scores— exists as part of two distributions: one for psychology and one for history. The distributions consist of the raw scores obtained by all the students who took these tests. If we can determine where John's scores fall in these distributions, we should be able to answer our question. First we need information that describes each distribution. As we now know, the mean and standard deviation are necessary to describe a distribution. Thus, if we have the mean and the standard deviation for each distribution, we should be able to answer our question. Let's add the information we need, but one piece at a time. First, we will add the means. The mean in psychology was

75, and the mean in history was 140. Before we go any further, let's organize our data and examine them carefully.

Psychology	***History***
$X = 85$	$X = 90$
$\overline{X} = 75$	$\overline{X} = 140$

We see that John's score was 10 points above the class mean in psychology and 50 points below the class mean in history. Clearly, he performed better compared with the rest of the class in psychology than in history. We have answered our question without even using the standard deviation of these distributions. Well, then, of what value is the standard deviation? As we will soon see, the standard deviation will enable us to pinpoint the percentage of scores above or below each of these scores. At first glance it may appear that John's history score is far below average, maybe even the lowest in the class. However, we don't know for sure because we have no idea how spread out or variable the history scores were. Consider the following illustrations:

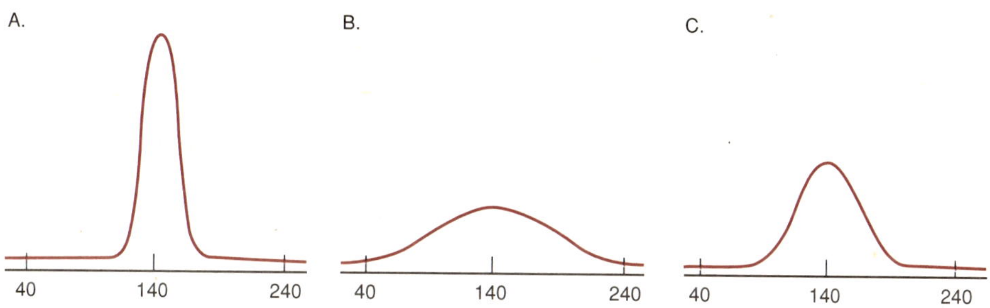

If the history scores are distributed as they are in A, then a score of 90 may indeed be the lowest in the class. If the distribution looks like B, 90 will not be the lowest score. In distribution C, we can expect a fair percentage of scores to be lower than 90. Similarly, we don't know if John's psychology score of 85 is far above average or only a little above average, simply because we don't know how spread out this distribution is. We will now add the standard deviations and pinpoint the locations of John's scores in their respective distributions.

The standard deviation in psychology was 10, and the standard deviation in history was 25. Again, let's organize our data before we do anything else.

Psychology	***History***
$X = 85$	$X = 90$
$\overline{X} = 75$	$\overline{X} = 140$
$SD = 10$	$SD = 25$

Next, let's construct curves to represent these data, assuming the scores are normally distributed.

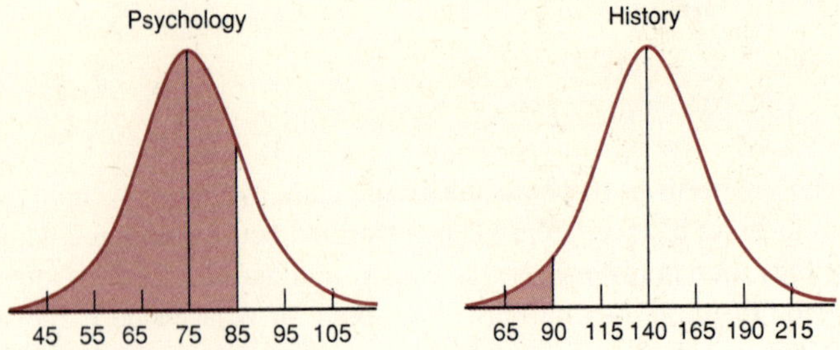

The shaded area in each distribution represents the proportion of scores below John's score. We can see that his psychology score is one standard deviation *above* the mean, and his history score is two standard deviations *below* the mean. To determine exactly what percentage of scores is lower than John's scores, all we need to do is consult the normal curve diagram to determine the percentage of cases lower than one standard deviation unit *above* the mean (for psychology) and two standard deviation units *below* the mean (for history).

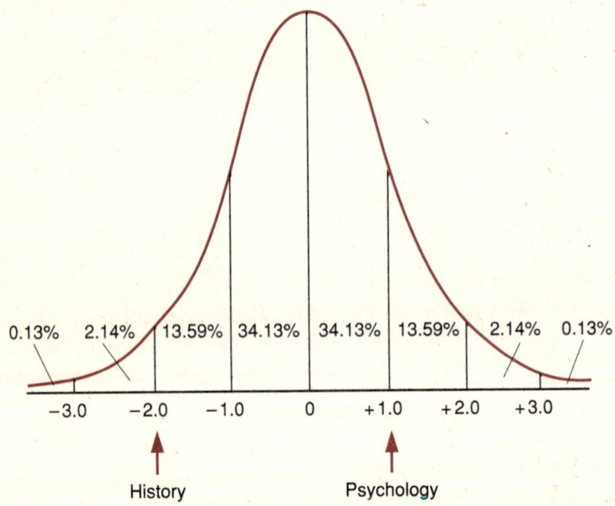

This diagram is identical to the normal curve presented in the section "Properties of the Normal Distribution." The Normal curve is used when we need a common basis on which to compare scores from distributions with different means and standard deviations. Examining this distribution we can see that about 84 percent of the class scored lower than John in psychology, while only about 2 percent scored lower in history. As compared with the rest of the class, his performance in psychology was far better than his performance in history. In psychology he scored at the eighty-fourth percentile, and in history he scored at the second.

Z-Scores

Now we have very specific information about John's performance. We had to collect the proper data (means and standard deviations for each distribution) and determine how far above or below the mean in standard deviation units each score was in order to determine the percentage of scores below (or above) the obtained raw scores. It took a while, but we got there! Fortunately, there is a mathematical shortcut. A relatively simple formula enables us to determine a score's exact position in the normal distribution quickly. The formula is called the z-score formula, and it converts raw scores into what are called z-scores. These are scores that tell us how far above or below the mean in standard deviation units raw scores lie.

$$z = \frac{X - \overline{X}}{SD}$$

where:

z = z-score
X = obtained raw score
$\overline{X}$ = mean score
SD = standard deviation

This formula enables us to convert raw scores from any distribution to a common scale, regardless of its mean or standard deviation, so that we can easily compare such scores. This eliminates the confusion that would ordinarily result from such comparisons. As we mentioned above, this formula is a shortcut method of doing what we just did in step-by-step fashion. In case you don't believe us, let's work through the same example, this time using the z-score formula.

> John obtained a score of 85 on his psychology midterm and 90 on his history midterm. On which test did he do better compared to the rest of the class?

The first thing we should do is to organize the relevant information. We already have the raw scores, the mean, and the standard deviation.

Psychology	***History***
$X = 85$	$X = 90$
$\overline{X} = 75$	$\overline{X} = 140$
$SD = 10$	$SD = 25$

Once we have all the necessary data—the obtained score, mean, and standard deviation for each distribution—we are ready to plug the data into the z-score formula, obtain z-scores for each raw score, and compare these using the z-score distribution:

Psychology

$$z = \frac{X - \overline{X}}{SD}$$

$$= \frac{85 - 75}{10}$$

$$= \frac{10}{10}$$

$$= +1.0$$

History

$$z = \frac{X - \overline{X}}{SD}$$

$$= \frac{90 - 140}{25}$$

$$= \frac{-50}{25}$$

$$= -2.0$$

As you can see, we were able to get the same results as before quickly using the mathematical formula. We can now use the properties of the normal curve to answer a variety of questions about these scores. For example:

What percentage of scores fall higher? Lower?

At what percentile do the scores lie?

How much better than average were the scores? How much poorer?

Just to make sure you understand the *z*-score concept, let's work through two examples.

EXAMPLE: On a 70-item test Mary obtained a score of 49. The test had a mean of 40 and a standard deviation of 3. What percentage of the class scored higher than Mary?

STEP 1: Organize the relevant information.

$X = 49$
$\overline{X} = 40$
$SD = 3$

STEP 2: Convert to *z*-scores.

$$z = \frac{X - \overline{X}}{SD}$$

$$= \frac{49 - 40}{3}$$

$$= \frac{9}{3}$$

$$= +3.0$$

STEP 3: Use the normal curve to answer questions about comparisons, percentages, or percentiles.

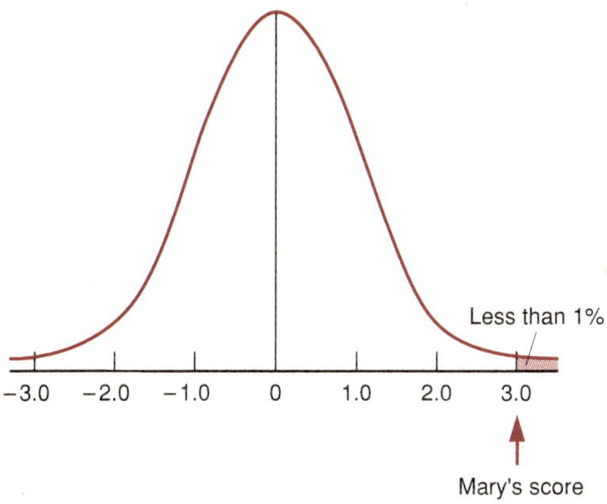

The shaded area in the *z*-score distribution indicates the percentage of obtained scores that were higher than Mary's. In other words, less than 1 percent (or, more accurately, less than 0.1 percent) of the individuals who took the test scored higher than Mary.

EXAMPLE: On the verbal portion of the Scholastic Assessment Test (SAT) Pete obtained a score of 350. The mean of the SAT-V is 500, and its standard deviation is 100. The college Pete wants to go to will not accept applicants who score below the eighth percentile on the SAT-V. Will Pete be accepted by this college?

Step 1:

$$X = 350$$
$$\overline{X} = 500$$
$$SD = 100$$

Step 2:

$$z = \frac{X - \overline{X}}{SD}$$

$$= \frac{350 - 500}{100}$$

$$= \frac{-150}{100}$$

$$= -1.5$$

Step 3:

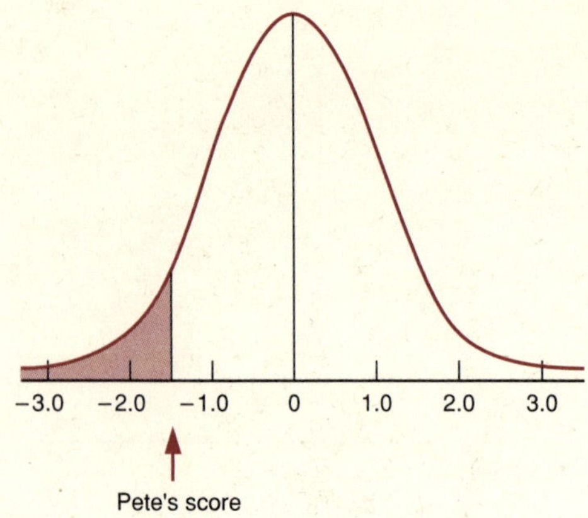

So far, we have not had to deal with *z*-scores containing decimals. We can see though that the shaded area in the curve represents the percentage of scores below Pete's score. The question is, does this shaded area represent at least 8 percent of the scores obtained by others? If it does, Pete's score is at or above the eighth percentile, and he will be accepted. If it represents less than 8 percent, Pete's score is below the eighth percentile, and he will not be accepted.

In an introductory statistics course you would learn to determine *exactly* what percentage of the *z*-score distribution falls below a *z*-score of 1.5, but we will settle for an estimate. Let's go ahead and estimate, considering the following illustration:

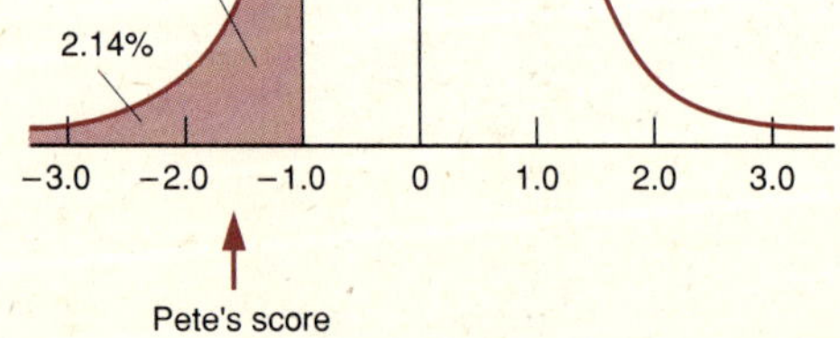

We know that about 2 percent of the scores fall below two *z*-score units below the mean and that about 14 percent fall between one and two *z*-score units below the mean.

A common mistake is to erroneously assume that since −1.5 is halfway between −1.0 and −2.0, about 7 percent of the scores fall between −1.0 and −1.5 and another 7 percent fall between −1.5 and −2.0. This reasoning would be correct *if* the proportions of the curve between −1.0 and −1.5 and between −1.5 and −2.0 were the same. The following illustration shows, however, that a greater proportion of scores falls between –1.0 and 1.5 than falls between −1.5 and −2.0.

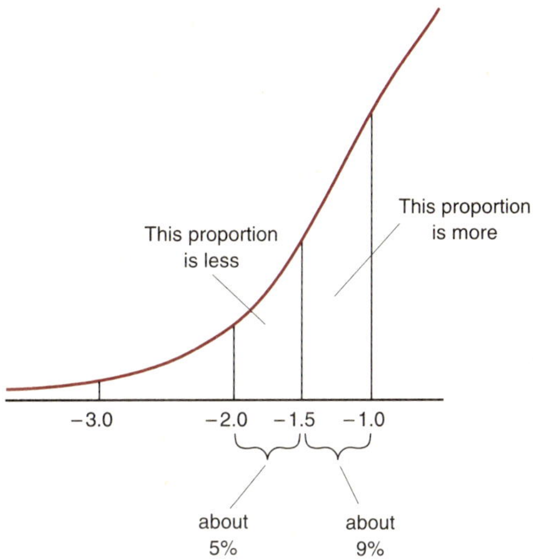

Remember, we are dealing with a curve, not with a histogram! If we were dealing with a histogram, then splitting the percentage in half would be correct. Since we are not dealing with a histogram, we must estimate the proportions any time we have a *z*-score that results in a decimal number.

Now, returning to our example, we see that about 7 percent (2 percent below $z = -2.0$, and 5 percent between $z = -1.5$ and $z = -2.0$) of SAT-V scores fall below 350. Pete's score is below the eighth percentile.

T-Scores

In working through this last example, you may have been confused about the negative numbers at times or may have forgotten that you were dealing with negative numbers. To avoid this difficulty, statisticians often convert *z*-scores to T-scores. T-scores are identical to *z*-scores, *except* that the T-score distribution has a mean of 50 and a standard deviation of 10. Our *z*, or normal curve distribution, had a mean of 0 and a standard deviation of 1.0. In the T-score distribution, negative numbers are eliminated except in those extremely rare cases where raw scores more than five standard deviations below the mean are obtained. To convert a raw score to a T-score you must first convert to a z-score. The formula for a T-score is:

$$T = 10z + 50$$

This formula says multiply the z-score by 10 and add 50 to this value to obtain the equivalent T-score. Let's convert John's psychology z-score of $+1.0$ and history score of -2.0 to T-scores.

Psychology	***History***
$T = 10z + 50$	$T = 10z + 50$
$= 10(1.0) + 50$	$= 10(-2.0) + 50$
$= 10 + 50$	$= (-20) + 50$
$= 60$	$= 30$

Thus, a z-score of 1.0 is equivalent to a T-score of 60, and a z-score of -2.0 is equivalent to a T-score of 30. Notice that the negative number has been eliminated. The following illustration shows the relationship between z-scores and T-scores:

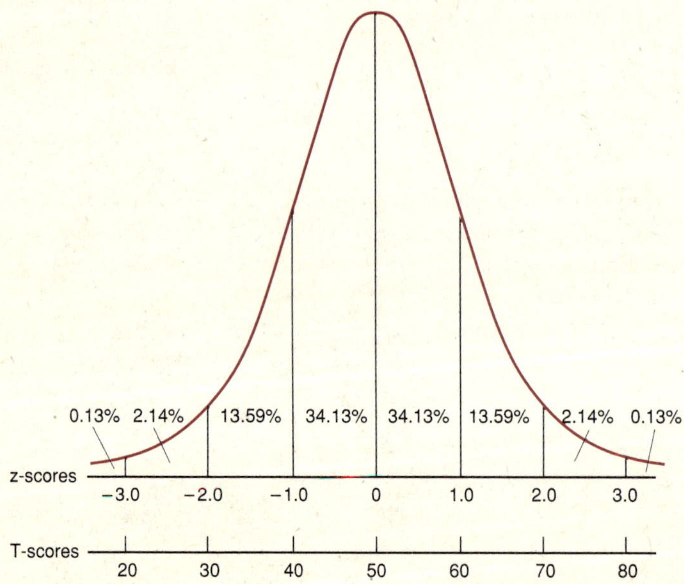

Thus far, we have considered statistical methods of tabulating and graphing data, the measures of central tendency and variability, and converted scores. In the next chapter we will consider another statistic, one that enables us to indicate how closely related or associated different sets of scores are.

SUMMARY

This chapter introduced you to the concept of score variability, methods to compute estimates of variability, the normal distribution, and converted scores. Its major points are:

1. *Variability* is the term we use to describe how spread out or dispersed scores are within a distribution.
2. The range, a gross estimate of variability, is determined by subtracting the lowest score from the highest score in the distribution.
3. The semi-interquartile range (SIQR), which is usually reported along with the median, is determined by subtracting the value for the first quartile from the value for the third quartile and dividing the remainder by 2.
4. The standard deviation (SD) is usually reported along with the mean and is our best estimate of variability. It is determined by subtracting the mean from each raw score to obtain a deviation score (x), squaring each deviation score, summing the squared deviation scores, dividing the total by the number of scores, and then determining the square root of this value.
5. Distributions with small standard deviations have a compressed appearance and are called *homogeneous distributions.*
6. Distributions with large standard deviations have a more expanded appearance and are called *heterogeneous distributions.*
7. The normal distribution is a specific type of symmetrical distribution that is mathematically determined and has fixed properties.
8. Although the normal distribution is hypothetical, it approximates the distribution of many test scores, enabling us to use it as a model on which to base statistical decisions.
9. We use the normal distribution as our basis for comparing scores from distributions with different means and standard deviations.
10. We do so by converting raw scores from different distributions to either z-scores or T-scores and using these converted scores as the baseline for the normal distribution. This enables us to compare scores from different distributions on a single distribution with a single mean and standard deviation.
11. Determine z-scores by subtracting the mean for the distribution from the raw score and dividing by the standard deviation of the distribution.
12. Determine T-scores by first computing the corresponding z-score for a raw score, multiplying the z-score by 10, and adding 50 to the product.
13. The main advantage of the T-score over the z-score is the elimination of negative numbers.

For Practice

*1. For this set of scores (5, 6, 6, 4, 5, 1, 2, 3, 5, 3), compute the following:

a. N

b. Mode

c. Median

d. Mean

e. Standard deviation

f. Variance

g. Range

*2. Given $\overline{X} = 100$ and SD = 10,

a. Convert these raw scores into *z*-scores: 120, 132, 140, and 145.

b. Convert these *z*-scores into raw scores: −2.5, 0.6, 1.25, and 2.15.

c. Convert these T-scores into raw scores: 75, 38, 35, and 28.

d. What percentages of scores lie between the following scores?

75–90

90–120

100–110

112–125

*3. A normal score distribution has a mean of 100 and a standard deviation of 15.

a. What *z*-score is the equivalent of a raw score of 120?

b. What raw score is most equivalent to a T-score of 33?

c. Approximately what percentage of scores lie below a score of 85?

*4. A pupil obtains a raw score of 82 on a test with a mean of 100 and a standard deviation of 12. His score corresponds to what T-score?

*5. The mean for the following distribution is 80 and the standard deviation is 12. Assuming a normal distribution, compute or determine the *z*-scores and T-scores for the following students:

Student	***Score***
John	68
Mary	104
Jim	86
Claire	62

*6. The following are the means and standard deviations of some well-known standardized tests, referred to as Test A, Test B, and Test C. All three yield normal distributions.

	Mean	*Standard deviation*
Test A	500	100
Test B	100	15
Test C	60	10

a. A score of 325 on Test A corresponds to what score on Test C? A score of 640 on Test A corresponds to what score on Test B?

b. The counselor told Sally that she had scored so high on Test A that only 2 people out of 100 would score higher. What was Sally's score on Test A?

*Answers for these questions appear in Appendix D.

CHAPTER 14

Correlation

Our last statistical topic is correlation. Thus far we have discussed statistics that are used to describe distributions and the position of individual scores within a distribution. There are times, though, when we are interested in the extent to which an individual's position or rank in one distribution is similar or dissimilar to his or her position or rank in a different distribution. That is, at times we want to determine how closely scores in *different* distributions are related to each other. Or, simply, we wish to know if individuals with high scores in distribution A tend also to obtain high scores in distribution B.

These and similar issues are concerned with the extent to which two different distributions of scores correlate. A statistic called a *correlation coefficient* (symbolized by r) helps us address general issues like those just mentioned or answer specific questions like those that follow:

Are athletes really poor scholars?

If you do poorly on the verbal portion of the SAT, are you likely to do poorly on the quantitative portion?

Do students with high grades in high school really tend to get high grades in college?

In this first question what is being asked is whether individuals who score high in a distribution of ratings pertaining to physical ability tend to score low in a distribution of ratings pertaining to intellectual ability. Using information gained from the previous chapter we can illustrate this as follows:

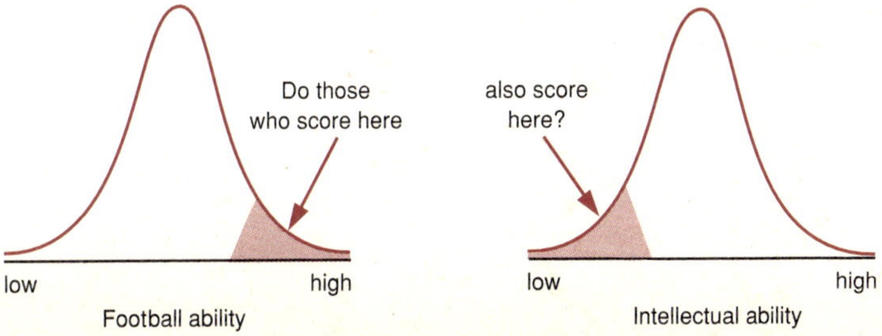

This question asks whether there is a *negative* correlation between the two. Are high scores in one distribution associated with low scores in the other?

The next question asks whether those who score low in the SAT-V distribution also score low in the SAT-Q distribution. Here, too, we can illustrate the question being asked, but note the difference from our previous illustration:

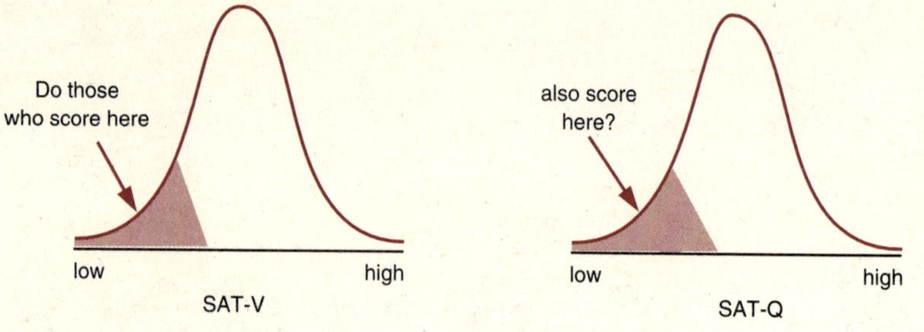

This question asks whether there is a *positive* correlation between the two distributions of scores.

Our last question asks whether students with high grades in high school tend also to receive high grades in college. This issue could be illustrated in the same manner as before:

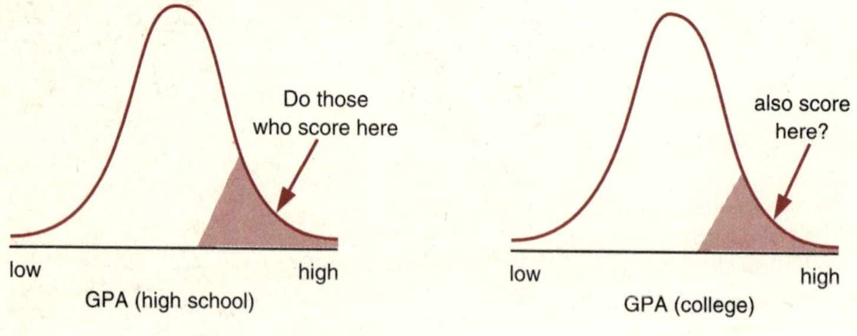

It asks whether there is a *positive* correlation between the two distributions. In other words, are high scores in one distribution associated with high scores in the other distribution?

THE CORRELATION COEFFICIENT

As we have seen, distributions can correlate positively or negatively. They may also not correlate at all! The correlation coefficient (r) tells us at a glance the strength and direction (positive or negative) of the relationship between distributions. Correlation coefficients range from -1.0 to $+1.0$. The closer a coefficient gets to -1.0 *or* to $+1.0$, the stronger the relationship. The sign of the coefficient tells us whether the relationship is positive or negative. The following examples are illustrative of correlation coefficients:

Coefficient	*Strength*	*Direction*
$r = -.85$	Strong	Negative
$r = +.82$	Strong	Positive
$r = +.22$	Weak	Positive
$r = +.03$	Very weak	Positive
$r = -.42$	Moderate	Negative

Strength of a Correlation

The previous coefficients are described as ranging from very weak to strong. You may ask yourself, "How high must r be for it to be strong?" Well, there is no cut-and-dried answer to this question, because an $r = .40$ may be considered strong for one set of data (for example, correlation of IQ scores and "happiness") and very weak for another (for example, correlation of scores from two standardized achievement tests). In other words, we must always consider the distributions with which we are dealing before deciding whether an r is weak, moderate, or strong. If our distributions are composed of scores arrived at by fairly objective means, such as standardized achievement tests, we require r's to be fairly high (for example, .80 or more) before we call them strong. When distributions are composed of scores arrived at by subjective means, such as ratings of happiness, job success, or maturity, we usually consider much lower r's (for example, .50 to .60) as indicative of the presence of a strong relationship between the distributions in question.

Direction of a Correlation

The following illustrates the possible relationships between distributions that will result in positive or negative correlation coefficients. A positive correlation exists when:

1. High scores in distribution A are associated with high scores in distribution B;
2. Low scores in distribution A are associated with low scores in distribution B.

A negative correlation exists when:

1. High scores in distribution A are associated with low scores in distribution B;
2. Low scores in distribution A are associated with high scores in distribution B.

An everyday example of a positive correlation is the relationship between height and weight. As people *increase* in height, they tend to *increase* in weight, and vice versa. A real-life example of negative correlation is the relationship between the number of cigarettes smoked per day and life expectancy. As the number of cigarettes smoked per day *increases*, life expectancy *decreases*, and vice versa. Fortunately, for those who are smokers, the correlation is not "very strong."

When there is no systematic relationship between two distributions, correlation coefficients around .00 are found. These indicate that high scores in distribution A are likely to be associated with *both* high and low scores in distribution B, and vice versa. In other words, there is no consistent pattern.

FIGURE 14.1
A Scatterplot Indicating a Perfect Negative Correlation

Player	*Rank in Touchdowns*	*Rank in GPA*
A	5 (lowest)	1 (highest)
B	4	2
C	3	3
D	2	4
E	1 (highest)	5 (lowest)

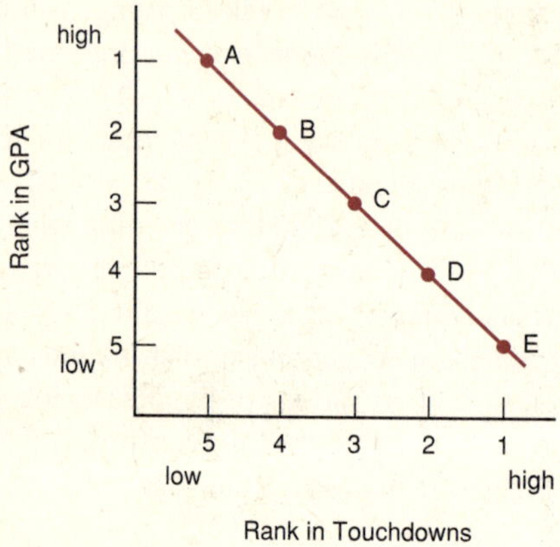

Scatterplots

As we have noted, the strength and direction of a relationship between two distributions can be determined by a correlation coefficient. Scatterplots also enable us to determine the strength and direction of a correlation, but in a less formal manner. A scatterplot is nothing more than a graphical representation of the relationship between two variables representing the scores in two distributions.

Suppose we are interested in determining whether there is a relationship between number of touchdowns scored and academic achievement. To do so, we randomly select five running backs from past football teams, count up the number of touchdowns they scored, and obtain copies of their transcripts. Although it is not necessary to do so, for illustrative purposes we will then rank each player on the two variables in question: touchdowns scored and GPA.* The results might look something like those in Figure 14.1.

This graph is a scatterplot of the data for each individual player. It indicates there is a *perfect negative* correlation ($r = -1.0$) between rank in touchdowns and rank in GPA. The player ranked highest in touchdowns is ranked lowest in GPA, and vice versa. There is a *perfect* correlation because all the plotted points can be connected by a straight line. We can tell it is a *negative* correlation because the slope of the scatterplot descends from left to right.

*We could also have used the unranked, or raw score, data. Our choice of data will determine the type of correlation coefficient that we compute and the symbol used to denote it, as we explain later.

FIGURE 14.2
A Scatterplot Indicating a Perfect Positive Correlation

Player	*Rank in Touchdowns*	*Rank in GPA*
A	5 (low)	5 (low)
B	4	4
C	3	3
D	2	2
E	1 (high)	1 (high)

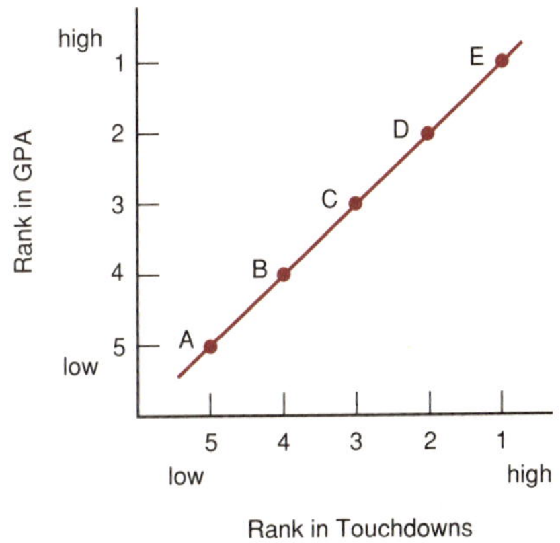

Let's collect the same data from another school, one that emphasizes academics and not football. These data are represented in Figure 14.2.

The scatterplot in Figure 14.2 indicates a *perfect positive* correlation ($r = 1.0$) between these variables. The player ranked lowest in touchdowns was also ranked lowest in GPA. The player ranked highest in touchdowns was also ranked highest in GPA. This is a *perfect* correlation because, again, the points are connected by a straight line. However, this time we can see the correlation is *positive* because the slope of the scatterplot ascends from left to right.

As you might have suspected, both of these examples are unrealistic. Perfect correlations, whether positive or negative, seldom occur. Normally one ends up with r's somewhere *between* -1.0 and $+1.0$. Consider in Figure 14.3 data collected from a third school. The scatterplot in this figure represents a *positive* correlation. However, it is not a perfect correlation, because the points are "scattered" around the line rather than falling on the line. The line drawn through the points, called the regression line, is mathematically determined and is included here only to highlight the degree to which the data points slope upward or downward.

These data yield an r of .42. You can estimate the position of a regression line by drawing a straight line through the scattered points that best fits the movement of data upward (positive correlation) or downward (negative correlation). This movement is actually the rate at which rank in touchdowns changes relative to rank in GPA as we move from one individual to another. You may also enclose scattered data points with an ellipse, as we have

FIGURE 14.3
A Scatterplot Indicating a Weaker Positive Correlation

Player	*Rank in Touchdowns*	*Rank in GPA*
A	5 (low)	5
B	4	2
C	3	4
D	2	1
E	1 (high)	3

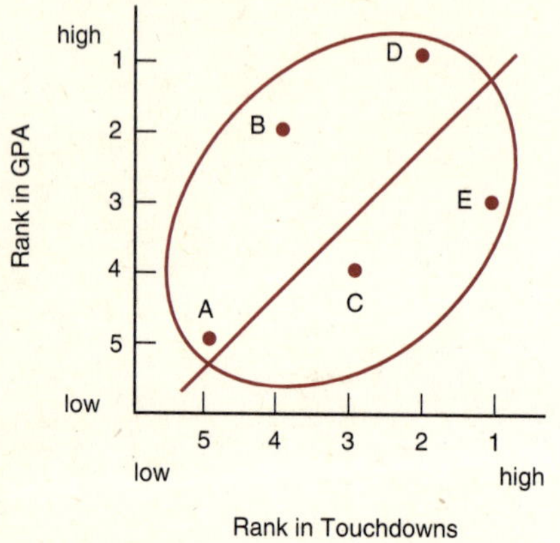

done, to highlight the *strength* of the relationship. As the data points form a tighter and tighter ellipse, the correlation gets stronger. This is illustrated by the scatterplots in Figure 14.4. Notice that when r approaches zero, a circle rather than an ellipse is needed to "capture" all the data points. As these examples illustrate, we often deal with correlations less than -1.0 or $+1.0$ because people do not conform to strict rules governing relationships among their abilities and other characteristics. Instead, relationships occur according to general trends with lots of exceptions. For example, there is a positive relationship between height and weight. Tall people tend to weigh more than short people. However, there are reversals to this trend (or exceptions to the rule): tall, skinny folks and short, stout folks. The more reversals or exceptions present in relationships, the weaker the correlation between the variables.

Where Does *r* Come From?

The correlation is determined through any one of a variety of mathematical formulas. One of these uses data that have been ranked, rather than raw scores-data like those presented in Figure 14.1. This type of correlation coefficient is called a rank difference correlation,* which has the formula:

*The rank difference correlation is one of several different types of correlations. The Greek letter rho (ρ) is used to identify a rank difference correlation.

FIGURE 14.4
Scatterplots for a Variety of Correlations

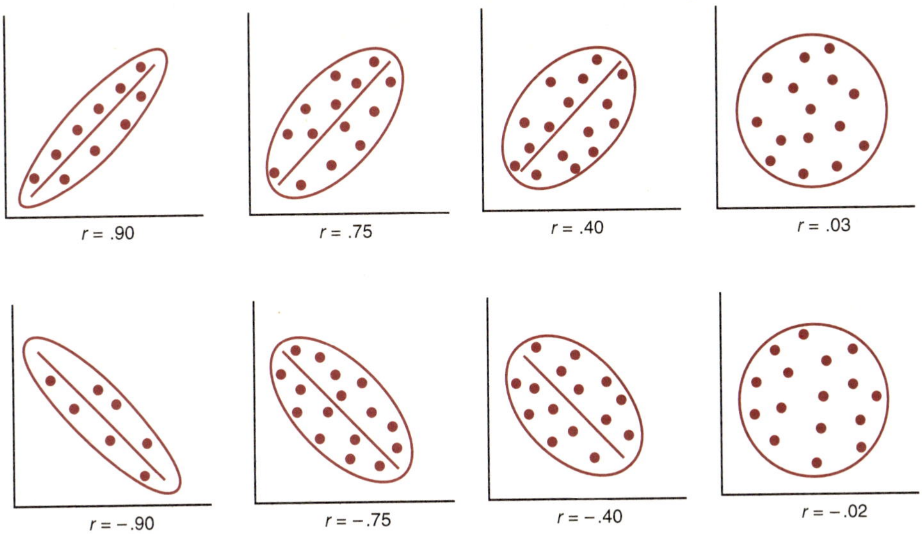

$$r_\rho = 1 - \frac{6\Sigma D^2}{N(N^2 - 1)}$$

where:

r_ρ = rank difference coefficient of correlation

Σ = sum of

D = difference between a pair of ranks

N = number of pupils

The results of this formula for the rank difference coefficient when applied to the data presented in Figure 14.1 are as follows:

Rank in touchdown	*Rank in GPA*	*Difference ranks*	*D^2*
5	1	4	16
4	2	2	4
3	3	0	0
2	4	2	4
1	5	4	16
			$\Sigma D^2 = 40$

$$r_\rho = 1 - \frac{6(40)}{5(25 - 1)}$$

$$= 1 - \frac{240}{120} = 1 - 2 = -1.0$$

The calculation of another type of correlation, called the Pearson Product-Moment Correlation, is illustrated with an example in Appendix B. The advantage of the rank difference correlation is that it can be used with small numbers of subjects, whereas the Pearson Product-Moment Correlation must be used with larger numbers of scores, usually thirty or more pairs of scores. Generally, when this number of scores is obtained, the Pearson Product-Moment Correlation (symbolized simply as r) is easier to use and more accurate. However, since few teachers are ever called on to actually compute a correlation coefficient, especially on large numbers of students, we will not concern ourselves with computations for the Pearson Product-Moment Correlation in this chapter. More important is your ability to understand and interpret correlation coefficients. Thus far we have described what a correlation is and we have considered the numerical and graphical representations of correlations. Next, let's consider a frequently misunderstood aspect of correlation.

Causality

Correlation does not imply causality. That is, a correlation only indicates that some sort of relationship or association exists between two distributions. It does not mean that one distribution of scores *causes* the other distribution of scores. This may seem perfectly logical and sensible to you. Yet, one of the most frequent misinterpretations in statistics (and in education) is to infer that because two variables are correlated with each other, one variable causes the other. It is possible that one variable may cause another, and thus account for the relationship between the two. However, it is just as possible, and usually more likely, that the two variables are correlated with each other because of the effects of some *third* unidentified variable. That is, a third variable is actually causing one or both conditions, thus making it only appear as though the first variable is causing the second.

For example, there is a negative correlation between air temperature and frequency of colds. As air temperature decreases, the number of people who catch colds increases. Thus, one might infer, incorrectly, that a drop in air temperature will cause colds. While this is a *possibility*, it is much more likely that the effect is the result of the effects of a third variable. That is, rather than a drop in air temperature causing an increase in colds, it may be that a drop in air temperature causes people to stay indoors and come in contact with each other more frequently, which causes an increase in colds. Figure 14.5 illustrates the probable sequence of events.

Two variables may also correlate with each other because a third variable affects them both. For example, head size correlates with mental age. However, this does not mean that increases in head size cause increases in mental age. Both of these are affected by a third variable, chronological age, shown in Figure 14.6.

To sum up, in and of themselves, correlation coefficients alone can never be used to prove causality. Now that we are aware of this common misinterpretation, let's consider some other cautions.

FIGURE 14.5
One Way a Third Variable May Affect Conclusions About Causality

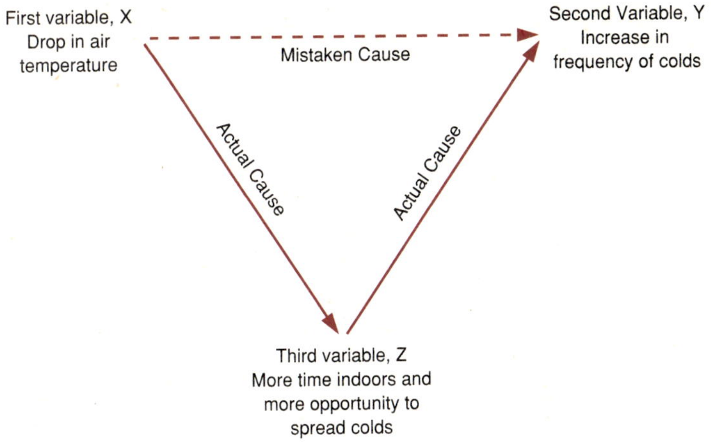

FIGURE 14.6
Another Way a Third Variable May Affect Conclusions About Causality

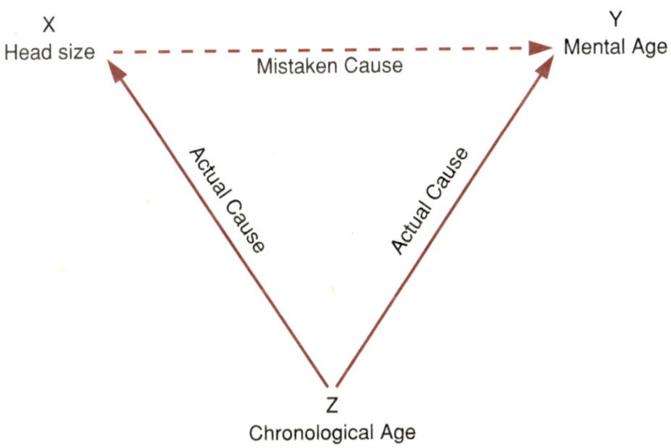

Other Interpretive Cautions

A correlation coefficient of .83 is referred to as "point eight three," *not* as 83 percent. Furthermore, to make comparative decisions about the relative strength of correlation coefficients, it is insufficient to simply compare the coefficients themselves. Instead, it is necessary to square the coefficient and multiply the result times 100. The result of this operation is called the *coefficient of determination*. The coefficient of determination is the percentage of variability (see Chapter 13) in one variable that is associated with or determined by the other variable. The following computations of the coefficient of determination demonstrate that a correlation coefficient of .80 is four times as strong as a coefficient of .40 and sixteen times as strong as a coefficient of .20.

Correlation Coefficient (r)	r^2	$r^2 \times 100$	*Coefficient of Determination*
.80	.64	64	64%
.40	.16	16	16%
.20	.04	4	4%

The coefficient of determination is an important concept in more advanced statistical operations. For our purposes we need to keep in mind only that correlation coefficients are not percentages and that we must convert correlation coefficients to the coefficient of determination *before* we can make decisions about their relative strength.

CURVILINEARITY. All the scatterplots we have discussed thus far are plots of variables that have *linear* relationships with each other. In a linear relationship, scores on variables A and B either increase or decrease at approximately the same rate throughout the entire range of scores. That is, they progressively move up or down together in the same way regardless of whether they are at the low end, middle, or high end of the score continuum. In a curvilinear relationship, scores on variables A and B may increase together at first and then decrease, or they may decrease at first and then increase, depending on whether the scores are at the low, middle, or high end of the score distribution. The curvilinear relationship between anxiety and test performance (Duffy, 1972) is depicted in the scatterplot here:

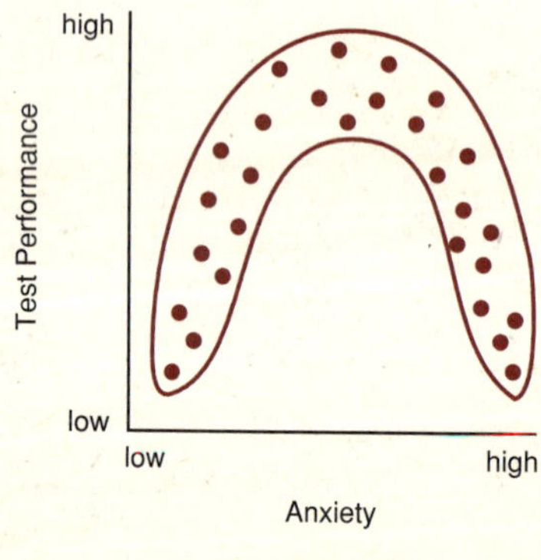

When data are related to each other in curvilinear fashion, a curved regression line, rather than a straight regression line, best fits the data. This curvilinear relationship indicates that increases in anxiety are positively associated with test performances up to a point, after which the association between anxiety and test performance is negative. When plotted, such data take on a boomerang shape. While it is possible to compute a correlation coefficient for such data, the coefficient is of a special type. For curvilinear data, computing a coefficient like that which we've been discussing will yield an artificially low r. Thus, it is always a good idea to plot data *before* computing a correlation coefficient. Otherwise, a falsely low r will result if the data are curvilinear.

TRUNCATED RANGE. Normally, we compute correlation coefficients across the range of all possible values for variables A and B. At times, though, we may desire or be forced to consider only a part of all the possible values (for example, just low-ranked or high-ranked individuals). Here we are dealing with a truncated range of scores. When only a portion of the entire range of scores is considered, the strength of the correlation coefficient *goes down*. The following scatterplots illustrate this conclusion. The first scatterplot illustrates the relationship between IQ scores and standardized test scores.

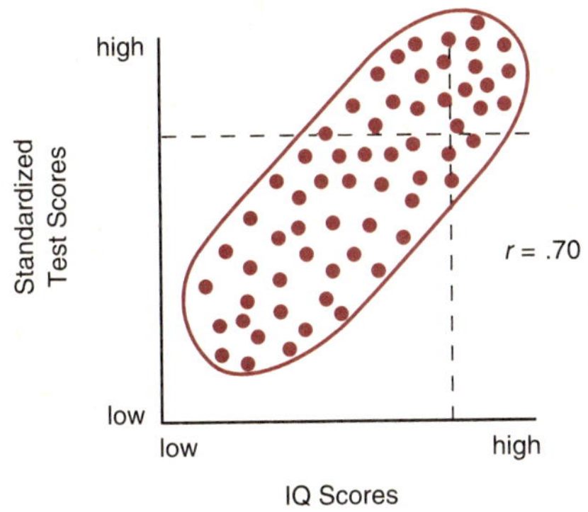

However, let's say that we are concerned only with the relationship between high scores on both tests (indicated by the broken lines demarcating the upper right-hand section of the scatterplot). The correlation between only the high scores is much weaker than the correlation between scores across the entire range. This is illustrated in the next scatterplot, which is an enlargement of the upper right-hand section of the previous scatterplot.

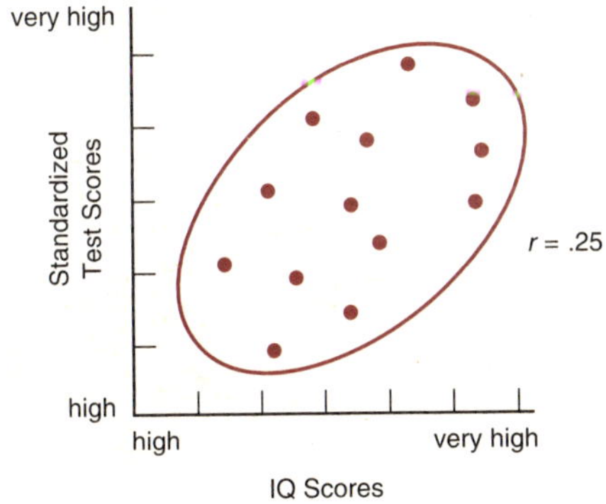

This completes our chapters on statistics. We trust you now have a good working knowledge of the concepts and methods presented. If so, you are ready to apply some of these concepts and methods in the following chapters. If not, now is the time to review. The remainder of the text will be a lot easier to understand if you take the extra time to review.

SUMMARY

In this chapter you were introduced to a number of considerations related to the topic of correlation. The major points are:

1. Correlation refers to the extent to which two distributions are related or associated. That is, it refers to the extent to which scores in one distribution vary depending on the variation of scores in the other distribution.
2. The extent of correlation is indicated numerically by a correlation coefficient (r) and graphically by a scatterplot.
3. When high scores in one distribution tend to be associated with low scores in another distribution, and vice versa, the correlation is negative.
4. When high scores in one distribution tend to be associated with high scores in another distribution (with the same being true for low and moderate scores), the correlation is positive.
5. Correlation coefficients may range from -1.0 (perfect negative correlation) to $+1.0$ (perfect positive correlation). A correlation of .00 indicates an absence of relationship or association.
6. The size of the number of the correlation coefficient indicates the strength of the correlation (higher numbers indicate stronger correlation), and the sign indicates the direction (positive or negative).
7. Scatterplots range from straight lines indicative of a perfect correlation to ellipses that approach circles. The tighter the ellipse, the stronger the correlation; the more circular the ellipse, the weaker the correlation.
8. The fact that two variables are correlated with each other does *not* necessarily mean that one variable causes the other. Often the correlation is the result of the effects of a third variable.
9. To compare the relative strength of correlation coefficients it is necessary to square the coefficients, resulting in coefficients of determination. Correlation coefficients are not percentages; coefficients of determination are.
10. When two distributions are linearly related, scores increase or decrease across the range of scores.
11. When two distributions have a curvilinear relationship, scores in one distribution may increase and then decrease, or vice versa, while scores in the other distribution consistently increase or decrease.
12. Since a linear correlation coefficient will underestimate the strength of a curvilinear relationship, it is wise to construct a scatterplot before computing a correlation coefficient.
13. When only a portion of the entire range of scores for a distribution is considered (for example, only high or low scores) in computing a correlation

coefficient, the strength of the correlation coefficient decreases. This effect is due to use of a truncated range of scores, rather than the entire range of scores.

For Practice

1. After pairing each X score with each Y score in the order given below, construct a scatterplot of the data.
   X: 15, 15, 15, 15, 30, 30, 30, 30, 45, 45, 45, 45, 60, 60, 60, 60, 75, 75, 75, 75
   Y: 1, 2, 1, 3, 12, 10, 13, 15, 19, 18, 20, 21, 15, 11, 12, 12, 2, 3, 1, 2

*2. Does the scatterplot in question 1 indicate that the data are linear or curvilinear? If X represents age and Y represents average annual income in thousands of dollars, describe this relationship in words.

*3. Using the formula given in Appendix B, compute a Pearson Product-Moment Correlation for the following data.
   X: 10, 8, 14, 6, 4, 8, 7, 3, 7, 10
   Y: 12, 7, 13, 8, 7, 6, 6, 4, 9, 11

   How would you describe the direction and size of this relationship?

*4. Compute the coefficient of determination for the data in question 3.

*5. In the following matching exercise, column A contains scatterplots and column B contains correlation coefficients. Indicate which of the correlation coefficients in column B most closely approximates the scatterplots in column A. Each of the options may be used only once or not at all.

Column A

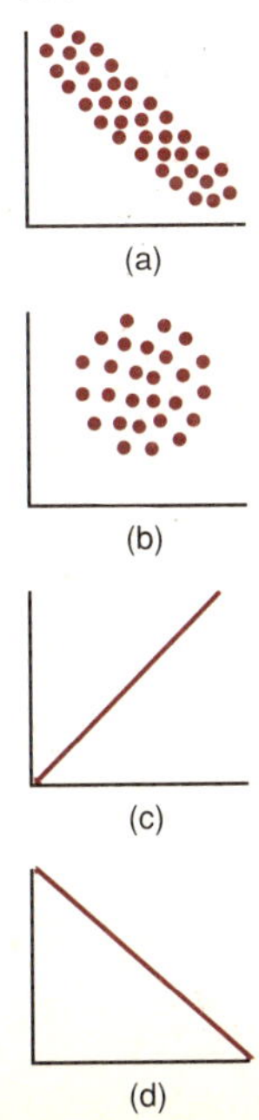

Column B

1. +1.0
2. −1.0
3. + .80
4. − .80
5. + .50
6. − .50
7. 0.0

*6. A researcher finds a high positive correlation between shoe size and vocabulary size in elementary-school pupils. The researcher concludes that "big feet cause big vocabularies." Do you agree or disagree? If so, why? If not, why not?

*7. Explain why the use of a truncated range of scores will result in a lower correlation between the variables in question than if the distribution were not truncated.

*Answers for questions 2 through 7 appear in Appendix D.

CHAPTER 15

Validity

In the last three chapters we introduced you to the field of statistics. In this and subsequent chapters we will show how to use some of this newly acquired knowledge to evaluate tests. In short, we will show you how statistical tools are applied to test results to determine the degree of confidence we can place in them.

WHY EVALUATE TESTS?

If a test shows that 60 percent of the students in our third-grade class are reading below grade level, should we be seriously concerned? Your initial response might be an unqualified yes, but we would say, not necessarily. We would be worried only if we had confidence in the results of our test. We have such confidence only when we are reasonably sure a test measures the skill, trait, or attribute it is supposed to measure; when it yields reasonably consistent results for the same individual; and when it measures with a reasonable degree of accuracy. That is, we should seriously consider using test results only from tests that are valid, reliable, and accurate. These terms can be defined as follows:

1. *Validity*—Does the test measure what it is supposed to measure?
2. *Reliability*—Does the test yield the same or similar scores (all other factors being equal) consistently?
3. *Accuracy*—Does the test approximate fairly closely an individual's true level of ability, skill, or aptitude?

To be a "good" test, a test ought to have adequate validity, reliability, and accuracy. In this chapter we will see how statistics help us determine the extent to which tests possess validity.

TYPES OF VALIDITY

A test is valid if it measures what it says it measures. For instance, if it is supposed to be a test of third-grade arithmetic ability, it should measure third-grade arithmetic skills, not fifth-grade arithmetic skills and not reading ability. If it is supposed to be a measure of ability to write behavioral objectives, it should measure that ability, not the ability to recognize bad objectives. Clearly, if a test is to be used in any kind of decision making, or indeed if the test information is to have any use at all, it is essential that the test be valid.

Content Validity

There are several ways of deciding whether a test is sufficiently valid to be useful. The simplest is content validity. The content validity of a test is established by examination. Test questions are inspected to see whether they correspond to what the user feels should be covered by the test. This is easiest when the test is in an area such as achievement, where it is fairly easy to specify what should be included in the content of a test. It is more difficult if the concept being tested is a personality or aptitude trait, as it is sometimes difficult to specify beforehand what a relevant question should look like. Another problem with content validity is that it gives information about whether the test *looks* valid, but not whether the reading level of the test is too high or the items are poorly constructed. A test can sometimes look valid but measure something entirely different than what is intended, such as guessing ability, reading level, or skills that may have been acquired before instruction. Content validity is, therefore, more a minimum requirement for a useful test than it is a guarantee of a good test.

Content validity answers the question "Does the test measure the instructional objectives?" In other words, a content-valid test matches or fits the instructional objectives.

Criterion-Related Validity

A second form of validity is criterion-related validity. In establishing criterion-related validity, scores from a test are correlated with an external criterion. There are two types of criterion-related validity: concurrent and predictive.

CONCURRENT CRITERION-RELATED VALIDITY. Concurrent criterion-related validity deals with measures that can be administered at the same time as the measure to be validated. For instance, the Stanford-Binet and the Wechsler Intelligence Scale for Children-III (WISC-III) are well-known, widely accepted IQ tests. Therefore, a test publisher designing a short screening test that measures IQ might show that the test is highly correlated with the WISC-III or the Binet, and thus establish concurrent criterion-related validity for the test. Unlike content validity, criterion-related validity yields a numeric value, which is simply a correlation coefficient, sometimes called a validity coefficient. The concurrent validity for a test is determined by administering both the new test and the established test to a group of respondents, then finding the correlation between the two sets of test scores. If there exists an established test (criterion) in which most people have confidence, criterion-related validity provides a good method of estimating the validity of a new test. Of course, usually there is some practical advantage of having a new test—it is cheaper to give, or shorter, or can be administered to groups. Otherwise, it would be easier simply to use the established test. The following example illustrates how concurrent validity might be established for a new third-grade math test.

The Goodly Test of Basic Third-Grade Math has been around a long time, but it takes 60 minutes to administer. Being pressed for teaching time, you develop another test that takes only 20 minutes to administer and call it the Shorter and Better Test of Basic Third-Grade Math. You send it off to a test publisher with visions of fame and wealth.

The publisher writes back to ask whether the test is as good as the Goodly Test: "No point marketing a test that isn't at least as good as the Goodly."

To address this challenge, you would determine the test's concurrent validity by giving both the Goodly and the Shorter and Better to the same group of students and calculating a correlation coefficient between scores on the two tests. If the same students score similarly on both tests, indicated by a high correlation, the new test could be said to have concurrent validity. Consider the following hypothetical data:

Student	***Scores on Goodly***	***Scores on Shorter and Better***
Jim	88	37
Joan	86	34
Don	77	32
Margaret	72	26
Teresa	65	22
Victor	62	21
Veronica	59	19
Wilson	58	16

Since the correlation in this instance is likely to be very high (notice that, for the data shown, everyone maintains the same rank across tests), the concurrent validity of the Shorter and Better Test has been established. The publisher will be impressed, and you are soon to be famous.

PREDICTIVE VALIDITY. Predictive validity refers to how well the test predicts some future behavior of the examinee. This form of validity is particularly useful for aptitude tests, which attempt to predict how well the test taker will do in some future setting. The Scholastic Assessment Test, or SAT, for instance, is frequently used to help decide who should be admitted to college. It would be desirable, therefore, for it to do a good job of predicting success in college. If a personality test is used to choose among various types of therapy for mental patients, then it is desirable that it have good predictive validity. That is, it should predict who will do well with what kind of therapy. The predictive validity of a test is determined by administering the test to a group of subjects, then measuring the subjects on whatever the test is supposed to predict after a period of time has elapsed. The two sets of scores are then correlated, and the coefficient that results is called a *predictive validity coefficient.*

If a test is being used to make predictions, then an effort should be made to find its predictive validity for the setting in which it will be used. High predictive validity provides a strong argument for the worth of a test, even if it seems questionable on other grounds. In such a situation you might argue about whether it is being used to predict something worthwhile, but you can't argue about whether the test does a good job of predicting. The following example illustrates the concept of predictive validity:

"Psychics predict blizzard for Houston on July 4th!" You have likely seen similar predictions on various tabloids while waiting in checkout lines at supermarkets. Are they valid? Initially, you'd probably say no, but how can you be sure? The only answer is to wait and see if the predictions come true. With a test, similar reasoning applies. Just because a test is named the Test to Predict Happiness in Life doesn't mean it can (or cannot). More likely than not, we would be inclined to say it can't. But again, the only way to be sure is to wait for a period of time and see if the individuals for whom the test predicts "happiness" are actually happy.

Both predictive and concurrent criterion-related validity yield numerical indices of validity. Content validity does not yield a numerical index, but instead yields a logical judgment as to whether the test covers what it is supposed to cover. However, all three of these indices—content, concurrent, and predictive—assume that some criterion exists external to the test that can be used to anchor or validate the test. In the case of content validity, it was the instructional objectives that provided the anchor or point of reference; in the case of concurrent validity, it was another well-accepted test measuring the same thing; and in the case of predictive validity, it was some future behavior or condition which we were attempting to predict. However, if a test is being developed to measure something not previously measured, or not measured well, and no criterion exists for anchoring the test, another kind of validity must be used. This type of validity is called *construct validity*.

Construct Validity

A test has construct validity if its relationship to other information corresponds well with some theory. A theory is simply a logical explanation or rationale that can account for the interrelationships among a set of variables. Many different kinds of theories can be used to determine the construct validity of a test. For instance, if it is supposed to be a test of arithmetic computation skills, you would expect scores on it to improve after intensive coaching in arithmetic. If it is a test of mechanical aptitude, you might expect that mechanics would, on the average, do better on it than poets. You might also expect that it would have a *low* correlation with scores on a reading test, since it seems reasonable to assume that reading ability and mechanical ability are not highly related. In general, any information that lets you know whether results from the test correspond to what you would expect (based on your own knowledge about what is being measured) tells you something about the construct validity of a test. It differs from concurrent validity in that there is no good second measure available of what you're trying to test, and from predictive validity in that there is no measure of future behavior available.

Already in this chapter we have had to introduce some new terms and concepts. Before proceeding, be familiar with these terms and concepts, and, if necessary, reread our presentation on validity. Before you do, though, let's try to understand at a commonsense level what we've been saying.

What Have We Been Saying? A Review

A test should ideally do the job it's written to do. That is, it should measure what it's supposed to measure. In other words, it should be valid. The following three questions are equivalent:

1. Is the test valid?
2. Does the test measure what it is supposed to measure?
3. Does the test do the job it was designed to do?

It makes no sense to prepare or select for the classroom a test designed to measure something other than what has been taught. If we want to measure someone's height, does it make sense to use a scale? A ruler, yardstick, or a tape measure would certainly be more appropriate. Similarly, if we are interested in knowing whether our students can multiply two-digit numbers, would it make sense to administer a test that focuses on addition of two-digit numbers? The appropriate measure would be a test that includes items on two-digit multiplication. Such a test would *do the job it's supposed to do*. It would have content validity.

For achievement tests, content validity is most important because the "job" of an achievement test is to measure how well the content taught has been mastered. The best way to ensure that a test's content is valid is to be sure its items match or measure the instructional objectives. Recall that in Chapter 5 we discussed ways to check whether items match objectives. Now, let's review predictive validity.

Consider a situation in which the purpose of a test is to identify those individuals who are likely to stay with a company for at least three years. A valid test in this case would accomplish this purpose. But just what is the purpose? Is it to measure how well certain concepts have been mastered? No, the purpose is to predict who will last three years and who won't. A different kind of validity is in order—predictive validity.

In this situation we are interested only in finding a measuring instrument that correlates well with length of time on the job. We don't care whether it is an IQ test, math test, reading test, vocational test, visual-motor integration test, or whatever. The purpose is to predict who will last three years. If the math test correlates .75 with length of time on the job and the vocational test correlates .40 with length of time on the job, which test has the *better predictive* validity? The math test, of course, because it would provide us with the most accurate predictions of future behavior.

In the case of concurrent validity, the purpose of a test is to approximate the results that would have been obtained had a well-established test been used. In other words, if the ranking of students with the new or shorter test *concurs* with the rankings of students on the older, standard test, then the new or shorter test has concurrent validity. Remember, unless a new test does something more easily or better than an established measure, there is no point in constructing a new test!

Finally, let's think about construct validity. Construct validity is important in establishing the validity of a test when we cannot anchor our test either to a well-established test measuring the same behavior or to any measurable future behavior. Since we do not have these anchoring devices to rely on, we can only create verbal and mathematical descriptions or theories of how our test behavior (called a construct) is either likely to change following or during certain situations, or likely to be related to other constructs. If a test of our theory reflects or demonstrates the relationships specified, then the new measure has construct validity. Unlike predictive and concurrent validity, not one but many correlation coefficients emerge from a construct-validation study. The actual process used to assess construct validity can be lengthy and complex and need not concern us here. Figure 15.1, Review of Validity, summarizes our discussion of validity thus far. Believe it or not, our presentation of test validity has been quite superficial as far as measurement theory goes. If you are interested in a more intensive discussion of any of these topics you can consult one or more of the measurement texts listed in Appendix C. Next, we will discuss the role of validity coefficients in evaluating tests.

INTERPRETING VALIDITY COEFFICIENTS

Now that we have discussed and reviewed the concepts of content, concurrent, and predictive validity, we can begin to put these concepts to use in evaluating tests. Remember, validity coefficients enable us to estimate the extent to which a test measures what it is supposed to measure. Let's consider the role of validity coefficients in making decisions about tests.

Content Validity

If you are wondering why content validity is included in this section, you are probably grasping more of what has been presented than you may realize. Procedures to determine a test's content validity do *not* yield validity coefficients. Content validity is established by comparing test items with instructional objectives (with, for example, the aid of a test blueprint) to determine whether the items match or measure the objectives. After such an examination takes place, a test is judged either to have or not to have content validity. No correlation coefficient is computed. Instead, human judgment is relied upon.

Concurrent and Predictive Validity

Concurrent and predictive validity require the correlation of a predictor or concurrent measure with a criterion measure. Thus, these types of validity *do* yield numerical coefficients. Using our interpretation of these coefficients, we can determine whether a test is useful to us as a predictor or as a substitute (concurrent) measure. In general, the higher the validity coefficient, the more valid the test will be. However, several principles must be considered in evaluating validity coefficients.

> PRINCIPLE 1: Concurrent validity coefficients are generally higher than predictive validity coefficients. This does *not* mean, however, that the test with the higher validity coefficient is more suitable for a given purpose.

FIGURE 15.1
Review of Validity

	Asks the question:	*To answer the question:*
• Content Validity	Do test items match and measure objectives?	Match the items with objectives.
• Concurrent Criterion-Related Validity	How well does performance on the new test match performance on an established test?	Correlate new test with an accepted criterion, for example, a well-established test measuring the same behavior.
• Predictive Criterion-Related Validity	Can the test predict subsequent performance, for example, success or failure in the next grade?	Correlate scores from the new test with a measure of some future performance.

Remember: Predictive validity involves a time interval. A test is administered and, after a period of time, a behavior is measured which the test is intended to predict. For example:

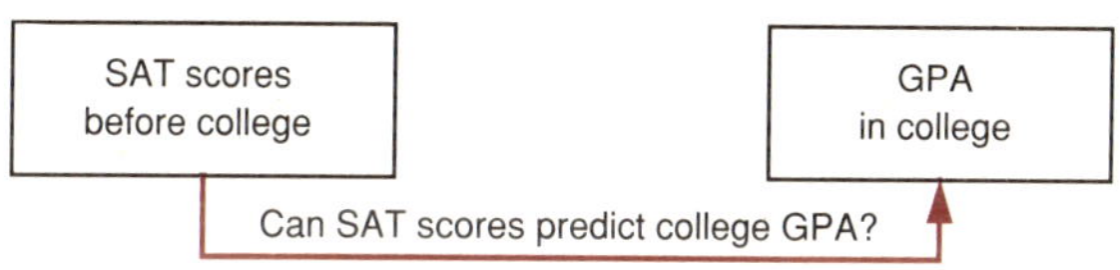

Remember: Concurrent validity does not involve a time interval. A test is administered, and its relationship to a well established test measuring the same behavior is determined. For example:

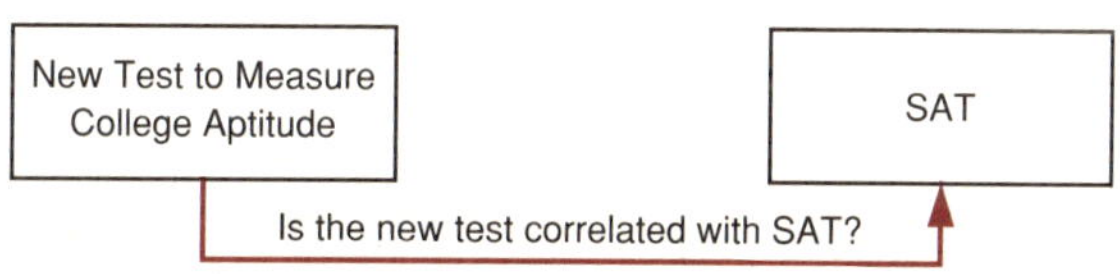

The rationale for this principle is that, in establishing concurrent validity, no time interval (or a very small time interval) is involved between administration of the new test and the criterion or established test. Thus, the chances that the behavior of individuals measured on both the new test and the criterion test has changed between testings is negligible. On the contrary, predictive validity coefficients are by definition susceptible to such changes. Lifestyle, personality, and attitudinal or experiential changes may alter an individual's rank on a criterion measure two years from now from what it was at the initial testing. Thus, a *decline* in the size of the correlation between the test and a measure of future performance would be expected as the time interval between the two testings increases.

Generally, concurrent validity coefficients in the .80-and-higher range and predictive validity coefficients in the .60-and-higher range are considered encouraging. Thus, if a new achievement test reports a concurrent validity coefficient of .60 with an established achievement test, we probably would not consider using the new achievement test. On the other hand, if a new college selection test correlated .60 with college GPA, the new test might be considered suitable for use as a college selection test. In other words, the *purpose* of the test as well as the size of the validity coefficient must be considered in evaluating the test.

PRINCIPLE 2: Group variability affects the size of the validity coefficient. Higher validity coefficients are derived from heterogeneous groups than from homogeneous groups.

If the college selection test mentioned before was administered to *all* high-school seniors in a district (a heterogeneous group) and if all these students went to the same four-year college, the obtained validity coefficient would be higher for this group than if the test were administered only to high-school seniors in the top 10 percent of their class (a homogeneous group). At first glance this may not seem to make sense. The picture becomes clear, however, if we think about how changes in the rankings of individuals on the two measures are affected by the variability of these distributions. In the heterogeneous group, students who are at the top of their high-school class are likely to score high on the test and have high college GPA's. Students at the bottom of the class are likely to score low and have low college GPA's. That is, the likelihood of major shifting in ranks occurring is small. It's not likely that students who score low on the test will have high GPA's and vice versa, as is illustrated in Figure 15.2.

Although some shifting in ranks or position might be expected, as indicated by the arrows in Figure 15.2, dramatic shifts would be unlikely. While it might be possible for our lowest-scoring student on the selection test (Student A) to obtain a 3.5 GPA, it would be unlikely. But what happens when the variability of the group is greatly reduced, creating a homogeneous group composed only of the top 10 percent of the high-school seniors? Now we would expect a pronounced shifting of ranks or positions to take place. This is likely to occur because the students are all ranked *so closely together* on the selection test that even small differences between their ranks on GPA will lower the size of the validity coefficient. This is illustrated in Figure 15.3.

Compare the overlap, or possible shifting in ranks, for this group to the possible shifting in ranks for the heterogeneous group. The width of the arrows has not changed, but their significance has. There is much more likelihood of dramatic shifts occurring among the students in this homogeneous group. They are so much alike in ability that the test is unable to discriminate among those individuals in the high-ability group who will rank low, middle, or high in their GPA's, since the range of GPA's for this group is only about 3.5 to 4.0. When test scores or criterion measures are more heterogeneous, however, the test is able to discriminate among those who will rank low, moderate, or high in GPA's. In such a case, GPA's might range from 0.0 to 4.0. Thus, in evaluating a test's validity coef-

FIGURE 15.2
Comparison of Probable Rankings Between College Selection Test Scores and College GPA for Four Students from a Heterogeneous Group

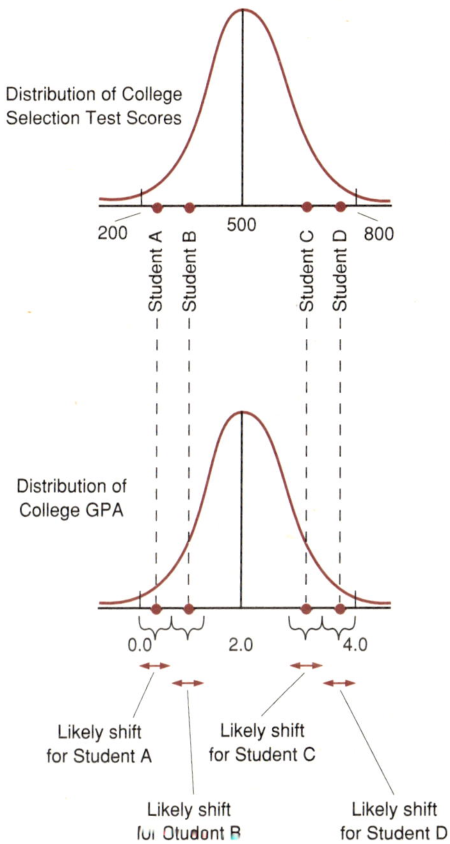

ficient, it is necessary to consider the variability of the group from which the coefficient was derived. For example, critics who discourage using the SAT as a criterion for college admission often point out that its predictive validity coefficient is only about .40. What they may fail to consider, however, is that the coefficient is not based on all high-school students, but only on those who took the test and actually went to college. This is a far more homogeneous group than the entire body of high-school students. Thus, its predictive validity coefficient is smaller than would be expected if it were based on *all* high-school students.

PRINCIPLE 3: The relevance and reliability of the criterion should be considered in the interpretation of validity coefficients.

FIGURE 15.3
Comparison of Probable Rankings Between College Selection Test Scores and College GPA for Four Students from a Homogeneous Group (Upper 10% of Senior Class)

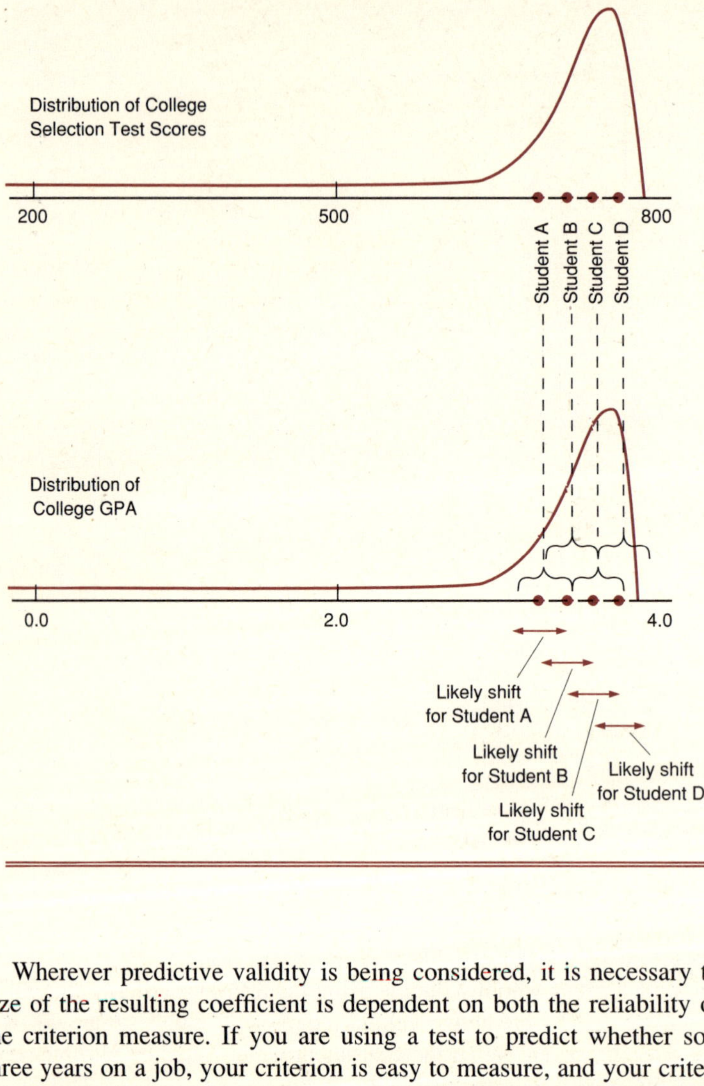

Wherever predictive validity is being considered, it is necessary to be aware that the size of the resulting coefficient is dependent on both the reliability of the predictor *and* the criterion measure. If you are using a test to predict whether someone will last for three years on a job, your criterion is easy to measure, and your criterion measure would be dependable. For this measure you need simply to determine whether someone is employed after three years. Unfortunately, in many cases criterion measures are not so clear-cut. For example, let's say you want to establish the predictive validity of a test to predict job success, rather than simply whether someone is or is not employed after three years. What does job success mean? Herein lies the problem of selecting a criterion measure. Is it best measured by salary scale? Number of promotions? Amount of sales?

Merchandise produced? Supervisor ratings? Peer ratings? All of these? We could probably go on and on, but the point is that criterion measures that are meaningful are often difficult to identify and agree upon. Each of the criterion measures mentioned may be an important *aspect* of job success, but none is *equivalent* to job success. Ideally, you would want to collect many measures of job success and determine their relationship to the test. In reality, however, such a thorough approach might be impossible due to financial or time constraints. What typically happens in a predictive validity investigation is that one or two of what are considered to be relevant criterion measures are selected and correlated with the predictor. Naturally, such a compromise limits somewhat the weight that one might attach to predictive validity coefficients, since not all relevant aspects of the criterion are considered.

If a test has a predictive validity coefficient of .60 with salary after three years, but coefficients of .20 with supervisor ratings and .16 with peer ratings, we would seriously question the test's validity. Since salary typically increases from year to year, often independent of success on the job, the correlation with salary might not be very meaningful, since salary may not be all that *relevant*. On the other hand, supervisor and peer ratings may be more relevant measures. However, our test's correlation with these measures is little more than what might occur by chance. Thus, since the test does not correlate highly with more relevant criteria, we might question its predictive validity. However, to do so without considering the dependability of the criterion measure we have chosen would be a mistake.

To correlate highly or even moderately with each other, measures must be dependable or fairly stable (that is, *reliable*). If ratings by supervisors or peers vary greatly from rating period to rating period, then any attempt to correlate such ratings with a predictor will yield low correlation coefficients—even if the predictor is highly reliable. Thus, if an employee gets a high rating from one peer or supervisor and a low rating from another, how can the predictor possibly predict a rating? The answer is that it can't. Some evidence of stability or reliability in a criterion measure is necessary before we can conclude that a predictor that correlates poorly with a criterion measure is actually a poor predictor and not the result of an unreliable criterion measure.

We have intended this discussion to alert you to the importance of studying carefully any and all statistical data presented in test manuals. Where predictive validity coefficients are reported, check the adequacy (the relevance) of the criterion measure and its dependability (the reliability) before drawing any conclusions about the validity of the predictor.

SUMMARY

This chapter introduced you to the major types of validity and some principles to be considered in interpreting validity coefficients. The major points are:

1. To be considered seriously, test results should be valid and reliable.

2. A valid test measures what it is supposed to measure.

3. Content validity is assessed by comparing a test item with instructional objectives to see if they match. Content validity does not yield a numerical estimate of validity.

4. Criterion-related validity is established by correlating test scores with an external standard or criterion to obtain a numerical estimate of validity.

5. There are two types of criterion-related validity: concurrent and predictive.
   a. Concurrent validity is determined by correlating test scores with a criterion measure collected at the same time.
   b. Predictive validity is determined by correlating test scores with a criterion measure collected after a period of time has passed.

6. Construct validity is determined by finding whether test results correspond with scores on other variables as predicted by some rationale or theory.

7. In interpreting validity estimates, the following principles should be kept in mind:
   a. The adequacy of a validity estimate depends on both the strength of the validity coefficient and the type of validity being determined.
   b. Group variability affects the strength of the validity coefficient.
   c. Validity coefficients should be considered in terms of the relevance and reliability of the criterion or standard.

For Practice

*1. A teacher who is a friend of yours has just developed a test to measure the content in a social studies unit you both teach. His test takes 30 minutes less time to complete than the test you have used in the past, and you decide this is a major advantage. You decide to evaluate the new test by giving it and the old test to the same class of students. Using the data below, determine if the new test has concurrent validity.

Scores on the new test: 25, 22, 18, 18, 16, 14, 12, 8, 6, 6
Scores for the same students on the old test: 22, 23, 25, 28, 31, 32, 34, 42, 44, 48

*2. Indicate how and with what types of tests you would evaluate the predictive and construct validity of the new social studies test in question 1.

*3. Examine the validity coefficients of the following tests and, assuming they are content-valid, determine which are suitable for use. State your reasons. What is unusual about Test C?

	Test A	*Test B*	*Test C*
Concurrent validity coefficient	.90	.50	.75
Predictive validity coefficient	.72	.32	.88

*4. Assuming the following tests measure the same content and assuming all other things are equal, rank them in terms of their overall acceptability for predicting behavior in upcoming years.

	Test A	*Test B*	*Test C*
Concurrent validity coefficient	.90	.80	.85
Predictive validity coefficient (one-month interval)	.50	.65	.60
Predictive validity coefficient (six-month interval)	.40	.10	.55

*5. What types of validity go with the following procedures?

a. Matching test items with objectives

b. Correlating a test of mechanical skills after training with on-the-job performance ratings

c. Correlating the short form of an IQ test with the long form

d. Correlating a paper-and-pencil test of musical talent with ratings from a live audition completed after the test

e. Correlating a test of reading ability with a test of mathematical ability

f. Comparing lesson plans with a test publisher's test blueprint

6. The principal is upset. The results of the four-year follow-up study are in. The correlation between the grades assigned by you to your gifted students and their college GPA is lower than the correlation between grades and college GPA for nongifted students. The principal wants to abandon the gifted program. How would you defend yourself and your program?

---

*Answers for these questions appear in Appendix D.

CHAPTER 16

Reliability

The reliability of a test refers to the consistency with which it yields the same rank for an individual taking the test several times. In other words, a test (or any measuring instrument) is reliable if it consistently yields the same, or nearly the same, ranks over repeated administrations during which we would not expect the trait being measured to have changed. For instance, a bathroom scale is reliable if it gives you the same weight after five weighings in a single morning. If the five weights differ by several pounds, then the scale is not especially reliable. If the five weights differ by 25 pounds, then it is extremely unreliable. In the same manner, educational tests may be very reliable, fairly reliable, or totally unreliable. For instance, if a multiple-choice test given to a class were so difficult that everyone guessed at the answers, then a student's rank would probably vary quite a bit from one administration to another, and the test would be unreliable.

If any use is to be made of the information from a test, then it is desirable that the test results be reliable. If the test is going to be used to make placement decisions about individual students, you wouldn't want it to provide different data about students if it were given again the next day. If a test is going to be used to make decisions about the difficulty level of your instructional materials, you wouldn't want it to indicate that the same materials are too difficult one day and too easy the next. In testing, as in our everyday lives, if we have use for some piece of information, we would like that information to be stable, consistent, and dependable.

METHODS OF ESTIMATING RELIABILITY

There are several ways to estimate the reliability of a test. The three basic methods most often used are called *test-retest*, *alternative form*, and *internal consistency*.

Test-Retest

Test-retest is a method of estimating reliability that is exactly what its name implies. The test is given twice and the correlation between the first set of scores and the second set of scores is determined. For example, suppose a math test given to six students on Monday is given again on the following Monday without any math having been taught in between these times. The six students make the following scores on the test:

Student	*First administration score*	*Second administration score*
1	75	78
2	50	62
3	93	91
4	80	77
5	67	66
6	88	88

The correlation between these two sets of scores is .96. Thus it could be concluded that this test is quite reliable. The main problem with test-retest reliability is that there is usually some memory or experience involved the second time the test is taken. That means that the scores may differ not only because of the unreliability of the test, but also because the students themselves may have changed in some way. For example, they may have gotten some answers correct on the retest by remembering or finding answers to some of the questions on the initial test. To some extent this problem can be overcome by using a longer interval between test administrations, to give memory a chance to fade. However, if the interval is too long, the students may have changed on the trait being measured because of other factors, for example, reading in the library, instruction in other courses, seeing a film, and so on. Thus, in considering test-retest reliability coefficients, the interval between testings must also be considered. Test-retest reliability is illustrated in Figure 16.1.

Alternate Forms

If there are two equivalent forms of a test, these forms can be used to obtain an estimate of the reliability of the test. Both forms are administered to a group of students, and the correlation between the two sets of scores is determined. This estimate eliminates the problems of memory and practice involved in test-retest estimates. Large differences in a student's score on two forms of a test which supposedly measures the same behavior would indicate an unreliable test. To use this method of estimating reliability, two equivalent forms of the test must be available, and they must be administered under conditions as nearly equivalent as possible. The most critical problem with this method of estimating reliability is that it takes a great deal of effort to develop *one* good test, let alone two. Hence, this method is most often used by test publishers who are creating two forms of their test for other reasons (for example, to maintain test security). Figure 16.2 illustrates alternate-forms reliability.

Internal Consistency

If the test in question is designed to measure a single basic concept, then it is reasonable to assume that people who get one item right will be more likely to get other, similar

FIGURE 16.1
Test-Retest Reliability

To determine test-retest reliability, the same test is administered twice to the same group of students, and their scores are correlated. Generally, the longer the interval between test administrations, the lower the correlation. Since students can be expected to change with the passage of time, an especially long interval between testings will produce a "reliability" coefficient that is more a reflection of student changes on the attribute being measured than it is a reflection of the reliability of the test.

This time interval reflects the reliability of the test.	January 1 Test A	February 1 Test A
	Correlation, $r = .90$	
This time interval reflects the reliability of the test plus unknown changes in the students on the attribute being measured.	January 1 Test A	June 1 Test A
	Correlation, $r = .50$	

FIGURE 16.2
Alternate-Forms Reliability

To determine alternate-forms reliability of a test, two different versions of the same test are administered to the same group of students in as short a time period as possible, and their scores correlated. Efforts are made to have the students complete one form of the test in the morning and another, equivalent form of the test in the afternoon or the following day.

June 1, morning Test A (Form X)	June 1, afternoon Test A (Form Y)

Correlation, $r = .80$

items right. In other words, items ought to be correlated with each other, and the test ought to be internally consistent. If this is the case, then the reliability of the test can be estimated by the internal consistency method. One approach to determining a test's internal consistency, called *split halves*, involves splitting the test into two equivalent halves and determining the correlation between them. This can be done by assigning all items in the first half of the test to one form and all items in the second half of the test to the other

FIGURE 16.3
Internal Consistency Reliability (Odd-Even Method)

The internal consistency of a test is determined from a *single* test administration. Hence, it does not involve a time interval as do the test-retest and alternate-form methods. The test is split into two equal parts and the total scores for each student on each half of the test are correlated. The internal consistency method of determining reliability is appropriate only when the test measures a unitary, homogeneous concept (for example, addition or finding the least common denominator) and not a variety of concepts.

Half of Test A (e.g., even-numbered items)	Half of Test A (e.g., odd-numbered items)

Correlation, $r = .75$

form. However, this approach is only appropriate when items of varying difficulty are randomly spread across the test. Frequently they are not. In these cases the best approach would be to divide test items by placing all odd-numbered items into one half and all even-numbered items into the other half. When this latter approach is used, the reliability is more commonly called the *odd-even reliability*.

SPLIT-HALF METHODS. To find the split-half (or odd-even) reliability, each item is assigned to one half or the other. Then, the total score for each student on each half is determined and the correlation between the two total scores for both halves is computed. Essentially, a single test is used to make two shorter alternative forms. This method has the advantage that only one test administration is required, and, therefore, memory or practice effects are not involved. Furthermore, it does not require two tests. Thus, it has several advantages over test-retest and alternate-form estimates of reliability. Because of these advantages, it is the most frequently used method of estimating the reliability of classroom tests. This method is illustrated in Figure 16.3.

Internal consistency calculated by this method is actually a way of finding alternate-form reliability for a test half as long. However, since a test is usually more reliable if it is longer, the internal consistency method *underestimates* what the actual reliability of the full test would be. Thus, the split-half (or odd-even) reliability coefficient should be corrected or adjusted upward to reflect the reliability that the test would have if it were twice as long. The formula used for this correction is called the Spearman-Brown Prophecy Formula. It is:

$$r_w = \frac{2r_h}{1 + r_h}$$

where r_w is the correlation for the *whole* test, and r_h is the correlation between the two *halves* of the test. The result of applying this formula gives the predicted split-half (or odd-even) reliability coefficient for a test twice as long as either of its halves. In almost all cases, it will increase the size of the reliability coefficient from that computed for the two half tests.

KUDER-RICHARDSON METHODS. Another way of estimating the internal consistency of a test is through one of the Kuder-Richardson methods. These methods measure the extent which items within one form of the test have as much in common with one another as do the items in that one form with corresponding items in an equivalent form. The strength of this estimate of reliability depends on the extent to which the entire test represents a *single*, fairly consistent measure of a concept. Normally Kuder-Richardson techniques will yield somewhat lower estimates of reliability than split halves, but higher than test-retest or alternate-form estimates. These procedures are sometimes called item-total correlations.

There are several ways to determine the internal consistency of a test using Kuder-Richardson procedures. Of these, two are frequently seen in test manuals. The first is more difficult to calculate, since it requires the percentage of students passing each item on the test. It is, however, the most accurate and has the name KR20 (Kuder-Richardson Formula 20). The resulting coefficient is equal to the average of all possible split-half coefficients for the group tested. The second formula, which is easier to calculate but slightly less accurate, has the name KR21. It is the least cumbersome of the KR formulas and requires a knowledge only of the number of test items (n), the mean of the test ($\overline{X}$), and its standard deviation(s). The formula for the KR21 is:

$$\text{KR21} = \frac{n}{n-1}\left(\frac{1-\overline{X}(n-\overline{X})}{ns^2}\right)$$

The KR21 formula tends to produce a smaller (less accurate) coefficient than KR20 but has the advantage of being easier to calculate. Test publishers often report a Kuder-Richardson coefficient, so it is important that you recognize it and know something about it.

Before leaving the topic of internal consistency we need to mention one other coefficient because of its frequent use. This coefficient, called coefficient Alpha, is closely related to Kuder-Richardson procedures but has the advantage of being applicable to tests that are multiple-scored, that is, that are not scored right or wrong or according to some other all-or-none system. For example, on attitude or personality surveys the respondent may receive a different numerical score on an item depending on whether the response "all," "some," "a little," or "none" is checked. In such cases our previous methods of determining internal consistency would not be applicable and the coefficient Alpha should be used. Coefficient Alpha is laborious to compute, so its computation is best left up to the test publisher. Its interpretation is not difficult, however, because it is interpreted the same as the Kuder-Richardson methods and therefore may be taken as an index of the extent to which the instrument measures a single, unified concept.

PROBLEMS WITH INTERNAL CONSISTENCY ESTIMATES. Internal consistency techniques are useful measures of reliability in that they involve only one test administration and are free from memory and practice effects. However, there are some problems with these methods. First, they can only be used if the entire test consists of similar items measuring a single concept. Thus, they *would* be appropriate for use on a spelling test, but *not* for a language test involving a spelling section, a reading comprehension section, and a composition section.

A second problem is that measures of internal consistency yield inflated estimates of reliability when used with *speeded* tests. A speeded test consists entirely of easy or relatively easy item tasks with a strict time limit. On such a test, test takers are expected to answer correctly most items attempted. Ranks or grades are usually assigned mostly on the basis of the number of items attempted (since the items are easy, most attempts are successful), rather than on mastery of the subject areas, written expression, and so forth. Examples of speeded tests are typing tests or such manual dexterity tests as screwing nuts on bolts or putting square pegs in square holes.

Speeded tests may be thought of in contrast to *power tests*. Power tests have difficult items, or items varying in difficulty, but have such generous time limits that most students have an opportunity to attempt most or all of the items. With a power test, ranks or grades are assigned based mostly on the quality or "correctness" of answers, rather than on the number of items attempted. Examples of power tests are essay tests, word problems, and reasoning tasks. In reality, *most* tests are a combination of power *and* speed tests. The typical classroom or standardized achievement test is partially a speeded test (for example, some easy items, fairly strict time limits) and partially a power test (for example, items range in difficulty, and most students are expected to attempt most items in the allotted time).

Why is this important? Recall that we said that measures of internal consistency yield inflated estimates of reliability when used with speeded tests. Therefore, since most achievement tests are partially speeded, estimates of internal consistency reliability that are computed for such tests will also be somewhat inflated. Naturally, they will not be as falsely high as they would be for a *pure* speeded test, but they will be high enough to suggest that the test is more reliable than it actually is. For this reason, it is always preferable to look for a second estimate of reliability (for example, test-retest, or alternate-form) rather than relying on the internal consistency method to evaluate a test's reliability.

INTERPRETING RELIABILITY COEFFICIENTS

In Chapter 15 we discussed several principles relevant to the interpretation of validity coefficients. These were provided to give you some guidelines with which to consider the validity of a test. In this chapter we will discuss several principles related to the interpretation of reliability coefficients, which should prove useful as guidelines in evaluating the reliability of a test.

Our first principle relates to the effect of group variability on the size of the reliability coefficient. It should sound familiar, since we considered this concept in discussing the interpretation of validity coefficients.

PRINCIPLE 1: Group variability affects the size of the reliability coefficient. Higher coefficients result from heterogeneous groups than from homogeneous groups.

Rather than present our rationale for this principle, you might want to refresh your memory by reviewing Principle 2 from the previous chapter. The concept applied here is exactly the same, except that it refers to repeated administrations of the same test, or to alternate forms of the same test, rather than predictor and criterion measures. Figures 16.4 and 16.5 illustrate Principle 1 applied to test-retest reliability.

PRINCIPLE 2: Scoring reliability limits test reliability.

If tests are scored unreliably, error is introduced that will limit the reliability of the test. A test cannot have reliability higher than the reliability of the scoring. Recall that in Chapter 7 we stressed how important it is to make essay scoring as reliable as possible. If

FIGURE 16.4
Comparison of Probable Rankings for Repeated Administrations of the Same Test (or Alternate Forms of the Same Test) for Four Students from a Heterogeneous Sample

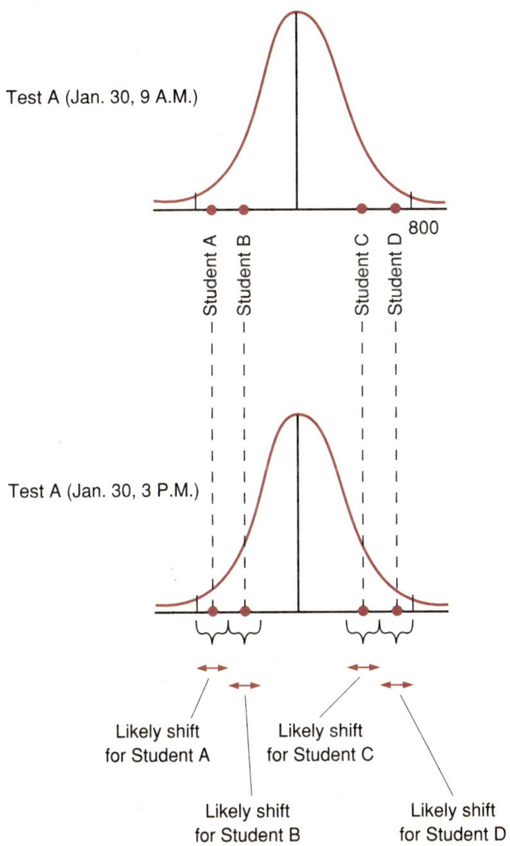

FIGURE 16.5
Comparison of Probable Rankings for Repeated Administrations of the Same Test (or Alternate Forms of the Same Test) for Four Students from a Homogeneous Sample

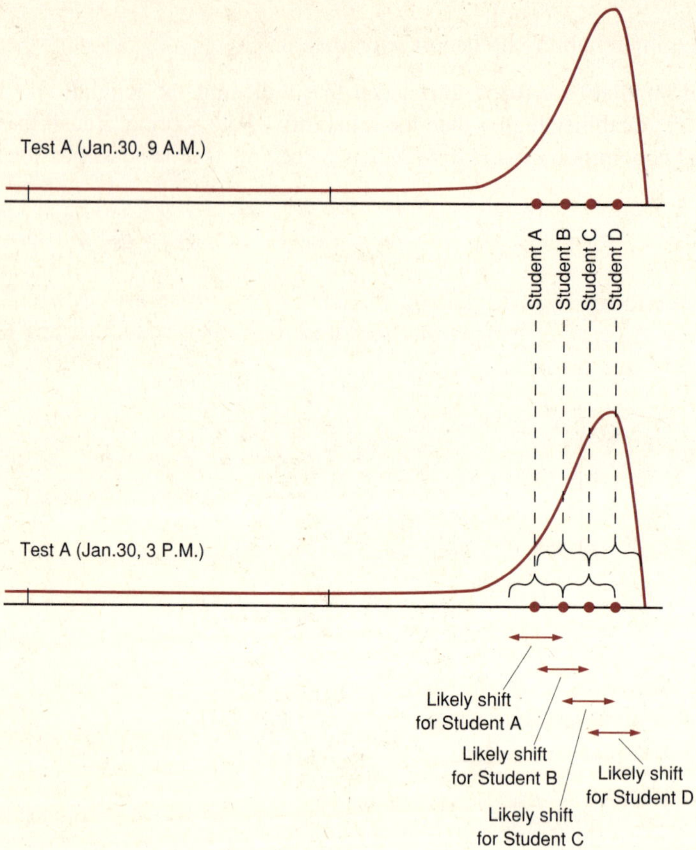

there is little agreement among scorers about the "correctness" of an answer, an otherwise good test may not have sufficient reliability. Stated another way, if scoring reliability is .70, then .70 becomes the *maximum* possible reliability of the test. In reality, it would be even lower, since other sources of error would add to the unreliability of the test. This is why objectivity in scoring and clerical checks are important. Thus, before dismissing a test as too unreliable for your purposes, check its scoring reliability. It may be that improvements in scoring procedures will result in a reliability increment large enough to make the test usable.

> PRINCIPLE 3: All other factors being equal, the more items included in a test, the higher the test's reliability.

There are several reasons for this principle. First, the number of items increases the potential variability of the scores (that is, group variability will increase). According to Principle 1, this will lead to an increase in the stability of ranks across administrations, and increased reliability. Second, when more items are added to a test, the test is better able to sample the student's knowledge of the attribute being measured. For example, a ten-item test about the presidents of the United States will provide a more reliable and representative sample of student knowledge of United States presidents than a two-item test. With a two-item test, a student might get lucky and guess correctly twice, earning a perfect score. Furthermore, such a limited sample may penalize better-prepared students, since its narrow focus may miss much of what they have mastered. It should be noted that Principle 3 is the basis of the Spearman-Brown Prophecy Formula we introduced earlier. A caution is in order, however. Simply increasing the number of items on a test will not *necessarily* increase a test's reliability. For example, if the extra items are ambiguous or otherwise poorly written items, then test reliability would likely *decrease*. Only if the added items are at least the equivalent of those in the original test will reliability *increase*. Thus, in interpreting a test's reliability, always consider its length. A very short test with a reliability of .80 may, with only a few more items added, turn out to measure some trait just as well as or better than a longer test with a reliability of .90.

PRINCIPLE 4: Reliability tends to decrease as tests become too easy or too difficult.

As tests become very easy (nearly everyone answers all of the items correctly) or very difficult (nearly everyone answers all of the items incorrectly), score distributions become homogeneous, which is illustrated by Figure 16.6.

By referring to Principle 1, we can conclude that when distributions are homogeneous, significant shifting of ranks and a lowering of the correlation coefficient will occur. Another factor worth considering is that when tests are made very difficult, guessing is encouraged. This is another source of error that serves to lower reliability even further. Hence, both very easy and very difficult tests will have low reliabilities. Because of error due to guessing, very difficult tests will be even less reliable than very easy tests.

FIGURE 16.6
Score Distributions for Very Easy and Very Difficult Tests

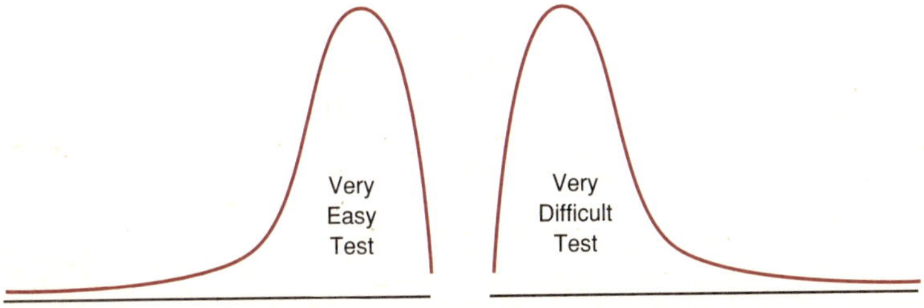

SUMMARY

This chapter introduced you to the concept of reliability, various methods of estimating reliability, and several principles to be considered in interpreting reliability coefficients. Its major points are:

1. Reliability refers to the stability of a test score over repeated administrations. A reliable test will yield stable scores over repeated administrations, assuming the trait being measured has not changed.
2. Test-retest estimates of reliability are obtained by administering the same test twice to the same group of individuals, with a small time interval between testing, and correlating the scores. The longer the time interval, the lower test-retest estimates will be.
3. Alternate-form estimates of reliability are obtained by administering two alternate or equivalent forms of a test to the same group and correlating their scores. The time interval between testings is as short as possible.
4. Internal consistency estimates of reliability fall into two general categories: split-half or odd-even estimates and item-total correlations, such as the Kuder-Richardson procedure. These estimates should be used only when the test measures a single or unitary trait.
5. Split-half and odd-even estimates divide a test into halves and correlate the halves with each other. Because these correlations are based on half tests, the obtained correlations underestimate the reliability of the whole test. The Spearman-Brown Prophecy Formula is used to correct these estimates to what they would be if they were based on the whole test.
6. Kuder-Richardson methods determine the extent to which the entire test represents a single, fairly consistent measure of a concept.
7. Internal consistency estimates tend to yield inflated reliability estimates for speeded tests.
8. Since most achievement tests are at least partially speeded, internal consistency estimates for such tests will be somewhat inflated.
9. In interpreting reliability coefficients the following principles should be considered:
   a. Group variability affects test reliability. As group variability increases, reliability goes up.
   b. Scoring reliability limits test reliability. As scoring reliability goes down, so does the test's reliability.
   c. Test length affects test reliability. As test length increases, the test's reliability tends to go up.
   d. Item difficulty affects test reliability. As items become very easy or very hard, the test's reliability goes down.

For Practice

*1. All other things being equal, which test—A, B, or C—would you use?

Type of Reliability	*Test A*	*Test B*	*Test C*
Split-half reliability coefficient	.80	.90	.85
Test-retest reliability coefficient	.60	.60	.75
Alternate-forms reliability	.30	.60	.60

*2. If the unadjusted odd-even reliability for a test is .60, what is its true reliability?

*3. What reliability coefficient would be *least* appropriate in each of the following situations?

a. The test is speeded.

b. The test measures heterogeneous topics.

c. Students can easily learn the answers from taking the test.

4. Assuming that the following tests all had exactly the same internal consistency reliability coefficient of .75, and assuming all other things are equal, which test—A, B, or C—would you use?

Aspects of test	*Test A*	*Test B*	*Test C*
Content	Homogeneous	Heterogeneous	Homogeneous
Test length	50 items	25 items	100 items
Difficulty	Average	Difficult	Average
Speed/power	Speeded	Speed and power	Power

*5. For each of the following statements indicate which type of reliability is being referred to from among the four alternatives which follow:

Test-retest	Alternate-forms (long interval)
Alternate-forms	Split-half

a. "Practice effects" could most seriously affect this type of reliability. _____

b. This procedure would yield the lowest reliability coefficient. _____

c. Requires the use of a formula to adjust the estimate of the reliability to that for a total test. _____

d. Should be used by teachers who want to give comparable (but different) tests to students. _____

e. Changes due to item sampling will not be reflected. _____

*6. Test A and Test B both claim to be reading achievement tests. Test A reports a test-retest reliability of .88, and Test B reports split-half reliability of .91. Test B has content validity with Mr. Burns's classroom objectives. Test A has concurrent validity with a recognized reading test, but measures several skills not taught by Mr. Burns. If Mr. Burns wishes to evaluate progress over his course of instruction, which test should be used for both his pre-test and post-test?

7. Test A and Test B both claim to be reading readiness tests for use in placing children in first-grade reading groups. Neither test reports validity data. Test A reports an internal consistency reliability of .86, and Test B reports a test-retest reliability of .70. If a first-grade teacher came to you for advice on test selection, what would be your recommendation?

---

*Answers for these questions appear in Appendix D.

CHAPTER 17

Accuracy and Error

When is a test score inaccurate? Almost always. Surprised? If you are, you have reason to be. We have learned (or have been "programmed") to put a great deal of faith in test scores. In fact, to some individuals test results represent the ultimate truth. Our position is that tests are fallible. They come with varying degrees of "goodness," but *no test* is completely valid or reliable. In other words, all tests are imperfect and are subject to error.

If most or all tests were perfectly reliable, then we could put a great deal of confidence in a person's score from a single test. If Student A scores 75 on a perfectly reliable test, then 75 is his or her "true" score. However, most tests are not perfectly reliable—in fact, most tests are a long way from being perfectly reliable. Therefore, when Student A scores 75 on a test, we only hope that his or her true score—his or her actual level of ability—is somewhere around 75. The closer the reliability of the test is to perfect, the more likely it is that the true score is very close to 75.

Later in this chapter we will introduce a special statistic that will enable you to estimate the *range* of scores within which lies an individual's true score or true level of ability. This is the extent of the precision we can realistically arrive at in interpreting test scores. In other words, a score from any test is our best guess about an individual's true level of knowledge, ability, achievement, and so forth, and, like all guesses, the guesses we make can be wrong.

All tests are subject to various sources of error that impair their reliability and, consequently, their accuracy. Logically, if we understand these sources of error in test scores, we should be able to minimize them in constructing tests and thereby improve test reliability. But, just what is "error" in testing?

ERROR—WHAT IS IT?

"I've made a mistake." We have all said this aloud or to ourselves at one time or another. In other words, we've made an error-we have failed to do something perfectly, or as well as we would like to have done it. The notion of error in testing is very similar. No test measures perfectly, and many tests fail to measure as well as we would like them to. That is, tests make "mistakes." They are always associated with some degree of error. Let's look at a test score more closely.

Think about the last test you took. Did you obtain exactly the score you felt or knew you deserved? Was your score higher than you expected? Was it lower than you expected? What about your *obtained* scores on all the other tests you have taken? Did they *truly* reflect your skill, knowledge, or ability, or did they sometimes underestimate your knowledge, ability, or skill? Or did they overestimate? If your obtained test scores did not always reflect your true ability, they were associated with some error. Your obtained scores may have been lower than they should have been, or higher than they should have been. In short, an *obtained score* has a *true* score component (actual level of ability, skill, knowledge) and an *error* component (which may act to lower or raise the obtained score).

Can you think of some concrete examples of a type of error that lowered your obtained score? Remember when you couldn't sleep the night before the test, or you were sick but took the test anyway, or the essay test you were taking was so poorly constructed it was hard to tell what was being tested, or the test had a 45-minute time limit but you were allowed only 38 minutes, or the time you took a test that had multiple defensible answers? Each of these examples illustrates various types of error. These and perhaps other sources of error prevented your "true" score from equaling your obtained score. Another way of saying this is simply that your obtained score equaled your true score *minus* any error.

Now, what about some examples of situations in which error operated to *raise* your obtained score above your actual or "true" level of knowledge, skill, or ability? In short, what about the times you obtained a higher score than you deserved? Never happened, you say! Well, what about the time you just happened to "see" the answers on your neighbor's paper, or the time you got lucky guessing, or the time you had 52 minutes for a 45-minute test, or the test that was so full of clues that you were able to answer several questions based on the information given in other questions? Remember the teachers we described in Chapter 1 who "helped" students taking standardized tests? Each of these examples illustrates error. Again, because of this error your true score was not reflected in your obtained score. You received a higher score than you deserved! In these cases your obtained score equaled your true score *plus* any error.

Then how does one go about discovering one's true score? Unfortunately, we do not have an answer. The true score and the error score are both theoretical or hypothetical values. We never actually know an individual's true score or error score. Why bother with them then? They are important concepts in that they allow us to illustrate some important points about test reliability and test accuracy. For now, simply keep in mind:

Obtained score = True score ± Error score

Table 17.1 illustrates the relationship among obtained scores, true scores, and error. In considering the table, remember that the *only* value in the table we are sure about is the obtained score value. We *never* know what the exact true scores are or what the exact error scores are. This is probably one of the most difficult concepts you have had to master.

According to Table 17.1, Donna, Gary, and Marsha each obtained higher scores than they should have. These students had error work to their advantage in that their obtained scores were higher than their true scores.

On the other hand, Jack, Phyllis, and Milton each obtained lower scores than they should have. These students had error work to their disadvantage in that their obtained scores were *lower* than their true scores. Unfortunately, as noted earlier, we never actually know what an individual's true and error scores are. The values shown in our table are

TABLE 17.1
The Relationship Among Obtained Scores, Hypothetical True Scores, and Hypothetical Error Scores for a Ninth-Grade Math Test

Student	*Obtained Score*	*True Score**	*Error Score**
Donna	91	88	+3
Jack	72	79	−7
Phyllis	68	70	−2
Gary	85	80	+5
Marsha	90	86	+4
Milton	75	78	−3

*Hypothetical values

hypothetical values used to impress upon you the fact that *all* test scores contain error. If you understand the notion of test error, you already have an intuitive understanding of our next topic, the standard error of measurement.

THE STANDARD ERROR OF MEASUREMENT

The standard error of measurement of a test (abbreviated S_m) is the standard deviation of the *error scores* of a test. In the calculations following, S_m is the standard deviation of the error score column. It is determined in the same manner you would determine a standard deviation of any score distribution. Review the following calculations to confirm this. We will use error scores from Table 17.1: +3, −7, −2, +5, +4, −3.

STEP 1: Determine the mean:

$$\overline{X} = \frac{\Sigma X}{N} = \frac{0}{6} = 0$$

STEP 2: Subtract the mean from each error score to arrive at the deviation scores. Square each deviation score, and sum the squared deviations:

$X - \overline{X} =$	x	x^2
$+3 - 0 =$	3	9
$-7 - 0 =$	−7	49
$-2 - 0 =$	−2	4
$+5 - 0 =$	5	25
$+4 - 0 =$	4	16
$-3 - 0 =$	−3	9
		$112 = \Sigma x^2$

STEP 3: Plug the x^2 into the formula and solve for the standard deviation.

$$\text{Error score SD} = \sqrt{\frac{\Sigma x^2}{N}} = \sqrt{\frac{112}{6}} = \sqrt{18.67} = 4.32$$

Thus, the standard deviation of the *error score distribution*, also known as the standard error of measurement, is 4.32. If we could know what the error scores are for each test we administer, we could compute S_m in this manner. But, of course, we never know these error scores. If you are following so far, your next question should be, "But how in the world do you determine the standard deviation of the error scores if you never know the error scores?"

Fortunately, a rather simple statistical formula can be used to *estimate* this standard deviation (S_m) without actually knowing the error scores:

$$S_m = SD\sqrt{1 - r}$$

where r is the reliability of the test.

Using the Standard Error of Measurement

Error scores are assumed to be random. As such, they cancel each other out. That is, obtained scores are inflated by random error to the same extent as they are deflated by error. Another way of saying this is that the mean of the error scores for a test is zero. The distribution of the error scores is also important, since it approximates a normal distribution closely enough for us to use the normal distribution to represent it. In summary, then, we know that error scores (1) are normally distributed, (2) have a mean of zero, and (3) have a standard deviation called the standard error of measurement (S_m). These characteristics are illustrated in Figure 17.1.

Returning to our example from the ninth-grade math test depicted in Table 17.1 we recall that we obtained an S_m of 4.32 for the data provided. Figure 17.2 illustrates the distribution of error scores for these data.

What does the distribution in Figure 17.2 tell us? Before you answer, consider this: The distribution of error scores is a *normal* distribution. This is important since, as you learned in Chapter 13, the normal distribution has characteristics that enable us to make decisions about scores that fall between, above, or below different points in the distribution. We are able to do so because fixed percentages of scores fall between various score values in a normal distribution. Figure 17.3 should refresh your memory.

In Figure 17.3 we listed along the baseline the standard deviation of the error score distribution. This is more commonly called the *standard error of measurement* (S_m) of the test. Thus we can see that 68 percent of the error scores for the test will be no more than 4.32 points higher or 4.32 points lower than the true scores. That is, if there were 100 obtained scores on this test, 68 of these scores would *not* be "off" their true scores by more than $\pm$ 4.32 points. The S_m, then, tells us about the distribution of obtained scores around true scores. Knowing an individual's true score, we can make predictions what his or her obtained score is likely to be.

FIGURE 17.1
The Error Score Distribution

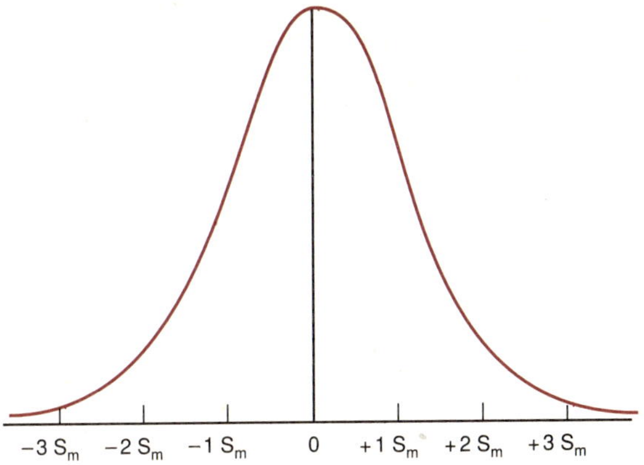

FIGURE 17.2
The Error Score Distribution for Test Depicted in Table 17.1

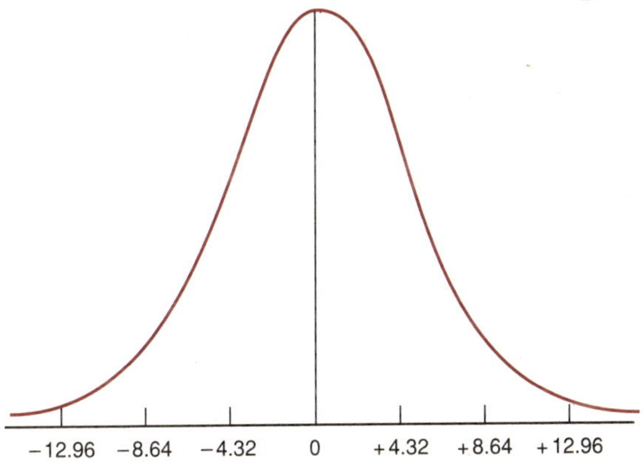

The careful reader may be thinking, "That's not very useful information. We can never know what a person's true score is, only their obtained score." And this is correct. As test users, we work only with obtained scores. However, we can follow our logic in reverse. If 68 percent of obtained scores fall within $1S_m$ of their true scores, then 68 percent of true scores must fall within $1S_m$ of their obtained scores. Strictly speaking, this reverse logic is somewhat inaccurate when we consider individual test scores. However, across all test scores, it would be true 99 percent of the time (Gulliksen, 1987). Therefore, the S_m is often used to determine how test error is likely to have affected

FIGURE 17.3
The Ninth-Grade Math Test Error Score Distribution with Approximate Normal Curve Percentages

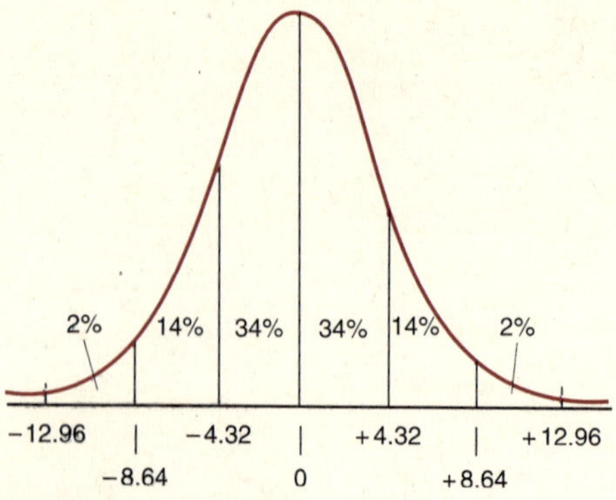

individual obtained scores. Let's use the following number line to represent an individual's obtained score, which we will simply call X:

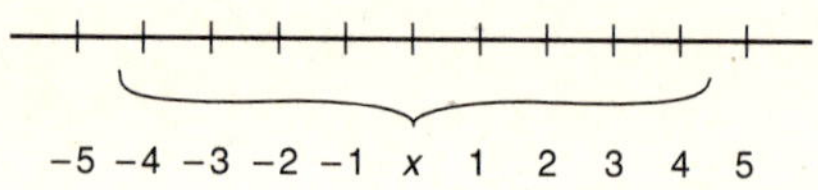

That is, X plus or minus 4.32 (± 4.32) defines the range or band, which we are about 68 percent sure contains this individual's true score. Extending this reasoning, we can construct a similar band around *any* obtained score to identify the range of scores that, at a certain level of confidence, will capture or span an individual's true score. Stated another way, if a student obtains a score of X on a test, the student's true score on the test will be within $\pm 1S_m$ of X about 68 percent of the time. We know this to be the case since error (the difference between obtained and true scores) is normally distributed. We can conceptualize what we have been describing by considering error to be normally distributed around any obtained score. Returning once again to our ninth-grade math test (Table 17.1), we see that Marsha had an obtained score of 90. We also know that the S_m for the test was 4.32. Knowing the data, and that error is normally distributed, we can graphically depict the distribution of error around Marsha's obtained score of 90, as shown in Figure 17.4. Figure 17.5 illustrates the distribution of error around an obtained score of 75 for the same test.

Why all the fuss? Remember our original point. All test scores are fallible; they contain a margin of error. The S_m is a statistic that estimates this margin for us. We are accustomed to reporting a single test score. Considering the S_m, that is, reporting a range of scores that spans or captures an individual's true score, helps us present a more realistic picture of someone's obtained scores. From our last two examples we could conclude with 68 percent certainty that for a distribution with a standard error of measurement of

FIGURE 17.4
The Error Distribution Around an Obtained Score of 90 for a Test With $S_m = 4.32$

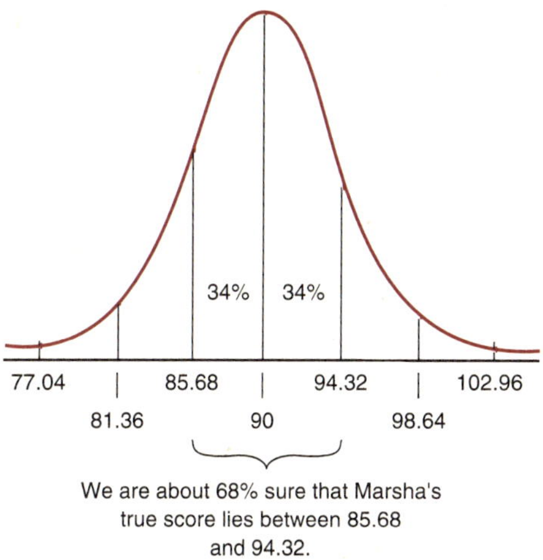

FIGURE 17.5
The Error Distribution Around an Obtained Score of 75 for a Test with $S_m = 4.32$

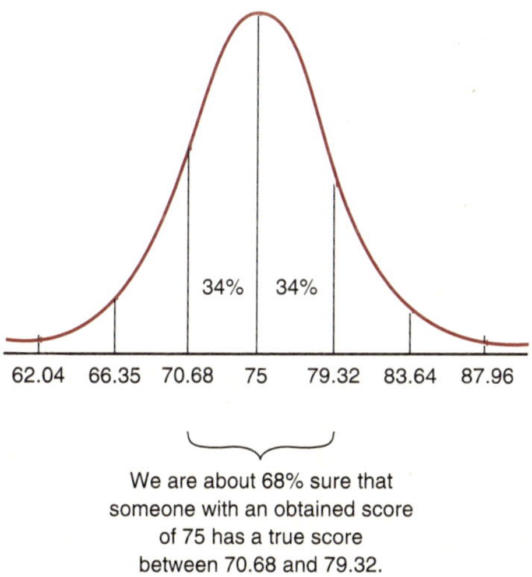

4.32, each student's true score would be captured by a range of scores ± 4.32 from his or her obtained score. Left unsaid was the fact that we would probably be wrong in drawing such a conclusion 32 percent of the time! Even though we report a band of scores 8.64

points wide around a single score, we will still draw an incorrect conclusion 32 percent of the time.

This is *not* an exceptional case. Even the *best* tests often have S_m of from 3 to 5 points (more or less, depending on the scale). In education we have long had a tendency to *overinterpret* small differences in test scores since we too often consider obtained scores to be completely accurate. Incorporating the S_m in reporting test scores *greatly* minimizes the likelihood of overinterpretation and forces us to consider how fallible our test scores are. After considering the S_m from a slightly different angle, we will show how to incorporate the S_m to make comparisons among test scores. This procedure is called *band interpretation*. First, however, let's sew up a few loose ends about S_m.

More Applications

Let's look again at the formula for the S_m:

$$S_m = SD\sqrt{1 - r}$$

We know that an obtained score, X, $\pm$ $1S_m$ will span or capture the true score 68 percent of the time. Extending this thinking further, we know that the range of scores covered by X $\pm$ $2S_m$ will capture the true score 95 percent of the time. Finally, we know that the range of scores covered by X $\pm$ $3S_m$ will capture the true score more than 99 percent of the time. Figure 17.6 illustrates these relationships.

FIGURE 17.6
The Area or Bands for a Given Obtained Score That Are 68%, 95%, and 99% Sure to Span the True Score

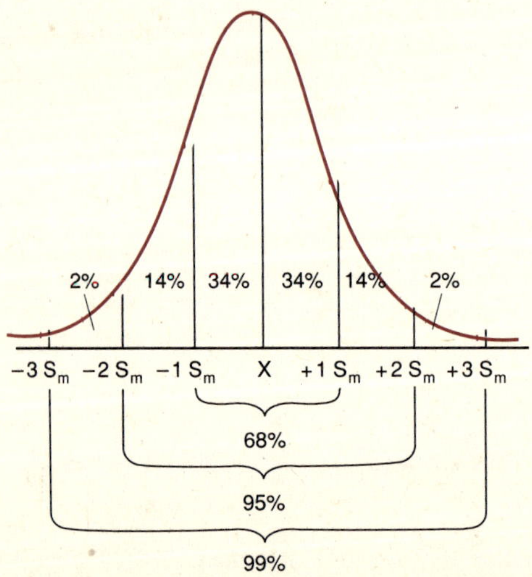

Let's work an example. A test has a standard deviation of 5 points and a reliability of .75. The standard error of measurement of the test is:

$$S_m = 5\sqrt{1 - .75} = 5\sqrt{.25} = 2.5$$

If a student obtains a score of 80 on the test, you know that his or her true score lies between:

77.5 and 82.5 (68% of the time)	$X \pm 1S_m$
75 and 85 (95% of the time)	$X \pm 2S_m$
72.5 and 87.5 (99% of the time)	$X \pm 3S_m$

The expressions "68 percent of the time," "95 percent of the time," and so on refer to the hypothetical situation in which the student is given the test many times. In this case, the student could expect that his or her true score would be within the interval a certain percentage of the total number of times the test was taken.

Here's another example. A teacher gets back the results of class IQ tests. The IQ test given to the students has a standard deviation of 15 and a test-retest reliability of .84. Therefore, the test has a standard error of measurement of 6. The teacher then knows that of the children who made an IQ score of 100, about 68 percent have a true score between 94 and 106; 95 percent have a true IQ score between 88 and 112; and 99 percent have a true IQ score between 82 and 118. For one particular child with an IQ of 100, the teacher knows that probably the true IQ is between 94 and 106, but 32 percent of the time (100% − 68% = 32%) it will be even further than that from 100. Thus, the teacher has some idea of just how much confidence to place in the score. That is, the teacher has an idea about the accuracy of the score.

If the test is perfectly reliable ($r = 1.0$), then a student will always get exactly the same score. In this case the S_m is 0, as can be seen by substituting a coefficient of 1.0 in the formula for S_m. If the test is very close to perfectly reliable, the S_m will be very small, and we can assume the student's obtained score is very close to his or her true score. If the test is not reliable, the S_m will be nearly as big as the standard deviation, and we can assume the student's obtained score is not a good approximation of his or her true score. The relationships among true scores, error scores, obtained scores, and reliability are illustrated next.

TEST K IS PERFECTLY RELIABLE (r = 1.00). In other words, a student's ranking on repeated administrations of Test K *never changes*. There is no error, and as a result the student's true score equals the obtained score *and* there is *no* error score distribution: Thus, S_m is zero. Proof:

$$\begin{aligned} S_m &= SD\sqrt{1 - r} \\ &= SD\sqrt{1 - 1.0} \\ &= SD\sqrt{0} \\ &= 0 \end{aligned}$$

Test L Is Totally Unreliable (r = .00). In other words, a student's ranking on repeated administrations of Test L is *likely to vary across the range of possible rankings*. If the student is ranked first on one administration, he or she could easily be ranked last on the next administration. Thus, because there is *so much error* present, the S_m will be the same as the SD of the test. Proof:

$$
\begin{aligned}
S_m &= SD\sqrt{1 - r} \\
&= SD\sqrt{1 - .00} \\
&= SD\sqrt{1} \\
&= SD\,(1) \\
&= SD
\end{aligned}
$$

In reality, neither of the examples presented here actually occur. So, the Sm typically takes on a value greater than 0 and smaller than the test's standard deviation. As reliability increases, Sm decreases, and as reliability decreases, the Sm increases. In summary, the Sm can be thought of as a measure of the accuracy of a test score. The larger the Sm, the less accurate the score. The smaller the Sm, the more accurate the score.

Standard Deviation or Standard Error of Measurement?

Until you have a working familiarity with these concepts, you can expect to confuse the standard deviation (SD) with the standard error of measurement (S_m). Don't despair! The two have some similarities, but they are very different. Both are measures of score variability, but of different kinds of scores. The standard deviation is a measure of variability of *raw* scores for a *group* of test takers. It tells you how spread out the scores are in a distribution of raw scores. You learned to compute and interpret standard deviations in Chapter 13. The standard error of measurement, however, is the standard deviation of the hypothetical *error* scores of a distribution. This is what you learned to compute and interpret in *this* chapter. Think about what you have just read:

Standard deviation (SD) is the variability of *raw* scores.

Standard error of measurement (S_m) is the variability of *error* scores.

The standard deviation is based on a group of scores that *actually exist*. The standard error of measurement is based on a group of scores that is *hypothetical*.

WHY ALL THE FUSS ABOUT ERROR?

In reality, an individual's obtained score is the best estimate of an individual's true score. That is, in spite of the foregoing discussion, we usually use the obtained score as our best guess of a student's true level of ability. Well, why all the fuss about error, then? For two reasons: First, we want to make you aware of the fallibility of test scores, and second, we want to sensitize you to the factors that can affect scores. Why? So they can be better controlled. Now you know how to determine how wide a range of scores around an obtained score must be to be 68 percent sure that it captures the true score. Controlling error can help narrow this range, thereby increasing the utility of test results. So, let's consider error more closely.

The sources of error can be classified into the following categories:

1. Test takers
2. The test itself
3. Test administration
4. Test scoring

Error Within Test Takers

This source of error could be called intra-individual error. Earlier, we talked about several within-student factors that would likely result in an obtained score lower than a student's true score. The examples we used were fatigue and illness. We also noted that accidentally seeing another student's answer could be a factor that might result in an individual's obtained score being higher than his or her true score. Situations such as these are undesirable since they have unpredictable effects on test performance, and as a result the reliability and accuracy of the test suffers. They are usually temporary situations, affecting a student on one day but not on another. Any temporary and unpredictable change in a student can be considered intra-individual error or error within test takers. Remember, we are *not* saying anything about actual errors or mistakes test takers make in responding to test items. Rather, we are talking about factors that change unpredictably over time and, as a result, impair consistency and accuracy in measurement.

Error Within the Test

We may refer to this source of error as an intra-test or within-test error. The poorly designed essay test that results in an obtained score lower than a true score and the poorly written test replete with clues that results in an obtained score higher than a true score are both examples of this source of error.

There are many, many ways to *increase* error within the test. The following is only a partial list:

Trick questions

Reading level that is too high

Ambiguous questions

Items too easy or too difficult

Poorly written items

To the extent that test items and tests are poorly constructed, test reliability and accuracy will be impaired.

Error in Test Administration

Misreading the amount of time to be allotted for testing is an example of error in test administration that could raise or lower obtained scores in relation to true scores. There are, however, a variety of other direct and indirect test administration factors to be considered, including physical comfort, instructions and explanations, and test administration attitudes.

PHYSICAL COMFORT. Room temperature, humidity, lighting, noise, and seating arrangement are all potential sources of error for the test taker.

INSTRUCTIONS AND EXPLANATIONS. Different test administrators provide differing amounts of information to test takers. Some spell words, provide hints, or tell whether it's better to guess or leave blanks, while others remain fairly distant. This is what the teachers we described in Chapter 1 did. Naturally, your score may vary depending on the amount of information you are provided.

TEST ADMINISTRATOR ATTITUDES. Administrators will differ in the notions they convey about the importance of the test, the extent to which they are emotionally supportive of students, and the way in which they monitor the test. To the extent that these variables affect students differently, test reliability and accuracy will be impaired.

Error in Scoring

With the advent of computerized test scoring, error in scoring has decreased significantly. However, even when computer scoring is used, error can occur. The computer, being a highly reliable machine, is seldom the cause of such errors. But teachers and other test administrators prepare the scoring keys and directions that are provided to the programmers and operators, thus introducing possibilities for error. And students sometimes fail to use no. 2 pencils or make extraneous marks on answer sheets, introducing another potential source of scoring error. Needless to say, when tests are hand-scored, as most classroom tests are, the likelihood of error increases greatly. In fact, you can be sure, because you are human, that you will make some scoring errors in grading the tests you give.

These four sources of error—the test takers, the test, the test administration, and the scoring—are factors that increase the discrepancy between an individual's obtained score and his or her true score. To the extent that these sources of error are present, individual and group scores will be prone to error, and therefore less accurate. We can take measures to minimize error within the test, the test administration, and the scoring, but we can never eliminate such error completely. Generally, error due to within-student factors is beyond our control.

These sources of error also affect the different types of reliability coefficients we have discussed. This notion is worth considering further, since different estimates of reliability may be spuriously high (if they fail to account for important sources of error) or spuriously low (if they account for unimportant sources of error). Next we consider the extent to which our four sources of error influence the test-retest, alternate-forms, and internal consistency methods of estimating reliability.

SOURCES OF ERROR INFLUENCING VARIOUS RELIABILITY COEFFICIENTS

Test-Retest

If test-retest reliability coefficients are determined over a short time, few changes are likely to take place *within students* to alter their test scores. Thus, short-interval test-retest coefficients are not likely to be affected greatly by within-student error. However, as the time interval involved increases, it becomes more and more likely that significant changes will occur in the test takers. Correspondingly, test scores will be increasingly affected by these changes and the test-retest reliability will be lowered. This lowered reliability may be more a result of new learning on the part of the students than it is an indication of the unreliability of the test.

Since the *same* test is administered twice in determining test-retest reliability, error within the test itself (for example, from poorly worded or ambiguous items) does not affect the strength of the reliability coefficient. Any problems that do exist in the test are present in both the first and second administrations, affecting scores the same way each time the test is administered. As long as similar administration and scoring procedures are followed, administration and scoring errors are likely to contribute only minimally to error. However, if there are significant changes in either or both, these can contribute significantly to error, resulting in a lower estimate of test-retest reliability.

Alternate Forms

Since alternate-forms reliability is determined by administering two different forms or versions of the same test to the same group close together in time, the effects of within-student error are negligible. Generally, students do not change significantly between morning and afternoon, or from one day to the following day. Granted, students may be more fatigued when taking Form B of a test immediately after taking Form A. However, these factors can be controlled by splitting the test administration across groups of students, as suggested in Table 17.2.

Error within the test, however, has a significant effect on alternate-forms reliability. Unlike test-retest reliability, error within the test is *not* the same between test administrations. Error within Form A combines with error within Form B to have an effect on alternate-forms

TABLE 17.2
Splitting Same-Day Alternate-Form Administrations Across Groups

A.M. Group	*P.M. Group*
Students whose last names begin with A–K get form A.	Students whose last names begin with A–K get form B.
Students whose last names begin with L–Z get form B.	Students whose last names begin with L–Z get form A.

reliability. By now you are aware of how difficult it is to construct one good test, much less two! Yet, this is just what is necessary for acceptable alternate-forms reliability.

As with test-retest methods, alternate-forms reliability is not greatly affected by error in administering or scoring the test, as long as similar procedures are followed. Since within-test error is considered by alternate-forms estimates, these estimates normally have the lowest numerical index of reliability.

Internal Consistency

With test-retest and alternate-forms reliability, within-student factors are taken into account by the method of estimating reliability, since changes in test performance due to such problems as fatigue, momentary anxiety, illness, or just having an "off day" are recorded by having two separate administrations of the test. If the test is sensitive to these problems, it will record different scores from one test administration to another, lowering the reliability (or correlation coefficient) between them. Obviously, we would prefer that the test *not* be sensitive to these problems. But if it is, we would like to know about it.

With internal consistency reliability, neither within-student nor within-test factors are taken into account by the method of estimation. Since there is a single test administered, no changes in students should occur, and any errors within the test will occur only once. Similarly, since there is but a single administration and scoring procedure, administration and scoring errors are held to a minimum.

Measures of internal consistency, then, are influenced by the fewest of four sources of error affecting test reliability. Thus, we would expect such measures to yield higher reliability coefficients than test-retest or alternate-forms estimates. This is important in evaluating test data presented in standardized test manuals. If a test publisher presents only internal consistency estimates of reliability, the publisher has failed to indicate how consistent the obtained scores from the test are likely to be over time. Also unknown is whether any parallel or alternative forms being offered are equivalent to each other. Simply *saying* there are two alternate, equivalent, or parallel forms is not sufficient. To evaluate their equivalence there must be an estimate of alternate-forms reliability.

By itself, then, an internal consistency reliability coefficient—high though it may be—does not provide sufficient evidence of a test's reliability. When you must have an estimate of a test's reliability and can give only a single administration (such as with a typical teacher-made test), measures of internal consistency can be useful. However, any well-constructed standardized test must provide more than just information on the test's internal consistency. Generally, there must be provided a measure of the test's reliability over time (that is, test-retest reliability) and, if it advertises alternate forms, an estimate of the equivalence of the forms being offered (that is, alternate-forms reliability).

The influence of the four sources of error on the test-retest, alternate-forms, and internal consistency methods of estimating reliability are summarized in Table 17.3.

BAND INTERPRETATION

Thus far, we have learned how to use the standard error of measurement, S_m, to more realistically interpret and report single test scores. In this section we will show you how

TABLE 17.3
Extent of Error Influencing Test-Retest, Alternate-Forms, and Internal Consistency Methods of Reliability

Reliability Measure	*Type of Error* *Within Student*	*Within Test*[1]	*Administration*	*Scoring*
Test-retest, short interval	Minimal	Minimal	Minimal[2] or moderate[3]	Minimal[4] or moderate[5]
Test-retest, long interval	Extensive	Minimal	Minimal[2] or moderate[3]	Minimal[4] or moderate[5]
Alternate-forms, short interval	Minimal	Moderate[2] or extensive[3]	Minimal[2] or moderate[3]	Minimal[4] or moderate[5]
Alternate-forms, long interval	Extensive	Moderate[2] or extensive[3]	Minimal[2] or moderate[3]	Minimal[4] or moderate[5]
Internal consistency	Minimal	Minimal	Minimal	Minimal

1. Assuming test is well constructed.
2. If test is standardized.
3. If test is teacher-made.
4. If test is objective.
5. If test is subjective.

to use the standard error of measurement to more realistically interpret and report groups of test scores. Let's consider the following example:

John obtained the following scores on an end-of-year achievement test:

Subtests	***Scores***
Reading	103
Listening	104
Writing	105
Social Studies	98
Science	100
Math	91

Note: $\overline{X}$ = 100 and SD = 10 for all subtests.

Now, suppose you have a parent conference coming up, and John's parents want you to interpret his scores to them. What would you say? Would you say that he did best in Writing and poorest in Math? Would you say that the differences among the scores are likely due to measurement error, or do they represent actual differences in achievement?

It seems likely that John's parents would know from looking at the scores what John did best in and what he did poorest in. If they had some statistical sophistication, as you now have, they might even be able to conclude that his Math score is at about the nineteenth percentile and that his Reading score is at about the sixty-ninth percentile—a difference between the two tests of 50 percentile points. This appears to be a rather dramatic difference indicating a real difference in achievement. But how can we be sure the difference is not due to error? Granted it seems to be so large a difference that it probably is a "real" difference rather than a "chance" (that is, due to error) difference. But what about the difference between Writing (sixty-ninth percentile) and Science (fiftieth percentile)? Is this difference a "real" or a "chance" one? In short, how large a difference do we need between test scores to conclude that the differences represent real and not chance differences? As you might have guessed, we can employ the standard error of measurement to help us answer these questions. The specific technique we will be discussing is called *band interpretation*. This technique lends itself quite well to the interpretation of scores from test batteries. Here is a step-by-step approach to band interpretation.

Technically, the approach we will be describing fails to consider the problem of the *reliability of the difference scores*. This advanced statistical concept basically states that in comparing scores from two tests (or subtests), the reliability of the difference between the two scores will be less than the reliability of each of the two scores. Thus, less confidence should be placed in the difference score than in either of the individual scores. For those who may be interested, the formula to compute the reliability of the difference score is as follows:

$$r_{Diff.} = \frac{(r_{11} + r_{22})/2 - r_{12}}{1 - r_{12}}$$

where r_{11} is the reliability of one measure,
r_{22} is the reliability of the other measure,
r_{12} is the correlation between the two measures.

Our approach, band interpretation, represents a practical compromise between this statistically correct approach and the all-too-common acceptance of difference scores as being reliable.

Steps: Band Interpretation

LIST DATA. List subtests and scores, and the $\bar{X}$, SD, and reliability (r) for each subtest. For purposes of illustration, let's assume that the mean is 100, the standard deviation is 10, and the reliability is .91 for all the subtests. Here are the subtest scores for John:

Subtests	***Scores***
Reading	103
Listening	104
Writing	105
Social Studies	98
Science	100
Math	91

DETERMINE S_M FOR EACH SUBTEST. Since in our example SD and r are the same for each subtest, S_m will be the same for each subtest.

$$S_m = SD\sqrt{1 - r}$$
$$= 10\sqrt{1 - .91}$$
$$= 10\sqrt{.09}$$
$$= 3$$

ADD AND SUBTRACT S_m. To identify the band or interval of scores that has a 68 percent chance of spanning or capturing John's true score, add and subtract S_m to each subtest score. If the test could be given to John 100 times (without John learning from taking the test), 68 out of 100 times John's true score would be within the following bands:

Subtest	*Scores*	*68% band*
Reading	103	100–106
Listening	104	101–107
Writing	105	102–108
Social Studies	98	95–101
Science	100	97–103
Math	91	88–94

GRAPH THE RESULTS. On each scale, shade in the bands to represent the range of scores that has a 68 percent chance of capturing John's true score.

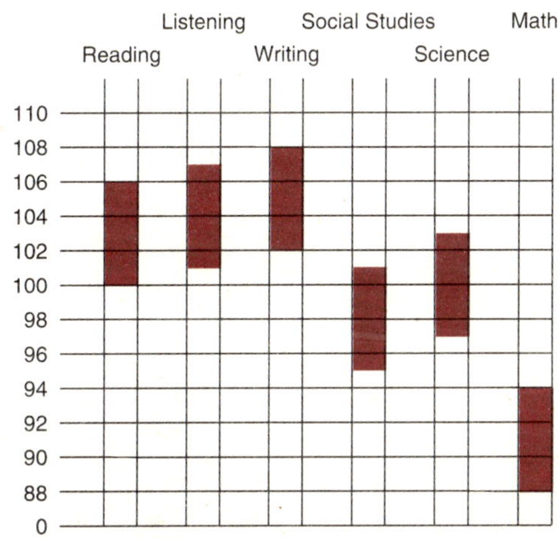

INTERPRET THE BANDS. Interpret the profile of bands by visually inspecting the bars to see which bands overlap and which do not. Those that *overlap* probably represent differences that occurred by *chance*. For example, Reading, Listening, Writing, and Science may differ from each other only by chance—in spite of the fact that John's Science score of 100 was 5 points lower than his Writing score of 105, a difference of half a standard deviation. We arrive at this conclusion because there is at least some overlap among the bands for each of these subtest scores. Thus, we could say John's level of achievement is similar in each of these subjects.

However, we can see a large difference in John's Math achievement compared to these same four subtests. Since there is no overlap, we will consider this difference a *real*, not a chance, difference. Social Studies shows a *real* difference compared to Writing (again, no overlap), but only a *chance* difference compared to Reading, Listening, and Science (again, because there is overlap).

Getting the hang of it? Band interpretation is one of the most realistic and appropriate ways to interpret scores from test batteries, since it considers the error that is always present in testing. Work with it and you will reduce the natural tendency to put too much weight on small or chance differences among scores.

So far we have used the subtest score plus and minus the standard error of measurement to identify whether a real difference exists among subtest scores. We have constructed ranges of scores around each obtained score in which we are 68 percent sure the individual's true score lies. Recall from our earlier discussion of S_m, though, that by adding and subtracting twice the value of S_m to the obtained subtest score, we can construct an interval or range of scores within which we are 95 percent sure the individual's true score lies. Naturally, this would create a much wider band for each obtained score, which has the effect of making overlap much *more* likely. This means "real" differences would be less likely to appear. That is, if we use the 95 percent rule by adding $2S_m$ to and subtracting $2S_m$ from each score instead of adding and subtracting only the standard error of measurement, we may have very different interpretations of the same test scores. Let's see what kind of difference this makes. Figure 17.7 compares and contrasts the 68 percent and 95 percent approaches.

Now let's compare conclusions. At the 68 percent level, we concluded that there was a significant discrepancy between John's math achievement and all his other subjects (there is no overlap between his math score interval and any other subtest score interval). We also concluded that there was a real difference (that is, no overlap) between John's social studies achievement and his writing achievement. All other differences were attributed to chance (that is, there was overlap).

Now look at the 95 percent profile in Figure 17.7. In essence we have doubled the width of each band in order to become more confident that we have really captured John's true score within each interval. As a result of this more conservative approach to test interpretation, the real differences decline sharply. We use the word conservative with the 95 percent approach since the odds of John's true score falling outside the band are only 1 in 20 or .05 with the 95 percent approach, but 1 in 3 or about .32 with the 68 percent approach. We are, therefore, *more confident* that John's true score is within the band with the 95 percent approach. Since the bands will be larger, the only real differences we find at the 95 percent level are between John's math achievement and his achievement in listening and writing. All the other bands overlap, suggesting that at the 95 percent level the differences in obtained scores are due to chance. Thus, if we employ the more conservative 95 percent approach, we would conclude that even though the difference between John's obtained reading and math scores is 12 points ($103 - 91 = 12$, a difference of 1.2 standard deviations), the difference is due to chance, not to a real difference in achievement.

Why bother with the 95 percent level, then? Well, if you are going to make important decisions about a student, a conservative approach appears warranted. In short, if you are

FIGURE 17.7
Comparison of the 68% and 95% Methods of Band Interpretation

Subtest	*Scores**	*68% range* ($X \pm 1S_m$)	*95% range* ($X \pm 2S_m$)
Reading	103	100–106	97–109
Listening	104	101–107	98–110
Writing	105	102–108	99–111
Social Studies	98	95–101	92–104
Science	100	97–103	94–106
Math	91	88–94	85–97

*$\overline{X} = 100$
SD = 10

Profiles
68% range

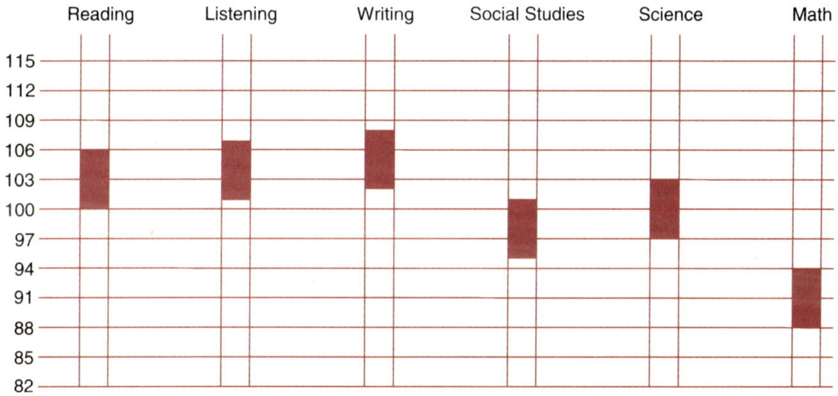

95% range

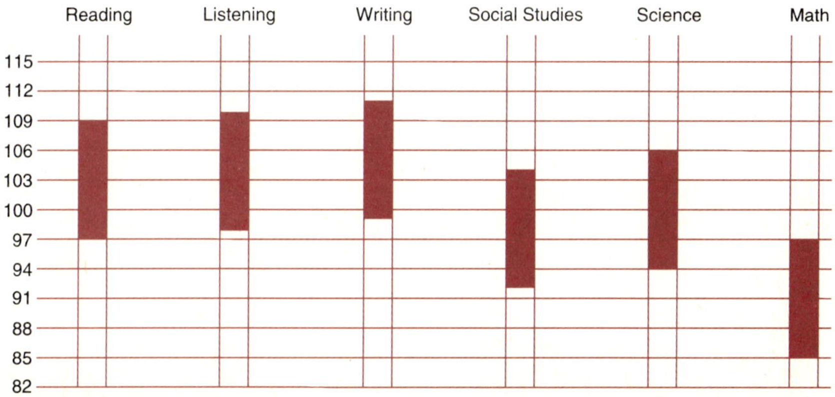

concerned about the effects of a "wrong" decision (that is, saying a real difference in achievement exists when it is really due to chance), take the conservative approach. On the other hand, if little is at risk for the student (or yourself), then the less conservative 68 percent approach is probably warranted. To make it simpler yet, let differences at the 68 percent level be a signal to you; let differences at the 95 percent level be a signal to school and parents.

In the next chapter, we will describe an application of band interpretation in which we believe the more conservative 95 percent approach should typically be employed. This will be in relation to determining real differences between a student's potential for achievement, called *aptitude*, and actual achievement.

A Final Word

Technically, there are more accurate statistical procedures for determining real differences between an individual's test scores than the ones we have been able to present here. These procedures, however, are time-consuming, complex, and overly specific for the typical teacher. Within the classroom, band interpretation, properly used, makes for a practical alternative to these more advanced methods, which is superior to simply comparing individual scores.

Before we complete this chapter, answer the questions—using the 95 percent approach—that we raised at the beginning of this section. To refresh your memory here they are:

Is there a real difference between John's Reading score and his Math score?
Is there a real difference between John's Writing score and his Science score?

SUMMARY

Chapter 17 presented the concepts of accuracy and error; the statistic used to represent error (the standard error of measurement); and the four sources of error in measurement. Its major points are:

1. No test is perfectly reliable, and therefore no test is perfectly accurate. All tests are subject to error.

2. Error is any factor that leads an individual to perform better or worse on a test than the individual's true level of performance.

3. An obtained score for a test contains two components: One reflects the individual's true level of performance, and the other reflects the error associated with the test that prevents the individual from performing at exactly his or her true level of ability.

4. An individual's true score and error score are hypothetical. We can never be sure exactly what they are.

5. The standard error of measurement (S_m) is the standard deviation of the error score distribution of a test.

6. The standard error of measurement for a test can be determined mathematically if we know the test's standard deviation and reliability.
7. The error distribution is normally distributed and has a mean of zero, and its standard deviation is the standard error of measurement.
8. We can be 68 percent sure an individual's true score lies in the range between one S_m above and one S_m below that individual's obtained score.
9. We can be 95 percent sure a true score lies in the range of scores between two S_m above and two S_m below the obtained score.
10. We can be 99 percent sure a true score lies in the range of scores between three S_m above and three S_m below the obtained score.
11. Using the S_m in interpreting scores helps us avoid overinterpreting small differences among test scores.
12. As reliability increases, accuracy increases and the S_m decreases.
13. The S_m refers to the variability of error scores; the SD refers to the variability of raw scores.
14. By controlling the sources of error in testing, we can improve test accuracy.
15. Error is classified into four categories, within:
    a. test takers
    b. the test
    c. the test administration
    d. scoring
16. Error within the test takers refers to changes in the student over which the test administrator has no control.
17. Error within the test refers to technical problems in the test. The test developer has considerable control over this source of error.
18. Error within the test administration refers to physical, verbal, and attitudinal variables that vary from administration to administration and affect test scores. By standardizing administration procedures, the administrator can minimize this source of error.
19. Error in scoring typically refers to clerical errors that influence test scores. The test administrator can control this source of error by using objective items and clerical checks or using computer scoring.
20. Different estimates of reliability are differentially affected by the various sources of error.
21. Test-retest reliability is most susceptible to error within test takers.
22. Alternate-forms reliability is most affected by error within the two forms of the test. As a result, it usually yields lower reliability estimates than test-retest or internal consistency estimates.

23. Since only one administration and one test are necessary for internal consistency estimates, this approach is least affected by error. As a result, internal consistency estimates of reliability typically will be higher for the same test than test-retest or alternate-forms reliability estimates.

24. Band interpretation is a technique that the teacher can use to help separate real differences in student achievement from differences due to chance. This approach helps prevent overinterpretation of small differences among subtests in achievement test batteries.

For Practice

*1. Calculate the standard error of measurement for a test with a standard deviation of 10 and a reliability of .84. Draw a normal curve picturing the error score distribution in units of the standard error of measurement.

*2. Suppose an individual received a score of 16 on the above test. Calculate the range or band within which we could be 95 percent sure that this individual's true score is contained. What would this range or band be if we wanted to be 99 percent sure this individual's true score is contained within it? To be 68 percent sure?

*3. What are the four sources of error that increase the discrepancy between an individual's obtained score and his or her true score? Give a specific example of each.

*4. Indicate the extent to which (a) within-student, (b) within-test, (c) admini stration, and (d) scoring error affects each of the following methods of determining reliability:
a. Test-retest, short interval
b. Test-retest, long interval
c. Alternate-forms, short interval
d. Alternate-forms, long interval
e. Internal consistency

*5. Construct a subtest profile with bands for each of the following subtests taken by a particular student. Assume the mean is 50, the standard deviation is 8, and the reliability is .91 for all the tests. Construct your bands so that they have a 68 percent chance of capturing this individual's true scores. How would you interpret the differences between subtests to this student's parents?

Subtests	***Scores***
Reading	56
Listening	50
Writing	61
Social Studies	35
Science	60
Math	56

*6. The following table lists the scores obtained on five different tests by Tom and Mary. At the 99 percent level, indicate which tests showed real differences in performance between Tom and Mary.

Test	S_m	***Tom***	***Mary***
A	5.5	80	60
B	16.0	150	165
C	3.4	32	35
D	30.0	620	679
E	8.0	89	103

*7. The following reliability coefficients were reported for a test administered to a single class. How do you account for the differences?

Test-retest (30 days)	$r = .90$
Alternate-forms	$r = .84$
Split-half (corrected using the Spearman-Brown formula)	$r = .93$

*8. Consider the following information from two tests:

Test	***Mean***	***Reliability***	***SD***
A	100	.91	20
B	100	.75	10

On which test would an individual's score fluctuate the most on repeated test administrations? Explain why.

*Answers for these questions appear in Appendix D.

CHAPTER 18

Standardized Tests

So far, we have limited our discussion of testing and measurement to teacher-constructed tests—and with good reason. The average teacher uses teacher-made tests for most classroom testing and decision making. However, teachers are also required at least once a year to administer *standardized* tests, evaluate the results of such tests, and interpret the results to interested and sometimes concerned parents. Thus, it is necessary that we spend time getting to know the advantages, limitations, and uses of standardized tests and how to interpret their results. Before we consider these issues, however, let's find out what a standardized test is.

WHAT IS A STANDARDIZED TEST?

Standardized tests are tests constructed by test construction specialists, usually with the assistance of curriculum experts, teachers, and school administrators, for the purpose of determining a student's level of performance relative to the performance of other students of similar age and grade. Such tests often take years to construct as opposed to a few days for a teacher-made test. They are called *standardized* because they are administered and scored according to *specific* and *uniform* (that is, standard) procedures. In other words, a standardized test administered and scored in Buffalo, New York, would be administered and scored in exactly the same manner in New York City, Chicago, Los Angeles, or anywhere else in the United States. Because of these standardization procedures, measurement error due to administration and scoring is reduced.

When the Round Rock, Texas, teachers we described in Chapter 1 decided to "help" some students taking a standardized test, they seriously compromised the utility of the test results for these students. Since the conditions under which these students took the test varied from the conditions under which other students took the test, we cannot validly compare performances. Did the actions of the teachers, while probably well-intended, really "help" these students by invalidating their test results?

When standardized tests are appropriately employed, test results from different students, classes, schools, and districts can be more easily and confidently *compared* than would be the case with different teacher-made tests. Imagine the difficulty in comparing teacher-made test results from Mrs. Smith's fifth-grade class in Orlando, Florida, with Mrs. Wilson's fifth-grade class in Portland, Oregon. Not only would the test items be different; the length of the test, the amount of time allowed, the instructions given by the teacher, and the scoring criteria would also be different. In short, there would be little or no basis for comparison. Table 18.1 compares standardized achievement tests with teacher-made achievement tests. We have emphasized the word

TABLE 18.1
A Comparison of Standardized and Teacher-Made Achievement Tests

	Standardized Achievement Tests	*Teacher-Made Achievement Tests*
Learning outcomes and content measured	Measure general outcomes and content appropriate to the majority of schools in the United States. They are tests of general skills and understanding that tend not to reflect specific or unique emphases of local curricula.	Well adapted to the specific and unique outcomes and content of a local curriculum; they are adaptable to various sizes of work units, but tend to neglect complex learning outcomes.
Quality of test items	Quality of items generally is high. Items are written by specialists, pretested, and selected on the basis of the results of a quantitative item analysis.	Quality of items is often unknown. Quality is typically lower than that of standardized tests due to the limited time of the teacher.
Reliability	Reliability is high, commonly between .80 and .95, and frequently above .90.	Reliability is usually unknown, but can be high if items are carefully constructed.
Administration and scoring	Procedures are standardized; specific instructions are provided.	Uniform procedures are possible, but usually are flexible and unwritten.
Interpretation of scores	Scores can be compared to norm groups. Test manual and other guides aid interpretation and use.	Score comparisons and interpretations are limited to local class or school situation. Few, if any, guidelines are available for interpretation and use.

Adapted with permission of Prentice-Hall, Inc. from *Measurement and Evaluation in Teaching*, Seventh Edition, by Norman E. Gronlund and Robert L. Linn.

achievement because there are actually various types of standardized tests. *Standardized test* is a general term that includes not only achievement tests, but also aptitude tests, interest inventories, and various personality assessment instruments, which we will discuss later. Now that we have a basic idea of what a standardized achievement test is, let's consider the uses of such tests.

USES OF STANDARDIZED ACHIEVEMENT TESTS

In Chapter 2 we discussed educational decision making. We concluded that teacher-made measurement instruments are useful for most educational decisions. In the classroom, standardized achievement tests are administered once, or perhaps twice, each school year. These tests are used when it is necessary to compare test scores over time or across students, classes, schools, or districts. In some cases standardized achievement tests are used diagnostically, to help educators identify student strengths and weaknesses or for evaluating specific programs and curricula. For the most part, though, standardized tests are used for comparative purposes. This is quite different from the main uses of teacher-made tests, which are to determine pupil mastery or skill levels, to assign grades, and to provide students and parents with feedback. Why, then, would the classroom teacher administer a standardized test? To compare this year's students with last year's? To compare class A with class B? Yes, but the most accurate answer is more likely that the classroom teacher administers standardized achievement tests because he or she is required to do so. This is the case in many, if not most, school districts in the country today. Furthermore, the trend is toward more rather than less standardized testing. Morrison (1992) reviewed statistics published by the U.S. Department of Education and found that revenue from standardized test sales increased by 150% between 1960 and 1989, while student enrollment only grew by 15%.

Part of the reason for this increase in standardized testing is the current trend toward increasing accountability. As teacher salaries and school taxes increase, taxpayers demand more justification for how their tax dollar is spent. By and large, taxpayers will support higher teacher salaries if teacher effectiveness increases, or at least remains constant. One indicator of teaching effectiveness, limited though it is, is standardized achievement test scores. As long as the public wants standardized achievement tests administered in the schools, the public will elect school-board members who feel similarly, who will in turn choose school administrators who feel similarly, and who will, in turn, require teachers to administer standardized achievement tests in their classrooms.

Accountability also includes evaluation of various federal and state programs. Most, if not all, such programs require that standardized achievement tests be administered as part of the program's evaluation. Further funding may depend on the results of these tests.

What this boils down to is that citizens, school administrators, special project personnel, and administrators of federal programs want to be able to compare students, schools, and districts with each other in order to make judgments concerning the effectiveness of school-wide or district-wide programs and practices. Standardized achievement tests enable them to do so. As long as this objective remains, standardized test administration and interpretation will be a necessary part of teaching. Hence, the classroom teacher must learn to administer and interpret these tests.

WILL PERFORMANCE-BASED ASSESSMENT MAKE STANDARDIZED TESTS OBSOLETE?

The status quo regarding the nationwide reliance on standardized tests to evaluate American education is changing. As we noted in Chapter 1 and Chapter 9, pressure is mounting to use performance-based assessments to supplement traditional tests, both standardized and teacher-made. And pressure to increasingly use performance-based assessments to evaluate students and programs is being felt at all levels—local, state, and national. Does this mean that the utility and employment of standardized tests will decrease? While some would say yes, we do not think so.

First, administering standardized performance-based assessments for all pupils would be extremely time-consuming and demanding on teachers, and far more expensive than traditional standardized testing. Second, for performance-based assessment to be useful in comparing schools or districts on a state or national level, procedures will need to be developed that meet appropriate psychometric standards. Since standards for performance-based assessments are currently unclear, it is likely to be some time until procedures can be established that adhere to them. And third, when performance-based procedures that meet appropriate standards are developed, they will provide a different kind of information than that provided by traditional standardized tests, rather than replace the information provided by standardized tests.

Thus, there will almost certainly be the room and the need for both assessment approaches—traditional standardized and performance-based—in the schools of the future. In the meantime, a primary need facing the new teacher will be to learn how to use and interpret traditional standardized tests. As will be discussed later in this chapter, this will also put you a step ahead when adequate standardized performance-based assessment systems become a reality.

ADMINISTERING STANDARDIZED TESTS

Recall our discussion of reliability and error in Chapters 16 and 17. We identified four major sources of error associated with measurement:

1. Within the student (illness, fatigue)
2. Within the test (poor items)
3. In administration (too little time, too many "hints")
4. In scoring (clerical errors)

A standardized test, because it has been carefully prepared over several years, generally will have carefully constructed items, thereby minimizing error within the test. Since such tests usually are machine-scored, clerical errors in scoring are minimized. Little

FIGURE 18.1
Directions Read Aloud to Students Taking the Comprehensive Tests of Basic Skills (CTBS)

Before the first test session, distribute to each student the copy of CTBS/S, *Level B, with his or her name on it and a pencil (No. 2 or softer) with an eraser attached.*

SAY: In this book are some tests. I will tell you a few things to remember while you are taking the tests.

Listen carefully to all directions I give and make sure you know what to do before you begin. Raise your hand if you do not understand. Do not begin to work on a test until I tell you to do so.

For some tests, I will read the questions out loud to you. On other tests, you will work by yourselves. When you are working by yourselves, work as fast as you can.

There may be some questions that you are not able to answer, because they test things you have not yet been taught. If you cannot answer a question, do not spend too much time on it. Make the most careful choice you can, and go on to the next one. When you come to the word "WAIT" or "STOP," do not go any farther. If you finish before I tell you to stop, you may go back over the test you have been working on.

Each question has only one right answer. Each answer choice has a circle that goes with it. When you have decided which answer is right, fill in the circle that goes with that answer. Mark only one answer for each question. Make your marks clear and dark. Do not let your marks go outside the circle.

Mark all your answers in your book, but do not make any other marks in the book. If you think you have made a mistake and want to change an answer, erase the first mark completely and then fill in the circle that goes with the one you think is right.

If you are not beginning the testing session with Test 1, see the Table of Contents for the page number of the test being given.

The directions in this manual for administering each test may also be used for the Reading tests as a separate measure; the page numbers are the same.

From *Comprehensive Tests of Basic Skills, Examiners' Manual, Form S, Level B.* Reproduced with permission of McGraw-Hill School Publishing Company.

can be done in standardized test situations to minimize within-student error, but standardized tests do minimize error in test administration. Figure 18.1 provides an example of how a standardized test minimizes error in test administration. Notice the specific directions that are given the test administrator as to what to say, how to give out pencils, and what to do during the test. The best way to guard against error in test administration is to instruct *everyone* to administer the test in exactly the same way. Instructions such as these attempt to promote uniformity in how the test is administered across teachers, schools, and districts. If performance-based assessment comes to be used for comparisons between students in different localities, similar standardized instructions and conditions under which performance must be demonstrated will be

FIGURE 18.2
Do's and Don'ts About Administering Standardized Tests

Do

- Read the manual *before* test administration day.
- Be sure you have been given the correct form for your grade level.
- Adhere strictly to the administration instructions.

Don't

- Try to minimize the achievement nature of the test.
- Deviate from the standardized administration instructions (i.e., do *not* allow more time, give hints, spell words, define words, etc.)

necessary. Figure 18.2 also provides some helpful hints to keep in mind when administering standardized tests.

The last point in the figure bears further emphasis. It is not uncommon for classroom teachers to "individualize" the test administration by helping slower students, or by pushing faster students. This is a violation of standardized testing procedure. The test and its administration and scoring are called *standardized* because everyone gets the same treatment. This sameness is what allows reliable comparisons to be made. Helping or pushing some students means those students are not getting the same treatment as other students. Teaching to the test, practicing with earlier versions of the test, and various other techniques to enhance overall test scores compromise the standardized test's validity. Thus, any comparisons we make will be less meaningful.

Unfortunately, such practices may be increasing as standardized test performance too often has come to be relied on as "the" indicator of teacher, school, or district efficacy. Haladyna, Aschbacher & Winters (1991) dubbed the term "test score pollution" to refer to the increasingly common practice of educators violating standardized test procedures in an attempt to increase standardized test scores. Just how common are such practices? Urdan and Paris (1994) surveyed 153 K–8 teachers. Their sample reported that four out of five "teachers they work with spend considerable time teaching to the test."(p.151). Furthermore, they found that teachers of minority students spent even more time teaching to the test (and therefore less time was spent in the regular curriculum) than did teachers of non-minority students. They also found that more experienced teachers were more likely to engage in appropriate preparation for standardized testing (i.e., they taught test-taking skills) than less experienced teachers. This study, the example of the Round Rock, Texas teachers, given in Chapter 1, and anecdotal reports from practicing teachers all indicate that there is a troubling tendency present among teachers in the field to violate standardized test preparation and administration procedures. Regardless of whether the teacher is naive or well-intended, such violations compromise the very reason the tests are administered, which is to allow reliable and valid comparisons of pupil achievement to be made.

TYPES OF SCORES OFFERED FOR STANDARDIZED ACHIEVEMENT TESTS

In this section we will consider the types of scores offered for standardized tests: grade equivalents, age equivalents, percentiles, and standard scores.

Grade Equivalents

Grade-equivalent scores are probably the most widely used vehicle to report test results. They are also likely to be those most often misinterpreted. Grade equivalents are deceptively simple to interpret, on the surface. Consider the following statement:

> Danielle obtained a Math Computation grade-equivalent score of 7.6 (seventh grade, sixth month) on the California Achievement Test (CAT). That means that even though she's only in fourth grade, she can do seventh-grade-level math!

Do you agree with this statement? If you do, you have fallen victim to the most common kind of misinterpretation regarding grade-equivalent scores. Danielle's obtained score is the score that the publisher *estimates* would be obtained by the average seventh-grader during the sixth month of school. It does *not* necessarily mean that Danielle is *ready* for seventh-grade math! She may not necessarily have mastered the prerequisites for success in seventh grade or even sixth grade! All we know for sure is that a fourth-grader who obtains a math grade equivalent of 7.6 is *well above average* in math. This is not the same as saying the student is ready for seventh-grade math work. In fact, we don't even know how seventh-graders would do on this test since it is unlikely that any seventh-grader took the test! To understand this statement, we must consider the way in which grade-equivalent scores are determined.

Usually a test is administered to the targeted grade (for example, fourth grade) plus the grades immediately below and above the targeted grade (for example, third and fifth grades). Thus, grade equivalents are based on actually obtained scores only for students one grade level below to one grade level above the grade being tested. Scores appearing in grade-equivalent norms tables that are more than one grade level below or above the grade being tested are *estimated*—they are extrapolated from the obtained scores. This is where the problem lies. Much higher or lower grade equivalents than average represent only relative degrees of performance. They say nothing about specific skills mastered or deficiencies.

Unfortunately, the problems related to grade equivalents do not end here. Others are listed below:

1. Apparently equal differences in scores do not necessarily reflect equal differences in achievement. For example, growth in reading comprehension from 2.6 to 3.6 will likely not mean the same degree or amount of growth as growth in reading comprehension from 7.6 to 8.6. It is likely that the one year's improvement is attributable to different factors in each case.

2. Grade equivalents are meaningless unless a subject is taught across all grades. Why report a physics grade equivalent of 6.2 when physics is taught only during the twelfth grade? What does it mean to say your performance in physics is equivalent to that of a beginning sixth-grader?
3. Grade equivalents are often misinterpreted as *standards* rather than norms. That is, teachers often forget that grade equivalents are averages—about half the students will score above and half below grade placement (depending on aptitude, of course!).
4. Grade equivalents may not be directly comparable across school subjects. That is, a fifth-grader who is one year behind grade placement in reading is not necessarily as far behind in reading as he or she may be in math, even though he or she is one year behind in math, too. This is because growth in different subjects occurs at different rates. Equal levels of growth or deficiency, as indicated by grade-equivalent scores, may mean quite different things.

In spite of these shortcomings, grade equivalents continue to be popular. Our recommendation is that if you use them, you should consider carefully the cautions we have outlined above. In general, they are more useful for the elementary grades, where they can be used to compare growth across a common core of subjects. In spite of this, remember that we cannot be very confident in the equality of the units, their equivalence across subjects, or their meaningfulness when grade equivalents far above or below grade placement are obtained.

Age Equivalents

Age-equivalent scores are very similar to the grade-equivalent scores just discussed. Age-equivalent scores are determined in a fashion similar to that described for grade equivalents. That is, samples of 7-, 8-, and 9-year-olds might be tested and average scores for each age determined. Scores for younger or older students would then be estimated or extrapolated from these scores. Problems similar to those affecting grade equivalents affect age equivalents, as outlined here:

1. Equal differences in scores may not reflect equal differences in achievement. In other words, does growth from age 6 to age 7 represent the same amount of growth as from age 10 to 11? It may or may not, depending on the trait being measured. Furthermore, growth in most traits slows down or stops during the teens or early twenties. In other words, a year's growth in reading after age 17 is likely to be very different from a year's growth in reading at age 7.
2. Age equivalents are only meaningful if subjects are taught across all grades. It makes little sense to say someone has an age equivalent of 16.9 in subtraction.
3. Age equivalents may be misinterpreted as standards, rather than averages or norms.
4. Growth across subjects may vary greatly, even if age equivalents show equal growth. A year's increase in language age equivalent does not necessarily mean the same thing as a year's increase in science age equivalent.

Unlike grade equivalents, age equivalents have *not* attracted widespread acceptance in the schools. Like grade equivalents, they are most useful in the elementary grades to compare growth across a common core of subjects. The above-mentioned shortcomings should always be considered in interpreting age equivalents.

Percentile Ranks

With grade- and age-equivalent scores we indicate the grade or age group in which a student's test performance would be considered average. That is, if a student obtains a grade-equivalent score of 4.5, we can say the student did as well on the test as an average fourth-grader during the fifth month of school. At times, however, we are not interested in making such comparisons. In fact, we would go so far as to say that in most cases we are more interested in determining how a student's performance compares with that of students in his or her own grade or of the same age. Percentile ranks enable us to make such comparisons.*

Percentile ranks are a substantial improvement over grade- and age-equivalent scores in that they do not suffer from the many limitations of the latter. Since comparisons are within-grade, it does not matter whether subjects are taught across grades, and since growth is only relative to others in the grade, the problem of growth being unequal at different grade levels is avoided. In addition, percentile ranks are less likely to be considered as standards for performance. However, percentile ranks do have two major shortcomings, which follow:

1. Percentile ranks are often confused with *percentage correct*. In using percentile ranks, be sure you are communicating that a percentile rank of 62, for example, is understood to mean that this individual's score was higher than 62 percent of the people who took the test or, conversely, that 62 percent of those taking the test received scores lower than this individual. Commonly, a score at the sixty-second percentile is misinterpreted to mean the student answered only 62 percent of the items correct. A score at the sixty-second percentile might be equivalent to a B or a C, whereas a score of 62 percent would likely be an F.
2. Equal differences between percentile ranks do *not* necessarily indicate equal differences in achievement. To refresh your memory, review the section on percentiles in Chapter 13. Briefly, in a class of 100 pupils, the difference in achievement between the second percentile and fifth percentile is substantial, whereas the difference between the forty-seventh and fiftieth is negligible—assuming a normal distribution. Interpretation of percentile ranks has to consider that units

*You may be wondering what the difference is between percentiles and percentile ranks. Percentiles and percentile ranks have slightly different meanings. In finding *percentiles*, one starts with the percentile desired (e.g., P_{25}, P_{50}, P_{75}, etc.) and then finds the score value below which there is that percentage of cases (e.g., 25 percent of the class scored below a score of 70). In finding *percentile ranks*, the reverse direction is taken: One starts with all the score values and then finds the percentage of cases falling below each value. Generally, percentile ranks are determined for all the scores in a distribution at the same time.

FIGURE 18.3
Normal Curve (Approximate Percentile Ranks Indicated Along Baseline)

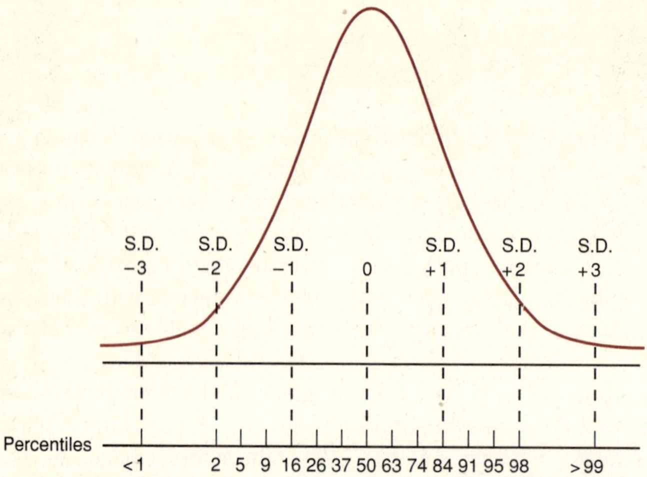

toward the tails of the distribution tend to be spread out, while units toward the center tend to be compressed, as illustrated in Figure 18.3.

As long as these limitations are considered, percentiles represent a useful type of score to employ in interpreting standardized test results.

Standard Scores

Like percentile ranks, standard scores compare a student's performance to that of other students at the same grade level. The problem of equal differences between units not representing equal differences in achievement is overcome through the use of standard scores. Computation of such scores was discussed in Chapter 13, and you might want to review the relevant sections of that chapter. Recall that the *z*-score is the basic type of standard score, and all other standard scores are derived from it. This is an important consideration to keep in mind since many test publishers "create" new types of standard scores with various means and standard deviations when they publish new tests (e.g., *Developmental Standard Scores* on the Iowa Tests of Basic Skills, or *Expanded Standard Scores* on the Comprehensive Tests of Basic Skills). You need not be overwhelmed by such scores since conceptually they are identical to *z*-scores.

Similar to, but different from, *z*-scores are a special type of standard score called *stanines*. Stanines are ranges or bands within which fixed percentages of scores fall. They are determined by dividing the normal curve into nine portions, each being one-half standard deviation wide. Stanines and the percentage of cases within each stanine are indicated here:

Stanine	*Percentage of cases*
1	4% (lowest)
2	7
3	12
4	17
5	20
6	17
7	12
8	7
9	4 (highest)

Stanines have a mean equal to 5 and a standard deviation equal to 2. Each stanine is one-half standard deviation wide. Interpreting stanines is straightforward in that a student is simply described as being "in" the second stanine, ninth stanine, etc. A major advantage of stanines is that, since they are intervals or bands, they tend to minimize overinterpretation of data. Also, since they only require single-digit numbers, they are useful for situations where recording space is limited.

Standard scores represent the ultimate in standardized test score interpretation. However, there is one factor that limits their widespread adoption—most educators, parents, and students do not understand how to use standard scores. As a result, few schools or districts request standard scores from test publishers. As we will demonstrate, however, standard scores can be time and effort savers in determining aptitude-achievement discrepancies. They also allow for easy comparison of scores both within and across pupils, either over time or across subjects.

Having had a course in tests and measurements, you are now able to make use of standard scores to make sense out of standardized test scores. Keep in mind that such scores are not understood by most parents and students and as a result are not a good medium to use in reporting standardized test results. What should you use, then? In our opinion, grade and age equivalents lend themselves too easily to misinterpretation and have too many limitations. As we mentioned, standard scores would be our choice but may be too complicated for use by the general public. We recommend, therefore, that you use percentile ranks when reporting and interpreting standardized test results to parents. Be sure, however, to consider the limitations we mentioned regarding percentile ranks in making such interpretations. Next, we will turn to the important topic of test interpretation and provide examples of standardized test score reports from publishers to familiarize you with the variety of reports available.

INTERPRETING STANDARDIZED TESTS: TEST AND STUDENT FACTORS

Standardized tests, although less useful for day-to-day instructional decision making than teacher-made tests, can be very useful for placement and diagnostic decisions and for providing feedback to parents and students. Unfortunately, standardized test interpretation is by no means a straightforward task. Standardized or not, tests are fallible and require thoughtful and considerate use. To acquire the skill of properly using standardized tests, you must consider certain factors. These factors can be classified into two categories: test-related and student-related.

Test-Related Factors

Test-related factors can limit the interpretability of the test's results due to problems inherent in the test itself, its use, or its administration. They can be addressed by asking the following questions: Does the test have acceptable reliability and criterion-related validity? Does the test have content validity for my instructional objectives? Was the test's norm group composed of students similar to my class? Were the standardized procedures followed? Let's consider each of these questions.

Does the test have acceptable reliability and criterion-related validity?

This question highlights the need to know how valid, reliable, and accurate a test is. In Chapters 15, 16, and 17 we discussed validity, reliability, and accuracy. We can determine whether a test is reliable, accurate, and valid from information contained in the administrator's manual or the technical manual accompanying the standardized test. Let's consider this information.

RELIABILITY. An acceptable standardized test should have reliability coefficients of about:

.95 for internal consistency

.90 for test-retest

.85 for alternate-forms

If your test has coefficients this high, you can feel confident that the test is reliable. Of course, there is nothing sacred about these particular coefficients. If your test has coefficients of .92 for test-retest reliability, .93 for internal consistency, and .82 for alternate forms, your test will still have good reliability.

ACCURACY. If the test is reliable, then it is also accurate. That is, it is likely to yield obtained results close to an individual's true level of achievement. In the administrator's or technical manual for a test under the section "Standard Error of Measurement" you will find a numerical value that will enable you to determine the range of scores within which an individual's true score is likely to lie. Recall from Chapter 17 that this range of scores can be determined at the 68, 95, and 99 percent levels of confidence.

CRITERION-RELATED VALIDITY. Recall that criterion-related validity may be of two types: predictive and concurrent. Since standardized achievement tests are used to assess past learning, it makes little sense to report predictive validity coefficients for them. However, concurrent validity coefficients are often reported. These are numerical estimates of the extent to which a test correlates with another established test or tests. However, using such coefficients to determine an achievement test's validity is difficult. Since the content and specificity of the different tests will vary, a valid achievement test may yield concurrent validity coefficients of .60 with Test X and .90 with Test Y, and still be a good achievement test. The reason for the discrepancy may reflect a closer match in content and specificity between your test and Test Y, and less of a match with Test X. For this reason, it *is most* important to evaluate the content validity of standardized achievement tests. Concurrent validity is of secondary importance. Of course, one would be very suspicious of an achievement test that yielded a concurrent validity coefficient of less than .50 with an established standardized achievement test.

Does the test have content validity for my instructional objectives?

A numerical estimate of validity, showing that Test A correlates highly with Test B, does *not* mean that either Test A *or* Test B has content validity for your instructional objectives. Only by matching items with your objectives can you determine whether a standardized achievement test has content validity for your class. Furthermore, remember that just because a test is reliable does not necessarily mean it is valid. If the test has several items covering dictionary skills and you have not taught such skills, the case for content validity of the test for your class has been weakened. That is, if the test does not measure or match your objectives and your instruction, the test's results will be ambiguous, regardless of that test's reliability or accuracy.

As the person on whom the burden of test interpretation is likely to fall, it is your responsibility to assess the test's content validity. You can do so by matching each item with your objectives. If there is a high degree of correspondence between your objectives and the test items, the content validity of the test has been affirmed.

Was the test's norm group composed of students similar to my class?

When the pilot or preliminary version of a standardized test is constructed, it is often administered to a test or pilot group of students. Revisions are made as indicated, and then it is administered to a *norming group* or *norming sample.* A norms table for the test is then compiled, based on the performance of this sample of the test.

A norms table provides you with a variety of kinds of information. It enables you to determine the proportion of test takers who scored above, at, or below the various scores possible on the test. In addition, norms tables enable you to convert raw scores to percentiles and percentile ranks and to a variety of standard scores. Table 18.2 is a norms table that enables conversion from raw scores on various subtests to expanded standard scores. Expanded standard scores are a variation of the *z*-scores discussed earlier. Most publishers of standardized tests develop their own versions of standard scores. However, all of these scores conform to the *z*-score interpretations presented earlier, albeit with different means and standard deviations.

Knowing what kind of students made up the norm group is of utmost importance. This is the group with which you will be comparing your students in interpreting their scores. If the test you administer to your upper-income class was normed on a sample of low-income children from impoverished backgrounds, and your class scored somewhat higher than 50 percent of the norm group, would you interpret the findings to mean exceptional performance? Hopefully not. Since children who were raised in impoverished, low-income families tend to score low on standardized tests, we would expect children from upper-income families to score considerably higher regardless of instructional method or the academic potential of the children involved. Such a comparison would be inappropriate. Similarly, it would be inap-

TABLE 18.2
Norms Table to Convert Raw Scores to Expanded Standard Scores for Fourth-Graders Who Take the CTBS from September to November

TABLE 6
RAW SCORE TO EXPANDED STANDARD SCORE (SCALE SCORE)

Form Q **Level 2**

RAW SCORE	READING			LANGUAGE				ARITHMETIC				TOTAL BAT-TERY	STUDY SKILLS			RAW SCORE
	VOCAB	COMPR	TOTAL	MECH	EXPR	SPELL	TOTAL	COMPU	CNPT	APPLI	TOTAL		REF	GRAPH	TOTAL	
00	186	132	127	163	179	175	132	211	195	187	176	108	177	182	140	00
01	214	167	143	201	216	211	145	228	220	231	186	112	236	214	160	01
02	233	188	156	236	239	239	155	242	240	265	194	116	277	235	176	02
03	248	202	166	268	258	261	165	254	259	294	201	119	309	253	191	03
04	261	215	174	295	277	280	174	264	276	319	207	122	336	272	205	04
05	274	228	182	319	297	296	182	272	291	341	213	125	360	292	219	05
06	287	242	189	340	316	310	190	280	306	361	218	128	381	312	234	06
07	299	258	196	358	335	322	198	287	319	378	223	131	401	331	249	07
08	310	274	203	373	352	333	207	293	332	393	229	134	418	349	263	08
09	321	291	211	387	367	343	216	300	344	406	234	137	434	366	278	09
10	332	307	219	400	381	352	224	306	354	418	239	139	449	380	292	10
11	341	323	227	412	394	361	233	311	364	431	244	142	464	392	306	11
12	349	337	236	423	405	368	242	317	373	443	249	145	479	403	319	12
13	356	349	245	433	417	376	251	323	381	456	254	147	496	413	331	13
14	363	360	254	443	428	383	260	328	388	471	259	150	514	422	343	14
15	369	370	262	454	439	391	269	334	395	487	265	152	534	431	353	15
16	375	378	271	464	450	399	277	339	403	505	270	155	554	440	363	16
17	381	385	280	476	462	408	285	344	410	524	275	157	576	449	372	17
18	386	392	288	488	473	417	293	349	417	549	280	160	601	458	380	18
19	392	398	296	502	485	427	301	354	425	581	285	162	631	467	388	19
20	398	404	304	518	497	438	308	359	434	628	290	165	673	477	395	20
21	404	410	311	538	510	450	314	364	443		295	167		488	402	21
22	410	415	318	562	524	463	321	368	453		299	170		500	408	22
23	416	421	325	594	540	477	326	373	464		304	173		513	414	23
24	423	428	331	635	556	493	332	377	476		308	175		528	420	24
25	429	434	336	689	575	510	337	381	490		312	178		546	426	25
26	435	440	342		594	530	341	385	506		317	180		566	432	26
27	442	447	347		616	554	346	389	524		321	183		590	437	27
28	449	453	351		641	582	350	393	548		324	186		620	443	28
29	456	460	355		674	618	354	397	578		328	189		657	449	29
30	464	467	359		722	665	358	401	619		332	191		709	455	30
31	472	474	363				361	405			335	194			461	31
32	482	482	367				365	410			338	197			467	32
33	492	490	370				368	414			341	200			474	33
34	503	500	374				372	419			345	203			481	34
35	516	510	377				375	424			348	205			488	35
36	530	522	380				378	430			351	208			497	36
37	546	535	383				382	436			353	211			505	37
38	566	550	386				385	443			356	214			514	38
39	593	566	390				389	450			359	217			524	39
40	630	585	393				392	459			362	220			535	40
41		605	396				396	468			364	223			546	41
42		629	399				399	480			367	225			558	42
43		659	402				403	493			369	228			570	43
44		696	405				407	509			372	231			583	44
45		748	408				410	527			374	234			598	45
46			411				414	549			377	237			615	46
47			414				418	574			379	240			635	47
48			417				421	605			382	243			660	48
49			420				425				384	245			693	49
50			423				429				386	248			738	50
51			426				433				389	251				51
52			429				436				391	254				52
53			433				440				393	256				53
54			436				444				396	259				54
55			439				448				398	262				55
56			442				452				400	264				56
57			446				456				402	267				57
58			449				461				404	270				58
59			453				465				407	272				59
60			457				470				409	275				60

propriate to compare the performance of low-income children to a norm group composed entirely of upper-income children. The low-income group would be expected to fare poorly in comparison, again, regardless of instructional methods or academic potential.

Fortunately, most norm groups are not composed of such homogeneous groups of students. Most standardized test publishers attempt to administer their tests to norm groups that are representative of the general United States population. This means the sample is scientifically chosen to be as similar to the general United States population as possible in terms of sex, ethnicity, region, and income. This increases the usefulness of the test for making comparisons with your class. Often a compromise must be reached in creating a norms table. In trying to closely represent the United States norm, we create a norms table that may not represent the unique characteristics of an individual classroom. To the extent your class fails to approximate the United States population in general, the comparisons you make to the norm will be less valid.

Trying to assess progress in a class for the intellectually gifted by comparing test scores to a national norm, therefore, would not be appropriate. All or most students would score high in comparison. This is *not necessarily* because the students are working hard, or because their teachers are effective. It may simply be the result of choosing an inappropriate standard for comparison, in this case a norm group composed of the general population of students, not gifted students. Although the gifted students may seem to be doing very well by comparison, it would be difficult to discriminate among them, since all or most would score at or near the "ceiling" for the test.

A similar case could be made for the inappropriateness of comparing a class composed entirely, or mainly, of low-income, low-achieving students to a norm group representative of the national population. Such a class would score very low by comparison—probably so low as to make discrimination among students in the class difficult.

Most teachers, however, do not have uniformly high- or low-achieving students in their classes. How, then, can teachers in such classes tell how appropriate the comparisons they make are? Fortunately, there is an answer.

The teacher knows approximately what his or her class composition is with respect to income and ethnicity. The teacher can then find the composition of the norm group by reading the "Norm Group" description section in the appropriate manual accompanying the standardized test. An example of such a description is presented in Figure 18.4. After studying the description, you can compare your class to the norm group. The closer the correspondence between the class and the norm group, the more confidence you can place in interpreting results using the norms table. The more the discrepancy between the table and the norm group, the less confidence you can place in interpretations based on the norms table. This is a judgment that one gets better at with time and practice.

But what if you decide there is a large discrepancy between the norm group and your class? Is there any way to interpret the standardized test results? Fortunately, the answer lies in the concept of local norms.

LOCAL NORMS. When a class, school, or district is atypical, that is, unlike the norming sample, or when comparisons among homogeneous local classes or groups are necessary, local norms can be used to make better use of test results. It should be noted, however, that we are not suggesting that local norms be substituted for national norms.

FIGURE 18.4
Norm Group Description from the Tests of Achievement and Proficiency

Standardization

In the fall of 1984, Form G of the *TAP* Multilevel Battery, Form G of the *ITBS* Multilevel and Primary Batteries, and the *CogAT* Primary and Multilevel Batteries were jointly standardized and scaled in Grades K–12. The fall sample consisted of approximately 15,000 students per grade from 49 of the 50 states. Criteria used in selecting and weighting the sample were geographic region, size of school district, and socioeconomic status (family education and income).

In the spring of 1985, empirical spring norms were obtained from all three batteries by readministering the batteries in a one-third subsample of schools that had participated in the fall standardization. In the spring, approximately one-half of the students tested with Levels 15–18 were administered Form G, the others Form H.

In addition, subsamples of students in the spring standardization in Grades 9–12 were also administered the *TAP* Listening and Writing supplements.

Norming Sample

Schools were selected at random prior to the time contacts were made for participation in the norming sample. Separate samples were identified for public school districts, Catholic school systems, and private non-Catholic schools. Each of these samples was chosen to be representative of the national population of schools according to type. The sampling procedure was designed to produce (1) a national probability sample representative of the nation's students; (2) a sample of the nation's school buildings to provide the basis for school building norms; and (3) the data on which to base special Catholic, large-city, and high and low socioeconomic norms.

The actual norming sample tested adhered closely to the target design; that is, a high proportion of first-choice schools and districts chosen randomly to represent cells specified by the design did actually participate in the standardization. First-choice schools comprised 62.3% of the participating schools, 22.9% were second-choice, 8.6% were third-choice, and 6.3% were fourth-choice or greater. Riverside test users made up 32% of the sample.

We are suggesting that local norms are useful tools that can, in some situations, increase the interpretability of test scores. They do so by enabling more meaningful comparisons to be made among similar students, classes, and schools. Since such norms are established on relatively homogeneous groups, they enable better comparisons within such

TABLE 18.3
A Comparison and Contrast of National and Local Norms

	National Norms	*Local Norms*
Composition	Large numbers of students of various ethnicity and income selected to represent U.S. population.	All students in a specific school or district.
Use	Compare local performance to a national norm.	Compare local performance to a local norm.
Advantage	Allows broad, general comparisons in areas of broad concern (e.g., college entrance, scholarships).	Allows comparisons in areas of local or immediate concern (e.g., academic gain within homogeneous groups, placement in local classes).
Disadvantage	Not useful in comparisons when relatively homogeneous groups are involved.	Not useful for making broad comparisons at a national level.

groups, but they do not allow broader or national comparisons to be made. Table 18.3 compares and contrasts national and local norms.

ESTABLISHING LOCAL NORMS. Although establishing norms generally will be the responsibility of the school district's support staff, they are fairly easy to develop. To construct a local norms table, use the following procedures:

1. Collect scores for all individuals in the local group.
2. Tally all the obtained scores.
3. Construct a simple frequency distribution (refresh your memory by rereading this procedure in Chapter 12).
4. Compute percentile ranks for each score in the table (see Chapter 13).
5. Refer to the table as you would a national norms table.

INTERPRETING A NORMS TABLE. A national norms table like the one shown in Table 18.2 can be confusing and intimidating at first glance. The key to successfully maneuvering through a norms table to convert raw scores to obtained scores is to first understand how the table is organized. Table 18.2 lists the CTBS subject areas across the top row. These include Reading, Language, Arithmetic, and Study Skills. Also listed is a column for the Total Battery, between the Arithmetic and Study Skills sections. Each of these major areas are separated from each other by double vertical lines.

Beneath each subject area section lie various subtest and total score columns. For example, the Reading subtests include Vocabulary and Comprehension columns, along with a Total column. The Language subtests include Mechanics, Expression, and Spelling columns, along with a Total column. Each of the other subject areas are arranged in similar fashion.

To convert a raw score to an Expanded Standard Score, find the student's subtest raw score in either the left or right columns, whichever is closest to the column for the subtest you are interested in, and look along a straightedge (e.g., a ruler) to find the Expanded Standard Score that corresponds to the raw score in question. For example, a student with a raw score of 25 in Reading Comprehension would have an Expanded Standard Score of 434, a student with a raw score of 25 in Spelling would have an Expanded Standard Score of 510, and a student with a raw score of 11 in Arithmetic Computation would have an Expanded Standard Score of 311.

Next, we will turn to the final question addressing test-related factors that influence standardized test interpretation:

Were standardized procedures followed?

Here, the teacher needs to think back to the day the test was administered. Were any required procedures or wording altered or omitted? Was extra time or too little time afforded? Was help made available above and beyond what was permissible according to the test manual? If no such violations occurred, no more need be done about this consideration. If one or more violations did occur, then the teacher must realize that the test's reliability has been affected to some unknown extent. Obviously, this reduces the confidence you can place in the test results. Since you will never be sure how reliability has been affected by such violations, or be certain the violations resulted in increased or decreased scores, there is little you can do to correct for such errors—except, of course, to prevent them.

This completes our discussion of test-related factors to be considered in interpreting standardized tests. Now, let's consider several equally important student-related factors.

Student-Related Factors

The variety of student-related factors that can affect test score interpretation can be divided into several categories: age, sex, and development; motivation; emotional state on the test day; disabilities; and aptitude.

AGE, SEX, AND DEVELOPMENT. An awareness of individual differences has influenced educational practice for many years. We read and hear about students being visual or auditory learners, high- or low-IQ, advanced or delayed, and so forth. Yet we sometimes fail to consider three of the most obvious of the individual differences among children—age, sex, and stage of development.

Typically, norms tables are broken into three or four sections to correspond to various times of the year. Students are expected to know more, and therefore answer more items correctly in May than in October, due to the effects of schooling. This makes sense, of course, but what about the case of a first-grader who turns *six* the day *before* school starts, compared to the first-grader who turns *seven* the day *after* school starts? Should both students, all other factors except age being equal, be expected to improve their test scores equally? If you are familiar with younger elementary-age children, your answer would likely be a firm no. Five-, six-, and seven-year-olds show very different rates of development in different areas. Furthermore, there are differences that correlate with sex. Girls tend to master verbal skills and reading earlier than boys. Norms tables for achievement tests generally do not take such factors into account. The reasons for academic performance are complex and, of course, involve more than just age, sex, and stage of development. Do not treat them as though they alone determine test performance, but do not neglect these factors in interpreting standardized test scores.

MOTIVATION. Ever find it hard to be "up" for a test? If you are like most of us, it happens from time to time. At those times your performance is less likely to reflect your actual level of achievement than if you were up for the test. Most pupils have little trouble getting ready for a teacher-made achievement test—they know that their grades depend on it. With standardized tests, however, motivation can be a problem.

Both pupils and their parents have made more sophisticated use of standardized tests over the last few years. Many parents realize that such tests do not affect a child's grades in school, but at the same time may not realize that such results are often used for instructional grouping and other instructional decisions that will affect their child later. Believing standardized tests are not important often leads pupils to take a "who-cares?" attitude toward standardized tests. Such an attitude is sometimes unintentionally transmitted by teachers in an effort to minimize the anxiety some pupils experience over tests. The result can be a decline in motivation and a consequent decline in performance.

EMOTIONAL STATE ON THE TEST DAY. Just as teachers get emotionally upset from time to time, so do their students. This does not simply refer to students who are nervous about the test, but also to students who may be undergoing severe stress for personal reasons, such as an argument before the test, a dispute at home, or some destabilizing event within the family. One cannot function at one's best when depressed, angry, or very nervous. When you find these characteristics exhibited by a student before or during the test, make a note of it and consider it when you interpret the student's test performance at a later date.

DISABILITIES. There is a sizeable percentage of students in the public schools who suffer from physical and/or emotional problems that hinder academic achievement. Naturally, such challenged students would not be expected to perform as well on standardized tests as students without such challenges. The implications for test interpretation depend on the type and severity of the challenge. Time and space prevent us from considering all of these. However, Chapter 20 will deal in detail with issues related to testing the challenged student.

APTITUDE. *Aptitude* and *potential* can be considered synonymous for our purposes. They refer to the "maximum" we can expect from a student, as indicated by a student's score on a test of academic aptitude or potential. Such tests are often referred to as IQ tests or intelligence tests. IQ tests will be discussed in more depth in Chapter 19. For now, all we need to know is that such tests provide us with a benchmark or standard against which to compare achievement test scores.

The academic aptitude test provides us with an estimated ceiling for a student's academic performance. The academic achievement test, on the other hand, measures actual academic performance. Traditionally, students have been labeled overachievers or underachievers based on the relationship between their academic aptitude and academic achievement. Figure 18.5 illustrates an underachiever, an overachiever, and a student achieving at expectancy.

Student A in Figure 18.5 is a student with considerable potential who is not achieving his or her potential. Student B is a student with moderate potential who is achieving above his or her potential. More accurately, this "overachiever" is a student whose obtained aptitude score (not necessarily true score) is lower than his or her obtained achievement score. Student C represents a student achieving at the level we would expect, given his or her aptitude score. The obtained aptitude score is equivalent to the obtained achievement score.

Obviously, it is necessary to have an aptitude score to enable you to determine whether a student is achieving at *expectancy* (the level you would expect, given the student's aptitude). However, school district policies vary in requiring the administration of aptitude tests. Depending on your district, you may have aptitude tests administered to students every few years, or only in the fourth and ninth grades, or not at all.

If you find aptitude test scores in your students' folders, you can use them to enhance your achievement test interpretation. However, be careful not to simply label your students underachievers or overachievers.

FIGURE 18.5
Relative Levels of Aptitude and Achievement for an Underachiever, an Overachiever, and a Student Achieving at Expectancy

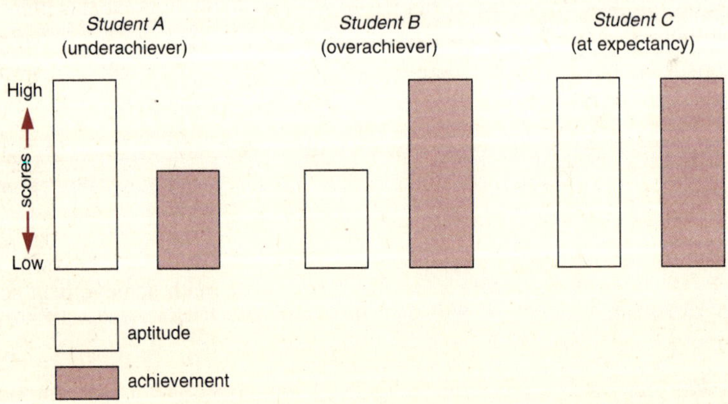

Most aptitude tests yield more than one overall IQ score. Many yield a *verbal* and *nonverbal* score, or a *language* and *nonlanguage* score, or a *verbal* and a *quantitative* score. Quantitative scores represent general math or number ability. When the aptitude or IQ test yields a verbal score and a nonverbal score or a quantitative score, more relevant comparisons are possible than when only one overall score is reported. Consider the following example:

> Donna, a new fifth-grader, obtained the following scores on the Cognitive Abilities Test (an aptitude test) at the beginning of fourth grade. (*Note*: $\overline{X} = 100$, SD = 15.)
>
> Verbal = 100
>
> Quantitative = 130
>
> Donna's scores on the California Achievement Test (CAT) given at the end of fourth grade are as follows:

	Percentile rank
Reading Vocabulary	66
Reading Comprehension	60
Reading Total	63
Math Concepts	99
Math Computation	99
Math Total	99

> Donna's parents have requested a conference with you. They want you to "push" her harder in reading until her reading scores match her math scores, which have been superior.

What would you do? How would you interpret Donna's scores? Would you "push" her in reading? Before you answer these questions, let's make Donna's data interpretable. We can do so by using bar graph comparisons to illustrate the concepts of underachievement and overachievement. This time we will add measurement scales to each histogram.

We know that an obtained IQ score of 100 is at the fiftieth percentile on an IQ test with a mean of 100 and a standard deviation of 15. We also know that on the same test an IQ score of 130 is at the ninety-eighth percentile, two standard deviations above the mean. In the graphs in Figure 18.6 our percentile scales do not correspond directly to each other, but this is of little consequence since we are not interested in comparing reading with math. Rather, we are interested in comparing verbal aptitude with reading total, both of which are on the same scale, and quantitative aptitude with math total, which are also on a common scale.

From the graphs, we would conclude that Donna's obtained math achievement score actually *exceeds* the obtained math aptitude score. According to our popular but somewhat misleading terminology, she is "overachieving" in math. Unless she is paying a high price socially or emotionally for working so hard at math, we see no problem here. Hence, the qualifier "over" in the word *overachiever* should not imply a negative valua-

FIGURE 18.6
A Comparison of Donna's Aptitude and Achievement Scores

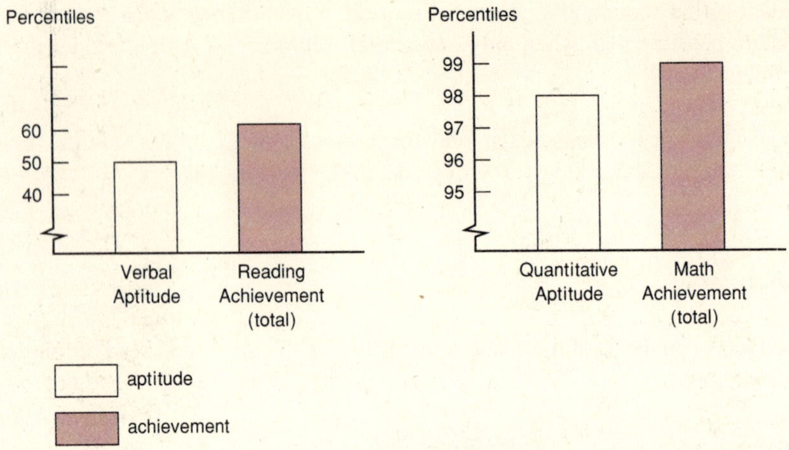

tion of what has been accomplished by this student. But Donna's parents are not concerned with her math achievement; they are concerned with her reading achievement. They want her "pushed," which suggests they feel she can do better than she has in the past. That is, Donna's parents feel she is underachieving in reading. Is she?

On the basis of a comparison of her obtained verbal aptitude score and her obtained reading achievement score, our conclusion would have to be no. In fact, Donna is "overachieving" in reading, too. That is, her obtained reading achievement score exceeds her obtained verbal aptitude score; she is actually performing above expectancy. Would you agree that she needs to be pushed? By now, we should hope not. In fact, you might suggest to Donna's parents that they ease up, using your skills in the interpretation of standardized test results to substantiate your suggestion.

Aptitude-Achievement Discrepancies*

What we have been doing is making a general or global decision about whether Donna is achieving at her expected level, as indicated by her aptitude score. In other words, are there any differences between her aptitude and her achievement? When these differences

*The following discussion assumes high difference score reliability. Unfortunately, difference scores often are less reliable than the reliability of the aptitude or achievement tests that are used to determine them. The formula for determining reliability of difference scores is presented in the section on band interpretation of scores in Chapter 17. The procedures described in this section are intended to provide the regular classroom teacher with an easy-to-use standard for identifying students who may be in need of further testing or diagnosis. They are not intended to classify a student on the basis of an aptitude-achievement discrepancy.

are large enough to indicate substantial variation in the traits being measured, we call them *aptitude-achievement discrepancies*.

But when is a difference a discrepancy? How large must the gap be before we call a difference a discrepancy? Does this begin to sound familiar? We hope so, but if it does not, this next question should help: How large a difference do we need between an aptitude score and an achievement score before we can conclude that the difference is due to a "real" discrepancy, rather than a "chance" difference? In Chapter 17 we learned how to use the standard error of measurement (S_m) and band interpretation to discriminate real from chance differences among subtests in an achievement test battery. This same principle can be applied to discriminate real discrepancies from chance differences when dealing with aptitude and achievement test scores.

We will consider an example in a moment, but first let's review one aspect of band interpretation. Recall that we can use the 68 percent (score $\pm$ $1S_m$) or 95 percent (score $\pm$ $2S_m$) methods, depending on how conservative we want to be regarding the educational decisions to be made. If such findings are kept within the classroom and little of consequence is to follow from a band interpretation, or if comparisons are limited to those among subtests on an achievement battery, the 68 percent approach may be appropriate. However, when student achievement is compared to student aptitude, often profound or at least important educational decisions or conclusions are reached. Indeed, aptitude-achievement discrepancies, when based on individual rather than group tests, are in many states one of the main criteria for determining if a child is to receive special educational services. While decisions such as placement in special education do not come about solely on the basis of aptitude-achievement discrepancies, the special education referral process often begins with a teacher recognizing such a discrepancy and becoming aware that a student is not achieving up to potential. Certainly such an important educational step should be approached with caution. Thus, we would strongly encourage you to use the more conservative 95 percent approach any time you search for aptitude-achievement discrepancies.

Let's turn to an example that illustrates how aptitude-achievement discrepancies are determined. Table 18.4 lists scores obtained by three students on the California Achievement Test and an aptitude test, the Cognitive Abilities Test. Inspect the table. Are there any aptitude-achievement discrepancies? Are you having trouble answering?

Before going any further, let's try to make some sense out of the table. Provided are three types of scores for the California Achievement Test: grade equivalents, percentile ranks, and standard scores. It is more often the case than not that several scores are reported for each student. However, aptitude scores, like those in our table from the Cognitive Abilities Test, are typically reported in standard scores only. The first step in determining aptitude-achievement discrepancies is to be sure both sets of scores are on the same scale. If for some reason standard scores are not included on your score report, request a copy of the test manual and convert the scores you do have (for example, either grade or age equivalents or percentiles) to standard scores. Such conversions normally require using only the appropriate table or tables in the manual. Instructions on how to perform the necessary operations will be provided in the manual, and they likely will differ somewhat from test to test.

After you have converted all scores to standard scores, the remaining steps are very similar to those we followed in the section on band interpretation in Chapter 17. Once our

TABLE 18.4
Scores for Max, Betty, and Robert Reported in Standard Scores (SS), Percentile Ranks (%), and Grade Equivalents (GE)

	*California Achievement Test**																		*Cognitive Abilities Test*	
	Reading Recognition			*Reading Comprehension*			*Reading Total*			*Math concepts*			*Math Computation*			*Math Total*				
Name	*GE*	*%*	*SS*	*GE*	*%*	*SS*	*GE*	*%*	*SS*	*GE*	*%*	*SS*	*GE*	*%*	*SS*	*GE*	*%*	*SS*	*Verbal*	*Quanti-tative*
Max	2.2	13	82	2.3	15	83	2.2	14	82	1.9	9	79	2.5	17	85	2.2	13	85	81	89
Betty	2.9	25	89	3.3	34	94	3.1	30	92	3.2	32	93	3.6	42	97	3.4	37	95	112	120
Robert	5.4	84	116	5.8	89	121	5.6	87	118	4.6	68	107	4.8	73	109	4.7	70	108	114	118
	$S_m = 3.5$			$S_m = 3.0$			$S_m = 3.3$			$S_m = 3.5$			$S_m = 2.5$			$S_m = 3.0$			$S_m = 3.5$	$S_m = 3.5$

*$\bar{X} = 100$, SD = 15.

Note: S_m is in standard score units. The values provided are illustrative estimates only. Actual values will differ somewhat.

scores are all on the same scale, determine the S_m for each subtest. This is important because each subtest will have a somewhat different S_m. Do not use the S_m for the whole test, as this would give an inaccurate or misleading interpretation in many cases. In Table 18.4 the S_m is listed under each subtest. While the S_m is usually not included in score reports, you can find the S_m for each subtest in the test manual. You could also compute the S_m for each subtest, using the formula $S_m = SD\sqrt{1 - r}$. To do so, you would need to look up the reliability of each subtest in the manual. However, most manuals will give you S_m for each subtest.

After determining the S_m for each subtest, add and subtract $2S_m$ to each obtained score. This gives us the range of scores for each subtest within which we are 95 percent sure the student's true score lies. Remember, we are advising use of the more conservative 95 percent approach in determining aptitude-achievement discrepancies. Using Table 18.4, here are the data for Betty's reading and verbal IQ scores:

Name	*Subtest*	*Obtained score*	S_m	*95% range*
Betty	Verbal IQ	112	3.5	105–119
	Reading Recognition	89	3.5	82–96
	Reading Comprehension	94	3.0	88–100
	Reading Total	92	3.3	85.4–98.6

Now we are ready to complete our band interpretation and identify any aptitude-achievement discrepancies. Transfer your data to a table like the one used in Chapter 17, as shown in Table 18.5.

TABLE 18.5
Band Interpretation of Betty's Verbal IQ and Reading Scores (95% Level)

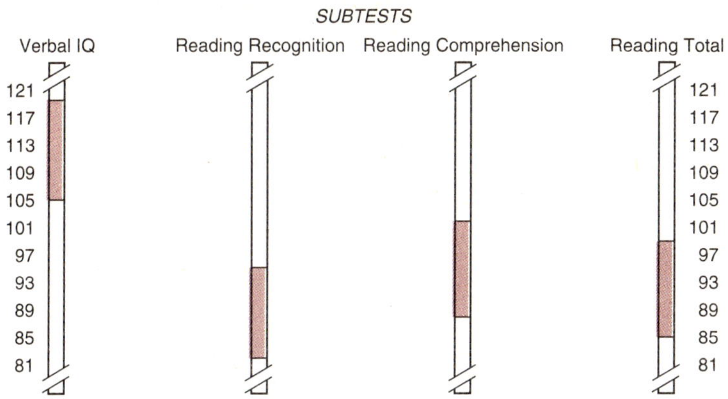

Inspection of the table reveals there are real differences between Betty's verbal aptitude or IQ and her reading achievement. Even though we have used the conservative 95 percent approach, there is no overlap between her verbal aptitude and her reading achievement. We could state with considerable confidence that a difference this large indicates a real discrepancy.

Keep in mind, however, that when an aptitude-achievement discrepancy is found, the teacher's task is only beginning. Why the discrepancy exists must be determined, and then appropriate steps taken to remediate it.

This concludes our discussion of aptitude-achievement discrepancies. Recall why we began this discussion: to consider comparing actual student achievement to individual potentials, not just to each other, or to a local or national norm. Students have differing levels of potential, and searching for aptitude-achievement discrepancies helps sensitize you to these differences. Grouping and instructional planning, not to mention standardized score interpretation, are facilitated and aided when student achievement is considered in relation to potential, not simply in relation to norms. The beneficiaries of such an approach to standardized test interpretation are likely to be both you and your students.

We have now discussed several test-related and student-related factors considered important to standardized test interpretation. It may seem as though these factors are too many and too complex to deal with every time you have to interpret standardized test scores. However, with time and practice they become second nature—if you make yourself consider them in your initial attempts at standardized test interpretation. We will present dialogues in the next section that illustrate this point. They will provide examples of how these factors can be vital to sound educational decision making in what sometimes can become emotion-laden parent conferences, and demonstrate how these factors can be integrated with marks or grades from teacher-made tests and performance-based assessments to clarify your students' performance to parents.

INTERPRETING STANDARDIZED TESTS: PARENT-TEACHER CONFERENCES AND EDUCATIONAL DECISION MAKING

Thus far in this chapter we have defined what standardized tests are; described their various uses; and discussed important considerations in administering standardized tests, the types of scores reported for standardized tests, and various test-related and student-related factors that can affect the reliability and accuracy of standardized tests. If it seems as though we have covered a lot of territory in this chapter, your perceptions are correct. In this section, we will integrate and apply this information to actual, real-world situations. As with our previous examples, these will not be exaggerated or hypothetical situations. They have occurred with one or both authors, and at some point you may be confronted by similar situations. Our intent in providing these examples is to provide you with information necessary to use test data effectively, and not to abuse it. Keep in mind our main point. Tests are tools that may be used correctly or incorrectly. The following examples show how they can work to your advantage as well as your disadvantage.

An Example: Pressure to Change an Educational Placement

(Miss Garza, the seventh-grade math teacher, is grading papers in her office when Jackie, one of her students in her Introductory Algebra class, walks in. Looking sad and forlorn, Jackie asks Miss Garza if she can speak with her.)

JACKIE: Miss Garza, can I transfer out of Introductory Algebra and get into Fundamentals of Math? (Introductory Algebra is the standard-level mathematics class for seventh grade; Fundamentals of Math is a remedial math class, designed for students with limited mathematical aptitude and achievement.)

MISS GARZA: You want to switch out of Algebra and into Fundamentals! Why, Jackie?

JACKIE: Well, you know that I barely passed Algebra for the first six weeks, and I'm failing it for the second six weeks. I just don't get it. It's too hard for me. I'm not good in math.

MISS GARZA: Well, Jackie, why is that? You have always done well in math in the past, as your record indicates, and that's both on standardized achievement tests and your grades in math up to this point. Are you studying? It sure doesn't look it from your test performance, and as you know, you failed to turn in most of the assignments.

JACKIE: The reason I don't turn in the assignments is because they are too hard. That's my whole point. I just can't understand algebra. It's too hard for me. It's really making me depressed. If I can't get out of Algebra I'm going to fail it. That means I'll not only be ineligible to play volleyball for the school, but I'll also be grounded until I bring my grades back up.

MISS GARZA: Jackie, how do you think transferring into Fundamentals is going to help you?

JACKIE: Well, I'll be able to play volleyball, and I won't be grounded, and then I won't feel depressed.

MISS GARZA: Well, Jackie, this is an important decision, and I think your parents should be involved. This decision has a big potential impact on your future, not just in terms of sports and whether you're grounded but on whether you take the right courses needed in high school and to get into college. So I'm going to give your parents a call and set up a conference to review this with them.

JACKIE: Why do you have to do that?

MISS GARZA: This decision is one that you and I should not make until we consult with your parents and review your entire record.

JACKIE: Well, I thought teachers were supposed to be here to help students. If you get my parents involved in this, it's not going to help at all. They're probably going to say they want me to stay in Algebra, because they don't care whether I pass or fail anyway. They just want something to complain about.

MISS GARZA: Well, that may or may not be the case, but the bottom line is that we're not making any decisions about transferring you out of Algebra until all the information is reviewed with your parents.

(Jackie grabs her books quickly and storms out of Miss Garza's room without saying goodbye. Miss Garza then contacts Mrs. Williams, Jackie's mother, and lets her know that she would like to get up a conference as soon as possible to review Jackie's math performance. A parent conference is arranged, and the next dialogue describes the interchange between Miss Garza and Mr. and Mrs. Williams.)

(After exchanging pleasantries, Miss Garza informs the parents about Jackie's request to switch from Algebra to Fundamentals.)

MR. WILLIAMS: Oh, why does she want to do that?

MRS. WILLIAMS: She's failing, isn't she?

MISS GARZA: Well, I'm afraid so. For the first six weeks she barely passed, and this six weeks her grades are well below passing. Unless she really gets down to work, gets her homework completed, and prepares properly for the tests, she's not likely to pass for this six weeks.

MR. WILLIAMS: Well, let's go ahead and transfer her into Fundamentals, then. As you know, with the present school policy, if she fails she'll be ineligible to play volleyball.

MISS GARZA: I realize that, Mr. Williams. However, I'm concerned that if we take this step, we may send her the wrong message for the future.

MRS. WILLIAMS: What do you mean? You want her to fail? She just loves to play sports, and it would kill her to have to sit out because of ineligibility.

MISS GARZA: Well, Mr. and Mrs. Williams, you're Jackie's parents, and I think you should have the final say on this matter. My concern is that Jackie has worked herself into a corner and is trying to take the easy way out, rather than putting together an effective plan to solve the problem herself. If this is the way she solves her problem now, I'm concerned she'll continue to do the same in the future.

MR. WILLIAMS: Maybe you just don't like Jackie. Is that it?

MISS GARZA: Mr. Williams, if I didn't like Jackie and if I wasn't concerned for her future, I wouldn't have called you, I wouldn't have set up this conference, and I wouldn't have collected all the information I've gotten for us to review. My hope is that we can review her records, including her report cards and standardized test results, and make an informed decision that is most likely to benefit Jackie in the long run, rather than a hasty and impulsive one based on emotion rather than reason.

MRS. WILLIAMS: Are you saying Jackie has emotional problems?

MISS GARZA: No, Mrs. Williams. I'm not qualified to make a diagnosis or decision about emotional problems. However, I have taught middle school for a number of years, and situations like this come up frequently. Adolescence is a difficult time, both for students and their parents, and the patterns that we put in place early in adolescence tend to repeat themselves later on. My concern is that Jackie has more than ample ability to handle Introductory Algebra, but she currently is unwilling to put in the time and effort required. If she lacked the mathematical or intellectual aptitude, or if it were evident that other factors might be contributing to her academic difficulties, I would not have suggested a conference.

MR. WILLIAMS: Okay, let's see what information you have. I know what her report card says, but I don't know anything about the standardized test scores she brought home.

(Miss Garza then describes how standardized tests are constructed and what their scores are designed to represent. Subsequently, she reviews scores from the group IQ test that Jackie took

FIGURE 18.7
Jackie Williams: Test Scores from First Through Sixth Grades

		Percentile Scores		
Grade	*Test*	*Math Computation*	*Concepts*	*Math Total*
1	ITBS	91	81	86
2	ITBS	94	90	93
3	ITBS	85	83	84
4	ITBS	32	14	24
5	CogAT	–	–	88
5	ITBS	90	85	87
6	ITBS	88	82	85

in fifth grade, as well as the year-end standardized test scores from first through sixth grade. Miss Garza then indicates these scores on a piece of paper, as illustrated in Figure 18.7.)

(After reviewing the data, Miss Garza points out that seven of the eight scores are above the eighty-fifth percentile. This, she says, indicates that Jackie's mathematical aptitude and achievement are well above average. Thus, there is no evidence that suggests that she should be unable to handle the Introductory Algebra course because of a lack of aptitude or ability.)

MR. WILLIAMS: Wait a minute! What about her scores in fourth grade? They're not at the eighty-fifth percentile; they're way down at the twenty-fourth percentile. How do you explain that? If she has such great aptitude and achievement, why did she do so badly on that test?

MISS GARZA: I really don't know, Mr. Williams. However, there are any number of reasons why a student may do poorly on a standardized test administration. (*She then shares with the Williamses a copy of Figure 18.8.*)

MISS GARZA: As you can see, interpreting standardized tests is not as simple as it might first appear. The reliability and validity of any score or group of scores depends on a number of factors related to the test and a variety of factors related to the student. Since the test was the fourth-grade version of the Iowa Test of Basic Skills, the same test that she took before and after fourth grade, we can pretty well rule out test-related factors as being contributory to her poor performance. If, on the other hand, for some reason the district had administered a completely different test, which may have had less direct applicability to the district's instructional objectives, that factor might explain the decline. I would conclude that some factor other than her ability was probably the cause.

FIGURE 18.8
Factors to Consider in Interpreting Standardized Test Scores

Test-related Factors

1. Does the test have acceptable reliability and criterion-related validity?
2. Does the test have content validity for my instructional objectives?
3. Was the test's norm group composed of students similar to my class?
4. Were standardized procedures followed?

Student-related Factors

1. Age, sex, and development
2. Motivation
3. Emotional state on the test date
4. Disabilities
5. Aptitude

MRS. WILLIAMS: Aren't these the tests that are administered over a three-day period in April?

MISS GARZA: Yes, that's right.

MR. WILLIAMS: (*looking empathically at his wife*) Wasn't it in April of Jackie's fourth-grade year that your mother died?

MRS. WILLIAMS: Yes, it was. And you know how devastated Jackie was when her grandmother died. (*looking at Miss Garza*) They were very close.

MR. WILLIAMS: Miss Garza, do you think that could explain why she did so poorly that year?

MISS GARZA: Well, I can't be sure, but it sounds reasonable.

MRS. WILLIAMS: Yes, it does. What other information do you have?

(Miss Garza then reviews with the parents Jackie's grades in math from her previous report cards. These range from straight A's from first through fourth grade, through A's and B's in fifth grade and sixth grade. Jackie's first D in math was in her first six weeks of seventh-grade Algebra. Miss Garza points out that, with the exception of the D, these grades are completely consistent with what would be expected from an individual with standardized test scores at the eighty-fifth percentile.)

MISS GARZA: So, from all the evidence we have available, we have a consistent pattern except for the fourth-grade standardized test. So you see why I'm concerned that we may be allowing Jackie to avoid responsibility and take the easy way out by transferring into Fundamentals. More important, this will put her behind her peers and make it difficult for her to have the same advantages they have in high school and college.

MR. WILLIAMS: What! How can that be? How can what you take in seventh grade affect you in college?

MISS GARZA: Well, if Jackie goes into Fundamentals now, that means she'll take Introductory Algebra or Consumer Math next year. As a result, during her first year in high school she will be enrolled in one of the lower or remedial math classes, such as Beginning Algebra or Math in Life, rather than Algebra 1.

MRS. WILLIAMS: This is confusing. Are you telling me that ninth-grade Beginning Algebra is a remedial class rather than the beginning or entry-level algebra class?

MISS GARZA: That's right, Mrs. Williams. Students who pass Introduction to Algebra in seventh grade will go on to Geometry in eighth grade, Algebra I in ninth grade, Geometry in tenth grade, Algebra II in eleventh grade, and either Trigonometry, Calculus, or one of the other options during twelfth grade.

MR. WILLIAMS: So if she gets off this track, she would end up basically being a year behind in math when she graduates.

MISS GARZA: That's right, Mr. Williams.

MR. AND MRS. WILLIAMS: (*together*) We'll talk to her!

The situation described above is not designed to provide a complete and detailed diagnosis or intervention plan for Jackie. Rather, it is to illustrate what has been presented in this and other chapters. Without examining the cumulative record of test scores, report cards, and the factors identified in Figure 18.8, neither Miss Garza, the parents, nor Jackie would be likely to make an informed decision. An individual grade, such as Jackie's grade in Algebra, or a standardized test score, such as her test score in fourth grade, should not be the basis on which important educational decisions are made. Instead, defensible educational decisions require that all sources of data be considered, including standardized test scores, report cards, and classroom grades. This is your best safeguard to an informed parent-teacher conference.

Obviously, Jackie will not be happy with the decision. However, Jackie is also a seventh-grader who is unaware of the long-term ramifications of transferring into the remedial class at this point. In her mind the transfer would clearly be the best option, since it would lead to resolution of all her problems and would require very little in the way of commitment on her part. All too often, educators find themselves in the position of making decisions in order to please parents or students, without considering the appropriateness of *all* the data on which the decisions are based as well as the short- and long-term consequences of these decisions. In a case such as this, it is likely that if Jackie's parents sit down with her and discuss the short- and long-term consequences of their decision and provide the proper support, the outcome will be a positive one.

A Second Example: Pressure from the Opposite Direction

Mr. Buckley is your school's teacher for talented and gifted (TAG) students. Each year, it is his job to review the parent and teacher nominations of students for this program, which is designed for students who have significantly above-average aptitude or achievement in language arts, math, or science. One of the main reasons Mr. Buckley was given this job was that he made a favorable impression on the principal and school board when they were interviewing for the position. He explained that his approach to making selections would be "data-based." That is, he planned to review each child's cumulative folder and would be looking for not just an isolated test score, grade, or assignment that was well above average but a consistent pattern across standardized tests, grades, and work samples that indicated high aptitude and/or achievement. District administrators and the school board, well aware of the district's high socioeconomic status, felt quite comfortable with his approach, since it would give them something to fall back on when parents complained that their child was not selected for the TAG program. The dialogue that follows took place between Mr. Buckley and Mr. and Mrs. Miller after the Millers found out that their son, Bart, was not selected for the TAG program.

MR. MILLER: Well, Mr. Buckley, since we called this meeting, I may as well lay out our agenda. We were very, very disappointed that Bart was excluded from the TAG program. We are his parents, and we know quite well Bart's exceptional capacity, not just in math, but in language and science as well. He was a straight-A student last year, you know! If that's not indicative of his appropriateness for your program, then I don't know what is. We were surprised when we heard he was excluded, and, quite frankly, we would like for you to show us exactly why he was excluded.

MRS. MILLER: By the way, Mr. Buckley, we may be new to this district, but we know how things like this are handled. We've heard from a lot of different people that in this district it's not what you know but who you know that counts. I want you to know in advance that we have already consulted with our attorney, who will be interested in what you have to say this afternoon. By the way, both my husband and I have a professional interest in what you have to tell us as well. I have a master's degree in education, and my husband teaches at the university.

MR. BUCKLEY: I didn't know that, but it should facilitate our ability to communicate. I'm glad to have individuals like you to talk with, since usually I have to spend a great deal of time explaining things and providing background information. In fact, let me just give you a copy of the criteria I use in selecting students for the TAG program. *(Mr. Buckley then gives Mr. Miller a checklist that illustrates the many objective criteria that students must meet to qualify for TAG.)*

MR. MILLER: *(with a wide-eyed look of surprise on his face)* Um, uh . . . um . . . um . . . Well, okay, let's get on with it.

MR. BUCKLEY: As you know, the TAG program is designed to provide an accelerated curriculum to students who have documented aptitude and/or achievement above the ninety-fifth percentile. For a measure of aptitude, we use the IQ or academic aptitude test scores that are in the student's file. For a measure of achievement, we use the standardized tests that are administered every April, and for a measure of day-to-day performance, we use grades and work samples from the classroom. Once nominations are received from teachers and parents, the process, although time-consuming, is straightforward. The student's file is reviewed, and if the student demonstrates consistent aptitude and achievement above the ninety-fifth percentile, with commensurate classroom grades and work performance, the student is selected for the TAG program. Since there is a lot of information in Bart's file, I have taken the liberty of summarizing his aptitude and achievement score performance and his grades in the various subjects. Here's what it looks like. *(Mr. Buckley then provides Mr. and Mrs. Miller with a copy of the summary sheet in Figure 18.9.)*

MR. BUCKLEY: As you can see, Mr. and Mrs. Miller, except for the straight A's he received for the last two grading periods last year, Bart's achievement has been in the average to slightly above average range. Consequently, it would be inappropriate and maybe even damaging to Bart to enroll him in the TAG program, since essentially he would be competing with students who are more advanced in achievement and aptitude. While we can't be sure, this likely would affect his self-confidence, self-esteem, social life, and a variety of other factors in a way that could actually slow his academic progress.

(Mr. and Mrs. Miller look at each other, with pained expressions on their faces.)

FIGURE 18.9
Bart Miller: Test Scores and Six-Week Marks from First Through Third Grades

		Percentiles		
Grade Level	*Test*	*Math*	*Language*	*Science*
1	SRA	60	52	49
2	SRA	68	46	53
3	SRA	58	59	63

	Grade Level	*1st Six Weeks*	*2nd Six Weeks*	*3rd Six Weeks*	*4th Six Weeks*	*5th Six Weeks*	*6th Six Weeks*
	1	B	C	B	B–	C	B
Math	2	A	B	B–	C	C	C
	3	C	C	B–	C	A	A
	1	A	B	B	B+	B	B–
Language	2	B	B+	A–	B	B–	C
	3	B	B–	C+	C	A	A
	1	A	B	C	D	D	C
Science	2	C	C	B–	C	C	C
	3	B–	B–	B	C	A	A

MRS. MILLER: *(clearing her throat)* Well, I . . . I see what you're saying, Mr. Buckley. But he got straight A's during those last two grading periods last year. I always thought that straight A's meant exceptional performance, and exceptional performance is what the TAG program is all about, isn't it?

MR. BUCKLEY: Yes, it is about exceptional performance, but it's also about exceptional demands being placed on students. That is, students in the TAG program are expected to do more work, complete it more quickly, and meet a higher level of expectations than students in the regular program. If there were any data that supported Bart's ability to profit from such a placement, I would have gone along with your recommendation.

MR. MILLER: Wait a minute—it wasn't just our recommendation. Miss Peterson, his teacher last year, recommended him, too!

MR. BUCKLEY: Yes, I realize that. I have the recommendation here. I also have 14 other recommendations from Miss Peterson for the TAG program. In addition, I've reviewed the grades given by Miss Peterson to all 25 students in her class during those two 6-week periods last semester.

MR. MILLER: And . . .

MR. BUCKLEY: Nearly every student in the class received straight A's during those last two 6-week grading periods. These data make it difficult to know how Bart would perform under different circumstances, such as the TAG program.

MRS. MILLER: I was hoping that starting to get A's like that meant Bart was a "late bloomer."

MR. BUCKLEY: I understand. But, as you can see from the data, with the exception of these two grading periods, Bart's performance is in the average to only slightly above average range. Rather than subjecting him to an accelerated program at this time, I believe keeping him in the regular class to give him more time to show his abilities might be more beneficial.

MR. MILLER: Thanks very much for your time and the reasonable approach you've taken. I guess I should have looked at the whole picture instead of just a part of it before getting angry.

How do you think these conferences would have ended if Miss Garza or Mr. Buckley had failed to consider all the data pertaining to aptitude, achievement, and classroom performance? Would Jackie have dropped out of algebra? Would Bart have been placed in TAG? How would the parents, teachers, and students have felt about the decisions? How would each child's psychological and/or social development have been affected by these decisions?

Of course, there may be many and varied responses to these questions. We are not implying that the proper use of test data will *ensure* a child's success. But we are saying that the proper use of tests will increase the likelihood of a child's success. At some point you may be in situations similar to the ones in which Miss Garza and Mr. Buckley found themselves. If you collect and organize *all* your data, and consider the relevant test- and student-related factors that may affect them, you are more likely to help parents and students make decisions that are to their benefit in the long run, rather than only in the short run.

Next, we will study a few of the many types of individual student score reports that are available from publishers of standardized tests. Each type of report provides different information and will be better suited for some decisions than for others. Knowing what each type of report provides, and how the data may be used, will enable you to "fine-tune" your feedback to parents at conferences, since, as you will see, certain reports can provide a wealth of information about a student's achievement.

INTERPRETING STANDARDIZED TESTS: SCORE REPORTS FROM PUBLISHERS

Test publishers offer a variety of reports for test users, ranging from the small press-on labels illustrated in Figure 18.10 containing only identification information and a single type of test score, to comprehensive reports such as those illustrated in Figures 18.11 and 18.12. The press-on labels are designed to be affixed to report cards or cumulative folders to provide a concise norm-referenced record of past or current achievement. Comprehensive individual score reports are designed to provide more specific, criterion-referenced information to help teachers diagnose a student's specific strengths and weaknesses. With proper interpretation they can also help students and parents understand how uniformly a child is achieving in the many subskill areas that are part of the child's curriculum.

Although individual score reports differ from publisher to publisher, they commonly report the following:

Identification information (pupil's name, birthdate, teacher's name, school, grade, test date)

Requested scores (raw scores, grade equivalents, percentile ranks, standard scores, scores developed by the publisher)

A breakdown of the student's performance by subskill areas (see Figure 18.11), or a bar or line graph profile to enable quick visual comparisons of performance across the many skill areas assessed (see Figure 18.12)

As was mentioned above, these standardized test reports can help you understand a pupil's strengths and weaknesses, especially when coupled with teacher-made tests. In addition to having diagnostic utility, such reports also provide helpful comparative, placement, and even mastery information. After analyzing the kind of data press-on labels provide, we will study the data provided in two examples of these detailed reports.

The Press-On Label

Figure 18.10 illustrates the simplest type of publisher score report, the press-on label. Typically, these labels are ordered by a district for each pupil and are attached to report cards and cumulative school folders. The label in Figure 18.10 includes Thomas's national percentile rank, compared to the norm group of ninth-graders, across the various subtests of the Tests of Achievement and Proficiency (TAP).

Any questions that Thomas or his parents have about his performance in the various subject areas compared to national standards should be fairly easy to answer based on this

FIGURE 18.10
A Press-on Label for the Tests of Achievement and Proficiency (TAP)

NAME JACKSON, THOMAS			Tests of Achievement and Proficiency				GRADE 09	TEST DATE 05/92
SCORES REPORTED	READING	WRITTEN EXPRESSION	MATH	CORE TOTAL	SOCIAL STUDIES	SCIENCE	INFO PROCESS-ING	COM-POSITE
NPR	53	59	70	61	53	45	50	56
COMPLETE EDITION. Key: NPR = National Percentile Rank								

information. However, just to be sure, let's consider a couple of possible situations. Try responding to the following interpretive exercise before looking at the authors' responses. After you have responded, compare your reactions with the authors' responses. If you have difficulty determining why the authors respond the way they do, review the relevant sections of this text before proceeding further.

Interpretive Exercise:

1. *Parent:* "Except for two of the subtests, this looks just like Thomas's score reports from previous years. Thomas has always done better in reading than writing until this test. We'd better get him a tutor in reading because this shows he's falling behind."
2. *Thomas:* "I was sick when I took the TAP, so the low score on Science must be because of that. I know all about science stuff and don't need to worry about it."

Authors' Responses:

1. Although Thomas's percentile rank in Reading (53) is lower than his percentile rank in Writing Expression (59), the difference is not large enough to be meaningful, due to the margin of error (i.e., standard error of measurement) that accompanies the test. This is an apparent rather than a real difference. It does not necessarily indicate a decline in reading achievement or the need for tutoring. Both scores indicate that Thomas is slightly above the national average in Reading and Writing Expression.
2. Illness is a student-related factor that bears consideration in interpreting standardized test scores. However, if Thomas was ill, his performance most likely would have been affected across all the tests rather than limited to the Science subtest. Thus, we would have expected low scores across the board, and scores lower than Thomas has obtained in the past. The latter is not the case, according to his parents, and only in Science is his percentile rank below 50.

The Press-on Label is helpful in comparing a pupil's performance to that of others nationwide, and in comparing performance from year to year. However, it tells us nothing about specific skills. That is, we can't tell whether Thomas has mastered geometric operations, or capitalization and punctuation, or any other specific skill. The detailed skills analysis reports illustrated in Figure 18.11 and Figure 18.12 will enable us to make these determinations, however.

A Criterion-Referenced Skills Analysis or Mastery Report

Figure 18.11 is the Criterion-Referenced Skills Analysis Report for Linda Adams. You can see the skills report is quite detailed. You may have felt a twinge of fear or concern due to the detail included. This is a fairly typical reaction to these types of reports, since they are often very confusing and intimidating to the casual test user (i.e., most parents

FIGURE 18.11
A Criterion-Referenced Skill Analysis for a Fourth-Grader for the Iowa Tests of Basic Skills (ITBS)

Iowa Tests of Basic Skills **B**
Service 1:
Student Criterion-Referenced Skills Analysis

	READING			LANGUAGE					MATHEMATICS			CORE TOTAL	SOCIAL STUDIES	SCIENCE	SOURCES OF INFO.			COMPOSITE	MATH COMPUTATION
	VOCABULARY	COMPREHENSION	TOTAL	SPELLING	CAPITALIZATION	PUNCTUATION	USAGE/ EXPRESS	TOTAL	CONCEPTS/ ESTIM.	PROBS/ DATA INTERP.	TOTAL				MAPS & DIAGRAMS	REF. MAT'LS	TOTAL		
Grade Equivalent	5.8	7.6	6.7	5.3	5.9	8.8	8.2	6.3	5.6	6.7	5.7	6.5	7.3	8.6	6.0	5.3	5.6	6.7	5.4
National Percentile Rank	73	86	83	62	67	87	82	79	69	78	72	81	86	90	69	62	65	84	64
National Stanine	6	7	7	6	6	7	7	7	6	7	6	7	7	8	6	6	6	7	6
Normal Curve Equivalent	63	73	70	56	59	74	70	67	61	66	62	68	73	77	61	56	58	71	57

* Includes Mathematics Computation

A

Student:	ADAMS, LINDA	Building:	JOHNSON ELEM	Sex:	F
I.D. No.:		Building Code:		Grade:	4
Class\Group:	COOPER	System:	RIVER FALLS ISD	Lvl/Form:	10/K
Norms:	SPRING 1992	Birth Date:	07/83	Test Date:	05/93
Order No.:	000-005926-001==	Age:	09-10	Page:	99

Skills	(Class N) **C**	Number of Items **D**	Number Attempted	Number Correct this Student	Percent Correct this Student	Class Average Percent Correct	National Average Percent Correct
Comprehension	(10)	38	38	30	79	56	55
Factual Meaning		12	12	10	83	63	55
Inferential Meaning		20	20	14	70	52	55
+Evaluative Meaning		6	6	6	100	55	56
Spelling		31	31	24	77	63	69
Root Words		20	20	15	75	56	68
Words with Affixes		6	6	5	83	47	57
Correct Spelling		5	5	4	80	53	81
Capitalization	(10)	27	27	25	93	55	67
Names and Titles		2	2	2	100	53	78
Dates and Holidays		3	3	2	67	56	69
Place Names		6	6	6	100	50	67
+Organizations/Groups		3	3	3	100	57	52
E Ling/Lit Conventions		8	8	9	63	66	66
Overcap/Correct Cap		5	5	3	60	56	68
Punctuation	(10)	27	27	21	78	47	52
Terminal Punctuation		10	10	6	60	63	56
Comma		6	6	4	67	54	55
+Other Punctuatn Mrks		5	5	5	100	54	44
Overuse/Correct Use		6	6	6	100	53	53
Usage and Expression	(10)	36	36	28	78	56	56
Usage		19	19	11	58	58	56
Verb Forms		8	8	3	38	47	55
Pronouns; Modifiers		3	3	3	100	61	48
Other Conventions		5	5	3	60	50	54
Correct Usage		3	3	2	67	73	68
Expression		17	17	17	100	58	57
+ Concise & Clear		3	3	3	100	61	51
Approp Language		8	8	8	100	73	56
Organization		6	6	6	100	56	63
Concepts & Estimation	(10)	40	40	31	78	57	62
Concepts		24	24	19	79	51	70
Number/Operations		8	8	5	63	68	72
Geometry		5	5	4	80	58	70
Measurement		3	3	2	67	52	64
Fract/Decml/Percent		3	3	3	100	59	65
Probability/Stats		1	1	1	100	62	61
Equations/Inequalts		4	4	4	100	63	75
Estimation		16	16	12	75	52	54
Standard Rounding		7	7	5	71	58	60
Order of Magnitude		4	4	2	50	53	64
+ Compensation		5	5	5	100	50	37

Skills	(Class N)	Number of Items	Number Attempted	Number Correct this Student	Percent Correct this Student	Class Average Percent Correct	National Average Percent Correct
Problems & Data Interp	(10)	27	27	21	78	57	60
Problem Solving		16	16	10	63	51	66
Single-Step: + & −		5	5	3	60	68	76
Single-Step: x & ÷		3	3	2	67	58	62
Multiple-Step		4	4	2	50	52	58
Prob-Solv Strategy		4	4	3	75	60	65
Data Interpretation		11	11	11	100	61	53
Read Amounts		3	3	3	100	58	65
+ Compare Quantities		6	6	6	100	60	48
+ Interprt Relatnshps		2	2	2	100	55	49
Social Studies	(10)	35	35	28	80	55	58
History		3	3	3	100	54	62
Geography		17	17	12	71	50	60
Economics		9	9	8	89	62	59
Political Science		4	4	3	75	79	56
Sociology & Anthro		2	2	2	100	58	53
Science	(10)	35	35	28	80	71	56
Nature of Science		7	7	4	57	52	59
Life Science		10	10	9	90	61	49
Earth and Space		10	10	8	80	56	59
Physical Sciences		8	8	7	88	62	58
Maps and Diagrams	(10)	26	26	20	77	52	63
Map Reading		13	13	13	100	55	64
Locate & Describe		6	6	6	100	54	71
+ Determine Direction		1	1	1	100	57	49
Determine Distance		3	3	3	100	55	52
Living Conditions		3	3	3	100	52	67
Diagrams and Charts		13	13	7	54	49	62
Locate Information		5	5	4	80	70	61
− Explain Relatnshps		3	3	0	0	46	68
Infer Processes		5	5	3	60	51	58
Reference Mat'ls	(10)	30	30	24	80	48	67
Alphabetizing		4	4	4	100	52	67
Table of Contents		6	6	6	100	71	63
− Dictionary		6	6	0	0	70	73
Card Catalog: Locate		4	4	4	100	65	67
Encyclopedia		4	4	4	100	60	56
Gen Refer Materials		6	6	6	100	62	74
Math Computation	(10)	37	37	29	78	55	66
Add Whole Numbers		9	9	6	67	57	74
Subtract Whole Nos		9	9	6	67	53	68
Multiply Whole Numbers		11	11	10	91	56	65
Divide Whole Numbers		8	8	7	88	52	57
Thinking Skills	(10)	27	27	19	70	61	66
Focus/Info-Gathering		26	26	23	88	58	66
Remembering		69	69	59	86	55	60
Organizing		136	136	105	77	57	60
Analyzing **F**		64	64	46	72	60	58
Generating		30	30	24	80	75	60
Integrate/Evaluate							

The Riverside Publishing Company
a Houghton Mifflin company

Actual size 8.5" x 11".

The Student Criterion Referenced Skills Analysis Report is available for *ITBS*, *TAP*, *ITED* and the achievement portion of combined achievement/ability testing.

This is an excellent report for individual student evaluation because it permits criterion-referenced interpretation of student performance.

A Plan 2 provides 2 copies of this report for each student. Scores reported are main score (GE or SS), NPR, and NS. Stanines can be suppressed.

B With custom reporting, up to any of four scores can be reported for each test, total, and composite, and as many additional copies as desired can be ordered by indicating your preferences on the OSS. This report may be obtained for any group of students by subpopulating.

C The number of students in the class who took each test is provided.

D For each test and skill category, the number of items, the number attempted, the number correct and percent correct for the student, the class and the nation are provided.

E Skill categories on which an individual student's performance is considerably above or below the student's overall score are flagged with a plus (+) or minus (–). These indicators of strengths and weaknesses can be suppressed by checking the appropriate box on the OSS.

F Performance on items measuring Thinking Skills is reported.

Adapted from *Riverside 95* Catalog. Copyright © 1995. Reprinted with the permission of the publisher, The Riverside Publishing Company, 8420 West Bryn Mawr Avenue, Chicago, Illinois 60631. All rights reserved.

FIGURE 18.12
An Individual Performance Profile for a Fourth-Grader for the Iowa Tests of Basic Skills (ITBS)

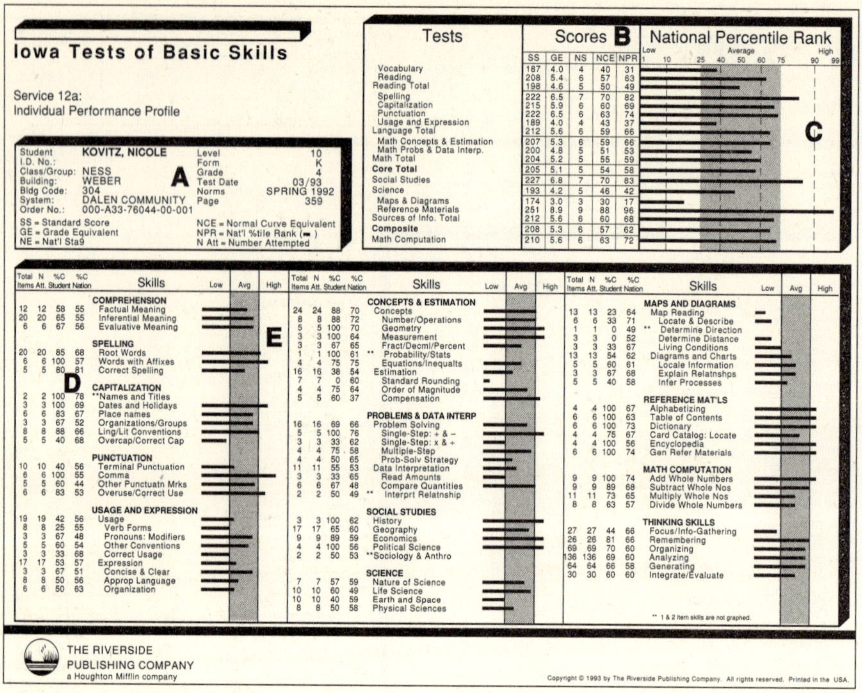

Iowa Tests of Basic Skills

Service 12a:
Individual Performance Profile

Student	KOVITZ, NICOLE	Level	10
I.D. No.:		Form	K
Class/Group:	NESS	Grade	4
Building:	WEBER	Test Date	03/93
Bldg Code:	304	Norms	SPRING 1992
System:	DALEN COMMUNITY	Page	359
Order No.:	000-A33-76044-00-001		

A

SS = Standard Score
GE = Grade Equivalent
NE = Nat'l Sta9
NCE = Normal Curve Equivalent
NPR = Nat'l %tile Rank (▬)
N Att = Number Attempted

B

Tests	SS	GE	NS	NCE	NPR
Vocabulary	187	4.0	4	40	31
Reading	208	5.4	6	57	63
Reading Total	198	4.6	5	50	49
Spelling	222	6.5	7	70	82
Capitalization	215	5.9	6	60	69
Punctuation	222	6.5	6	63	74
Usage and Expression	189	4.0	4	43	37
Language Total	212	5.6	6	59	66
Math Concepts & Estimation	207	5.3	6	59	66
Math Probs & Data Interp.	200	4.8	5	51	53
Math Total	204	5.2	5	55	59
Core Total	205	5.1	5	54	58
Social Studies	227	6.8	7	70	83
Science	193	4.2	5	46	42
Maps & Diagrams	174	3.0	3	30	17
Reference Materials	251	8.9	9	88	96
Sources of Info. Total	212	5.6	6	60	68
Composite	208	5.3	6	57	62
Math Computation	210	5.6	6	63	72

National Percentile Rank: Low — Average — High; 1 10 25 40 50 60 75 90 99

C

D **E**

Total Items	N Att.	%C Student	%C Nation	Skills
				COMPREHENSION
12	12	58	55	Factual Meaning
20	20	65	55	Inferential Meaning
6	6	67	56	Evaluative Meaning
				SPELLING
20	20	85	68	Root Words
6	6	100	57	Words with Affixes
5	5	80	81	Correct Spelling
				CAPITALIZATION
2	2	100	78	**Names and Titles
3	3	100	69	Dates and Holidays
6	6	83	67	Place names
3	3	67	52	Organizations/Groups
8	8	88	66	Ling/Lit Conventions
5	5	40	68	Overcap/Correct Cap
				PUNCTUATION
10	10	40	56	Terminal Punctuation
6	6	100	55	Comma
5	5	60	44	Other Punctuatn Mrks
6	6	83	53	Overuse/Correct Use
				USAGE AND EXPRESSION
19	19	42	56	Usage
8	8	25	55	Verb Forms
3	3	67	48	Pronouns: Modifiers
5	5	60	54	Other Conventions
3	3	33	68	Correct Usage
17	17	53	57	Expression
3	3	67	51	Concise & Clear
8	8	50	56	Approp Language
6	6	50	63	Organization

Total Items	N Att.	%C Student	%C Nation	Skills
				CONCEPTS & ESTIMATION
24	24	88	70	Concepts
8	8	88	72	Number/Operations
5	5	100	70	Geometry
3	3	100	64	Measurement
3	3	67	65	Fract/Decml/Percent
1	1	100	61	** Probability/Stats
4	4	75	75	Equations/Inequalts
16	16	38	54	Estimation
7	7	0	60	Standard Rounding
4	4	75	64	Order of Magnitude
5	5	60	37	Compensation
				PROBLEMS & DATA INTERP
16	16	69	66	Problem Solving
5	5	100	76	Single-Step: + & –
3	3	33	62	Single-Step: x & ÷
4	4	75	58	Multiple-Step
4	4	50	65	Prob-Solv Strategy
11	11	55	53	Data Interpretation
3	3	33	65	Read Amounts
6	6	67	48	Compare Quantities
2	2	50	49	** Interprt Relatnship
				SOCIAL STUDIES
3	3	100	62	History
17	17	65	60	Geography
9	9	89	59	Economics
4	4	100	56	Political Science
2	2	50	53	**Sociology & Anthro
				SCIENCE
7	7	57	59	Nature of Science
10	10	60	49	Life Science
10	10	40	59	Earth and Space
8	8	50	58	Physical Sciences

Total Items	N Att.	%C Student	%C Nation	Skills
				MAPS AND DIAGRAMS
13	13	23	64	Map Reading
6	6	33	71	Locate & Describe
1	1	0	49	** Determine Direction
3	3	0	52	Determine Distance
3	3	33	67	Living Conditions
13	13	54	62	Diagrams and Charts
5	5	60	61	Locale Information
3	3	67	68	Explain Relatnshps
5	5	40	58	Infer Processes
				REFERENCE MAT'LS
4	4	100	67	Alphabetizing
6	6	100	63	Table of Contents
6	6	100	73	Dictionary
4	4	75	67	Card Catalog: Locate
4	4	100	56	Encyclopedia
6	6	100	74	Gen Refer Materials
				MATH COMPUTATION
9	9	100	74	Add Whole Numbers
9	9	89	68	Subtract Whole Nos
11	11	73	65	Multiply Whole Nos
8	8	63	57	Divide Whole Numbers
				THINKING SKILLS
27	27	44	66	Focus/Info-Gathering
26	26	81	66	Remembering
69	69	70	60	Organizing
136	136	69	60	Analyzing
64	64	66	58	Generating
30	30	60	60	Integrate/Evaluate

** 1 & 2 item skills are not graphed.

THE RIVERSIDE PUBLISHING COMPANY
a Houghton Mifflin company

The Individual Performance Profile (Service 12a) and Group Performance Profile (Service 12b) are available for *ITBS, TAP, ITED* and the achievement portion of combined achievement/ability testing.

Teachers and parents are the primary users of the 12a Individual Profile. The 12b Group Profile is most often used by administrators and cirriculum specialists. Both are useful to analyze relative strengths and weaknesses, and to develop strategies for groups or individuals.

A Two copies of 12a are provided for each student and two copies of 12b are provided for each class, building, and system with Plans 4 and 5. On the 12b Group Profile, a summary profile by class, by building, and by system is provided.

B Reports main score (GE or SS as selected in step 4 on the OSS), NPR, and NS (unless NS is suppressed in step 4) for both services. With custom reporting, up to any four scores can be selected for each test, total and composite, and as many additional copies as desired can be ordered by indicating your preferences on the OSS.

C Local or national PRs and predicted achievement may be graphed on Service 12a using a bar graph. A 50% confidence interval band may be selected if NPRs are reported. Choose by checking the appropriate box on the OSS.

D For 12a, the number of items, number attempted, and the percent correct for the student and the nation for each skill category are reported. The 12b Group Profile reports average class, building, or system percent correct for each skill category in place of the student data.

E On 12a, a graph highlights the student's strengths and weaknesses by comparing the student to the national percent correct for each skill category. On the 12b Group Profile, the percentage of local students scoring Low, Average, and High for each skill is calculated and reported. The local percentages can be compared with the national norm group percentage.

and students and some teachers). This is unfortunate, because much information relevant to sound educational decision making may be gleaned from such reports if they are approached in a systematic way. Let's see how this can be done.

Read the text adjacent to the large letters A, B, C, D, E, and F in Figure 18.11 to orient yourself to the information being reported. The ITBS, and other standardized tests, have become increasingly flexible in recent years in allowing districts to request breakdowns like those indicated on this report in order to better match and assess local educational goals and objectives. Thus, while not a substitute for teacher-made tests, such custom score reports from standardized tests can now provide information relevant to classroom and local decision making as well as provide a basis for normative, national, and longitudinal comparisons.

Similar reports are increasingly being sent home to parents. Unfortunately, adequate interpretive guidelines are often not provided to parents and students (or even teachers). As a result, reports like these are often misinterpreted, ignored, or devalued by educators and parents alike. Our position, however, is that these reports can be useful in "fine-tuning" parent-teacher conferences and in helping you make better classroom decisions. As you did with the Press-on Label in Figure 18.10, use Figure 18.11 to respond to the following interpretive exercise before looking at the authors' responses.

Interpretive Exercise:

1. *Parent:* "I can't believe it! It says right here that this test is for tenth-grade level students. How can you people give a tenth-grade test to a fourth-grader and expect valid results?
2. *Parent:* "Mrs. Cooper, I'm appalled at Linda's performance on the ITBS. She's never had a grade below C and yet she got two zeros, a 38, and several 50's and 60's on this test. I don't want her to be promoted if she doesn't know her basics. What do you suggest I do with her? Should we retain her?"

Authors' Responses:

1. Looking at the section identified by the large "A" we can see how a parent might come to this conclusion. The third line from the bottom on the right of the box reads "LVL/Form: 10/K". If read quickly, this may look like a tenth-grade test! Standardized tests typically have multiple levels, versions, and forms. Often these are indicated by numbers rather than letters or other symbols. Thus, the level and the grade can be confusing to the casual reader. In this case we would explain to the parent that her fourth grader took Level 10 of the test, but that this is the correct level for a fourth-grader, pointing out that it does indicate "Grade: 4", just below the level information.
2. We would suggest that you explain to Linda's parent that it is not unusual for even top students to show some irregularity in skill achievement when such a detailed analysis is done. Point out that 71 separate skills were assessed. Be careful, however, not to minimize the fact that Linda did miss all the items on the Maps and Diagrams: Explain Relationships subtest, and the Reference

Materials: Dictionary subtest. Point out though that this finding, while significant, needs to be viewed in a larger context; 77 percent of the items in the Maps and Diagrams skill cluster and 80 percent of the items in the Reference Materials skill cluster were answered correctly. This indicates that her weaknesses are specific and not indicative of a broad-based skills deficit. Further reassurance that Linda does not suffer from broad deficits may be provided by referring to the national percentiles included at the top of the report. These indicate that Linda obtained national percentile ranks of 69 for Maps and Diagrams and 62 for Reference Materials. A similar approach could be taken to address the 38 percent correct score Linda obtained on the Usage and Expression: Verb Forms subtest, and the other subtest where she obtained less than 70 percent correct. This should help minimize the parent's concerns and answer the question of retention.

An Individual Performance Profile

Detailed criterion-referenced skills cluster and mastery reports which also include norm-referenced information like the one in Figure 18.11 are becoming increasingly common. Sometimes they are offered with subtest profiles like the report illustrated in Figure 18.12. This report, also for the ITBS, is called an Individual Performance Profile. The bar graph profile of subtests and skill scores can ease interpretation, especially for those who tend to be intimidated by numbers.

However, this report also provides less comparative detail regarding the various skill areas than the report illustrated in Figure 18.11. Omitted are the "Number Correct This Student" and "Class Average Percent Correct" columns from the report in Figure 18.11. Whether or not the omission of this information is offset by the added interpretive ease of the profiles illustrated by Figure 18.12 is a decision you may need to make.

Decisions about the types of standardized test reports to purchase from test publishers are sometimes based on teacher input. Since it is usually teachers who are called on to make these interpretations, this seems to make good sense! If you have the opportunity to provide such input be sure to study carefully the various score reports available from standardized test publishers. Remember, the reports you select should help you, your students, and their parents understand test performance, not confuse or frustrate. Only by investing adequate time up front, before reports are ordered, will this goal be realized.

Regardless of the type of feedback provided to parents by your district, you will be asked to interpret test scores for parents and students. When these questions come up, refer to Figure 18.8 to help you consider the test- and student-related factors that may influence standardized test scores, and use whatever individualized score reports are available to fine-tune and personalize your interpretation. Once you have done this a few times, you will join the ranks of informed, intelligent test users.

Other Publisher Reports and Services

The three examples of score reports covered above are only the tip of the score report iceberg. A host of other reports are readily available, for example, alphabetical lists with scores for classes, grade levels, schools, and the district; similar lists ranked by performance and indicating each student's percentile rank; and histograms and line graphs which include the standard error of measurement for each subtest to facilitate band interpretation. In the highly competitive standardized test market, publishers have had to become increasingly creative and flexible in meeting the needs of educators at the classroom, school, and district levels. Requests for custom scoring services are given serious consideration and support. Frequently, larger districts will enjoy not only telephone contact and support from test publishers, but personal visits, training, and consultation as well.

PERFORMANCE-BASED ASSESSMENT AND STANDARDIZED TESTS. Many, if not all, standardized test publishers are either involved in the development of standardized performance assessments or are at least closely watching developments around the country related to performance-based assessments. With the advent of CD-ROM multimedia applications (see Chapter 21) for the personal computer, the development of standardized simulations for classroom performance assessment appears imminent. Will this prove to be the death knell for traditional standardized testing? While some would hope so, we doubt that this will happen.

More likely, in our opinion, performance-based assessment will join standardized and teacher-made tests in educational evaluation. Should standardized performance-based assessments become mandatory, standardized test publishers will be among the first to begin offering standardized performance-based assessment systems. Fortunately, when this becomes a reality, your background in standardized test theory and practice will enable you to assimilate their systems with little difficulty. Just as we now use both teacher-made and publisher-constructed tests, we envision that both teacher-made and publisher-constructed performance assessment procedures and systems will be employed increasingly in the future.

Chapter 9 has given you a head start on this movement, from the teacher-made end. If performance-based assessment becomes mandatory in your district, you have the tools needed to begin implementing such measures. This chapter on standardized test theory, application, and practice will need only minimal modification to be applicable to standardized performance-based assessment procedures and systems. By mastering the content and procedures covered in this chapter, you are learning how to properly use standardized tests, which will be a benefit to you as soon as you begin to teach; in addition, you are preparing yourself to properly use standardized performance-based assessments in the future.

In this chapter we have described various aspects of standardized test construction, administration, and interpretation. In the next chapter we will discuss the various types of standardized tests, describe some of these, and provide a step-by-step approach to follow in planning and implementing a comprehensive standardized testing program in your school district.

SUMMARY

This chapter introduced you to the use, administration, and interpretation of standardized tests. Its major points are:

1. Standardized tests are carefully constructed by specialists, and they carry specific and uniform, or standardized, administration and scoring procedures.
2. Standardized tests may be achievement, aptitude, interest, or personality tests.
3. Standardized achievement tests facilitate comparisons across districts and regions because of uniformity of content, administration, and scoring and a common basis for comparison—the norms table.
4. Standardized achievement tests are frequently used to make comparisons over time or across students, schools, or districts.
5. Although standardized achievement tests are not as useful to the classroom teacher as teacher-made tests, accountability requirements have made it necessary for teachers to administer and interpret them.
6. When administering standardized tests, all administrators should uniformly follow instructions in order to minimize error in test administration.
7. Although grade-equivalent scores are commonly used, they have several limitations, including the following:
   a. They tend to be misinterpreted as indicative of skill levels, rather than relative degrees of performance.
   b. Equal differences in units do not reflect equal changes in achievement.
   c. They have limited applicability except where subjects are taught across all grade levels.
   d. They tend to be seen as standards rather than norms.
   e. Comparability across subjects is difficult.
8. Age equivalents are much less commonly used and suffer from limitations similar to those of grade equivalents.
9. Percentile ranks compare a student's performance with that of his or her peers. Although percentile ranks are superior to grade and age equivalents, they suffer from the following two disadvantages:
   a. They are often confused with percentage correct.
   b. Equal differences in units do not reflect equal changes in achievement.
10. Standard scores also compare a student's performance with that of his or her peers. In addition, equal differences in units do reflect equal differences in achievement. Standard scores are superior to percentile ranks for test

interpretation, but they tend to be not well understood by many educators and much of the general public.

11. Percentile ranks are recommended for interpreting standardized test results to the public. However, their limitations must be kept in mind.
12. Both test-related and student-related factors should be considered in interpreting standardized test results.
13. Test-related factors require the teacher to assess the test's reliability and validity, the appropriateness of the norm group, and the extent to which standardized procedures were adhered.
14. When a class is considerably different in composition from the norm group, the appropriateness of comparison to the norm group becomes questionable. In such situations local norms may be established to enable more valid comparisons to be made.
15. Differences in student-related factors require the teacher to consider the child's age, sex, and development; motivation; emotional state on the test day; disabilities; and aptitude in interpreting standardized test scores.
16. Students whose obtained achievement scores are lower than their obtained academic aptitude scores are said to be below expectancy.
17. Students whose obtained achievement scores are higher than their obtained academic aptitude scores are said to be above expectancy.
18. Students whose obtained achievement and academic aptitude scores are equivalent are said to be achieving at expectancy.
19. Students whose obtained achievement scores show "real" discrepancies when compared with their obtained academic aptitude scores have aptitude-achievement discrepancies. Band interpretation using 95 percent levels is recommended for such comparisons.
20. Interpreting standardized test scores by comparing students to their individual potential or aptitude can lead to more effective educational decision making than comparing students to the norms.
21. Consider the various test- and student-related factors that can affect performance on standardized tests, along with other available information (e.g., grades, cumulative folders), in consulting with parents about important educational decisions. Considering all sources of data before making a decision decreases the likelihood that test results will be over- or underinterpreted.
22. Standardized test publishers provide a wide variety of score reports. Depending on district policy, students and parents may receive reports that are fairly straightforward or are complex and require careful scrutiny. In any case, the

classroom teacher who is skilled in their interpretation will be the one most likely to use these reports in the best interests of the students.

23. As the push for performance-based assessment gains momentum, standardized test publishers will likely begin marketing standardized performance-assessment systems. The teacher skilled in standardized test theory, application, and interpretation will have little difficulty incorporating performance-based assessment tools into the decision-making process.

For Practice

1. "Our principal is so insensitive," said Donna. "He knows Billy Brown has trouble reading, but he won't let me help him read the test questions when we give the California Achievement Test next week." Should the principal allow Donna to read the questions to Billy? Support your decision with arguments based on points made in this chapter.

2. "Blanketiblank Public Schools Again Score Below National Average on CTBS—Mayor Calls for Freeze on Teacher Pay Until Scores Reach National Average." As a teacher in the Blanketiblank Public Schools, how would you respond to such a newspaper headline? In your response, critique the assumption underlying the headline and suggest an alternative way to measure student progress.

*3. Consider the following data obtained from the Wechsler Intelligence Scale for Children–Revised (WISC–R) and the Stanford Achievement Test at the end of fourth grade.

Student	*Verbal IQ*	*Reading Vocabulary*		*Reading Comprehension*	
		GE	SS	GE	SS
Bonnie	107	5.9	113	6.5	119
Chris	94	4.5	93	4.0	88
Jack	125	5.8	112	5.6	110
	$S_m = 3.0$	$S_m = 2.5$		$S_m = 3.5$	

$\overline{X} = 100$, $SD = 15$

After inspecting the data above, answer the following questions:

a. Is each student's achievement about what we would expect? If not, who is not achieving at expectancy?

b. Are there any aptitude-achievement discrepancies?

4. Check your work in question 3 above by constructing a table like Figure 17.7 and subject the scores to a band interpretation. Now answer the same questions again.

5. Mr. Simpson "simply can't understand" why his third-grade son can't skip fourth grade. "After all," he says, "your own test scores show he's reading and doing math at a fifth-grade level." Tactfully explain to Mr. Simpson why his son may not really be ready for fifth-grade reading and math.

6. Mr. Gregg, fresh out of college (and a tests and measurements course), is constantly extolling the virtues of standard scores over other types of converted scores. Parent conferences are coming up and he feels confident that the parents he meets with will "finally get a clear and precise interpretation of their children's test results," because he will interpret the tests using standard scores, not grade or age equivalents or percentiles. As a "seasoned veteran," what advice would you give to Mr. Gregg?

*7. Thomas, a fourth grader in your class, obtained the following raw scores on the CTBS. Using Table 18.2, convert his raw scores to Expanded Standard Scores.

SUBTEST	*RAW SCORES*
Vocabulary	36
Comprehension	19
Mechanics	12
Expression	9
Spelling	24
Computation	29
Concepts	18
Application	11
References	8
Graphical	13

*The answers for questions 3 and 7 appear in Appendix D.

CHAPTER 19

Types of Standardized Tests

In the first part of this chapter we will describe various types of standardized tests with which classroom teachers frequently come into contact. First, we will consider the achievement test battery, the single-subject achievement test, and the diagnostic test. Next, we will consider individual and group tests of academic aptitude. Finally, various personality tests that sometimes appear in student records will be described. Our intention is *not* to evaluate or recommend any of these tests. Each of the tests we describe is simply an "accepted' test with satisfactory psychometric (mental measurement) properties. At the same time we do not mean to imply that the tests we have selected are the *only* tests with acceptable psychometric properties. The question is how appropriate is a test for you, your school, or your district. The answer to this question depends on a variety of factors. Several of these test-related factors were discussed in Chapter 18. They will be referred to again in this chapter when we describe a step-by-step process that can be used to evaluate standardized tests and to develop a comprehensive school-wide or district-wide testing program.

STANDARDIZED ACHIEVEMENT TESTS

The first standardized tests came into existence around the turn of the century. These tests were tests of a single achievement area, such as spelling. Single-subject achievement tests are still used today, although they are largely confined to the secondary grades.

A variation of the single-subject achievement test is the diagnostic achievement test. However, use of the diagnostic test is normally limited to those elementary and secondary school pupils who are experiencing academic difficulty. These tests are administered to "diagnose" or indicate the specific cause or causes of a problem (for example, faulty letter identification) in some general academic area (for example, reading recognition). Seldom are such tests administered to an entire class or grade. Typically, students are selected for diagnostic testing after a single-subject test or an achievement battery has indicated a problem in some general academic area.

The most frequently used type of achievement test is the achievement test battery, or survey battery. Such batteries are widely used, often beginning in the first grade and administered each year thereafter. There are several reasons survey batteries are more popular than single-subject achievement tests. The major advantages of survey batteries over single-subject achievement tests are identified here:

1. Each subtest is coordinated with every other subtest, resulting in common administration and scoring procedures, common format, and minimal redundancy.
2. Batteries are less expensive and less time-consuming to administer than several single-subject tests.
3. Each subtest is normed on the same sample, making comparisons across subtests, both within and between individuals, easier and more valid.

This last point is probably the major reason batteries have come into such widespread use. Recall that we often use standardized tests to compare students, classes, or schools. It takes less time to make these comparisons when a single norm group is involved than when several are involved. Furthermore, the likelihood of clerical errors is minimized when single, comprehensive score reports from a battery are used to make comparisons, as opposed to several single-subject score reports.

Of course, batteries have their disadvantages, too, and these are:

1. The correspondence (content validity) of various subtests in the battery may not be uniformly high.
2. The battery, emphasizing breadth of coverage, may not sample achievement areas in as much depth as a single-subject achievement test.

Nonetheless, most districts conclude that these limitations are offset by the advantages of an achievement battery. Next, we will describe briefly some of the more popular achievement test batteries.

Achievement Test Batteries, or Survey Batteries

CALIFORNIA ACHIEVEMENT TEST (CAT). This battery is published by CTB/McGraw-Hill and is appropriate for students in grades 1.5–12. It has five levels appropriate for various grades, and two alternate forms of the test are available. Scores are provided for Reading (vocabulary and comprehension); Language (mechanics, usage, structure, and spelling); and Mathematics (computation, concepts, and problems). The CAT has been standardized simultaneously with the Short Form Test of Academic Aptitude, facilitating identification of aptitude-achievement discrepancies.

COMPREHENSIVE TESTS OF BASIC SKILLS (CTBS). Like the CAT, the CTBS is published by CTB/McGraw-Hill. However, it is appropriate for students in grades K–12. Seven levels of the test are available for students in the various grades, and an alternate form can be obtained. Level A is considered a preinstructional or readiness test and provides scores for Letter Forms, Letter Names, Listening for Information, Letter Sounds, Visual Discrimination, Language, Sound Matching, and Mathematics. Level B provides scores for Reading, Language, Mathematics, and Total Battery. Level B is designed to be administered to pupils who have completed their first year of instruction. The remaining levels, C, 1, 2, 3, and 4, yield scores in Reading, Language, Mathematics, Reference Skills (except for Level C), Science, and Social Studies. A Total Battery score is also provided, composed of Reading, Language, and Mathematics scores. Like the CAT, the CTBS has been standardized simultaneously with the Short Form Test of Academic Aptitude.

IOWA TESTS OF BASIC SKILLS (ITBS). This battery is published by the Riverside Publishing Company. It is appropriate for students in grades K–8. The ITBS was normed on the same sample as the Cognitive Abilities Test (CogAT), an academic aptitude test. Thus, determination of aptitude-achievement discrepancies is facilitated when these two tests are used. Scores are provided for Listening, Word Analysis, Vocabulary, Reading, Comprehension, Language (Spelling, Capitalization, Punctuation, and Usage), Visual and Reference Materials, Mathematics (Concepts, Problem Solving, Computation), Social Studies, Science, Writing and Listening Supplements, and Basic and Total Battery.

METROPOLITAN ACHIEVEMENT TESTS (MAT). Harcourt Brace Jovanovich publishes this battery, which is appropriate for students in grades K–9. Six levels span the various grades, and two alternate forms of the Primer level and three alternate forms of the other five levels are available. The Primer level includes scores for Listening for Sounds, Reading, and Numbers. The next level, Primary I, includes scores for Word Knowledge, Word Analysis, Reading, Mathematics Computation, and Mathematics Concepts. Primary II includes these plus Spelling and Mathematics Problem Solving. The remaining levels all provide scores for Word Knowledge, Reading, Language, Spelling, Mathematics Computation, Mathematics Concepts, and Mathematics Problem Solving. In addition, Science and Social Studies scores are available for the two highest levels.

SEQUENTIAL TESTS OF EDUCATIONAL PROGRESS (STEP). This battery is published by the Educational Testing Service. It is appropriate for grades 4–14 and consists of four levels and two alternate forms. Scores are provided at the lowest three levels for English Expression, Reading, Mechanics of Writing, Mathematics Computation, Mathematics Basic Concepts, Science, and Social Studies. The highest level of the STEP does not include the Mechanics of Writing and Mathematics Basic Concepts Subtests.

SRA ACHIEVEMENT SERIES (SRA). Published by Science Research Associates, the battery is appropriate for students in grades 1–9. Five levels cover the grade range, and no alternate forms are available. The two lowest levels include subtests for Reading (Word Picture Association, Sentence-Picture Association, Comprehension, Vocabulary), Mathematics (Concepts and Computation), and Language Arts (Alphabetization, Capitalization, Punctuation, Spelling, and Usage). The three highest levels include subtests for Reading (Comprehension, Vocabulary, Total); Language Arts (Usage, Spelling, Total); Mathematics (Concepts, Computation, Total); Social Studies; Science; and Uses of Sources.

STANFORD ACHIEVEMENT TEST SERIES. Like the MAT, this battery is published by Harcourt Brace Jovanovich. It is appropriate for grades 1.5–9.5. Six levels are provided for the various grades and two alternate forms are available. Subtests for Reading,

Mathematics, and Language Arts are available at all levels. Except for the lowest level, scores are also provided for Science, Social Studies, and, except at the highest level, Listening Comprehension. A unique feature of the Stanford Achievement Test is that the test is available as either a basic battery, including only the Reading, Mathematics, and Language Arts subtests, or as a complete battery, including all the subtests. Practice tests are also available for all but the highest level.

TESTS OF ACHIEVEMENT AND PROFICIENCY (TAP). Published by Riverside Publishing Company, the TAP is appropriate for students in grades 9–12. The TAP is designed to allow for continuity with the ITBS, and also has been normed concurrently with the Cognitive Abilities Test (CogAT), an academic aptitude test. Thus identification of aptitude-achievement discrepancies is facilitated when these two tests are used. Scores are provided for Reading Comprehension, Mathematics, Written Expression, Using Sources of Information, Social Studies, and Science. Listening and Writing supplements are also available.

Single-Subject Achievement Tests

GATES-MACGINITIE READING TESTS. This test is published by Riverside Publishing Company. It is appropriate for grades K–12 and uses nine levels to cover these grades. Two alternate forms are available for the six highest levels. The upper seven levels include subtests measuring Vocabulary and Comprehension. The formats vary across the levels, with stimuli ranging from pictorial at the lower levels to increasingly complex prose at the higher levels. Items measure recognition rather than recall.

MODERN MATH UNDERSTANDING TEST (MMUT). Published by Science Research Associates, this test is designed for grades 1–9. The three areas of mathematics measured at each level are Foundations, Operations and Geometry, and Measurement. Each of these areas is broken down further into the following: knowledge and computation, elementary understanding, problem solving and application, and structure and generalization.

NELSON READING TEST, FORMS 3 AND 4, AND THE NELSON-DENNY READING TEST, FORMS C AND D. These tests are published by Houghton-Mifflin. Forms 3 and 4 are appropriate for grades 3–9, and Forms C and D for grade 9 through college/adult. Each form includes a Vocabulary and a Reading Comprehension subtest. An optional Word Parts test for Form 3 yields scores for Sound-Symbol Correspondence, Root Words, and Syllabication. A Reading Rate subtest is included for Form 4 and Forms C and D.

Diagnostic Achievement Tests

DIAGNOSTIC TESTS AND SELF-HELPS IN ARITHMETIC. This test is published by CTB/McGraw-Hill and is designed for use in grades 3–12. The test actually consists of three components: Screening Tests, Diagnostic Tests, and Self-Help exercises. Three screening tests cover Whole Numbers, Fractions, and Decimals and help identify which area or areas require further diagnostic testing, while a fourth screening test is more general and also consists of more difficult items. Its use is generally restricted to secondary students. Dependent on a student's errors in the screening tests, one or more of the following 23 diagnostic tests would be administered:

Addition Facts
Subtraction Facts
Multiplication Facts
Division Facts
Uneven Division Facts
Addition of Whole Numbers
Subtraction of Whole Numbers
Multiplication of Whole Numbers
Division of One-Place Numbers
Division of Two-Place Numbers
Regrouping Fractions
Addition of Like Fractions
Subtraction of Like Fractions
Addition of Unlike Fractions
Subtraction of Unlike Fractions
Multiplication of Fractions
Division of Fractions
Addition of Decimals
Subtraction of Decimals
Multiplication of Decimals
Division of Decimals
Percent
Operation of Measures

Each diagnostic test is also cross-referenced to the others to assist in isolating the difficulty. That is, missing an item such as "414 × 361 = " may be due to an error in adding, placing, or multiplying. By cross-referencing with related diagnostic tests, the examiner is able to determine where in the process the breakdown occurred. The Self-Helps are linked to the diagnostic test items. These provide examples of similar problems worked out in detail and indicate the steps involved in arriving at the correct answers. Pupils are advised to study the examples and then attempt the exercise.

GATES-MCKILLOP READING DIAGNOSTIC TEST. Published by Teachers College Press, this text is designed for use at all grade levels. Two forms of the test are available. It is administered individually, and the pupil responds orally. Scores are provided for Oral Reading, Word Perception, Phrase Perception, Blending Word Parts, Giving Letter Sounds, Naming Letters, Recognizing Visual Forms of Sounds of Nonsense Words, Initial Letters, Final Letters, Vowels, Auditory Blending, Spelling, Oral Vocabulary, Syllabication, and Auditory Discrimination. Like the Diagnostic Tests and Self-Helps in Arithmetic, cross-referencing of subtests helps pinpoint weaknesses. However, no estimate of reading comprehension is available, and all scores depend on the pupil's *oral* reading level. At times a pupil's oral reading achievement may be significantly different from his or her silent reading achievement.

STANFORD DIAGNOSTIC READING TEST. Published by Harcourt Brace Jovanovich, this test is designed for grades 2.5–8.5. Unlike the Gates-McKillop, this test can be group administered with pupils responding on paper. Two levels are provided. The lower level provides scores for Reading Comprehension, Vocabulary, Auditory Discrimination, Syllabication, Beginning and Ending Sounds, Blending, and Sound Discrimination. The higher-level battery provides scores for Reading Comprehension (literal, inferential, and total); Vocabulary; Syllabication; Sound Discrimination; Blending; and Rate of Reading.

STANDARDIZED ACADEMIC APTITUDE TESTS

Thus far in this chapter we have discussed tests that are used to measure past achievement. The intent of these tests is to identify what students have learned. At times, however, we are also interested in measuring an individual's potential for learning or an individual's academic aptitude. Such information is useful in making selection and placement decisions and to determine whether students are achieving up to their potential, that is, to indicate aptitude-achievement discrepancies. In short, aptitude tests are used to predict *future* learning. Achievement tests are used to measure *past* learning.

The History of Academic Aptitude Testing

The development of tests to predict school achievement began in France at the beginning of the twentieth century. France had embarked on a program of compulsory education, and the minister of public instruction realized that not all French children had the cognitive or mental potential to be able to benefit from instruction in regular classes. "Special" classes were to be established for the instruction of such children. Admission to these "special' classes was to be dependent on the results of a medical and psychological evaluation. However, no tests were available at the time that could be used to identify children who had the cognitive or mental potential to benefit from instruction in regular classes. In 1905 Alfred Binet and his assistant, Theo Simon, were commissioned to develop such a test. The aim of their test was to measure a trait that would predict school achievement.

They revised their test in 1908 and again in 1911. The concept of mental age (as opposed to chronological age) as an index of mental development was introduced with the first revision and refined with the second. Since Binet was commissioned to develop a test that would predict school achievement, he was concerned with the predictive validity of his scale and repeatedly studied its validity for use in the public schools.

By the time of his death in 1911, Binet's scale was widely used and heralded as an "intelligence" test. English translations of the 1908 and 1911 revisions were made, and in 1916 a Stanford University psychologist, Louis Terman, standardized the Binet test on American children and adults. This version of the test became known as the Stanford-Binet Intelligence Scale or IQ test, and was revised and/or restandardized again in 1937, 1960, 1972, and 1985. Hence, what had begun as a test designed to predict *school achievement* had evolved into a test of intelligence.

Since Binet's seminal work, several other "intelligence" or IQ tests have been developed. Some, like the Stanford-Binet, are designed to be administered individually (for example, Wechsler Intelligence Scale for Children-III, Wechsler Adult Intelligence Scale-Revised, Slosson Intelligence Test); others are designed for group administration (for example, Cognitive Abilities Test, Otis-Lennon Mental Ability Test, Kuhlmann-Anderson Intelligence Tests). While each of these tests is different from the Binet, each also has similarities and correlates strongly with the Binet. Recall that tests that correlate strongly measure much the same thing. Recalling that Binet's test predicts school achievement, it is no surprise that both individually and group administered "intelligence" tests also predict school achievement. In short, a test developed to predict school achievement has come to be considered as a test of intelligence.

Why all the fuss? There would be no need for such a fuss if we knew that the tests *actually* measured intelligence. We *do* know they predict academic achievement. But do they measure intelligence? To answer this question, we would need first to define intelligence and then determine whether people who score high on intelligence tests possess more of this "stuff " than people who score low on intelligence tests. Unfortunately, we can't agree on what the "stuff " of intelligence is. For example, one of the most recent conceptions of intelligence (Sternberg, 1989) is that it can be defined by its underlying components and altered through instruction. Thus, traits previously thought inherited and unalterable could be taught. Theorists have been hypothesizing and arguing for decades about what intelligence is, and the debate will likely go on for decades more. Consequently, since we do not agree on what "intelligence" is, we cannot be sure we are measuring it. Discussions of definitions and theories of intelligence may be found in most graduate-level measurement tests. For our purposes, we will conclude that the tests mentioned here, and others like them, do predict school achievement. We are not at all sure, however, that they are measuring intelligence. Since we are not sure they are measuring intelligence, we are reluctant to call them intelligence tests. We can use such tests intelligently, though, by restricting their application to what we know they can do—predict school achievement. Before we review some of the more common of these tests, we will consider two important aspects of the scores such tests yield: their stability, and other characteristics they predict.

Stability of IQ Scores

In general, IQ scores tend to increase in stability with increases in age. In other words, IQ scores for younger children are less reliable or more subject to error than IQ scores for older children and adults. Furthermore, test-retest reliabilities tend to decline as the time interval between test and retest increases. Table 19.1 illustrates these relationships.

TABLE 19.1
Approximate Correlations Between Individual IQ Tests and Retests

Age at First Test	*Age at Second Test*	*Approximate Correlation*
2	14	.20
4	14	.55
6	14	.70
8	14	.85
10	14	.90

As Table 19.1 indicates, little is gained in terms of predicting later performance by administering IQ tests to children less than four years of age. Once children reach the age of about six, their IQ scores tend to remain fairly stable. Remember, this is *not* to say that an individual's obtained score is not likely to change at all, only that changes are likely to be small and not affect much the individual's overall percentile rank in the general population.

What Do IQ Tests Predict?

ACADEMIC ACHIEVEMENT. We have said that IQ tests, or tests of academic aptitude, predict school achievement. But just how well they do predict school achievement depends on what we use as an outcome measure. Correlations between IQ tests and standardized achievement tests generally range from .70 to .90. However, correlations between school IQ tests and grades generally range from .50 to .60. Standardized achievement tests tend to be carefully constructed and measure outcomes similar to those measured by academic aptitude tests. Keeping this in mind and realizing that grades tend to be considerably more subjective, it is no surprise that the correlation with grades is somewhat lower. As might be expected, IQ scores also correlate highly with the highest level of schooling completed.

JOB SUCCESS. In any criterion-related validity study, the size of the obtained correlation will depend on the particular outcome measure or criterion measure employed. Ghiselli (1966) reported that when completion of a training program is considered as a criterion for job success, moderately strong correlations are found (.38 to .53). However, when the criterion was defined as on-the-job performance, considerably lower correlations were found. These ranged from −.10 for sales clerks to .33 for salesmen. In short, tests of academic aptitude appear to be far less effective in predicting job success than they are at predicting academic achievement. Part of the reason for this may be the often subjective nature of the criteria used to rate job success (for example, supervisor's ratings). Just as subjectivity in teacher-assigned grades may lead to a lower correlation between IQ and school performance, subjectivity in determining job success may be responsible for the lower correlation between ratings of job success and IQ test scores.

EMOTIONAL ADJUSTMENT. No firm conclusion may be drawn about the relationship between IQ and emotional adjustment. At the beginning of the century, it was commonly held that very high-IQ individuals tended to have more severe emotional and adjustment problems than individuals with more "normal" IQs. However, a long-term follow-up (over several decades) of high-IQ individuals begun by Terman in 1921 did much to dispel this myth. Current thinking suggests that high-IQ individuals have emotional difficulties about as frequently as low- to moderate-IQ individuals.

HAPPINESS. Perhaps in part because we do not have a suitable definition or measure of happiness, we do not really know the extent to which IQ scores may predict happiness. Since they do predict school achievement and to a lesser extent job success, we might infer there would be a positive correlation between IQ and happiness. However, such a position is not supported by research and assumes that school and job success are themselves correlated with happiness.

In summary, the characteristic that IQ tests predict most strongly is school achievement. Recall that the first IQ test was developed to predict school achievement. Ninety years later, in spite of repeated attempts to modify and improve on the IQ test, we find that it still does best just what it was designed to do. Although it has been used in a variety of ways, the IQ test remains, first and foremost, a good predictor of school achievement. Whatever else it measures or predicts, it does so far less effectively and efficiently. Our recommendation is to recognize IQ tests for what they are—predictors of school achievement—and avoid the tendency to make them into something they are not. In the next section we will describe briefly some of the commonly used group and individually administered IQ tests.

Individually Administered Academic Aptitude Tests

STANFORD-BINET INTELLIGENCE SCALE: FOURTH EDITION. This test published by Houghton Mifflin is appropriate for ages 2 through 23. As mentioned above, it was originally developed in France in 1905 and revised for American use in 1916. The Fourth Edition appeared in 1985 and represents a significant revision and renorming effort. It is a substantial improvement over previous editions. Stimuli are now contemporary, and the test now has fifteen subtests organized into four areas: Verbal Reasoning, Quantitative Reasoning, Abstract/Visual Reasoning, and Short-Term Memory. Subtest scores are standard scores with a mean of 50 and a standard deviation of 8. Area scores and a composite, overall IQ score have means of 100 and standard deviations of 16. The Fourth Edition has considerably more utility than the previous version, but does require longer to administer than the Wechsler scales and other individually administered IQ tests.

WECHSLER INTELLIGENCE SCALE FOR CHILDREN–III (WISC–III). This test is published by the Psychological Corporation. It is appropriate for students between six and sixteen years of age. Along with its companion tests, the Wechsler Preschool and Primary Scale of Intelligence–Revised (WPPSI–R) and the Wechsler Adult Intelligence Scale–Revised (WAIS–R), the Wechsler scales are the most popular individually administered IQ tests. They yield Verbal IQ scores, Performance (nonverbal) IQ scores, and Full-Scale IQ scores. Thirteen WISC–III subtest scores are also provided:

Verbal	**Performance**
Information	Picture Completion
Similarities	Coding
Arithmetic	Picture Arrangement
Vocabulary	Block Design
Comprehension	Object Assembly
Digit Span (optional)	Symbol Search
	Mazes (optional)

The Verbal IQ score is the average of the first five verbal subtest scores. The Performance IQ score is the average of the first six performance subtest scores. The Full-Scale IQ score results from all eleven of the subtest scores.

Group Administered Academic Aptitude Tests

COGNITIVE ABILITIES TESTS (COGAT). Published by Riverside Publishing Company, this test is appropriate for children in grades K–13. It includes a nonreading test at the lowest two levels and eight multilevel tests that provide Verbal, Quantitative, and Nonverbal scores. This test was normed simultaneously with the Iowa Tests of Basic Skills and Tests of Achievement and Proficiency, facilitating aptitude-achievement comparisons. The nonreading test has four subtests: Oral Vocabulary, Relational Concepts, Multimental, and Quantitative. The Verbal test includes Vocabulary, Sentence Completion, Verbal Classification, and Verbal Analogies subtests. The Quantitative test measures Quantitative Comparisons, Number Series, and Equation Building. The Nonverbal subtests eliminate reliance on reading ability entirely. They consist of items to measure Figure Analogies, Figure Classification, and Figure Synthesis.

OTIS-LENNON MENTAL ABILITY TESTS (OLMAT). This test is published by Harcourt Brace Jovanovich and is appropriate for grades K–12. An earlier version of this test is called the Otis Quick-Scoring Mental Ability Test. The test requires as little as 30 minutes to administer at the lower levels and up to 50 minutes at the higher levels. Although this test compares favorably with other IQ tests, a disadvantage is that only a Total IQ score is provided.

SHORT FORM TEST OF ACADEMIC APTITUDE (SFTAA). Published by CTB/McGraw-Hill, this test is appropriate for grades 1.5–12.0. Five levels of the test cover the grade range. The SFTAA is a revision of an earlier test called the California Test of Mental Maturity. It yields Language, Non-Language, and Total scores and consists of four subtests: Vocabulary, Analogies, Sequences, and Memory. This test was standardized simultaneously with both the California Achievement Test (CAT) and the Comprehensive Test of Basic Skills (CTBS), thus facilitating aptitude achievement comparisons.

STANDARDIZED PERSONALITY ASSESSMENT INSTRUMENTS

Of the types of standardized tests with which the classroom teacher comes in contact, personality tests are probably the least used and the least understood. Perhaps this is the way it should be, since teachers are mainly concerned with academic development and are not trained in personality development or assessment. Nonetheless, teachers cannot help but have some impact on and ideas about personality development, and results from such tests do show up in pupil folders. Interpretation of such tests is beyond the scope of this text and the training of classroom teachers. Thus, we will limit ourselves to considering briefly what personality is, discussing the two major approaches to personality assessment, and describing briefly several examples of personality tests.

What Is Personality?

As in the case of intelligence, no one has arrived yet at a definitive, universally accepted definition of personality. We do know that people tend to behave in certain relatively fixed ways across various situations. One such pattern of typical and expected behavior may be considered to be a personality *trait*. For example, individuals who tend to become nervous or anxious when speaking in front of groups tend to become anxious in any public speaking situation—large or small. A personality trait for such individuals would be anxiety. All of an individual's traits or characteristics, taken together, comprise an individual's personality. Thus, perhaps we can define personality as the typical or characteristic ways individuals behave. This is a deceptively simple definition, however. Allport and Odbert (1936) estimated that the number of typical ways individuals behave is in the *thousands*. If we accept this definition, then, we must admit that the task of measuring these traits would be an enormous one. Nevertheless the task has been approached with considerable success over the last eighty years. Essentially, the efforts to measure personality have moved in two directions: objective personality assessment and projective personality assessment. We will describe each of these and then some examples of each type of assessment instrument.

OBJECTIVE PERSONALITY ASSESSMENT. Objective personality assessment usually employs self-report questionnaires. Items are often based on questions used in psychiatric interviews. The first instrument of this type appeared during World War I. Since then, they have gained considerable popularity among psychologists, the military, and industry. This approach provides a lengthy list of statements, adjectives, or questions to which examinees respond. A variety of formats have been employed, including checklists, true-false, and multiple-choice. Some items are obviously indicative of serious psychopathology; others are much more subtle. In most cases *individual* responses are not that meaningful in the interpretation. Instead, patterns of responses or a profile of scores is relied on for interpretation.

Objective personality instruments have the advantage of being economical to administer. They can be group administered and monitored by a clerk rather than requiring the time and training of a psychiatrist or psychologist for valid administration. Major disadvantages include their sometimes questionable validity, a tendency to mark answers in a safe or socially desirable fashion (thereby perhaps masking certain traits), or attempts to fake a normal or pathological response pattern. This latter point has received extensive attention by personality test developers, and validity scales have been built into some instruments to inform the examiner that responses have been faked.

PROJECTIVE PERSONALITY ASSESSMENT. Projective personality assessment involves requiring examinees to respond to unstructured or ambiguous stimuli (for example, incomplete sentences, inkblots, abstract pictures). The basic theory underlying projective personality testing can be summarized as follows:

1. With the passage of time, response tendencies in various situations tend to become resistant to change and tend to reproduce themselves in the presence of various stimuli.

2. When presented with suggestive or ambiguous stimuli, examinees will respond to them in ways that relate to conscious or unconscious motives, beliefs, or experiences.
3. Projective tests, by presenting stimuli that are suggestive of various aspects of the individual's life (for example, mother-father relationships, the need for achievement) or are ambiguous, will make individuals respond in ways that reflect their conscious or unconscious motives, beliefs, or experiences.

A major advantage of projective over objective tests is that the stimuli are often sufficiently abstract to allow scoring criteria to detect a variety of appropriate and inappropriate behavior. Such techniques may uncover a broader range of psychopathology and allow for the use and interpretation of unique responses. Major disadvantages of projective techniques include questionable validity related to their often complex scoring rules and their expense. Projective personality tests always require administration and scoring by an appropriately trained psychologist or psychiatrist.

Objective Personality Tests

ADJECTIVE CHECKLIST. Published by the Consulting Psychologists Press, this instrument is appropriate for individuals in ninth grade through adults. It consists of an alphabetical list of adjectives and is usually completed in about 15 minutes. The subject checks those adjectives that are applicable. Scores can be obtained in 24 variables, including self-confidence, self-control, counseling readiness, and various needs and aspects of personal adjustment.

EDWARDS PERSONAL PREFERENCE SCHEDULE (EPPS). This instrument is published by the Psychological Corporation and is appropriate for college students and adults. It is normally completed in 45 to 50 minutes. Subjects respond by choosing one of a pair of statements that apply to them. Each statement represents a need, and each of these needs is assessed by nine pairs of statements.

MINNESOTA MULTIPHASIC PERSONALITY INVENTORY–2 (MMPI–2). Published by the Psychological Corporation, this instrument is appropriate for individuals over 18 years of age. It generally takes about one hour to complete. The MMPI–2 is the most widely used of the objective personality tests and has been in use for over sixty years. It requires individuals to respond to 567 statements presented in true-false format. Responses are scored on several scales, including validity scales and scales measuring concern for bodily functioning, depression, hysteria, psychopathological tendencies, paranoia, anxiety, schizophrenia, level of mental activity, and social comfort. The MMPI–2 is widely used as a screening instrument in psychiatric, educational, military, industrial, and government institutions. A modified version of the MMPI–2, called the MMPI–A, was published in 1992 and is appropriate for adolescents.

MYERS-BRIGGS TYPE INDICATOR (MBTI). This instrument is published by the Educational Testing Service. It is appropriate for ninth grade through adult and requires about one hour to complete. The format is forced-choice and scores are provided for introversion versus extroversion, sensation versus intuition, thinking versus feeling, and judgment versus perception. The MBTI has been in use for over fifty years and enjoys widespread popularity.

Projective Personality Tests

RORSCHACH INKBLOT TECHNIQUE. This test is published by Hans Huber Medical Publisher, Berne, Switzerland. It consists of ten cards or plates. Each card contains an inkblot, some black-and-white, some colored. Examinees are asked to describe what they "see" in the ambiguous blot. Responses are scored according to location, content, and a variety of other factors, including whether form or color was used to construct the image, whether movement is suggested, and whether shading or texture was considered. Scoring is complex, and although acceptable validity data are scant, the Rorschach has been one of the most popular projective tests used by clinical psychologists. In the hands of a skilled clinician it can yield a surprising variety of information.

THEMATIC APPERCEPTION TEST (TAT). Published by the Harvard University Press, the TAT is designed for individuals age 10 through adult. Adaptations of the test for younger children (Children's Apperception Test) and senior citizens (Senior Apperception Test) are also available. The subject is presented with a series of pictures (usually 10 or 12 of the total of 30) and asked to make up a story to fit each picture. The pictures vary in degree of structure and ambiguity. The record of stories is then examined to determine the projection of the subject's personality, as indicated by recurrent behavioral themes, needs, perceived pressures, and so on. Interpretation is often complex and requires an appropriately trained psychologist or psychiatrist.

This concludes our discussion of the types of standardized tests. By no means all-inclusive, our presentation of various types of tests has focused on those tests which the average classroom teacher is most likely to come into contact with. In the remainder of this chapter we will discuss how these tests, or tests like them, are evaluated in planning and implementing a comprehensive school- or district-wide testing program.

PLANNING A SCHOOL- OR DISTRICT-WIDE TESTING PROGRAM

In the past, the average classroom teacher could be expected to have little, if any, input into the development of a district-wide testing program. In many cases administrators design testing programs without considering the needs and limitations of local schools. Unfortunately, when local school personnel do not have input into decisions concerning a district-wide testing program, are not apprised of the reasons for decisions, and yet are forced to abide by these decisions, resistance is usually encountered. Such resistance may take a variety of forms, including decreased motivation for the testing program—an attitude that may easily be transmitted to students. Furthermore, with the passage of time, an adversarial rather than a collegial relationship often develops between test administrators and local school personnel. The effect of this can be an increase in error in testing and a subsequent decline in the reliability and validity of the assessment.

Fortunately, more and more school districts are working to minimize this us-against-them attitude and are soliciting input from local school personnel in developing and implementing district-wide testing programs. In the future it is more likely than in the past that you will be asked to serve on a committee that will decide your district's testing program. Below we provide a brief, logical approach to guide your participation on such a committee. In fact, it may be the case that you are one of the few individuals on the committee who has a knowledge about the selection of a comprehensive and efficient test battery.

Step 1: Ask the Right Question

All too often the first question asked is "What tests should we use?" In reality such a question is quite premature. The first question to ask is "What is the purpose of our testing?" Defining the purpose makes the remaining steps go much more smoothly and efficiently. A good testing program *matches* the purposes of testing—just like a good item matches the objective it is measuring. Asking the right question also decreases the likelihood that you will simply "borrow" another district's program. While this option is tempting and appears to be a timesaver, it can also backfire in the long run. Not all districts have the same needs or are interested in answering the same questions. Therefore, no one testing program can be all things to all districts. First and foremost, then, consider the purpose or purposes of the testing program, using the selections offered in Table 19.2.

Step 2: Decide on the Purposes for Your Testing Program

At this stage the committee decides which of these purposes are to be filled by the testing program. Obviously, standardized tests need not be included for everyday instructional decisions or grading, as these purposes are already being served by tests constructed within the classroom. In your school or district, one of the other purposes or uses listed in Table 19.2 may not be necessary. For example, there is no point in going through the time and expense of administering a reading readiness test at the end of kindergarten for placement purposes if there is no difference in instructional methods or grouping in the first grade. On the other hand, if students are placed into different groups, depending on readiness scores, and instruction is altered accordingly, then your test is useful for placement, grouping, and instructional planning.

Once the uses or purposes of testing have been identified, the focus of the committee begins to shift to considerations about the tests themselves. These considerations are general, relating to the integration of the overall testing program, as well as focused, relating to the specific tests.

TABLE 19.2
Purposes of Educational Testing and Types of Tests Appropriate for Each Purpose

Purpose	*Appropriate Test* Teacher-made tests	*Appropriate Test* Standardized tests
Classroom:	x	
Grading	x	
Achievement gains	x	x
Diagnostic	x	x
Grouping	x	x
Instructional planning	x	x
Aptitude-achievement discrepancies		x
Academic potential		x
Guidance		x
Administrative:		
Selection		x
Placement		x
Special education placement		x
Program evaluation	x	x
Public relations		x

Step 3: Consider the Program's Integration

REDUNDANCY. Frequently a district finds itself administering more than one test to measure the same thing or for the same purpose. Such overtesting or redundancy is more likely when tests are required by funding agencies at several levels: district, regional, state, and national. Funding for programs often comes from one or some combination of these sources, and each source wants data to support its funding efforts. Usually, these data take the form of test scores which districts are required to provide to ensure continued funding. To be helpful, each of these sources usually recommends a test or variety of tests that are "acceptable." All too often, schools and districts feel they must use a different test for each source. In reality, the results from a single survey battery may meet the requirements of several funding sources, as well as district feedback and accountability needs. For example, a district may administer the California Achievement Test to determine which schools qualify for Chapter I funding and the Iowa Test of Basic Skills to meet district needs for feedback about achievement levels. The purpose in each case is to obtain data about achievement levels. There is no reason to administer both batteries. Either one would provide the necessary information.

In other cases, districts get overly test-conscious and seem to test regardless of whether they need it. An example would be districts in which achievement batteries are administered at the beginning *and* at the end of the year. In general, if test results are *not* used, only filed away, overtesting is likely. Worksheet A has been developed to help you minimize redundancy and overtesting.

To use Worksheet A in Figure 19.1, first list the main purposes of testing identified in step 2. Next, indicate the grade levels for which the purpose is appropriate (e.g., a reading readiness test would be appropriate in late kindergarten or early first grade). Then indicate the test you currently use or plan to use for each purpose. Afterward compare the various tests to the purposes to determine whether any of them may serve more than one purpose at the appropriate grade level. After doing so, indicate the test you will retain for each purpose. If you succeed in eliminating even one test, you will save your district much time and money, as well as adding to the amount of time that teachers can spend in teaching rather than testing.

TIMING. A test should fit the purpose of testing, but it should also be administered at the right time to allow maximum use of the test results. If information is needed prior to the beginning of the school year, the right test ought to be administered toward the end of the previous school year, not after school has started. This rather obvious fact is not always considered when testing programs are being planned. The following general guidelines may be referred to in planning a program:

Time of school year	*Purpose of testing*
Early	Selection Placement/grouping Diagnostic
Late	Program evaluation Achievement gains Guidance

Time considerations also relate to the frequency of testing. Should tests be administered each year or only in selected years? Nowadays, it is common for districts to administer yearly achievement batteries, readiness tests in kindergarten or first grade, academic aptitude tests in third or fourth grade and again in fifth or sixth grade, and a general aptitude test and interest inventory in eleventh grade.

CONTINUITY. A well-integrated program will also consider testing as a whole from grades K–12. When test data are accumulated over several years on a pupil, these data become increasingly useful for interpretive purposes. This is especially true if these data are collected from the same battery or batteries of tests. While it is possible to convert scores from the California Achievement Test to equivalent scores from the Iowa Tests of Basic Skills, it is certainly less time consuming and costly to use scores from the same battery for a period of years. Comparisons also are facilitated by retain-

FIGURE 19.1
Worksheet A: Minimizing Redundancy

Purpose of testing	*Grade levels*	*Original test used for this purpose*	*Possible tests for this purpose*	*Test retained*	*Comments*

ing the same battery since the comparisons are in relation to the same norm group. Naturally, as tests become dated, or district goals and objectives change over the course of time, it may be necessary to switch batteries to maintain relevance and content validity. We are not advocating sticking with the same battery for 50 years, only that careful thought and consideration be paid to issues like content validity, relevance, and the likelihood of revision in the near future. This latter point is a very practical one. If you are seriously considering switching tests, and the test you want to switch to will be revised in the next year or two, it is probably worth postponing the switch until after the revision. This way you will avoid having to adjust old scores to new scores after the revision. You will have a fresh start and not have to be concerned about revision for several years.

Step 4: Evaluate and Select the Specific Tests

At this stage we are *finally* ready to answer the question "Which tests should we use?" Having completed Worksheet A, we have eliminated redundancy in our program, but now we want to evaluate each test remaining in our program to see not just that it fits the relevant purpose(s) of testing, but that our final selection actually has acceptable psychometric and practical characteristics. Worksheet B will guide us in our evaluation. Should we find that our "final selection" from Worksheet A fails to get acceptable ratings on psychometric or practical grounds, do not despair! This simply means that other comparable tests will have to be evaluated until we find one that has acceptable ratings. Once this is determined, this more appropriate test may be substituted for the "final selection" from Worksheet A and should still meet the purpose(s) of testing met by the previous test. Before considering Worksheet B, however, let's consider where the information necessary to complete the worksheet comes from.

There are several sources of information about standardized tests available, including publishers' test catalogs, *Tests in Print, Mental Measurements Yearbooks,* and specimen sets.

PUBLISHERS' TEST CATALOGS. Test catalogs include all tests a publisher offers, usually with a variety of descriptive information, such as subtest names, content covered, appropriate age and grade levels, administration time, number of forms and levels, cost, scoring services and reports available, and limited psychometric information. Publishers' catalogs are designed to present tests favorably and are often less than objective in their presentations. Nonetheless, they are one way to familiarize yourself with the variety of tests available and get an idea of whether a test is likely to fit your district's instructional emphasis.

TESTS IN PRINT. *Tests in Print* is a reference book that lists most of the tests in use today, the names and addresses of the publishers, and somewhat less descriptive information than is available from publishers' catalogs. However, it is unbiased in presenting this information. *Tests in Print* is a comprehensive reference. Much of the practical information you may need about tests is available in this single volume, saving you the trouble of having to leaf through many catalogs.

MENTAL MEASUREMENTS YEARBOOKS. *Mental Measurements Yearbooks* is a set of comprehensive reference books about tests, covering virtually all tests published over the last several decades. The yearbooks are revised every few years and contain critical reviews of the tests by knowledgeable and respected reviewers, such as measurement specialists and educational psychologists. They also contain summaries of test reviews published in professional journals and other sources. The reviews give you the benefit of an expert's appraisal of each test's strengths and weaknesses. This probably is the best source for accurate and critical information about both the test's psychometric and practical characteristics.

SPECIMEN SETS. A specimen set includes a copy of the test booklet, answer sheet, administrator's manual, and technical manual. These enable you to examine firsthand the test format, content validity for your school or district, and other factors. Before ordering hundreds or thousands of tests, it makes sense to order an inexpensive specimen set for any tests under consideration.

Usually, information will be gleaned from several or all these sources in evaluating a standardized test. Let's turn to Worksheet B.

Worksheet B, in Figure 19.2, is almost self-explanatory. First jot down the purpose for testing, then put down the name of the test under consideration. Completing the remainder of the form involves rating the test for each column. How you rate the tests on each dimension is up to you. You might use a two-point scale (acceptable/not acceptable) or some five-point scale. What is important is that you consider each dimension, especially content validity. To provide the information that will enable you to rate the test, use one or more of the sources already described. Remember, should your "final selection" from Worksheet A be rated unacceptable, substitute another comparable test (the tests we reviewed earlier in this chapter might provide you with some possibilities) and rate it. After reviewing several tests, you may find that none is acceptable in all dimensions—but

FIGURE 19.2
Worksheet B: Test Evaluation/Comparison Form

Purpose: ____________________

Test name from Worksheet A	*Content validity*	*Reliability*	*Norms*	*Costs*	*Time and ease of administration*	*Alternative form*	*Chance of revision*

certainly one will be more acceptable than the others. This should be your final choice for the purpose stated.

Step 5: Develop a Specific and a District-Wide Testing Schedule

Although you have evaluated your tests and selected your final package, you still need to plan the specific testing schedules for each test and a general coordinated testing schedule for the district. Such planning should be completed long *before* the beginning of the school year. This will enable copies of the schedule to be sent out to school personnel for their consideration and input at the beginning of the school year. Remember our initial point—all too often such input and consideration is neglected, resulting in resistance to the testing program. If you've gone through all the time and effort of planning such a program, take a bit more time to check it out with other local school personnel, which should result in better cooperation and a smooth test administration and collection period. While no particular format is perfect for all specific and district-wide schedules, Worksheet C, in Figure 19.3 on page 410, is offered as one example. All you need to do is fill in the tests and dates.

This completes our step-by-step approach to planning a comprehensive and efficient school- or district-wide testing program. It also completes our discussion of standardized tests. Next, we will turn to testing and evaluating the exceptional child in the regular classroom.

FIGURE 19.3
Worksheet C: District-Wide and Specific Testing Schedule

District-wide testing schedule

Grade	*Test*	*Test materials to school*	*Testing dates*	*Answer sheets collected*
1				
2				
3				
4				
5				
6				
7				
8				
9				
10				
11				
12				

Specific Testing Schedule—Test

Task	*Due date*
1. Order tests and materials.	
2. Distribute materials and instructions.	
3. Distribute general testing schedules.	
4. Train testers and proctors.	
5. Arrange for scoring.	
6. Train teachers in interpretation.	
7. Administer tests.	
8. Collect tests and score them.	
9. Distribute results.	
10. Prepare and distribute reports.	

SUMMARY

This chapter has described various types of standardized tests, reviewed briefly examples of each type, and presented you with a step-by-step approach to follow in planning a school- or district-wide standardized testing program. Its major points are:

1. The survey battery is the type of achievement test most frequently used today.
2. The main advantages of a survey battery over several single-subject tests are:
   a. Coordinated subtests

b. Savings in time and expense

c. A common norm group

3. The disadvantages are that:

   a. Content validity may vary across subtests.

   b. Depth of coverage may be less than that obtained with a single-subject test.

4. Single-subject achievement tests are mainly used in the secondary grades.

5. Diagnostic achievement tests are usually administered only to selected students who have already exhibited difficulties in achievement.

6. Academic aptitude or IQ tests are used to predict future learning; achievement tests measure past learning.

7. Academic aptitude tests were initially developed about ninety years ago to predict school performance, but came to be known as intelligence tests. Today, they still do a good job of predicting school performance.

8. After about age six, IQ scores tend to be fairly stable for the remainder of an individual's life. Prior to age six, and especially during the first few years of life, they tend to be unstable.

9. One definition of *personality* is the typical and characteristic ways people behave.

10. The objective approach to personality assessment relies on self-report questionnaires that are economical but suffer from questionable validity, test takers' perception of the social desirability of answers, and faking.

11. Projective personality assessment is based on the theory that when individuals are presented with suggestive or ambiguous stimuli, these stimuli will elicit responses that are fairly rigid and reflective of conscious or unconscious motives, beliefs, or wishes.

12. Projective tests are more flexible than objective personality tests but suffer from questionable validity and greater expense.

13. In planning a school- or district-wide testing program, the following steps are recommended:

    a. Ask the right question (What are the purposes of testing?).

    b. Decide on the purposes of testing.

    c. Consider the program's integration (redundancy, timing, and continuity).

    d. Evaluate and select specific tests.

    e. Develop a district-wide testing schedule.

For Discussion

1. Identify two advantages and two disadvantages of standardized tests.

2. Discuss some of the ways IQ scores should be used and some of the ways they should not be used. Give specific examples.

3. Describe the advantages and disadvantages of objective versus projective personality tests. If your personality were being measured, which would you choose?

4. For two standardized achievement tests of your own choosing, find the information that is required to complete Worksheet B (see Figure 19.2). Which of these two tests would you recommend as the better one for the purpose stated?

CHAPTER 20

Testing and Measuring the Special Learner in the Regular Classroom

At first glance you may wonder why we have included a chapter about testing and measuring special learners. You might say, "That's the responsibility of the school psychologist or educational diagnostician," "Special learners are in special ed classrooms, not regular ed classrooms," or "I won't have to deal with special learners if I'm going to be a regular ed teacher." These statements have some validity, but they are less accurate descriptions of the regular classroom teacher's involvement with special education with each passing day.

The laws and policies governing the education of children with disabilities now require that the regular classroom teacher be more actively involved than ever before in the work of the special educator, including the early childhood special educator. The traditional special education "pull-out" system, in which the special learner is taught in a self-contained classroom for at least part of the day, has been criticized as discriminatory, ineffective, and inefficient (Davis, 1989). Indeed, the National Council on Disabilities (1989) reported that the intent of the Education for All Handicapped Children Act (PL 94–142) never was to segregate special learners, even those with multiple or severe disabilities.

Legal decisions are increasingly requiring the inclusion of special learners in the regular education classroom. A 1993 decision by the U.S. Court of Appeals found that a New Jersey school district failed to make a reasonable effort to meet a student's special learning needs when it excluded him from the regular classroom (Viadero, 1993). The trend for the future is toward even greater inclusion of special learners in the regular classroom (Cannon, Idol & West, 1992; Conte, 1994; Hale & Carlson, 1992). Not everyone believes that full inclusion is in the best interests of special and regular education students, however, especially experienced teachers (Coker & Griffith, 1994). Nonetheless, the predominant view is that the regular classroom teacher may expect to be called on increasingly to collaborate and cooperate with the special educator in both teaching and evaluating the special learner's academic, physical, and behavioral progress (Bauwens, Hourcade & Friend, 1989; Cannon, Idol & West, 1992; Friend & Cook, 1992).

To put these recent developments into context we begin this chapter by reviewing some of the events in the field of special education that have led to current laws and policies for educating the special learner. We then indicate how the testing and measurement skills of the regular classroom teacher play a role in their implementation. More specifically, we hope to familiarize you with the ways in which the measurement and testing practices you have learned in this text can guide you in the identification and evaluation of special learners in your class. We also will discuss the trend toward regular class inclusion of severely and multiply challenged learners (i.e., those who previously received services in self-contained classrooms) who are taking one or more medications that may affect their learning and behavior. The implications of the recent movement to assess the safety and efficacy of these medications based on increased feedback from classroom teachers will be described. Some examples of the measurement instruments used by the classroom teacher to assist in the evaluation of the safety and efficacy of such medications will also be presented.

Finally, we will discuss the issue of special education for gifted and talented students. Like students with disabilities, this segment of the population may comprise from 2 to 5 percent of the school population. This means that classroom teachers may expect to have one or more gifted or talented students in their classes at any given time. As a result, we will identify relevant issues related to the definition of giftedness, describe some of the more commonly used methods of identifying the gifted student, and discuss the implications of the identification process for the regular education teacher.

SPECIAL EDUCATION: RECENT HISTORY

A variety of social, political, and legal developments have shaped special education's history. One effect of both world wars was to promote greater social acceptance of the disabled. As disabled (i.e., challenged) veterans returned home to resume productive and socially respectable roles, federal and state programs grew to facilitate their readjustment and employment. These programs were eventually extended to other, nonveteran groups, laying the foundation for our modern era of special services for challenged populations.

Along with the postwar relaxation of social stereotypes of the physically and mentally challenged came the establishment of organizations for parents of challenged children. Previously, parents of such children were beleaguered not only with the psychological problems of adjusting to the presence of the child with disabilities, but also with the anxieties and guilt accompanying negative social valuation of the challenged child. Parents organized specifically for the purpose of obtaining recognition of and appropriate educational services for their children. Out of these organizations grew strong national movements, such as the National Association of Retarded Citizens and the United Cerebral Palsy Association, which remain influential in stimulating the allocation of federal and state resources. Today, parent associations remain powerful in influencing services to practically every special learner subgroup.

Between 1948 and 1958, the number of children identified with mental retardation in public schools more than doubled, as did the number of programs for these pupils. By 1956, all states had laws pertaining to education of exceptional children and were engaged in funding local school programs. The Council for Exceptional Children, founded in 1922, underwent rapid growth and supported the development of programs and services at the national level. During the 1960s, additional federal legislation was enacted and financial support provided for research, demonstration programs, and teacher training. This growing federal involvement was highlighted in 1968 with the establishment of the Bureau of Education for the Handicapped, a separate federal agency with its own budget and programs.

CRITICAL COURT CASES. In the decades of rapid expansion and change in special education, conflicts inevitably arose among parents, professionals, and governing authorities regarding the most effective and appropriate programs. These conflicts moved special education into the arenas of litigation and legislation, and several important court cases since 1950 have significantly shaped the present pattern of services. Initially, these cases brought needed attention to special learners. Subsequent legislation has transformed the role of general education to require increased instruction and evaluation of the efficacy of that instruction to special learners.

Although specific litigation relating to educational rights of challenged children did not emerge until the early 1970s, the foundation for interpretation of constitutional principles in special education cases was laid in what may be the landmark civil rights case of this century. *Brown vs. Board of Education of Topeka* represented the Supreme Court response to four similar cases brought on behalf of black children seeking admission to the public schools of their community on a nonsegregated basis. The Court ruled that requiring children to attend racially segregated schools was in violation of their Fourteenth Amendment rights.

Over a decade of social action and litigation was required before relatively stable mechanisms existed to guarantee Fourteenth Amendment rights of minority children in schools across the country, and even more time elapsed before these rights were extended to special learners. As activism on behalf of challenged children grew in the decades of the 1950s and 1960s, schools were beginning to come to grips with constitutional equal opportunity and due process issues relating to the educational rights of children.

Prior to the 1970s, most state and local public school programs exercised the option of serving or not serving children with disabilities in their programs. As a result, segregation or outright exclusion of such children was common on the grounds that no services were available that could benefit them in the public schools. A gradual reversal of this trend, on the basis of Fourteenth Amendment principles, was initiated in 1971 in the case of *Pennsylvania Association of Retarded Children vs. Commonwealth of Pennsylvania.* The decision in this case held, in essence, that the state was obligated to provide children with mental retardation an appropriate program of public school education and training. The decision was based on equal protection and due process provisions.

Immediately following the *Pennsylvania* decision in 1972, a similar case was brought from the District of Columbia. *Mills vs. the Board of Education* sought to extend the right of free and appropriate education to all children with disabilities, not just the mentally retarded. These included children labeled as behavioral problems, emotionally disturbed, blind, deaf, and speech or learning disabled. The plaintiffs argued that the school district had denied such children not merely an equal education, but in fact any education at all, while providing free education to other children of the District. Of particular concern was the reassignment or expulsion of children without a hearing, as required by due process standards. The court ruled in favor of the plaintiffs, thus including all types of children with disabilities in the judicial interpretation of the Fourteenth Amendment.

Public Law 94–142

It remained for Congress to put the piecemeal statements of exceptional children's educational rights derived from the courts into a coherent national legislative program. A major issue were the millions of special learners in the country who were excluded from public education, receiving educational services in inappropriate settings, or receiving services at the expense of their families. Also at issue were the futures of children perhaps destined for institutional care at great taxpayer expense, children who might otherwise become self-sustaining with the provision of appropriate education. The result of all these concerns was Public Law (PL) 94–142, the Education for All Handicapped Children Act of 1974, or EAHCA. Today, PL 94–142 is known as the Individuals with Disabilities Education Act, or IDEA.

This new law greatly extended the scope and impact of all previous legislation regarding special learners. Specifically, it added new provisions mandating the provision of free public education to all children, the expansion of the federal role in financing special education, and the creation of enforcement machinery to assure compliance with the law. For the first time it was made clear that failure to comply with, or to work toward compliance of, the provisions of PL 94–142 would result in the loss of all federal funds to a school system. Furthermore, the law placed enforcement responsibility not in the hands of the U.S. Office of Education, but in the hands of the U.S. Office of Civil Rights, which is empowered to investigate complaints and arbitrate compliance issues. Thus, PL 94–142 was vastly strengthened over preceding legislation and is considered to be landmark legislation for challenged learners.

Public Law 99–457

As far-reaching as the implications of PL 94–142 have been, in 1986 Congress passed a major set of amendments to the law. This action, which has come to be referred to as PL 99–457, extends all rights and protections of the law to preschoolers. Under this legislation, all states were required to provide a free and appropriate public education to children with disabilities, ages 3 through 5, by the 1990–1991 school year. This act also provided funding to states to provide educational services to infants and toddlers requiring special services and their families. In essence, the bill provided incentives to encourage school districts to begin serving children with disabilities from birth throughout their school years. PL 99–457 also specifies that a multidisciplinary assessment of the challenged child be conducted and an IFSP (Individualized Family Service Plan) be developed for each child identified as in need of special services. The result of PL 99–457 is evident in many schools today. Preschool children of all ages, identified as being challenged or at-risk, can be seen in both special and regular education classes (e.g., kindergarten, P.E.).

Thus, while PL 94–142 was the landmark legislation of the 1970s, the passage of PL 99–457 underscored congressional and legislative commitment to the enforcement of the principal features of PL 94–142 and reinforced the trend toward increasing, rather than decreasing, involvement of regular education in the identification of children in need of special services and provision of appropriate educational services, including evaluation of their progress. Obviously, since PL 99–457 is specifically geared toward the preschool population, its impact on the regular classroom teacher beyond the primary grades will be limited, but important. Through parent conferences and informal contact with younger siblings, teachers are expected to recognize and refer pre-schoolers who may be at-risk.

Section 504 of the Rehabilitation Act

Since the late 1980s Section 504 of the Rehabilitation Act of 1973 has been interpreted as broadening special education eligibility standards beyond those established by PL 94–142 (Hakola, 1992). PL 94–142 requires that a student's behavior or learning be seriously or severely affected by one of the twelve categories of disability it delineated before a student is eligible to receive special educational services. However, Section 504 establishes a broader standard of eligibility. It defines a person with a disability as anyone with a physical or mental impairment which substantially limits one or more major life activities. This law also empowers the Office of Civil Rights to enforce Section 504 compliance.

In recent years Section 504 has generated considerable controversy, in part because of the "ambiguity and brevity of Section 504 in regard to requirements for elementary and secondary schools" (Gammel, 1992, p. 298). One example of the lack of clarity involves funding for services. When a child qualifies for special educational services under Section 504 (i.e., "504 only") the child is not eligible for funding through federal PL 94–142 monies. This means that local or state funds must then be used to fund special services. Needless to say, such funds are scarce in most districts. Thus, provision of special services for "504 only" challenged children is likely to be within the less expensive regular classroom setting. This also is in keeping with the intent of Section 504, which, like PL 94–142, is for services to be provided within the least restrictive environment. While the funding and eligibility issues of Section 504 will continue to be clarified in coming years through legal interpretation and/or legislation, it appears reasonable to conclude that the involvement of the regular education teacher with "504 only" students may be expected to increase in the future.

We believe that PL 94–142, PL 99–457, and Section 504 of the Rehabilitation Act should send a loud and clear message to educators that governmental and legislative involvement in education is not decreasing. As mentioned in Chapter 1, it is likely to increase in the future as the inclusion of special learners in the regular classroom becomes the norm.

THE SPECIAL EDUCATOR, THE REGULAR EDUCATOR, AND FULL INCLUSION

While PL 94–142 required placement of special learners in the least restrictive educational environment, many special learners were nevertheless segregated into resource or self-contained classrooms on the assumption that they could not benefit from regular class instruction. This was especially true for students who were viewed as more severely mentally, physically, emotionally, and behaviorally challenged. The common wisdom for decades was that it was not only in the best interests of such severely challenged children to be in segregated classrooms, but that this was also essential to protect the regular educational process from disruption due to the presence of such challenged students.

However, recent literature reviews (Halvorsen & Sailor, 1990; Stainback & Stainback, 1992) document improved educational and social outcomes for special learners, even those who were severely challenged, who were in integrated placements (i.e., placements which included contact with regular education students and curriculum as well as special education services) as compared to peers in segregated placements (i.e., self-contained special education only). These reviews led Sailor, Gee & Karasoff (1993) to conclude that "The body of research literature is sufficient to demonstrate that educators need no longer spend energy and resources debating the issue of whether or not to integrate or include students with severe disabilities in the learning environments of their non-disabled peers but can concentrate instead on how best to do it" (p.2).

These findings have led many special and regular educators to accept and adopt "full inclusion" as a goal for all special learners. Sailor et al. (1993) identified the following key elements of full inclusion for special learners:

- Full general education class membership.
- Full perception of "ownership" from both special and general education.
- Individual outcomes-based decision making.
- Student-based services with team curriculum design.
- Site-team coordination of services and educational support.

Even before full inclusion came to be as accepted as it is today, it was clear that, in keeping with the non-segregatory intent of PL 94–142, the trend was already toward increased mainstreaming of the challenged learner. For example, Figure 20.1 illustrates that in the 1987–1988 school year approximately 75 percent of all challenged children received their *primary* educational services in the regular classroom or in a combination of the regular classroom with one or more periods in a resource room. The movement toward full inclusion, when fully implemented, will increase this percentage.

Categories of Challenged Learners

Over the past few decades challenged students have been classified and defined in a number of ways. New definitions of challenging conditions will continue to evolve as more and more becomes known about this subgroup of school children. However, before the significance of a challenging condition for public school instruction can be discussed, the question that must be asked is "What kind of challenge?" For this question, a number of categories of challenging conditions have been identified to indicate the types of special services and instruction most appropriate to a challenged child. These categories usually include children with physical disabilities, hearing impairments, visual impairments, mental retardation, emotional or behavioral disorders, learning disabilities, communication disorders, autism, and multiple disabilities, which are described in Figure 20.2.

The purpose of these categories is not to label or stigmatize the challenged child but to identify learners in need of specialized assistance. That is, these categories enable a shorthand way of communicating about those learners whose physical, emotional, and/or cognitive functions are so impaired from any cause that they cannot be adequately or safely educated without the provision of special services. While these special services are the direct responsibility of the special education program within a school, the regular classroom

FIGURE 20.1
Evironments in Which 6- to 21-year-old Disabled Students Were Served During the 1987–88 School Year

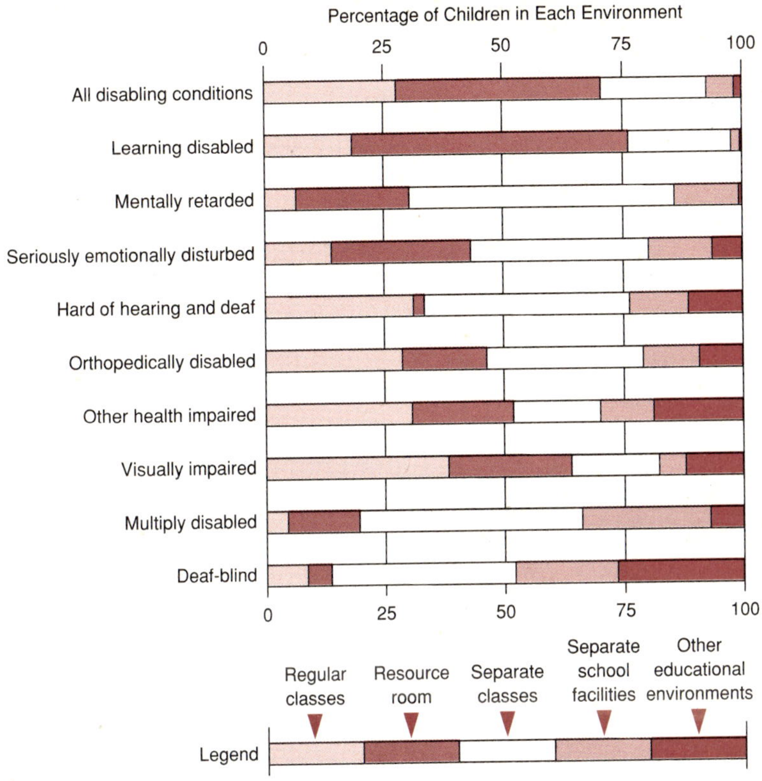

SOURCE: U.S. Department of Education, Office of Special Education and Rehabilitation Services, *Twelfth Annual Report to Congress on the Implementation of the Education of the Handicapped Act*, 1989.

teacher is expected to play an increased contributory and supportive role in both the provision and evaluation of these services.

FULL INCLUSION AND ITS IMPACT ON THE CLASSROOM TEACHER

Under full inclusion one of the main functions of the classroom teacher is the acquisition, interpretation, and reporting of data pertaining to the performance of special learners in the regular classroom. The regular classroom teacher may be called upon to collect and evaluate a variety of data about special learners in the classroom. This may include completing portfolios and authentic assessments, conducting structured observations, keeping anecdotal records, completing one or more questionnaires or rating scales, and administering and interpreting both teacher-made and standardized tests.

FIGURE 20.2
Categories of Disabling Conditions

Physical Disabilities	Students whose body functions or members are impaired by congenital anomaly and disease, or students with limited strength, vitality, or alertness due to chronic or acute health problems.
Hearing Impaired	Students who are hearing impaired (hard of hearing) or deaf.
Visually Impaired	Students who, after medical treatment and use of optical aids, remain legally blind or otherwise exhibit loss of critical sight functions.
Mental Retardation	Students with significantly subaverage general intellectual functioning existing concurrent with deficiencies in adaptive behavior. Severity of retardation is sometimes indicated with the terms *profound, trainable,* and *educable.*
Emotionally/Behaviorally Disordered	Students who demonstrate an inability to build or maintain satisfactory interpersonal relationships, who develop physical symptoms or fears associated with personal or school problems, who exhibit a pervasive mood of unhappiness under normal circumstances, or who show inappropriate types of behavior under normal circumstances.
Learning Disabled	Students who demonstrate a significant discrepancy between academic achievement and intellectual abilities in one or more of the areas of oral expression, listening comprehension, written expression, basic reading skills, reading comprehension, mathematical calculation, mathematics reasoning, or spelling, which is not the result of some other disability.
Communication Disordered	Students whose speech is impaired to the extent that it limits the communicative functions.
Autistic	Students with severe disturbances of speech and language, relatedness, perception, developmental rate, or motion.
Multiple or Severe Disabilities	Students who have any two or more of the disabling conditions described above.

Testing or Assessment?

Note that only some of the data we have referred to come from formal tests (i.e., teacher-made or standardized). This is intentional. Remember, tests are fallible, and the decision to identify a child as a special learner has significant implications for that child's educational and future opportunities. Thus, many and varied forms of data are collected to obtain as diverse and accurate a picture of the child's performance as is possible. Thus, the classroom teacher's role in the identification and evaluation process should not be construed as only "testing," but more broadly as "assessment."

The term assessment has been defined as "the process of collecting data for the purposes of (1) specifying and verifying problems and (2) making decisions about students" (Salvia & Ysseldyke, 1991, p. 3). The regular classroom teacher plays a significant role in the ongoing and varied process by which a student is assessed and determined to be eligible for special education services. Once this occurs the regular education teacher continues to be actively involved in decision-making and assessment of the special learner. The many levels at which regular classroom teachers are involved in this process have been organized into a flow chart by Ysseldyke & Algozzine (1990), shown in Figure 20.3. This flow chart illustrates how the assessment skills of regular education teachers are instrumental in every step of the special education identification, instruction, and evaluation process.

Next we will consider in more depth the ways the classroom teacher's assessment skills are required to comply with PL 94–142 and, increasingly, Section 504. These data are all important in provision of the following services required by PL 94–142 and implied by Section 504: child identification, individual assessment, Individual Educational Plan (IEP) development, individualized instruction, and review of the IEP.

Child Identification

Child identification consists of a school or school district's procedures for identifying challenged children in need of special education, including pre-school children as now required by PL 99–457. Students needing special education services may never have entered school or could be among those students attending school in need of special services but who have not been identified as having special needs. It is in the identification of these students that you may be expected to play an important role.

One stage of this identification is the referral. While referrals may be made by parents, physicians, community agencies, and school administrators as a result of district-wide testing or screening, students may also be recommended for special services by you as a teacher. For students who are currently enrolled in regular education, you will be the most likely individual to identify students with needs for special services. In such cases you will become a liaison between the child and the special education staff within a school. In this capacity it will be your responsibility for accumulating and reporting to qualified personnel data that can accurately portray:

1. The student's current educational status, including attendance records, grades, achievement data (including portfolios and authentic assessments), and written

FIGURE 20.3
Teacher Participation throughout the Special Learner Identification, Instruction, and Evaluation Process

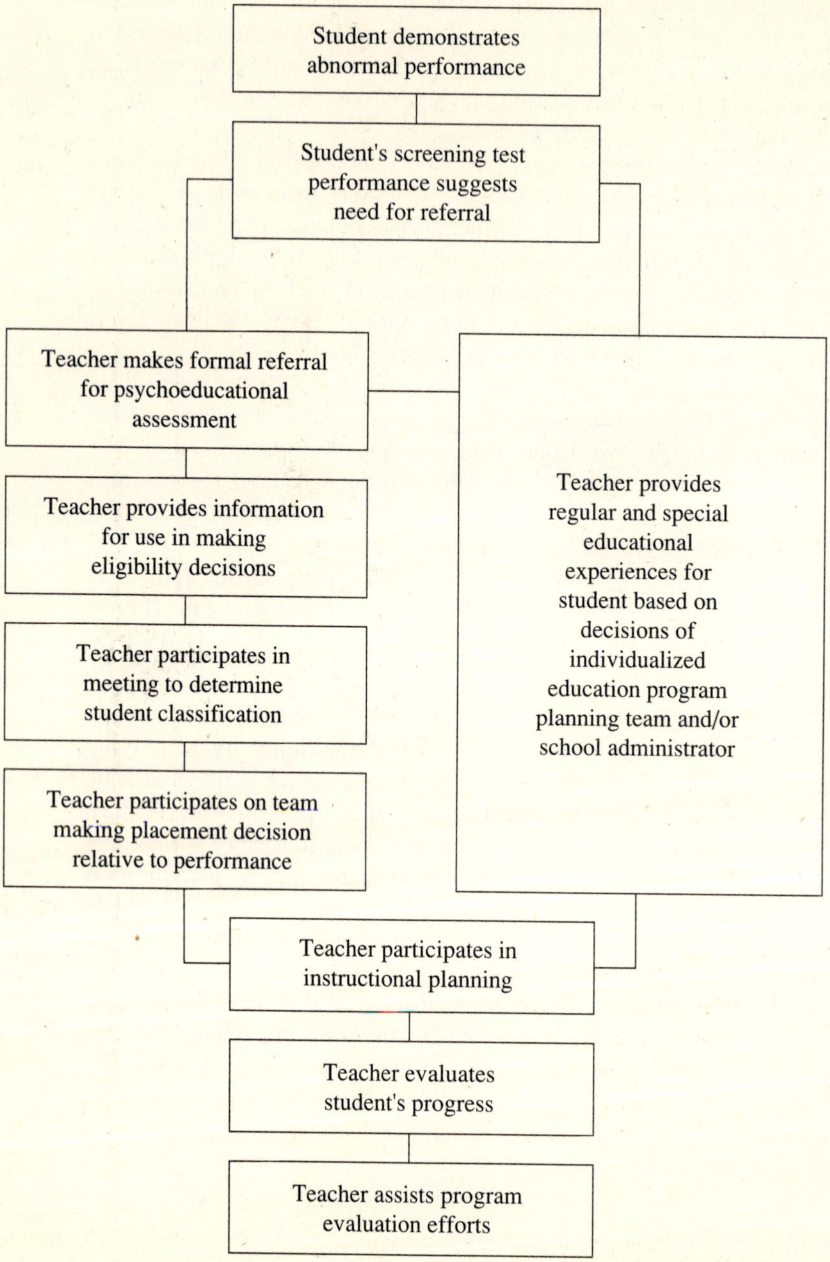

SOURCE: James E. Ysseldyke and Bob Algozzie, *Introduction to Special Education,* 2nd ed. (Boston: Houghton, Mifflin, 1990), p.312. Reprinted by permission.

accounts of classroom observations or systematically collected anecdotal records;
2. Previous instructional efforts and strategies provided the student and the result of those efforts;
3. Data about the child reported or provided to the teacher by parents.

Under PL 94–142 referrals are processed through a referral committee which usually includes the professional who recommends the child for special services, the building principal or designated representative, a special educator, a school psychologist and/or educational diagnostician, and the classroom teacher or any other individual who has knowledge of the student's performance and the placement alternatives available. The purpose of the committee is to reach a decision (usually in writing) regarding the educational alternatives appropriate to the child. Obviously, it is important that you not only play a prominent role on this committee when you are recommending a child for special services but that the data provided by you in support of special services be valid, reliable, and accurate. This can only be accomplished by applying sound measurement principles and by selecting the data that most accurately characterize the child's need for particular kinds of services.

Individual Assessment

A second process to which you may be expected to contribute is individual child assessment. Individual assessment is the collecting and analyzing of information about a student in order to identify an educational need in terms of the following:

1. The presence or absence of a physical, mental, or emotional disability;
2. The presence or absence of a significant educational need;
3. The identification of specific learning competencies of the student together with specific instructional or related services that could improve and maintain the student's competencies.

Although the individual assessment of a child's capabilities falls within the responsibilities of certified professionals who have been specifically trained in assessing students with disabilities, you can and often will be expected to corroborate the findings of these professionals with performance data from the classroom. The corroborative data you can be expected to provide fall into the following categories:

Language

Physical

Emotional/behavioral

Sociological

Intellectual

In this text you have been exposed to measurement techniques that will enable you to present systematic, useful data about a referred child that address each of these five areas. We will describe this in more detail after considering the example of an individual assessment report shown in Figure 20.4.

This report is from a multidisciplinary admission, review, and dismissal committee. First and foremost among these data are formal and informal indications taken from portfolios, workbooks, homework assignments, weekly and unit tests, and classroom observation as to the student's primary language and proficiency in both the expressive and receptive domains. Often, your observation and recording of these data will suggest to special educators the validity of the standardized tests that may have been given to the student and whether they may have been given in a language other than that in which the child is dominant.

Corroborative data pertaining to the physical attributes of the student can also be recorded. Only you may be in a position to observe on a daily basis the ability of the child to manipulate objects necessary for learning, to remain alert and attentive during instruction, and to control bodily functions in a manner conducive to instruction. In some instances you may provide the only data available as to the physical ability of the child to benefit from regular class instruction.

You can also provide useful data about the emotional behavior of the exceptional child. These data may be derived from standardized behavior checklists, in-class structured observations, anecdotal records, adaptive behavior scales, sociograms, and student-teacher interactions that have been designed either to corroborate the need for special services or to monitor the progress of the child in the regular classroom. Several of these sources of data were discussed in Chapters 9 and 11.

A fourth area in which you may be expected to provide data pertains to the sociological and environmental influences on the child which may, in part, influence the child's classroom behavior. Sociological data about a child are often obtained through communications with the family and knowledge of the circumstances leading up to and/or contributing to the student's intellectual and emotional behavior. The extent to which the child's home life and out-of-school support and services contribute to the educative function can provide an important adjunct to in-school data.

Finally, there is the student's intellectual functioning as demonstrated by verbal and nonverbal performance and by the child's behavior. Although verbal and nonverbal behavior are usually assessed by professionals certified in special education, you may be asked to provide corroborating data pertaining to the child's adaptive behavior. *Adaptive behavior* is the degree to which the student meets standards of personal independence and social responsibility expected of his or her age and cultural group. Within the context of the classroom, you will have many opportunities to observe the social functioning of the child and gain insights into the appropriateness of this functioning, given the age range and cultural milieu in which the child operates. In fact, you may be the only individual in a position to provide trustworthy data about this side of the special learner's social and interactive behavior.

All of the data discussed here are the responsibility of certified teaching and support personnel within a school or school district. These personnel may include educational diagnosticians, school psychologists, counselors, special educators, and, of course, the regular classroom teacher. Each of these individuals has responsibility for only those parts of the overall assessment to which he or she is assigned and qualified. As we have

FIGURE 20.4
Individual Assessment Data from the Admission, Review, and Dismissal Committee Report

Admission, Review, and Dismissal (ARD) Committee Report
Page 3

Student *Miller, Jeremy*

ID# *072431*

II. INDIVIDUAL EDUCATIONAL PLAN
(as noted on page 1 of this report)

A. Present Levels of Competencies:
(Complete AREAS as appropriate)

*Specify name as appropriate; may include Norm-Referenced Tests, Curriculum/Performance-Based and Criterion-Referenced Tests, and Teacher Observation(s).

	Eval. Date	Eval. Method Data Source*	Grade/Age Level	Severe Discrep.	Information on Current Functioning (include information on strength/weakness as appropriate)
MATHEMATICS CALCULATION					*Jeremy is functioning on grade level in math. He is currently learning subtraction of 2-digit numbers with borrowing. This is an area of strength for him.*
REASONING					
READING BASIC SKILLS	*10/15/92*	*Woodcock/Johnson Teacher Informal Inventory*	*1.0*	✓	*Reading is an area of weakness for Jeremy. He is currently functioning below grade level in both comprehension and skills in reading.*
COMPREHENSION	*10/15/92*	*Woodcock/Johnson Teacher Informal Inventory*	*1.0*	✓	
SPELLING/WRITTEN EXPRESSION	*10/15/92*	*T.O.W.L. Brigance*	*P*	✓	*Jeremy has difficulty both orally and manually producing correct spelling. He is unable to write a complete sentence with correct capitalization and punctuation.*
OTHER: ______					
PRE-VOC/ VOCATIONAL				Indicate skills which may be prerequisite to participation in vocational education.	
PHYSICAL	*10/16/92*	*Health History Inventory O.T. Assessment*	*Below Age Level*	Indicate physical abilities/disabilities which would affect participation in instrucional settings or in P.E. *Jeremy's fine motor coordination is not adequately developed for his age. It hinders his ability to learn writing skills.*	
SPEECH/LANGUAGE	*10/16/92*	*Language Sample-Speech Therapy Assessment*	*Below Age Level*	*Jeremy's language development is below average. He has a significant need for articulation instruction. This weakness currently impedes his performance in oral expression.*	
INTELLECTUAL/ DEVELOPMENTAL	*10/15/92*	*WISC-R*	*Average Range*	*Jeremy's performance on the WISC-R indicates that he is of average intelligence for his age.*	
SOCIAL/ BEHAVIORAL	*10/15/92*	*Informal Assessment Parent & Teacher Reports*	Indicate behaviors which would affect educational placement, programming or discipline. *Jeremy is a cooperative student. He gets along well with both peers and adults. This is an area of strength for him.*		

FOR EMOTIONALLY DISTURBED STUDENTS ONLY - AS NOTED IN THE ASSESSMENT REPORT (Date:______________) one or more of the following characteristics have been exhibited over a long period of time, have occured to a marked degree, and have adversely affected his/her educational performance:

__an inability to learn which cannot be explained by intellectual, sensory or health factors:
__an inability to build or maintain satisfactory interpersonal relationships with his peers/teachers:
__inappropriate types of behavior or feelings under normal circumstances;
__a general pervasive mood of unhappiness or depression; or
__a tendency to develop physical symptoms or fears associated with personal or school problems.

Date of meeting: *10-23-92*

SE-605-83 Page 3 of *4*

seen, however, it is not an overstatement to say that with PL 94–142 and Section 504, contributions of the regular classroom teacher to the overall assessment of the child will not be taken lightly. The regular classroom teacher will be expected to make a considerable contribution to determining the educational needs of children whose constitutionally guaranteed right to education may require special services. This contribution may be in the form of either corroborating the findings of other professionals or as a source of data whose unique day-to-day contact with the child allows for observation and assessment unequaled by other school personnel.

Individual Educational Plan Development

A third stage in which you may become involved in the implementation of PL 94–142 is in helping develop the Individual Educational Plan (IEP) for each challenged student within your classroom. A student receives special education services only after a multidisciplinary team has reviewed data from the comprehensive assessment. As noted, data from this assessment are expected to address the language, physical, emotional/behavioral, sociological, and intellectual functioning of the child. If from this assessment it is determined that the student has a physical, mental, or emotional disability that establishes his or her eligibility to receive special education services, an IEP is written to state short- and long-term objectives for the instructional and related services to be delivered to the child and to specify the least restrictive environment in which the instruction is to take place. A portion of an Individual Educational Plan is shown in Figure 20.5.

The IEP developed for each student by the multidisciplinary team generally includes the following:

1. A statement of the student's present competencies taken from the overall assessment data, which generally includes:
   a. The competencies of the student in academic content areas or his or her developmental skills level.
   b. The physical abilities and disabilities exhibited by the student which could affect his or her participation in instructional settings, including, for example, physical education and vocational education.
   c. Social, emotional, and psychological behaviors demonstrated by the student and which affect his or her educational program.
2. A statement of long-term (annual) and short-term (weekly, monthly) instructional objectives. Short-term instructional objectives represent intermediate steps designed to lead the student to the achievement of end-of-year objectives. The statement of these objectives generally is accompanied by a designation of the person or persons responsible for implementing the activities designed to help the student achieve the objective and may include a statement of special materials, resources, or methods used in achieving the objective.
3. A statement of the specific educational services to be provided the student within the least restrictive environment designated. These services should relate directly to the long- and short-term objectives for the student.

FIGURE 20.5
Portion of an Individual Educational Plan

Individual Educational Plan: Educational Priorities Stated as Annual Goals and Short-term Objectives
Page 4 of 4

Goal: *Jeremy will demonstrate reading comprehension and word attack skills at the 2.0 grade level.*

Objectives	Criteria	Evaluation Procedure	Date of Review	Code
Complete all reading skills assignments in the 1st grade text and workbook. *Answer detail recall, sequence, and conclusion questions re: a 2.0 grade level selection.*	*85% accuracy average of assignments* *95% accuracy*	*Record of completion and grades for text and workbook assignments.* *Informal reading inventory.* *Brigance Criterion referenced Inventory*	*6/2/92*	

Goal: *Jeremy will write complete sentences of at least 5 words with correct capitalization and punctuation.*

Objectives	Criteria	Evaluation Procedure	Date of Review	Code
Capitalize the beginning word of each sentence. *Capitalize proper nouns.* *Use period, question mark, or exclamation mark as end punctuation correctly.*	*Write 5 sample sentences without any punctuation or capitalization errors.*	*Written Sample:* *Informal test of written expression.*	*6/2/92*	

Goal: *Jeremy will spell words orally and in written form correctly at the 1.5 grade level.*

Objectives	Criteria	Evaluation Procedure	Date of Review	Code
Complete all spelling units with weekly spelling tests.	*80% accuracy average of test scores.* *1.5 grade level on inventories*	*Informal spelling inventory based on the spelling test word list.* *Brigance Criterion-referenced Inventory Test of written spelling.*	*6/2/92*	

Related Service Goal: *Jeremy will correctly articulate "l" and "r" sounds and express himself in complete, descriptive sentences of at least 6 words in length.*

Objectives	Criteria	Evaluation Procedure	Date of Review	Code
Read orally a passage containing 10 words with beginning, medial, and final "r" and "l" sounds. *Orally describe a current activity in complete, descriptive sentences of at least 6 words in length*	*100% accurate pronunciation* *Can perform this task upon request.*	*Language sample* *Informal assessment by the speech therapist.*	*6/2/92*	

Related Service Goal: *Jeremy will write legible capital and lowercase letters in word and sentence form upon request in manuscript.*

Objectives	Criteria	Evaluation Procedure	Date of Review	Code
Write all alphabet letters in uppercase form correctly in manuscript. *Write all alphabet letters in lowercase form correctly in manuscript.*	*Legibility of writing of all manuscript letters, both upper and lowercase*	*Written sample* *Informal assessment by occupational therapist.*	*6/2/92*	

4. A statement of the dates for the initiation of the services, the approximate amount of time to be spent providing each service, and a justification for the services and settings in which they will be provided.
5. A statement of the criterion for and time of evaluating each long- and short-term objective.

As should now be obvious, writing the IEP is a complex and comprehensive process. Under full inclusion the regular classroom will increasingly be the special learner's placement. Thus, the IEP cannot be written without the assistance and cooperation of the regular classroom teacher. It should be obvious as well that you will have to play a significant role in monitoring and reporting the progress the student is making toward fulfilling the objectives of the IEP. As progress data must be reported back to the multidisciplinary team at regularly scheduled intervals for decision-making purposes, its reliability, validity, and accuracy is of utmost importance. Since you may be the sole link between the child and the team for relatively long periods of time, your measurement skills to systematically observe, record, and monitor the performance of the challenged child become of paramount importance with respect to the effective implementation of the student's IEP.

Individualized Instruction

A fourth stage in which you may become involved in the implementation of PL 94–142 is in providing individualized instruction to the challenged student. Individualized special education instruction is the day-to-day instruction provided to this student based on the objectives set forth in the student's IEP. This program of individualized instruction should be consistent with the needs of the special learner and your curriculum. Your activities may include providing any or all of the following:

- Specific instructional objectives based on student needs as stated in the IEP.
- Learning activities appropriate to each student's learning style and presented as specifically and sequentially as needed for the student to progress toward attainment of each instructional objective.
- Instructional media and materials used for each learning activity selected on the basis of the student's learning style.
- An instructional setting that provides multiple arrangements for learning.
- A schedule of teaching time assuring the provision of instruction to each exceptional student in individual or group arrangements.
- Procedures by which the teacher measures, records, and reports each exceptional student's progress.

You may be responsible for documenting the provision of an individualized instructional program for each special learner in your classroom as well as for monitoring and recording the success of the individualized program. The writing of specific instructional objectives in accord with the student's IEP and the preparation and administration of teacher-made tests to record student progress toward these objectives are tasks for which you also may be responsible.

Reviewing the IEP

In general, school districts will have an established set of procedures or a system for reviewing each special learner's progress based on the objectives stated in the student's IEP. The purpose of this review is not only to determine the student's progress toward the objectives of the plan but also to determine the need for modifying the plan and for further special services. A critical aspect of this review is documenting the movement of a student to either a more or less restrictive environment or release from all special educational services.

Recommendations for major changes in the IEP, including changes in the student's placement (for example, to a more or less restrictive environment), are the responsibility of the multidisciplinary team. However, all persons involved in implementing the student's IEP are likely to be involved in this review. For example, some of the many pieces of information that must be gathered prior to a major change in a student's placement include:

- The number of instructional options that have been attempted, including those within the regular classroom.
- The appropriateness of the long- and short-range educational objectives, including those written by the regular classroom teacher.
- The reliability, validity, and accuracy of the testing that led or contributed to a review of the student's current placement, including testing completed within the regular classroom.

A student may only be moved to a more restrictive environment, even temporarily, if sufficient data exist documenting that the student's behavior warrants such action. These data generally attempt to establish:

- The student's behavior being examined was not solely caused by the disabling condition.
- Adjustments in the student's IEP, including alternative educational programs, were tried in an attempt to prevent the recurrence of the undesirable behavior leading to reconsideration of the child's placement.

In each of these areas, data provided by the classroom teacher are often critical, since you may be in the most advantageous position to make these assessments about the everyday performance of the student. Here, as elsewhere with the implementation of PL 94–142, the reliability, validity, and accuracy of the data you provide will be a direct reflection of the testing and measurement skills you have acquired. While the specific measurment and testing requirements of Section 504 remain to be determined, it appears reasonable to conclude that a similar set of expectations for the role of the classroom teacher in identifying and evaluating "504 only" children with disabilities will be developed.

MONITORING SPECIAL LEARNERS ON MEDICATION

As the movement toward full inclusion becomes more widespread, the regular classroom teacher may expect to see increased numbers of severely and multiply challenged students in the regular classroom. Many of these special learners will have significant emotional and behavioral disorders that are believed to require medication therapy. Whatever your beliefs may be about the use of medication for the management of challenged children, recent literature reviews are unanimous in concluding that the use of psychiatric (i.e., psychotropic or psychoactive) medications such as stimulants, antidepressants, antianxiety agents, and antipsychotics is rapidly increasing. This is in spite of lack of objective, empirical support for their safety and efficacy with children and adolescents, with the exception of stimulants for the child with Attention Deficit Hyperactivity Disorder, or ADHD (Barkley, Conners, Barclay, Gadow, Gittleman, Sprague & Swanson, 1990; Biederman & Steingard, 1990; Gadow, 1992; Gadow & Pomeroy, 1993; Kubiszyn, Brown, DeMers, Landau & Reynolds, 1992).

ADHD is a relatively common disorder characterized by impairments in attention and concentration, distractibility, impulsivity, and sometimes hyperactivity. Estimates indicate that from 3 to 5 percent of children have symptoms consistent with a diagnosis of ADHD (DSM-IV, 1994), and most of these are treated with psychoactive medications, typically stimulants. Thus, even without full inclusion it is likely that the classroom teacher will see one or more students with ADHD in any given class. ADHD has been defined as a handicapping condition under PL 94–142 as Other Health Impaired (OHI) and under Section 504.

All medications prescribed for the management of emotional or behavioral problems (i.e., psychotropic or psychoactive medications), and many that are prescribed for other difficulties (e.g., anticonvulsants, antihypertensives) have potential for unexpected side effects, such as impairments in concentration, memory, awareness, coordination, consciousness, respiration, heart rate and rhythm, and other vital functions (Brown & Borden, 1989; Brown, Dingle & Landau, 1994; Bukstein, 1992; Gadow, 1992). Thus, it is important to monitor those children taking psychoactive and other powerful medications for such side effects. Assessment of the safety and efficacy of any medication will require your vigilance to provide valid and reliable school-based assessment of the therapeutic and side effects of these medications (Fisher & Newby, 1991; Forness & Kavale, 1988).

Traditionally, however, psychiatrists, pediatricians, and other physicians who prescribe these medications have relied on parent report or student self-report, typically in the practitioner's office, to make important decisions about initiating, adjusting, or terminating a child's medication. Since the reliability and validity of data obtained in this way may be questioned, school- and teacher-based data are increasingly being requested to help make these decisions (Brown & Borden, 1989; Barkley et al. 1990; Fisher & Newby, 1991; Kubiszyn et al. 1992).

Historically, the classroom teacher's involvement in a student's medication regimen was passive and minimal. However, as the practice of prescribing psychoactive medications to school-age children has increased dramatically in recent years, the extent of their use and safety have been questioned in the professional literature by psychologists and educators (Forness & Kavale, 1988; Gadow, 1991; Kratochwill, 1994), and more recently by task forces of the Child Clinical (Barkley et al. 1990) and School Psychology (Kubiszyn et al. 1992) Divisions of the American Psychological Association.

In response, and in hopes of ensuring the safety and efficacy of medicated special learners, practitioners are increasingly beginning to ask teachers to complete one or more of a variety of medication-related and behavior rating scales and questionnaires (Brown & Borden, 1989; Fisher & Newby, 1991; Gadow, 1992). Thus, the classroom teacher may expect to play a more and more active and important role in collecting and validating the data prescribers must have before making decisions about medication for special learners.

In addition, psychologists and child and family therapists also are recognizing the importance of obtaining classroom data to help assess the efficacy of their interventions with special learners and their families. They, too, are increasingly asking, either directly or through parents of special learners, for teachers to provide a variety of types of classroom data (e.g., from observations, anecdotal records, sociometrics, and questionnaires or rating scales). The bottom line is that both physicians and mental health professionals are increasingly recognizing the importance of obtaining reliable and valid data from the classroom teacher to assess the safety and efficacy of their interventions. With the movement toward full inclusion of special learners, classroom teachers can expect more severely and multiply challenged learners in their classrooms, and more requests for classroom data from non-school professionals.

To familiarize you with some of the data collection tasks you may be asked to perform, we present some examples of several of the more commonly used medication and behavior rating scales. Our mention of these instruments does not represent an endorsement of them; these are simply examples of several instruments in use.

Scales Used to Assess Medication and Psychosocial Interventions

Probably the most commonly used questionnaire is the Conners Teacher Rating Scale-Revised (Goyette, Conners & Ulrich, 1978). Also known as the CTRS–28, this is a relatively short, 28 item questionnaire that is widely used to evaluate the effects of medication and other therapies on children with a variety of emotional and behavioral problems including ADHD. A similar rating scale for parents called the Conners Parent Rating Scale-Revised (CPRS–28) also exists. The CTRS–28 appears in Figure 20.6.

A 10-item version of the CTRS called the Abbreviated Symptom Questionnaire-Teachers (ASQ–T) is even more commonly used (Goyette et al. 1978). It is also known as

FIGURE 20.6
The Conners Teacher Rating Scale-Revised, or CTRS–28

CHILDREN'S HOSPITAL NATIONAL MEDICAL CENTER
111 Michigan Avenue, N. W.
Washington, D. C. 20010

Teacher's Questionnaire

Name of Child ______________________ **Grade** ________

Date of Evaluation ______________________

Please answer all questions. Beside *each* item, indicate the degree of the problem by a check mark (✔)

	Not at all	Just a little	Pretty much	Very much
1. Restless in the "squirmy" sense.				
2. Makes inappropriate noises when he shouldn't.				
3. Demands must be met immediately.				
4. Acts "smart" (impudent or sassy).				
5. Temper outbursts and unpredictable behavior.				
6. Overly sensitive to criticism.				
7. Distractibility or attention span a problem.				
8. Disturbs other children.				
9. Daydreams.				
10. Pouts and sulks.				
11. Mood changes quickly and drastically.				
12. Quarrelsome.				
13. Submissive attitude toward authority.				
14. Restless, always "up and on the go."				
15. Excitable, impulsive.				
16. Excessive demands for teacher's attention.				
17. Appears to be unaccepted by group.				
18. Appears to be easily led by other children.				
19. No sense of fair play.				
20. Appears to lack leadership.				
21. Fails to finish things that he starts.				
22. Childish and immature.				
23. Denies mistakes or blames others.				
24. Does not get along well with other children.				
25. Uncooperative with classmates.				
26. Easily frustrated in efforts.				
27. Uncooperative with teacher.				
28. Difficulty in learning.				

the Hyperactivity Index and is useful for assessing the day-to-day changes that often are helpful in making medication adjustments for ADHD. The ASQ–T has a companion form for parents called the ASQ–P. A copy of the ASQ-T is included in Figure 20.7.

The Child Behavior Checklist–Teacher Rating Form, or CBCL–TRF (Achenbach, 1991) is the teacher version of a similar questionnaire for parents. It is longer than the Conners questionnaires (118 items) and is useful in identifying a variety of emotional and behavioral disorders. It is often used in conjunction with the parent version (CBCL) to

FIGURE 20.7
The Abbreviated Symptom Questionnaire-Teacher (ASQ–T), also known as the Hyperactivity Index

ASQ-T
C. Keith Conners, Ph.D.

Child Rated:____________________ **Rater:**____________

Day:__________ **Date:**__________ **Time:**______ *am pm*

Instructions

Read each item below carefully, and decide how much you think your student has been bothered by this problem today/this week/this month. For each behavior described below, circle one number to indicate how much of a problem that behavior was for your student.

Not at All	Just a Little	Pretty Much	Very Much	
0	1	2	3	Restless in the "squirmy" sense
0	1	2	3	Temper outbursts, unpredictable behavior
0	1	2	3	Distractibility or attention span a problem
0	1	2	3	Disturbs other children
0	1	2	3	Pouts and sulks
0	1	2	3	Mood changes quickly and drastically
0	1	2	3	Restless, always up and on the go
0	1	2	3	Excitable, impulsive
0	1	2	3	Fails to finish things
0	1	2	3	Easily frustrated in efforts

MHS

Your school psychologist or counselor will complete the reverse side.

Reproduced by permission of Multi-Health Systems, Inc., 908 Niagra Falls Boulevard, North Tonawanda, NY 14120-2060.

compare teacher and parental perceptions of the same child for screening, diagnosis, and ongoing evaluation of both medication and psychosocial interventions. Page three of the four page TRF is reproduced in Figure 20.8.

The School Situations Questionnaire (SSQ) is a brief, 12-item questionnaire devised by Barkley (1987). It is designed to identify situations in which children manifest various behaviors. It is used to aid in the diagnosis of ADHD and other behavior problems and is sensitive to the effects of stimulant medication. A similar version for parents called the

FIGURE 20.8
The Child Behavior Checklist-Teacher Rating Form, or CBCL–TRF

Below is a list of items that describe pupils. For each item that describes the pupil **now or within the past 2 months**, please circle the 2 if the item is **very true** or **often true** of the pupil. Circle the 1 if the item is **somewhat** or **sometimes true** of the pupil. If the item is **not true** of the pupil, circle the 0. Please answer all items as well as you can, even if some do not seem to apply to this pupil.

0 = Not True (as far as you know) 1 = Somewhat or Sometimes True 2 = Very True or Often True

0 1 2 1. Acts too young for his/her age
0 1 2 2. Hums or makes other odd noises in class

0 1 2 3. Argues a lot
0 1 2 4. Fails to finish things he/she starts

0 1 2 5. Behaves like opposite sex
0 1 2 6. Defiant, talks back to staff

0 1 2 7. Bragging, boasting
0 1 2 8. Can't concentrate, can't pay attention for long

0 1 2 9. Can't get his/her mind off certain thoughts; obsessions (describe): ______________

____

0 1 2 10. Can't sit still, restless, or hyperactive

0 1 2 11. Clings to adults or too dependent

0 1 2 12. Complains of loneliness

0 1 2 13. Confused or seems to be in a fog
0 1 2 14. Cries a lot

0 1 2 15. Fidgets
0 1 2 16. Cruelty, bullying, or meanness to others

0 1 2 17. Daydreams or gets lost in his/her thoughts
0 1 2 18. Deliberately harms self or attempts suicide

0 1 2 19. Demands a lot of attention
0 1 2 20. Destroys his/her own things

0 1 2 21. Destroys property belonging to others
0 1 2 22. Difficulty following directions

0 1 2 23. Disobedient at school
0 1 2 24. Disturbs other pupils

0 1 2 25. Doesn't get along with other pupils
0 1 2 26. Doesn't seem to feel guilty after misbehaving

0 1 2 27. Easily jealous
0 1 2 28. Eats or drinks things that are not food—*don't* include sweets (describe): ______________

____

0 1 2 29. Fears certain animals, situations, or places other than school (describe): ______________

____

0 1 2 30. Fears going to school

0 1 2 31. Fears he/she might think or do something bad
0 1 2 32. Feels he/she has to be perfect

0 1 2 33. Feels or complains that no one loves him/her
0 1 2 34. Feels others are out to get him/her

0 1 2 35. Feels worthless or inferior
0 1 2 36. Gets hurt a lot, accident-prone

0 1 2 37. Gets in many fights
0 1 2 38. Gets teased a lot

0 1 2 39. Hangs around with others who get in trouble
0 1 2 40. Hears sounds or voices that aren't there (describe):

____

0 1 2 41. Impulsive or acts without thinking
0 1 2 42. Would rather be alone than with others

0 1 2 43. Lying or cheating
0 1 2 44. Bites fingernails

0 1 2 45. Nervous, high-strung, or tense
0 1 2 46. Nervous movements or twitching (describe):

____

____

0 1 2 47. Overconforms to rules
0 1 2 48. Not liked by other pupils

0 1 2 49. Has difficulty learning
0 1 2 50. Too fearful or anxious

0 1 2 51. Feels dizzy
0 1 2 52. Feels too guilty

0 1 2 53. Talks out of turn
0 1 2 54. Overtired

0 1 2 55. Overweight
56. Physical problems without known medical cause:
0 1 2 a. Aches or pains (*not* headaches)
0 1 2 b. Headaches
0 1 2 c. Nausea, feels sick
0 1 2 d. Problems with eyes (describe): ______________

____

0 1 2 e. Rashes or other skin problems
0 1 2 f. Stomachaches or cramps
0 1 2 g. Vomiting, throwing up
0 1 2 h. Other (describe): ______________

____

____

PAGE 3

Please see other side

From Achenbach, T. (1991), *Manual for the teacher's report form.* Burlington: University of Vermont, Department of Psychiatry.

FIGURE 20.9
The School Situations Questionnaire, or SSQ

SCHOOL SITUATIONS QUESTIONNAIRE

Child's name ______________________________ Date __________
Name of person completing this form ______________________________

Does this child present any behavior problems for you in any of these situations? If so, indicate how severe they are.

Situations	*Yes/No* (Circle one)		*If yes, how severe?* (Circle one) Mild								Severe
While arriving at school	Yes	No	1	2	3	4	5	6	7	8	9
During individual desk work	Yes	No	1	2	3	4	5	6	7	8	9
During small group activities	Yes	No	1	2	3	4	5	6	7	8	9
During free playtime in class	Yes	No	1	2	3	4	5	6	7	8	9
During lectures to the class	Yes	No	1	2	3	4	5	6	7	8	9
At recess	Yes	No	1	2	3	4	5	6	7	8	9
At lunch	Yes	No	1	2	3	4	5	6	7	8	9
In the hallways	Yes	No	1	2	3	4	5	6	7	8	9
In the bathroom	Yes	No	1	2	3	4	5	6	7	8	9
On field trips	Yes	No	1	2	3	4	5	6	7	8	9
During special assemblies	Yes	No	1	2	3	4	5	6	7	8	9
On the bus	Yes	No	1	2	3	4	5	6	7	8	9

.... For Office Use Only ....

Total number of problem settings __________ Mean severity score __________

From Barkley, R. A. (1987), The school situations questionnaire. *Defiant Children: A Clinician's Manual for Parent Training*. Reproduced by permission of The Guilford Press.

Home Situations Questionnaire (Barkley, 1987) is used to compare the child's behavior in home and school settings. The SSQ is reproduced in Figure 20.9.

How often these or similar instruments come across your desk depends in large part on the practices of medical and mental health professionals in your area. Our perception is that it is increasingly likely that you will be asked to participate in these data collection efforts due to the effects of full inclusion and increased efforts to obtain classroom data to assess the efficacy of both pharmacological and non-pharmacological interventions. Next, let us turn to a discussion of the gifted and talented special learner.

AT THE OTHER END OF THE CURVE: THE GIFTED CHILD

As you have seen, much attention at the federal and state levels has been directed toward improving educational opportunity for the challenged child. Recalling our discussion of the normal distribution, we recognize that roughly 2 percent of the population will fall into an area defined as two standard deviations below the mean, and this is typically the cutoff that is used for identifying children as having disabilities. But remember, there are also children at the other end of the curve. They score in the upper 2 percent on IQ, aptitude, and achievement tests. Are there any school programs or special instructional techniques for them? Since these students are also two standard deviations away from (in this case, above) the mean, won't they be shortchanged by an educational system designed to educate children who are "average"? Do these learners have special needs that should also be addressed? In this section we will expose you to some of the measurement approaches and instruments that currently exist to at least identify those children who are far above average in creative and intellectual ability.

Defining "Gifted"

Definitions of giftedness vary, just as philosophies vary about how we should teach the gifted. Generally speaking, the term *gifted* has given way to the term *gifted and talented* or some other description that expands the definition to include not just those who score in the upper 2 percent on IQ tests, but also those who have achieved exceptionally in some academic or other area, those who are excelling in art or music, or those who score in the upper ranges on a test of creativity. Lest you think that the federal government has forgotten about the gifted and talented population, let's review the definition of gifted and talented children provided by the U.S. Office of Education:

> Gifted and talented children are those identified by professionally qualified persons who by virtue of outstanding abilities are capable of high performance. These are children who require differentiated educational programs and services beyond those normally provided by the regular program in order to realize their contribution to self and society. Children capable of high performance include those with demonstrated achievement and/or potential ability in any of the following areas: (1) general and intellectual ability, (2) specific academic aptitude, (3) creative or productive thinking, (4) leadership ability, (5) visual and performing arts, (6) psychomotor ability (Marland, 1972, p. 10)."

Except for the "tail" of the normal curve that one is referring to and the specific areas of giftedness, we see little difference between this definition and the one that provides the rationale for the provision of proper educational experiences to the disabled learner.

Assessment and Identification

Although perhaps the most commonly used method to identify a gifted student has been an individually administered IQ test, it is by no means the only method. As we have discussed, IQ tests are designed to measure theoretical models of intelligence, and no specific IQ test can claim that it actually does measure "intelligence," in large part because we fail to agree on just what intelligence is. Therefore, to use only an IQ test to identify gifted children excludes those individuals whose particular gift or talent may lie outside the realm of the theories or concepts that define the IQ test. For this reason, it has become increasingly popular for several other criteria to be used in identifying potentially gifted and talented children. Let's look first at the role of IQ, then at some of these other characteristics that define giftedness.

INTELLIGENCE. Most formulas for defining giftedness include general intelligence. This is particularly true in the elementary grades; it is believed that although schoolchildren are still developing their specialized intellectual capacities, their general intelligence is almost completely formed in the critical preschool years. The emphasis on general intelligence for aiding identification of giftedness at the elementary level also is a function of the difficulty of measuring specific aptitudes at that age, when many of the words and concepts required for accurately testing specific aptitudes have yet to be taught.

At the junior high and secondary levels, measures of specific intelligence are more likely to be substituted for general intelligence. The most common are verbal and mathematical aptitude, scores for which can be derived from most general IQ tests. For example, a sufficiently high score on verbal intelligence could qualify a learner for gifted English but not for gifted math, and vice versa; this gives greater flexibility to the definition of giftedness.

How high must a student score on tests of general or specific intelligence to be considered gifted? This depends on the school district's criteria. However, it is known how intelligence is distributed among individuals in the entire population. Recall that intelligence is distributed in a bell-shaped curve, with most individuals scoring around the middle of the curve, which represents an IQ score of 100. From the shape of this curve, we also know that less than 1 percent of the population scores 145 or higher, about 2 to 3 percent scores 130 or higher, and approximately 16 percent scores 115 or higher.

Although these percentages vary sightly depending on the test used, they are a useful guideline for selecting gifted learners. An IQ score of about 130 or higher generally makes one eligible for gifted instruction (Dembo, 1981). However, in practice, because giftedness almost always is defined in conjunction with at least several other behaviors, admission to gifted programs and classes usually is far less restrictive. It is not uncommon to accept scores below 130 as eligible for gifted instruction (of course, this is highly variable among schools and states). Sometimes IQ is not considered at all in determining giftedness, in which case the learner must exhibit unusual ability in one or more other areas.

Because IQ tests rely greatly on standard language usage that predominates in the middle class, a school district with a high concentration of students from lower socioeconomic strata may not require a high level of tested intelligence (at least not as measured by standardized tests). In most cases, general intelligence is only one of several behaviors that are defined as constituting giftedness. Rarely is general intelligence used as the only index of giftedness, nor should it be.

While general intelligence is the most frequently used measure of ability, other components of intelligence have also been hypothesized. For example, Gardner & Hatch (1989) propose seven different "intelligences" based upon skills found in a modern technological society. Their seven abilities, along with some representative individuals who would be expected to possess high levels of these abilities, are identified in Table 20.1.

TABLE 20.1
Gardner's Multiple Intelligences

Dimension	*Example*
Linguistic intelligence: Sensitivity to the meaning and order of words and the varied uses of language	Poet, journalist
Logical-mathematical intelligence: The ability to handle long chains of reasoning and to recognize patterns and order in the world	Scientist, mathematician
Musical intelligence: Sensitivity to pitch, melody, and tone	Composer, violinist
Spatial intelligence: The ability to perceive the visual world accurately, and to recreate, transform, or modify aspects of the world based on one's perceptions	Sculptor, navigator
Bodily-kinesthetic intelligence: A fine-tuned ability to use the body and to handle objects	Dancer, athlete
Interpersonal intelligence: The ability to notice and make distinctions among others	Therapist, salesperson
Intrapersonal intelligence: Access to one's own "feeling life"	Self-aware individual

SOURCE: Adapted from Gardner & Hatch, 1989.

Gardner and his associates have developed instructional materials and modules to teach some of these abilities.

Their theory derives from the observation that many individuals who are successful in life do not score high in traditional indicators of ability, such as verbal or mathematical reasoning. Gardner and his associates suggest that these individuals, to be successful, used other abilities, such as those in Table 20.1, to minimize their weaknesses and accentuate their strengths. Their theory may have particular relevance for teaching gifted learners, some of whom may not learn from school in the traditional classroom setting using the traditional curriculum. These researchers reason that alternative forms of learning could "tap into" other dimensions of intelligence that in the traditional classroom may go unnoticed or underutilized.

ACHIEVEMENT. Among other behaviors frequently used to determine giftedness is the learner's achievement, usually in the areas for which gifted instruction is being considered. Achievement is measured by yearly standardized tests which cover areas such as math, social studies, reading comprehension, vocabulary, and science. Cut-off scores in the form of percentile ranks are determined in each subject area, with a percentile score of 90 to 95 representing a typical cutoff. Although cutoff percentiles differ among school districts, a cutoff percentile of 90 means that a learner is eligible for gifted instruction if his or her score on the appropriate subscale of a standardized achievement test is higher than the scores of 90 percent of all those who took the test.

CREATIVITY. In addition to intelligence and achievement, indices of creativity often are considered in selecting gifted learners. Inclusion of this behavioral dimension has broadened the definition of this type of learner to include both the gifted and the talented. The significance of this addition is that not all gifted learners are talented, nor are all talented learners gifted. The phrase "gifted and talented," which is widely used, can mean talented but not gifted, gifted but not talented, mostly talented with some giftedness, mostly gifted with some talent, or both gifted and talented.

These alternative categorizations are made possible by inclusion of creativity indices in the eligibility standards. Because creative behaviors generally are considered in selecting gifted students, this type of learner more appropriately might be called "gifted and/or talented." Some observable signs of creativity in a learner include:

- Applying abstract principles to the solution of problems
- Being curious and inquisitive
- Giving uncommon or unusual responses
- Showing imagination
- Posing original solutions to problems
- Discriminating between major and minor events
- Seeing relationships among dissimilar objects

In identifying the gifted and talented learner, the creative component is usually composed of recommendations from teachers based upon these and other signs of creativity from performance assessments and any observable creative products from portfolio assessments (e.g., sculpture, painting, musical score, science fair project, short story). It is interesting to note that studies have shown only a modest relationship between intelligence and creativity, indicating that creativity is fairly independent of both IQ and achievement.

TASK PERSISTENCE. A fourth behavior sometimes used in selecting gifted and talented learners involves recommendations from teachers and other knowledgeable sources concerning a learner's task persistence. This behavior is difficult to evaluate, but it is often considered indispensable for satisfactory achievement in a gifted and talented program, because both the quantity and quality of the work are likely to be considerably higher than what is expected in the regular classroom. Obviously, this trait alone would not be sufficient for qualifying a learner for gifted instruction, but if such instruction is indeed geared to the extremely able student, students will need unusual levels of task persistence to succeed. Behaviors that teachers look for in determining task persistence include:

- Ability to devise organized approaches to learning
- Ability to concentrate on detail
- Self-imposed high standards
- Persistence in achieving personal goals
- Willingness to evaluate own performance, and capability to do so
- Sense of responsibility
- High level of energy, particularly in academic tasks

Implicit in these four characteristics of giftedness—intelligence, achievement, creativity, and task persistence—is the assumption that not all gifted children are equally gifted in every area of their functioning (intellectual ability, academic achievement, social skills, artistic accomplishment, etc.). Indeed, it would be no surprise to the average classroom teacher to find that he or she may have a child in the classroom who is gifted or talented in mathematics, or science, or music, but not necessarily in any other academic area. Furthermore, gifted children are not immune to physical, emotional, or neurological deficits that can reduce their capacity to demonstrate or express their gifts or talents consistently or frequently enough to obtain recognition and attention. Rather than assume that "gifted" always means the child is able to cope and excel, it is far better to keep in mind that the label usually applies to some specific subset of an individual's thoughts or behavior rather than the entire person, and that a gifted and talented person is not immune to the frustrations and feelings that are evident in others.

Nonetheless, neither the federal nor state governments fund programs for the gifted and talented at levels comparable to funding for children with disabilities. This does not mean, however, that giftedness, happiness, success, and acceptance necessarily go hand in hand. The gifted child, if identified, may respond well to relatively inexpensive interventions that may provide you with unanticipated rewards for your efforts.

Current Trends in Teaching and Assessing the Gifted and Talented

Gifted and talented education has taken on added prominence in recent years as a result of the increase in alternatives by which the gifted learner can accelerate, or move, through the traditional curriculum.

There is little evidence to support the claim that homogeneously grouped, or tracked, classes increase overall school achievement relative to heterogeneously grouped classes (Slavin, 1990; Gamoran, 1992; Kerckhouf, 1986). However, this research specifically excluded gifted learners who represent about the top 3–5 percent of the school population. Research tends to support programs and classes specifically targeted to the gifted and talented when they are allowed to pursue accelerated programs, where a grade can be skipped and/or advanced courses taken—such as Advanced Placement (AP) courses for college credit (Slavin, 1990). Other gifted and talented programs which simply enrich or add to existing curriculum by allowing students to pursue games and simulations to promote creativity and problem-solving, conduct individual investigations, or are simply given the use of computers or other technology, tend to be less successful in increasing the achievement of these learners (Kulik & Kulik, 1984). Gifted and talented programs that are exclusively enrichment programs have been criticized for providing few activities that would not benefit all learners. Their primary advantage tends to be that they provide beneficial opportunities for learners who can master the regular curriculum rapidly enough to take advantage of them.

This has led to the increasing popularity of "magnet schools" whose primary purpose is to provide curriculum in specialized areas—such as science, language arts, and the creative arts—to a broad range of students whose interests and abilities qualify them. Some magnet schools are schools within a school, thereby promoting heterogeneous interactions among learners while providing advanced and accelerated coursework leading to college credit and/or early high school graduation to those who can master the curriculum more quickly. The magnet school concept, as well as other alternatives, such as early graduation, that move the gifted learner more rapidly through the school curriculum are coming to define programs for the gifted and talented.

SUMMARY

This chapter has acquainted you with the field of special learners and its relationship to the regular classroom teacher. Its major points are:

1. The field of special education has undergone tremendous growth with respect to its programs and services as well as significant change with respect to the laws and policies governing the education of the disabled.

2. The most significant of these laws and policies has been PL 94–142 and the policies resulting from it. PL 94–142 guarantees the right of every child of school age to receive free public education appropriate to his or her needs. PL 99–457 extended these rights to children three years of age and older and provided incentives to schools to identify and provide services to infants and toddlers with disabilities. Recent interpretations of Section 504 of the Rehabilitation Act have broadened special instruction eligibility for students with disabilities.

3. The special education profession and the public schools have chosen to interpret "education that is appropriate to the needs of a child with disabilities" as education that not only matches and builds upon the child's current level of intellectual and/or emotional functioning, but that also is provided in the least restrictive environment conducive to meeting the intellectual and emotional needs of the child.

4. The recent movement toward full inclusion in the educational mainstream of students with multiple and severe disabilities indicates that the regular classroom is increasingly being viewed as the least restrictive alternative. Thus, for most students with disabilities the regular classroom will be the least restrictive environment.

5. The role of the regular classroom teacher in implementing PL 94–142 includes responsibilities in:

   a. child identification

   b. individual assessment

   c. Individual Educational Plan (IEP) development

   d. individualized instruction

   e. review of the IEP

   Similar responsibilities appear to be evolving as a result of legal interpretations of Section 504.

6. An example of the measurement skills needed by the regular classroom teacher for child identification is documenting the difficulties of the child through observation, informal and formal tests and authentic assessments, and instructional strategies that have not been effective.

7. An example of the measurement skills needed by the regular classroom teacher for individual assessment is collecting and analyzing information pertaining to the learning competencies of the student and the effects of specific instructional activities on these competencies.

8. An example of the measurement skills needed by the regular classroom teacher for IEP development is writing short- and long-term instructional objectives for the student, specifying both the outcome to be reached and the instructional activities to be implemented.

9. An example of the measurement skills needed by the regular classroom teacher for individualized instruction is documenting the implementation of an individualized instructional program for each exceptional child and monitoring and recording the success of this program.

10. An example of the measurement skills needed by the regular classroom teacher to review the IEP is determining the reliability, validity, and accuracy of the measurement procedures used to indicate the need to change the child's placement to either a more or a less restrictive environment.

11. As a function of full inclusion of multiply and severely disabled children on medication in the regular classroom coupled with increased awareness of the need for more reliable and valid assessment of the safety and efficacy of such medications, teachers will increasingly be called upon to collect data from a variety of sources for evaluation by prescribing professionals.

12. While the field of special education typically focuses on those individuals within the lower 2 percent of the normal curve, those individuals at the upper 2 percent of the normal curve, sometimes referred to as gifted and talented, have received at least some federal, state, and local attention in terms of their particular needs.

13. Some learner characteristics that have been used to identify students as gifted and/or talented are intelligence, achievement, creativity, and task persistence.

14. Magnet schools, early graduation, and Advanced Placement courses for college credit are increasingly being used to meet the educational needs of the gifted and talented.

For Discussion

1. List four implications of Public Law 94–142 for how you will construct tests for use in your classroom.

2. Describe at least two methods for identifying challenged learners in your classroom.

3. Assume you are asked by a multidisciplinary team to monitor and collect data on one of your students who may be mildly retarded. What types of information would you collect, and in what form would you report these data to the multidisciplinary team?

4. Twelve years after PL 94–142 was passed, Congress passed PL 99–457. Speculate about how special education services for preschoolers may affect you in working with such children when they enter elementary school.

5. What effect will recent interpretations of Section 504 of the Rehabilitation Act have on you as a classroom teacher? What are the costs and benefits of these interpretations to teachers, students, and society?

6. Imagine that you are asked to complete questionnaires like those presented in this chapter on two or three students taking medication in your class on several occasions over the school year. Do you feel this is time well spent? If so, why? If not, why not?

7. What four characteristics are typically used to identify a learner as gifted and/or talented? What kind of information would you try to obtain to assess a student in each of these areas?

8. What has the research told us about the relative merits of homogeneous grouping, accelerated programs, enrichment programs, and magnet schools as they apply to the gifted and talented?

CHAPTER 21

The Personal Computer (PC) in Testing and Measurement

Today most, if not all, schools have personal computers (PCs) in the classroom, a personal computer lab, and PCs available for faculty and staff use. In some innovative programs the PC is integral to novel pedagogy. Teachers in these programs move students along at their own pace using multimedia software, instead of providing direct instruction (Piper, 1994). Swan & Mitrani (1993) estimate that today there are over 2 million computers in the schools. From their perspective, the appropriate use of computers will eventually transform the structure of our schools, with more individualized learning for students and teachers who are facilitators rather than purveyors of knowledge.

While PCs have been in place in most schools for a decade or longer, this technology is underutilized, and perhaps most underutilized in applications for tests and measurements. This is unfortunate, since the PC's greatest usefulness in today's classroom may be in the area of testing and measurement. Put another way, classroom teachers, always strapped for time, could save significant time and effort when performing important but tedious and/or repetitive measurement tasks by utilizing relevant test construction, test analysis, item analysis, test scoring, and grade storage computer programs, or by adapting existing word processing, database, and spreadsheet programs.

In keeping with our main objective for this text, we want you to become skilled and proficient test users. Appropriate use of PCs can greatly assist you in achieving this objective by helping you make the most of your tests and the information they provide. In this chapter, we will assume no prior knowledge of computers and will keep our presentation focused on readily understandable aspects of PC operation and use. First, we will consider some of the possible reasons for PC underutilization.

WHY ARE PCs UNDERUTILIZED?

PCs have not been unique in enjoying initial enthusiastic support but failing to achieve mainstream status in our schools. Cuban (1986) reported that a similar phenomenon characterized the introduction of other technological alternatives into education (e.g., radio, film, television, and video). This finding has led Cuban (1989) and others (LaFrenz & Friedman, 1989) to conclude that technology alone, regardless of its promise, is not enough to sustain pedagogical change without the support of rank and file teachers.

While PCs have been around for some time, there are still teachers, trained before the 1980s, who have had little exposure to and training on PCs. Even those who are more recently trained often have little formal training in PC use for measurement purposes and typically have not been exposed to test and measurement-related software. While many teachers are now more computer literate (i.e., familiar with basic PC operations), few have been formally trained in computer programming or in ways to adapt word processing, spreadsheet, database management, and other software programs to the classroom. This lack of training and exposure is perhaps one of the main reasons why the use of the PC for classroom measurement tasks continues to be the exception rather than the rule.

Without sufficient training and experience it is not a surprise that some teachers are at least apprehensive, if not outright phobic about working with PCs. Often they fear, unrealistically, that they will make mistakes which will do permanent harm to the PC or the program they are utilizing. Others, fearful of appearing foolish, shy away after limited exposure and resist investing the time and effort necessary to save significant time and effort later. At times these underlying fears and misconceptions may manifest themselves differently; some teachers may appear hostile or aloof to the use of technology in the classroom. In any case, unrealistic fears and lack of training remain major deterrents to widespread teacher use of PCs.

Unfortunately, there is no consensus as to how to address widespread computer anxiety. Studies that report a decrease in anxiety following increased exposure to computers (Heinssen, Glass & Knight, 1987; McInerney, McInerney & Sinclair, 1994) are offset by studies that report an increase in anxiety following increased exposure (Rosen, Sears & Weil, 1987; Mahmood & Medewitz, 1989).

Another factor interfering with PC acceptance and use in the schools relates to trust. Since their introduction, overzealous and often short-sighted salespeople "sold" PCs to educators as "high-tech," easy to use, cure-alls for educational problems. However, once PCs were purchased, all too often suppliers' promises were found to be without substance. Many suppliers failed to provide even minimal installation and utilization support. Calls to suppliers' technical support lines, usually long distance and at the purchaser's expense, more often than not resulted in busy signals, or long waits on hold. When calls were answered many users were confronted with either poorly trained, or impatient technicians, who only added to their frustration. Other suppliers made support available, but at prohibitively expensive rates, especially for public school personnel. Today, most suppliers have made progress in providing technical support to purchasers and users, but it may take a long time for users to rebuild trust in an industry that left many purchasers "high and dry" once a sale was finalized.

Another important factor inhibiting computer utilization relates to the software or the computer programs that have been written for educational purposes. Initially, many of these programs were unimaginative, slow to execute, and poorly written. Often the accompanying documentation (i.e., the "directions") was cryptic, incorrect, or poorly organized. As a result, such poorly designed and documented applications failed to meet expectations, were difficult to understand and to operate properly, and led to significant frustration for both professionals and students.

The result of all these factors was that the early promise of PCs for educational use was never realized. Administrators, teachers, parents, and students expected great things from PCs, only to see them often relegated to status as dust gatherers, or rather expensive "toys" used only to reward students who behaved appropriately in class.

In this chapter we will help you avoid these impediments to the use of the PC and show you how to use it as a practical tool in managing test and measurement data in your classroom. In order to be able to use the PC effectively, however, it is necessary that you learn something about the PC. In the first part of this chapter we will familiarize you with PCs in general. We will discuss what a PC is, describe the components of a PC system, and explain how a PC works. Next, we will describe how many of the measurement activities described in this text can be facilitated or improved through the use of a PC. Finally, we will provide you with a step-by-step guide that can be used to ensure that you and your school purchase the right PC and, thereby, join the ranks of those who are effectively using this promising addition to the classroom.

WHAT IS A COMPUTER?

The computer is a tool used to manage or process written or numerical information more effectively and efficiently than human beings. It is an information processor. The kinds of processing it can perform include filing information (much like a manual system in a filing cabinet); subjecting information to statistical procedures (much like a statistician with a hand calculator); and, perhaps of greater relevance to us, generating and analyzing tests and test items. Other uses of the computer include writing music; creating art; creating graphics (pictorial representations); performing simulated experiments; and providing instruction directly to the student in the form of exercises, problem sets, and assignments requiring both reading and writing. In this chapter, we will consider the role of computers in test and test-item construction and analysis, and the recording and assignment of grades. In short, we will show you how a computer can help you more efficiently construct, score, and evaluate written tests and sum, average, or analyze class or individual test or assignment grades.

TYPES OF COMPUTERS

There are three major types of computers: the mainframe computer, the minicomputer, and the microcomputer, or personal computer.

Mainframe Computer

Remember when you went through registration and the computer made a mistake in your registration? This was not the work of a PC but the work of a *mainframe computer*. These are the large computers that are housed in the computer center at your university or college. In the past this is what we typically associated with the term *computer*. These are huge pieces of machinery which are very much subject to variations in temperature and humidity. This is why they are often housed in separate buildings where temperature and humidity can be maintained at precise levels. Because they are extremely expensive, they are primarily owned or shared by large institutions.

Minicomputer

Another type of computer is the *minicomputer*. These computers are often used by large businesses. They are smaller and less complex than a mainframe computer. These computers are found most often in offices and are used by computer programmers or operators to manage the large amounts of information and clerical tasks generated by a company or business. These computers are also quite expensive but are less costly than mainframe computers.

Personal Computers

The third type of computer is the *personal computer*. Personal computers come in two varieties: desktop and portable (i.e., laptop, notebook, and subnotebook). These are the computers you see in use in schools, homes, business offices, airports and on airplanes, and virtually any setting in which information management is important. They are sold by a variety of manufacturers including Apple (Macintosh), IBM, and a variety of IBM clones (Compaq, Dell, Gateway, Packard-Bell, etc.). These computers sell for anywhere from a few hundred to several thousand dollars, depending on how they are configured (examples of different configurations will be provided in the next section). These are the computers that have the most potential for the classroom, since they are affordable and can easily perform the tasks that educators most often need done. Furthermore, PCs can be linked together through electronic networks. These will be described next.

LOCAL AREA NETWORKS (LANS). PCs are rapidly reaching the point where their power and storage capacity is on a par with minicomputers. Indeed, many now believe that with the rapid spread of the *Local Area Network,* or LAN option, minicomputers will soon die out. A LAN allows multiple computers located within 200 to 1,000 feet of each other (e.g., in an office building or complex, or in a school) to share resources such as programs, storage, files, printers, and electronic mail. This cuts costs and enables different users to work with common or compatible software, reducing the compatibility problems common when different users use different software packages.

E-MAIL. Electronic mail enables members of a LAN or other network to "E-mail" messages to each other electronically and almost instantaneously. While the memo and the Post Office are not yet dead, the rapid growth of E-mail indicates it is becoming an increasingly viable option to sending memos or mail.

THE INTERNET, OR INFORMATION SUPERHIGHWAY. LANs enable multiple PCs in a limited area to be electronically linked. Could PCs in different parts of town, or in different towns, states, countries, or continents be similarly linked to exchange information, including E-mail? The answer to this question is that they already are! The term "Information Superhighway" is used to describe the worldwide network, or Internet, that makes this interchange possible. If you are able to E-mail your parents, or friends (not necessarily the order of priority!), from a computer at your college or university you are doing so through the Internet. As information available on the Internet increases (and this is happening very rapidly), you will probably find yourself spending more and more time on the "net," and doing much more than E-mailing.

PC World (1994), a widely regarded PC information source, reported that 51 percent of all PCs used in North America by business, education, or government were already networked in LANs, and that 85 percent will be networked by 1998. A recent survey by *Multimedia Schools* (1994) revealed that 24 percent of K–12 schools are already accessing the Internet worldwide network. Now, let's turn to a description of the various components involved in a PC system.

PC SYSTEM COMPONENTS

PC system components can be divided into two major categories: hardware and software. Software may be permanently stored within a PC (e.g., the operating system that tells the various hardware components how to interact with each other). More commonly, however, the term software is used to describe the many different word processing, spreadsheet, database management, game, educational, and business programs that are available for purchase from computer stores or computer magazines. This is the software that actually carries out the computer user's information management wishes.

When the first edition of this text was published in 1984, several different types of PCs were in existence. These included PCs made by Apple, Atari, Commodore, Radio Shack, Texas Instruments, and many others. Fierce competition during the 1980s saw the field narrow by 1990 to only two major types of PCs: those sold by Apple Computer Company (e.g., Macintosh) and those sold by International Business Machines (IBM), and what are referred to as IBM clones. IBM clone manufacturers, such as Compaq, Dell, Gateway, and Packard-Bell all produce PCs that are compatible with IBM PCs and vice-versa. However, neither IBMs nor IBM clones currently are compatible with Apple PCs, and vice-versa. This is because there are significant differences between them in hardware, operating systems, and software. There is hope for future compatibility, however. Apple and IBM announced a plan in 1991 to develop compatible hardware, operating systems, and software. However, release of the first Apple and IBM/IBM clone compatible computers, currently scheduled for 1995, has been repeatedly delayed. Next, we will provide descriptions of the various components of a PC system to help introduce you to computer jargon, which will enable you to understand better how a personal computer works and allow you to intelligently select and use PCs.

Hardware

The basic hardware components of a desktop PC system consist of a keyboard, a central processing unit (called a CPU), and a video-display monitor. Additional hardware units, called *peripherals*, often include some combination of the following: a modem or fax/modem, a printer, a floppy disk drive or two, and a hard drive. Many PCs have the capability to be upgraded by the addition of plug-in circuit boards (usually called cards). Extra memory (the area where information is stored) is a common add-on. For example, you may purchase a PC with 8 megabytes (commonly referred to as 8 megs) of memory, which means the computer's memory can hold 8,000,000 characters of information. Each letter, number, punctuation mark, or space in a sentence, for example, is a character.

If you are using an Apple Macintosh PC, 8 megs of memory will probably be sufficient for most programs you run. However, as more IBM and IBM clone users have switched from the reliable but intimidating DOS operating system to the more user-friendly but memory-hungry graphical Windows operating system, memory requirements for Windows-based software have skyrocketed. When this book was first published in 1984 average memory requirements for DOS-based programs were in the 256K–512K range. Today, more and more IBM compatible Windows-based computer programs or applications now require as much as 8 megs of memory just to operate, with twice as much or more needed to operate with reasonable efficiency. Macintosh memory requirements, while increasing over the years, have not done so as dramatically as have Windows-based programs. Next, let's discuss how programs and data are stored and accessed.

Data and Program Storage and Access

CASSETTES. You may still find computers in schools that rely on audiocassettes for programs and data storage. While they may be useful for some classroom purposes, they are antiquated for measurement uses.

DISKETTES. Disk drives now take the place of the cassette. Disk drives may be either part of the CPU housing or external and have the advantage of accessing and storing data much more quickly than cassettes. Thus, the use of disks or diskettes has increasingly become the standard for storage of programs and data in the schools. Disks are more efficient and can hold many times more information than cassettes. Disks come in two sizes: the flexible 5 ¼" size and the rigid plastic-cased 3 ½" size. Regardless of the size and flexibility of the case, both the 5 ¼" and 3 ½" sizes are referred to as floppy disks or diskettes. But just because they are referred to by the same generic name, don't think they are interchangeable! A 5 ¼" diskette cannot fit into or be read by a 3 ½" disk drive, and vice-versa. Thus, before you buy a program for your school (or home) computer, be sure the program is on the proper size diskette for your computer. Complicating matters further, different computers with the same size disk drive (either the 5 ¼" or the 3 ½") will not necessarily have the same format. The format refers to the way information is coded or stored on the diskette. Apple and IBM/IBM compatible computer manufacturers have different ways of storing and retrieving information from diskettes. Until Apple and IBM release a compatible system, Apple computers will read information only from disks that have an Apple format while IBM/IBM compatible computers will read only disks that have an IBM format.

Unfortunately, there is yet another important consideration to be aware of with diskettes. This refers to the diskette's density. Both 3 ½" and 5 ¼" diskettes can be found in single density (SD), double-density (DD), and high-density (HD) format. Simply put, this means that different amounts of information may be stored on a disk, depending on whether it has been formatted as a single-, double-, or high-density disk, For example, a single-density 5 ¼" diskette will hold only about 360K of data, whereas a high-density 5 ¼" diskette will hold 1.2 meg. Similarly, a single-density 3 ½" disk will hold about 360K; a double-density 3 ½" disk will hold roughly 720K; and a high-density 3 ½" disk will hold about 1.44 meg. To make matters worse, without carefully reading the label it is impossible to determine a diskette's density. Fortunately, however, most computers produced today are downward compatible. This means that they typically include high-density disk drives in 3 ½", 5 ¼", or both sizes. Consequently, they can read from and write to diskettes in single-, double-, or high-density format. Problems can and will arise, however, if you purchase a program that is shipped on a double- or high-density diskette and attempt to either read from or write to this program from an older computer (i.e., like those found in many schools) with a single-density 3 ½" or 5 ¼" disk drive.

Thus, there are three major considerations in purchasing software, or computer programs on diskette. You must first identify the program in which you are interested, and, then, when you are ordering or purchasing it, be sure it is of the proper disk size and proper format (i.e., IBM or Apple), and that its density is compatible with your disk drive.

HARD DISKS. Another type of storage is the hard disk. Hard disks may be either internal or external. That is, a hard disk drive, like a floppy disk drive, may be housed separately and connected to the computer by a cable, or may be housed internally so there is no external cable or housing. Most modern PCs include internal hard drives, but some produced in the mid-late 1980s included external hard drives. Many of these are still in use in the schools. Hard disks have two major advantages over floppy disks. They can store fifty to more than a thousand times as much data as may be stored on a single floppy disk, and the use of a hard disk significantly increases the speed with which computer programs will operate. On the negative side, all the data may be lost if the hard drive fails. Thus, it is important that all information stored on hard disks is also stored (i.e., backed-up) on floppy disks or a tape drive backup unit, so that your information is not lost in the event of a hard drive or computer failure.

TAPE BACKUP DRIVES. A tape backup should not be confused with the antiquated cassette tape storage system described earlier. Tape backup units can quickly and completely copy a 40–250 meg hard drive's data in from 10–20 minutes, when floppy disk backups may require more than an hour. Most individuals in businesses rely on hard disks because of the great volume of information that these disks can contain. If your school computer has a hard disk you will be able to store years of measurement data on it and enjoy speed of operation. However, be advised to discipline yourself to create backup disks or tapes on a daily or weekly basis. Too often, computer users fail to do so until they learn this lesson the hard way.

CD-ROM. No, we are not talking about your collection of music CDs. However, a compact disc (CD) that is used for storage of computer data looks just like an audio CD. The major advantage of this mode of storage over floppy and hard disks is its capacity. A CD-ROM can store up to 650 meg (650,000,000 characters) of information. Furthermore, the speed with which programs are accessed and loaded has been described as mind-boggling and astounding, given the volumes of data that can be stored on one CD-ROM. With their tremendous storage capacity, CD-ROMs can store the contents of entire encyclopedias, collections of books, dictionaries, almanacs, etc. Like floppy and hard disk drives, CD-ROM drives may be internal or external to the computer.

CD-ROM technology is developing at the same pace as other PC-related technology. The original CD-ROM drives were single-speed units, which were quickly eclipsed by double-speed drives (the minimum standard today) that speeded up access times. Today, triple-speed and quad-speed drives are available, and eclipse the access time of double-speed drives, for two to three times the price of double-speed drives. However, as has been the case with everything else in the computer area, prices will come down. Storage capacity on a CD will soon increase from the 650 meg standard to 3 gigabytes (3,000 megs, or 3,000,000,000 bytes). These high density CDs will not be able to be read by existing CD-ROM drives. They are expected to hit the market sometime in 1996 and will be very expensive initially, so contemporary CD-ROM drives will continue to serve you well for years to come.

CD-R. At the time of this writing the first CD-R units had just appeared. The R in CD-R stands for recordable, which means that you can now write or store data, including multimedia data, on CD disks. However, this technology is expensive, with CD-R drives selling for $2500–$7000. In addition, installing and operating the software necessary to accomplish this task is currently time-consuming and complex.

Once prices come down and operational difficulties are resolved, CD-R drives may be a boon to educators. CD-R technology may hold particular promise for educational measurement. As the trend toward full inclusion of special learners in the regular classroom increases (see Chapter 20), and as the trend toward increased authentic assessment and performance assessment (see Chapter 9) grows, exciting possibilities incorporating CD-R technology are apparent. Teachers could develop not only learning modules, but multimedia, interactive assessment modules as well that could emphasize practical, authentic, and performance assessment tasks. Furthermore, once such assessment modules have been developed they can be repeatedly used to provide a semi-standardized "test" that can free the teacher from having to come up with new simulations each year, or for similar students. Only time will tell, of course, whether such promise is ever translated into day-to-day practice, but it is not too early to begin considering this possibility.

MULTIMEDIA. By adding a CD-ROM drive, 16 bit stereo sound card, and speakers to IBM/IBM compatible PCs, or a CD-ROM drive to Macintoshes (sound cards and speakers are already included with modern Macs), PCs become multimedia platforms. Simply put, this means that modern PCs (i.e., large on-board memory, giant hard drives, powerful CPUs) can be used to enjoy the increasingly sophisticated text, animated, sound, and graphics software that began to appear in the early 1990s. This is an exciting new arena for PC software developers.

There has been an explosion in new CD-ROM/Multimedia titles since the early 1990s. Developers have expanded beyond the original and still very useful encyclopedic and other text-based reference CDs to multimedia CDs that employ text, graphics, sound, and video to help you to learn a variety of subjects including foreign languages (pronunciation included), art, music, history, medicine, and various sciences. Business-related CD-ROM software has become an alternative to purchasing word processing, spreadsheet, and database management programs on diskettes. These versions now enable you to perform all the functions diskette-based versions did, and often provide additional utilities and multimedia tutorials (CD-ROM can tell and show you what to do, rather than requiring you to read and comprehend a tutorial!). To top things off, CD-ROM versions can be less expensive than their disk-based counterparts. To date, however, the potential for effective use of CD-ROM/multimedia for measurement purposes has not yet been realized. As you might expect, most of the CD-ROM/Multimedia software development thrust has been toward the highly profitable game market.

Software

Software refers to the computer programs, or list of step-by-step instructions, that tell a computer what to do. If you have ever played a home video game, you probably had to plug a cartridge into the video game unit. When you did, you were actually plugging a computer program into the video game unit. This program, or software, tells the computer how to play the video game with you. The cartridge you plugged in is one example of software. In educational settings software may be stored on cartridges such as these. Usually, it is stored on diskettes. Increasingly, it will be found on CD-ROM.

A tremendous amount of education-oriented software is available. Software packages (computer programs) useful to teachers range from programs designed to teach students how to read or how to add, subtract, multiply, and divide to programs that provide simulations of various situations, which require students to actively problem-solve or plan solutions to the problems presented. Software packages also have been developed that help teachers construct objective tests, score these tests, and analyze the test data as well as help the teacher manage such clerical functions within the classroom as keeping grades and recording homework, attendance, and tardiness.

The kinds of software and hardware available to you will be largely dependent on the insight and expertise of the individual or committee that selects the hardware and software for your particular school. In too many cases, individuals in schools have purchased hardware without first evaluating their software or program needs. This can be a costly mistake, since software from one manufacturer created for a particular type of computer (e.g., for the Macintosh) will not operate on another computer (for example, an IBM or IBM clone). Thus, you may find yourself in a position where, although your school has PCs available, the software programs that are available are either inappropriate or inadequate for your needs. Purchasing a PC hardware package without first evaluating school, classroom, or district instructional and evaluation software needs is like purchasing a textbook without knowing what subject you will teach.

Over the last several pages we have provided you with a lot of information about PCs and their potential for enhancing classroom procedures. Several important historical and technical factors to consider about this relatively new technology were reviewed. Keep in mind what we warned you about at the outset, however. While the information provided was current at the time of this fifth edition, the only constant in the PC industry is change! We turn now to how a PC processes information. Later we will provide you with a checklist you can use to guide you through the PC selection maze.

HOW A PC WORKS

A PC stores, alters, combines, and compares information. That is, it processes information. Just what is this process? Let's look at the three stages involved—input, processing, and output—as they might apply to measurement uses.

Input: The Program and the Measurement Data

The program is the how-to-do-it manual for a PC. It is a step-by-step set of specific directions that tells the central processing unit of the computer what it is to do with the information you give it. In order for the computer to be able to "listen" to the program, the program must be entered into the computer's memory. This can be done by inserting a floppy 3 ½" or 5 ¼" diskette, or a CD-ROM on which the program is written, by "calling up" the program from the hard drive if it has been stored (i.e., saved) there, or by actually writing a program into the computer's memory by typing in the instructions at the computer's keyboard.

Although writing a computer program yourself may never be necessary, should you need to write one, it will require knowledge of one of several computer languages. These languages comprise special words that have specific meanings that the computer understands. You may have learned (or will learn) one or more of these languages in a computer literacy course. If you did, you probably learned a computer language called BASIC (Beginner's All-Purpose Symbolic Instruction Code). BASIC is a widely used interactive programming language that can be used for testing and measurement tasks and most school-related instruction. It is simple and fun to learn, and it is flexible enough to be used for almost any testing and measurement problem (computing reliability, validity, test scoring and recording, etc.) and any instructional problem (teaching vocabulary or arithmetic, solving social studies problems, conducting simulated chemistry and physics experiments, etc.). If you were to write a simple program in BASIC, telling the computer to find the mean of four student scores, the program would look like the following:

```
5 REM CALCULATE THE MEAN OF 4 NUMBERS

10 PRINT "ENTER THE 4 NUMBERS FOR WHICH

15 PRINT YOU WISH TO CALCULATE THE MEAN"

20 INPUT A, B, C, D

25 LET X = (A + B + C + D)/4

30 PRINT "THE MEAN IS"; X

40 END
```

Here is a translation of some of the words that appear in the program:

REM	allows you to add remarks within a program for your information to help whoever uses your program
PRINT	allows you to print a variable or expression
INPUT	allows you to input data from the keyboard
LET	allows you to assign a new value to a specified variable
END	is the last statement in every BASIC program

When you use the program written here, only the second, third, and sixth lines (lines 10, 15, and 30) cause anything to appear on the video screen. The mean you requested would appear in place of the X in line 30. Of course, BASIC can be used to solve far more complicated problems than this, including word problems, such as the teaching of reading or vocabulary. This short example should give you a feel for the simple procedures that need to be learned in order for you to write your own programs.

Since you are likely to hear of them, here are some other computer languages often used with PCs:

COBOL. (COmmon Business-Oriented Language). A computer language designed mainly for programming business applications.

PASCAL. A high-level, general purpose programming language, similar to BASIC but allowing more sophistication.

FORTRAN. (FORmula TRANslator). A computer language designed primarily for programming scientific applications.

APL. (A Programming Language). A computer language designed primarily for programming mathematical applications.

LOGO. A simple-to-learn computer language which emphasizes graphic applications.

PILOT. A simplified computer language, PILOT is one type of "authoring program" that enables an individual without training in BASIC or any other formal computer language to develop instructional and measurement programs.

Unless you have had training in one of these computer programming languages, you will likely be using commercial programs on diskette or CD-ROM, or programs already stored on your computer's hard drive. Whether you use commercial software packages or program the computer yourself, you will need to input the data, or the information, you want the computer to process. For classroom measurement purposes, these data may be in the form of text (for example, instructional objectives, test items, or complete tests) or numbers (test scores, item analysis data). Fortunately, inputting data to the PC is straightforward and knowledge of a programming language is not necessary. The software you are using will tell you what to input and when. In short, if you can type, you can operate a PC software package. Loading a program into a PC's memory and feeding the data into memory in accord with the directions the program gives you constitute the input.

Processing: The Central Processing Unit (CPU)

Once the data have been entered via the keyboard, the CPU begins processing the data according to the instructions it gets from the program. The CPU or chip is often referred to as the "brain" of the microcomputer. This is an unfortunate choice of words, since the CPU or chip is really not very "brainy." It cannot think, it cannot feel, it cannot be creative. However, it is an extremely obedient and fast processor of information. The CPU does exactly and only what it is told to do by the program, that is, by the human programmer—no more and no less. Thus, a "smart" program will make the computer appear smart, and a "dumb" program will make it appear dumb.

Intense competition and dizzying technological advances over the last few years have led to significantly more powerful chips for both the Macintosh and IBM and IBM compatible computers. More powerful IBM/IBM compatible chips in particular have been emerging, on average, every 18–24 months. The first IBM and compatible computers utilized a chip known as the 8086 or "XT" chip. Since then the "86" family of chips has evolved through the 80286 or "AT" chip, the 386SX and 386DX chips, to the 486SX chip to what is currently considered an "entry level" PC processor, the 486DX chip. At the time of this revision even the 486DX chips are headed for obsolescence as the 586 or "Pentium" chip is rapidly becoming the standard. For Macintosh users the "state of the art" chip is the 68LCO40 66/33.

Unlike the often cosmetic changes that accompany a "new" model year in the auto industry, the evolution of these chips has brought with it dramatic improvements in CPU power and flexibility. The newer 486 and 586 or Pentium chips are processing at "clock speeds" (i.e., processing speeds) of 100 mhz and more. By comparison, the 8086 or XT chip processed at 4 mhz. This suggests that today's chips process 25 times faster than the older chips. This is misleading, however. The newer chips are so technologically superior to the older chips that they are not only more than 25 times faster, they are also capable of multitasking (i.e., running more than one program simultaneously) and of handling computational tasks that were simply impossible for the older chips.

Beyond speed and power, the newer chips enable technological advances that were once considered science fiction. Some PCs can now recognize voice commands, accept input in writing from special input "pens," suggest alternatives for awkward grammar, and correct misspellings. These innovations, at the time of this writing, are in their infancy, but progress and promise are clearly present. Nonetheless, a PC still cannot do your thinking and planning for you. Correctly inputting data and instructions remains vital to the computing success. As computerphiles are inclined to say, "garbage in, garbage out."

After the CPU completes processing the data according to the program's directions, it sends the results of its processing to the video monitor, to a printer, or to a memory storage center for future access. This may be on a diskette or a hard disk. In the future this may also be a CD-R. The result of the CPU's processing is called *output*.

Output (Video, Printed Copy, Storage)

Output is the end result of the CPU's processing. Output is the product we want the computer to produce. Most often this will be processed information. Output for measurement purposes may be in a variety of forms, including item analysis and statistical data, test items, tests, student names, grades, objectives, and even the identification of student strengths and weaknesses.

Typically, output is first viewed on the video monitor. Afterward, decisions are made whether to eliminate, save, or print all or parts of the output. If it is to be printed, a special command is used to activate the printer. This will provide what is called *hard copy* of the output. If you decide to save the information on diskette or hard disk, another command is used to accomplish this. The output may then be obtained as needed at any time from the diskette or hard disk. If the output (tests, items, test scores, grades) will be used more than once, it is saved to avoid having to input it at a later time.

Monitor Evolution

As with chips, there have been manifold technological advances in monitors, printers, and hard drives. When our first edition was published, monochrome and color CGA monitors were the standard. These early color monitors were crude by today's standard and were impossible for serious text or graphics work. Thus, business and text-based users used only monochrome monitors. Over the years the clarity and flexibility of color monitors improved through EGA and VGA technology, but these remained poor choices for text-based applications. The typical PC today comes equipped with a Super VGA (SVGA) color monitor with 256 color combinations and one or two megs of its own memory to assist in rapid refreshment of its increasingly detailed and complex graphics screens. In addition, these monitors often have a .28 dot pitch, which means that the monitors are as sharp and clear as monochrome monitors for working with text and numbers. Modern SVGA monitors are also "non-interlaced." Simply put, this means they have significantly less screen flicker than the older generation of interlaced SVGA monitors. Thus, they are much easier on the eyes over long periods of time. Older VGA, EGA, and CGA monitors were fine for games and some graphics, but with dot pitches in the .51 or even larger range, the characters they formed often were too fuzzy to allow for prolonged text-based work without eyestrain and frustration.

Printer Evolution

In the past choosing a printer meant deciding between a relatively fast but noisy and fuzzy 9-pin dot-matrix printer and noisy, slow but typewriter-quality daisy wheel printers. Today, daisy wheel printers have become dinosaurs, like audiocassette recorders and 8086 chips. While a few inexpensive 9-pin dot-matrix printers can still be found, they have been replaced by 24-pin dot-matrix printers capable of creating near letter quality print at high speeds. Even these, however, are rapidly being replaced by laser printers and less expensive ink-jet and bubble-jet printers. All these produce letter quality text as fast or faster than the 24-pin dot-matrix printers, and they do it almost silently, by comparison. In addition, a new generation of color ink-jet and bubble-jet printers is now available for \$100–\$200 more than a comparable black and white printer. While the color-printed output from these printers does not match that of color printers costing thousands of dollars more, being able to add color to transparencies, tests, and handouts can add a high interest dimension to teacher-produced measurement and curriculum materials. Today, the picture for printers parallels that for PCs: better quality for less cost.

Hard Drive Evolution

Early PC users eagerly embraced the first hard drives because they made it unnecessary to engage in the repetitive disk-swapping required by early non-hard drive 8086s and Macintoshes. These early hard drives came in 5 meg, 10 meg, and 20 meg capacities, which at the time seemed gargantuan. A 20 meg drive was more than adequate to store multiple programs and data files. Today, however, a single Windows-based program can use more than 20 megs of disk space, and the trend toward huge programs will continue in the foreseeable future. Thus, hard drive capacity has increased by leaps and bounds in recent years. Today, an entry level IBM compatible PC should have at least a 500 meg hard drive, if it is to be used by a single user for typical use. However, hard drives with 600 meg to 1000 meg (i.e., 1 gigabyte) are now common, and even these may be inadequate in the not-too-distant future. For the Macintosh, a hard drive with 300 meg storage can be considered the minimum acceptable standard.

Over the last few pages we have tried to bring you "up to speed" regarding the latest technological advances at the time this edition was being written. We have no doubt, however, that much of what we have provided will be outdated by the time we are working on our next edition. Lest you despair about trying to keep up with this rapidly evolving technology, let us put these developments in a different, more pleasant perspective.

As potent as today's PCs are compared to those available in the early 1980s, their prices have not increased! In fact, today's PCs, even equipped with the latest chips, monitors, huge hard drives, fax/modems, CD-Rom/multimedia and a quiet letter-quality printer can be purchased for less than typical IBM or Apple PCs a decade ago.

Now that you have a better understanding of what PCs are and how they operate, let's consider how they can facilitate classroom measurement.

PC APPLICATIONS IN CLASSROOM MEASUREMENT

In this section we will describe how PCs can facilitate and improve various aspects of measurement practice. We will consider the various ways in which a PC can assist the classroom teacher with instructional objectives; test items; test development and analysis; scoring or grading and recording of in-class and homework assignments, projects, and tests; assignment of final marks; and various statistical analyses. A caution regarding the security of our electronic data will also be offered.

Instructional Objectives

One of the measurement tasks teachers find tedious is the writing of instructional objectives. Educational software will not minimize the necessary skills and time initially needed to construct good instructional objectives, but a word processing program (a program that allows you to add, delete, shift, or revise written information quickly and efficiently) enables teachers to modify their objectives from year to year to reflect changing educational trends and goals. This minimizes clerical time and increases the amount of time you have available for instructional or other measurement tasks. Saving instructional objectives on a diskette or hard drive facilitates analysis of objectives and sharing of well-written objectives among teachers at the same grade level, saving still more time and leading to better-written objectives, thereby improving measurement practice. Finally, printing the objectives and distributing them to your students, especially in the secondary grades, will help students focus on the most relevant content areas. Changing the lists as your goals change is simplified, and printing the new list requires minimal time and effort.

Test Items

Similar reasoning applies to test items as applies to instructional objectives. With a word processing program, you can easily make minor or major modifications to test items or even whole tests. You can print new versions much more quickly than you or a typist could make changes with a typewriter. This could be a major time saver. Similarly, sharing of well-written items is facilitated if they are stored on a diskette or hard drive and available to all teachers, either by sharing diskettes and hard drives or through a LAN. Software is available that assists the teacher in constructing test items. By indicating common faults of a test item, these programs minimize the chances that you will construct and use poor items. Programs are also available that will generate alternate forms of tests according to instructional objectives and difficulty levels. Given a pool of test items and their difficulty levels, the computer could be instructed to make a number of shorter tests based on common objectives and at prespecified difficulty levels, thereby ensuring that different tests would be comparable.

As the trend increases toward full inclusion (see Chapter 20) of special learners into the regular classroom, the need for a broader range of item difficulties and formats will increase. The PC may be helpful in this regard, allowing easier and more accurate item storage, modification, and incorporation into tests of varying lengths and difficulties. Being able to use a PC to efficiently "customize" tests designed for a classroom of regular education students to fit the needs of the special learners who will increasingly show up in your classes will enable you to devote more time to instructional activities, and minimize the frustration of having to "start from scratch" with each new addition to your class.

Tests

Software is available that will guide the classroom teacher through the entire test construction process, from writing instructional objectives, through matching items to objectives, to assembling and analyzing the test. It is in this last area, test and item analysis, that the PC's power and convenience may prove most beneficial. Programs to compute item difficulty levels and discrimination indices are available, and quantitative item analyses of objective test items are now a reality for the busy classroom teacher. Also available are programs that enable the teacher to determine the reliability of classroom tests.

Statistical packages and data management programs make it possible for classroom teachers to keep accurate and comprehensive records of student performances over the course of the year, and over several years. This enables the teacher to compare classes, tests, and curricula; to identify aptitude-achievement discrepancies; and to evaluate the effects of new instructional techniques on test performance. For the first time, the classroom teacher is able to objectively and scientifically analyze data from classroom tests without all the hand calculation that otherwise would be necessary. When these data are considered along with standardized test data, they enhance instruction and increase the satisfaction of pupils, parents, and administrators with the measurement process.

Grades

Just as some PC programs enable teachers to collect and analyze test scores, other programs enable teachers to do the same with grades. Trends like grade inflation or declines in basic skills are easier to identify and correct if these data are stored for ready reference. Software is available that can automatically keep track of student performance for an entire class as students work their way through an instructional program. When used as an adjunct to more traditional educational methods, such an approach can go far toward providing an extra dose of drill and practice or tutorial assistance to students in need (e.g., special learners included in the regular classroom) without adding to the teacher's already heavy instructional and record-keeping burden.

Statistical Analysis

While we have already mentioned several ways in which the statistical power of the PC can be used in measurement applications, a variety of other applications also exist. These include computing summary statistics for grade-level, school, or PTA meetings and the preparation of reports for parent conferences. Before describing how software can help us with these measurement tasks, we will caution you about the security of electronic data.

Electronic Security

With the advent of LANs, which were described earlier, sharing of goals, objectives, and other measurement data can be greatly facilitated. However, as described by Spetalnick (1994), the advantage of easy data access and sharing afforded by LANs brings with it a potentially serious downside. What is shared in a LAN is electronic, intangible data, rather than printed data. Thus, in allowing for greater flexibility the LAN also compromises the security of the data accessible through it. Unless password regulated, anyone on the LAN may access any information processed or stored on any PC that is part of the LAN. Thus, issues of program security and personal data privacy and integrity are a concern. If you are part of a LAN it may be useful to keep Spetalnick's (1994) caveat in mind: "electronic communications are about as private as a postcard" (p.40).

We do not believe the previous list of PC applications to testing and measurement is exhaustive. At the same time, we hope we have not overwhelmed you or presented too rosy a picture of what we believe can be the potential impact of PCs on testing and measurement in the classroom. We believe these applications will save teachers time, lead to better measurement practice, and provide the teacher with important data regarding instructional methods that ordinarily would not be available at the time they are needed.

PCs are not, however, panaceas for every classroom or every teacher; like tests, they can be used or abused. Our hope is that you use them.

MEASUREMENT-RELATED SOFTWARE

In past editions of this text we have reviewed a variety of measurement-related software packages to provide you with a reference in purchasing software once you enter the classroom. However, in this edition we have decided to eliminate this section, for the reasons that follow, and instead provide suggestions for you to follow in finding measurement-related software appropriate to your needs.

Volume and Updates

The sheer volume of educational and measurement-related software titles today make a review or even a listing of them impractical in the space we have available. Furthermore, software is constantly being updated, with new features added that may at times have significant bearing on a purchaser's decision. These revisions often take place annually, whereas our text is revised on a three-year basis.

Installed Programs and LANs

By now, many schools and districts have already purchased measurement and classroom management software packages and either require teachers to use these packages to maintain uniformity, or these have been installed on the hard drives of the computer(s) made available to teachers. Similarly, if your school has installed a LAN, you may be limited to accessing only the software installed on the server (i.e., the main computer that all other PC "stations" access to obtain programs and data).

Developer Turnover

In the hotly competitive software marketplace it is not unusual for a piece of software to be marketed commercially by one company for a few months or a year, only to see that company be purchased or merged with another company. Alternatively, the publisher may go bankrupt, and the software may then be marketed under a different name or manufacturer, or the software may "disappear" while an update is completed. It can be very frustrating to purchase a piece of commercial software, then call the manufacturer's technical support number for an installation or operations problem only to hear the telephone company's ear piercing triple tone followed by the message "That number has been disconnected and is no longer in service."

Shareware and Electronic Bulletin Boards (BBS)

Many excellent measurement-related software packages are being developed by private individuals and offered for use as "shareware" through one of many electronic bulletin board services (BBS). Using a modem, a PC user "calls up" a BBS and "downloads" a program. This involves transferring the file from the mainframe bulletin board computer to your PC through the electronic link your modem provides. Once you download this program into your PC's hard drive, usually you are allowed several uses free of charge to "try out" the program. After several free uses you are asked to register for the program by sending a fee (usually around $25) to the developer. If you do not pay, the program will usually lock itself up to prevent further unauthorized use.

On-line Services and the Internet

Shareware programs are added to various BBS on an almost daily basis and are of varying quality. Because of their rapidity of release and their great variability there is no way to keep up with them. Thus, instead of trying to review them, we have listed and described briefly in Appendix E several of the more popular "on-line" or "cyberspace" services that enable you to most easily access the electronic bulletin boards and the shareware they contain. Each of these services charges a monthly fee, with additional fees assessed for "premium" services. By joining one of these services you will be able to access these programs directly and evaluate their appropriateness for your needs. On-line services provide on-line help for your search, as well as telephone support services. In addition, these services either already, or soon will, allow access to the world-wide "Information Superhighway" or Internet at an additional cost to their regular on-line services. Whether or not this will allow you an advantage over the existing BBS system to evaluate shareware or obtain other educational and measurement-related information remains to be seen.

Shareware Catalog

As an alternative to scanning ("surfing" to cyberspace junkies) the many BBS or the Internet for measurement software, you can call Public Brand Software at 1-800-426-3475 and order a catalog of public domain shareware. Once you have perused the catalog you can order the software you want to "test drive," usually for $5 or less per disk. Often the disk will contain more than one program.

The final section of this chapter concerns the process of selecting a microcomputer. We believe this section to be one the most important, since purchasing the wrong computer will likely do little more to improve educational measurement than would selection of the wrong standardized test.

STEPS IN SELECTING A PC

In Chapter 19 we presented a step-by-step approach to the design and implementation of a school-wide testing program.

In this section we will present a similar step-by-step approach to the selection of a PC. As a classroom teacher, you may not have much to say about the kinds of software and hardware your school selects. As with standardized test selection, too often it is the case that such decisions are made at administrative levels without soliciting input from classroom teachers. However, you may be asked for input, and if you are, the decision-making steps presented in this chapter should help organize your thinking and perhaps the thinking of the selection committee. Furthermore, there is no reason you could not use this same process to select a PC for yourself.

As mentioned, the exploding popularity of PCs has brought with it some resistance. Part of this negative reaction stems from the underutilization of PCs once they are brought into a school setting. Unfortunately, all too often they are relegated to the category of typewriters or game machines. Even more disconcerting, the authors have seen many simply gather dust. By following these guidelines, you will minimize the likelihood that these valuable resources will be wasted in your school.

Step 1: Identify Objectives

Identify specific objectives for the use of the PC. This is probably self-evident, but this step is too frequently overlooked. Sometimes the only objective seems to be "get a PC" or "get as many PCs as we can." When such objectives dominate thinking, the end result is all too often a PC that fails to run the software needed to achieve your educational goals. Indeed, the authors are aware of situations wherein naive school personnel have fallen prey to beeps, blinking lights, high-technology jargon, and a high pressure sales pitch, ending up with a PC but without software that is suitable to their purposes.

Our first recommendation, then, is that specific objectives be identified. "To aid in testing" is not specific enough. "To generate alternate forms of multiple-choice tests" or "to maintain records of student achievement in resource rooms," or "to weight and combine scores for class work, homework, reports, and tests into six-week and semester marks" are specific objectives. In formulating objectives, consider the following:

WHAT ARE THE USES TO WHICH THE PC WILL BE PUT? PC programs are available to assist in test construction, administration, scoring, analysis, and storing of records. Other education-related uses for the PC include administrative (accounting, attendance, grading, word processing, recordkeeping, planning, and projecting); instructional (drill and practice in basic skills, tutorial, and simulations); programming (teachers and students learning computer languages); instructional management (classroom recordkeeping); guidance; and research applications.

WHAT FUTURE USES CAN BE ANTICIPATED? Plan hardware and software applications for your school and school district as they will be five years from now. If enrollment is increasing, project what it is likely to be in five years and use these data in helping determine how many PCs may be needed. Most important, try to determine how specific subject matter specialists in math, chemistry, English, social studies, and so on, see the future role of the PC in their disciplines. Will science instructors be turning to more specialized multimedia applications of the PC for graphic simulations of lab experiments? Will language arts teachers be using the computer almost exclusively for word processing and tutorial training in composition writing?

With the increasing emphasis being placed on performance assessment (see Chapter 9), will computer-generated scenarios, simulations, and multimedia presentations be needed? Finally, will your school or district begin to establish LANs? If so, what kind of performance capabilities of different LAN options (there are several) will be needed to obtain maximum performance from the linked PCs? These trends and requirements should play an important role in the types of hardware and software that are purchased. They also speak for the need for any specific recommendations to be developed by an interdisciplinary team of teachers. Finally, will your school be accessing a BBS and/or the Internet? If so, then a high speed (i.e., 14,400 baud or more) modem will decrease long-term costs and short-term time wasted waiting for information to be sent and received.

WHAT GRADE LEVELS ARE BEING CONSIDERED FOR PC USE? Since the tasks required of the computer differ considerably by grade level, so should the type and complexity of the computer. Computer literacy can be accomplished adequately on older PCs that are no longer capable of running modern memory-hungry programs. Sophisticated problem-solving simulations that might be standard fare in high-school social studies, computer science, and science classes require a more powerful and flexible PC (i.e., one with a 486DX or newer chip, CD-ROM/multimedia, modem or fax/modem and 8 megs or more of memory). Most schools or school districts need a mix of PCs, but that mix can be very different depending on whether the school is lower elementary, upper elementary, or secondary; whether PCs must serve both students and teachers; and whether the PCs must serve all subject matter areas or only certain ones.

Step 2: Identify Software

Identify the software necessary to meet your specific objectives. If step 1 looked complicated and time-consuming, wait until you get to step 2! As we mentioned earlier, there are literally thousands of educational programs on the market. For measurement purposes, the supply of educational software is somewhat smaller. However, you still must evaluate each software program individually to determine whether it meets your needs. Unfortunately, there is a great deal of variability in the quality of software. How does one go about reviewing such software? Fortunately, many reputable software distributors will make available to school personnel examination copies of their programs. In some cases representatives will be sent to the school upon request. These requests should be written on school or district letterhead to elicit the distributors' cooperation. If a manufacturer or distributor refuses to cooperate, avoid purchasing their wares. Reputable firms will not shy away from making their programs available to schools on an examination basis. As we mentioned earlier, explore what is available as shareware through a BBS. This public-domain software is nearly always available for limited uses at no charge. Take shareware for a "test drive," only paying the registration fee for the shareware that does the job you want it to. Once you have screened the software that is available for your purposes and made your selection, then you are ready for the next step.

Step 3: Identify Special Features

Using your objectives and the software you have selected, identify the features you will need in your PC and related components. This is important if the software and hardware is to be compatible, that is, if the PC is to have sufficient memory to run the software or the color or graphics capability called for by the software. Some of the features to consider include the chip's processing power, a math co-processor (i.e., a second chip that is devoted to processing mathematical functions and which dramatically speeds up computational time in 8086, 286, 386, and 486SX computers—486DX and Pentium-based computers already have math co-processors built into their chips), memory, peripherals, keyboard, video monitor and video memory, modem or fax/modem, hard drive, CD-ROM/multimedia, graphics, color, sound and music, language, and cost and service.

MEMORY. In general, the more memory, the better. White (1994) reported that the most cost-effective way to upgrade a PC's performance is to add memory. Be sure you know how much memory your software requires. Your PC must have at least that amount, and more memory will speed up processing time. Minimum for older PC programs is about 128K to 512K. Modern programs will often require 4 megs or more for Macintosh-based programs and 8 megs or more for IBM and IBM compatible programs, especially if they are designed for the graphical Windows interface. With modern Windows programs 16 megs is often recommended to avoid frustrating waits for the screen to refresh itself.

PERIPHERALS. What kind and how many peripherals will you need to meet your objectives? Printers (dot matrix, laser or ink-jet); hard disk, tape backup and CD-ROM drives; sound card and speakers for multimedia; light pens to provide input by pointing to a place on the video display; scanners that can copy text or graphics into the computer's memory; voice synthesizers to hear programs that "speak"; voice recognition cards that translate a human voice into a set of PC instructions, modems or fax/modems to connect your PC to other computers (e.g., BBS mainframes or colleagues in other towns) or fax machines; and PC-based answering machines or voice mail all ought to be considered. Finally, keep in mind that LANs can provide your school with the option of sharing expensive peripherals amongst multiple PCs housed in different classrooms on campus. Look for hard disks with capacities of 500 megs or more and modems/fax-modems with speeds of 14,400 baud or higher.

KEYBOARD. If your PC is to be used by young children, a transparent, resilient keyboard cover can be used with standard keyboards to afford protection from debris and grimy fingers in the younger grades. If your objectives include teaching programming or word processing, the cover can be removed since the standard keyboard would then be easier to work with. Keyboards should include a separate number pad, which is useful for mathematical data entry.

VIDEO MONITOR. Much has changed in the visual display area over the last several years. When PCs were first developed, television sets often were used as monitors. Today, however, the situation has reversed itself. PCs equipped with sound cards and television receiver cards are now serving double duty as televisions when they are not being used as computers! Newer computers do not even offer the black-and-white or green phosphorous screens that were common in the 1980s, and which may still be used in your school. As video displays have increased in speed, detail, and clarity over the years, the benefits of larger monitors have become evident. The 14" monitor, standard in the late 1980s, is quickly being replaced by 15" monitors and 17" and larger monitors are now available. The development of non-interlaced monitors with dot pitches of .28 or less has reduced eyestrain and made modern SVGA color monitors acceptable for word processing and text-based applications.

VIDEO MEMORY. No, this is not a misprint. Modern video cards require their own memory separate from the memory required by the CPU. The video display cards that drive or operate the monitors now include their own memory in order to more quickly renew or refresh screens. Just as with the "main body" of the PC, the more memory you can get, the better and faster your monitor will operate. Minimum should be one meg, with two or more megs better.

SOUND OR MUSIC. This capability enables you to provide an auditory cue or signal to students at various points in a testing program. Others may use it for entertainment or creative purposes. All modern PCs include sound as a standard feature, although standard sound on a Macintosh is superior to an IBM or compatible PC. However, a variety of add-on speakers and sound cards (e.g., Sound Blaster) are available for the IBM and compatible market. This enables the sound quality on these machines to exceed that of the Macintosh. Sound cards should be 16 bit stereo at least.

CD-ROM/MULTIMEDIA. Coupled with a sound card and speakers, the addition of a CD-ROM drive enables you to enjoy the increasingly broad selection of books, art, music, games, and other applications now available on this format. Look for a double speed CD-ROM, although triple and quadruple speed drives were just beginning to appear as this fifth edition was being prepared.

LANGUAGES. Determine which languages are best suited to your needs. For most testing and instructional uses, BASIC is adequate. Other languages may be needed to meet special needs.

COST AND SERVICE. Don't forget your budget, and don't forget someone will have to set up and maintain your system. Shopping for the best price can be a false economy if you cannot get quick and reliable service after the usual 90-day warranty runs out. Mail-order prices are usually better than retail, but may prove more expensive in the long run. While most manufacturers provide a "help" line number to call for support, these lines are often busy. Furthermore, they are often not toll free. Thus, a hidden cost of a PC can be time spent waiting on hold for an out of state long-distance call. Contacting the sales representative at the local outlet that sold your system may be much simpler, less time consuming, and less frustrating.

Step 4: Compare

Once you've identified the features you need, compare the different machines and rate them. To facilitate this step, use the rating chart in Table 21.1. Once you have identified the units that best meet your needs, get hands-on experience with each unit before making your final selection. Too often individuals fail to put in the necessary hands-on time and purchase on impulse or recommendation from someone who may have different

TABLE 21.1
Rating PCs by Features

Features	*PCs Considered* 1	2	3	4	5
Available software (list for your objectives)					
Chip (486DX or Pentium for IBM compatibles) (68LCO40 66/33 for Macintosh)					
Memory (8 megs minimum, 8–16 megs for Windows applications) (4 megs minimum for Macintosh)					
Peripherals (hard and tape drives; modem or fax/modem; CD-ROM/multimedia; scanner; dot-matrix, laser, ink-jet, or bubble-jet color, or black and white printer; voice synthesizer; light pen; television receiver card)					
Keyboard (transparent overlay)					
Video monitor (size at least 14", dot-pitch of at least .28, non-interlaced SVGA color, at least one meg of video memory)					
Languages (BASIC, COBOL, PASCAL, LOGO, FORTRAN, APL, others)					
Cost					
Service (warranty service availability)					

needs. In such cases, dissatisfaction or disgust may be the outcome. Now perhaps you can see why so many PCs sit unused or are underused in schools. No tool, no matter how good, is helpful if it's not used. When the opportunity presents itself, use the PC to make your teaching easier and more effective.

SUMMARY

In this chapter we have introduced you to issues related to testing and the personal computer (PC). Its major points are:

1. The PC is a tool that manages and processes information. As such, it can be used by the classroom teacher to generate test items and tests; perform item and test analyses; create, update, and maintain instructional objectives; and store, compute, and analyze grades.
2. In spite of their time-saving potential, PCs often are underutilized, usually due to unwarranted fears on the part of untrained teachers.
3. A mainframe computer is a large and expensive machine housed in a specially prepared facility where temperature and humidity can be maintained at precise levels.
4. A minicomputer is a smaller and less expensive machine than a mainframe, used primarily by businesses to manage large amounts of information and to perform clerical tasks. As PCs have become increasingly powerful they have come to replace minicomputers.
5. A PC is the smallest and least expensive computer that is applicable to the instructional, measurement, and other data processing needs of schools.
6. Components of a PC system can be divided into hardware and software.
7. Hardware components consist of a keyboard, a central processing unit (called a CPU), a video-display terminal, and additional hardware components (called peripherals).
8. Software consists of the computer programs that give step-by-step directions to the computer.
9. Generally, computer software is not interchangeable from one brand of PC to another. This necessitates the careful matching of software and computer before making a purchase.
10. The work of a PC can be divided into three stages: input, processing, and output.
11. The PC can be used for:
    a. Storing, updating, and printing instructional objectives
    b. Randomly selecting test items from a large pool of items according to objective, difficulty level, or some other criteria
    c. Calculating quantitative item analyses, indicating test item faults
    d. Keeping records of student performance over different tests
    e. Calculating, averaging, and storing grades
    f. Tracking changes in pupil test performance as a result of new teaching methods, instructional materials, or curricula
    g. Summarizing large amounts of data by grade level and school
12. Because of rapid technological advances PCs today are many times more powerful than those placed in service even a few years ago. For maximum

benefit from modern software, CD-ROM/Multimedia, BBS, Internet, and LAN applications, modern PCs are required (i.e., the newest chips, large memories and large capacity hard drives, high speed modems).

14. Steps in selecting a PC consist of the following:
    a. Identifying your specific objectives for the use of a PC
    b. Identifying the software available to meet your specific objectives
    c. Identifying the features you will need in your computer and related software to meet your objectives
    d. Comparing the different computers and rating them according to the features listed in Table 21.1

For Discussion

1. The terms *hardware* and *software* come up repeatedly when educators discuss PCs. Imagine you are talking with a teacher who is totally unfamiliar with such jargon. How would you explain the difference between these terms? What examples could you give of each?

2. You have helped another teacher become familiar with computer hardware and software. Now the teacher asks, "How does a computer work?" Assume you can't run and hide. How would you respond to this question? (*Hint*: Try to organize your answer around the terms *input, processing,* and *output.*)

3. Imagine that you have access to a PC at your school. To what measurement-related uses could you put the computer? (*Note*: Respond in terms of your own area of specialization—reading, math, science, special education, and so on.)

4. Because of your recent completion of a course in tests and measurements that included PC selection and use, your principal designates you to be your school's representative at the district's Committee for Computer Acquisitions. At the first meeting the chairperson asks whether anybody has any objections to "simply getting as many ABC Computers as our budget allows, and then building our computer training around them." How would you respond? What would your alternative recommendation(s) be?

*5. Mr. Joseph is the chair of your school's newly formed Multimedia Committee. He wants to spend $300 of the $6000 allocated to the committee on a CD/ROM Multimedia kit to upgrade the school's 386SX–25 IBM Clone with 2 megs of memory and an 80 meg hard drive since it was purchased just two years previously. He wants to spend the rest on CD-ROM/Multimedia software to "bring us into the 21st century." Why may Mr. Joseph, other teachers, students, administrators, and parents be disappointed if this course of action is followed? What alternative course might be suggested?

*Answer to Question 5 appears in Appendix D.

CHAPTER 22

In the Classroom: A Summary Dialogue

The following is a dialogue between Ms. Wilson, a sixth-grade teacher, and some of the school staff with whom she works. Ms. Wilson is three months into her first teaching assignment at a middle school in a medium-sized metropolitan school district. We begin our dialogue with Ms. Wilson on a Friday afternoon as she wraps up the final class session before a quarterly testing period is to begin.

MS. WILSON: I know you all feel we've covered a tremendous amount this year. Well, you're right. We have. And now it's time to find out how much you've learned. It's important for you to know how well you're doing in each subject so you can work harder in the areas where you might need improvement. It's also nice to know in what areas you might be smarter than almost everyone else. So, next week, I want you to be ready to take tests over all the material we have covered so far. (*A few students groan in unison.*) Remember, this will be your chance to show me how smart you are. I want you to get plenty of sleep Sunday night so you'll be fresh and alert Monday. (*As the bell rings, Ms. Wilson shouts over the commotion of students leaving the classroom.*) Don't forget, I'll be collecting homework on Monday!

(*As Ms. Wilson collapses into her chair, Ms. Palmer, an experienced teacher, walks in.*)

MS. PALMER: Glad this grading period is just about over. Next week will be a nice break, don't you think? Just reviewing and giving tests. It'll sure be nice to have this weekend free without any preparations to worry about.

MS. WILSON: You mean you won't be making up tests this weekend!

MS. PALMER: No. I have tests from the last three years which I've been refining and improving. With only a few modifications, they'll do fine.

MS. WILSON: You're awfully lucky. I'm afraid I haven't had a chance to even think about how I'm going to test these kids. All these subjects to make tests for, and then all the scoring and grading to do by next Friday. I think I'm going to have an awful weekend.

MS. PALMER: Will you be giving criterion-referenced or norm-referenced tests?

MS. WILSON: Umm . . . well . . . I don't know. I remember hearing those terms in a tests and measurement class I once took, but I guess I just haven't had time to worry about those things until now. I suppose I'm going to have to get my old textbook out tonight and do some reviewing. Gosh! I hope I can find it.

MS. PALMER: Well, if you use norm-referenced tests, there are some available in Ms. Cartwright's office. You know, she's the counselor who is always so helpful with discipline problems. In fact, she has a whole file full of tests.

MS. WILSON: Will *you* be using norm-referenced tests next week?

MS. PALMER: Not really. For these mid-semester grades, I like to make my tests very specific to what I've been teaching. At this point in the year it seems to provide better feedback to the kids and parents—especially the parents. Anyway, the parents aren't really interested in where their kid scores in relation to other students until later in the semester, when I've covered more content and the kids have had a chance to get their feet on the ground.

MS. WILSON: You mean these norm-referenced tests don't cover specifically what you've taught?

MS. PALMER: (*trying to be tactful*) Well, no. Not exactly. I guess you have forgotten a few things since you took that tests and measurement course.

MS. WILSON: I guess so.

MS. PALMER: Why don't you make a test blueprint and compare it to some of the items in Ms. Cartwright's test file?

MS. WILSON: A test *what* print?

MS. PALMER: A test blueprint. You know, where you take the objectives from your lesson plans and construct a table that shows the content you've been teaching and the level of complexity—knowledge, comprehension, application—that you're shooting for. Then, see how Ms. Cartwright's tests match the test blueprint.

MS. WILSON: But what if I didn't write down all my objectives? I had objectives, of course, but I just didn't write them down all the time, or when I did, I usually didn't keep them for long. You know what I mean? (*No comment from Ms. Palmer.*) And I don't think I wrote them so they included levels of complexity according to that taxonomy-of-objectives thing I think you're referring to.

MS. PALMER: But I'm afraid that without objectives, you won't know if the items on Ms. Cartwright's tests match what you've taught. Would you believe that last year a teacher in this school flunked half his class using a test that didn't match what he taught? Boy, what a stir that caused!

MS. WILSON: (*looking worried*) I guess I'll have to start from scratch, then. It looks like a very long weekend.

MS. PALMER: Of course, you might consider giving some essay items.

MS. WILSON: You mean long-answer, not multiple-choice questions?

MS. PALMER: Yes, but you'll have to consider the time it will take to develop a scoring guide for each question and the time you'll spend grading all those answers. And, then, of course, only some of your objectives may be suited to an essay format.

MS. WILSON: (*trying to sort out all of what Ms. Palmer just said without sounding too stupid*) By scoring guide, do you mean the right answer?

MS. PALMER: Well, not quite. As you know, essay items can have more than one right answer. So, first you will have to identify all the different elements that make an answer right and then decide how to weight or assign points to each of these elements, depending on what percentage of the right answer they represent.

MS. WILSON: How do you decide that?

MS. PALMER: (*trying to be polite and being evasive for the sake of politeness*) Well . . . very carefully.

MS. WILSON: I see. (*long pause*) Well, maybe my old tests and measurement book will have something on that.

MS. PALMER: I'm sure it will.

MS. WILSON: Sounds as though I have my work cut out for me. I guess I'll just have to organize my time and start to work as soon as I get home.

(Ms. Palmer and Ms. Wilson leave the classroom and meet Mr. Smith, another teacher.)

MR. SMITH: You won't believe the meeting I just had with Johnny Haringer's parents!

MS. PALMER AND MS. WILSON: What happened?

MR. SMITH: Well, they came to see me after Johnny missed an A by two points on one of my weekly math tests. It was the first time that he had missed an A the entire semester.

MS. WILSON: Were they mad?

MR. SMITH: They were at first. But I stayed calm and explained very carefully why two points on the test really should make a difference between an A and a B

MS. WILSON: What kinds of things did you tell them?

MR. SMITH: Well, luckily I keep student data from past years for all my tests. This allows me to calculate reliability and validity coefficients for my tests using one of the PCs in the math lab. I simply explained to Johnny's parents, in everyday, commonsense language, what reliability and validity of a test meant, and then gave them some statistical data to support my case. I also explained the care and deliberation I put into the construction of my tests—you know, all the steps you go through in writing test items and then checking their content validity and doing qualitative and quantitative item analyses. I think they got the idea of just how much work it takes to construct a good test.

MS. WILSON: And?

MR. SMITH: And after that they calmed down and were very responsive to my explanation. They even commented that they hadn't realized the science of statistics could be so helpful in determining the reliability and validity of a test. They even commended me for being so systematic and careful. Can you believe that?

MS. WILSON: Umm . . . reliability and validity? Do you mean we have to know the reliability and validity for every test we use?

MR. SMITH: Ever since that lawsuit by the parents of some kid over at Central for unfair testing, the school board has made every teacher individually responsible for using reliable and valid tests.

(Looking surprised, Ms. Wilson turns to Ms. Palmer and Ms. Palmer slowly and painfully nods to indicate her agreement with what Mr. Smith has been saying.)

MS. WILSON: Boy! I don't think I could explain reliability and validity that well—at least not to parents—and I know I wouldn't have the slightest idea of how to compute them.

MR. SMITH: Well, I guess we won't have any preparations to worry about this weekend ..nothing but review and testing next week. You have a nice weekend.

MS. PALMER: Well, it may not be all that bad. You've got that tests and measurement text at home, and next quarter, who knows? You may have time to plan for all this ahead of time.

MS. WILSON: (*being purposely negative*) That's if I don't have to explain reliability and validity to some irate kid's parents, construct a test blueprint, learn the difference between norm-referenced and criterion-referenced tests, make a scoring key for an essay test, and, of course, compute some test item statistics I probably can't even pronounce!

MS. PALMER: Let's get to our cars before the roof falls in. (*To Ms. Wilson under her breath*) Speaking of the roof.

(The principal approaches them.)

PRINCIPAL: Ah, Ms. Wilson. I'm glad I ran into you. How'd things go for you this quarter?

MS. WILSON: Very well, thank you. I really like my classroom, and the parents I've met have been very nice. All my students—well, almost all—have made me feel at home.

PRINCIPAL: Good. I've had good reports about your teaching, and your classroom discipline and management seem to be improving. I suppose you're all set for the end of this grading period. It's only a week away, you know. (*The principal looks at Ms. Wilson for some kind of response.*)

MS. WILSON: (*after a brief pause, she responds almost inaudibly*) Yes.

PRINCIPAL: Well, that's excellent, because you know how much emphasis our parents place on grades. All of our teachers spend a lot of time on grading. We've never had a serious incident in this regard like they've had over at Central. I'd like to think it was because of my policy that every teacher be responsible for using reliable and valid tests and for interpreting test scores to parents. I only wish that all teachers in the state would have to prove themselves competent in tests and measurement to be certified, like they do in some other states. I'm sure there would be a lot fewer angry students and parents, if this were the case. Well, Ms. Wilson, glad things are going so well. Have a nice weekend now. You too, Ms. Palmer.

MS. WILSON: Thank you.

MS. PALMER: You too.

MS. WILSON: I don't think I've had a more miserable Friday afternoon. I can only guess what the weekend will be like.

MS. PALMER: Maybe I can help. (*Ms. Wilson looks directly at her.*) I have a tests and measurement book called *Educational Testing and Measurement: Classroom Application and Practice,* which covers the kinds of things that might be helpful in preparing your tests for next week. If you're not busy, why don't I bring it over and help you with those tests?

MS. WILSON: (*straining to be reserved and matter-of-fact*) I guess that would be . . . OK. (*then, with a sigh of relief*) Yes, I think that would be fine.

You might think this scenario is a bit farfetched. It may come as a surprise, but we are willing to bet that something like this will happen to you long before the end of your first grading period. The incidents we have described repeat themselves thousands of times each school day in schools across the country. Unlike the preceding story, some have unhappy endings. Let's examine the testing issues that confronted Ms. Wilson.

CRITERION-REFERENCED VERSUS NORM-REFERENCED TESTS

One of the first issues that Ms. Wilson had to deal with was whether to use criterion-referenced or norm-referenced tests. Of course, she hardly knows the difference between them, so it should be no surprise later if there are misunderstandings between her, her pupils, and their parents over the meaning of her grades. Recall that criterion-referenced tests report test scores in relation to the test. That is, they are graded in terms of the number or percentage of items a student gets correct. Grades—such as A, B, C, etc.—are usually assigned indicating the level of knowledge or skill that was attained. These grades should reflect estimates of the level of performance necessary to do well according to certain criteria, for example, to divide and multiply four-digit numbers with decimals, to divide and multiply fractions, or to square whole numbers. It is these types of criteria that Mr. Smith is likely to have related to Johnny Haringer's parents in order to explain why the two-point difference in Johnny's test score should make a difference. In other words, Mr. Smith's grades were based on real performance skills that Johnny's parents could understand and appreciate. For most interim grades from which teachers are expected to diagnose learning difficulties and prepare remedial instruction, criterion-referenced tests are, generally, the most useful. Unfortunately, Ms. Wilson forgot or never knew that one of the first steps in preparing a test is to determine the *purpose* of the test.

If Ms. Wilson's purpose (and the school's) for this grading period was to determine where each student stood in reference to other students, an existing norm-referenced test might have been perfectly adequate. Needless to say, this testing purpose might have saved Ms. Wilson's weekend. Generally, however, interim grading periods are used for the purpose of providing feedback to students, their parents, and the teacher as to how well students have learned and teachers have taught specific skills. This objective usually calls for the use of a criterion-refenced test.

Even if Ms. Wilson had decided beforehand to use criterion-referenced tests, Ms. Palmer's suggestion of looking at Ms. Cartwright's norm-referenced tests was a good one. This is especially true in light of Ms. Palmer's suggestion that a test blueprint be used to determine which, if any, items from these tests matched the specific content that Ms. Wilson taught. As long as these norm-referenced tests were not to be given to these students at a later time, items from them might be effectively used in a criterion-referenced test, saving Ms. Wilson from preparing every item from scratch.

INSTRUCTIONAL OBJECTIVES

Another issue raised in the course of this dialogue concerned the proper use of instructional objectives. One implication should be clear. Instructional objectives not only help teachers organize their teaching—they help them write tests, too. However, Ms. Wilson took a careless approach to writing instructional objectives, so they could not be used to help construct her tests. It's likely that some failed to specify the level of behavior or the conditions under which the behavior could be expected to be performed. This would prevent her from matching her instruction to the items in Ms. Cartwright's test files. It also means that Ms. Wilson must rely only on her memory as to what was and was not covered during the grading period. Let's hope Ms. Wilson's tests don't ask her students questions that were never formally taught or that were taught at a level different than that represented by her test items.

Lawsuits involving unfair testing stem from situations similar to that in which Ms. Wilson now finds herself. Settlements against teachers and districts can occur if it can be shown that some harm has come to the student as a result of the neglect of proper testing procedures. Ms. Wilson seems to be in such a precarious position on this issue that we can only hope her weekend makes up for the effort that was missing earlier in the semester. Given that this is an interim grading period in which formal decisions about a student's progress are not likely to be made, Ms. Wilson will probably avoid any serious problems—this time.

THE TEST BLUEPRINT

We've already discussed the use of the test blueprint, but a few more points about this important tool can be made. Recall from Chapter 5 that a test blueprint is simply a table that lists the important objectives to be taught and the levels of student behavior that can be expected from these objectives. In the cells of the table are placed the number or percentage of items that cover each topic at a particular level of behavior. The test blueprint can be an important device for planning a test. It is used in deciding the number of items that should be written for each major objective and, in evaluating an existing test, it is used to determine how well a test compares in types and numbers of items with what has been taught.

Ms. Wilson had the opportunity of using a test blueprint in both of these ways. Had a test blueprint been prepared, Ms. Wilson could have quickly sorted through Ms. Cartwright's test file to determine if the content of any test items matched the content of any of the cells in the test blueprint. This might have precluded the need for Ms. Wilson to personally write every test item needed. The key to preparing a test blueprint is the preparation of behavioral objectives that include the level of behavior that is being taught. Unfortunately, Ms. Wilson now must pay for failing to properly prepare behavioral objectives with the more arduous task of constructing all new test items and the uncertainty of whether these test items accurately and fairly reflect the content she has taught.

ESSAY ITEMS AND THE ESSAY SCORING GUIDES

Recall that another suggestion given by Ms. Palmer was that some of the items Ms. Wilson needed could be essay items. Ms. Palmer's suggestion was probably based upon the notion that a large block of content could be tested with one or a few essay items. While the implication here is that some time could be saved in the test preparation process for some content areas by writing essay items, Ms. Palmer was correct in suggesting that essay items will only be appropriate for some content areas and some teaching objectives (for example, where rote recall and memorization of facts were not the primary objectives). Also, it should be recognized that the time needed to prepare scoring guides and to grade essay items might outweigh the fact that the initial essay question might be easy to write. Ms. Wilson seemed to be unaware of the need for scoring guides, presumably thinking that essay items are simply scored right or wrong as multiple-choice items are. But, as was seen in Chapter 7, this is not the case. Points are assigned to essay items in relation to the extent to which the student includes in his or her answer the elements of a good response. The scoring of essay items requires specifying these elements before the grading begins and identifying examples of the different alternatives that might adequately represent the elements of a good response. All this takes considerable time and effort, which Ms. Wilson did not expect.

Like many new teachers, Ms. Wilson probably saw the essay item as an easy way out of having to write many different test items. As Ms. Palmer pointed out, though, scoring essays reliably is time-consuming. Nevertheless, Ms. Wilson *should* have considered essay items. We say this because it is entirely likely, even probable, that some of the content Ms. Wilson has taught during the semester should be tested with essay items. Since Ms. Wilson will have to cram all of her test construction into a single weekend, it is unlikely that time can be spent in identifying which content is best tested with an essay format and in preparing scoring guides. Here again, an earlier start on a test blueprint might have paid rich dividends in time saved later.

RELIABILITY, VALIDITY, AND TEST STATISTICS

Mr. Smith raised the important issues of reliability and validity. Nothing could be more fundamental to a good test than its reliability and validity—that is, its capacity to consistently give the same or a similar score over repeated testings and to measure what it is supposed to measure. These two terms have technical meanings, which were presented in Chapters 15 and 16, but they also have practical, commonsense meanings, and these should be second nature to any beginning teacher.

The practical or commonsense notions that lie behind the concepts of reliability and validity are far more present in our everyday lives than is frequently believed. These two words, *reliability* and *validity,* appear in all types of writing—from newspapers and weekly newsmagazines to popular books—as well as in the language of businesspeople, engineers, nurses, social workers, people from all walks of life. The significance of this fact for the teacher is that parents and even some of your students will be aware of these concepts and will not hesitate to confront you with them (albeit sometimes inaccurately) when they feel they may be used to their advantage. It is unfortunate that many parents have only a partial or limited knowledge of these concepts as they apply to testing. But it is even more unfortunate that some teachers are unable to correct the misunderstandings that parents sometimes have about these concepts. It is not that most teachers lack textbook definitions for these terms, but that they are unable to convert these definitions to the practical language that students and their parents are likely to understand. Of course, the main advantage for the teacher knowing practical ways to discuss the concepts of reliability and validity is that they can be invaluable tools in communicating the meaning of test scores to parents and in justifying and defending decisions based upon these test scores.

Mr. Smith's interaction with Johnny Haringer's parents provided some evidence of a practical as well as technical knowledge of reliability and validity. Mr. Smith was able to defuse a potentially difficult meeting with Johnny's parents essentially because he could talk *their* language. He described reliability and validity with words that *they* could relate to. This is how Mr. Smith was able to strike a responsive chord, to get beneath the emotional issue that brought him together with Johnny's parents, and to communicate a commonsense understanding of the characteristics of a good test. This commonsense understanding went a long way toward turning a potentially nasty confrontation into a useful and productive meeting about Johnny's progress.

Recall also that Mr. Smith went beyond the simple commonsense notions of reliability and validity to actually show Johnny's parents some statistics indicating his test's reliability and validity. While most standardized tests will have these statistics already calculated and displayed for the teacher in the test manual, the teacher will have to understand the test manual and give parents a faithful interpretation of what all the statistics mean, if the situation requires. Most of what was covered in Chapters 12 through 18 was intended to prepare the teacher for this task. On the other hand, Mr. Smith's test probably was not standardized, and, therefore, Mr. Smith needed to calculate these statistics. Here, the availability of a computer program for calculating test statistics (Chapter 21) and his knowledge of the uses of a PC made this easy.

Any first-year teacher, particularly in the first quarter of teaching, could not be expected to be prepared as well as Mr. Smith. But note that Mr. Smith made a point of saying that he always kept his test scores on file, probably in the PC's memory. When time permitted, he used the PC to calculate the necessary statistics to show a test's reliability and validity. This foresight paid off handsomely in his meeting with Johnny's parents. It would have been impossible for Mr. Smith to have calculated these statistics on the spot and probably even unlikely that they could have been calculated between the time Johnny's parents called for an appointment and the actual time the meeting took place. Instead, Mr. Smith used the PC to calculate reliability. The computer program he used might have computed reliability using the odd-even or Kuder-Richardson method, and validity by correlating a test's scores with end-of-semester or end-of-year test scores as was described in Chapters 15 and 16.

Even though Mr. Smith's reliability and validity statistics were not determined with student data from Johnny's test, they were calculated with student data from past semesters in which students similar to Johnny took the same test. As long as Mr. Smith's data were not too dated, they are acceptable evidence of the test's reliability and validity. Mr. Smith's foresight is within the reach of every teacher, and, if we are to take seriously the principal's admonition that parents and teachers place a great deal of emphasis on testing in this school, we suspect Ms. Wilson should plan on having some of this same foresight.

GRADES AND MARKS

There is no better way in which to end this chapter, and indeed this book, than by reinforcing the critical role that grades and marks play in the testing process. As the most visible sign of the testing and measurement process, grades and marks stand as the end products that can make or break a test. Since Ms. Wilson had not thought about whether a criterion-referenced or norm-referenced strategy was appropriate, it is unlikely that she had given much thought about what marks or grades would be used in reporting the results of her tests to parents and students. Would she simply have used the school's formal reporting system to convey all the pertinent facts about a student's performance, or would there be other marks that might make finer distinctions and interpretations of a student's strengths and weaknesses? Would Ms. Wilson even know the strengths and weaknesses of her students at the end of this testing? And, if so, how would they be communicated to students and parents?

It was apparent from Mr. Smith's discussion with Johnny's parents that information was available from his tests that separated students into more than simply A's, B's, C's, and so on. Specific differences between an A and a B presumably were recorded or at least could be retrieved from the test score data for the parent-teacher conference. Perhaps Mr. Smith's test was divided into a certain number of competencies, each of which could be marked "pass" or "fail." Then, maybe an A was based upon a student achieving "passes" on all competencies, a B based upon a student achieving "passes" on 9 out of 10 competencies, and so on.

By making further differentiations across letter grades, Mr. Smith armed himself with some powerful ammunition as to why Johnny deserved a B, even though he missed an A by only two points. Mr. Smith learned the important point that grades are meaningless to students and parents unless some criterion can be attached to them that is seen as being of value to parents and teachers. Telling Johnny's parents that Johnny does not know how to divide and multiply two-digit numbers that have decimals—such as those that occur on end-of-year examinations, balancing a checkbook, in homework assignments in the next grade, and in finding the best buy per ounce among competing products in a grocery store—goes a lot further to convince his parents that Johnny has a weakness that must be remedied than simply telling them that Johnny deserves a B, not an A.

These are only a hint of the many problems involved in choosing grades and marks, which were covered in Chapter 10. Even if a test is meticulously constructed, has high reliability and validity, and has been carefully administered and graded, it still can be considered a poor test, unless the grades that are based upon it can be communicated meaningfully to parents and students. While Mr. Smith has obviously given some thought to this aspect of testing, Ms. Wilson still has this lesson to learn.

SOME FINAL THOUGHTS

In the previous discussion of issues related to our dialogue, we admittedly have been pretty hard on Ms. Wilson. Even in this seemingly small slice of classroom life, Ms. Wilson has been confronted with more problems than she can possibly deal with in the time available to her for constructing the following week's tests. But if you think this brief dialogue has been hard on Ms. Wilson, you will be surprised to learn that these are not all the problems that she would need to confront in the real world. We believe we have been kind to Ms. Wilson by limiting her distress and discomfort to one Friday afternoon and to only the few measurement concepts we chose to discuss in our dialogue.

The real world of the classroom is not so accommodating. It presents testing and measurement problems every day of the week and each week of the school year. Also, the cast of characters will be larger in the real world than the few who were included here. And we haven't even begun to characterize the different responses of students and parents, each of whom produce a unique challenge to the teacher who must explain and justify testing decisions.

After reading this book, you should have a better understanding of the practical side of testing and maybe even some insights into how to handle yourself should similar situations arise. But real life is not easily portrayed on the pages of a book. For you, the reader, and for us, the authors, it occurs only in classrooms, and this of course is why we have chosen to spend the better part of our lives in those classrooms. Our advice is to use this book to prepare for that real world. Review its contents often and keep this book close at hand for future reference. Combine the skills you have learned with your own good judgment and experience and you will be sure to continue to learn as you teach.

APPENDIX A

Math Skills Review

This review of math skills covers all operations necessary to complete the calculations in this text. The Self-Check Test and answer key that appear at the end of the appendix can help you determine which skills you may need to review.

ORDER OF TERMS

The order of terms in addition is irrelevant.

$$2 + 3 = 3 + 2 = 5$$

The order of terms in subtraction is important.

$$3 - 2 \neq 2 - 3$$

The order of terms in multiplication is irrelevant.

$$3(2) = 2(3) = 6$$

There are several ways to write "multiplied by."

$$3 \times 2 = 3(2) = 3 \cdot 2 = 6$$

The order of terms in division is important.

$$6/2 \neq 2/6$$

There are several ways to write "divided by."

$$4 \div 2 = 4/2 = 2\overline{)4} = 2$$

ORDER OF OPERATIONS

When multiplying (or dividing) the sum (or difference) of several numbers by another number, you may either multiply (divide) or add (subtract) first.

$$2(3 + 4) = 2(7) = 14 \quad \text{or} \quad 2(3 + 4) = 6 + 8 = 14$$

$$3(5 - 1) = 3(4) = 12 \quad \text{or} \quad 3(5 - 1) = 15 - 3 = 12$$

$$\frac{6 + 4}{2} = \frac{10}{2} = 5 \quad \text{or} \quad \frac{6 + 4}{2} = \frac{6}{2} + \frac{4}{2} = 3 + 2 = 5$$

$$\frac{9 - 6}{3} = \frac{3}{3} = 1 \quad \text{or} \quad \frac{9 - 6}{3} = \frac{9}{3} - \frac{6}{3} = 3 - 2 = 1$$

The operations within parentheses are completed first. Within the parentheses, multiplication and division are completed before addition and subtraction. After math in the parentheses is finished, other multiplications and divisions are completed before additions and subtractions.

$$\begin{aligned}(3 - 2) - 4(6 + 1) + 8 &= \\ 1 - 4(7) + 8 &= \\ 1 - 28 + 8 &= -19\end{aligned}$$

$$\begin{aligned}(6 + 4) - 6(3 - 2) + 11 &= \\ 10 - 6(1) + 11 &= \\ 10 - 6 + 11 &= 15\end{aligned}$$

$$\begin{aligned}(4/2) + 3(2 + 6) - 3 &= \\ 2 + 3(8) - 3 &= \\ 2 + 24 - 3 &= 23\end{aligned}$$

FRACTIONS

For addition and subtraction, fractions must have the same denominator. If a common denominator is not obvious, multiply the two denominators to get a common denominator. In order to keep the value of the new fractions equal to that of the original fractions, multiply each numerator by the denominator of the other fraction (cross-multiplying).

$$\frac{1}{2} + \frac{1}{4} = \frac{4}{8} + \frac{2}{8} = \frac{6}{8} = \frac{3}{4}$$

$$\frac{2}{3} - \frac{2}{5} = \frac{10}{15} - \frac{6}{15} = \frac{4}{15}$$

$$\frac{1}{5} + \frac{1}{2} = \frac{2}{10} + \frac{5}{10} = \frac{7}{10}$$

This could also be accomplished by multiplying both the numerator and the denominator of each fraction by the denominator of the other fraction.

$$\frac{1}{2}+\frac{1}{4}$$

$$\frac{1}{2}\times\frac{4}{4}=\frac{4}{8} \quad \text{and} \quad \frac{1}{4}\times\frac{2}{2}=\frac{2}{8} \text{ so } \frac{4}{8}+\frac{2}{8}=\frac{6}{8}=\frac{3}{4}$$

$$\frac{2}{3}-\frac{2}{5}$$

$$\frac{2}{3}\times\frac{5}{5}=\frac{10}{15} \quad \text{and} \quad \frac{2}{5}\times\frac{3}{3}=\frac{6}{15} \quad \text{so} \quad \frac{10}{15}-\frac{6}{15}=\frac{4}{15}$$

$$\frac{1}{5}+\frac{1}{2}$$

$$\frac{1}{5}\times\frac{2}{2}=\frac{2}{10} \quad \text{and} \quad \frac{1}{2}\times\frac{5}{5} \quad \text{so} \quad \frac{2}{10}+\frac{5}{10}=\frac{7}{10}$$

To multiply two fractions, simply multiply across the numerators and across the denominators.

$$\frac{3}{4}\times\frac{1}{2}=\frac{3}{8} \qquad \frac{2}{7}\times\frac{1}{3}=\frac{2}{21} \qquad \frac{3}{6}\times\frac{1}{3}=\frac{3}{18}$$

To divide two fractions, invert the divisor and then multiply.

$$\frac{3}{8}\div\frac{1}{2}=\frac{3}{8}\cdot\frac{2}{1}=\frac{3}{4} \qquad \frac{2}{3}\div\frac{3}{4}=\frac{2}{3}\cdot\frac{4}{3}=\frac{8}{9}$$

$$\frac{1}{2}\div\frac{3}{5}=\frac{1}{2}\cdot\frac{5}{3}=\frac{5}{6} \qquad \frac{3}{4}\div\frac{4}{5}=\frac{3}{4}\cdot\frac{5}{4}=\frac{15}{16}$$

To simplify multiplication and division of fractions, you may cancel out equal amounts in the numerators and denominators.

$$\frac{1}{2}\cdot\frac{2}{3}\div\frac{1}{9}=\frac{1}{2}\cdot\frac{2}{3}\cdot\frac{9}{1}=\frac{1}{\cancel{2}^{1}}\cdot\frac{\cancel{2}^{1}}{\cancel{3}^{1}}\cdot\frac{\cancel{9}^{3}}{1}=\frac{3}{1}=3$$

$$\frac{3}{24}\cdot\frac{8}{9}\div\frac{1}{2}=\frac{3}{24}\cdot\frac{8}{9}\cdot\frac{2}{1}=\frac{\cancel{3}^{1}}{\cancel{24}_{3}}\cdot\frac{\cancel{8}^{1}}{\cancel{9}_{3}}\cdot\frac{2}{1}=\frac{2}{9}$$

$$\frac{1}{32}\div\frac{1}{16}\cdot\frac{3}{4}=\frac{1}{32}\cdot\frac{16}{1}\cdot\frac{3}{4}=\frac{1}{\cancel{32}_{2}}\cdot\frac{\cancel{16}^{1}}{1}\cdot\frac{3}{4}=\frac{3}{8}$$

MIXED NUMBERS

In addition and subtraction, it is only necessary to have the denominators of the fractions the same.

$$2\frac{1}{4} + 3\frac{1}{3} = 2\frac{3}{12} + 3\frac{4}{12} = 5\frac{7}{12}$$

$$8\frac{2}{3} - 3\frac{2}{7} = 8\frac{14}{21} - 3\frac{6}{21} = 5\frac{8}{21}$$

$$6\frac{2}{3} + 4\frac{1}{4} = 6\frac{8}{12} + 4\frac{3}{12} = 10\frac{11}{12}$$

In subtraction it is sometimes necessary to "borrow" from the whole number in order to subtract the fractional part.

$$4\frac{1}{2} - 2\frac{2}{3} = 4\frac{3}{6} - 2\frac{4}{6}$$

You cannot subtract the fractions, but since $1 = \frac{6}{6}$ you can convert $4\frac{3}{6}$ to $3\frac{9}{6}$, so

$$3\frac{9}{6} - 2\frac{4}{6} = 1\frac{5}{6}$$

An easier way to convert mixed numbers is to multiply the whole number by the denominator of the fraction, then add the numerator.

$$3\frac{1}{2} = \frac{(3\cdot 2) + 1}{2} = \frac{6 + 1}{2} = \frac{7}{2}$$

$$2\frac{3}{4} = \frac{(2\cdot 4) + 3}{4} = \frac{8 + 3}{4} = \frac{11}{4}$$

$$8\frac{1}{3} = \frac{(8\cdot 3) + 1}{3} = \frac{24 + 1}{3} = \frac{25}{3}$$

DECIMALS

To convert a fraction to a decimal fraction, perform simple division.

$$\frac{3}{8} = 8\overline{)3.000} = .375 \qquad \frac{1}{2} = 2\overline{)1.0} = .5 \qquad \frac{3}{4} = 4\overline{)3.00} = .75$$

The number of decimal places is not changed by addition or subtraction.

$$\begin{array}{r} .2 \\ +.5 \\ \hline .7 \end{array} \qquad \begin{array}{r} .68 \\ -32 \\ \hline .36 \end{array} \qquad \begin{array}{r} .374 \\ -.234 \\ \hline .140 \end{array} \qquad \begin{array}{r} .949 \\ +.055 \\ \hline 1.004 \end{array}$$

In multiplication, the number of decimal places in the answer is equal to the total of the number of places in the numbers you are multiplying.

$$\begin{array}{r} .42 \\ \times .003 \\ \hline .00126 \end{array} \qquad \begin{array}{r} .81 \\ \times .2 \\ \hline .162 \end{array} \qquad \begin{array}{r} .5 \\ \times .5 \\ \hline .25 \end{array} \qquad \begin{array}{r} .24 \\ \times .02 \\ \hline .0048 \end{array}$$

In division, the divisor is converted to a whole number by moving the decimal point to the right as many places as necessary. The decimal point in the number you are dividing into must be moved the same number of places to the right.

$$\begin{array}{lll} .25\overline{)1.000} & \text{becomes} & 25\overline{)100.0} = 4.0 \\ .32\overline{)6.4} & \text{becomes} & 32\overline{)640} = 20. \\ .482\overline{)14.46} & \text{becomes} & 482\overline{)14460} = 30. \end{array}$$

SQUARES AND SQUARE ROOTS

Squaring a number is multiplying it by itself.

$$3^2 = 3(3) = 9 \qquad 4^2 = 4(4) = 16$$

Taking a square root is finding a number which, when multiplied by itself, equals the number of which you are taking the square root.

$$\sqrt{4} = +2 \text{ or } -2 \text{ since } 2(2) = 4 \text{ and } -2(-2) = 4$$
$$\sqrt{16} = +4 \text{ or } -4 \text{ since } 4(4) = 16 \text{ and } -4(-4) = 16$$
$$\sqrt{9} = +3 \text{ or } -3 \text{ since } 3(3) = 9 \text{ or } -3(-3) = 9$$

ALGEBRA

To solve equations, you must get the unknown (usually symbolized by x) on one side of the equation, and all other numbers on the other side. This is done by adding, subtracting, multiplying, or dividing both sides of the equation by the same number.

$$2x = 4$$

Divide both sides by 2 $\qquad \dfrac{2x}{2} = \dfrac{4}{2}$

$$x = 2$$

$$\frac{x}{6} = 3$$

Multiply both sides by 6 $\quad \frac{6x}{6} = 3(6)$

$$x = 18$$

$$x + 3 = 9$$

Subtract 3 from both sides $\quad (x + 3) - 3 = 9 - 3$

$$x = 6$$

$$x - 4 = 6$$

Add 4 to both sides $\quad (x - 4) + 4 = 6 + 4$

$$x = 10$$

This procedure can also be done in combinations of the above.

$$2x + 4 = 10$$

Subtract 4 from both sides $\quad (2x + 4) - 4 = 10 - 4$

$$2x = 6$$

Divide both sides by 2 $\quad \frac{2x}{2} = \frac{6}{2}$

$$x = 3$$

$$3x + 15 = 75$$

Subtract 15 from both sides $\quad (3x + 15) - 15 = 75 - 15$

$$3x = 60$$

Divide both sides by 3 $\quad \frac{3x}{3} = \frac{60}{3}$

$$x = 20$$

$$4x + 10 = 110$$

Subtract 10 from both sides $\quad (4x + 10) - 10 = 110 - 10$

$$4x = 100$$

Divide both sides by 4 $\quad \frac{4x}{4} = \frac{100}{4}$

$$x = 25$$

SELF-CHECK TEST

DIRECTIONS: SOLVE THE FOLLOWING PROBLEMS.

______1. $13^2 =$ ______

______2. Convert $\frac{1}{4}$ to a decimal______

______3. $\sqrt{144} =$ ______

______4. $24(380 + 20) =$______

______5. $\frac{2}{5} + \frac{3}{15} =$ ______

______6. $144 \div .048 =$ ______

______7. $16x + 10 = 330 \quad x =$ ______

______8. $\frac{2}{3} \div \frac{7}{10} =$ ______

______9. $1.32 \times .07 =$ ______

______10. $2\frac{2}{3} + 6\frac{1}{12} =$ ______

______11. Convert $\frac{1}{5}$ to a decimal ______

______12. $\frac{2}{3} \div \frac{14}{15} \times \frac{2}{5} =$ ______

______13. $(24 - 15) - 2(17 + 4) + 32 =$ ______

______14. $1.375 + .139 =$ ______

______15. $9x + 72 = 342 \quad x =$ ______

Answers: **1.** $13 \times 13 = 169$; **2.** .25 **3.** 12 or −12 **4.** 9,600 **5.** $\frac{3}{5}$ **6.** 3,000 **7.** 20 **8.** $\frac{20}{21}$ **9.** .0924 **10.** $8\frac{3}{4}$ **11.** .2 **12.** $\frac{2}{7}$ **13.** −1 **14.** 1.514 **15.** 30

APPENDIX B

Pearson Product-Moment Correlation

The following example illustrates the raw score method for computing the Pearson Product-Moment Correlation Coefficient (*r*). Listed in the X and Y columns are pairs of raw scores for each student. The X^2 column lists the square of each X score. The Y^2 column lists the square of each Y score. The XY column lists the cross products of the X and Y columns (X multiplied by Y).

Name	*X*	*Y*	X^2	Y^2	*XY*
Art	10	14	100	196	140
Ben	7	12	49	144	84
Cathy	5	7	25	49	35
Debbie	9	12	81	144	108
Eugene	6	9	36	81	54
Fred	11	15	121	225	165
Glenda	2	5	4	25	10
Henry	2	4	4	16	8
Mary	5	14	25	196	70
Sharon	4	7	16	49	28
	61	99	461	1125	702

To compute a Pearson Product-Moment Correlation Coefficient for the above data, follow these steps:

1. Square each X score and each Y score.
2. Multiply each person's X score (not the squared X score) times the same person's Y score (again, not the squared Y score).
3. Sum the X, Y, X^2, Y^2, and XY columns.
4. Plug the values into the following formula:

$$r = \frac{\Sigma XY - \dfrac{(\Sigma X)(\Sigma Y)}{N}}{\sqrt{\Sigma X^2 - \dfrac{(\Sigma X)^2}{N}}\sqrt{\Sigma Y^2 - \dfrac{(\Sigma Y)^2}{N}}}$$

where ΣXY is the sum of the XY column
ΣX is the sum of all X scores
ΣY is the sum of all Y scores
N is the number of persons observed
ΣX^2 is the sum of the X^2 column
ΣY^2 is the sum of the Y^2 column

$$r = \frac{702 - \dfrac{(61)(99)}{10}}{\sqrt{461 - \dfrac{(61)^2}{10}}\sqrt{1{,}125 - \dfrac{(99)2}{10}}}$$

$$= \frac{702 - \dfrac{6{,}039}{10}}{\sqrt{461 - \dfrac{3{,}721}{10}}\sqrt{1{,}125 - \dfrac{9{,}801}{10}}}$$

$$= \frac{702 - 603.9}{\sqrt{461 - 372.1}\sqrt{1{,}125 - 980.1}}$$

$$= \frac{98.1}{\sqrt{88.9}\sqrt{144.9}}$$

$$= \frac{98.1}{(9.43)\,(12.04)}$$

$$= \frac{98.1}{113.54}$$

$$= .86$$

There is a strong positive relationship between X and Y.

APPENDIX C

Statistics and Measurement Texts

Anastasi, A. (1989). *Psychological Testing* (6th ed.). New York: Macmillan.

Bartz, A. E. (1988). *Basic Statistical Concepts* (3rd ed.). New York: Macmillan.

Cronbach, L. J. (1990). *Essentials of Psychological Testing* (5th ed.). New York: HarperCollins.

Downie, N. M., & Heath, R. W. (1983). *Basic Statistical Methods* (5th ed.). New York: Harper & Row.

Ebel, R. L., & Frisbie, D. A. (1991). *Essentials of Educational Measurement*. Englewood Cliffs, NJ: Prentice-Hall.

Gronlund, N. E., & Linn, R. L. (1990). *Measurement and Evaluation in Teaching*. New York: Macmillan.

Lyman, H. B. (1986). *Test Scores and What They Mean* (4th ed.). Englewood Cliffs, N.J.: Prentice-Hall.

Mehrens, W. A., & Lehman, I.J. (1991). *Measurement and Evaluation in Education and Psychology*. New York: Holt, Rinehart & Winston.

Nitko, A. (1983). *Educational Testing and Measurement*. New York: Harcourt Brace Jovanovich.

Oosterhof, A. C. (1990). *Classroom Applications of Educational Measurement*. Columbus, Ohio: Charles E. Merrill.

Payne, D. A. (1992). *Measuring and Evaluating Educational Outcomes*. New York: Macmillan.

Stahl, S. M., & Hennes, J. D. (1980). *Reading and Understanding Applied Statistics: A Self-learning Approach* (2nd ed.). San Francisco: W. H. Freeman.

Thorndike R. M., Cunningham, G., Thorndike, R. L., & Hagan, E. (1991). *Measurement and Evaluation in Psychology and Education*. New York: Macmillan.

Young, R. K., & Veldman, D. J. (1981). *Introductory Statistics for the Behavioral Sciences* (4th ed.). New York: Holt, Rinehart & Winston.

APPENDIX D

Answers for Practice Questions

CHAPTER 4

3. (a) B (b) E (c) B (d) E (e) B (f) B (g) E (h) B
5. (1) c (2) d (3) d (4) g

CHAPTER 5

4. (1) d (2) a (3) b (4) e (5) f
5. (a) 2 comprehension, 1 application (b) 30% multiplication, 30% division

CHAPTER 6

3. (a) The "a" should be "a/an."
   (b) National origin of the names in the stem provides a clue to the answer.
   (c) Contains an absolute; opinionated.
   (d) Multiple defensible answers; lacks specificity.
   (e) Begins with a blank; lacks specificity.
   (f) Lists should be titled and arranged in some logical order. Too wide a variety of concepts being measured, making some answers obvious (i.e., nonhomogeneous lists).

CHAPTER 8

1. p = .22 (a difficult item), D = .64 (an excellent discriminator)
2. p = .40 (moderately difficult), D = −.33 (poor item, delete or modify)
3. (a) ambiguity (b) miskeyed (c) ambiguity (d) guessing (e) miskeyed
4. p = .25; D = 10. The key discriminates positively, but not all distractors discriminate negatively. Probably some guessing and/or ambiguity.

CHAPTER 9

1. Conventional tests are given to obtain data on which to base grades, indicate how much has been learned, make decisions about instructional placement, talk to parents about, and help others make employment decisions. Performance

assessments are given to stimulate higher-order thinking in the classroom and simulate real-world activities.

2. By refocusing the curriculum on thinking, problem-solving, and student responsibility for learning.
3. An indirect measure, such as knowledge shown in a multiple-choice test, will only suggest that something has been learned. A direct measure, such as a problem solving activity, requires that acquired knowledge can be applied and exhibited in the context of a real-world problem.
5. For example, the Darwin School records percentage of words read accurately during oral reading, number of sentences read with understanding, and number of story elements learners can talk about on their own. The West Orient School requires portfolios of poetry, essays, biographies, and self-reflections.
8. Scoring rubrics are model answers against which a learner's performance is compared. They can be a detailed list of what an acceptable answer must contain or a sample of typical responses that would be acceptable.

CHAPTER 10

5. Numerical mark = 74.75, letter grade = C, both approaches yield the same result because they differ only in the point at which the equating procedure is applied.

CHAPTER 11

6. 4.0
7. (a) AV; (b) AP; (c) AV; (d) AV; (e) AP; (f) AP; (g) AP; (h) AP; (i) AV
8. (a) Too many thoughts (double-barreled)
   (b) Uses a negative; factual
   (c) References the past
   (d) Uses an absolute
   (e) Not direct or clearly written

CHAPTER 12

1. Grade 1, positively skewed; grade 3, normal; grade 5, negatively skewed
2. Group 1: N = 10, R = 13 (inclusive R = 14), $\overline{X}$ = 93.3, MDN = 94.0, mode = 90, 94, and 97
   Group 2: N = 10, R = 36 (inclusive R = 37), $\overline{X}$ = 89.6, MDN = 92.5, mode = 97
   The difference in means is caused by the score of 61 in Group 2. For Group 1 the mean would be the best measure of central tendency. For Group 2 the median would be the best measure of central tendency.
3. Use from 8 to 10 intervals. Choose the number that best demonstrates variations in the frequency of scores.

4. (1) c (2) c (3) a (4) b (5) b
5. $P_{25} = 93.5$; $P_{50} = 99$
6. (a) Normal; (b) negatively skewed; (c) positively skewed
7. (a) Simple frequency distribution; small number and range of scores
   (b) List, small number but large range
   (c) Grouped frequency distribution; large number and range of scores

CHAPTER 13

1. N = 10; mode = 5; median = 4.5; mean = 4.0; standard deviation = 1.61; variance = 2.6; range = 5 (inclusive R = 6)
2. (a) 2.0, 3.2, 4.0, 4.5
   (b) 75, 106, 112.5, 121.5
   (c) 125, 88, 85, 78
   (d) About 15%; 82%; 34.13%; about 11%
3. (a) 1.33 (b) 74.5 (c) about 16%
4. 35
5. John, −1.0, 40; Mary, +2.0, 70; Jim, +.5, 55; Claire, −1.5, 35
6. (a) 42.5, 121 (b) 700

CHAPTER 14

2. Curvilinear. Income goes up until age 60, then income decreases with age.
3. .844; positive and strong
4. 71.2%
5. (a) 4 (b) 7 (c) 1 (d) 2
6. Disagree. A third variable, yet unmeasured, could cause both big feet and large vocabularies in the same individuals, making the relationship only appear causal. More likely, however, since such a variable probably could not be identified, it would be appropriate to regard the high correlation as erroneously caused by insufficient N or sampling.
7. It restricts the variability of scores and, hence, cannot reveal the covariation of X and Y scores in the larger distribution of scores.

CHAPTER 15

1. The concurrent validity coefficient is −.97. The test has no concurrent validity when compared with the old test.
2. Predictive validity: Correlate the test scores with scores on a subsequent test in social studies, or with end-of-quarter grades in social studies. Construct validity: Correlate the test scores with ratings on citizenship, scores on a test of social awareness, or any test which measures a part of what the new test measures. Conversely, it would also be correlated with the exact opposite of what the test measures.

3. Both Test A and Test C would be acceptable. Test C is unusual because predictive validity is higher than concurrent. Normally the opposite is true.
4. Test C is most acceptable, followed by Test A and Test B.
5. (a) content (d) predictive
   (b) predictive (e) concurrent
   (c) concurrent (f) content
6. A lower correlation is expected since your gifted group is homogeneous. Therefore, the strength of the correlation is limited due to the truncated range of scores involved.

CHAPTER 16

1. Test C
2. $r = .75$
3. (a) internal consistency; (b) internal consistency; (c) test-retest
4. Test C
5. (a) test-retest (d) alternate-forms
   (b) alternate-forms (long interval) (e) test-retest
   (c) split-half
6. Test B
7. Use neither test, unless acceptable validity can be established.

CHAPTER 17

In the problem at the end of Chapter 17, there is a real difference between John's Reading and Math scores, but not between his Writing and Science scores.

1. $S_m = 4.00$

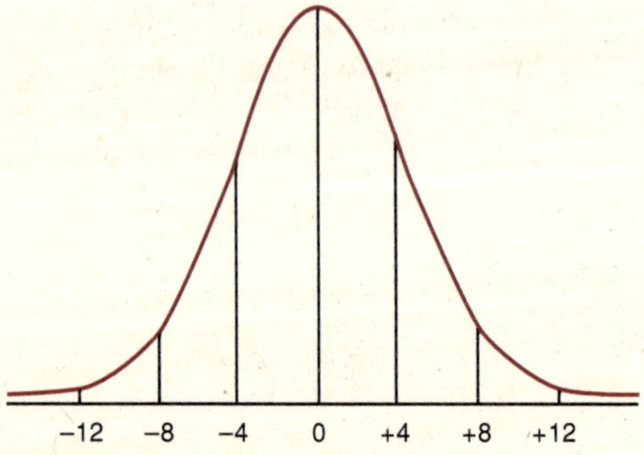

2. 95% = 8 − 24; 99% = 4 − 28; 68% = 12 − 20
3. Within-student (illness); within-test (poor items); within-administration (timing); within-scoring (miskeys)
4. (a) Most subject to administrative and scoring; least subject to within-test
   (b) Most subject to within-student; least subject to within-test

(c) Most subject to within-test; least subject to within-student
(d) Most subject to all sources
(e) Least subject to all sources

5. The following subtest profile shows bands for 68 percent certainty.

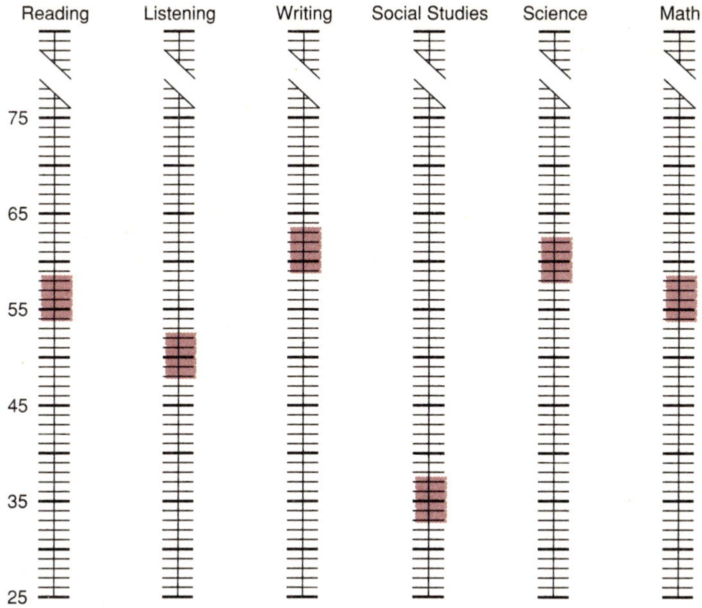

Subtest	*Band*
Reading	53.6–58.4
Listening	47.6–52.4
Writing	58.6–63.4
Social Studies	32.6–37.4
Science	57.6–62.4
Math	53.6–58.4

$$S_m = SD\sqrt{1 - r}$$
$$= 8\sqrt{1 - .91}$$
$$= 8\sqrt{.09}$$
$$= 8(.3)$$
$$= 2.4$$

Social Studies is significantly lower than all others. Listening is significantly lower than all but Social Studies. Writing is significantly higher than all but Science. Other differences are due to chance.

6. None shows real differences.
7. Differences of this size and direction are expected since each method is affected by different sources of error.
8. S_m for A = 6 and S_m for B = 5; scores from A would fluctuate most.

CHAPTER 18

3. (a) Jack is achieving below expectancy, Bonnie is above, and Chris is at expectancy.

(b) There is an aptitude-achievement discrepancy between Jack's Verbal IQ and his Vocabulary and Comprehension achievement.

7.

Subtest	***Expanded Standard Scores***
Vocabulary	530
Comprehension	398
Mechanics	423
Expression	367
Spelling	493
Computation	397
Concepts	417
Application	431
References	418
Graphical	413

CHAPTER 21

5. Adding only a CD-ROM/Multimedia kit to a 386SX–25 with 2 megs of RAM and an 80 meg hard drive will be a major disappointment. Some CD-ROM/Multimedia software may operate on such a platform, but would be very slow, and many features (the reason for going with CD-Rom/Mutimedia) will be unavailable. A better option would be to spend about $1500–$2000 of the money on a new 486DX–66 or Pentium-based machine with an integral double-speed CD-ROM drive, sound card, speakers, 8–16 megs of RAM and at least a 400 meg hard drive. While this would leave only $4000–$4500 available for software, the software will run, and with all its capacity, thereby increasing the likelihood the software will be used, and increasing everyone's satisfaction in the long run.

APPENDIX E

On-Line or Cyberspace Services

The following services all charge a monthly access fee, with additional surcharges added for selected services. Be sure to clarify these charges before subscribing. The services are listed alphabetically, and none is specifically recommended by the authors.

America Online: over 900,000 users, has an easy to use graphical interface, call 800–827–6364.

Compuserve: over 1,500,000 users, graphical interface, oldest online service, call 800–848–8199.

Delphi: over 150,000 users, full access to the Internet, call 800–695–4005.

GEnie: over 400,000 users, known for data-base and games, call 800–638–9636.

Prodigy: over 2,700,000 users, extensive multimedia features, call 800–776–3449.

SUGGESTED READINGS

Chapter 1

American Psychological Association (1985). *Standards for educational and psychological tests.* Washington, DC: APA.

Bloom, B. S., & Madaus, G. F. (1981). *Evaluation of student learning.* New York: McGraw-Hill.

Daly, J. L. (1982). *Let's talk testing. Small School Forum, 3,* no. 3, 23–24.

Holmes Group. (1986). *Tomorrow's teachers.* East Lansing, MI: The Holmes Group, Michigan State University.

National Assessment of Educational Progress. (1987). *Learning by doing: A manual for teaching and assessing higher order thinking in science and mathematics* (Report 17-HOS-80). Princeton, NJ: Educational Testing Service.

Resnick, L., & Resnick, D. (1989). *Assessing the thinking curriculum: New tools for educational reform.* Pittsburgh: Learning Research and Development Center, University of Pittsburgh.

Valente, W. D. (1980). *Law in the schools.* Columbus: Merrill.

Vernon, L. (1982). Don't take away our tests, but . . . *New Directions for Testing and Measurement,* no. 16, 67–71.

Ward, J. G. (1980). The news on testing: The good, the bad, and the useful. *American Educator: The Professional Journal of the American Federation of Teachers, 4,* no. 3, 24–27.

Chapter 2

Collier, M. (1986). A specific investigation of relative performance of examination markers. *Assessment and Evaluation in Higher Education, 11,* no. 2, 130–137.

Cronbach, L. J. (1990). *Essentials of psychological testing* (5th ed.). New York: HarperCollins, Chapter 2.

Green, K. E., & Stager, S. F. (1987). Differences in teacher test and item use with subject, grade level taught, and measurement coursework. *Teacher Education & Practice, 4,* no. 1, 55–61.

Gullickson, A. R., & Ellwein, M. C. (1985). Post hoc analysis of teacher-made tests: The goodness-of-fit between prescription and practice. *Educational Measurement: Issues and Practice, 4,* no. 1, 15–18.

Hall, B. W., et al. (1985). How beginning teachers use test results in critical education decisions. *Educational Research Quarterly, 9,* no. 3, 12–18.

Linn, R. L. (1983). Testing and instruction: Links and distinction. *Journal of Educational Measurement, 20,* no. 2, 179–189.

McKillip, W. D. (1979). Teacher-made tests: Development and use. *Arithmetic Teacher, 27,* no. 3, 38–43.

Smith, C. W. (1987). 100 ways to improve and use teacher-made tests. *Illinois Schools Journal, 66,* no. 3, 20–26.

Stiggins, R. J. (1985). Improving assessment where it means the most: In the classroom. *Educational Leadership, 43,* no. 2, 69–74.

Stiggins, R. J. (1988). Make sure your teachers understand student assessment. *Executive Educator, 10,* no. 8, 26–30.

Ward, J. G. (1980). The news on testing: The good, the bad, and the useful. *American Educator: The Professional Journal of the American Federation of Teachers, 4,* no. 3, 24–27.

Chapter 3

Collier, M. (1986). A specific investigation of relative performance of examination markers. *Assessment and Evaluation in Higher Education, 11,* no. 2, 130–137.

Green, K. E., & Stager, S. F. (1987). Differences in teacher test and item use with subject, grade level taught, and measurement coursework. *Teacher Education & Practice, 4,* no. 1, 55–61.

Gronlund, N. E. (1987). *How to construct achievement tests* (5th ed.). Englewood Cliffs, NJ: Prentice-Hall.

Linn, R. L. (1983). Testing and instruction: Links and distinction. *Journal of Educational Measurement, 20,* no. 2, 179–189.

Mehrens, W. A., & Lehmann, I. J. (1987). Using teacher-made measurement devices. *NASSP Bulletin, 71,* no. 496, 36, 38–44.

Mehrens, W. A., & Lehmann, I. J. (1991). *Measurement and evaluation in education and psychology* (4th ed.). New York: Holt, Rinehart and Winston.

Neeb, Karl-Ernst, et al. (1984). Empirical evaluation of different procedures for the construction of criterion-referenced items and instructional tasks. *Studies in Educational Evaluation, 10,* no. 2, 191–197.

Popham, W. J. (1988). *Educational evaluation* (2nd ed.). Englewood Cliffs, NJ: Prentice-Hall.

Secolsky, C. (1983). Using examinee judgments for detecting invalid items on teacher-made criterion-referenced tests. *Journal of Educational Measurement, 20,* no. 1, 51–63.

Stiggins, R. J. (1988). Make sure your teachers understand student assessment. *Executive Educator, 10,* no. 8, 26–30.

Chapter 4

Gronlund, N. (1990). *Measurement and evaluation in teaching* (6th ed.). New York: Macmillan.

Hall, B. W., et al. (1985). How beginning teachers use test results in critical education decisions. *Educational Research Quarterly, 9,* no. 3, 12–18.

Linn, R. L. (1983). Testing and instruction: Links and distinction. *Journal of Educational Measurement, 20,* no. 2, 179–189.

Neeb, Karl-Ernst, et al. (1984). Empirical evaluation of different procedures for the construction of criterion-referenced items and instructional tasks. *Studies in Education Evaluation, 10,* no. 2, 191–197.

Popham, W. (1981). *Modern educational measurement.* Englewood Cliffs, NJ: Prentice-Hall.

Rudman, H. E. (1987). Testing and teaching: Two sides of the same coin? *Studies in Educational Evaluation, 13,* no. 1, 73–90.

Stiggins, R. J. (1985). Improving assessment where it means the most: In the classroom. *Educational Leadership, 43,* no. 2, 69–74.

Stiggins, R. J. (1988). Make sure your teachers understand student assessment. *Executive Educator, 10,* no. 8, 26–30.

Chapter 5

Ball, D. W., et al. (1986). Level of teacher objectives and their classroom tests: Match or mismatch. *Journal of Social Studies Research, 10,* no. 2, 27–31.

Bloom, B. S., & Madaus, G. F. (1981). *Evaluation of student learning.* New York: McGraw-Hill.

Choppin, B. (1985). Item banking using sample free calibration. *Evaluation in Education: An International Review Series, 9,* no. 1, 81–85.

Dwyer, C. A., & Dwyer, F. M. (1987). Effect of depth of information processing on students' ability to acquire and retrieve information related to different instructional objectives. *Programmed Learning and Educational Technology, 24,* no. 4, 264–279.

Green, K. E., & Stager, S. F. (1987). Differences in teacher test and item use with subject, grade level taught, and measurement coursework. *Teacher Education & Practice, 4,* no. 1, 55–61.

Gullickson, A. R., & Ellwein, M. C. (1985). Post hoc analysis of teacher-made tests: The goodness-of-fit between prescription and practice. *Educational Measurement: Issues and Practice, 4,* no. 1, 15–18.

Linn, R. L. (1983). Testing and instruction: Links and distinction. *Journal of*

Educational Measurement, 20, no. 2, 179–189.

Mager, R. (1975). Preparing instructional objectives (2nd ed.). Palo Alto, CA: Fearon.

Neeb, Karl-Ernst, et al. (1984). Empirical evaluation of different procedures for the construction of criterion-referenced items and instructional tasks. *Studies in Education Evaluation, 10,* no. 2, 191–197.

Nimmer, D. N. (1984). Measures of validity, reliability, and item analysis for classroom tests. *Clearing House, 58,* no. 3, 138–140.

Thibodeau, G. P., et al. (1986). Answering the reading level question. *Academic Therapy, 21,* no. 3, 267–273.

White, J. D. (1988). Who writes these questions, anyway? *College Composition and Communication, 39,* no. 2, 230–235.

Zeidner, M. (1987). Essay versus multiple-choice type classroom exams: The student's perspective. *Journal of Educational Research,* 80, no. 6, 352–358.

Chapter 6

Bloom, B. S., & Madaus, G. F. (1981). *Evaluation of student learning.* New York: McGraw-Hill.

Choppin, B. (1985). Item banking using sample free calibration. *Evaluation in Education: An International Review Series, 9,* no. 1, 81–85.

Ebel, R. L. & Frisbie, D. A. (1986). *Essentials of Educational Measurement* (4th ed.). Englewood Cliffs, NJ: Prentice-Hall, Chapter 7.

Frary, R. B. (1985). Multiple-choice versus free-response: A simulation study. *Journal of Educational Measurement, 22,* no. 1, 21–31.

Frisbie, D. A. (1988). Instructional module on reliability of scores from teacher-made tests. *Educational Measurement: Issues and Practice, 7,* no. 1, 25–33.

Green, K. E., & Stager, S. F. (1987). Differences in teacher test and item use with subject, grade level taught, and measurement coursework. *Teacher Education & Practice, 4,* no. 1, 55–61.

Gronlund, N. E. (1987). *How to construct achievement tests* (5th ed.). Englewood Cliffs, NJ: Prentice-Hall.

Karras, R. (1985). A realistic approach to thinking skills: Reform multiple-choice questions. *Social Science Record, 22,* no. 2, 38–43.

Kolstad, R. K., & Kolstad, R. A. (1982). Applications of conventional and nonrestrictive multiple-choice examination items. *Clearing House, 56,* no. 4, 153–155.

Mehrens, W. A., & Lehmann, I.J. (1991). *Measurement and evaluation in education and psychology* (4th ed.). New York: Holt, Rinehart & Winston, Chapter 10.

Royer, J. M., et al. (1987). The sentence verification technique: A practical procedure for testing comprehension. *Journal of Reading, 30,* no. 5, 414–422.

Smith, C. W. (1987). 100 ways to improve and use teacher-made tests. *Illinois Schools Journal, 66,* no. 3, 20–26.

Stanley, J. C., & Hopkins, K. D. (1981). *Educational and psychological measurement and evaluation* (6th ed.). Englewood Cliffs, NJ: Prentice-Hall, Chapter 10.

White, J. D. (1988). Who writes these questions, anyway? *College Composition and Communication, 39,* no. 2, 230–235.

Zeidner, M. (1987). Essay versus multiple-choice type classroom exams: The student's perspective. *Journal of Educational Research, 80,* no. 6, 352–358.

Chapter 7

Blok, H. (1985). Estimating the reliability, validity and invalidity of essay ratings. *Journal of Educational Measurement, 22,* no. 1, 41–52.

Braun, H. I. (1988). Understanding scoring reliability: Experiments in calibrating essay readers. *Journal of Educational Statistics,* 13, no. 1, 1–18.

Coker, D. R., et al. (1988). Improving essay tests: Structuring the items and scoring responses. *Clearing House, 61,* no. 6, 253–255.

Ebel, R. L. (1986). *Essentials of educational measurement* (4th ed.). Englewood Cliffs, NJ: Prentice-Hall, Chapter 6.

Green, K. E., & Stager, S. F. (1987). Differences in teacher test and item use with subject, grade level taught, and measurement coursework. *Teacher Education & Practice, 4,* no. 1, 55–61.

Kemerer, R., & Wahlstrom, M. (1985). An alternative to essay examinations: The interpretive exercise, how to minimize test time and save dollars. *Performance and Instruction, 24,* no. 8, 9–12.

Royer, J. M., et al. (1987). The sentence verification technique: A practical procedure for testing comprehension. *Journal of Reading, 30,* no. 5, 414–422.

Smith, C. W. (1987). 100 ways to improve and use teacher-made tests. *Illinois Schools Journal, 66,* no. 3, 20–26.

Sweedler-Brown, C. O. (1985). The influence of training and experience on holistic essay evaluation. *English Journal, 74,* no. 5, 49–55.

White, J. D. (1988). Who writes these questions, anyway? *College Composition and Communication, 39,* no. 2, 230–235.

Zeidner, M. (1987). Essay versus multiple-choice type classroom exams: The student's perspective. *Journal of Educational Research,* 80, no. 6, 352–358.

Chapter 8

Anastasi, A. (1989). *Psychological testing* (6th ed.). New York: Macmillan, Chapter 8.

Collier, M. (1986). A specific investigation of relative performance of examination markers. *Assessment and Evaluation in Higher Education, 11,* no. 2, 130–137.

Gullickson, A. R., & Ellwein, M. C. (1985). Post hoc analysis of teacher-made tests: The goodness-of-fit between prescription and practice. *Educational Measurement: Issues and Practice, 4,* no. 1, 15–18.

Kolstad, R., et al. (1984). The application of item analysis to classroom achievement tests. *Education, 105,* no. 1, 70–72.

Luecht, R. M. (1987). Test pac: A program for comprehensive item and reliability analysis. *Educational and Psychological Measurement, 47,* no. 3, 23–26.

Mehrens, W. A., & Lehmann, I. J. (1991). *Measurement and evaluation in education and psychology* (4th ed.). New York: Holt, Rinehart & Winston, Chapter 11.

Nimmer, D. N. (1984). Measures of validity, reliability, and item analysis for classroom tests. *Clearing House, 58,* no. 3, 138–140.

Secolsky, C. (1983). Using examinee judgments for detecting invalid items on teacher-made criterion-referenced tests. *Journal of Educational Measurement, 20,* no. 1, 51–63.

Smith, C. W. (1987). 100 ways to improve and use teacher-made tests. Illinois Schools Journal, 66, no. 3, 20–26.

Woodrow, J. E. J. (1986). Using the Apple Macintosh and Multiplan spreadsheet to analyze tests. *Journal of Computers in Mathematics and Science Teaching, 5,* no. 3, 34–45.

Chapter 9

Bransford, J. D., & Vye, N. J. (1989). A perspective on cognitive research and its implications for instruction. In L. B. Resnick & L. E. Klopfer (Eds.), *Toward the thinking curriculum: Current cognitive research.* 1989 ASCD Yearbook (pp. 173–205).Alexandria, VA: Association for Supervision and Curriculum Development.

Fuhrman, S. (1988). Educational indicators: An overview. *Phi Delta Kappan, 2,* 486–487.

Gardner, H. (1990). Assessment in context: The alternative to standardized testing. In B. R. Gifford & M. C. O'Connor (Eds.), *Future assessments: Changing views of aptitude, achievement and instruction.* Boston: Kluwer Academic Publishers.

Nitko, A. J. (1989). Designing tests that are integrated with instruction. In R. L. Linn (Ed.), *Educational measurement* (3rd ed.) (pp. 447–474). New York: American Council on Education, Macmillan.

Popham, W. J. (1987). The merits of measurement driven instruction. *Phi Delta Kappan, 68,* 9, 679–682.

Resnick, L., & Resnick, D. (1990). Assessing the thinking curriculum: New tools for educational reform. In B. R. Gifford & M. C. O'Connor (Eds.), *Future assessments: Changing views of aptitude, achievement and instruction.* Boston: Kluwer Academic Publishers.

Resnick, L. B. (1987). *Education and learning to think.* Washington, DC: National Academy Press.

Shepard, L. A. (1989). Why we need better assessments. *Educational Leadership, 46,* 4–9.

Chapter 10

Collier, M. (1986). A specific investigation of relative performance of examination markers. *Assessment and Evaluation in Higher Education, 11,* no. 2, 130–137.

Gronlund, N. E. (1990). *Measurement and evaluation in teaching* (6th ed.). New York: Macmillan, Chapter 19.

Hills, J. R. (1982). *Measurement and evaluation in the classroom* (2nd ed.). Columbus, OH: Merrill, Chapters 14–19.

Luecht, R. M. (1987). Test pac: A program for comprehensive item and reliability analysis. *Educational and Psychological Measurement, 47,* no. 3, 23–26.

McKillip, W. D. (1979). Teacher-made tests: Development and use. *Arithmetic Teacher, 27,* no. 3, 38–43.

Millman, J., et al. (1983). Does grade inflation affect the reliability of grades? *Research in Higher Education, 19,* no. 4, 423–429.

Nottingham, M. (1988). Grading practices—watching out for land mines. *NASSP Bulletin, 72,* no. 507, 24–28.

Chapter 11

Aiken, L. R. (1980). Attitude measurement and research. *New Directions for Testing and Measurement,* no. 7, 1–24.

Anastasi, A. (1989). *Psychological testing* (6th ed.). New York: Macmillan, Chapter 17.

Cronbach, L. J. (1990). *Essentials of psychological testing* (5th ed.). New York: HarperCollins, Chapter 17.

Gardner, P. L. (1987). Measuring ambivalence to science. *Journal of Research in Science Teaching, 24,* no. 3, 241–247.

Grimes, M. D., & Hansen, G. L. (1984). Response bias in sex-role attitude measurement. *Sex Roles: A Journal of Research, 10,* no. 1–2, 67–72.

Lull, J., & Cappella, J. (1981). Slicing the attitude pie: A new approach to attitude measurement. *Communication Quarterly, 29,* no. 2, 67–80.

Markus, E. J. (1980). Mapping the social structure of a class: A practical instrument for assessing some effects of mainstreaming. *Journal of Special Education, 14,* no. 3, 311–324.

Meredith, V. H., & Williams, P. L. (1984). The testing issue. Proceedings of a conference held at Alabama State. *Educational Measurement: Issues and Practice, 3,* no. 1, 15, 35.

Ruth, L., & Murphy, S. (1984). Designing topics for writing assessment: Problems of meaning. *College Composition and Communication, 35,* no. 4, 410–422.

Schibeci, R. A. (1982). Measuring student attitudes: Semantic differential or Likert instruments? *Science Education, 66,* no. 4, 565–570.

Walker, D. K. (1973). *Socioemotional measures for preschool and kindergarten children.* San Francisco: Jossey-Bass.

Chapters 12–14

See Appendix C.

Chapter 15

Anastasi, A. (1989). *Psychological testing* (6th ed.). New York: Macmillan, Chapter 6.

Blok, H. (1985). Estimating the reliability, validity, and invalidity of essay ratings. *Journal of Educational Measurement, 22,* no. 1, 41–52.

Frisbie, D. A. (1973). Multiple-choice versus true-false: A comparison of reliabilities and concurrent validities. *Journal of Educational Measurement, 10,* 297–304.

Nimmer, D. N. (1984). Measures of validity, reliability and item analysis for classroom tests. *Clearing House, 58,* no. 3, 138–140.

Chapter 16

American Psychological Association (1986). *Standards for educational and psychological tests.* Washington, DC: APA.

Anastasi, A. (1989). *Psychological testing* (6th ed.). New York: Macmillan, Chapter 5.

Blok, H.(1985). Estimating the reliability, validity, and invalidity of essay ratings. *Journal of Educational Measurement, 22,* no. 1, 41–52.

Braun, H. I. (1988). Understanding scoring reliability: Experiments in calibrating essay readers. *Journal of Educational Statistics, 13,* no. 1, 1–18.

Costin, F. (1972). Three-choice versus four-choice items: Implications for reliability and validity of objective achievement tests. *Educational and Psychological Measurement, 32,* 1035–1038.

Frisbie, D. A. (1988). Instructional module on reliability of scores from teacher-made tests. *Educational Measurement: Issues and Practice, 7,* no. 1, 25–33.

Luecht, R. M. (1987). Test pac: A program for comprehensive item and reliability analysis. *Educational and Psychological Measurement, 47,* no. 3, 23–26.

Millman, J., et al. (1983). Does grade inflation affect the reliability of grades? *Research in Higher Education, 19,* no. 4, 423–429.

Nimmer, D. N. (1984). Measures of validity, reliability, and item analysis for classroom tests. *Clearing House, 58,* no. 3, 138–140.

Oosterhof, A. C., & Glasnapp, D. R. (1974). Comparative reliability and difficulties of the multiple-choice and true-false formats. *Journal of Experimental Education, 42,* 62–64.

Rudner, L. M. (1983). Individual assessment accuracy. *Journal of Educational Measurement, 20,* no. 3, 207–219.

Chapter 17

American Psychological Association (1986). *Standards for educational and psychological tests.* Washington, DC: APA.

Anastasi, A. (1989). *Psychological testing* (6th ed.). New York: Macmillan, Chapter 5.

Nimmer, D. N. (1984). Measures of validity, reliability, and item analysis for classroom tests. *Clearing House, 58,* no. 3, 138–140.

Rudner, L. M. (1983). Individual assessment accuracy. *Journal of Educational Measurement, 20,* no. 3, 207–219.

Chapter 18

American Psychological Association (1986). *Standards for educational and psychological tests.* Washington, DC: APA.

Anastasi, A. (1989). *Psychological testing* (6th ed.). New York: Macmillan, Chapter 4.

Choppin, B. (1985). Item banking using sample free calibration. *Evaluation in Education: An International Review Series, 9,* no. 1, 81–85.

Cronbach, L. J. (1990). *Essentials of psychological testing* (5th ed.). New York: HarperCollins, Chapter 3.

Daly, J. L. (1982). Let's talk testing. *Small School Forum, 3,* no. 3, 23–24.

Dreher, M. J., & Singer, H. (1984). Making standardized tests work for you. *Principal, 63,* no. 4, 20–24.

Green, D. R. (Ed.). (1974). *The aptitude achievement distinction.* Monterey, CA: CTB/McGraw-Hill.

Hills, J. R. (1983). Interpreting stanine scores. *Educational Measurement: Issues and Practice, 2,* no. 3, 18–27.

Lyman, H. B. (1986). *Test scores and what they mean.* Englewood Cliffs, NJ: Prentice-Hall.

Stiggins, R.J. (1985). Improving assessment where it means the most: In the classroom. *Educational Leadership, 43,* no. 2, 69–74.

Thibodeau, G. P., et al. (1986). Answering the reading level question. *Academic Therapy, 21,* no. 3, 267–273.

Chapter 19

Anastasi, A. (1989). *Psychological testing* (6th ed.). New York: Macmillan, Chapter 14.

Cronbach, L. J. (1990). *Essentials of psychological testing* (5th ed.). New York: HarperCollins, Chapter 7.

Guilford, J. P. (1967). *The nature of human intelligence.* New York: McGraw-Hill.

Karmel, L. J. (1978). *Measurement and evaluation in the schools* (2nd ed.). New York: Macmillan, Chapter 2.

Katz, M. (1973). *Selecting an achievement test: Principles and procedures.* Princeton, NJ: Educational Testing Service.

Lanyon, R., & Goodstein, L. D. (1982). *Personality assessment* (2nd ed.). New York: Wiley.

Mehrens, W. A., & Lehmann, I. J. (1987). *Using standardized tests in education* (4th ed.). New York: Holt, Rinehart and Winston, Chapter 3.

Samuda, R. J. (1975). *Psychological testing of American minorities: Issues and consequences.* New York: Dodd, Mead.

Chapter 20

Bricker, D., & Gumerlock, S. (1988). Application of a three-level evaluation plan for monitoring child progress and program effects. *Journal of Special Education, 22,* no. 1, 66–81.

Davis, G. & Rimm, S. (1989). *Education of the gifted and talented.* Englewood Cliffs, NJ: Prentice-Hall.

Fetterman, D. (1988). *Excellence and equality: A qualitatively different perspective on gifted and talented Education.* Albany, NY: State University of New York Press.

Gronlund, N. E. (1974). *Individualizing classroom instruction.* New York: Macmillan.

Howell, K. W., Kaplan, J. S., & O'Connell, C. Y. (1979). *Evaluating exceptional children: A task analysis approach.* Columbus, OH: Merrill.

Miederhoff, J. W., & Wood, J. W. (1988). Adapting test construction for mainstreamed mathematics students. *Mathematics Teacher, 81,* no, 5, 388–392.

Milgram, R., Dunn, R. & Price, G. (1993). *Teaching and counseling the gifted and talented adolescent: An international learning style perspective.* Westport, Conn.: Praeger.

Schwartz, Lita L. (1994) *Why give "gifts" to the gifted? Investing in a national resource.* Thousand Oaks, CA: Corwin press.

Valente, W. D. (1980). *Law in the schools.* Columbus, OH: Merrill.

Wood, J. W., & Aldridge, J. T. (1985). Adapting tests for mainstreamed students. *Academic Therapy, 20,* no. 4, 419–426.

Yoshida, R. K. (1976). Out-of-level testing of special education students with a standardized achievement battery. *Journal of Educational Measurement, 13,* 315–331.

Chapter 21

Angus, J. (1989). *Infoworld consumer product guide.* New York: Prentice-Hall.

Birnes W., Woodall, W., & Hayfield, N. (1989). *The McGraw-Hill personal computer programming encyclopedia.* New York: McGraw-Hill.

Bowker, R. R. (1989). *The software encyclopedia—1989.* New York: Reed.

Coburn, P. (1985). *Practical guide to computers in education* (2nd ed.). Reading, MA: Addison-Wesley.

Eager, B. (1994). *Using the Internet.* Indianapolis, IN: Que Corporation.

Hillman, H. (1984). *Macmillan complete computer buyer's checklist.* New York: Macmillan.

Lodish, E. (1986). Test writing made simple: Generate tests and worksheets electronically. *Electronic Learning, 5,* no. 5, 28, 30, 68.

McCallum, L. W. (1985). CATGEN: A computer assisted test generator. *Teaching of Psychology, 12,* no. 1, 45–46.

Microcomputer index, published bi-monthly. Palo Alto: Database Services.

Nelson, L. R. (1984). Using microcomputers to assess achievement and instruction. *Educational Measurement: Issues and Practice, 3,* no. 2, 22–26.

Peterson, R. (1991). *The PC-SIG encyclopedia of shareware* (4th ed.). Sunnyvale, CA: PC-SIG, Inc.

Software reviews on file, published monthly. New York: Facts on File, Inc.

Spencer, D. (1986). *The illustrated computer dictionary* (3rd ed.). Columbus, OH: Bell and Howell.

Truett, C. (1990). *Microcomputer software sources.* Englewood, CO: Libraries Unlimited, Inc.

Woodrow, J. E. J. (1986). Using the Apple Macintosh and Multiplan spreadsheet to analyze tests. *Journal of Computers in Mathematics and Science Teaching, 5,* no. 3, 34–45.

REFERENCES

Achenbach, T. (1991). *Manual for the teacher's report form.* Burlington: University of Vermont, Department of Psychiatry.

Allport, G. W., & Odbert, H. S. (1936). Trait-names: A psycho-lexical study. *Psychological Monographs, 47,* 1–171.

Bauwens, J., Hourcade, J. & Friend, M. (1989). Cooperative teaching: A model for general and special education integration. *Remedial and Special Education, 10 (2),* 17–22.

Barkley, R. A. (1987). The school situations questionnaire. From: *Defiant Children: A Clinician's Manual for Parent Training.* New York: Guilford Press.

Barkley, R. A., Conners, C. K., Barclay, A., Gadow, K., Gittleman, R., Sprague, R. L. & Swanson, J. (1990). Task Force Report: The appropriate role of clinical child psychologists in the prescribing of psychoactive medication for children. *Journal of Clinical Child Psychology, 19 (Suppl.),* 1–38.

Biederman, J. & Steingard, R. (1990). *Psychopharmacology of children and adolescents: A primer for the clinician.* (Technical Paper No. 27). Washington, DC: World Health Organization.

Bloom, B., Englehart, M., Hill, W., Furst, E., & Kratwohl, D. (1956). *Taxonomy of educational objectives: The classification of educational goals. Handbook I: Cognitive domain.* New York: Longmans, Green.

Brown R. T. & Borden, (1989). Neuropsychological effects of stimulant medication on children's learning and behavior. In C.R. Reynolds & E. Fletcher-Janzen (Eds.), *Handbook of Clinical Child Psychology* (pp. 443–474), New York: Plenum.

Brown, R. T., Dingle, A. & Landau, S. (1994). Overview of psychopharmacology in children and adolescents. *School Psychology Quarterly, 9(1),* 4–25.

Bukstein, O. (1992). Overview of pharmacological treatment. In V.B. Van Hasselt & M. Hersen (Eds.), *Handbook of behavior therapy and pharmacotherapy for children* (pp. 213–232). Boston: Allyn & Bacon.

Cannon, G. S., Idol, L. & West, F. J. (1992). Educating students with mild handicaps in general classooms: Essential teaching practices for general and special education. *Journal of Learning Disabilities, 25(5),* 314.

Coffman, W. E. (1971). Essay examinations. In R. J. Thorndike (Ed.), *Educational measurement* (2nd ed.). Washington, DC: American Council on Education.

Coker, D. R. & Griffith, P. (1994). Collaboration in the classroom: Joint responsibilities for teachers for specified instruction. *Journal of Instructional Psychology. 21(1),* 3–7.

Conte, A. E. (1994). Blurring the line between regular and special education. *Journal of Instructional Psychology, 21(2),* 103–113.

Cuban, L.(1986). *Teachers and machines: The classroom use of technology since 1920.* New York: Teachers College Press.

Cuban, L. (1989). Neoprogressive visions and organizational realities. *Harvard Educational Review, 59(2),* 217–222.

Davis, W. (1989). The regular education initiative debate: Its promises and problems. *Exceptional Children, 55(5),* 440–446.

Diagnostic and Statistical Manual of Mental Disorders-IV (DSM-IV) (1994). Washington: American Psychiatric Association.

Duffy, E. (1972). Activation. In N. S. Greenfield and R. A. Sternbach (Eds.), *Handbook of psychophysiology.* New York: Holt, Rinehart and Winston.

Fisher, M. & Newby, R. F. (1991). Assessment of stimulant response in ADHD children using a refined multimethod clinical protocol. *Journal of Clinical Child Psychology, 20,* 232–244.

Forness, S. R. & Kavale, K. A. (1988). Psychopharmacological medication: A note on classroom effects. *Journal of Learning Disabilities, 21,* 144–147.

Frazier, D. & Paulson, F. (1992). How portfolios motivate reluctant learners. *Educational Leadership, 49 (8),* 62–65.

Friend, M. & Cook, L. (1992). The new mainstreaming. *Instructor,* 30–36.

Gadow, K. D. (1991). Clinical issues in child and adolescent psychopharmacology. *Journal of Consulting and Clinical Psychology, 59,* 842–852.

Gadow, K. D. (1992). Pediatric psychopharmacology: A review of recent research. *Child Psychology and Psychiatry, 33,* 153–195.

Gadow, K. D. & Pomeroy, J. C. (1993). Pediatric psychopharmacology: A clinical perspective. In T. R. Kratochwill & R.J. Morris. (Eds.), *Handbook of psychotherapy with children and adolescents* (pp.356–402). Boston: Allyn & Bacon.

Ghiselli, E. E. (1966). *The study of occupational aptitude tests.* New York: Wiley.

Gullikson, H. (1987). *Theory of mental tests.* Hillsdale, NJ: Erlbaum.

Goyette, C. H., Conners, C. K. & Ulrich, R. F. (1978). Normative data on Revised Conners Parent and Teacher Rating Scales. *Journal of Abnormal Child Psychology, 6,* 221–236.

Haladyna, T., Nolen, S. B. & Haas, N. S. (1991). Raising standardized achievement test scores and the origins of test score pollution. *Educational Researcher, 20(5),* 2–7.

Hales, R. M. & Carlson, L. B. (1992). *Issues and trends in special education.* Lexington, KY: Federal Resource Center for Special Education.

Halvorsen, A. & Sailor, W. (1990). Integration of students with severe and profound disabilities: A review of research. In R. Gaylord-Ross (Ed.), *Issues and Research in Special Education* (Vol 1)(pp. 110–172). New York: Teachers College Press.

Harrow, A. J. (1972). *A taxonomy of the psychomotor domain.* New York: David McKay.

Hebert, E. (1992). Portfolios invite reflection from students and staff. *Educational Leadership, 49 (8),* 58–61.

Heinssen, R. K., Glass, C. R. & Knight, L. A. (1987). Assessing computer anxiety: Development and validation of the Computer Anxiety Scale. *Computers in Human Behavior,* Vol. 3, 59–69.

Holmes Group (1986). *Tomorrow's teachers.* East Lansing, MI: The Holmes Group, Michigan State University.

Honzik, M. P., McFarlane, J. W., & Allen, L. (1948). The stability of mental test performance between two and eighteen years. *Journal of Experimental Education, 17,* 209–324.

Keillor, G. (1985). *Lake Wobegon days.* New York: Penguin.

Kratochwill, T. R. (1994). Psychopharmacology for children and adolescents: Commentary on current issues and future changes. *School Psychology Quarterly, 9(1),* 53–59.

Kratwohl, D. R., Bloom, B. S., & Masia, B. B. (1964). *Taxonomy of educational objectives. Handbook II: Affective domain.* New York: David McKay.

Kubiszyn, T., Brown, R., DeMers, S., Landau, S. & Reynolds, C. (1992) *APA Division 16 Task Force Report: Psychopharmacology and the schools.* Paper submitted to the Division 16 Executive Committee.

Kubiszyn, T. (1994) Pediatric psychopharmacology and prescription privileges: Implications and opportunities for school psychology. *School Psychology Quarterly, 9(1),* 26–40.

LaFrenz, D. & Friedman, J. E. (1989). Computers don't change education, teachers do! *Harvard Educational Review, 59(2),* 222–225.

Likert, R. (1932). A technique for the measurement of attitudes. *Archives of Psychology,* 140.

Lord, F., & Novick, M. (1968). *Statistical theories of mental test scores.* Reading, MA: Addison-Wesley.

Mahmood, M. A. & Medewitz, J. N. (1989). Assessing the effect of computer literacy on subjects' attitudes, values, and opinions toward information technology: An exploratory longitudinal investigation using the Linear Structural Relations (LISREL) model. *Journal of Compter-Based Instruction, 16,* 20–28.

McInerney, V., McInerney, D. M. & Sinclair, K. E. (1994). Student teachers, computer anxiety and computer experience. *Journal of Educational Computer Research, 11(1),* 27–50.

Miller, G. A. (1956). The magic number seven, plus or minus two: Some limits on our capacity for processing information. *Psychological Review, 63,* 81–97.

National Assessment of Educational Progress (1987). *Learning by doing: A manual for teaching and assessing higher order thinking in science and mathematics* (Report 17-HOS-80). Princeton, NJ: Educational Testing Service.

National Council on Disability. (1989). *The education of students with disabilities: Where do we stand?* Washington, DC: National Council on Disability.

National Education Goals Panel. (1992). *Resolutions of the National Education Goals Panel: Future of the NAEP* (Goal 3). Washington, D.C.

National Education Goals Report. (1992). Executive Summary: *Building a Nation of Learners*. Washington, D.C.

Osgood, C. E., Suci, G. J., & Tannenbaum, P. H. (1957). *The measurement of meaning.* Urbana: University of Illinois Press.

Paulson, P. & Paulson, F. (1991). Portfolio: Stories of knowing. In P.H. Dryer (Ed.), *Claremont Reading Conference 55th Yearbook.*

Pemberton, H. (1994). News of the latest products and technology for K–12. *Mutimedia Schools.* Volme 1 (2).

Pitler, H. A technology magnet school emerges. *Multimedia Schools* (1994). Volume 1 (2).

Pollock, J. (1992). Blueprints for social studies. *Educational Leadership, 49 (8),* 52–53.

Redding, N. (1992). Assessing the big outcomes. *Educational Leadership, 49 (8),* 49–53.

Resnick, L., & Resnick, D. (1989). *Assessing the thinking curriculum: New tools for educational reform.* Pittsburgh: Learning Research and Development Center, University of Pittsburgh.

Rosen, L., Sears, D. & Weil, M. (1987). Computerphobia. *Behavior Research Methods, Instruments and Computers, 19,* 167–179.

Sailor, W., Anderson, J., Halvorsen, A.T., Doering, K., Filler, J. & Goetz, L. (1989). *The comprehensive local school: Regular education for all students with disabilities.* Baltimore: Paul H. Brookes.

Sailor, W., Gee, K. & Karasoff, P. (1993). Full inclusion and school restructuring. In M. Snell (Ed.). *Instruction of Students with Severe Disabilities* (4 Ed.). Macmillan: New York.

Salvia, J. & Ysseldyke, J. E. (1991). *Assessment* (5th Ed.). Boston: Houghton-Mifflin.

Sax, G. (1989). *Principles of educational and psychological measurement and evaluation: Third edition.* Belmont, CA: Wadsworth.

Shavelson, R. & Baxter, G. (1992). What we've learned about assessing hands-on science. *Educational leadership, 49 (8),* 20–25.

Shavelson, R., Gao, X. & Baxter, G. (1991). *Design theory and psychometrics for complex performance assessment.* Los Angeles: UCLA.

Spetalnick, T. (1993). Privacy in the electronic community. *EDUCOM Review.* Volume 28(3), 38–40.

Sternberg, R. (1986), *Intelligence applied.* New York: Harcourt Brace Jovanovich.

Swan, K. & Mitrani M. (1993). The changing nature of teaching and learning in computer-based classrooms. *Journal of Research on Computing in Education, 26(1),* 40–54.

Szetela, W. & Nicol, C. (1992). Evaluating problem-solving in mathematics. *Educational Leadership, 49 (8),* 42–45.

Thorndike, R. M., Cunningham, G., Thorndike, R. L., & Hagen, E. (1991).

Measurement and evaluation in psychology and education. New York: Macmillan.

Tuckman, B. W. (1975). *Measuring educational outcomes.* New York: Harcourt Brace Jovanovich.

Urdan, T. C. & Paris, S. G. (1994) Teachers' perceptions of standardized achievement tests. *Educational Policy, 8(2),* 137–156.

Viadero, D. (1993). Disabled New Jersey boy must be placed in regular classroom, court rules. *Education Week, XIII,* 37, 12.

White, R. (1994). Upgrades that pay. *PC Computing, 7 (11),* 196–211.

Wiggins, G. (1992). Creating tests worth taking. *Educational Leadership, 49 (8),* 26–34.

Ysseldyke, J. E. & Algozzine, B. (1990). *Introduction to Special Education,* (2nd Ed.), Boston: Houghton-Mifflin.

INDEX

ISBN: 978-1-951161-01-9

Table of Contents

How to Use this Workbook For Enhance Knowledge.

Complete beginners can begin using this Workbook for Where the Crawdads Sing by Delia Owens to get immediate help of the major lessons and Summary of the book.

The goal of this Workbook is to help answer all your problems by providing all the juicy details in the bestselling novel; Where the Crawdads Sing by Delia Owens, which will help you understand the authors true meaning in this novel.

By using this Workbook, readers will find summary, quotes etc which we believed were major in defining the crucial messages of the author in the book.

There are Spaces to jot down your thoughts at the end of each Section. Take out a pencil, pen, or whatever digital technology you would put to use to jot down your thoughts and feelings, while you read.

And don't forget to have fun - While at it. *This Where the Crawdads sing Workbook* reminds us that we are forever shaped by the children we once were, and that we are all subject to the beautiful and violent secrets that nature keeps.

About the Author

Delia Owens is a globally acclaimed best-selling author of a number of books about wildlife science in Africa. & Zoologist

She has won lots of awards including the Award for Nature Writing, John Burroughs award and has had her works published influential media outlets such as the African Journal of Ecology, the nature and a host of others.

Born 1949, M - Mark Owens

22 years living in AFRICA - living close to the land & working in wildlife conservation. They wrote about these experiences in 3 memoirs.

- They have been advised to never return to Zambia because they are wanted for questioning in a murder that took place there decades ago. That murder, victim remains unidentified, was filmed & broadcast on nat'l TV - US. Delia not suspected - her husband & stepson Christopher have been implicated by some witnesses. An ABC camera crew filming a segment program for Turning Point on the Owenses' conservation work in Zambia. Also it was the subject of the 2010 18,000 word article written by Jeffrey Goldberg pub - the New Yorker. George "controversial killer of a poacher in Zambia" [illegible] Similarity between = Delia Owen's true life exp. and the story of a Southern loner, a noble naturalist, who gets away with what is described as a righteously motivated murder in the remote wild.

Noted

PART ONE: THE MARSH

Chapter One: Ma

The novel starts in 1952 with Kya, a six-year who is in the process of noticing her mother, referred to as Ma, leave the house as usual. Such departure usually brings meat at the end of it, but she noticed something strange, which was how Ma slammed the door on her way out and the fact that she leaves with a case in her hand.

The absence of the customary wave from Ma further raised little Kya's suspicion that something might be wrong. This foreboding is increased by the tightness in her small chest, and after Ma makes a quick exit without looking back, she rushes back to the steps to wait, in the hope that all was well.

Stepping out from the house, her elder brother; Jodie- who is seven years older reassures her that their mother would come back, there was no way she would abandon them. He seemed skeptical himself, so Kya brings up the story of the fox that left her babies for which Jodie explains that it only happened because the mother was wounded and could not cater for her young family.

Their Ma was neither wounded nor starving and could not just up and leave them. That's not what mothers do, and theirs was just incapable of such cruelty, even though she was wearing her gator shoes and carried a blue case on her way out like she was headed somewhere essential and could take a while. Kya wasn't so sure either, yet she had to believe her brother.

In the marsh that is their environment and habitation, not much has changed since the 1500s, as those who needed spacious lands had to move away as the marsh was covered by a shoreline which led to a few killed by malaria and others swallowed by the

swamp. The survivors usually disappear at intervals until 200 years later when runaway slaves known as Maroons came in contact with the environment

Their Ma didn't come back that day. This would not be the first time she left after a fight, but unlike the other times, she didn't come back that day which worried Pa more than the children except Kya who sat at the house steps in anticipation that Ma would magically show up

Early the next day, Kya resumed her wait for Ma, but she didn't come back. Jodie who normally didn't play with Kya came out, and they had a fun moment playing games in the hopes that it would take her mind off things, but that didn't happen either. After a while, Kya came back to the steps, but Ma didn't come home that day.

Thoughts

Chapter Two: Jodie

It had been weeks since their Ma left and the children, after doing their best to coexist peacefully with Pa albeit unsuccessfully slowly drifted away and left home one at a time until it was just Jodie and Kya left. She was gradually forgetting their names and after a quick breakfast with her remaining sibling, ventured out of the house until the angry and lean frame of their Pa came running after them.

Later that same day, Kya had her heart shattered, even more, when Jodie announced that he could not put up with their Pa anymore and had to leave the house the same way others did. Catching a glimpse of his shadow walking away, Kya felt alone for the first time, and as she firstly warmed leftovers for supper and later laid down to sleep, the reality of her situation, its helplessness dawned on her even more.

Three days later, Pa came back with a bottle in his hand, drunk. He then proceeded to burn Ma's things to the utter dismay of Kya who then learned that the only way to live with him was to disappear from the house before he woke up and only come back at night when he must have gone to sleep.

For the first time, Kya had to go grocery shopping in the market and after almost being hit by some boys, made it back in one piece only to discover that cooking as she had seen Ma do was virtually impossible. She made sorry meals that hardly passed her throat. Keeping the house in order was slightly more doable.

On Kya's birthday, she had no doubt Ma would come back. Ma never missed her birthdays, but as the day went by, it dawned on her that Pa either never remembered or didn't care. Ma never came.

Thoughts

Chapter three: Chase

In the fall of 1969, two boys found a local named chase in the sand near the swamp, presumed dead. Running off, they quickly informed the sheriff who came along with the local doctor to pronounce him dead. This was strange by all means, as there was no other footprint to indicate anyone retreating after he had fallen.

It didn't matter that the boys weren't supposed to be out there in the first place; they had to get help. The sheriff would rather not meddle in such but after hearing the name of the person involved, had no choice but to race over and get a better understanding of the situation

It was widely believed that he had fallen from the tree and had been dead for at least 10 hours before the time they found him

The sheriff quickly pointed out that people usually come here in packs and the fact that there were no footprints meant there was more than met the eyes at the scene.

Thoughts

Chapter Four: School

Back in 1952, it was time for little Kya to get some formal education and her chaperone in the person of Mrs. Culpeper arrived to take her to school. It didn't matter that she wore heels that would make running after Kya impossible, the more critical factor was the hunger churning Kya's stomach which made her get out of her hiding place at the mention of free lunch at school.

Dressing up in the only dress she had left and walking without shoes, Kya promptly slid her Hands into the older Woman's and moved along. It didn't become easier that she could not spell dog and was either mocked or ignored by all; she was determined to learn as much as possible from them over time, no matter how they felt about her.

A few weeks later, little Kya jumped from a tree only to land squarely on a nail. The pain shot through her whole body and after Pa never came to help, she yanked the nail out and hoped to get a tetanus shot within two days to avoid dying slowly like Jodie always said.

The fear that enveloped her only reduced after she made it through the required 48 hours. It wasn't easy seeing as she had no help from Pa, but the times of dipping her foot in the freshly dug hole for comfort finally paid off or so it would seem.

Though she still hoped for Ma's return, Kya slowly accepted that it would never happen as days turned into months weeks and months.

Thoughts

Chapter Five: Investigation

Forward to 1969, the sheriff is dumbfounded at the turn of events. Sending the doctor into town for an ambulance, he did not know what to make of the lack of evidence, nor did he want to have the whole town in panic. To this effect, he ordered the boys to stay in the crime scene to avoid the spread of the news. After all, the just-deceased Chase was the best quarterback the town had ever seen.

A few minutes later, the deputy sheriff arrived on the scene and after about ten minutes of combing the area for clues to no effect, put them into more confusion as to how this issue would be resolved.

Soon enough, the ambulance came racing down, and before they loaded in, the sheriff noticed that the leg was bent in the wrong way and pictures were taken for further investigation.

The first clue that this death might be a murder and not an accident was gotten in the form of the back gate, which is usually closed but was left open. Both sheriff and his deputy agreed that this was indeed odd and was most likely done by someone who pushed Chase to his death and left it open to cover his tracks.

They both agreed that Chase's reputation as a philanderer might have ruffled a few feathers and could have led to a spat husband or boyfriend pushing him to his death. It was agreed that there are indeed a few men capable of driving Chase to the ground without many problems.

Thoughts

Chapter Six: A boat and a boy

Kya was startled when Pa came up one day to tell her that he was leaving town and would be back in four days. This was never the case as he didn't ever disclose his movements or whereabouts to her, so much that she waved hard when he turned from the road and got a dismissive hand gesture in return, much more than Ma did.

Stepping out behind the house, she found Pa's boat which she usually didn't enter, yet the urge to explore was high, not minding the possibility of getting a real beating if Pa ever found out she had gone to his boat.

Getting in, she slowly brought the boat to life, and after revving the engine, set sail without a care in the world. Sailing at an even speed, little Kya moved farther into the swamp, taking mental notes so she would not get lost.

A while later, she ran into another person, a young boy of about twelve who was fishing. They exchanged bows, and she moved on. Later on, she thought to go back home but could not remember which way she had come. Getting to where the boy was, he offered to help her, since he knew her brother Jodie. Kya followed him and quickly found her way home, thanking him as Ma had taught her. His name was Tate.

Thoughts

Chapter Seven: The Fishing Season

As time went on, it dawned on Kya that she had fewer people to interact. Pa barely says a word to her which leaves Tate and the market lady who she buys supplies from, a very nosey individual who is never able to mind her business.

Usually, Pa ran regular errands in his boat since he didn't have a car, combining this with his regular fishing expeditions and frequent visit to the gambling table.

Seeing as she could not ask Pa to lend her the boat, little Kya tried to please him by cleaning the house, and after he left, she headed to the local gas store to get some gas and groceries. After getting what she came for, Kya slowly made her way home, emptying the contents of the gas container in the tank, cleaning the boat afterward

The next day, Pa came home to cheap food from Kya, which was much better than the junks he ate outside. Having his fill, she took the opportunity to ask that he take her fishing sometime and after a loud laugh, agreed, and they subsequently made it a habit, sailing together at different times.

Thoughts

Chapter Eight: Negative Data

The sheriff and his deputy had to practically drag Chase's mother and widow out of the morgue where they had come to see his body and say goodbye. A few days later, the first results from the coroner came in, and it indicated that there were no fingerprints anywhere in the vicinity which raised their suspicion that this was a murder with an immaculate cover-up.

Making up their minds, the law enforcement officers decided to scan the area again in the hope that they had missed something earlier.

At the diner, the sheriff and deputy made to keep their ears on the ground as the local folk would generally talk about such events and perhaps they would pick up a valuable clue or two.

Approaching a group, they heard the men whisper that a suspect in the murder case should be Lamar Sands who had a bone to pick with the deceased due to the affair he had with his wife and the fact that he had a criminal record made it easy to point fingers at him.

Further forward, a group of women suspected it might be the lonely woman who lived alone at the marsh, a weird soul who was more than capable of committing such an act.

Shaking their heads, the sheriff and deputy moved on to get their dinner.

Thoughts

Chapter Nine: Jumpin

A black older man who is known as Jumpin due to his famed habit of springing up anytime anyone came to the gas station and smiling at them, greeted Kya and Pa warmly as they sailed towards him. After the customary greetings which involved an introduction of Kya, Jumpin duly filled their tank while making small talk and generally being a happy fellow.

Sailing further, Pa stopped at a restaurant for them to grab a bite which was both exciting and scary for Kya, seeing as she had never been in one. After disapproving glances from already seated customers, Pa ordered so much food that Kya genuinely thought she would fall sick afterward.

A few months later, Kya was shocked to see a letter from Ma. While she was eager to tear it open and read its contents, her inability to read anything else but her name made her wait for Pa to come back. He did, swiftly burning the letter to ashes before Kya could save anything else but the charred remains, stored in a little bottle and placed on the side of her bed.

Pa finally came back in what has become his default state-drunk, staggering through the door. Kya gained the needed confidence and asked him about the letter to which he barked and told her it was not her business as she was never coming back.

Thoughts

Chapter Ten: Just Grass in the Wind

At the crime scene, the sheriff and his deputy scoured for clues to aid their working theory. They noticed tracks made by different kinds of animals at different times but never found any that was man made

Walking along the shore close to the bay, they noticed shattered glass for which the sheriff insinuated must have come from a boat but his partner waved it off as just grass in the wind

Thoughts

Chapter Eleven: Croker Sacks Full

When Kya was ten, her Pa came home even less, sometimes being away for weeks at a time. Presently, it dawned on Kya that he most likely won't be coming back ever again and even though she still had the house and boat, there was no way she would survive for much longer on the thin supplies in the house.

The thought of surrendering herself to the authorities quickly faded away as she was not in a hurry to give up the marsh; the last thing she had in the world.

Sailing back up, she headed straight for jumpin with two sacks of fresh mussels for which he exchanged one for gas and the other for 50 cents which were enough to get her supplies.

They struck a business deal that would require her bringing in a few bags ahead of others very early in the morning or risk having the first ones gat all the cash. She promised never to be late after sending greetings from Pa.

Thoughts

___

___

___

___

___

___

Chapter Twelve: Pennies and Grits

As time went on, Kya finally believed that Pa would never come back home, same as Ma. Having to fend for herself, she would always set sail, always seeing Tate a distance away but never having the courage to go near him or utter a word. The hard thump of her heart against her ribs wouldn't let her.

She heard the sound of chatter all over, which signaled that she wasn't alone anymore. Dashing into a nearby bush to get a better look, she noticed five boys and four girls; Chase Andrews, one of them as they got ready to play football, all laughing and giggling.

The next morning, she sailed back up to jumping to make some money but was disappointed for the second time in a row as other people had already beaten her to it. He advised her to find other means of making money, and she took to fishing, spending the next eight hours gathering fishes

She then spent time, smoking them and delivering to jumping, who didn't pay but promised to display them for sales and give her proceeds or return the fishes if no one buys.

Thoughts

Chapter Thirteen: Feathers

At fourteen, Kya had become sufficiently grown. Lanky, but a young adult by all means, albeit one that had to get food from trash and digging of holes. One day, she noticed the presence of another person, a boy slightly older than her and she did the one thong se always did; run.

This little activity prevented her from catching and smoking any fishes that day, as she spent the rest of it hiding that meant she couldn't get any money as she had planned.

Seeing a feather stuck in a tree trump, Kya thought to pluck it at first but later changed her mind, only to wake up to a different one every day, which meant they were put there by someone, perhaps the mystery boy she had seen earlier.

One night a few days later, several boys came through the woods, bellowing on her while, making strange noises. Seeing as there was literally no door and they could walk in and cause her harm, Kya tried to retreat through the back only to see them go as they had come. To her relief.

Seeing a new feather the next day, convinced her that whatever game was being played is still on.

Thoughts

____

____

____

____

Chapter Fourteen: Red Fibers

Moving forward, deputy sheriff Joe informed Sheriff Ed that further report had come in which points to the fact that Chase had indeed fallen from the tree but the fall was not enough to kill him. There was definitely someone else on the crime scene as suggested by the red wool materials found on his clothing which weren't part of it in the first place.

Thoughts

Chapter Fifteen: The Game

Time and again, Kya gladly continued their game of feathers, until one morning that she came out and discovered that he had upped the stakes by including a carton which included some seeds and an engine plug; just what she needed, accompanied by a handwritten note which she could not read

The next day, Tate came in person to say a few words and convinced her not to run away this time, she obliged. He mentioned that he felt she needed the items she brought and gave them to her, seeing as he had spares himself.

She thanked and reminded him that she could not read and he told her that the content was that he felt the need to give her those items and departed by promising to come to see her at intervals and teach her to read if she didn't mind.

Thoughts

Chapter Sixteen: Reading

Seeing as Tate never came around to start the reading lessons, Kya decided to go into the village and share a few words with Jumpin and Mabel, two people who have always been kind to her. A while later, she noticed two boys taunting Jumping by throwing racial slurs at him and even rocks. For this, she aimed and hit one of the boys hard in the head while the other took off.

She wondered why jumpin never said or did anything to them on her way home, no longer interested in human interaction.

The next day, Tate arrived promptly and apologized for his initial absence. He immediately got into teaching her and showed a fantastic level of patience until she could pronounce a few words, after which he felt so much pride and encouraged her to try even harder.

After more practice, she improved significantly and was able to read out words accordingly, even the bible.

Thoughts

Chapter Seventeen: Changing the Threshold

Growing even more, Kya discovered from jumpin, that a few people from social services had been looking for her and in order to stay out of sight, went back home and pleaded with Tate that they learn elsewhere, in hiding.

He obliged her request and together, they went as far into the mash as possible, Kya retreating that she was not scared of wild animals, bears included.

A few days later, she reached womanhood while sailing and was found by Tate as he helped reach out to Mabel who encouraged her that there was nothing wrong with her. Then next day, Tate came to her with cakes, and after they played for a while, he kissed her, and she agreed to be his girlfriend, not minding that she was only fifteen at the time.

A second kiss followed, which was much better than the first and made Kya happy.

Thoughts

Chapter Eighteen: White Canoe

Tate and Kya made it a habit to spend as much time together as they could, always sailing across in happiness and playing like children. It didn't matter the day or time; their primary focus was to be with each other, generally having a good time.

One afternoon, however, Tate came with some items which were wrapped in a blanket and beckoned on Kya to sail with him. After they had gotten to a particular part, he unveiled the details to be a massive cake with her name on it and other gift items to celebrate her fifteenth birthday.

She was genuinely moved by this gesture since nobody but Ma remembers her birthday. On inquiry, she found out that he knew the date by going through her bible. She could read now and do little sums, which explains the scribblings too.

Tate's father; Saunders, had to ask his son about all the rumors going on about how he was involved with a marsh girl and made him realize it would not be wise to start a family with her at this point. In his defense, Tate pointed out that she was the best human he had ever met and was practically teaching her to read and write

On some nights, Tate would fantasize about her breasts and the growing urge in him to touch them, so much that he finally got the chance to after Christmas that year. She was trying to bathe, and he just walked up to her from behind and ran his hands all over her body and breasts, awakening a longing within her.

He finally got the chance to make love to her one day, their clothes are taken off, and bare bodies revealed, only for him to realize that it should not be this way, she was too young, much to her disappointment.

He had to leave for college soon, which left her heartbroken. His promise to come back to her fast enough didn't change much as she saw one more person she love walk away. He said goodbye, and she stood after he had left, a hand to her heart.

Thoughts

Chapter Nineteen: Something Going on

It had been eight days since the body of Chase Andrews was found and the sheriff and his deputy tried to get more clues to which the former stated that he heard a rumor that the deceased was making frequent but secret trips to the marsh

This led to the belief that he must have gotten involved with someone from there, most likely a woman which gave the law enforcement officers a place to start from in digging for more clues.

While waiting for the mother of Chase to come to speak to them about some clue she had, they ordered lunch.

Thoughts

Chapter Twenty: July 4

The day Tate promised Kya had finally come and she went excitedly to the water bank to wait for him. She would wait till evening before undressing and going into the water for a swim, eager to have her body cooled after the hotness she felt all over and would come out and wait for her body to dry before picking up her clothes and going back to the house.

This became her daily ritual for days on end, yet there was no sign of Tate or his boat and just as she was about to go in after waiting for him another day, felt something pull her from behind, she shouted and screamed.

Thoughts

Chapter Twenty-One: Coop

After waiting in vain for Tate, it became clear to Kya that everyone would always disappoint, to which she made a mental note never to love or trust again. Kya didn't want any form of human interaction in the nearest future, but as her supplies wore thin, she had to go to Jumpin to get a few things without being warm to him or standing around to chat.

Months later, her life went back to the routine before Tate came around and months turned into a year, and another and no matter how hard she tried, the vacuum in her heart remained.

Thoughts

PART TWO: The Swamp

Chapter Twenty-Two: Same Tide

At nineteen, Kya had grown into a young woman, though she still lived in the marsh and survived on scraps and other things. One day at the beach, she noticed the impending approach of people and quickly went to hide, only to see Chase Andrews and his band of friends run in to play football and she noticed how they had been friends for years, and her loneliness tugged at her heart. Chase eventually saw her hiding and held her gaze for a little while before smiling and going back to join the group.

This gave her hope that perhaps, there was hope for social interaction, which led her to always come back to the beach in the hope that she would catch another glimpse of him.

Days later, while in town and feeling more social than average, she ran into him and after a stiff introduction, invited her for a picnic on his boat. She accepted, and he gave her the rendezvous point.

Unknown to Kya, Tate had made effort to see her on the 4th of July as agreed but could not make it as his professor asked him to come along on a trip for which he was the only student chosen.

Two weeks later, he was on his way to say sorry and explain himself when he noticed her far off and after observing how unashamedly timid she was, made the cold calculated decision to walk out of her life for good without saying goodbye.

Thoughts

Chapter Twenty-three: The Shell

On the day of the picnic, Kya dressed up in denim shorts and cotton top and looked normal like every young woman her age. After they met and said stiff hellos, Chase helped her onto the boat, and they sailed to the spot he had chosen, coming to shore to lay a blanket and make small talk.

A while later, he kissed her and immediately made for her clothes, removing her top and positioning himself between her thighs when she jerked up suddenly, offended that all he wanted was to be her first; that was his goal after all, but perhaps he should have spent more time wooing her. She was the trashy marsh girl but was worth more than a soft picnic.

Retreating, she walked and ran the many miles to her boat, rejecting his suggestion to convey her. On getting to where her boat was, she got in and went home, disappointed

Thoughts

Chapter Twenty-Four: The Fire Tower

Ten days after their last encounter, Kya ran into Chase again, albeit knowingly, holding his gaze and circling back toward him after he called to her. Chase apologized again, promising such would never repeat itself between them.

He took her to a fire tower at another spot from where she could see most of the town and swamp, and after coming down, he asked to see where she lived. Reluctantly, she took him to her shack, and he was both interested and impressed that she has been able to live alone in this place for over ten years.

Turning around, she took him down to the beach, and he watched her feed birds, amazed at the beauty that was both outside and lay within this often maligned marsh girl.

After the got back in, he promised to come to visit her often, which led her to ask what he wanted with her. He responded by saying that all he wanted was to be close to and get to know her better without doing anything she didn't want.

She agreed.

Thoughts

Chapter Twenty-Five: A visit from Patti Love

On the agreed day, Patti Love Andrews arrived at the sheriff's office to give her own insight into the murder of her son. Once inside, she duly sat down and got right into it, telling the officers about a special necklace her son always wore which was given to him by the marsh woman. According to Patti, that same necklace was not around her son's neck, neither was it part of his belongings as collected by the coroner.

She concluded by informing them that chase had been involved with the marsh girl but broke it off before marrying Pearl, and since the former couldn't have him, she killed him.

The officers, eager to tread lightly told her that while this might be another angle, it wasn't a concrete lead and they would include it in among the possibilities and take a good look, just as they were doing at the time. She thanked them and left.

The next day, they decided to track her to the marsh and ask a few questions but after hitting several dead ends, arrived only to notice that her boat wasn't tied to the log which signaled she wasn't around

They came back the next day and found the boat tied, but call as they did, they got no answer which led them to believe that she was probably around and watching them that instant.

Thoughts

Chapter Twenty-Six: The Boat Ashore

Kya had become very comfortable around Chase and spent several hours a day with him, either exploring the marsh or just laying at the beach, taking in the sights.

While she had seen Tate a few times from a distance over the years, she was not prepared for the near run-in she had with him. He was there, about 40yards away but before he could see her, she quickly turned and went back the way she had come.

Tate finally made up his mind to seek Kya out and explain things before asking for her forgiveness. Life had made it possible that he would be moving back to the marsh to work at a soon to be established research Centre by the federal government, armed with a Ph.D. and Kya as his wife if she would have him.

To his utter surprise, he saw her just before getting to her lagoon and quickly noticed that she indeed was with Chase which confirmed the rumors. Seeing them kiss tore into him more than he cared to admit and he did what he had been doing, he turned his boat and went away.

While Chase longed to make love to Kya, she wasn't sure and made him wait by rejecting several advances. While she appreciated the company, she didn't want to give in and have him walk away from her afterward. After running into his parents and getting a cold stare, she asked when she would meet them officially. He said it would be soon; his eyes turned away from her.

Thoughts

Chapter Twenty-Seven: Out the Hog Mountain Road

On one of their times together a particular night, Chase made mention of his hopes for the future; getting married to Kya, building a two-story on the outskirts of town so she would not have to worry about so much contact with people. She had recently begun to harbor thoughts of a life with Chase but never dared hope, but here he was, speaking life to her innermost desires and even convincing her that his parents would not be a problem.

A few days later, he was able to convince her to come with him while he bought supplies in a nearby town and as they rode out in his pickup truck, she took in the scenery and let her mind get filled with all the possibilities with him.

In town, Chase checked them into a local motel and made another advance at her which was well received this time, as talks of marriage had knocked away all her inhibitions. The pain shot through her, and he told her to relax as it was normal, then lay beside her afterward, grinning.

Weeks later and after several other sex bouts, she breached the topic of meeting his people, he convinced her to wait for the right time after which he disappeared for a few days, increasing the longing within her.

A few days later, she heard the sound of a boat coming and she rushed to receive him, only to realize it was Tate. After hurling a few rocks at him, she listened to his story of how Chase was never loyal to her but actually sleeps with a number of women in town, knowing Kya would most likely not come to. After a bit more of apologies, she let him come in to take a look at his collections, marveling at how detailed they are and taking a few samples to show a publisher. Finally, he left and Chase

came back a week after Christmas, with a lot of questions in Kya's mind

Thoughts

Chapter Twenty-Eight: The Shrimper

The sheriff and deputy walked into their favorite diner to eat and most importantly, listen to what people were saying. While down the line, a man named Hal walked up to the sheriff and asked for a word in private for which he readily obliged.

At a private tale, he told the sheriff of how he and another man had seen the marsh girl in her boat, sailing towards the same area where Chase's body was found sometime after midnight.

The sheriff agreed that it was a clue and after Hal left, confided in his deputy that they now had grounds to seek for a warrant to interrogate her and search her house.

Thoughts

Chapter Twenty-Nine: Seaweed

Two days to the birthday of Chase, Kya went into town to get some unique supplies with which she would bake him a caramel cake; her first time in attempting such and spend a lot of time as possible with him on this special day.

On alighting from her boat, she saw him with his friends just a few feet away and knew that there was no way she could pass without being seen by them. Surprising to her was the fact that Chase had his hand around another girl and she wondered what that meant

After stiff introductions which barely got any reply from said friends, Kya spent her savings buying what she came for and went home to prepare. Additionally, she bought a newspaper which talked about the soon to be established research Centre and Chase's engagement to a girl known as Pearl Stone.

Outside, she noticed his boat stop close by and did the first thing that came to mind; she ran to hide and only came out to feed the galls after he left.

Thoughts

Chapter Thirty: The Rips

Trying to get rid of the pain lodged in her heart, Kya sailed out at night, getting into the water and waiting for a tide to perhaps cause some harm to her or make her feel fear. There were several instances where that could have happened but no matter how hard it tried, the wave could not have the effect she was looking for.

Ultimately, she was not mourning the betrayal from Chase, but her stupidity in believing that someone could stay with her. As far as she was concerned, love is a fallacy and one she would never associate with, ever.

Chase had played his game well by talking about marriage and making love to her, then going on his merry way by actually choosing and getting engaged to another. The pain stayed, but her determination to stay away from all form of human contact deepened even more.

Thoughts

Chapter Thirty-One: The book

Kya never bothered to check her mailbox, because she never gets any letters from anyone but a year after Chase got engaged to pearl, she regularly checked the mail and was delighted when a brown envelope was deposited with the contents revealing the first installment of her book from the publisher and a $5,000 early payment

The publisher assured her of further book projects along the line and more royalties to come every six months, which should always be in thousands of dollars.

To make sure, she went to the local directory to check if her land belonged to her family and after being informed that it was indeed theirs but needed to offset a backlog of taxes, did the needful and took home, a deed in her name.

She wrote a letter to Tate, inviting him over and he came and was given a signed copy of her book with a promise to never hide from him again

Thoughts

Chapter Thirty-Two: Alibi

The sheriff and his deputy were at a crossroads at this point. While they considered getting a warrant, there came the story from Jumpin and Tate that Kya was actually out of town the night Chase died and was in Greenville for two days.

Just as they were exploring other options, a woman walks in to confirm the story by stating that she and a handful of others saw her get on the bus on the said day and got back two days later.

Almost convinced, the sheriff came up with a theory that maybe Kya actually got on a bus but came back at night to commit the said act before getting on another bus on the same day.

The bus schedules confirmed the possibility of this, as there were several round tips made on the day and this convinced them further on the need to get that warrant.

Thoughts

Chapter Thirty-Three: The Scar

Sitting alone one late afternoon, Kya heard a truck pull up and though she wanted to take to her heels through the backdoor, the army uniform worn by the stranger coming towards her was fascinating, so she stood.

At the door, she realized that this person that had come to her shack was none other than her brother Jodie who had seen her book and decided to track her down. A brief moment of apology followed the news that Ma had died only two years earlier after suffering from physical and mental illness for days.

Ma had made an effort through the letter she sent, but Pa callously burnt it to ashes before going back to his drinking habit at first and finally leaving home.

She made him coffee first and later a sumptuous meal for dinner, and they spent a few moments reminiscing on the past and what could have been had things been any different.

Jodie had enlisted in the army as a form of punishment for how badly he treated her by abandoning her with Pa for all these years, knowing what he was capable of. He needn't apologize, as she did alright for herself and things were looking good for the future.

On his way out, he encouraged her to go after Tate, seeing as he was a good man.

Thoughts

Chapter Thirty-Four: Search the Shack

On getting to the shack, both the sheriff and his deputy found out that Kya was nowhere to be found, which was what they expected. Armed with a search warrant, they decided to comb through her belongings without scattering anything.

After a few minutes, the deputy found a red hat which was the exact color and texture with the wool found on Chase's corpse. To this, the sheriff declared that they send the materials to the lab and if indeed they matched, would have to invite Kya in for questioning

Thoughts

Chapter Thirty-Five: The Compass

Seven months after Jodie's visit, Kya excitedly got another of her books in print. Smiling as she ran her hand through it, she read a handwritten note from Tate with a compass attached to it, encouraging her to make good use of it.

Though a part of her heart still skips when she sees him, another part loathes him for abandoning her the way he did, and she wished one part would overshadow the other to give her the peace she needs, not minding the outcome.

Stepping out on this day, she saw him again in his boat, golden hair well covered with a red baseball cap and instead of calling to him like agreed, she hid until he passed before walking down to the beach to recite poems.

Thoughts

Chapter Thirty-Six: To Trap a Fox

The lab result came back and confirmed that the hat and wool samples match perfectly, which led to both men being convinced that it was time to bring her in for questioning.

As they were ringing out the potential charges and motive, a man walked in and after spending five minutes, gave them a substantial purpose for murder to run with.

Thoughts

Chapter Thirty-Seven: Gray Sharks

Doing her best to avoid the sheriff and his deputy, Kya now came at first light to get whatever supplies she needed from Jumpin. On this fateful day, she came as usual but surprisingly, Jumpin didn't acknowledge her wave like he always did. Only then did she notice a swam of boats racing towards her with the sheriff at the helm.

She sailed away quickly, eager to get away from them immediately by making use of her extensive knowledge of these parts. Just as she was about to escape, their superior boats caught up with her, and she was arrested for the murder of Chase, here rights read out loud.

Thoughts

Chapter Thirty-Eight: Sunday Justice

In the two months that Kya was incarcerated before the murder trial, she never made any effort to speak to anyone or even seek the services if a lawyer. A veteran who had retired before decided to take up her defense pro bono and try as he did, she neither showed interest in responding to anything he said nor even look at him.

Finally, the trial day came, and the judge declared that the case would not be moved to another county as the defense attorney had asked for The jury was mostly made up of people Kya knew as she took a little time to look at their faces, as the judge called for lunch recess.

Thoughts

Chapter Thirty-Nine: Chase for Chance

One morning while Kya was out on the beach, she heard a voice nearby and immediately stood up to stand face to face with Chase. Turning to walk away, he grabbed her and apologized for the way things ended between them, opining that it would never have worked out between them and suggesting things go back to the way it was between them.

Not wanting to hear any more of what the drunk Chase had to say, she tried to free herself before he made an attempt to force himself on her, eventually beating her down while he removed his trousers and her shorts.

At the last second, she gathered all the strength possible and hit him hard enough that he fell to the side. To make sure, she struck him in the groin and a few times in the kidney before getting on her boat and going home as two men stared at her.

Thoughts

Chapter Forty: Cypress Cove

The prosecutor called a Mr. Rodney to the stand as a first witness; he went ahead to tell the story of how himself and another friend heard Kya scream at Chase on that fateful morning that she would kill him if he ever came near her again, running away while pulling her shorts up.

The defendant was next, as he established that it was possible that Chase was trying to rape his client before she kicked him that way in self-defense before zooming off, Mr. Rodney agreed.

Thoughts

Chapter Forty-One: A Small Herd

After that encounter with Chase, Kya only thought of her swollen face and the need to stay away from him now and always. To make it easier, she packed a few things and went to her secret hideout where he would never find her.

She knew those men would never defend her, and Jumpin would encourage her to call the sheriff where it would be her word against that of Chase Andrews where nobody would ever believe her.

A few days later, she made sure to sail in areas where nobody would see her, least of all Jumpin as he would see the damage to her face and pity her or worse, seek redress. While doing this, she subtly planned her escape for a while.

Thoughts

Chapter Forty-Two: A Cell

Being locked up and threatened with the death penalty didn't scare Kya. The only terrifying thought was the possibility of being killed by another at a scheduled date. That wasn't how she wanted to go out.

The cell should have been called a cage, or so Kya thought, its structure and wooden beds which provided little or no comfort weren't much of a concern to her as none of her current predicament scared her.

Thoughts

Chapter Forty-Three: A Microscope

While on her regular habit of sailing out, Kya stumbled on Tate who was bent over and taking water samples, neither wanting him to see her purple eye or even talk to him at all, she made to get away before he quickly called to her to look into his new microscope and see an amoeba.

She talked of her editor wanting to meet up at Greenville though she was reluctant to go. He nudged her to try, mentioning that all she had to do was get to the main bus stop, and the driver would know how to assist her.

Curiosity got the better of her as she went closer and took a look, amazed at what she saw before taking several looks. He invited here for coffee which she declined, not wanting to get close to him for fear of losing herself to him again.

He offered her a jacket due to the weather, but she turned him down before he flung his cap at her which she did same, and they went back and forth until she suddenly caught herself and bade him goodbye.

Thoughts

Chapter Forty-Four: Cell Mate

A cat known as Sunday justice came in with the guard who brought supper into Kya's cell one night and stayed with her till morning, becoming a useful company in such a desolate place.

Her attorney came in to see her, reading out other options, such as a plea bargain for manslaughter and perhaps ten years behind bars, as against life in jail or the capital punishment if convicted of murder. She refused to explore any angle that would give the slightest inkling that she was indeed guilty and made him promise to get her out, one way or another.

The next morning, she finally decided to see Tate, who had visited over a dozen times but never got to see her as she refused. While he offered hope, she besought him to forget about her as she was a point in life where hope was useless

Thoughts

Chapter Forty-Five: Red Cap

The coroner was called onto the stand as the second witness, and cross-examination by the prosecutor ensued, where it was proven beyond all doubt that the red wool found on the jacket of the deceased did belong to the accused.

Afterward, the defendant asked questions of his own where it was established that there was neither any evidence to suggest that Chase was pushed, neither was there any way to determine that the said wool was deposited on the said night as it could have been there for over four years.

Back at her cell, her lawyer told her it had been a good cross examination and she thought of calling Jodie before folding up the paper where his number was written and instead picked up a textbook

Thoughts

Chapter Forty-Six: King of the World

Coming to town, Kya finally met jumpin to ask about the bus schedule to better decide if she would make the trip. On sighting her, he quickly noticed the bruise around her eye, which was already a month old but still visible.

After querying her a little, Kya opened up that Chase was indeed responsible but couldn't do anything else to here. Jumpin threatened to deal with the fellow, but Kya asked that he let the matter be as she was not ready to face the sheriff and have to relive that same day all over again.

He made her agree to always come to town so he would see her or he would be forced to come to look for her.

Thoughts

Chapter Forty-Seven: The Expert

The prosecutor called Sheriff Joe to the stand to get testimony. The sheriff proceeded to tell all present that there were no fingerprints found on the body of the deceased, so that angle would not be strong enough to make a proper case. On hearing this, the prosecutor discontinued his line of questioning as the defense attorney took over.

From what the sheriff said already, the defense only had to establish to the jury that there was no physical evidence linking her to the crime. He goes further to state that the lack of footprints in the sand is made possible by the rise of the tide which washes away all footprints every few hours or so, and not that Kya removed the evidence.

In conclusion, the defense attorney provided a document which was written by the sheriff a few months ago, complaining to the authorities that the grate needed urgent attention before it leads to serious injury or even death, further confirming the fact that Chase could well have died by accident.

Thoughts

Chapter Forty-Eight: A Trip

On the agreed day in October, Kya came to tell Jumpin about her trip to Greenville to meet with the editor and he pointed her in the right direction, wishing her well. On getting to the bus stop, Kya did her best not to return the stares coming her way by focusing on the driver who sold her the ticket and put her luggage in the right place.

Two days later, she returned from her trip to meet a lot more people staring at her. The thought to tell Jumpin of her coming back into town quickly evaporated when she found several boats waiting for gas and felt it was better to return the next day.

The next day, she met a solemn Jumpin who informed her that Chase had died the previous night and all the rumors going on in town that there was foul play involved. Silently, he was thankful that she was away on the night it happened, else they pin the whole thing on her. In shock, she walked away.

Thoughts

Chapter Forty-Nine: Disguises

Calling on the next witness, the prosecutor grilled him on the movement of passengers in and out of the bus on the said date to determine if there was the possibility of Kya coming back into town at night. He said that there was indeed a disguised man who fit the exact body type of the accused with their head kept down all through the ride.

The defendant simply asked if there was any way to be certain it was his client to which he responded in the negative, revealing that the possibility of this scenario came up after the sheriff suggested it.

The second witness also gave an account of a disguised old lady on the bus who would match the description of Kya but also narrated that it was impossible to tell if it was her, rendering his testimony void.

Thoughts

Chapter Fifty: The journal

Calling Patti Love to the stand, the prosecutor asked her about the handmade necklace which her son had worn for four years before his death. She confirmed that it must have been given to him by Kya as stated in the journal which she gave chase at one time.

Kya did not deny knowledge of the journal, as she had indeed given it to Chase and felt good that she was able to provide him with a gift that contained drawings of them, made by her.

Going forward, she confirmed that Chase had been wearing the said necklace on the last night she saw him at dinner in her house and noticed that it was missing the next morning she had to come to identify his body.

Thoughts

Chapter Fifty-One: Waning moon

Moving forward, the next witness; Mr. Miller, who worked as part of a boat crew, was called up and asked questions relating to the night Chase died at about past midnight. Giving a detailed description of someone who had the same features as Kya seen at that time, sailing without lights, he concluded that there was no other destination in that area apart from the fire tower where Chase was pushed down.

In response, the defense asked what exactly Kya was wearing on the said night, and he responded by saying that he was not close enough to see. On this note, it was brought to the attention of the court that this witness was nowhere near to determine if indeed it was Kya that he saw correctly.

Thoughts

Chapter Fifty-Two: Three Mountains Motel

The next witness was the potter at the hotel where Kya checked in during her stay in Greenville. He gave an account of how she came and stayed in her room for the two days she was in town, only stepping out briefly to meet with her editor.

The editor; Mr. Foster was called in next, and he admitted to dropping Kya off at the motel after their meeting, going further to reveal that an offer for her to stay in a four-star hotel was rejected by Kya, who specifically requested the three mountains motel, the closest one to the bus station.

The sheriff was the next witness called up, opining that while it was possible for Kya to have come back to town that night to commit the crime, there was simply not enough time for her to kill Chase and equally make it back to the bust in time. Another theory was brought up by the prosecuting counsel, stating that perhaps the riptide or waves aided her while sailing, yet was unable to provide proof to that effect.

Thoughts

Chapter Fifty-Three: Missing Link

Another witness in the person of Mr. O'Neal was called to the stand by the defense to give an account of what he saw on the same night Chase died, he convinced everyone present that it was too dark to assert that the boat his employees saw was actually that of Kya or that it was her to begin with.

In closing, the prosecutor stated that one of the illustrious sons of the town had been murdered and there were a motive and red wool on his jacket which sufficiently links the marsh girl to the murder.

The defense counsel admonished the jury and all present of their inability to adequately cater for an abandoned little girl who grew up to become a fantastic author through self-efforts and there was no evidence to show that she was in any way linked to the death of Chase and it was vital that they don't fail her again.

Thoughts

Chapter Fifty-Four: Vice Versa

While the jury went in to discuss and deliver their verdict, Tom, Tate and a few other friends of Kya gathered in a small room where they eagerly waited, though it seemed the future was bleak, Tom convinced them that if convicted, he would file and appeal based on mistrial due to prejudice.

Twice, Tom came in to inform them that the jury had asked to see the bus drivers' testimony and that of the coroner, which meant they were actually mulling things over and there was still hope.

A while later, he informed them that the jury had indeed reached a verdict and the court must reconvene. Once the judge came in, a small paper was shown to him and read out to declare that Miss Catherine Clark (Kya) had been pronounced not guilty by the jury and was free to go.

Though the judgment was not accepted by several people, there was nothing they could do, as the prosecutor cannot charge her twice with the murder.

Thoughts

Chapter Fifty- Five: Grass Flowers

Back home, it became a herculean task for Kya to open up to Jodie, try as he did to make her talk. All she did was yell out about how she didn't hate anyone but had to deal with so much hatred from people that she learnt to live without them; Jodie, Ma, everybody!

A while later, she heard an unfamiliar boat speed up before noticing the sheriff, his deputy, and another man pull up beside Tate, and after a few heated words from them, he was led into their boat as it sped away.

She wondered what must have led to such an action, as Tate was the one person she was looking to talking to.

Thoughts

Chapter Fifty-Six: The Night Heron

Slowly walking among people both familiar and unfamiliar, Tate had his head bowed as he moved to the graveyard to pay his last respect to his father whom the sheriff had come to inform him was dead. It didn't hurt that he thought more of Kya than his deceased dad, seeing that his feelings for her never faded.

Not expecting her to show up at the funeral, he quickly drove to her place and continued knocking until she opened the door. After that, he waited for her to walk to him before he professed his undying love to her and promised never to leave her again.

As if on cue, she opened up by telling him that she always loved him, even when she was a kid and didn't know what love meant.

Thoughts

Chapter Fifty-Seven: The Firefly

After the whole incident, Kya and Tate became even closer that the moved in with her and they got married in their own way.

One morning later, Tate came back with the terrible news that Jumpin had died in his sleep the previous night, and this led to a few tears being shed by Kya. She didn't attend his funeral as everyone had done but made out time to go to his yard to see Mabel and mourn with her.

They never had any children though they wanted one desperately. One day at the age of 64, Kya didn't return as expected, which led to Tate sailing out for her immediately.

He saw her laid down in her boat, laid back in death and a searing pain shooting through his heart.

At her burial, everyone in the town converged, and as she was laid in her designated place close to the sea, Tate knew his life would never be the same. His only consolation was that she had lived a good life and could finally rest.

Thoughts

References and Other Notable Workbooks

You are a Badass Workbook >> ISBN: 1950171868

WORKBOOK for The Longevity Paradox>> ISBN: 1950171795

A JOURNAL For Becoming | A Gratitude & Self Journal (Becoming By Michelle Obama Quotes)>> ISBN: 1098520211

A JOURNAL For Daring Greatly>> ISBN: 195017185X

A Journal The Subtle Art of Not Giving a F*ck>> ISBN: 1950171833

WORKBOOK for The Subtle Art of Not Giving A F*ck >> ISBN: 1950171779

WORKBOOK for Dare to Lead By Brene Brown >> ISBN: 1950171973

Workbook For Daring Greatly>>ISBN: 1950171906

Workbook For How To Win Friends and Influence People>> ISBN: 1950171892

71747786R00044

Made in the
USA
Middletown, DE

WORKBOOK

For

WHERE THE CRAWDADS SING

DELIA OWENS

BY

TIMELINE Publishers

Meditation

Consider some definitions of the word *meditation* ***from the Greek and Hebrew languages:***

Ponder	Imagine	Converse	Murmur
Muse	Ruminate	Reflect	Revolve in the mind

How does Christian meditation differ from New Age or Hindu meditation?

___

___

What are some things I can do to help me to meditate on Scripture?

___

___

___

___

The Eleventh Step helps us not to play god in our own lives or the lives of our loved ones. Instead, it encourages us . . .

- To seek God.
- To pray.
- To meditate.
- To improve our constant contact with God.
- To ask for his will and his power.

PHYSICAL FOCUS

Why is it God's will for us to turn from compulsive overeating and to eat in a healthy way instead? What does each verse below say on the subject?

Proverbs 23:1–3—When you sit to dine with a ruler, note well what is before you, and put a knife to your throat if you are given to gluttony. Do not crave his delicacies, for that food is deceptive.

___

Deuteronomy 8:3—He humbled you, causing you to hunger and then feeding you with manna, which neither you nor your fathers had known, to teach you that man does not live on bread alone but on every word that comes from the mouth of the Lord.

___

John 6:35—Then Jesus declared, "I am the bread of life. He who comes to me will never go hungry, and he who believes in me will never be thirsty."

Matthew 6:24a-b—[Jesus said] "No one can serve two masters. Either he will hate the one and love the other, or he will be devoted to the one and despise the other."

PRACTICING THE PRINCIPLES
(Homework)

1. How have you played god this week?
2. Refer to the section on ways to seek God. Are there ways listed that you haven't tried or haven't tried in a long time? Try at least three this week.
3. Memorize Step 8 and Step 9.
4. Study the ways to meditate on Scripture. Utilize as many new ones as you can when you meditate on the following Scriptures as they relate to the Eleventh Step:
   - Hebrews 11:6
   - Matthew 26:39
   - Proverbs 3:21-26
   - Ephesians 1:17-19
   - Psalm 145:1-5, 15

Julie's Thoughts to Munch On

Session 8:

How Do I Know What You Really Want, God?

GUIDING PRINCIPLE: *I can find God's will if I know where to look.*

APPLICATION QUESTION

How have you played god this week?

- Telling others what to do
- Judging others—focusing on their sins
- Not bothering to stop and spend time with God
- Feeling responsible to convict others of their sin
- Not relying on God's power, but your own
- Not obeying God's Word
- Not seeking God's will, thinking you know best
- Not confessing your sins
- Not giving thanks to him
- Worrying about the future
- Other

What are you going to do about it?

PRINCIPLES FROM THE WORD

Share your meditations on Scripture as they relate to the Eleventh Step: "Sought through prayer and meditation to improve our conscious contact with God through Jesus Christ, praying for knowledge of his will for us and the power to carry that out." Of the ways to meditate on Scripture that we discussed last week, which did you use?

STEPPING STONE SURVEY

Of the following ways to seek God, check the one that has been the most meaningful to you this week. Why? Was a Stepping Stone involved in this?

____ Being still before him, listening

____ Thanksgiving and praise

____ His Word

____ Nature

____ Talking to other Christians

____ Church

____ Asking God specific questions

____ Obeying him

____ Christian books

____ Singing to him

____ Using the Stepping Stones

____ Working the steps

SPIRITUAL FOCUS

Continue the Eleventh Step by discussing five ways to know God's will:

- ***Prayer***

James 1:5—If any of you lacks wisdom, he should ask God, who gives generously to all without finding fault, and it will be given to him.

What attitude should we have when we ask God? What does the following Bible verse say about that?

> ***Matthew 26:39b–c***—Jesus fell with his face to the ground and prayed, "My Father, if it is possible, may this cup be taken from me. Yet not as I will, but as you will."

___

If I feel that God has made his will for me evident, can I try to persuade him to change his mind?

> ***Numbers 22:18–19***—But Balaam answered them, "Even if Balak gave me his palace filled with silver and gold, I could not do anything great or small to go beyond the command of the Lord my God. Now stay here tonight as the others did, and I will find out what else the Lord will tell me."

Do you remember the story of Baalam, the false prophet? What led up to this statement?

___

___

What did he say here that was so bad?

___

What was the outcome?

___

What does this tell me about my life?

___

What do I do if I get no answer when I ask God what his will is for me?

Jeremiah 29:11–13—"For I know the plans I have for you," declares the LORD, "plans to prosper you and not to harm you, plans to give you hope and a future. Then you will call upon me and come and pray to me, and I will listen to you. You will seek me and find me when you seek me with all your heart."

___

• *Scripture*

Psalm 119:105—Your Word is a lamp to my feet and a light for my path.

What are some questions, obviously answered in Scripture, that I shouldn't ask God?

What are some questions that Scripture won't answer directly?

What does Scripture say generally about God's will for us?

> ***Micah 6:8***—He has shown you, O man, what is good. And what does the LORD require of you? To act justly and to love mercy and to walk humbly with your God.

What does "to act justly" mean to you?

What does "to love mercy" mean to you?

What does "to walk humbly with your God" mean?

When trying to make a decision, how do I know that a certain Scripture is God's answer for me?

• *Circumstances*

1 Thessalonians 5:18—Give thanks in all circumstances for this is God's will for you in Christ Jesus.

What does this mean to me in determining God's will?

How can circumstances help me to know God's will?

If I have prayed over something and have done what I really felt was God's will, is it wrong to feel regretful if it doesn't turn out as I desired?

____

____

- ## *Counsel of Others*

Proverbs 15:22—Plans fail for lack of counsel, but with many advisers they succeed.

Can anyone give me godly counsel?

____

What if someone says to you that God told them you should do something. What should you do?

> ***1 John 4:1***—Dear friends, do not believe every spirit, but test the spirits to see whether they are from God, because many false prophets have gone out into the world.

____

- ## *Feelings*

Psalm 37:4—Delight yourself in the LORD, and he will give you the desires of your heart.

Does this verse mean that I will always get what I want?

____

Does this mean that I will always be happy about God's will for me?

____

Can I trust my feelings to tell me what God's will is?

____

When I hear a "still small voice," is it always God? What can it be?

____

How do I know if God is speaking to me?

____

PHYSICAL FOCUS

How are you doing? Complete this questionnaire to see how you are stepping forward.

A. How is your eating?

1. I try to eat according to the healthy food plan I have chosen.
2. I try to eat under 1,000 calories a day and less than 20 grams of fat.
3. I have occasional slips, but usually stick to my plan.
4. I try to eat right, but I still binge frequently.
5. I am not trying.

B. How is your weight?

1. I am at a healthy weight according to my doctor.
2. I am overweight but only by 10 pounds or less.
3. I am overweight by 20-30 pounds
4. I am extremely overweight.

C. How is your exercise?

1. I exercise 4-5 times a week for at least 20 minutes.
2. I'm not able to exercise.
3. I could do more but I make up excuses.
4. I never exercise.

D. How are you working program?

1. I am *stepping forward*, losing weight, and learning new things about God.
2. I come to the meetings and do a little homework, but I'm not really trying.
3. I am too busy to come to Step Forward much of the time.
4. I am auditing Step Forward.

E. How is your weight affecting your health?

1. I feel great because I am losing weight or am near goal weight.
2. I feel a little sluggish because of the extra pounds.
3. I feel exhausted.
4. I have trouble breathing when I walk up stairs.

•••••

A. What do you think God's will is for your eating?

1. A healthy food plan.
2. Not restricting calories, but cutting down on fats.
3. I don't think it's important to him.
4. Other________________________________

B. What do you think God's will is for your weight?

1. Getting to a healthy weight and staying there.
2. Wearing the same size I wore when I was 18.
3. I don't think it's important to him.
4. Other________________________________

C. What do you think God's will is for your exercise?
1. Exercising 4-5 times a week for at least 20 minutes.
2. I'm not able to exercise.
3. I don't think it's important to him.
4. Other________________________________

D. What do you think God's will is for your program?
1. Continue to *step forward* next term.
2. Find a good diet and stick to it this time.
3. Lose weight by myself.
4. Other________________________________

•••••

How are you willing to *step forward*?

A. In your eating
1. I'm willing, one day at a time, to eat according to a healthy food plan.
2. I'm willing to try to quit bingeing.
3. I'm willing to give up my trigger foods one day at a time.
4. I don't want to try to *step forward* in my eating now.

B. In your exercise
1. I'm willing to exercise 4-5 times a week for at least 20 minutes.
2. I'm willing to quit making excuses and try to exercise 2 times a week for 10 minutes a time. I will also pray for willingness to double that.
3. According to my doctor, I'm really not able to exercise.
4. I'm still not willing to exercise.

C. In your program
1. I am willing to continue *stepping forward* and take my program very seriously, doing all of my homework and using many of the Stepping Stones every day.
2. I am willing to make coming to Step Forward a priority every week and to do 15 minutes a week of homework and write one short meditation on a Scripture.
3. I am willing to make coming to Step Forward a priority every week and pray for willingness to work program.
4. I am auditing Step Forward and too busy to work program.

Compare what you are doing with what you know God's will is for you, then pray for willingness to *step forward*.

Consider signing this covenant with God according to your willingness.

Dear God,
I want to *step forward* by ______________________________________

____

____

I'm not doing this to try to earn your favor, but to show you how much I love you by trying to be more obedient to you. I know you don't command me to do anything that you don't empower me to do, so help me to cooperate with you every day, whether I feel like it at the time or not.

Signed:____

PRACTICING THE PRINCIPLES

(Homework)

1. Do you have a decision to make? Use all five ways given in this week's lesson to see if you can determine God's will in this.
2. List the times when you have felt that God was definitely directing you. Did you obey him?
3. What are the things you are doing that you know are in God's will? What things are you doing that you know are not in God's will?
4. Write an Eleventh Step Prayer asking God to give you knowledge of his will and the power to carry that out.
5. Prayerfully consider filling out and signing the covenant with God in this week's lesson. Write the date and the specific covenant in your prayer journal and pray daily for God's help to do his will.
6. Meditate on the following Scriptures that pertain to the will of God:
   - Ephesians 5:17-21
   - Romans 12:2
   - Psalm 32:8, 9
   - Psalm 25:4-5, 8-9
   - Psalm 23:3

Julie's Thoughts to Munch On

Session 9:

Am I Sleepwalking Spiritually?

GUIDING PRINCIPLE: *Step 12: I can wake up to the Lord's presence if I don't doze.*

APPLICATION QUESTION

What decision do you have to make? How are you using the five ways to know God's will to make your decision?

- Prayer
- Scripture
- Circumstances
- Counsel of other Christians
- Feelings

Share your Eleventh Step prayer.

The Eleventh Step is: "Sought through prayer and meditation to improve our conscious contact with God through Jesus Christ praying for knowledge of his will for us and the power to carry that out."

PRINCIPLES FROM THE WORD

Share your Scripture meditation from homework as it relates to knowing God's will.

STEPPING STONE SURVEY

How do the Stepping Stones help you to do your Eleventh Step?

SPIRITUAL FOCUS

This week we will begin the Twelfth Step: "Having had a spiritual awakening, we tried to carry this message to compulsive overeaters, and to practice these principles in all our affairs."

What is a spiritual awakening?

____

____

How many spiritual awakenings can we have?

____

____

What is a spiritual awakening like? (Check the ones you have experienced.)

____ I experienced a breakthrough in my understanding of God and felt a new intimacy with him.

____ I saw him answer my prayer in a miraculous way and this increased my faith.

____ I knew something was missing in my life and confessed Jesus as my Lord and Savior, and gradually things began to get better.

____ When I called out to Jesus, I suddenly felt brand new, cleansed, and energized.

____ In a crisis I panicked and turned to God, and he helped me in unimaginable ways.

____ I had drifted from God and became awakened to his presence again after coming to Step Forward.

____ I met a Christian who shared his or her faith with me, and I realized that a closer relationship with God was possible.

____ I stepped out in faith and did what I thought God was leading me to do and felt great joy.

How are my spiritual awakenings hindered if I don't take the steps?

The Twelve Steps	How My Spiritual Awakenings Are Hindered If I Don't Take Each Step
1. We admitted that we were powerless over food and that our lives had become unmanageable.	1. If I don't admit my need for help, it is impossible to rely on God.
2. Came to believe that God, through Jesus Christ, could restore us to sanity.	2. If I don't realize that God can help me, it is harder to experience his help.
3. Made a decision to turn our will and our lives over to the care of God through Jesus Christ.	3. If I refuse to turn my will and my life over to God, it is impossible to have a close relationship with him and receive his help.
4. Made a searching and fearless moral inventory of ourselves.	4. If I do not look at my sins and vicious cycles and recognize that they are a barrier to God, walls build up between us.
5. Admitted to God, to ourselves, and to another human being the exact nature of our wrongs.	5. If I don't confess my wrongs to myself, God, and someone else, and if I pretend that they don't don't matter, my relationship with God is harmed.
6. Were entirely ready to have God remove all these defects of character	6. If I don't want to let go of my sins, walls remain between us.
7. Humbly asked him to remove our shortcomings.	7. If I don't have an attitude of humility with God and ask for him to help me to become the person that he would have me to be, we cannot be close.
8. Made a list of all persons we have harmed, and became willing to make amends to them all.	8. If I harm other people and refuse to face that fact, it interferes with my relationship with God and others.
9. Made direct amends to such people wherever possible, except when to do so would injure them or others.	9. If I refuse to make amends to others when I have harmed them, then I am not truly repentant for my sins, and they remain a barrier between God and me.
10. Continued to take personal inventory and when we were wrong, promptly admitted it.	10. If I don't stop briefly every day to see if I am continuing to walk closely with the Lord, I can drift away from him and not even realize it.
11. Sought through prayer and meditation to improve our conscious contact with God, through Jesus Christ, praying for knowledge of his will for us and and the power to carry that out.	11. If I don't continue to seek God and pray to him several times a day, my old nature will take over, and we will grow apart.
12. Having had a spiritual awakening, we tried to carry this message to compulsive overeaters, and to practice these principles in all our affairs.	12. If I rely only on the fact that I am saved from hell and don't seek to be awakened more and more to God, I won't experience him fully. If I don't share with others the wonderful blessings that he has given me, and if I don't practice these new ways I have learned, I will soon lose the progress I have made. If I don't do my Twelfth Step, I can live my entire life asleep to God's wonderful potential bursting inside of me.

Now that I am awake, what are some concepts that I am learning that are changing my life and enabling me to awaken more and more to all that God has for me?

Psalm 16

Verse 1—Keep me safe, O God, for in you I take refuge.

What is a refuge?

How can I take refuge in God?

---

*Verse 2***a***—I said to the Lord, "You are my Lord . . ."*
Even though he's the creator and sustainer of the entire universe and the King of Kings and Lord of Lords, he loves me just as much as any person he has ever made. He always has time for me.

*Verse 2***b***—Apart from you I have no good thing."*
I can work my fingers to the bone, but if I'm not doing God's will and relying on his power, nothing truly good will result.

Verse 3—As for the saints who are in the land, they are the glorious ones in whom is all my delight.
Other Christians (saints) give me much delight. If I try to fit in with people who don't know the Lord and do things their way, I won't have much pleasure.

Verse 4—The sorrows of those will increase who run after other gods. I will not pour out their libations of blood or take up their names on my lips.
I won't run after other gods: food, acceptance, material things, other people, success and so many other things. All of them can take God's place in my heart when I am devoted to them; therefore, I won't even pretend to play the games of the world or participate in its ungodly rituals.

*Verse 5***a** *— Lord, you have assigned me my portion and my cup . . .*
God has shown me what to eat, and he encourages me to eat it.

*Verse 5***b***–6***a***—You have made my lot secure. The boundary lines have fallen for me in pleasant places.*
As I walk with God, I feel secure and have an attitude of gratitude because I realize that nothing happens to me that doesn't filter through God's fingers first.

*Verse 6***b***—Surely I have a delightful inheritance.*
I know for a fact that I am going to heaven. I can't earn this reward. It is given to me by my Heavenly Father. I also know that I will have many blessings on earth if I walk closely with the Lord and am obedient to him.

***Verse 7**—I will praise the Lord, who counsels me; even at night my heart instructs me.*
God tells me his will. He warns me of danger. He convicts me of sin. He gives me encouragement. At night, when I sleep or lie awake, he gives me insights and understanding. He counsels me through a still small voice, through his Word, through the counsel of other Christians, through my circumstances and through my feelings.

***Verse 8a**—I have set the Lord always before me.*
I now realize that I have choice — to keep God constantly in my mind and heart or to turn my back on him and do things my own way.

***Verse 8b**—Because he is at my right hand, I will not be shaken.*
When I remember that God is always next to me, no matter what happens in my life, my world won't fall apart.

***Verse 9**—Therefore, my heart is glad and my tongue rejoices, my body also will rest secure,*
I have serenity and joy. I want to tell others about God and praise him. I feel better physically and am able to face the future without so much fear when I remember how good he is. I can relax even though I don't know what the future holds because I know who holds the future.

***Verse 10**—Because you will not abandon me to the grave, nor will you let your Holy One see decay.*
Heaven is real. I will not die. Jesus will return and all of God's promises will come to pass.

***Verse 11**—You have made known to me the path of life; you will fill me with joy in your presence, with eternal pleasures at your right hand.*
When I am on the path of recovery God has provided for me, I experience one spiritual awakening after another. With God by my side, my life is filled with joy and eternal pleasures.

PHYSICAL FOCUS

Read this letter of warning from a recovering bulimic so you'll think twice about going down that path:

Dear Step Forward members:

As I sit here and write this letter to you, I really don't know where to start. Addictions are as individual as the person affected. There are many complicated levels and feelings that remain buried deep inside. I often ask myself, "Why did this happen to me? Why did God allow this to happen to me?" Was there some lesson to be learned later in life? Let's face it, bad things happen to good people and this disease has captured many. I can still remember being a trusting, loving, caring, not to mention healthy, young woman.

For me, the trust factor was one of the first things to go. I became very secretive and felt that the majority of the people around me did not understand me, much less understand what I had become. My once outgoing personality had dwindled down to my almost becoming a recluse. I didn't want my very private disease to be found out. I wanted others to think that I was effortlessly perfect and beautiful. If my family and friends only knew all the horrible, self-abusive things that I had done to myself!

Then there was love. As the years rolled on. I had convinced myself that I was not worthy of love unless I looked a certain way. My self image, by this time, was totally distorted. My addiction had consumed me. I had forgotten what love and friendship were all about. I sent a lot of wonderful people, who loved me, running for cover during those years. All I cared about was looking great and staying thin. I was no longer myself. I had become an image in my own mind. I was out of control.

Fourteen years have passed and I still struggle daily. All those years of self-abuse have finally caught up with me in ways I never thought about. I never once thought about health issues and all the damage that I was doing. My mindset was "as long as I look good, life is good." But, the reality is, I have done severe damage to myself. I'm only in my early 30's and I have a heart condition, severe colon damage, anemia, severe body cramps, blackouts, and the list goes on and on.

My free and caring spirit that once flew high was crippled by this disease. I did not want this to be my destiny. I had to search deep within myself and decide if I wanted to live or die. I had slowly chipped away many years of my life and I decided I wanted to fly again. I wanted to be whole with the universe once again. I wanted to be among the living. Life has a lot to offer; besides, the alternative was death. No, my body will never be the same. I will never be able to go back in time and erase what I have done to myself, family, and friends. Lucky for me, there was still time to change my future.

Today, I'm still clawing my way out of my private hell. But, I know I will make it. When I look back on all those wasted years, I am lucky I'm alive. The damage has been done, and my search for inner peace is going to be an ongoing process for the rest of my life. But, at the moment, life is good and during my search I have learned how to love and to be loved once again. —Anonymous

A note from Julie:

I am so thankful that there is hope for people like this precious girl. Recovery is hard work, but it's possible. God is restoring her, just as he is restoring us. I know that he is turning her misery to ministry as she reaches out to us to warn us about the dangers of bulimia. Let's take a minute after reading her letter to pray for her recovery!

Love,Julie

PRACTICING THE PRINCIPLES

(Homework)

1. Refer to the section on spiritual awakenings. Describe your greatest spiritual awakenings. If you feel that you have not had a spiritual awakening, call your group leader or coach and talk to them about it. (Don't feel embarrassed. Just talk to someone about it.)
2. Reread Psalm 16 and the list of life-changing concepts following each verse. Circle ones that you hadn't thought of before or that you have problems accepting. Call your coach or group leader and discuss these things this week.
3. Try to memorize the Stepping Stones and all 12 Steps. Ask your accountability partner or a friend in the group to quiz you.
4. Meditate on the following Scriptures as they relate to the Twelfth Step:
   - Psalm 17:14c–15
   - Romans 13:11–14
   - Isaiah 50:4–5
   - Psalm 139:17–18
   - Ephesians 2:3–6

Julie's Thoughts to Munch On

Session 10:

You're Making Me Better, and I'm Telling!

GUIDING PRINCIPLE: *I can carry the message if I'm willing.*

APPLICATION QUESTION

Of the following concepts we discussed from Psalm 16 last week, which one do you need to be reminded of most?

____ God is my refuge. I am safe in him, no matter my circumstances.
____ I am just as important to God, and he loves me just as much as anyone in the world.
____ I can work my fingers to the bone, but if I'm not doing God's will and relying on him, it's worth nothing.
____ Fellowship with other Christians gives me more delight than trying to fit in with those who don't know the Lord.
____ When I play the games of the world and run after worldly pursuits, I will have great sorrows.
____ God has shown me what to eat.
____ Nothing happens to me that doesn't pass through God's fingers first. When I remember this, I feel secure.
____ I really am going to heaven!
____ God really does counsel me.
____ I have a choice: to focus on God or turn my back on him.
____ No matter what happens to me, I will not be shaken because God is next to me.
____ I can rejoice and rest secure because, although I don't know what the future holds, I know who holds the future.
____ I will never die.
____ If I continue to stay close to God, I will have joy and eternal pleasure.

PRINCIPLES FROM THE WORD

Share your Scripture meditation from homework as it relates to spiritual awakenings.

STEPPING STONE SURVEY

This week's Stepping Stone focus is on Coaching (Accountability).

Who is qualified to coach?

____

What are my responsibilities as a Coach?

- **To work the program to the best of my ability.**

____

- **To be supportive.**

- **To be honest.**

Some possible guidelines for Coaches:

- **Watch for codependency.**

- **Direct the conversations.**

- **Don't enable ineffective behavior.**

- **Don't encourage reliance on you.**

- **Don't be their policeman, but their cheerleader.**

- **Don't let them put you on a pedestal.**

Rewards of Coaching

How can each sentence in this Scripture passage remind us of a promise for coaches?

Isaiah 58:10–12*—If you spend yourselves in behalf of the hungry and satisfy the needs of the oppressed.*
If you're a coach!

Then your light will rise in the darkness,
Others will see God's qualities reflected from you.

And your night will become like the noonday.
You will have direction and won't stumble.

The Lord will guide you always;
When you don't know what to do with someone you are coaching, the Lord will guide you.

He will satisfy your needs in a sun-scorched land
You will be given all that you need to help someone (when the heat is on!): patience, love, compassion and wisdom.

And will strengthen your frame.
Your program will be stronger.

You will be like a well-watered garden, like a spring whose waters never fail.
You will experience God's restoration and serenity in your life.

Your people will rebuild the ancient ruins and will raise up the age-old foundations;
Many of your coachees will rebuild their faith in God and his Word.

You will be called Repairer of Broken Walls, Restorer of Streets with Dwellings.
You will be appreciated (usually!).

SPIRITUAL FOCUS

We will continue the Twelfth Step: "Having had a spiritual awakening, we tried to carry this message to compulsive overeaters, and to practice these principles in all our affairs."

Why carry the message particularly to other compulsive overeaters?

How can we carry the message by modeling the steps to recovery?

The Twelve Steps	How We Model the Twelve Steps
1. We admitted that we were powerless over food and that our lives had become unmanageable.	1. We admit honestly when we can't do something. We don't fall into helplessness and hopelessness.
2. Came to believe that God, through Jesus Christ, could restore us to sanity.	2. We remember that God can help us with anything.
3. Made a decision to turn our will and our lives over to the care of God through Jesus Christ.	3. We turn our lives over to God, desire his will, and rely on him in every situation.
4. Made a searching and fearless moral inventory of ourselves.	4. We recognize our sins and shortcomings.
5. Admitted to God, to ourselves and to another human being the exact nature of our wrongs.	5. We confess openly our imperfections.
6. Were entirely ready to have God remove all these defects of character.	6. We are ready and willing to change when we recognize a shortcoming.
7. Humbly asked him to remove our shortcomings.	7. We are humble, teachable, and rely on God to change us.

8. Made a list of all persons we have harmed, and became willing to make amends to them all.	8. We recognize how we harm others.
9. Made direct amends to such people wherever possible, except when to do so would injure them or others.	9. We make amends and retribution when we harm someone.
10. Continued to take personal inventory and when we were wrong, promptly admitted it.	10. We are aware of our behavior and are quick to admit a mistake.
11. Sought through prayer and meditation to improve our conscious contact with God through Jesus Christ, praying for knowledge of his will for us and the power to carry that out.	11. We seek God and his will in every situation, relying on his power to do what he is leading us to do.
12. Having had a spiritual awakening, we tried to carry this message to compulsive overeaters, and to practice these principles in all our affairs.	12. We become spiritually awakened to God's presence, growing, reflecting his love to others, and practicing what we are learning so we can be good examples to those around us.

We can carry the message by coaching, by modeling the steps, and by telling others.

Look at ***1 Peter 3:15b***—Always be prepared to give an answer to everyone who asks you to give the reason for the hope that you have. But do this with gentleness and respect.

Is your hope in Step Forward, your Food Plan, your quiet time, Fellowship with others, or the other Stepping Stones?

____

How do the Stepping Stones and the steps help you to recover?

____

What can you say to someone when they ask you how you lost weight or why you seem so much happier?

____

How do you show gentleness and respect to others as you are sharing your story?

____

____

PHYSICAL FOCUS

What would you say if asked to tell a Step Forward newcomer about healthy eating?

____

____

____

____

____

PRACTICING THE PRINCIPLES

(Homework)

1. Write a short description of what you were like, what brought you to Step Forward and what you are like now. Pray that God will give you the opportunity to share with others what he has done in your life.
2. Are you willing to coach others? Why or why not? Talk to your group leader about this.
3. What are you modeling to your family/coworkers? Recovery or relapse? Describe.
4. Read "A Coach's Prayer" (see next page).
5. Meditate on the following verses as they relate to sharing the message of recovery with others.
   - Matthew 5:14-16
   - Mark 5:18-20
   - 1 Timothy 1:15-16
   - 2 Corinthians 1:3-4
   - Timothy 4:9-11

A Coach's Prayer

Dear God,

Help me to be a good Step Forward coach. Use my words to encourage others to work their program and learn to rely on you more each day.

Help me to work my own program well so that I will be a good example of recovery to each of my coachees. Inspire me to use the Stepping Stones to work the steps in new and exciting ways. Give me the ability to do what you are leading me to do. I know that, without your help, I can't do anything. But I also know that you do help me when I ask.

Help me not to be codependent with the people I am coaching. God, don't let me give unasked-for advice or try to fix anyone. Let me realize that my responsibility is to point them to you and the program, and you will heal their hurts. Help me not to get frustrated or angry if they refuse to work program or don't make the progress that I desire for them. Help me to remember that I am only their cheerleader, not their policeman, and if they choose not to work program or to do half-measures, it isn't my responsibility. When one just quits calling me after days or weeks of sharing and caring, help me not to feel used or hurt.

Help me to prioritize my time wisely with my coaching. With each call, help me to remember to pray for guidance before picking up the phone. Help me to focus on program and not just on circumstances, on recovery and not just on slips. Help me, dear God, to direct the conversation so that I will not just be a place to unload burdens, but one who points them to where their recovery really is . . . in you.

I am so grateful for this opportunity you have given me to share my recovery with others. It is a true example of your taking my weakness and using it for good as I turn it over to you. Please, God, help me to do it well.

In Jesus' name, Amen.

Julie's Thoughts to Munch On

Session 11:

I'm Practicing The Principles!

GUIDING PRINCIPLE: *I can practice the principles if I get up when I fall.*

APPLICATION QUESTION

Briefly share what your greatest spiritual awakening was like. What circumstances led up to it?

PRINCIPLES FROM THE WORD

Share your meditations from Scripture as they relate to Step 12 and to carrying the message.

STEPPING STONE SURVEY

The focus of this week's Stepping Stone Survey is Accountability. Share *steps forward* that you have made because your coach or accountability partner has helped you.

SPIRITUAL FOCUS

This week we will continue the Twelfth Step: "Having had a spiritual awakening, we tried to carry this message to compulsive overeaters, and to practice these principles in all our affairs."

Practice the Principles

What does the word** practice **in "practice the principles" imply?

____

____

____

____

At the end of this lesson we will have studied all 12 Steps.

Step 1: We admitted that we were powerless over food and that our lives had become unmanageable.

Step 2: Came to believe that God, through Jesus Christ, could restore us to sanity.

Step 3: Made a decision to turn our will and our lives over to the care of God through Jesus Christ.

Step 4: Made a searching and fearless moral inventory of ourselves.

Step 5: Admitted to God, to ourselves, and to another human being the exact nature of our wrongs.

Step 6: Were entirely ready to have God remove all these defects of character.

Step 7: Humbly asked him to remove our shortcomings.

Step 8: Made a list of all persons we have harmed, and became willing to make amends to them all.

Step 9: Made direct amends to such people wherever possible, except when to do so would injure them or others.

Step 10: Continued to take personal inventory and when we were wrong, promptly admitted it.

Step 11: Sought through prayer and meditation to improve our conscious contact with God through Jesus Christ, praying for knowledge of his will for us and the power to carry that out.

Step 12: Having had a spiritual awakening, we tried to carry this message to compulsive overeaters, and to practice these principles in all our affairs.

Can you memorize all 12 Steps? Sure, you can! Here are a couple of techniques:

Find a key word (or two) in each one. If you can choose and memorize a key word for each step, it's easier to remember the steps.

Step 1: ____________________	Step 7: ____________________
Step 2: ____________________	Step 8: ____________________
Step 3: ____________________	Step 9: ____________________
Step 4: ____________________	Step 10: ____________________
Step 5: ____________________	Step 11: ____________________
Step 6: ____________________	Step 12: ____________________

Find a shorter, catchy way to say each one. Here are some suggestions:

Step 1: I can't!
Step 2: God can!
Step 3: I'll let him!
Step 4: What needs changing?
Step 5: I confess!
Step 6: Help me want to change.
Step 7: Change me, Lord!
Step 8: Who have I hurt?
Step 9: I'm sorry!
Step 10: How am I doing?
Step 11: Help me to know you!
Step 12: You're making me better, and I'm telling!

How do you summarize the purpose of the 12 Steps?

Deuteronomy 8:10-14 gives us biblical admonition to practice the principles. Look at the application that follows each line.

1. When you have eaten and are satisfied
When you have been eating in a healthy way and your compulsion with food starts to subside . . .

2. Praise the Lord your God for the good land he has given you.
Thank God for his power at work in you bringing about your recovery.

3. Be careful that you do not forget the Lord your God
Don't think you are doing it on willpower . . .

4. Failing to observe his commands, his laws and his decrees that I am giving you this day.
Do not fail to use the Stepping Stones and work the steps because they help you to walk in God's ways.

5. Otherwise, when you eat and are satisfied, when you build fine houses and settle down, and when your herds and flocks grow large and your silver and gold increase and all you have is multiplied,
Otherwise, when your compulsion is gone and you are at goal weight and feel serene and secure,

6. Then your heart will become proud and you will forget the Lord your God, who brought you out of . . . slavery.
You will relapse because of your pride and, once again, you will become a slave to your compulsion.

Can you recognize the step in each of the following verses?

1. Step ____ ***1 John 1:9***—If we confess our sins, he is faithful and just and will forgive us our sins and purify us from all unrighteousness.

2. Step ____ ***2 Corinthians 12:9***—My grace is sufficient for you for my power is made perfect in weakness.

3. Step ____ **James 4:10**—Humble yourselves in the presence of the Lord, and he will exalt you.

4. Step ____ ***Romans 12:1***—I urge you, brethren, by the mercies of God, to present your bodies a living and holy sacrifice, acceptable to God, which is your spiritual service of worship.

5. Step ____ ***Psalm 96:2-3***—Sing to the Lord, praise his name; proclaim his salvation day after day. Declare his glory among the nations, his marvelous deeds among all peoples.

6. Step ____ ***Matthew 4:23-24***—If, therefore, you are presenting your offering at the altar, and there remember that your brother has something against you, leave your offering before the altar, and go your way; first be reconciled to your brother, and then come and present your offering.

7. Step ____ ***Romans 7:19 (Living Bible)***—When I want to do good, I don't, and when I try not to do wrong, I do it anyway.

8. Step ____ ***Psalm 119:30***—I have chosen the way of truth; I have set my heart on your laws.

9. Step ____ ***Philippians 4:6***—Do not be anxious about anything, but in everything, by prayer and petition with thanksgiving, present your requests to God.

10. Step ____ ***Proverbs 14:8-9***—The wisdom of the prudent is to give thought to their ways, but the folly of fools is deception. Fools mock at making amends for sin, but goodwill is found among the upright.

11. Step ____ ***Proverbs 28:13***—He who conceals his sins does not prosper, but whoever confesses and renounces them finds mercy.

12. Step ____ ***Hebrews 2:1***—We must pay more careful attention, therefore, to what we have heard, so that we do not drift away.

PHYSICAL FOCUS

Which Step Forward principle helps you most to stay away from compulsive overeating? Check the principle that most applies to you. Put a star beside the ones of which you want to be more aware.

____ I don't allow myself to get too hungry by skipping meals or eating too late.

____ I don't allow myself to graze. If I am going to have a snack, I sit down with it and eat it. Having second and third helpings sets me up for a binge.

____ If I have more than just a slip or two, I contact my accountability partner and tell him or her. Sometimes I ask if I may report my food for a few days.

____ I take care of myself by getting away alone every morning to have a quiet time. I stay away from restaurants that make me want to overeat. I refrain from having trigger foods in my house.

____ I know that eating too much sets me up for a binge. It's almost like there's a hunger mechanism in my stomach that is activated when my stomach gets too full.

____ It's important for me to identify the behaviors that cause my eating to get out of control (for example, eating while standing, eating while watching television, driving, or when upset).

____ My appetite is like a spiritual and emotional barometer for me. When I am ravenous, it is often because I am drifting from the Lord or have an emotion that I don't want to feel.

____ Recovery doesn't just happen to me. I must work at it.

____ Step Forward did not get its name accidentally. It means that we aim to make progress, but we aren't trying to be perfect.

____ Overeating is just a symptom of my dis-ease. I need to treat the cause of my dis-ease, not just the symptom, by working the 12 Steps and by learning how to turn my compulsive overeating over to the Lord.

PRACTICING THE PRINCIPLES
(Homework)

1. List the ways that you have changed as a result of this program. Write God a thank-you note!
2. Meditate on the following Scriptures as they relate to the Twelfth Step.
   - Psalm 96:2-3
   - Deuteronomy 8:6-8
   - John 6:35
   - 2 Corinthians 5:16-17
   - Psalm 141:4
3. Memorize Deuteronomy 8:10-12.

Julie's Thoughts to Munch On

Session 12:

I'm Growing Inside While Shrinking Outside!

GUIDING PRINCIPLE: *I can keep on stepping forward if I continue working program.*

APPLICATION QUESTION

What is the most significant way that you have changed spiritually as a result of working the Step Forward program?

____

____

____

What is the most significant way that you have changed emotionally as a result of working the Step Forward program?

____

____

____

PRINCIPLES FROM THE WORD

Share your meditations from Scripture as they relate to Step 12 and practicing the principles in all our affairs.

STEPPING STONE SURVEY

Which one of the Stepping Stones do you want to use more effectively next year? How do you think it will help you?

____

____

SPIRITUAL FOCUS

Review how we practice the principles of the steps:

Look at this fictitious example of working through a problem by using the 12 Steps:

Sally's 25-year-old son has married someone she doesn't like.

1. We admitted that we were powerless over food and that our lives had become unmanageable.

2. Came to believe that God, through Jesus Christ, could restore us to sanity.

3. Made a decision to turn our will and our lives over to the care of God through Jesus Christ.

4. Made a searching and fearless moral inventory of ourselves.

5. Admitted to God, to ourselves, and to another human being the exact nature of our wrongs.

6. Were entirely ready to have God remove all these defects of character.

7. Humbly asked him to remove our shortcomings.

8. Made a list of all persons we have harmed, and became willing to make amends to them all.

9. Made direct amends to such people wherever possible, except when to do so would injure them or others.

10. Continued to take personal inventory and when we were wrong, promptly admitted it.

11. Sought through prayer and meditation to improve our conscious contact with God through Jesus Christ, praying for knowledge of his will for us and the power to carry that out.

______

12. Having had a spiritual awakening, we tried to carry this message to compulsive overeaters, and to practice these principles in all our affairs.

______

How would you work through a problem using the steps?

1. ______
2. ______
3. ______
4. ______
5. ______
6. ______
7. ______
8. ______
9. ______
10. ______
11. ______
12. ______

PHYSICAL FOCUS

What is the most significant way that you have changed physically as a result of working the Step Forward program?

______

______

PRACTICING THE PRINCIPLES

(Homework)

1. Ask God to continue to teach you as you prepare to start over at Step 1.
2. Invite newcomers to *step forward* with you as you begin Unit 1.

Dear Step Forward Members,

It has been a joy to share the Step Forward program with you.

Please write to me and let me know how you have *stepped forward*. It will encourage me and others in our groups to hear your stories. I am writing a new book and will include some of your stories in it.

I'm looking forward to hearing from you!

Love,
Julie

Julie Morris
2663 Valleydale Rd.
Suite 266
Birmingham, AL 35244

Julie's Thoughts to Munch On